# Sensus Fidelium
## The Use of a Concept in the Post-Vatican II Era

Daniel J. Finucane

# SENSUS FIDELIUM
## THE USE OF A CONCEPT IN THE POST-VATICAN II ERA

DANIEL J. FINUCANE

WIPF & STOCK · Eugene, Oregon

Wipf and Stock Publishers
199 W 8th Ave, Suite 3
Eugene, OR 97401

Sensus Fidelium
The Use of a Concept in the Post-Vatican II Era
By Finucane, Daniel J.
Copyright©1996 by Finucane, Daniel J.
ISBN 13: 978-1-4982-8400-4
Publication date 2/15/2016
Previously published by International Scholars Publication, 1996

To Laura,

whose faith and good sense

have deepened my understanding of each

# CONTENTS

Foreword     xi

Preface     xix

Acknowledgments     xxiii

### CHAPTER 1: INTRODUCTION     1

Differences in Approaches and Appropriations *1*
The Question of Lay Involvement *3*
Historical Dimensions of the Sense of the Faithful *4*
Modern Antecedents for the Contemporary Pluralistic Context *9*
The Need for Contemporary Criteria for Discerning the *Sensus Fidelium* *12*
The Approach of the Present Study *14*

### CHAPTER 2: HISTORY OF THE CONCEPT: NEW TESTAMENT THROUGH THE COUNTER-REFORMATION     17

The Sense of the Faithful and the New Testament *19*
New Testament Communities *22*
The Sense of the Faithful and the Patristic Era *40*
Responsibility for the Tradition *40*
Election of Bishops *47*
*Seniores Laici* *59*
Consensus and the Expression of Doctrine *60*
The Sense of the Faithful in the Fathers *72*
The Sense of the Faithful and the Middle Ages *73*
The Community and Reception *78*
The Reformation *89*
Trent and the Counter-Reformation *96*
*Epikeia* and Reception *108*
The Historical Roots of a Modern Agenda *124*

## CHAPTER 3: HISTORY OF THE CONCEPT: MODERN PERIOD TO VATICAN II     127

The Seventeenth and Eighteenth Centuries *127*
Gallicanism *130*
The Sense of the Faithful and the Nineteenth Century *135*
Tuebingen *137*
John Henry Newman and the "*Rambler* Affair" *148*
The Context of Vatican I *172*
The First Vatican Council *181*
The *Sensus Fidelium* and Vatican I *195*
Modernism *197*
The *Sensus Fidelium* before Vatican II *202*
The Modern Agenda for Understanding the *Sensus Fidelium 208*

## CHAPTER 4: INTERPRETATION OF THE *SENSUS FIDELIUM* WITHIN THE CONTEXT OF VATICAN II     211

Vatican II and the Sense of the Faithful *211*
Key Characteristics of the Sense of the Faithful *222*
Use of the Criteria *251*

## CHAPTER 5: THEOLOGICAL TREATMENTS OF THE *SENSUS FIDELIUM* SINCE VATICAN II     253

Theological Perspectives on the *Sensus Fidelium 253*
Historical Focuses *258*
Systematic Treatments *275*
"Practical" Concerns and the Sense of the Faithful *379*
Perspectives on the *Sensus Fidei 379*
The Sense of the Faithful and Moral Theology *388*
Democratization of the Church *401*
Reception *403*
Liberation Movements *410*
Strategies for Developing the Sense of the Faithful *415*
Perspectives from within the Magisterium *419*

CHAPTER 6: ADEQUATE AND INADEQUATE USES OF THE TRADITION OF
THE *SENSUS FIDELIUM* IN POST-VATICAN II THEOLOGY       441

Recovering a Historical Perspective *442*
The Post-Conciliar Context *449*
Emphasis on the Magisterium *453*
Related Issues *458*
Emphasis on the Faithful *463*
Related Issues *467*
Emphasis on Interaction of the Magisterium and the Faithful *469*
Practical Issues 476
Interrelated Issues *480*
Issues of Interpretation *483*
Practical Directions *484*
Conclusion *489*

| | |
|---|---|
| Notes | 493 |
| Works Cited | 655 |
| Subject Index | 691 |
| Index of Authors | 697 |

# FOREWORD

At the close of the twentieth century, the Roman Catholic Church exhibits substantial tension, which is rooted in swift historical change. There was a 400 year interval between the conservative changes effected by the Council of Trent and the renewal of the Catholic tradition at the Second Vatican Council. Yet, there was a mere 15 year period between the progressive changes made by Vatican II and the emergence of an authoritarian reaction to those changes. Movement between conservative and progressive moments within an essentially developmental religious tradition is natural and even desirable. Yet, when the swings are closely spaced and rapidly paced, the faithful become disoriented, anxious, and often angry.

Daniel J. Finucane's study of *Sensus Fidelium* is a useful and very timely contribution to the Church's approach to institutional self-understanding at a critical turning point. As the Church struggles to, on the one hand, appropriate and realize the inspired vision of Vatican II, and on the other hand, in an almost contradictory fashion, to reinterpret and circumscribe its application, the *sensus fidelium* takes on particular importance. Today, perhaps more than ever the critical role of the laity's involvement in the development and reception of Church teaching cannot be ignored. Even if one could argue that there is need to reign in the tradition at this point in history, Vatican II's unequivocal empowerment of the laity demands an open, if not entirely democratic, process. Indeed, as Cardinal Joseph Ratzinger has noted, the Church is not a democracy; but it is a community of believers who, despite differing responsibilities and gifts, share the selfsame gift of the Spirit.

Finucane provides a thorough historical review of the *sensus fidelium* which is essential to an informed appreciation of this powerful concept. Moreover, he has eschewed the tendency to produce a disconnected catalogue of historical precedents in favor of a synthetic treatment that draws attention to unifying interpretations that have evolved over time. His most important and highly original contribution, though, is his elaboration of a set of criteria to identify and apply the *sense of the faithful* for the post-Vatican II era. His criteria promote a holistic approach that does justice to both the theological import and the practical impact of this essential feature of the Church's living tradition. The contemporary relevance of Finucane's *tour de force* is unquestionable. His work will serve as a welcome and instructive resource in the Church's struggle to remain faithful.

>Laurence J. O'Connell, Ph.D., S.T.D.
>President and CEO
>The Park Ridge Center for the Study of Health, Faith and Ethics
>Chicago, Illinois

# FOREWORD

"The Church would look foolish without them." Thus John Henry Newman was reported to reply when Bishop Ullathorne asked, "Who are the laity?" implying that, when it came to matters of doctrine, laity were not of very much account. It was in this context that Newman composed his famous essay "On Consulting the Faithful in Matters of Doctrine," destined to be the classic modern discussion of the role of the faithful generally, the *sensus fidelium*, in the identification and unfolding of Christian belief. In Newman's day, as for the whole of Catholic theology virtually up to the eve of the Second Vatican Council, the task of naming and articulating doctrine was thought to be exclusively the task of the hierarchy, meaning the pope and the bishops, the *ecclesia docens*, the Church teaching; the role of the rest of the Church, the *ecclesia discens*, the Church learning, essentially the laity, in matters of doctrine was that of docile assent. The laity actively believe what they passively receive from the hierarchy.

Newman believed the matter was more complicated. Years earlier, reflecting particularly on the fourth century Arian controversy, Newman observed that what came to be defined as Catholic faith in trinitarian questions was more firmly held by the Catholic community generally in their life of prayer than it was in the official positions of many bishops inclined to use Arian language. The fifth century christological definitions of Ephesus too, which affirmed the full divinity and full humanity of Jesus, were to no little extent supported or even dictated by popular devotion to Mary as theotokos, God-bearer. Newman cited other examples of cases where the faith life of the Christian community generally had been the primary theological *locus* or principle leading to dogmatic definitions.

culminating in the Roman Catholic definition of the Immaculate Conception of Mary in his own day. In many cases, if not in all, it seemed that the motive force fueling the development of doctrine was in fact the faith life of the whole Church.

The concept of the *sensus fidelium,* the sense of the faithful, and its importance in the life of the Church, has come to be universally recognized in Catholic theology. Vatican II explicitly referred to the prophetic office of the People of God and to the "supernatural sense of the faith which characterizes the People as a whole" *(Lumen gentium,* n. 12), but the problem is defining exactly what the concept means and what its exact role is in the evolution of ecclesial faith. Church authorities are understandably nervous about claims that beliefs widely held by the faithful are automatically normative doctrines. What an average Sunday congregation actually thinks it believes about various traditional doctrines would probably astonish theologians, not to mention bishops. Not only orthodox doctrines but also all manner of wild heresies have emerged in the midst of the Church down through its history and even in our own day. Opinions in matters of doctrine have to be weighed, as they say, not just counted. Church leaders need to discern what in the welter of Church life bears the mark of the action of the Holy Spirit and what comes from some other spirit of the times.

This is where Daniel Finucane's thorough study, *"Sensus Fidelium": The Use of a Concept in the Post-Vatican II Era,* makes its signal contribution. Finucane painstakingly traces the story of the notion of the implicit life of faith in the Church as an earnest of doctrinal identity from the New Testament up to our own times. He then carefully analyzes the evolution of the concept from Newman's famous nineteenth century essay to its virtual canonization at the Second Vatican Council. The intricate interplay of a wide variety of theological uses of the concept of *sensus fidelium* in the years since Vatican II is sorted out with admirable clarity in the final and central section of Finucane's work. At the conclusion of this wide-ranging and fair-minded exposition, it is possible to catch the outlines of an emerging consensus: the sense of the faithful involves the whole church, is a multi-dimensional source for theological reflection, requires a reciprocal relationship between the whole Church and the magisterium, is at the heart of the Church's inner life and the ground of its missionary task, cannot be adequately understood as merely passive, and has implications for each believer. Furthermore, the intrinsic importance and validity of appeal to the *sensus fidelium* also means that the simple fact of conflict in the Church does not automatically imply an absence of a sense of the faithful and that any contemporary assessment of the sense of the faithful is linked to the hermeneutic of doctrine generally.

In addition, Finucane's work makes it clear that *sensus fidelium is* intimately connected with two other master principles of contemporary Catholic theology: the development of doctrine and the reception of doctrine. The very notion that doctrine develops has been one of the most dynamic theological insights of the last several centuries. Certainly the Church rightly insists that there is a deposit of faith, a revelation given once and for all in biblical revelation and especially in the person of Jesus Christ and in his life and work, but the Church's apprehension of that revelation and its unfolding in the experiences of each generation of Church history imply a certain real change or development of that revelation. The organic living out of Christian faith in the context of new human insights and challenges is then articulated in theological reflection and eventually taken up by the active teaching ministry of the magisterium. The development of doctrine is not just the life of faith of believers, but this doctrinal development is unthinkable without its roots in the life of the Church.

Reciprocally, *sensus fidelium* is closely linked to what theologians today call the reception of doctrine. When one looks back over Church history one sees that some teachings have simply lapsed or have become moot, largely because the faithful generally couldn't see their continuing validity as expressions of Catholic faith. Think of how the solemn teaching of *Unam Sanctam* (1302), that it was necessary for salvation for every human creature to be subject to the Roman Pontiff, is understood today in comparison with how Boniface VIII apparently originally expected it to be received. Or consider how the Vatican I definition of papal primacy and infallibility were originally conceived by their most enthusiastic promoters and how these concepts actually entered into the life of the Church and were even eventually balanced by Vatican II's emphasis on episcopal collegiality a century later. How the teachings of Trent on biblical inspiration came to be adapted in the faith life of the Church in the face of historical and scientific discoveries of later centuries would be another example of how the sense of the faithful received official Church teachings and how then theology and later doctrinal pronouncements took these adaptations into account.

Of course, the sense of the faithful, how it should be understood and how it should be used in the development and reception of doctrine, is not just some sort of interesting historical question. The most hotly contested issues in contemporary Catholic Church life are intimately connected with how this concept should come into play. Think of the debates about reproductive ethics: birth control, artificial insemination, and the like. Are the convictions of faithful lay believers of no account when it comes to deciding such questions? Or on ecclesiastical questions, like clerical celibacy or the integration of women into the Church's sacramental ministry, is the *sensus fidelium* on such matters irrelevant? Surely on these topics, as on many others troubling the Church today, one must not just count noses to arrive at Catholic doctrine. The Church and its leaders must be faithful to the revelation entrusted to it by Jesus. But as the centuries, and now the millennia, unfold, the Church must not only be attentive to the letter of the message handed down to us by our Fathers and Mothers in the faith, but the Church must also be listening to the voice of the Spirit who continues to instruct the Church about the contemporary implications of that revelation given once and for all in Jesus. It was not just to Church leaders but to the whole Church that

*Foreword*

Jesus addressed these words on the eve of his passion: "I still have many things to say to you, but you cannot bear them now. When the Spirit of truth comes, he will guide you into all the truth" (John 16:12-13).

Francis W. Nichols, D.èsTh.
Saint Louis University
Saint Louis, Missouri

# PREFACE

I first heard the phrase, *sensus fidelium*, during a lecture on the history of moral theology. It was included as one of the sources for theology, along with the Scriptures, the magisterium, the theologians, and the philosophers. When I offered it as such a source later, during my master's oral, I was greeted with a chuckle by one examiner, who asked if I thought it really was much of a factor "these days." (And he was a fan of the concept.) The topic wove its way in and out of my theological reflection during my doctoral course work. Its meaning expanded as I studied history and the importance for modern ecclesiology of doctrinal development and hermeneutics, and it was deepened especially as I worked during the same period of time as a campus minister, musing over the dismissal and recognition, the active existence and unawareness, of the *sensus fidelium* in "regular" believers both on and off campus. In what way do believers make up not just the body of Christ, but the theological "sense" of the body of Christ?

Many authors have taken up the concept of the sense of the faithful, especially since Vatican II, and many point to it as an important resource in probing and resolving debates in the church. The Council has challenged the modern Christian; each baptized believer, and each group within the church with its many gifts and tasks, is called to grow in the faith, and to live faithfully in the modern world. Challenges and controversies make this a difficult calling. A living sense of the faith is foundational for the successful use of these challenges. Yet, it is especially in the middle of challenges and controversy that discernment is both needed and made more difficult.

The *sensus fidelium* proves to be a slippery resource in contemporary debates over morality, theology and practice. How do we know when and where the sense of the faithful is speaking? Is this common sense of believers available among all of the faithful? How do we find it out? Should we consult opinion polls? Which faithful should be counted? Are all those "consulted" suitably faithful or suitably able to articulate their faith as a theological source? How is the sense of the faithful related to the magisterium? Should the church as a whole merely reflect the official teachers of the body of Christ? Should these teachers merely voice what is commonly held or agreed to by the body? Is the sense in the Church ever independent of the statements of bishops and popes? Does the sense of the faith ever have to "simmer" for a while, developing insights of the faith in new contexts, able only to offer new statements after a suitable distancing and time of interpreting?

How should the sense of the faithful be understood, in order for it to function as an active resource as the church lives in the world, as it challenges the world, as it presents the Gospel to the world? There is a long, honored role for *sensus fidelium* in the tradition of the church. Where do we look for the sense of the faithful today?

This study surveys theological literature, mostly published after the Second Vatican Council, that pertains to the *sensus fidelium*. The material is chosen first to illustrate historical questions and the long history of the use of the concept. Then the writings of a number of key postconciliar authors who explore specifically theological aspects of the sense of the faithful are examined. No claim is made to a comprehensive treatment, but important voices are taken up in a way that is intended to be at least representative. Clearly, hermeneutical issues are ripe for further development and study in relation to this topic (as is suggested in several specific parts of this text).

If it is not possible to include all the material that should be taken into account for a full treatment of such a foundational concept, it is possible, nonetheless, to establish a historical backdrop on a sufficiently wide basis, to examine the sense of the faithful as a historical phenomenon and to show its characteristics as a received tradition. The issues presented by this tradition are considered here in the light of Vatican II. The Council's documents are themselves an ecclesiological phenomenon that presents both a wider foundation of insights for approaching ecclesiological questions than the official teachings that preceded it, and an (even dissonant) array of ecclesiologies and of possible sources for critiquing ecclesiological concerns and the sense of the faithful in particular. Vatican II, many have observed, offers an unfinished agenda for ecclesiology.

Genuine warrants for insight and development are embedded in the documents of Vatican II, however. An increased respect for and understanding of roles of the laity, an acceptance of historicity, the recognition of subsidiarity and conciliarity in church affairs, and the need to take up "the joys and the hopes, the griefs and the anxieties" of our time can now inform reflection on the long history of the sense of the faithful (*Gaudium et Spes*, # 1).[1] It is through the lens of Vatican II that this study focuses its criteria for understanding and evaluating theologies of the *sensus fidelium* in the post-Vatican II era.

Examples of theological treatments of the *sensus fidelium* collected here come from the period roughly a quarter of a century after the Council. Interest in its many facets continues, of course. A significant source of new writings has occurred with the centenary of John Henry Newman's death; theological literature abounds with articles and books that explore Newman's ongoing influence on modernism, morality, development of doctrine, lay spirituality, conscience, and the sense of the faithful. The bibliography of the present study has been supplemented to reflect ongoing works specifically on the *sensus fidelium*.

Several should be noted in particular. Recent works by James Heft and Patrick Hartin develop the ecumenical potential of the tradition of the *sensus fidelium*.[2] Paul Crowley has pursued the notion that a focus on this concept must become hermeneutical rather than epistemological if it is to be used to communicate a Catholic faith in different inculturated forms. He draws specifically on the work of Hans-Georg Gadamer.[3] John Burkhard does a thorough job of considering the multi-dimensional aspects of the sense of the faithful in a series of articles that takes up many of the same issues treated here. He surveys the history of the concept, the context of Vatican II, and the practical and theological implications of stressing the *sensus fidei* as an active element in the whole church.[4]

In the last few years a variety of issues and specific papal and episcopal writings have drawn attention to the teaching authority of the magisterium and the responses found in the church as a whole, especially with respect to the rights and responsibilities of the laity. The parameters shaping how the clergy are called from within the larger body of the faithful as pastors are themselves a matter of intense discussion among the faithful. Reactions in the theological community and the church generally, indicate that the issues related to the sense of the faithful—reception, dissent, the roles of the laity, the hermeneutics of magisterial teachings, the expression of authority in the church, the need for interaction and dialogue of pastors and people—all remain lively and important. Especially with the large number of voices speaking on such issues, the temptation is great to reduce conclusions prematurely to those weighted on only one portion of the church or to one set of voices within it.

The *communio* and the active *conspiratio* of pastors and faithful sought by Newman must still be built, even painfully, today, so that the church may be served by the process and content of a healthy sense of the faithful.

# ACKNOWLEDGMENTS

I am grateful to many people at Saint Louis University and elsewhere for their help in bringing this study to its current form. Among them are Edwin Lisson, S.J. who early in my theological course work introduced me to the concept of the *sensus fidelium*; Gerard Magill who helped me clarify an early version of my dissertation proposal and who suggested resources on the topic; Anne T. Mulcahy who read and critiqued an early draft of the manuscript; William M. Shea who has encouraged my work in this and other projects; and J. J. Mueller, S.J. who has consistently encouraged me to write, and to publish the dissertation, and who introduced me to Robert West and Catholic Scholars Press. Rosemary Jermann critiqued a portion of the text and endured early brainstorming sessions. Special support throughout the dissertation stage was shown to me by Betty Andrews, Donald Sutton, Patricia Munz and Carol Boerding.

I could not have given research and writing the time and energy they require without the endurance and support of my wife, Laura, nor without the generous computer time allowed to me by our sons, Danny and Michael.

I am very much indebted to the readers of my dissertation committee, Francis W. Nichols and Bernhard Asen, who before, during and after the original project and through this current version, provided support, critique and friendship far surpassing normal academic commitments.

Finally, without the encouragement, mentoring, and friendship of my doctoral advisor, Laurence J. O'Connell, this study would have been neither begun nor finished.

# CHAPTER 1

# INTRODUCTION

Plurality characterizes current treatment of the *sensus fidelium*. Throughout the Church's history the sense of the faithful has been recognized as a *fons theologiae*.[1] In its earliest uses it has served specifically as that aspect of the Church's reflections that speaks for the catholicity of a doctrine.[2] The variety in current understandings and uses of this concept thus present a problem.[3]

## DIFFERENCES IN APPROACHES AND APPROPRIATIONS

Church historians have recently examined several specific ecclesial issues to argue for a reappropriation of practices that involved the laity in the past. Election of bishops, the reception of canon law, and the reception of doctrine are areas where the faithful played an important role in previous eras, and where advocates for an active laity today look for models to use in changing current practices.[4]

Theologians differ. particularly in the way they regard the relationship between official magisterial statements and the laity's involvement in the development or reception of such statements. Arguments range from those who claim that the Church ought to be a democracy, with prior deliberations among the faithful feeding important decisions by hierarchical representatives,[5] to those who hold that the collective sense of the faithful is by nature a principle of conservation. with any changes in doctrine based on the insights of the faithful requiring an appeal to a superior authority to give them credibility.[6]

Some theologians examine the possibility of new insights being initiated by the laity, and even ask if there is a "magisterium of the faithful."[7] Others suggest looking to sociological tools such as surveys to find the collective sense of the faithful on specific doctrinal matters.[8] Yet, one who speaks for the official magisterium, Cardinal Joseph Ratzinger, has insisted that the introduction of insights from the faithful should not be modeled on standards that are "appropriate to civil society or the workings of democracy."[9] Ratzinger writes,

> Actually, the opinions of the faithful cannot be purely and simply identified with the *sensus fidei*.[31] The sense of the faith is a property of theological faith; and as God's gift which enables one to adhere personally to the truth, it cannot err. This personal faith is also the faith of the church, since God has given guardianship of the word to the church. Consequently, what the believer believes is what the church believes. The *sensus fidei* implies then by its nature a profound agreement of spirit and heart with the church, *sentire cum ecclesia*.[10]
>
> 31. Cf. John Paul II, *Familiaris Consortio*, 5: AAS 74 (1982), 85-86.

Determining when the faithful are thinking with the Church remains difficult when the question is raised of whether a teaching has been definitively formulated, or when a teaching is in an area where further development is definitely needed. Moral theology in general and medical ethics in particular, offer numerous cases where the magisterium has taught on questions that may yet expand into new, uncharted areas. Technical developments as well as continued reflection on such questions by experts and others may affect changes in these areas.[11]

## THE QUESTION OF LAY INVOLVEMENT

Such issues raise a number of practical as well as theological questions about how or whether to include lay involvement in decisions, and how to introduce and educate lay people to the tasks of reflecting or forming consensus in areas where they have lacked involvement in the recent past. Yet, even where the inclusion of the laity in decision making is considered to be a vital part of church dynamics, it is not immediately clear how this group, which has played a key role in Christian history, should be appropriated in the present.[12]

The very idea of involvement is one that would be foreign to many of the faithful. Before the Second Vatican Council, standard works on doctrine could separate the roles of pastors as active teachers, and of lay people as passive receivers of tradition.[13] Vatican II challenged the laity to an active role in many areas.[14] Yet, the post-conciliar response of both lay people and pastors to this challenge has been mixed. Confusion and frustration have been experienced by many lay people who have sought more involvement in the Church, especially where that involvement has challenged the established ways in which authority has been exercised. The response of some lay people has been apathy or a desire to return to the pre-Vatican II Church.[15]

The impetus of Vatican II toward an active, responsible laity has given the Church problems which lack immediate precedents from which to draw solutions. This is true of the practical challenges of working in the world, as well as the reflection needed by lay persons and pastors to support and inspire such work. Diversity in both the experiences of lay people and the current theological discussions about the *sensus fidelium* illustrate that it is not clear how to involve all believers in the *sensus Ecclesiae* today. Avery Dulles has written about the lack of agreement among those proposing appeals to the *sensus fidelium*: "In no significant case do we find a truly universal consensus. Whenever this criterion is invoked, there has actually been a clash of opinions."[16]

If the current views on the *sensus fidelium* were merely an array of interpretations isolated from each other, they might produce an interesting debate, but the lack of agreement itself would not necessarily be noteworthy. Plurality in theological views on topics in the post-Vatican II Church is not rare.

Nevertheless, interpretations of the sense of the faithful are bound together by necessity, in both their resources and their goals. Any serious attempt to understand or apply the sense of the faithful must be linked to the historical precedents that are part of the tradition. Any such attempt must also maintain, as part of its definition of the sense of the faithful, this theological source's established role as a key to unity and consensus. Genuine disagreements which occur concerning the nature of the *sensus fidelium* require a deeper look by participants in the discussion into both the use of sources, and the emphasis given to consensus itself.

## HISTORICAL DIMENSIONS OF THE SENSE OF THE FAITHFUL

In the study undertaken here, the history of the sense of the faithful will be examined. Criteria will be developed from the long tradition that can be used to evaluate the current situation. Interpreting the *sensus fidelium* with this method involves a certain circularity. The history of the sense of the faithful will be reviewed with an eye to developing criteria for assessing current approaches. These current views draw on the historical examples which, in fact, supply the key cases used to develop the history. Though this circularity is unavoidable, it may also contain within it a self-correcting mechanism. Each different aspect of the sense of the faithful that has been developed and accepted in subsequent theology will widen the understanding possible concerning this concept. The collection of such aspects combined with the unifying interpretations that have also developed, can guard against parochial reading that might come from using one element at the expense of others.

Before reviewing this history in detail, a brief look at some classical examples of the *sensus fidelium* will be given to illustrate key problems that have characterized past controversies in which it has played a role. Of particular interest in the establishing of criteria are the interplay of laity and hierarchy, the resolution of diverse viewpoints, and the presence of active or passive qualities in the contributions of the laity.

It might be suggested that the diversity of views on the sense of the faithful could be resolved quite simply by an appeal to authoritative judgment. Cardinal Ratzinger's remarks might be claimed in support of this approach, although they need not be read with such an emphasis. To resolve the issue in this way would be to collapse the sense of the faithful into the judgment of the hierarchy, rendering input from the body of believers meaningless in any practical sense. It will also become clear that such a reduction would be inconsistent with the functioning of the *sensus fidelium* in the past. This theological source has been a distinct indicator of the apostolic tradition, though it has always worked in conjunction with the magisterium in the process of deepening the understanding of doctrines.

Historians cite Tertullian as the first of the Fathers to employ the notion that the agreement of the whole people of faith on an issue is a guarantor of the truth of the issue in question.[17] Tertullian uses this argument from consensus among believers to deny to the heretics of his day the right to interpret the Bible.[18] The interpretation of the Scriptures themselves are thus realized in the general practice of the Church's members. The authority of the New Testament writings comes from their apostolic roots, yet these roots themselves are demonstrated in their acceptance by all the churches.

With the "Vincentian Canon," the agreement of the whole Church was recognized as proof that a doctrine was orthodox, that it was, in fact, catholic. A teaching that was believed "everywhere, at all times, by everyone" was thus established as part of the faith that is both "prophetic" and "apostolic."[19]

Universal agreement was a sign of the Church itself and of a doctrine that was rooted in apostolic origins, as well as being a safeguard against novelty and innovation. It was not for that reason a sanction for stagnation, however. A teaching can develop and still remain true to its identity. St. Vincent writes, that to a simple beginning of a belief may be added "appearance, beauty and distinction."[20]

Worth noting is the further discussion of the possibility of progress by St. Vincent, also in his *Commonitoria*:

> It is necessary, therefore, that understanding, knowledge, and wisdom grow and advance strongly and mightily as much in individuals as in the group, as much in one man as in the whole Church, and this gradually according to age and the times.[21]

From its beginnings, appeal to the *sensus fidelium* involved the insights of the faithful as a vital part of a living tradition. It served both to identify doctrines and to establish hermeneutical practices in the development of the tradition. It has functioned in contexts where a plurality of views on Church teaching have eventually borne fruit in agreement on new doctrinal expressions, though resolution has required new insights into interpretation. The content of tradition and the process of tradition have been forged in the same fires.

William Thompson has shown how the sense of the faithful has been considered under different emphases as it has been appropriated in different periods. In the Patristic period, the truth of Christ was identified with both the faith of the Church and the faith of the individual believer. The Fathers stressed the *consensus fidelium* as an indicator of Christ's presence. Because Christ could not fail, the Church could not fail. Moreover, this connection of the Church to the truth was no spiritualized concept; it was based on no "magical" union with Christ. It was an actual, living faith, held in practice by the Church as a whole, and by any true believer. The realization of the life of Christ in the body of believers was proven in the consensus found among them.[22]

Commenting on the work of Thomas Aquinas, Thompson notes Aquinas's concentration on the *sensus fidei*. Thomas and other scholastics of his period were less interested in the ecclesial aspects of consensus in regard to the sense of the faith, and more occupied with understanding the *sensus* itself. The personal and intellectual aspects of belief are not separated from the communal; one becomes a heretic by removing oneself from the belief of the Church. Yet, the focus is on the effect of the truth in the believer, and the capacity of the believer to respond to it.[23]

Thompson also discusses the emphasis on the *sensus fidelium* that develops in the Counter-Reformation with its explicit focus on ecclesiology. He examines the relationship of the faithful to the exercise of the infallibility of the Church, and he thus develops at length the later focus on the *sensus fidelium*, or the theological content in the faith of the believing Church, that has characterized the modern period.[24] His contribution to the current theological discussion will be considered later. In his methodology, Thompson consciously takes up Newman's agenda of drawing on historical precedents to understand the possibility of an active role of the *sensus fidelium*. In many ways, Newman's work not only begins the modern discussion, but sets its continuing agenda.

In the nineteenth century, the hierarchy moved decidedly toward centralization, following a pattern emphasized since the Council of Trent. Less and less authority was left in the hands of local ordinaries.[25] In this period the laity as a whole were not expected to be active participants in the reflections of the Church in this period. It was in this context that Newman discussed the legitimacy of "consulting the faithful."[26] Newman came to the defense of an author in the lay journal, the *Rambler*, who initiated a controversy by suggesting that the bishops consider the views of the laity in making decisions on a practical, political issue involving education.[27] Newman wrote that he understood the writer to mean by consulting,

> that the *fidelium sensus* and *consensus* is a branch of evidence which it is natural or necessary for the Church to regard and consult, before she proceeds to any definition, from its intrinsic cogency; and by consequence that it ever has been so regarded and consulted.[28]

In his now classic article, *On Consulting the Faithful in Matters of Doctrine*, Newman drew on a variety of cases that illustrate the role played by the laity in preserving orthodox belief during controversial periods of the Church's history.[29]

In Newman's historical illustrations, this "sense" may indeed be seen as being "natural or necessary." It is also relatively easy to see it in operation. In such examples, historical hindsight allows those of a later vantage point to see the *sensus fidelium* as an agent in the development of specific doctrines that are now accepted as part of the tradition. Still, Newman's attempt to defend the consulting of the faithful on specific issues in his own day met with misunderstanding and a lack of success.[30] Contemporary authors who use the approach of reviewing historical material to bring clarity to current issues involving the laity, may expect difficulties too. Interpreting one's own context is inherently problematic. A "hermeneutical distancing" is needed to bring both historical texts and contexts into full perspective.[31] At the same time, a contemporary understanding is not only possible but vital to the active appropriation of a living tradition.

Newman's difficulties are also understandable in more practical terms, however. The authorities of his time in England were not in agreement with his ideas; the laity did not gain the status of partners in their deliberations on educational policy. Even more importantly, in a wider context Newman did not win support for his notion that the laity should be brought into the deliberations of the church officials as active, informed contributors.

A decade later the First Vatican Council defined the trend toward centralization and strong papal authority that clearly did not intend to distribute responsibility for doctrine to the laity. The concepts of authority that developed in the Church, continuing up until Vatican II, remained focused on centralized authority and were unsympathetic to such insights as Newman's, even when the notion of the *sensus fidelium* itself was accepted. Difficulties in the current Church are in many ways extensions and complications of the issues that concerned Newman.[32]

## MODERN ANTECEDENTS FOR THE CONTEMPORARY PLURALISTIC CONTEXT

Jan Walgrave has pointed out that Newman's treatment in *On Consulting the Faithful on Matters of Doctrine* was designed to deal with the plurality of views and emphases concerning the *sensus fidelium* in his day. The characteristics he cites as defining the phenomena are linked to the views of particular advocates for different perspectives. For instance, in explaining that the *consensus fidelium* is a testimony to the fact of apostolic dogma, he seeks to make a connection with the emphasis of Giovanni Perrone who represented the Roman scholastic approach to doctrine of the time. Walgrave notes that Newman does not make this connection explicit. Perrone intended that believers should express their commitment to apostolic doctrine by adhering to the dogmas of the faith. Newman's own view was more nuanced. In another point, when referring to the sense of the faithful as an instinct or *phronema*, he follows Moehler in his *Symbolik*.[33] This *phronema* lies "deep in the bosom of the mystical body of

Christ," and is to be regarded as linked to apostolic dogma, as a direction of the Holy Spirit, as an answer to prayer, and as a jealousy of error.[34] Owen Chadwick notes how Newman's historical instincts were never reconciled with the scholastic approach of Perrone, even though the two remained friends.[35] The lack of acceptance of Newman's views is a precursor of the lack of reconciliation of such perspectives that continues today.

In the time between Vatican I and Vatican II, acceptance of a role to be played by the *sensus fidelium* was part of standard Roman Catholic descriptions of tradition. Yet its operation was linked to a particular view of the role lay involvement plays in doctrinal development. In 1912 Jean Bainvel wrote of the "deposit of faith":

> The deposit of faith is not an inanimate thing passed from hand to hand; it is not, properly speaking, an assemblage of doctrines and institutions consigned to books or other monuments. Books and monuments of every kind are a means, an organ of transmission, they are not, properly speaking, the tradition itself. To better understand the latter it must be represented as a current of life and truth coming from God through Christ and through the Apostles to the last of the faithful who repeats his creed and learns his catechism.[36]

Bainvel describes the tradition as living in the spirit and heart of actual believers, and yet it is in these individuals only in so far as they are possessors of the common sentiment of the Church. He asserts that the Church, through its members, and guided by grace, "recognizes as by instinct" what is truly part of the tradition.[37]

This instinct serves as the root of Newman's description of the sense of the faith. He does not claim, however, a role for the faithful that is autonomous from the influence of God, history or the magisterium. His argument is for the *conspiratio* of pastors and laity in the Church, working as a unit to express the movement of the Spirit. Yet, Newman describes a role for the laity that is distinct, though not autonomous.[38] Without recognition of a genuine instinct and expression of doctrine in the large body of believers, the students of tradition would look in vain for the uninterrupted carrying on of the faith in the history of the Church. In the foundational case described by Newman, many bishops would have been found in error in the Arian crisis. Though some pastors were faithful, the body of ordinary believers was the site of orthodoxy in a controversial and confusing period.[39]

In more recent times, dependence on the faithful to support a doctrine claimed for the tradition was cited by Pius XII in his promulgation of the dogma of the Assumption of Mary.[40] As Pius IX had done in Newman's own time, when defining the Immaculate Conception, the pope found in the consensus of believers living proof for a doctrine, where the Bible and history offered limited support.

Vatican II spoke in several places of the role of the sense of the faithful. Its link with the infallibility that Christ gives his Church was reiterated in the Dogmatic Constitution on the Church, *Lumen Gentium*, where the Fathers affirm, "The body of the faithful as a whole, anointed as they are by the Holy One (cf. 1 Jn. 2:20, 27), cannot err in matters of belief." The passage adds that this supernatural sense characterizes the people as a whole "when, 'from the bishops down to the last member of the laity,' it shows universal agreement in matters of faith and morals."[41] With the Second Vatican Council, responsibility for the faith was given to all, with the "division of labor" between the *Ecclesia docens* and the *Ecclesia discens* being challenged, even where hierarchical language and office were retained.[42] Interest in the faith of the people as a whole has not, in fact, been limited to pastors or to theologians, however. A growing number of the laity may now be expected to initiate input, and not wait to be consulted.[43]

## The Need for Contemporary Criteria for Discerning the *Sensus Fidelium*

The post-Vatican II Church has inherited a dual legacy. The sense of the faithful is accepted as a theological source and has received authoritative use in recent memory. Yet, there is disagreement as to how the laity should be involved in developing and expressing, as well as living, Church teaching.[44] This disagreement is tied to the question of whether the laity are to be consulted as active or passive contributors, or indeed, whether they may initiate input rather than waiting to be asked. The facts of the legitimacy of the *sensus fidelium*, and the impulse toward an active laity since Vatican II are yet to be harmonized.

The sense of the faithful has not been invoked by more recent popes to support infallibly declared statements in the post-conciliar Church, but contemporary studies that relate it to official Church teachings are not lacking. Several authors concerned with the *sensus fidelium* have written about it in reference to the response received by Paul VI's *Humanae Vitae*.[45] John Paul II has himself cautioned that the sense of the faithful is not to be equated with a majority opinion.[46] Following Vatican II in describing the vocation of the laity as "interpreting the history of the world in the light of Christ" and as a call to "illuminate and organize temporal realities according to the plan of God, Creator, and Redeemer," he yet emphasizes the role of pastors in leading the people in the process of discernment and providing an authoritative judgment of the "genuineness of its expressions."[47]

It is now clearly necessary to reexamine the way in which the *sensus Ecclesiae*, the insight of the Church, is discovered and expressed through all of its members. Whether or not the faithful are specifically aware of having an active role as a theological source, theologians have begun identifying the reactions of the laity to Church teaching, including disagreement with or even dissent to doctrinal pronouncements, as legitimate activities of the people that should be recognized and allowed to influence Church teaching.[48] The *sensus fidelium* is being presented as a tool for theology, as an active agent, with a conscious contribution to offer. If such a contribution is to be made, new criteria to identify and apply the sense of the faithful must be developed.[49]

The few examples introduced here challenge the notion that the plurality of approaches to the sense of the faithful could be resolved by choosing only one dimension of the tradition. Accumulating the insights from its multifaceted history would do more justice to its meaning, and perhaps provide a key to its ongoing use. These facets will thus be explored as a foundation on which to develop criteria.

New expressions and understandings of the faith of the Church must be in continuity with its tradition. John W. O'Malley has pointed out that Vatican II was distinguished by its awareness of history and of the historical precedents that can serve current issues. At the same time, the Council clearly recognized the reality of change in the world. The continuity that the Church can find with the past in this context is a "developmental continuity."[50] O'Malley states that the Council, particularly in *Gaudium et Spes*, accepted the themes of growth, progress and development as positive contributions developed in the temporal order, and under the inspiration of Pope John XXIII himself, applied these to the Church.[51]

Remaining honest to both the resources of past tradition and current challenges is perhaps more difficult, but no less important after Vatican II than immediately before it when Yves Congar wrote,

> Tradition is ultimately synthetic in its method of growth: it contains both documents and objective facts, both original data and life given through the Holy Spirit, an objective external norm together with a living subject. We could not give an adequate account of Tradition if we were to reduce it to any single one of these constitutive elements.[52]

Vatican II recognized the interplay of objective and subjective elements that fuels the growth of tradition, and it called laity as well as pastors to "contemplation and study" to reach an "intimate sense of spiritual realities which they experience."[53]

## THE APPROACH OF THE PRESENT STUDY

This interplay of objective and subjective, as well as the intertwined responsibilities of laity and pastors contribute to the difficulties in defining the *sensus fidelium*. Additionally, in the historical process through which the sense of the faith forms among believers and develops into a consensus that can then be expressed in doctrinal statements, there are inherent qualities that make interpretation difficult. The underlying philosophical issues that would be necessary for a complete hermeneutical discussion of this process will not be examined here. What will be attempted is an examination of how resources, including the faith of the laity, have been used in the past to bring clarity and expression in doctrinal matters. Past uses may shed light on present reflection on how the faithful contribute to the carrying on of the Church's faith. An attempt will thus be made to develop a sense of the process of tradition that can illuminate the treatment of questions even when their final resolutions can not be known. The focus will be on the way authors in the post-Vatican II Church draw on historical resources. These resources seem to connect them at their roots, and yet separate them in the uses they make of them.

The thesis of the present study is that the plurality of understandings of the *sensus fidelium* may be linked to a selective, partial use of its tradition. When different authors reduce this source of reflection in the Church to any of its single aspects, conflict between them is unavoidable. A wholistic approach to the *sensus fidelium* is necessary in order to reclaim the historical meaning of this concept and to make it available today as a dynamic element in the Church's ongoing tradition.

The post-conciliar context will be considered here in the light of the historical treatments of the sense of the faithful that are available in current scholarship. In Chapters Two and Three the long history of this theological source will be examined to identify the basic elements that have characterized the sense of the faithful as it has been appropriated in the past. The emphasis in Chapter Two will be on recalling the key examples of doctrine and praxis in the Church's history that have come to be recognized as part of the tradition of the sense of the faithful. Chapter Three will identify questions that have been introduced since the Reformation on the nature of tradition itself and the resources within it that are needed for its full appropriation by the Church.

An analysis of the historical issues raised will be given after this overview has been presented. In Chapter Four specific criteria for identifying the sense of the faithful will be derived from its history considered in the light of Vatican II. These criteria will later be used to examine the post-Vatican II discussion. Chapter Five will offer an overview of the descriptions of the sense of the faithful that have developed in the two and a half decades since the Council.

Chapter Six will identify and discuss four major focuses found among these post-conciliar authors. The first three will consist of authors who stress historical issues, a central role of the magisterium, or an extended role for the faithful. The fourth group will be comprised of those who seek a balance between an active body of all the faithful and the Church's leaders. Some reflection will be offered on the ambiguities and difficulties that seem inherent in the approaches of the authors in this last group. Additionally, however, the perspectives offered by those who pursue this fourth "interrelational" focus will be seen to suggest renewed possibilities for understanding the process by which the *sensus fidelium* may be discerned in the contemporary Church.

# CHAPTER 2

# HISTORY OF THE CONCEPT: NEW TESTAMENT THROUGH THE COUNTER-REFORMATION

Any examination of the historical expressions of the sense of the faithful involves sifting a collection of terms that vary in specific meanings, while clustering around a core reality.[1] That core is the ongoing lived instinct of believers that grasps and is penetrated by the truth of the Gospel. Different eras of the Church's history have presented to the faithful, to both its leadership and its larger body of members, those particular challenges, theological problems, and practical problems, that have drawn out diverse aspects or nuances in understanding the faith. These have given rise to an array of expressions associated with the sense of the faithful.

Thus, if contemporary authors do not draw on the sense of the faithful in the same way, this may be partially rooted in the variety of functions this source has served historically. As described previously, not only different names, but differences in nuance have come in succeeding eras; the Patristic age saw an emphasis on the *consensus fidelium*, the Middle Ages on the *sensus fidei*, and the time from the Counter Reformation to the present has emphasized the *sensus fidelium*. Yet, if controversy surrounds current usages, it is not inaccurate to say also, that the appropriation of the sense of the faithful historically has normally not occurred in the Church, until controversy made its functioning necessary. The role played by controversy or a plurality of views will be of key interest in the present historical examination of those situations that have emerged as examples where the sense of the faithful was at work.

This connection between *sensus fidelium* and the conflict that drives doctrinal development is illustrated by those examples that are most commonly recognized as indicating the sense of the faithful.[2] Standard citations of the sense of the faithful often identify it first in Tertullian's *Prescription Against the Heretics* (from around the year 200), where he argued for the use of the Scriptures against heretics. In his study of the *sensus fidei* in Vatican II's *Lumen Gentium*, Jesús Sancho Bielsa claims that the actual words are first found in Vincent of Lerins.[3] The first explicit theological appropriation of the *sensus fidelium* is generally attributed to Melchior Cano. The rise of the field of ecclesiology, of which this appropriation was a part, occurred to remedy the need for definition and support of church identity in response to the Reformation.[4] The active nature of the sense of the faithful in the Church is aptly described in the study of Gustave Thils, *L'Infallibilité du peuple chrétien "in credendo,"* which examines the sense of the faithful in the post-Tridentine era.[5] Newman's five main examples were all from eras where controversy led to new theological expressions in regard to doctrine.

Earlier we saw indications that the theological identification and understanding of the sense of the faithful in contemporary discussion might be colored by the use authors wish to make of it. Historical understandings of the sense of the faithful, and particularly the ways in which it is identified in the past by authors in the modern era, especially since the nineteenth century, are linked to theological issues. Thus, the sense of the faithful falls prey easily to anachronistic interpretations. In modern discussion, this "sense" has been named and described in distinct theological contexts that are connected with the issues and theological interests of authors with specific historical agendas. This examination of the *sensus fidelium* in the various periods of Church history will attempt to consider the issues that give rise to its expression in the original context, as well as take into account the identification of it made by contemporary authors.

## THE SENSE OF THE FAITHFUL AND THE NEW TESTAMENT

A historical examination of this theological source must begin by asking how or if the sense of the faithful was operative in the Church in its earliest communities. Certainly, many authors have drawn on the New Testament to support the notion of the *sensus fidelium*, and to define its meaning.

Modern standard works that predate Vatican II describe the nature and characteristics of the sense of the faithful while drawing on a variety of texts. M. Seckler, in his article "Glaubenssinn," in *Lexicon fuer Theologie und Kirche* cites texts that encourage growth in discernment among believers (Col. 1:9; Phil. 1:9; Eph. 1: 17 f) , the assurance of truth (1 Cor. 2: 17) the presence of the Spirit (John 14:17; 16:13) and an ongoing instinct for the truth (1 John 2:27).[6]

M. Dominikus Koster uses Rom. 12:3ff and 1 Cor. 12:4ff; in his *Volk Gottes in Wachstum des Glaubens* to describe how a body of believers may express many different gifts and still be drawn into unity by the presence of the Spirit.[7]

Clément Dillenschneider in *Le Sens de la foi* discusses some of these same passages, emphasizing the active quality of faith which is demanded by the message of the apostles. Following St. Paul, he writes about how the spiritual sense must be developed; it is not enough to be an infant in the Christian life (1 Cor. 3:1-3). A faith that is fully informed by love is needed in order for the believer to gain that discernment necessary to penetrate what God has revealed.[8]

The Second Vatican Council draws on the standard descriptions of the sense of the faithful and its Scriptural warrants while developing a focus on an active laity. *Lumen Gentium* (# 12) commends to the whole people of God, the prophetic office and responsibility of witnessing to Christ. It notes the role of the laity as it cites 1 John 2:20 and 27 to illustrate the anointing received by the whole body of the faithful which keeps the Church safe from error. This passage speaks of the "supernatural sense of the faith which characterizes the People as a whole, [which] manifests this unerring quality when, 'from the bishops down to the last member of the laity,' it shows universal agreement in matters of faith and morals." This *sensus fidei* is "aroused and sustained by the Spirit of Truth."[9] 1 Thess. 2:13 is quoted to remind readers that it is the word of God and not that of other human beings that is received by believers, while Jude 3 is cited to add that this word was delivered to the saints—to human recipients. The Council Fathers thus link the responsibility for the work which was given to the apostles, to the ministry of those who now have responsibility for it as heirs to their original witness. The Fathers write that the Church "penetrates it more deeply by accurate insights, and applies it more thoroughly to life . . . under the lead of sacred teaching authority to which it loyally defers."[10]

At the same time, *Lumen Gentium* immediately adds that the Holy Spirit sanctifies and leads the People of God through a variety of gifts, and not exclusively through sacraments and Church ministries. 1 Cor. 12:11 and 12:7 are quoted to support the importance of the gifts given to all, in great variety, by the one Spirit. The section is then completed with the reminder that such gifts are to be judged as to their "genuineness and proper use" by those who preside over the Church.[11]

Kevin McNamara has observed that the Council sought here to return to a Pauline doctrine that is aware of and accepting of the reality of a variety of gifts given to the people. Some may be extraordinary, and the passage warns against the rash seeking or use of these. Yet, most importantly, a variety of common gifts are recognized and encouraged.[12] McNamara notes that in describing the infallibility of the Church in this passage, the Fathers recognize those in the hierarchy as members of the whole body of believers, and write to encourage a "harmonious cooperation" of the faithful and the hierarchy.[13] McNamara notes too, that in stressing the prophetic role of all believers, the Council opened a path to better ecumenical relations with the Protestant tradition which has stressed the prophetic role, and with the Eastern Christians who place great importance on *sobornost*.[14]

In a later passage, *Lumen Gentium* returns again to discuss how Christ fulfills his prophetic office through the Church in both laity and the hierarchy. The authors here draw on support from Acts 2:17-18 and Rev. 19:10.[15] These conciliar passages accept again the depth and variety of gifts of the Spirit that characterize the People of God, and the direct connection that exists between the living testimony to Christ and the living out of social and familial responsibilities by the faithful. Several passages are presented to offer support and direction for those responsibilities that each believer has (Eph. 5:16; Col 4:5; and Rom. 8:25), as well as to make clear the opposition involved (Eph. 6:12). Finally, the goal and the hope that leads believers to claim that goal are recalled in Rev 21:1 and Heb. 11:1.[16]

Another document which bears directly on the importance of Scripture in the living tradition of the Church and the sense of the faithful that animates its members in that tradition, is *Dei Verbum*. In an important passage, the active relationship between the tradition and all believers is described (# 8). Luke 2:19 and 51 are cited to describe the response of those who are called to "contemplate and study" and to "treasure" the tradition in their hearts. The connection of these verses to a Marian foundation recalls the significant connection with the Marian devotion and specific doctrines that have been the basis for official appropriations of the sense of the faithful in modern times. One commentator identifies this passage as a description of development of dogma, and notes that the "first medium" of development is contemplation by the faithful, with attention then given to the "preaching of those who have received through the episcopal succession, the sure gift of truth."[17]

In the next section (# 9), the document emphasizes the connection between Scripture and tradition, stepping away from the "two source" understanding which had dominated discussions of revelation after Trent. The work of the Spirit in revealing and sustaining the Gospel message is seen by the Council in wholistic terms.

The Vatican II documents that directly discuss the *sensus fidelium* employ Scripture to support a nuanced relationship of hierarchy and the body of believers considered as a whole. The contemporary discussions that examine the relationship of laity and pastors have found an important guide in these treatments.

## NEW TESTAMENT COMMUNITIES

Certainly, the Scriptures can be mined to support those understandings that have been established historically for the sense of the faithful. Still, the influence of New Testament communities is not limited to their being suppliers of scriptural texts that can give insight into themes that were developed later in the Church's history. The impact of the earliest Christian communities was felt directly in the sub-apostolic and Patristic ages in the body of issues and agendas that were delivered to the next generations by living believers. The churches that immediately followed the apostolic age were contexts for both passing on the Gospel, and for creating the forms that this passing on would take. The acceptance of teachers and the clarification of their roles, the identification of the laity itself as a distinct group in the Church, and the determination of a canon of Scripture were all developments that occurred in the churches over a period of decades and eventually centuries. When the Christian community began it had a variety of roles within it. As it developed variety continued to characterize its structure.[18] The churches that rooted themselves in apostolicity drew their foundations from the first century. In many ways, however, they had to create their own tools for handing on their traditions. One key development was in the office of *episkopos*. The term carries early importance in the New Testament, being attributed to Christ himself (1 Pet. 2:25).[19] Other "overseers" of the flock took their charism from him. At first the leaders who served in this capacity were wandering, charismatic preachers."[20] Yet from the start, the office carried an "impulse" toward permanency. First in the Pauline communities and then more strongly in the churches of the Pastoral letters, the role became an office with specific duties and criteria.[21]

The bishops soon came to hold a clear position of leadership and authority in the community. Bas van Iersel has argued that the community in the New Testament era retained control over the individual leaders, especially through the deliberations of councils. He sees the indications of growing episcopal authority in the Pastorals as exceptions to the norm exhibited in the churches.[22] Some would even go so far as to argue that the New Testament communities' structures would be most effectively translated into contemporary terms, as a democracy.[23] Rudolf Pesch asserts the New Testament emphasis on ministry as service.[24] The principle that governs ministry is, that "service performed in order to build up the Christian community is always official service."[25] He adds that all services done in the Church were seen as "collegial offices."[26] This emphasis on community responsibility and the plurality that characterized the communities even at the end of the New Testament period, is offered to support his judgment that a democratic structure, informed by fraternity and partnership was the norm.[27]

An assessment of the early churches that moves to very different conclusions is offered by Claude Dagens.[28] He finds that the early Church community is most appropriately expressed in modern terms as a hierarchical structure with a strong head. His argument is founded in what he calls the "principle of totality."[29] When the community is attacked, it is not challenged in its parts, but as a whole. To protect the whole, the representative of the community is the key actor. Dagens argues that, "The hierarchy is only *for* communion in the Church."[30] But in relying on the symbolic, representative role of the bishop, he moves from an argument about the bishop's suitability and sufficiency in acting for the community, to his necessity. He shifts from the genuine role exercised on behalf of the group, to one that is offered as the sole voice sufficient to protect and guide them. No role is left to the community itself. The data from the early communities has been interpreted in almost opposite ways. The indications are clear, however, that the evolution of office eventually moved from leaders (like Paul) who led by charismatic gifts, drawing the community as a whole to work and act together in key decisions, toward a system which developed by the second century, where individuals held responsibility for upholding apostolic tradition in the face of false teaching.[31]

Even when the bishop's role was clarified and strengthened, the congregation retained its importance. This occurred in a context where the authority of civil magistrates was absolutized. At the same time, in the parallel ecclesial setting, the bishop remained responsible to the people, and they retained both a freedom and responsibility in the community.[32]

Thomas Rausch has discussed the development of ministry into the three-fold structure of bishop, presbyter and deacon, which found acceptance by the end of the second century.[33] He points out, however, that not all communities were quick to accept this structure as the best way to resolve the challenges of gnosticism and montanism. Rausch cites a loss of the "Pauline concept of the multiplicity of charisms" as one casualty in the development of the churches' uniform ministerial structure. Another was the availability of ministry of women.[34]

Two communities are examined by Rausch that are important to current discussions of co-responsibility in the Church. The experiences of both are found in the New Testament texts that are often cited in the defining of the sense of the faithful. Both illustrate important issues in their resistance to the structure that was eventually accepted in the early churches.

Corinth is one community which faced schism, and received correction in the form of the letter of Clement of Rome around 96 A.D. Rausch notes that this church "which has become for some the paradigm of the charismatically structured community," had experienced problems regarding unity in Paul's day, and faced them again forty years later.[35] He observes that in the church's acceptance of leaders according to the advice Clement gave, the community accepted the principle of apostolic succession of Clement.[36]

This succession is characterized by the link of the bishop and the tradition in Clement's statement:

> The Apostles preached to us the Gospel received from Jesus Christ, and Jesus Christ was God's Ambassador. Christ, in other words, comes with a message from God, and the Apostles with a message from Christ. . . . From land to land, accordingly, and from city to city they preached, and from among their earliest converts appointed men whom they had tested by the Spirit to act as bishops and deacons for the future believers. And this was no innovation, for, a long time before the Scripture had spoken about bishops and deacons; for somewhere it says: I will establish their overseers in observance of the law and their ministers in fidelity.[37]

Interestingly, in the previous paragraph, Clement writes, "Each of us, brethern, must in his own place endeavor to please God with a good conscience, reverently taking care not to deviate from the established rule of service" (1 Clement 41: 1).[38] Each believer has a distinct place, yet this believer must find expression in the rule of service that is subject to overseers in the community. Good conscience is already an aspect that is central to this service.

The Johannine community serves as another example of grudging acceptance of the three-fold structure. Rausch describes it as the community that "may come closest to being an egalitarian discipleship."[39] He draws heavily on the insights of Raymond Brown as he examines the movements in this group from a "community of disciples guided by the Spirit" to one that fell into schism around the year 100, which left part of it gnostic.[40] Brown maintains that with the dissolving of the community the members addressed by the Johannine epistles learned the importance of an authoritative teaching office.[41]

Solutions in each case were found by recourse to identifiable leaders who could be linked to the authority of the apostles, but who had to exercise authority in new, stronger ways, in order to meet emerging problems. Clearly, these ministries were seen as needed for the sake of the community.

One of the key contributions made by the New Testament churches to succeeding generations was a strong emphasis on community, or *koinonia*. Friedrich Hauck describes the important, practical meaning this fellowship held in the early churches, particularly as it is apparent in the writings of St. Paul.[42] The association of a believer with the community is a participation in fellowship with Christ himself. This is not done in some "mystical absorption" but through the identification of the believer's life with Christ's. in a present personal possession of salvation, with a further fulfillment to be found in the future.[43] Paul uses the word also in his salutations to describe the firmness and "good standing" of those he addresses in the faith.[44]

He builds on this use to connect this faith with the table fellowship of the Eucharist. Hauck remarks that it is self-evident to Paul that participants in a cultic meal "become companions of the god" evoked. Those who take part in pagan meals are associated with the pagan gods; hence, in 1 Cor. 10: 21, his readers are warned to avoid the sacrifices made to idols. The meal celebrated as a communion with Christ is similarly a union with both the exalted Christ and the "earthly and historical Christ who had body and blood."[45] This union necessarily entails a fellowship and bond with the others at the table, and this is much more than a "mere bond of friendship."[46] Other structures pale in comparison. In Phlm. 17, Paul refers to the bond between himself and a slave, whose most important relationship to him is as a brother in the faith. In Romans (15:27) Paul calls on mutual sharing among Jewish and Gentile converts, in concrete, material terms as an expression of *koinonia*.[47]

The connection between the apostle and the community he serves is especially telling in connection with the collections that Paul discusses.[48] These collections represent and carry out a reciprocal relationship. The community receives spiritual gifts from the apostle, and returns to him the material gifts he needs. The sharing of fellowship is given practical expression in this giving, and in the collecting done for other communities. Hauck further examines how in 1 John, *koinonia* describes a "living bond" that characterizes Christian fellowship, which is in fact fellowship with God. The communion with Christ that begins in the present world extends into eternity where it will be fulfilled completely.[49]

J. Coppens describes the difficulties that scholarly treatments have encountered in understanding the nature of the community described in Acts.[50] The early Christian community has been characterized as having a unanimity of heart and spirit in the Lord. The members held their property in common, certainly in the sense that what they had was offered for the use of others, but in a more radical sense as well, as some gave up what they had completely, to serve the community.[51] He notes that the idealization of the community has been attributed to projection upon it the Greek "ideal of friendship." Comparisons with other models have also been offered to explain the image that is given in Acts.

Coppens speaks for a balance, an awareness of the pressures and the strengths that were particular to the new faith community in its context.[52]

This historically rooted, practical faith is discussed by Yves Congar as the "principle or norm of allegiance" that was to be described as the "rule of faith" in the early Church.[53] The faith is *"that which* the apostles handed down, having received it from Jesus Christ, and the Church has handed down after them, in so far as it is normative for belief." He adds that "tradition also transmits cultic rules, disciplinary elements in regard to which legitimate differences may exist between Churches."[54] Congar describes the norms by which the faith of the Church was linked to the faith of the apostles as being:

> (a) its conformity to what was handed down by the primitive authors, who had themselves received it, and thus back to the very start; (b) the succession of presbyters or episcopes who teach the Church; (c) recourse to the Scriptures, which contain all wholesome truth.[55]

Congar goes on to argue that it was not the bishops themselves who were the guarantors of truth or faithfulness; many in history have been connected with heresy or schism. Rather, the substance of what is handed down—the *paradosis* is the object of appeal found in the bishops themselves. This *paradosis* has the Spirit as its support. The bishops find their authority in the tradition; the tradition does not take authority from them.[56]

In the earliest centuries, the faith handed on from the first witnesses was understood as the focus and source of life for the community. The community created by it was then responsible for it, and the structures of understanding (*paradosis*) and leadership (bishop/presbyter/deacon) existed as source and guide respectively, of its life of faith. Unity was the product of these elements serving the ongoing faith of a living community.

Ludwig Hertling writes that this *koinonia* or *communio* (in Latin) is key to understanding the early Church.[57] He writes,

> *Communio* is the bond that united the bishops and the faithful, the bishops among themselves, a bond that was both effected and at the same time made manifest by eucharistic communion. *Communio* very often means simply the Church itself.[58]

Hertling goes on to describe the close connection and even identification of this concept with the concept of peace. The bond that made community could be otherwise described as a living together in the peace of fellowship. He notes how St. Augustine later, in writing to St. Jerome, referred to a young man who came to him in "Catholic peace," meaning that the man was "a member of the Church, a Catholic and not a heretic."[59]

When modern authors look to the early Church for evidence of a "sense" of the faith, they find it in expressions of *consensus*. This is quite consistent with the focus of the New Testament communities and their immediate successors. The way in which the community carried and handed on its own tradition was tied to its concern for unity in fellowship and belief.

Friedrich Buechsel notes that in the New Testament, *paradosis* "means 'tradition' only in the sense of what is transmitted, not of transmission."[60] He notes that the key point in St. Paul's use of the word, is that the tradition which he speaks has been handed down from the Lord (e.g., 1 Cor. 15:3). Any "tradition" begun by him or any source other than Christ has no validity (Col. 2:8). The churches should hold fast to the teachings that have been handed down; at the same time Bueschel states that Paul saw "no antithesis between pneumatic piety and the high estimation of tradition."[61]

The faith given to the apostles is thus the source of energy in the momentum of tradition. Yet, to consider this primacy is not to separate it from the concepts of community or ministry, but to distinguish it as the result of the Spirit that makes their existence meaningful. The faith of the first Christians was lived in communities. Marie-Louis Gubler has described how these communities were characterized by diversity.[62] In Paul's view the *ekklesia* was the local church, and in a given city there could be several house churches.[63] This is illustrated in Acts 16 by the churches in Phillipi led by Lydia and the jailor, and again in Acts 12 where several churches are seen to exist in Jerusalem, Gubler sees the insistence of Luke on unity in Acts (2:44-47, 4:32) as an exhortation and prescription. The living out of the Gospel in its communities created from the start, the issue of keeping diverse groups unified. The central importance of unity is illustrated by the way Paul dealt with the member of the church at Corinth who was living in an incestuous relationship (1 Cor. 5:3-5), where the apostle teaches that the entire community should be involved in the decision of excommunication.[64] Yet, Gubler argues forcefully that unity did not demand uniformity. The Jerusalem assembly described in Acts, that met to settle the dispute concerning the practices of Gentile and Jewish Christians was resolved with some differences left intact.

Gubler writes that the judgment of the assembly gave a powerful example of sensitivity in saying. "For it seemed good to the Holy Spirit and to us to lay upon you no greater burden . . ." (Acts 15:28).[65] She adds. "From that time on there were different approaches in the Christian *eucumenë*, but a guarantee of solidarity with and for one another."[66]

Gubler goes on to describe the "drift" away from sensitivity and tolerance in the churches which saw a growing mistrust and submission of women, and their loss as possible leaders. She speculates that this may have led to the movement of women into heretical gnostic communities, where they could continue to act as preachers and prophetesses. Gubler sees in the early churches' grappling with unity and diversity a challenge to contemporary practice. She sees the limiting of leadership to men as a move away from the unity in diversity in the early Church, to a mere uniformity.[67]

Many authors illustrate the intimate relationship between the expression of the faith tradition and the leadership structures.

In other authors, the contemporary discussion of the roles played by believers in relation to the roles of bishops and other clergy, draws on the early Church for precedents. Because of the evolving nature of ministry in the New Testament Church, these early communities may indeed offer insight into the crucial issues that relate to leadership. Several authors examine these issues with a specific interest in the sense of the faithful.

Jean-Louis D'Aragon considers the role of the *sensus fidelium* in the light of such Gospel passages as Mt 18:18 and John 20: 21-23, which have become standard supporting texts for the exercise of authority by ordained leaders in the Church.[68] D'Aragon argues for balance in the relationship between leaders and the body as a whole, by contrasting a hierarchical model with one that takes as its foundational image the Body of Christ, an image that he presents as being at once more Scriptural and more in keeping with the renewing of ecclesiology at Vatican II. Though respecting the importance of the historically developing magisterium in the Church, he maintains a key distinction between the leaders considered as individuals with power associated with them, and as representatives of the whole body. It is the latter focus that Scripture supports. In the passages in both Matthew and John he finds Jesus' instructions to be more appropriately understood as directed to the body of disciples—to all those given the Spirit, If the decisions made in the Church must be exercised by individual leaders, they are made on behalf of the body. As the Spirit is given to all, so does responsibility fall on all.[69]

In a similar way, Schillebeeckx examines the responsibility for teaching in the early Church. Contrasting first the technical meaning of magisterium—an office legitimately claimed by specific leaders in the Church—and teaching authority, he too maintains that the general authority for teaching resides in the whole Church.[70]

He notes that those given the specific role of teaching in the time of the Apostles could base their authority in charismatic gifts, and were not appointed in any official way by church leaders (Acts 13: 1-3).[71] It is interesting to compare the instructions given in the *Didache* (circa 100 A.D.) which advises the Christian community to examine those who come "in the name of the Lord."[72] Visitors who propose to teach or prophesy are to be welcomed, and then tested for the genuineness of their teaching. Discretion is recommended as a tool for recognizing true teaching among potential candidates.

Schillebeeckx remarks that on into the third century teachers could be ordained or not ordained. He cites the *Traditio* of Hippolytus from the early third century, which refers to *doctores*, teachers of the tradition who could be either lay or clergy.[73]

Alexandre Faivre points out that the term *laikos* is absent from New Testament documents and first appears in Christian writing only in the second century with the first letter of Clement of Rome to the Corinthians.[74] Faivre acknowledges that there are specific titles in the New Testament to describe leaders in the churches. Yet, he argues, the further organization of church structure into a hierarchical system, with laity distinguished specifically from the presbyters, came in Clement's response to a Corinthian church that experienced conflict and even scandal in its leadership. Faivre argues that Clement's main interest is to urge order and stability in Corinth. His distinguishing of laity is no more than an organizational tool that stems from the examples which he takes from the exercise of authority in the military and from the cultic hierarchy of the Old Testament.[75]

Faivre describes the lay person as "a strange being, subject to mutation, born the prisoner of an analogy, conditioned by a climate of conflict, and formed in a cultic environment."[76] He adds that Clement's way of distinguishing substrata in the Christian flock remained dormant, in fact, for another century, until Clement of Alexandria and Tertullian next employed it.[77] Faivre cites 1 Peter in remarking that the focus of the early Church was on the whole people as kleros. In the early Church, particular functions were distinguished within the one body, for the service of the whole.[78]

This whole body was responsible for carrying the tradition, and for living out the implications of the Gospel. The practical terms in which this living tradition was expressed are illustrated again by the instructions that are directed to the members of the Christian community in the *Didache*:

> Accordingly, elect for yourselves bishops and deacons, men who are an honor to the Lord, of gentle disposition, not attached to money, honest and well-tried; for they, too, render you the sacred service of the prophets and teachers. Do not, then, despise them; after all, they are your dignitaries together with the prophets and teachers.
> Furthermore, correct one another, not in anger, but in composure, as you have it in the Gospel; and when anyone offends his neighbor, let no one speak with him—in fact, he should not even be talked about by you—until he has made amends. As regards your prayers and alms and your whole conduct, do exactly as you have it in the Gospel of Our Lord.[79]

George MacRae examines some of the same sources as D'Aragon and Faivre in arguing for a balanced relationship between hierarchical and community based exercise of authority in the early Church.[80] He finds in Mt. 18 a clear warrant for Petrine primacy, yet expresses a view like that of D'Aragon, that Mt. 18: 18 is directed to the entire *ekklesia*, and not only to the disciples.[81] MacRae nuances his discussion of the New Testament churches carefully by first offering four theses that should mitigate a tendency toward prooftexting, or a tendency to see the churches of the New Testament period as all of the same time.[82] There were clearly differences in order in the early Church communities, as illustrated by the differences between the Pauline Epistles and the Pastorals, or again, in the difference in emphasis on local community in 1 Corinthians and on the universal Church in Ephesians.[83]

An ambiguity in Church descriptions has, in fact, led to divergent views of the types of structures that dominated Church leadership and authority. MacRae chooses the church at Corinth as a representative of the complexity that characterizes our view of authority in the early Church. In advising the Church at Corinth in the matter of the incestuous relationship in its midst (1 Cor. 5: 3-5) Paul directs the church to confront the man involved on the strength of the assembled community, in union with his own spiritual authority. MacRae argues that Paul sought not to impose a solution, but to draw out a strong decision in the community. It is a shared responsibility which "rests on the interaction between Paul and the Corinthians, between apostolic authority and local communitarian decision-making," that must deal with the problem in the community.[84]

An opposite position is taken by Myles Bourke.[85] He identifies the Corinthian incident (focusing on 1 Cor. 5: 8-13.) as "the only example of co-responsibility in decision-making furnished by the Pauline corpus."[86] Bourke discusses how the passage where Paul advises the Corinthians is ambiguous, and after discussing several exegetes on matter, argues a preference for a more "dictatorial" Paul.[87] The reference to the community is "hardly more than parenthetical"; Bourke compares the passage to other parts of the letter in claiming that Paul was not hesitant to use his own authority.[88]

Bourke qualifies his own judgment by saying that there is no reason to resolve the passage's ambiguity leniently, on the basis of an *a priori* view that Paul would hesitate to act apart from the consensus of the community. He is apparently contrasting his approach with those who hold such a view. Yet, he adds that Paul did want the community to join him in passing judgment; there is a concern for a "collegial exercise of authority."[89] Bourke thus finds in this case a concern for co-responsibility, though one in which the weight of the community's initiative is qualified. He borrows a phrase from W. D. Davies, in saying that Paul wanted the community to share his judgment, based in a "common climate of thought."[90]

In a similar argument, Bourke examines Mt. 18:15-20 as an example of church authority operating in the context of the whole community, to discipline a member of the community. He argues that verse 18:18 was originally connected to neither the verses immediately before nor after it, and that the passage is a church-formulation that should not be attributed to Jesus. Bourke asserts that reading 18:18 in the context of the entire Gospel, with its emphasis on the twelve, and particularly 28:16-20, where Jesus commissions the eleven to exercise authority, leads to the conclusion that "it is hard to think that the saying of 18:18 did not apply only to them and to those who would continue their mission in the church."[91]

Thus, while Bourke notes that the procedure used by the community to reach its decisions is not spelled out in the text, it is most likely that these occurred by the authorities leading the others in making such decisions.[92] Some interaction is likely, but Matthew does not give "a broad basis on which to build a theory of co-responsibility in decision-making."[93]

Bourke also takes up the issue of co-responsibility as illustrated in the account of the "Council" of Jerusalem, in Acts 15: 1-35. He argues that the Council speeches are literary constructions of Luke, with limited historical weight. Yet, the acceptance of Luke's account as canonical literature, as part of the New Testament, significantly demonstrates the Church's acceptance of the author's understanding of how decisions should be set in a context of co-responsibility.[94]

In this account, the Council advises the Church at large, on behalf of "the apostles and presbyters, together with the whole church" (Acts 15:22). Bourke points out that the decree itself that follows in Acts 15:23 is sent from the leaders with no mention of the whole Church. He adds that it is not certain that this omission is significant; the concern of Luke here is to show that the Gentile mission was accepted by the Jerusalem church. The process is clearly indicated in verse 22, as one in which the entire community played a part.[95]

Bourke concludes that a church assembly that excludes the active participation of the laity "does not meet the standards set by Luke" in this account.[96] He adds that in the exercise of authority the Church should be particularly careful to include theologians, those teachers who like the *didaskoloi* of 1 Cor. 12:28 rank after apostles and prophets. He argues that the charisms that exist outside of the hierarchy must be drawn on now as they were in New Testament churches.[97]

MacRae recounts how the charismatic gifts are described in the New Testament, as linked to both the laying on of hands in the case of ministers (2 Tim. 1: 6-7) and to the reception of some spiritual gift by each believer (1 Cor. 7:7).[98] He adds, "It is the common possession of the gifts of the Spirit *for a common purpose* which grounds our principle of shared responsibility in the church."[99] The possession of the Spirit is the first of two theological warrants that MacRae finds in the New Testament for this notion of shared responsibility. He describes a second in the Pauline image of the Body of Christ. Four implications for the members of the body come from this image. There is an emphasis on unity of all members, since all share the same Spirit. There is an interdependence of the members. All members have a dignity that comes from their sharing of the Spirit. The authority functioning in the body is Christ's.[100]

MacRae notes that this doctrine of the church was created by Paul to describe the local church. He observes that this local responsibility "must not be sacrificed to a total concern for central authority in the universal church."[101] The link of local churches to each other can not be reduced to "merely an organizational structure." That link rather, is the bond that identifies each community, the oneness of Christ. MacRae notes that it is with this understanding that Paul addresses his letters to "the church *of God* which is at Corinth."[102]

MacRae emphasizes the tentative quality in his study and stresses that clear evidence concerning the structures and functions of church order in the earliest churches is "singularly lacking." He notes too, that while "the danger of the argument from silence" is great, "in theology that argument has been used "nowhere so frequently as in New Testament ecclesiology."[103]

These concerns are shared by Jeremy Moiser in his study of the role played by the laity in the establishment of the New Testament canon.[104] Moiser examines both the Eastern and Western sources from the first four centuries that have had an impact on the issue of the establishment of a canon of Scripture.[105] His specific purpose is to determine the "contributions of the clergy, individually and synodically" and those of the laity "as individuals and as depository of the '*sensus fidelium.*'"[106] Interestingly, Moiser defines the *sensus fidelium* "in contradistinction" to the clergy.[107]

After a discussion of the primary sources in the first centuries, Moiser concludes that the "impetus" toward an official canon appears to have come from bishops, with occasional input from "other individuals in positions of clerical or academic authority."[108] He adds that "nothing specific can be deduced concerning the degree to which the clergy relied on the faithful" in determining the canon, "beyond general considerations on the nature of church authority in the early centuries."[109]

MacRae, in sifting the New Testament evidence, recognizes the absence of proof of any connections, and relies on principles of New Testament interpretation that admit the plurality of ecclesiologies and the developing methods for recognizing authority in the period.[110] He emphasizes a Pauline ecclesiology based in "building up the body of Christ."[111] Moiser traces the variety of views on the acceptance of a canon and the developing roles of bishops as the bearers of authority in these first centuries, though interestingly, he adds in a note that in a later age, Melchior Cano supported the idea that the pope and bishops alone could determine canonicity.[112] Moiser does observe, "It is doubtful whether one can intelligibly maintain that the expression of the *sensus fidelium* is to be sought precisely in the episcopal and presbyteral pronouncements we have considered."[113]

MacRae and Moiser both note the silence in their respective texts and illustrate a need to find a principle of interpretation that might give a clue as to lay involvement, or specifically, the sense of the faithful, in its relationship to official authority. Moiser ends his discussion by noting that the Christian canon is formed at the same time that episcopal authority was becoming defined and accepted. He finds the chronological closeness of these two developments to be important.

MacRae finds the image of the Body of Christ in Paul's writings compelling. Both authors draw precedents for a modern stance on the sense of the faithful from sources that are silent on the specific issue of lay involvement and multi-voiced on related issues. From the expressions that derive from these communities and that are extant now in the writings of early church leaders, it is not possible to discern the process, or more likely, the processes, that served as background to the forming of those expressions. The existence of some variety in known structures and the evidence of development in structures even with the New Testament itself add importance to understanding the themes that were more obviously important to the early churches.

The themes of unity, apostolicity and catholicity that came to be central in the *communio* are tied to central concerns of a living community confronted with challenges from within and without. Thomas Rausch describes well the early stages of development in the Christian communities, as they grappled with the responsibilities left to them as the apostolic age ended.[114] In the Pastoral epistles there is a move to concern for the "objectified" understanding and expression of the faith, which was now seen in terms of a "deposit."[115]

A key element of the living community has been discussed by George Tavard, who has noted that modern exegetical work has shown the vital link between liturgy and the New Testament. He states that it can be maintained "with considerable probability" that the canon of the New Testament was selected "partly for a liturgical purpose and according to principles borrowed from a liturgical experience."[116] Tavard describes the transmitting of apostolic tradition as one work with several expressions.[117] Tradition certainly includes the handing on of doctrine. Yet, it is expressed most centrally in worship, in the reading of Scripture at Mass and in "the *traditio corporis et sanguinis Christi*, the breaking of the bread and the drinking of the wine."[118] The liturgy also carries a "*traditio Spiritus*, a 'tradition' or communication of the Spirit."[119]

Tavard describes how the living tradition is found specifically in the liturgical living of the community. This foundation illustrates the need to understand the role of liturgical leaders, their selection, and the extent of activities for which the individual "ordinary" believers were responsible. Yet, it focuses these questions on what appears to be much surer ground: the importance of community itself, as bearer of tradition.

## The Sense of the Faithful and the Patristic Era

Biblical ecclesiologies, and in particular those elements of Scripture that are adduced to support a strong role for the *sensus fidelium* in the post-Vatican II Church, emphasize that responsibility for truth in the Church is given to the body, with its head, Christ. The active agent in this "sense" is the Holy Spirit. Among the various roles played by members of the body the tasks of leadership are not lacking; the role of apostle that is the foundation for the ordained ministry of today is given pride of place in Pauline theology and is emphasized as ministries evolve in the Pastoral Epistles and later works.

To look back into the earliest centuries for signs of the *sensus fidelium* as it might stand in relationship to magisterium, or even to look for the nature of co-responsibility operating between laity and clergy is a questionable strategy at best. The documents that survive from these churches do not show explicit concern for these issues.

Monika Hellwig has pointed out that the handing on of tradition throughout most of Christian history, and certainly in this early period, was spontaneous. At least part of this responsibility was not reflected upon, but "was taken very much for granted."[120]

## Responsibility for the Tradition

Worship and the ongoing life of faith were the means by which the tradition was carried on in the early communities. Led by the Spirit, preceded by the Apostles, and acted out in the liturgy and common life of believers, the understanding of the Gospel was presented and developed in the context of each new generation of hearers. Hellwig notes that "in the reflection and self-conscious formulation of preachers, teachers, and writers," emphasis was given to "the authoritative handing on of the 'rule of truth' or the 'interpretation of

Scripture.'" There was not the same interest in "the process of formulation of the rule or interpretation."[121]

This process was itself born of necessity in what has been called a "crisis" of authority. Gerald Bray identifies the early churches' efforts to understand their own use of sources for tradition as what current theology would call a "hermeneutical debate."[122] Issues of how to claim historical roots, what role to give human reason, and how to understand the "finality" of the apostles' original preaching were fuel for this crisis and ongoing debate.[123] The nature of ministry and particularly the role of bishops were defined in the early centuries, but these were always informed by the "popular feeling" in the Church.[124] Bray asks what may be seen as a circular hermeneutical question: how was popular feeling to be determined? He asks too, "Why was Athanasius right and everybody else wrong?"[125] Bray maintains that the struggle for clarity was governed by the idea of the *regula fidei*. He emphasizes the point that it was trust in the rule of faith, rather than the location in Scripture of any particular formulas that might express it, that was vital. The belief that the faith could be encapsulated in a short rule later fueled the development of the creeds themselves in the great councils.[126] What this dependence on the rule of faith demonstrates clearly, is the importance placed by the early Church on the faith as its foundation, even while it found tools in office and expressions to organize and identify itself in the midst of controversy.

When the community and its faith were challenged by persecution, division, or heresy the key focuses for the theologizing of the Church were the unity of the body and the roots of the apostolic faith.

Robert Eno vividly describes the context of plurality and change that characterized the early Christian centuries. The second century saw a movement from the first descriptions of structure by Ignatius of Antioch to the acceptance of the standard ministry of bishops, presbyters and deacons in nearly all churches by the end of the century.[127] A diversity of structures of ministry in the various Christian churches moved toward standardization in response to pressure from without.

Yet just as important as the challenges from without that would feed the development of understanding of who should carry authority, were the conflicts and dissensions from within the communities. Eno notes that descriptions of the idyllic, loving Christian community appear in apologetic literature such as Tertullian's *Letter to Diognetus* while pagan contemporaries of the Church saw conflict as a "built-in" aspect of Christianity. He quotes the emperor Julian's view that the best way to combat Christianity was to let it be destroyed by its own inner turmoil.[128] Eno quotes Augustine's later observation that "many who wish to become Christians are compelled by their dissensions to hesitate."[129]

It was in a climate of conflict that the Church examined the issue of who had the authority to express the tradition of the Apostles.[130] Eno argues that it was an effort to maintain the historic reality of the Gospels in the face of the challenges of the Gnostic mythological framework, that Irenaeus, Tertullian and others emphasized the office of monarchical bishop. This office grew in importance as a focus for understanding apostolic succession.

Within a context of controversy and innovation, the Church sought to conserve the truths of the Gospel. The identifying of the bearers of the tradition of the Apostles was linked to the local churches founded by the Apostles. Those persons in the churches who were identified as responsible for preaching and teaching these traditions were stressed as the focus of authority "in the pragmatic need to avoid schism."[131] According to Eno, the episcopate originated "from the church's own realization of its need to maintain order through structure to survive the threat of anarchy."[132] The growing attention to the problem is illustrated by some who found the emphasis on structure to be too great, as in the case of the rising Montanist controversy.[133]

The development of the episcopate, and the recognition of its role in passing on the apostolic tradition is discussed by Johannes Remmers, as he describes an intrinsic link of bishops to the identity of the whole Church.[134] The core of what has been received from the Apostles is their mission.[135] The evangelization of the whole world is not limited to the apostles, but must be carried on by others who come after them. Remmers describes their particular office by citing two characteristics that he takes from Edmund Schlink; "(1) eyewitness to the resurrection of Jesus Christ and (2) a mission given by the risen one."[136] The community that has come into existence through the work of the apostles has, through baptism, been handed a responsibility for the Gospel.[137]

This responsibility has its root in the call of the Gospel. The Christ event is the "seed" which is planted in history, which has an impact that goes through history to transform lives, and which transcends history by its eschatological nature.[138] Remmers emphasizes that the early Church's concept of *paradosis* held this Christ event, this realization of God's plan of salvation, as the central reason for the continuation of the apostolic mission. Importantly, this concept of *paradosis* predated that of succession.[139] The Christ event established a community of persons which continues to invite others to enter it.[140]

Remmers goes on to observe that Irenaeus connected the idea of tradition in the form of doctrine with a more general view of apostolicity. Remmers states that, "Irenaeus even more than the other Pre-Nicene Fathers, sees all of Christianity from the very beginning as the transmission and the unfolding of a single reality."[141] This single reality is expressed by the community. Remmers draws on Cyprian's description of that same community and comments. "It is not an amorphous mass of loosely connected believers; it is a structured community with various services and offices."[142] Peter Stockmeier has noted that the connection of tradition and apostolic succession is based in a "historically unfounded" view that truth is passed directly to each bishop from his predecessor.[143] The community is responsible, yet this responsibility becomes more and more focused in the bishop.

In a letter cited by Remmers, Cyprian speaks of the role of the bishop, saying:

> You ought to know, then, that the bishop is in the Church and the Church in the bishop; and if someone is not with the bishop, he is not in the Church. They vainly flatter themselves who creep up, not having peace with the priests of God, believing that they are secretly in communion with certain individuals. For the Church, which is One and Catholic, is not split nor divided, but is indeed united and joined by the cement of priests who adhere one to another.[144]

Unity is obviously the key theme here, and Cyprian argues that the bishop is at the core of that unity. Remmers states that the Church met the Gnostic challenge of around 175 A.D. with the systematic development of the understanding of apostolic succession in the hierarchy. This hierarchy is seen precisely to serve this unity. It is the responsibility of the whole Church to be one, and to bear the tradition in a unified way. Remmers thus observes that "the agreement of the whole community [was] the proof and the criterion" of the authenticity of the traditions expressed.[145]

Remmers emphasizes that the work of the Spirit in bringing the Church to truth does not happen "through mediation of the hierarchy." He quotes J.C. Groot in saying, "In the Church as 'communio', the presence of the Spirit is the fruit of a direct, immediate sending as happened at Pentecost."[146] The whole Church has an active responsibility for the truth. Remmers here recognizes the impact on the modern issue of infallibility, and adds, "The Church as a whole, therefore, does not have a secondary, passive share in the gift of infallibility—simply obeying what she hears from the hierarchy."[147]

He notes that the notion of a passive role is inconsistent with Vatican II, as he draws on the passage in *Lumen Gentium* (# 12) which describes the universal belief of the faithful. He assesses this universal belief then, from a historical perspective;

> Although the infallible teaching and guidance of the official magisterium is included here too, one cannot make the *consensus fidelium* entirely dependent on the teaching activity of the hierarchy. To do this would be to contradict the primacy and normative character of the community as a whole.[148]

From this historical assessment, Remmers argues for a returned emphasis on the Church's unity and the integration of roles. Specifically, Remmers charges that the early Church's insights have not been received.[149]

Remmers argues for an understanding of the Church that recaptures an insight seen previously in Faivre, "The People of God, to which the laity and clergy belong, is neither lay nor clerical itself."[150] He maintains that to be true to the Church's history, apostolic succession of the whole community should be given precedence over . . . hierarchical succession."[151]

One area that remained central to the identity of the community from the time of the New Testament communities through the following centuries was the expression and creation of identity in its liturgical life. Here too, diversity has been the common experience. Bruno Kleinheyer has described that most foundational of Christian liturgical events, the Eucharistic prayer, as an example of diversity and development.[152] He cites the *Apologia* of Justin Martyr as evidence that at an early stage in development, the celebrant created the prayer himself. Yet, Kleinheyer adds, it is most likely that such celebrants "did not follow their own inclinations, but prayed so that the community could recognize its faith in the prayer said on behalf of all."[153] The "Amen" voiced by the congregation was a living witness to the reality of the event occurring.

Hippolytus in the *Apostolic Tradition* emphasizes too, that the words of the prayer are not as vital as the connection with the faith of the community which they are to express.[154]

Controversy could also be expressed in liturgical contexts. The Eucharistic prayer contained the names of those bishops who led the churches which were in communion with the one celebrating the Eucharist. When sufficient disagreements occurred, the bishop's name was removed from the list of those to be included in the prayer.[155]

*Communio* continued to be a primary concern of the Church as it developed the strategies of office and practice that gave it identity in Patristic times. This was vividly expressed in the controversy over Easter. Peace was brought to the Church following the conflict of the bishops Anicetus of Rome and Polycarp of Smyrna, not by their resolving the debate over the dating, but by their agreeing to be at peace. Unity of heart was considered more important that ritual observance.[156] One commentator has observed, that while documents that would give the details of reconciliation are not extant, we have been left with evidence of a strong tradition that peace was achieved in the face of very real difficulties.[157] To achieve a genuine unity in the Church, uniformity was sacrificed.[158]

Even during periods where the Church enjoyed great unity, plurality characterized both its teaching and practice. Jean-Marie Tillard has examined this abiding plurality with an eye to the underlying issues.[159] When discussing the controversy over the dating of Easter, he notes that Irenaeus claimed that differences in the practice of fasting between Christian communities was evidence for a common faith. The intensity of disagreement illustrated a passion for living the faith—a faith that was held in common.[160]

Appeals to unity or consensus in the body led to an explicit rule for supporting the faith during the early centuries. As a response to crises, the responsibility for defending the faith became the role of "experts."[161] Yet, those with this responsibility held it in relation to the community. It is to the community's faith, the *dogma populare*, that St. Augustine appeals—to the faith held "from the bishops to the last lay believer."[162]

With the "division of labor" that occurred with a hierarchy of ministers came the rise of the exercise of co-responsibility. The expression of this ecclesial characteristic is illustrated in the way in which bishops were selected and by the activities that were undertaken by lay people.

## ELECTION OF BISHOPS

The election of bishops in the first centuries has received significant attention in the wake of Vatican II, whose ecclesiology has drawn on the recovery of patristic insights that preceded the Council and supported much of its renewal. The importance of historical studies on the work of the Council is described by John W. O'Malley, who views the approach of Vatican II to doctrine as unique in church history.[163] He writes, "For the first time in an ecumenical council, therefore, doctrinal positions had to formulated with as much concern for historical context and process as for their validity in terms of traditional metaphysics."[164] Of specific interest here is the way in which contemporary authors draw on the election of bishops as an illustration of the sense of the faithful.[165]

As noted before, explicit understanding of the sense of the faithful in a developed ecclesiological sense is not to be found in the Fathers.[166] Yet, the election of bishops illustrates that the whole Church was involved in the first century, in an area that has come to be recognized in current ecclesiology as an expression of the *sensus fidelium*.

Julio Eugui has studied the election of bishops in the first five centuries at length, with an emphasis on the role of local communities in the process. He first looks to the selection of Matthew to take the place of Judas among the twelve and the establishment of the first deacons as illustrations of the criteria used by the earliest communities to select their leaders.[167] In the first case, he notes that the apostles take the actual choice of a successor out of the hands of humans and place it under the direct will of God, by casting lots. In both this case and the selection of deacons, prior to any selection of candidates, was the establishment of the criteria of their good reputation in the community and their solidarity in the Gospel. Reputation was a key factor in the qualifications of these leaders. Eugui notes that in these cases, and again in the ministries of Paul and other leaders in the Church, the members of the local communities were called on to judge the suitability of candidates.[168]

Hard historical information on early elections is scarce.[169] Up until the third century the only sources extant on the topic are found in Clement of Rome and in the *Didache*.[170] In examining the case of Clement (letter to the Corinthians, 44), Eugui points out that while there is disagreement among translators and commentators concerning the understanding of the office of bishop and its relationship and weight in comparison to apostolic authority, it is clear that Clement understood the consent of the whole community to be essential to the acceptance of bishops and presbyters in their ministries. Unfortunately, Clement does not describe how this consent of the community was expressed. His purpose in writing, was to emphasize the divine origin of the offices discussed.[171] Eugui notes that in the key passages on election of bishops in the *Didache* there is a strong warrant for the involvement of the whole community, while there is little said about process.[172]

Robert Eno cites the selection of ministers by the people as a key example of shared responsibility in the early Church. He observes that episcopal elections that are better documented from the third and fourth centuries exhibit variety in their methods. The principle of popular involvement, however, was seen as important in churches in all areas.[173]

This general acceptance of co-responsibility is discussed by Raymund Kottje.[174] He notes that there is "clear evidence" that in the election of the bishop of Rome in the third century everyone in the community was allowed to vote. He is quick to add, however, that this right should not be confused with "the universal suffrage of a modern democracy."[175] Peter Stockmeier takes up this point also, in his overview of the history of episcopal election.[176] He finds it unfortunate that the discussion of election of bishops has been too closely tied to the ideas of democratization of the Church. The question of election thus has "incurred guilt by association."[177] He notes in particular the criticism made by Joseph Ratzinger, of those who see an ostensible identity of the sociological concept 'people' with the 'people of God.'"[178] Stockmeier emphasizes that in the election of bishops in the early Church there was no view that the office was "conferred 'from below.'" The central notion was that the Holy Spirit worked through the actions of the whole Church.[179]

This acceptance of the Spirit's role is not expressed in a passive way. Lay initiative played a key role in the process of selecting bishops. Eusebius recounts a third century event, where the bishop of Jerusalem, Narcissus, was seen to be growing too old to continue his responsibilities. When a Cappadocian bishop, Alexander, came into the area on a pilgrimage, members of the community prevailed on him to replace the bishop. Other local bishops consented to the change.[180]

Cyprian is by far the most important source for information on the election of bishops in the third century Church.[181] Though Cyprian was tireless in his work for orthodoxy, as demonstrated in the controversy over the *lapsi*, he tolerated "diversity, change of mind, even dissent," in the church under his care.[182] His desire for unity was evident in his inclusion of any channel through which the

Spirit might be expressed, whether such sources were lay or clerical. According to the writings of Cyprian himself, the practice of popular elections was the normal process over a wide geographical area, including Spain, Africa and Rome.[183]

Patrick Granfield connects Cyprian's own treatment of the topic to that of Hippolytus' *Apostolic Tradition*. The translation of the *Tradition* into Arabic, Coptic and Ethiopic languages may suggest that elections occurred not just in the West, but in Egypt and Syria as well. Granfield also notes that Origen apparently indicates the existence of elections in the Egyptian Church in his letter, *Homilia in Leviticum* (6,3).[184] Granfield notes that Cyprian did not consider lay participation in elections of bishops a condition of their validity, yet he argued for it "in strong terms" as "an ideal." His letters contain material concerning elections in his day as well as the expression of his own strong advocacy.[185]

In Cyprian's descriptions of episcopal elections, terms are used which designate specific roles for clergy (*cleri suffragium* and *clericorum testimonium*), laity (*suffragium* and *testimonium et iudicium*), and bishops (*collegarum testimonium et iudicium* and *coepiscoporum consensus*). Granfield adds that the most important term was the *divinum iudicium*. He states, "the divine judgment was seen as the final confirmatory seal on the community's choice."[186] Operating in an unstable and confusing period in which Roman persecution had led to the "lapse" of many into heresy, Cyprian sought a wide base of stability and unity in establishing leadership for the church.[187] Eugui describes the involvement of the community in selecting bishops as a guarantee of the suitability of those chosen. This, he says, was Cyprian's sole motivation for placing importance in popular elections.[188] Granfield finds that Cyprian desired the "open participative procedure conducted in the presence of all" as the best method of keeping unsuitable candidates out of the episcopate, and as a way of uniting community choice and divine judgment.[189]

Commentators are far from agreeing on the exact meanings of terms and the understanding of the process given by Cyprian concerning elections.[190] Assessments vary from those that see the laity and even the clergy as having only a nominating capacity or a right to give "public testimony" concerning candidates, to those who find evidence of a right to vote.[191]

In the light of the material from Cyprian himself, and the diverse views of his commentators, Granfield identifies three different aspects of the election of bishops: *testimonium*, *suffragium*, and *iudicium*.[192] *Testimonium* was the responsibility of the entire community. Public testimony was meant to uncover both positive and negative qualities in candidates. In *suffragium* the clergy and the people demonstrated their choice for bishop. Whether this was done by balloting, acclamation or some other method is not now clear.[193] In *iudicium* the whole electing body, including the other bishops, gave public approval to the choice of the *suffragium*.[194]

Cyprian himself did not give details of the functioning process, perhaps because the tradition involved was known to his contemporaries.[195] There is much speculation on the process, and comparison to the Roman voting methods of the time is often sought. Granfield notes that Roman practices too were changing in the third century, and expresses doubt that Cyprian would have followed any secular process that may have been left behind.[196]

Granfield draws a careful distinction between a view that regards a formal system of voting as unlikely, and one that sees the popular *suffragium* as a "mere formality." He sees a voice "vote" as a possible practice. What is clear is that the approval of the people was an essential part of the process of electing and giving a mandate of responsibility to bishops.[197]

Raymund Kottje discusses three aspects of the descriptions of Cyprian concerning the selection of bishops: the *populi suffragium*, *coepiscoporum consensus*, and *divinum iudicium*. Divine discernment is seen as revealed in the choice of the people that is also confirmed by other bishops. As the bishop's role evolved to that of a representative figure for the community, there is the realization that the selection of particular candidates for the position of bishop is properly done in the context of that community. The larger ecclesial community voices its acceptance visibly, through the other bishops who similarly represent the people as a whole.[198]

Ambrose describes this integrated process in his Epistle 63. The members of the community are described as having the responsibility of requesting a candidate, with the local bishops and metropolitan then deciding on the candidate. This role of the people is illustrated in Ambrose's own election.[199] Kottje notes that this process was not always smooth. There are records of many disagreements prior to such elections. These could be quite dramatic, even giving rise to violence.[200]

The theological problems in "the 'democratic' misunderstanding" of the Church are discussed by Hervé-Marie Legrand, who contrasts the relationship of bishop and church with democracy as it is understood in the modern sense.[201] He observes, "the reciprocity which exists between him and the church is not one of contract, but is based upon a confession of faith which cannot be judged by majority vote."[202] He cautions against a simplistic reading of the history of episcopal elections and warns that a "mechanical restoration of elections . . . would lead to theological confusion."[203]

Legrand also claims that the modern method of ordaining a bishop outside of his diocese would have appeared anomalous to the early Fathers.[204] He analyzes the selection of bishops in terms of the theological import of the process.[205] He finds three key elements. First, the community called the bishop. This was done at times, even against the candidate's will. He notes that this practice provided the church with "the greatest bishops of antiquity."[206] Secondly, the local community could take the responsibility of determining "that the bishop-elect held the apostolic faith, and bore witness to this fact." Legrand notes that the "scrutiny" by the community which was a part of the rites that were used for ordination is particularly evident in *Apostolic Constitutions VIII*. He emphasizes that this aspect of the rite illustrates that holding the apostolic faith was the responsibility of every believer. The role of those ordained to represent the church was precisely to express the "apostolicity" of the whole community.[207] Finally, the church "received" the bishop. Legrand cautions that claiming that "the local church *gave itself* its bishop" would not properly represent the understanding of the early Church.[208] Rather, acceptance by the whole community of the one selected was seen as acceptance of the action of the Holy Spirit.[209]

The theological importance of the community in the process was expressed liturgically, as pointed out by Francis Sullivan.[210] In the *Apostolic Tradition* of Hippolytus, dating from the end of second century, Sullivan identifies three steps in the ordination of bishops; "the choice of the candidate, the laying on of hands, and the prayer for the Holy Spirit." The local community has a great responsibility, in that the candidate must be "chosen, proposed, and found acceptable by all."[211] Yet, Sullivan shows that the liturgy illustrates that the local community is not "self-sufficient." Other bishops are called in to lay on hands. Just as the local church needs the other churches, its bishop must be linked to the other bishops. Additionally, only the bishops take part in laying hands on the candidate. giving "practical recognition of the collegial nature of the episcopate." Finally, the prayer for the Holy Spirit emphasizes the recognition of the source of life for ministry in the community.[212] In his discussion of the *Apostolic Tradition*. Sullivan draws on the translation of Gregory Dix.[213] He notes that Dix sees in this work of Hippolytus indications of the practices in the Rome of his own time. The liturgical descriptions could thus show what was happening as early as 180 A.D.[214]

Some disagreement exists about the meaning of the term "election" in Hippolytus. Eugui notes that it may mean, not the active choice of a candidate, but the expression of the approval or disapproval of the community as a whole prior to the ordination ceremony.[215]

Eno notes that the assent of the community was commonly given in public assemblies by "acclamation." In regard to this practice, he relates an event that is described in a letter of St. Augustine's. In the context of choosing his own successor, Augustine first tells of an earlier incident where the bishop of Milevis caused difficulties when he named his own successor, and told his clergy, but not the rest of the community. Augustine himself named a priest, Eraclius, to follow in his place. His letter reports, however, how he interacted with the people: "'Therefore that no one may complain of me, I make known to all of you my choice.' ... The people raised a shout: 'Thanks be to God! Praise to Christ! ... It is right and just!'" When Augustine added, "I need your assent to this; show me some agreement by your acclaim," he received the response, "So be it."[216]

Just what form acclamation of consent took is not clear. The documents that describe episcopal election often use the Latin words *electio* or *eligere* to describe the role of the people, yet at other times, the same term could indicate the participation of clergy from the local community or bishops from outside of it.[217] In the fourth century *consensus* and *consentire* also appeared in common use. From the beginning of the fifth century onwards, *consensus* became, in fact, a technical term. Bartelink claims that its connection with the acclamation of the people in the later elections of Roman emperors is likely to have affected Christian understanding.[218] In Gaul, the *consensus* of the church took on a particularly juridical emphasis, retaining the meaning "consent," but adding that of "'charter,' 'decree' or 'written, unanimous petition' ... sent to the prince for his confirmation."[219] This legal emphasis would later be found in other areas as well.[220]

It is clear that the role of the people as initiating agents in the choice of bishops waned in Patristic times. In 366 riots and the killing of 137 people occurred with the election of Pope Damasus.[221] Eno conjectures that it is possibly because of these sorts of events that a canon of "the so-called council of Laodicea" stipulated that "the election of those who are to be appointed to the priesthood (episcopate) is not to be committed to the multitude."[222] This fourth century canon indicates a tendency that was to become more widespread by the fifth and sixth centuries.[223]

Eno notes that "factionalism" played an important part in the decline of lay participation. Some expression of lay input was retained in the involvement of secular rulers in the selection of bishops. Yet, Eno states that such lay involvement was a mere "caricature" of the earlier practice of participation.[224] He adds,

> Faced with this growing abuse in which the Church became one more pawn on the chessboard of the rich and powerful, it is understandable that the hierarchy would struggle that the Church might regain something of its independence. In the process, however, over the long centuries, shared ecclesial responsibility became one of the victims.[225]

In the early Church, the involvement of the community in the selection of bishops was not seen as a juridical necessity or "sovereign right." However, where a majority of the people were in agreement this was recognized as the work of the Spirit expressed in the collection of believers that were rooted in a common baptism.[226] Yet this vision was eventually to become clouded by mundane concerns. Granfield finds three main reasons for the falling off of the practice of popular participation in elections; lack of education on the part of the laity, abuses in the election process, and the interference of secular rulers.[227]

A new expression of lay influence is found in the deposition of Paul of Samosata. In 268 a synod at Antioch sought his removal from office for both theological reasons and for having had a throne built in his own honor.[228] However, because he had served in a governmental capacity under the current Queen Zenobia of Palmyra, he was protected from actually vacating the office. When, however, she herself lost her position, the case was taken to Emperor Aurelian, who removed Paul. Here for the first time, the community of the faithful was not the cause of a bishop's removal, but rather the responsibility was taken by a secular authority.[229]

In the early Church, as the bishop's role evolved to that of the key figure for representing the community, the community's involvement was recognized as central to the power of representation of that office. This was true particularly in the case of the *lapsi*. In a time of confusion and crisis, the laity were recognized as an important vehicle for the expression of the Spirit; not, certainly in a necessary, juridical sense, but as a logical expression of ecclesial dynamics.

Whether the laity initiated a request for a candidate or ratified one proposed by other bishops, their involvement was an active one. This process is described by Ambrose in his Epistle 63 (A.D. 396), where the members of the community are described as having the responsibility of requesting a candidate, with the local bishops and metropolitan then deciding on the candidate. If the bishops did not agree with the popular choice, they then proposed another nominee, which the people then were asked to agree upon. A similar process is stipulated in a document of Pope Leo I from 458/59.[230]

The assent of the people eventually became merely a liturgical formality, but not until at least after the fifth century. Often the people expressed the wishes of the community by rejecting candidates. The councils of Ancyra (314) and Antioch (341) both included canons that described what to do with ordained bishops that were rejected in this way. Eno cites an example from the fifth century where this sort of popular decision still carried weight.[231]

In the fifth century several popes insisted on the inclusion of the community in the selection of bishops. Pope Boniface I in 422 found it "uncanonical" to exclude the clergy, nobility, or people from the process.[232] Both Pope Celestine I and Leo the Great wrote to the bishops in Gaul to remind them that bishops were to be elected by all.[233] Lynch describes the distinctions that were to be retained; "The clergy ought to subscribe to the election, the dignitaries give their testimony, and the rest of the people give consent." Yet, Pope Leo later criticized African bishops for a poor choice, claiming that they had fallen prey to the "presumption of intriguers" and the "rioting of the populace."[234] His successor, Pope Hilary, wrote that the will of the people should be set aside if the will of God would otherwise be undermined.[235]

Granfield notes that lay participation in the selection process waned as the control of bishops grew.[236] He notes that lay members lost all control to the clergy and bishops before the sixth century, and that at the Fourth Lateran Council (1215) any popular lay involvement was excluded as elections became the responsibility of the cathedral chapters.[237]

Lynch observes that during the pontificate of Gregory the Great, the laity had retained some "voice" in episcopal elections. Yet the writings of Gregory also show evidence of the arrival of a new element in the process. He describes the privileged place given to the preferences of princes, in contrast to their subjects, with regard to the choosing of bishops. This movement toward influence of secular rulers bore notorious fruit in the investiture controversy.[238]

Thus in the persons of rulers, some of the laity retained influence in the selection of bishops well into the Middle Ages.[239] Those who exercised such influences even used physical force at times, and mired the process in political entanglements that led to the eventual repudiation of lay involvement by the

Church as a whole, and particularly by the papacy.[240] These developments bore little connection to the earlier forms of lay influence that can be properly recognized as illustrating the consensus of the faithful.

It is not unreasonable to view the movement away from participation by the laity as being caused by a choking off of the means through which an active life of the Spirit could be nurtured and then expressed. The power of bishops grew, understandably, to meet serious problems that faced the Church, yet the structures that came to dominate Church decisions were developed without the contribution of an element of the Church that had also proven its merit. Common lay persons were less and less equipped to take part in a meaningful way. Yet, the lack of involvement on the part of the laity was due to particular circumstances and not to any inherent ecclesial inability or to any innate inappropriateness of including the laity.

After a detailed examination of records pertaining to the processes of selecting bishops in the first five centuries, Eugui acknowledges again, the ambiguity that remains in many cases concerning the process of election. He adds, however, that even with the lack of complete records, it is clear that there was community involvement.[241]

Eugui speaks of a "hierarchy of consents" in the process of nominating candidates for bishop.[242] Those with the power to ordain would have had the responsibility for making a final judgment on those proposed. A realistic treatment of the process must also include the influence exercised in actual practice by the previous bishop and the civil authority.[243]

Eugui sees the community's "unique claim" as its capacity to witness to the qualifications of the candidate that made him suitable or unsuitable for the episcopate. He adds that this moral witness could also be important to the success of the bishop after taking office. Obedience would be more likely where a genuine acceptance of him by the community existed.[244]

Eugui finds that the motivation to find the best possible candidate for bishop, that led to greater and then complete hierarchical control of the process is, in fact the same motivation that allowed full community participation in the early centuries.[245] The main criterion was the suitability of the candidates for episcopal office, and the historical structures that developed to serve that purpose are secondary to the goal itself.[246]

## SENIORES LAICI

In addition to the influence lay people might have through participation in the community's selection of its leaders, the Patristic period saw the emergence of other forms of leadership North Africa was the location of an "apparently anomalous" lay office in the fourth and fifth centuries, called the *seniores laici*. W. H. C. Frend has commented that these lay leaders "provide a striking exception to the otherwise universal decline of the role of the laity in the administrative and liturgical functions of the Church during the fourth century."[247] He notes, however, that these lay people served an important role in both the Donatist and Catholic churches in North Africa. They held administrative positions, serving churches and their bishops by supervising or protecting property, and in some areas they were organized into councils. They served in some disciplinary capacities and at times were even responsible for monitoring the actions of their bishops.[248] Frend remarks that, "they seem to have acted as watchdogs over the conduct of the clergy on behalf of the congregation."[249]

The *seniores laici* are linked to origins in the Jewish synagogue, and were likely in existence in other Western churches in earlier centuries. Ambrosiaster writes of the office as having existed in Italy. Tertullian distinguishes *seniores* from presbyters and records that these elders could excommunicate others in their churches. Cyprian, who often consulted those under his care, spoke of *seniores ex plebe*, in a way that Frend sees as support for the notion that those lay leaders held a form of representational office.[250] Frend sees strong similar ties between the "oligarchy of lay and priestly officers" that existed in North Africa, and the organization of Jewish groups that were concurrent or that predated the churches.[251] He speculates that the structure may even have a forerunner in the early Jewish-Christian church of Palestine.[252]

The responsibilities of the *seniores laici* are also discussed, and distinguished from those of presbyters by John Lynch.[253] He cites St. Augustine's writings where the *seniores* ranked between the clergy (*clerici*) and the common believers (*universa plebs*). He adds that an inscription from Hippo dating to Augustine's time suggests that the *seniores* were chosen by the people, and not the bishop.[254]

Lynch cautions that the *seniores* should not be seen as holding "all the real power of jurisdiction," with the clergy having only sacramental responsibilities. Yet, neither should they be regarded as the sort of elders that are respected in "primitive" communities.[255]

Frend sees the functions of the *seniores* as being absorbed by the bishops And other clergy who represented the established ecclesial structure as persecutions ended. It a peaceful climate the governance of the Church was carried on by "those who represented administrative and sacramental continuity."[256]

## CONSENSUS AND THE EXPRESSION OF DOCTRINE

The people in the early Christian communities who, as has been seen, were actively involved in selecting the guardians of tradition, were no less involved in understanding and expressing the content of the tradition.

To meet the challenges of schisms and heresy, the early communities drew on the teachings which they linked to the original Apostles. New revelation was not possible; the Church's task was to hand on the *depositum fidei*. The tool which surfaced to identify the genuine expressions of this received faith was consensus.[257]

The practices of Origen's time give a good indication of the nature of lay involvement in doctrinal concerns.[258] The people were to be present with the bishop when disputed issues were considered. Issues were clarified and broken down into a form that could be understood even by "unsophisticated" lay people, to allow the whole church to be involved in the process. At the same time such reformulation did not result in a simplistic treatment. The people's assent was needed, and this required of them an "attentative, probing and judicious listening."[259]

The response of the people could be quite dramatic in Origen's view:

> If I, who appears to be your right hand, who beats the name priest and who has proclaimed God's word, contravene the church's teaching and the norm of the gospel so that I become a scandal to you, church, then the entire church by unanimous resolution has the right to cut me, its right hand, off and cast me away.[260]

The degree of lay involvement that can be seen in early disputes is subject to much of the same ambiguity and lack of direct information that has been encountered in other areas. As Granfield shows, Cyprian again provides a somewhat clearer picture, at least in regard to the north African churches. General indicators of lay involvement occur in his various writings.[261] His *Epistle* 17 written in the context of turmoil over the *lapsi* indicates his regard for lay involvement. Cyprian assures, "the wishes of each one (of the *lapsi*) shall be looked into in your presence and with your judgment."[262] Granfield regards Cyprian's "theology of shared decision-making" to be "remarkable" particularly when placed in the light of his strong views on the authority of the bishop. Cyprian believed that the bishop "was independent, responsible only to God" in his judgment, and that heresy and schism were the results of disobedience. His writings on involvement also come in the midst of a great deal of stress.[263] Granfield writes that while he was bishop Cyprian faced

> widespread schism and apostasy among his clergy and laity; two major Roman persecutions (Decian and Valerian); a severe plague; fifteen months of voluntary exile and one year of imposed exile; major theological debates on the *lapsi* and rebaptism of heretics; and a bitter confrontation with the Bishops of Rome.[264]

It was in the face of tremendous turmoil and threats to the community and its faith, that Cyprian developed both a strong stand on the bishop's role and a clear theology and practice of lay involvement in decision making. Granfield comments that Cyprian's overriding motivation in his use of consultation was that it would give the church unity. A living unity was of the highest importance and was to be achieved by practical exercises of inclusion.[265]

In considering the ways tradition was viewed in the Patristic period, Avery Dulles sees an important shift occurring in the middle of the third century.[266] Before this time, the "general climate" is much like that of the Pastoral Epistles; the works of Clement of Rome, Irenaeus, and Tertullian battle Gnosticism and emphasize the continuity of apostolic office. He notes that the Alexandrian church may have been somewhat different. With its "strong speculative theology" it did not regard the ministerial offices as having such central responsibility for carrying the tradition. Yet, Dulles sees this church too as being of the same "traditionalist" approach, inasmuch as it limited speculation itself to that which had been "reliably handed down."[267]

Dulles observes that the strict method of linking interpretation to the material available from the apostles themselves as limited today; the questions grappled with today were beyond the apostles' limited scope. At the same time, the approach of this traditionalist time can serve to remind contemporary theologians that Christianity cannot be created by individuals on their own. It is rooted in the experience of eyewitnesses, and can only be properly understood in the context of the community of faith. This requires a "submission to the community and its leaders."[268]

In Cyprian, Dulles sees a change. Here he finds a move away from historical continuity with the apostles' oral tradition and the growth of the view that "the faith has been authentically planted in every local church."[269] Cyprian's treatise on the church, *De ecclesiae catholicae unitate* is the earliest extant treatment of ecclesiology.[270] In it he stresses the unity of the church and the impossibility of there being more than one bishop to represent it. Adalabert Davids states that for Cyprian, heresy and schism were synonymous.[271] For Cyprian, it was thoroughly consistent that disagreements were to be resolved through consensus. Dulles refers to this period when the integrity of the faith was connected to unanimous belief in the churches as the "Patristic golden age." It found its classical statement in the Vincentian Canon.[272]

Elsewhere, Dulles has observed that Patristic thinkers like Tertullian "imported" a Stoic view, following Cicero and Seneca, who taught that the "common consent" of all people in regard to an issue is an infallible guide to truths. Thus if believers from different lands with different languages held a belief in common, it must be included as part of the apostolic tradition.[273]

Interestingly, Origen contrasts the fruits of the Church's consensus and those of its "secular counterparts."[274] He writes in *Contra Celsum*:

> Whereas the Churches of God which are instructed by Christ, when carefully distinguished from the assemblies in the districts in which they are assembled, are as beacons in the world: for who would not admit that even the inferior members of the Church, and those who in comparison with the better are less worthy, are

nevertheless more excellent than many of those who belong to the (secular) assemblies in those cities. (3:29)[275]

In the third century, bishops came to be seen less as links to the apostles, and more and more as the heads of their churches. When joined together in councils, they were seen to have authority in defining the truth.[276]

Jakob Speigl has argued that lay influence in such early church councils was not significant. The role of consent illustrated by Cyprian's description of the Council of Carthage is one example of an important lay role.[277] Speigl notes, that although general lay participation was not challenged, it still died out. In the early councils, lay involvement was greater in ecclesial groups than it was in the civil gatherings of the same time. As the Church's councils began to be patterned after Roman secular models of governance, lay participation decreased. Certainly, where councils were called by the emperor, a significant "lay" influence was present. However, inasmuch as the emperor did not enter conciliar debates, it is not accurate to speak of lay involvement in doctrinal matters.[278]

Robert Eno identifies three different emphases held by the early Church in considering consensus. In Vincent of Lerins he identifies the consensus of the past, in Augustine he sees stress on the consensus of the present, and in papal letters he finds a consensus developed by and subject to Roman tradition.[279]

As precursors to Vincent's important contribution, both Irenaeus and Tertullian responded to Gnostic thinkers by invoking the established, widespread beliefs of the Church at large. The clear expressions of orthodox church teaching were contrasted with the secretive and inconsistent teachings of the Gnostics. Eno cites Irenaeus's *Adversus Haereses*, to show his reliance on the careful safeguarding of what is handed on. Nothing was to be added or subtracted (I. 3.). Further, apostolic foundation of a church secured its place as focal point for future teaching (III. 3).[280]

Of interest to the present study is Irenaeus's linking of the tradition to the process that included the interaction of Rome and Corinth in the sort of controversy that resulted in the correspondence of Clement of Rome. Irenaeus traces the successors of Clement up to his own day. Eno describes the *De Praescriptione Haereticum* of Tertullian as being developed completely along the model of Irenaeus. He describes the process of linking up with the apostolic sees as an effort of bishops to "trace their pedigrees" to show direct succession, and of synthesizing the teaching into "short, creedlike statements, the *reguli fidei*."[281]

If this sort of appeal was simple in the second century, it did not remain so in the fifth, the context of Vincent of Lerin's *Commonitoria*.[282] Eno cites the development of doctrine that attended the conciliar expressions of new creeds as a source of new complications. Eno contends that while Vincent argued for the importance of consensus, for dependence on the whole in contrast to a wayward "part," his norm for making this appeal was the ancient faith.[283] Innovation was the source of all problems in doctrine. Eno describes Vincent's stance:

> *Novitas* was the enemy. The following was his summary of the outcome of the rebaptism controversy of the third century: "Retenta antiquitas; explosa novitas" (6.9). Even spirituality played its part: the more pious a person was, the quicker he was to reject innovations (*Ibid.*). [284]

This connection noted by Eno of Vincent's key methodological ruler for consensus, and his view of the role played by an individual's piety exhibits an interesting early insight into the connection of the issues that would later be described as *consensus fidelium* and *sensus fidei*.

Monika Hellwig has noted that Vincent's views were motivated by his stance that Scripture was not an adequate basis for determining doctrine, because of the variety of interpretations that could be given to it. He thus seeks a foundation in the universal Church.[285] To find expression of consensus, Vincent found the surest sources in the great councils. These, of course were not available for consultation on all issues. In other cases then, he recommended dependence on the teachings of the ancient doctors, which taken together could have the same authority as a council.[286]

Augustine likewise drew on the approach of Irenaeus and Tertullian in citing antiquity against heresy in the teachings of the Donatists. Yet, Augustine's attack was much more dependent on present practice than that of the earlier apologists. The Donatists had, in fact, an ancient ally in Cyprian, whose holiness was unquestioned, and who had stood against Stephen, the Bishop of Rome, in the controversy over rebaptism. Augustine appeals to the well known holiness of Cyprian, and claims that this and his love of unity in the Church would have led him toward the generally accepted position of Augustine's day, if he had not been hampered by the confusion in his own.[287] Current consensus in Augustine's time gave him a tool for interpreting the route that orthodox thought took to its current catholic state, and for "cleaning up" key figures along that route.

Eno notes that Augustine was aware of new issues and new expressions of the faith in the first centuries of development of the tradition.[288] It is in this awareness that he draws heavily on contemporary consensus as the indicator of what new expressions were consistent with the ancient faith. This dependence on conciliar expressions was itself used with an eye for the widest possible consensus. The Donatists cited an earlier council of Carthage in support of rebaptism. To this assertion, Augustine could respond that more recent councils with greater scope had more authority, and that their deliberations might improve on the efforts of prior ones.[289]

In assessing the emphasis on Roman authority in interpreting tradition, Eno notes the dependence on ancient sees that grew in the early centuries, but adds that their prestige could be linked significantly to their prominence in secular matters. Rome alone "developed a theological rationale for its de facto leadership in the West and its claims to more than a primacy of honor in the universal Church."[290] Eno adds that the East maintained an active dependence on consensus. With the growth in strength of the claims of Roman authority, Western dependence on consensus waned.[291] The intent expressed by the Roman approach was, as in the other cases, a desire to preserve the *depositum fidei*. Eno observes that this intent was carried out with an attention to detail in practice which allowed for no deviation, and which was dependent on an unhistorical assumption that the Apostles, and especially Peter, had left the Church directives that were complete even in non-doctrinal matters.[292]

A contemporary Orthodox commentator has discussed consensus as expressed in the link of individual bishops to each other. Metropolitan Emilianos Timiadis observes, "There was never any such thing as an 'independent' episcopate, a set of 'episcopal monads.'"[293] He cites Cyprian's *De unitate*, where he writes, "The episcopate is one, of which each bishop holds his part within the undivided structure."[294] This authority reaches its fullness in the ecumenical council. These councils are, in fact, the fullest expression of the Vincentian Canon. They define the faith that is rooted in the Bible and carried by the tradition.[295] Timiadis observes that this view is itself expressed in the councils.[296]

Timiadis takes pains to include the laity as full participants of the Church in consensus. Citing many New Testament (especially Pauline) texts on the gifts that are given to all members, he claims that phrases like "official Church" or "teaching Church" are "used only by custom and are inaccurate from a dogmatic standpoint if taken literally."[297] The laity have had a genuine role in the carrying on of the tradition, and even in the expression of doctrine in the Church's councils. Timiadis stresses, however, that the people do not "sanctify" the councils, and that the bishops do not "define doctrine in the name of the people."[298] He comments that "some Russian theologians" appear to assert that the bishops serve as mere representatives of the people's judgment.[299] He writes,

> The Councils define doctrine in their own right "with the assistance of the Holy Spirit, *ipso et divino jure*"; the faithful people subsequently recognize these definitions as not exceeding their destination, but as interpreting practically and formulating infallibly the truth.[300]

The controversy and lack of immediate reception that attended the promulgation of doctrines by the Councils of Nicaea I, Chalcedon, and Nicaea II, in particular, illustrate this fact, according to Timiadis. The views of the faithful were not merely recited at the councils. Consensus was formed by the official teachings, which were promulgated with conciliar weight.[301]

Timiadis makes a clear distinction between the roles of the laity and the bishops. Receiving and preserving the faith is the duty of the whole Church, while defining and proclaiming it is the task of the ministers.[302]

Dulles observes that as the fifth century approached, a "more explicit" recognition was made that the Holy Spirit is active in the Church as a whole, especially when its faith is expressed through a council.[303] He adds that the desire for consensus did have the negative effect of forcing some members out of the remaining communion following conciliar definitions. He speculates that in an age less apt to demand uniformity, those with views like the Nestorians and Monophysites might have remained in union with Catholic believers.[304]

Timiadis and Dulles express the perspective commonly accepted in the Church in both the east and the west, that the doctrinal expressions of the great councils were the work of the Holy Spirit. The practical details of conciliar history often more clearly exhibit the human characteristics of their members. Dulles describes the process of striving for consensus as "inordinately politicized."[305]

Another Orthodox commentator, John Meyendorff, has put the matter in even stronger terms. Councils were not perceived as settling issues democratically by a "majority rule." Consensus was an indicator of the work of the Spirit, and thus a group in disagreement, one that went against consensus, had to chose between giving in and excommunication.[306] The council was perceived as carrying out the Biblical role of "witness" to the Gospel. The Spirit was recognized as more present in the consensus of a region than in the teaching of a single bishop, and a consensus of universal scope was the most authoritative witness possible. In this understanding, the council came to be recognized as "a *sign* of the will of God," when it met to address a specific issue in dispute. Its testimony was to be checked by the Church with the "other 'signs' of Scripture, Tradition, and other councils."[307]

Just as lay participation in the selection of bishops evolved away from the practice of accepting input from the whole Church, the work of councils themselves moved away from lay involvement, and into a mode where episcopal control was more and more direct. This was itself aided by the specialized "lay participation" that existed in the activities of secular rulers. Faivre notes that prior to the Councils of Carthage (411), Ephesus (431) and Chalcedon (451) the reigning emperors issued instructions banning the involvement or even attendance of lay people or monks.[308]

Meyendorff states that the councils' attitude toward minority views did not imply that a council, in its majority stances, was considered "infallible *ex sese*."[309] Reception by the Church was necessary for a conciliar teaching to be accepted as part of the tradition. He points out that in certain cases (such as the Council of Chalcedon), whole Christian bodies "risked" schism in the name of Christian truth rather than receive a councils teaching. Reception is not a matter of "referendum" or "an expression of lay 'democracy.'"[310] Rather its function is to indicate that the human risk that is always a part of faith is also present in the witness of conciliar teachings. It indicates that the real authority governing the whole Church is the Holy Spirit.[311] Dulles links the lack of reception of some council teachings to "unhealthy pressures" that pushed for consensus.[312] He states that "hasty settlement of complex speculative questions" made it difficult for churches and the people to receive some teachings.[313]

The beliefs of the laity did not, in fact, always mirror the teaching of the bishops. It is important to note that in many cases, the laity have been wrong in beliefs that were widespread among them. Granfield notes that on several historical occasions such as the rise of Islam in the seventh century or the Protestant Reformation in the sixteenth, the faithful have not upheld the faith in the face of challenges.[314] Yet, at times the faithful as a whole were instrumental in keeping the Church as a whole from falling away from the truth. Here the role of the *sensus fidelium* specifically expressed through the lay faithful is seen serving the *sensus Ecclesiae*, although as one source.[315]

Newman drew two cases from the Patristic period to illustrate the reality of the sense of the faithful. He found a key example in the Arian crisis. Newman was concerned to see the work of the Spirit expressed continuously in the life, teaching and worship, and the tradition of the Church. In his study of the Council of Nicaea, he came to recognize that the laity played a vital role in ensuring that the faith of the Council was not compromised.[316] In the fourth century a considerable number of bishops embraced Arian views, prompting Jerome's famous line, "The whole world groaned when, to its astonishment, it discovered that it was Arian."[317] Athanasius and others remained true to the position that would eventually be recognized throughout the Church as orthodox. Yet, for a considerable time, it was mainly the common people who maintained the orthodox Christology.

It is important to note that the importance of the Arian crisis for understanding the *sensus fidelium* is clearer after the fact than it was at the time. The debates and confusions of the period itself were the focus of theological reflection, and were in the hands of those whose roles as debaters and decision makers were commonly accepted. It is in retrospect that the role of the faithful has been seen to have been important in the fourth century. Coulson points out Newman's own view that the *consensus fidelium* is clarified "only when required for use."[318]

Newman's second Patristic example afforded him a case with more immediate imaginative appeal. He closes his *On Consulting the Faithful on Matters of Doctrine* by quoting an account of the common people awaiting the decision of the Council of Ephesus in the fifth century, regarding the orthodoxy of the *theotokos*. Newman quotes Bernard Dalgairns's *The Devotion to the Sacred Heart of Jesus* (1853):

> The day wears on, and still nothing issues from the church; it proves, at least, that there is a difference of opinion; and as the shades of evening close around them, the weary watchers grow more anxious still. At length the great gates of the Basilica are thrown open; and oh, what a cry of joy bursts from the assembled crowd, as it is announced to them that Mary has been proclaimed to be, what every one with a Catholic heart knew that she was before, the Mother of God! . . . Men, women, and children, the noble and the low-born, the stately matron and the modest maiden, All crowd round the Bishops with acclamations. They will not leave them; they accompany them to their homes with the long procession of lighted torches; they burn incense before them, after the eastern fashions to do them honor. There was but little sleep in Ephesus that night; for very joy they remained awake; the whole town was one blaze of light, for each window was illuminated.[319]

Newman cites with approval this image of the faithful bursting forth with consent to the expression of what they held dear, and in a spirit of communion and intimacy of agreement among lay people and bishops that rivals the ideal community life described in Acts.

If the actual historical situation was filled with confusion and debates while the faith of the Church was clarified, at times through the efforts of several assemblies, the desire for clarity and unity were a goal that was certainly at the heart of the work of the councils. The controversies born from the thought of Arius and Nestorius were not, in fact, settled until reception of conciliar teachings was eventually expressed in the faith and worship of the Church. The process of reception of doctrine has long been recognized as a key element in doctrinal formulation.

As an expression of the role of the faithful, reception is vital to the development of doctrine in the Church. Its function has been identified in the early centuries as well as in medieval times, and continues to be seen as an important theological issue today. A description of its role including its Patristic component will be taken up in a later section.

## THE SENSE OF THE FAITHFUL IN THE FATHERS

Contemporary theological assessments of the sense of the faithful regularly select examples from the Fathers to support the claim that the concept is common in the first centuries even if the exact words are not. Congar has listed examples in the oft cited appendix to his *Lay People in the Church*. He includes, Gregory Nazianzen, Basil, And Jerome on the notion that those who do not "believe as Catholics believe nullify the faith of the whole people." Epiphanius and Nicephorus are shown as offering support for the importance of "communal practice and belief." Augustine is cited in numerous texts, and his influence is seen also in Paulinus of Nola, Vincent of Lerins, and Cassian. These authors are offered specifically in respect to the *sensus fidelium*.[320]

Dillenschneider sees this "sense" in the words first of Clement of Rome and then in the Alexandrians. Clement and Origen after him are cited as teaching the importance of the spiritual growth that is necessary to developing the "sense" of the faith that is given through grace.[321]

Fathers of the East such as Gregory of Nyssa, Cyril of Jerusalem, John Chrysostom, and others are all quoted in their teachings on the work of the Spirit in bringing clarity and purity to the believer.[322] The insight of the faith that is encouraged by the Fathers may at times have been construed as spiritualized vision; St. Augustine's formula, *Crede ut intelligas*, has drawn the accusation of fideism.[323] Dillenschneider notes that Leo the Great contrasted the wisdom of the world with the wisdom of faith. This sort of argument was made to establish that the sense of the faith that is developed in the believer is superior to ordinary human wisdom. Dillenschneider observes that the teachings of the Fathers on the "eyes of faith" and "the spiritual sense" had an important impact on the reflections that developed during the Middle Ages and throughout scholastic thought.[324] This later work would focus particularly on the *sensus fidei*.

## THE SENSE OF THE FAITHFUL AND THE MIDDLE AGES

Pierre Boglioni has pointed out the difficulties in determining the characteristics of popular religion in the Middle Ages.[325] Sources are difficult to select. To some extent all aspects of the culture were affected by religion. Boglioni himself examines written materials that are extant from ecclesial synods, legal activities, penitentials, sermons, literature and liturgy.[326] Yet, even these documents that speak of lay experience cannot directly express the views of an overriding number of believers throughout these centuries who remained illiterate. The documents that are available are the work of the educated clerics.[327] The issue of documents renders any treatment of the religiousness of the common people either unwieldy or anecdotal.

The discussion attempted here will examine the Middle Ages, as it did the previous periods, from the standpoint of the sources within it that have motivated and informed the modern understandings of the sense of the faithful. A continually more centralized hierarchy in this period delineated the roles of pope, bishops and theologians more and more distinctly, and thus clarified the conditions under which the whole body of believers might affect expressions of doctrine or law.[328] Theological reflection blossomed in this period too. St. Thomas Aquinas, found particular significance in the *sensus fidei*, and developed the sense of the faithful in the light of this focus on the individual believer.

The route taken by the issue of co-responsibility in the Middle Ages is described succinctly by Robert Benson, as a movement from the view of Pope Leo the Great in the mid-fifth century, "He who governs all should be elected by all," to that of Pope Innocent IV in the middle of the thirteenth, "Election belongs to the cathedral chapter and not to individuals, and nevertheless individuals elect together."[329] Not only does the shift describe a move from a large group of electors to a smaller one, but also a conceptual shift from a practice influenced by Roman civil models to one that was based in the "revival of scientific jurisprudence" that had been growing since the early twelfth century.[330]

If the Patristic period shows some ambiguity in the role of the laity in "electing" the bishop, allowing interpretations that have ranged from seeing actual voting to those only affirming the choice of clerics or bishops (yet where even in the latter, an active involvement in the selection process was maintained), in the eleventh century there was a clear distinction between the *electio* of the clergy and the *expetitio* or approval of the laity. Chronological order in the "requesting" of the laity was reversed too, so that the role of the laity was merely one of ratifying the completed election.[331] Certainly, lay people with secular power were highly involved. Because of abuses, the Gregorian Reform sought to strengthen the supervision of episcopal appointments by the ecclesial authorities.[332] At the same time, in this period the role of the laity as a group came to be clearly distinguished from that of the clergy.[333]

Benson notes that this distinguishing did not mean a split was seen between clergy and laity; rather each was seen as connected to a specific arena of responsibility. Both groups were important to the Church.[334] These two parts of the body were linked to the spiritual and the secular. Benson cites Hugh of Saint Victor,

> This universe consists of two orders, laymen and clerics, like two sides of a single body. . . . There are two lives: one terrestial, the other celestial; one corporeal, the other spiritual. . . . In both powers (that is, terrestial and spiritual), there are different grades and orders of power, on both sides distributed under one head and, as it were, derived from one origin. . . . The early power has the king as head. The spiritual power has the supreme pontiff.[335]

If both parts of the body were important in this ecclesiology, the predominance of one over the other in church decisions was clear cut. In his *Decretum*, Gratian compiled laws that covered the practices of seven centuries.[336] Benson cites the passage that describes the reconciliation of conflicting texts on episcopal selection: "From the foregoing authorities, it is clear to everyone that election belongs to clerics."[337]

Lay involvement on the part of rulers in episcopal elections remained active enough to generate serious problems, inasmuch as that involvement was often motivated by political concerns and specifically by the struggle for power between civil and ecclesial leaders. The long period of continued lay involvement that followed the initial attempts of the Gregorian Reform is evidence of the intricate positioning for power that characterized much of the Medieval practice of choosing bishops. The continued claims to authority among secular rulers renders understandable the growth of ecclesial and especially papal power in the period, even if this growth occurred at the cost of any lay involvement.[338]

Jean Gaudemet notes that within two centuries of Gratian's *Decretum*, elections moved from the "electoral college" which included lay members to the cathedral chapter which did not.[339] Gratian quoted Pope Celestine I (429) in saying, "The people must be taught, not followed," to which he adds, "The people must not go ahead, but must follow."[340] Yet Gratian also maintains,

> It is clear that layfolk must not be excluded from an election and that princes must not be kept out. However, the fact that the people have a part to play in the election does not mean that it is called to conduct it; but it must give its consent to the election made by the clergy.[341]

Gaudemet points out that there is no warrant in Gratian for papal intervention. However, the inherent hierarchical nature of elections coupled with political turmoil and "the spirit of chicanery" exhibited within the chapters led to the electors looking to Rome for mediation.[342]

In its move to a more hierarchical ecclesiology the Church saw the authority to make judgments concerning the tradition placed more and more at the top of its structure. Congar notes that in the Patristic period, the transmission of tradition was linked to the deposit of faith, which was seen not as "a formal principle of authority," but as *"what* the Church believes."[343] Following B. Haeggelund he says that in this period the *regula fidei* was not seen as "a rule for faith," but rather as "the rule which is faith."[344] Further, even though there were disputes between "pastors" and "doctors," there was no formal distinction between the two.[345]

With the Middle Ages, this changed. There was now a distinction between the magisterium of doctors and that of pastors. With this distinction between types of teachers, their areas of concern could be distinguished, and then separated. Bishops were seen as teaching by authority and jurisdiction. Doctors were recognized for public exhibition of scholarly competence.[346] The focus in the understanding of the tradition shifted from what was taught with authority, to what it was that authority taught.

Congar notes the growth of papal authority in particular, in both its practical activities and its theological standing.[347] He sees the developing understanding of papal magisterium as encompassing four elements. First, "a broad sense of 'heresy'" developed after the Gregorian reform, which equated disagreement with the Roman Church with error.[348] Secondly, there was "repeated affirmation that the Roman Church has never erred in faith." Congar notes that this church is not to be identified necessarily with the *"sedes Romana"* or the Pope himself. Thirdly, there was a growing insistence that papal judgment ended theological debate. This authority to settle disputes came to be seen as taking precedence over "preaching and witness." Finally, there was a developing stress on the role of the pope with regard to councils, that was supported somewhat by the *False Decretals*. Congar notes that when the pope was considered to have the authority to "authorize," "convoke," "preside over" and "confirm" councils, it was not a great step to say that it was by his judgment that disputed points of dogma were settled as well. It was then his role both "to 'finaliter determinate ea quae sunt fidei' (decide finally those things which are part of faith) and to 'novum symbolum edere' (declare a new article of faith)."[349]

Within his analysis, Congar draws on one of his own previous treatments of St. Thomas's understanding of infallibility.[350] Here he elaborates on the distinction in Aquinas between the teaching of the theologians, and the role of judgment exercised by the pope.[351] In regard to the question of whether the pope ratified the authority of a council or gave it its authority, Congar finds a nuanced position. Thomas saw the authority of the pope and that of a council operating in a co-supportive rather than competitive relationship.[352] He sees inerrancy as belonging to the *Ecclesia universalism*. The pope is inerrant only "insofar as he is a personification or a figure of the universal Church."[353] Congar notes that in

Thomas's context, this sort of representational or symbolizing function was understood to be "effected under the aegis of the public authority joining together a given community and personifying it."[354] Congar sees this as the "very spirit of Catholicism, with its organic vision of the Church," where qualities of the community were "translated" into the person at its head. It is in this way that the infallibility of the whole is understood as "incorporated" in the pope.[355]

Congar argues that Thomas does not reduce the papal magisterium to an "unreasonably juridical" power. He notes that some role of "judicial and doctrinal competence" is given generally to priests. Yet, because the pope holds the highest office among those responsible for juridical decisions and has the highest authority to speak publicly for the Church, the papal prerogative does include the highest form of juridical power.[356]

## THE COMMUNITY AND RECEPTION

In the hierarchically and juridically focused context of the Middle Ages, the contribution of the larger body of faithful can be seen in terms of reception. Contemporary authors see a significant part being played by the laity in its reception of councils doctrine and law.

Reception bridges the Patristic era and the Middle Ages as an expression of the *sensus Ecclesiae*. The warrants for placing importance on reception are rooted in the New Testament itself.[357] The terms used by Paul to describe the "receiving" and "accepting" of the Gospel are Greek equivalents for the rabbinical terms for "handing on" and "receiving" tradition.[358] Rausch identifies the same dynamic in the reception of the apostolic message by the earliest converts, the establishment of the New Testament and the later acceptance of liturgy, laws and customs that developed in one place and were adopted by other churches.[359]

Rausch describes reception in terms of both classical and ecumenical perspectives. The classical view can be considered in terms of two phases separated by the time of Constantine.[360] In the earlier stage, reception referred to the acceptance of local synods by other churches. This practice illustrated that a church's identity is tied to its communion with other ecclesial bodies. Miguel M. Garijo Guembe describes the process in this period as a "direct reception."[361] From Constantine's time on, reception came to be understood as a description of the process by which the teachings of ecumenical councils were accepted.[362] Rausch's discussion of the ecumenical concept of reception here relates the early model of a "communion of churches" to efforts in the current ecumenical dialogues to develop consensus among separated churches.[363]

As seen above, the reception process could lead, not only to acceptance, but also to rejection of doctrine. During the first millennium, with its emphasis on the Church as a communion of bodies, the concept of reception that prevailed included the expectation that interaction and debate would be a significant part of actual reception. Rausch points out that with the rise of hierarchical ecclesiology in the late Middle Ages and even more solidly after the Council of Trent (1545-1563) reception became "a purely juridical category."[364] He adds that where a strong stress has been placed on hierarchical authority, a sense of reception may have been dismissed altogether.[365]

Edward Kilmartin states that the models of reception that developed in the West in the second millennium "are not adequate to the task of explaining the process and significance of reception as an ecclesiological reality."[366] He elaborates by saying that in the Middle Ages, the Church was seen as a "universal corporation" where the clergy and laity could advise the Pope through representatives. The Roman legal notion, "*Quod omnes tangit, ab omnibus tracteri et approbari debet*," was given the status of canon law by Pope Gregory IX in 1234.[367] Kilmartin notes that when ecclesial representatives agreed "on matters of doctrine and discipline . . . it was considered to be the expression of the inspiration of the Spirit and the consensus of the faithful." Submission to the decision was then required, and "no other form of reception was considered."[368] Significantly, a pattern where the desire for consensus forced a choice of conformity or rejection and separation from the group, is exhibited in parallel ways in the area of conciliar understanding in the first millennium and in the area of individual responsibility in the second millennium in the West.

The historical importance of the distinction between reception that is linked to communion and that which is governed by a hierarchical model and is thus expressed juridically, takes on a significant theological meaning when it gives rise to the distinction of reception considered as an expression of an active *sensus fidelium* or as an expression of obedience to authority.[369]

Kilmartin offers an analysis of the relationship between the practical process of reception in the earlier councils and the spiritual issues at stake.[370] Where "significant spiritual goods" were at stake, but where these were already seen as important to the community in question, reception was simple. With councils like Nicaea I and Chalcedon where the issues involved were subject to controversial interpretations, the reception process was more complex. Most importantly, Kilmartin asserts that reception was "never in fact, nor [was it] understood by the churches to be" a matter of "a merely juridical act of acceptance by church officials."[371] He adds "rather, the juridical act was viewed as *initiating* a spiritual process of reception by the whole community."[372] Kilmartin observes that from the late Middle Ages on, reception has been treated in terms of constitutional law. When this approach was combined with a dichotomy of an active teaching church and a passive learning church, the "original rich meaning" of reception was left behind. He adds that some post-Reformation Roman Catholic writers specifically reduced the notion of reception to a matter of "religious obedience."[373]

The difference between the first and second millennia understandings of reception is seen as key by Garijo. He considers the most important issue in understanding Catholic dogma in its historical context to be in how to regard the "ecumenicity" of the councils.[374] The manualists establish this in terms of formal aspects; as rendered by the functioning of the council delegates or by the authority of the pope. Modern historians, however, find that the ecumenical nature of the councils of the first millennium was founded in a set criteria that were different from those recognized in later centuries. The most important guide for the first councils was reception.[375]

Garijo points to the Arian crisis as a key example in direct regard to reception.[376] The turmoil that followed Nicaea illustrates the fact that the Church needed a significant amount of time and effort to receive what is recognized now as a central part of its faith.[377] In its own time, the Council was seen to be offering an "innovation."[378]

Garijo describes the era of the great councils as one where reception occurred in a process that was both stressful and critical.[379] The historical intricacies of several conciliar theologies have been examined by Congar.[380] Early on, councils came to be recognized as the vehicles responsible for carrying the *paradosis* received from the apostles.[381] Congar insists that the continuity of tradition was understood as tied to the work of the councils not in a juridical sense, but rather by the recognition that the content of the faith expressed in them was in continuity with apostolic faith. Universal belief was expressed in the conciliar decrees, and even the work of smaller councils could be raised to universal levels of importance in the Church, by the operation of reception.[382]

Congar notes the key role of reception in forming the canon of Scripture, in serving the unity of the Church which resulted from synodal letters sent to important churches like Rome and Alexandria, in liturgy, where local practices were extended into larger areas, in the canonization of saints, and in matters of law and discipline.[383] Congar points out that the centralizing of judgment concerning the tradition in the Roman Church and particularly in the pope himself became possible as the pope came to be identified with the church of Rome, and this church came to be identified with the universal Church.[384] Rome thus claimed the authority to canonize saints, in practice following Alexander II (d. 1073) and by law with Gregory IX in 1234.[385]

In this centralization of authority over such decisions, it was still the judgment of the whole Church which was at stake. Congar illustrates how the larger body has continued to operate in making judgments up until modern times. He notes the non-reception of the teaching of Chalcedon, the non-reception in the East of the *filioque* clause in the creed and later the union of East and West decreed at Florence, the lack of acceptance of Pius II's *Execrabilis* (1460) forbidding appeals to councils, and even the response to Pope John XXIII's *Veterum sapientia* on the use of Latin in seminaries.[386]

Congar describes several theories of reception that are no longer maintained. One taught by Cardinal Francesco Zabarella (1335-1417), Nicholas of Cusa, and others, saw the reception of the community as a necessary element for the truth of laws.[387] Nicholas saw reception as certain when a church council decided on an issue. In its Gallican form, this sort of view led to the belief that reception was a juridical necessity.[388] Congar points out that within a strongly juridical context, the Gallican refusal to have higher authority imposed on a local church was motivated by a concern to protect the validity of the local community. "Blind obedience" was unacceptable. He observes that those who saw the issues involved in strictly legalistic terms could not appreciate the attempts to maintain a legitimate pastoral structure.[389] He points out that the texts adduced by the Gallicans, including St. Isidore, Gratian, and St. Thomas Aquinas supported the view that mere power could not override the reasonable response of Christian freedom to "despotic" authority.[390] Congar notes that these same notions, based in

2 Cor. 13,10, were use by sixteenth and seventeenth century authors "who had not a whiff of Gallicanism about them, sometimes even in order to justify the non-obligatory nature of 'non-received' law."[391] This same verse was used also in the disputes at Vatican I between those who supported and those who omitted a clarifying of the limits on the pope's power.[392]

The role of the whole Church in accepting the doctrinal teachings of councils is strongly emphasized by Kilmartin, when he describes the early Church. At stake was the valid transmission of tradition, and around this task grew the notions of *consensio antiquitas et universitas*.[393] A vertical consensus had to be shown by a council, to establish that what it taught followed upon the ancient faith.[394] Showing such a vertical consensus entailed establishing arguments and finding support for its claims. This was difficult to do and was tied to the need to establish "horizontal" consensus. The doctrinal expressions of a council had to be received by the whole Church as evidence that it had fulfilled its task of teaching.[395] Kilmartin writes,

> In short, in the ancient Catholic Church the problematic of the universal council, under both aspects of consensus, was inseparably linked with the problem of reception. The fact that the success of the council was not automatically guaranteed from the outset points to the awareness of the primacy of the content of the conciliar decisions over whatever formal juridical authority it could claim.[396]

The vertical consensus took precedence over the horizontal, inasmuch as the tradition was something passed on to subsequent generations. Kilmartin relates that reception was also clearly connected to the importance of the content in question for the lives of those in the receiving community. Nicaea II, for instance, found an adverse reaction among Frankish theologians, since it did not present a teaching that was important in their particular context.[397]

Kilmartin uses the early councils as indications that unity of faith could become possible in the relations between East and West today. As a model, he suggests the Council of Florence, where if only for a short time, differences in "dogmatic formulations" did not prevent unity on the "intention of faith."[398] Ironically, the lack of reception of this council in the East and the change of heart on the part of many Eastern bishops provides a poignant example of how the sense of the faithful found the efforts of their pastors for the sake of unity unacceptable.

As has already been indicated, in the West the Middle Ages saw a decline in lay involvement even of a representative nature on the part of leaders, and certainly in the participation of the body of believers as a whole. Jan Walgrave describes the centuries immediately following the fifth with its important councils and doctrinal controversies, as "living on traditional formulas, and no longer enlivened by creative thought."[399] The Church in its theological and philosophical leaders, continued to hand on the received tradition, but Walgrave observes that little innovation in expressing it was to be found during this time. Citing St. Gregory the Great and St. Bede, he states that even its best representatives "were not conspicuous for their originality."[400] Thus, it is not surprising that while the *consensus fidelium* involved an active and even initiating role for lay people in the first five centuries, the expressions of the sense of the faithful in the centuries that followed was passive or reactive.

Very significant examples of "reactions" certainly occurred. Newman cited two examples from the Middle Ages as classic expressions of the *sensus fidelium*. Each involved an area of worship or piety where the people had retained an active interest in doctrinal expression. The ninth century saw controversy rise over the doctrine of the Real Presence. Newman observes,

> when the learned Benedictines of Germany and France were perplexed in their enunciation of the doctrines of the Real

Presence, Paschasius was supported by the faithful in his maintenance of it.[401]

Walgrave notes that the theological debates in this period "were nearly all about words and expressions."[402] The sources employed by the theologians of the time were the Scriptures and documents attesting to later tradition compiled in the *floregia*. Here texts from the early Fathers, Councils, liturgies and decretals were all listed without the benefit of historical context.[403] Rather, the "science of language" was used to interpret them.[404] Paschasius's *De Corpore et Sanguine Domini* (831, revised in 844) thus discusses whether the Eucharist occurs "*in mysterio*" or "*in veritate*," and the debate which followed his treatment revolved around the proper understanding of these phrases.[405] Paschasius himself was attacked by his contemporaries as "crude and materialistic" in his interpretation.[406]

Newman sees popular lay support for the views of Paschasius as an indicator of the sense of the faithful. David Knowles cites this first treatise on the Eucharist from the ninth century thinker as a "herald" of future theologizing and an indicator of the ability of theologians in the Carolingian culture to "seize the essential points" in a concept.[407] He claims the controversy subsided because the parties in the dispute did not have the tools needed for "analysing and redefining" the issues.[408] From the contemporary perspective, it might be considered that the reaction of the people in support of the Real Presence was not so much the ratification of a theological construct as an instinctive response to an insight embedded in Paschasius's concrete expressions, even if they might have been "crudely" stated.

Newman's second Medieval case involves the understanding of the communion of saints in the fourteenth century. In this area of "religious *cultus*," Newman sees the faithful indicating clearly to Pope John XXII their collective belief that the faithful in heaven enjoyed true beatitude, even if the Fathers were not in agreement on the issue and the Pope himself was perceived as heterodox.[409]

This case is examined at some length by Decima Douie.[410] He finds it odd that such a controversy should have existed at all, over the pope's views on the Beatific Vision.[411] Douie recalls the strengths of John in reforming the Curia and giving the Church financial stability as well as the considerable trouble that characterized his dealings with the Franciscan Order. The pope's speculations at the end of his life on the state of the saints in heaven departed from his previous legal and administrative interests, and when faced with controversy at large, and the criticisms of clerics at close hand, he repudiated the disputed views.[412]

Douie recounts that two days before he died, John XXII "summoned his cardinals to his bedside and solemnly declared, 'that the holy souls see God and the divine essence face to face and as clearly as their condition as souls separated from their bodies allows.'"[413] Douie claims that the insistence on the pope's part that his teachings were always private and not given as the Vicar of Christ, and his request that his successors speak to the issue, should not be used as an example against the power of papal teaching, but as evidence in support of papal infallibility. John had taken care to show he was not speaking heresy in his official teaching.[414]

Other historians are less enthusiastic about the zeal in the pope's retraction, and point at any rate to the effects of the initial sermons on the Church and to the theological reaction he provoked. J. N. D. Kelly notes the "modified retraction" and points out that the pope's ideas had been condemned at the University of Paris in 1333, and by the majority of theologians that John consulted.[415] Certainly the wording of the final retraction seems designed to invite further analysis and teaching, and this occurred with Benedict II's *Benedictus deus* (1336). This response taught that the souls "see the divine essence intuitively and ever face to face, not through the intervention of any other being, but through the divine essence itself."[416]

Douie maintains that the criticisms that John XXII encountered were connected with the positions he took concerning evangelical poverty. When the condemnations of John on this matter "had become somewhat stale," his teachings on the Beatific Vision "condemned by the universities and the general opinion" provided another avenue for his detractors.[417] Whatever political motivations there may have been in the criticism of the pope's position on this issue, and however thoroughly he may have presented his position or repudiated it, the critical response to his view seems rather clearly to have been influenced by the popular rejection of his views. If theological criticism then and now has been concerned with the strength and authority with which John XXII held his view, Newman's point seems well taken. The view of the people was held strongly in response to the pope, even if it was based in an instinctive sense of scandal.[418]

Expression of the *consensus fidelium* in decision making and the exercise of the *sensus fidelium* in doctrinal matters both found the laity in a more passive role in the Middle Ages than in the earlier centuries. Yet the most important contribution of this period to the understanding of the sense of the faithful came in the theological focus on the *sensus fidei*. The key medieval figure for contemporary reflection in this matter is St. Thomas Aquinas.

Avery Dulles describes Aquinas as giving an "Aristotelian turn" to the sense of the faithful. Thomas approached the issue in terms of the "connaturality," a sort of "existential affinity" that each believer possesses in regard to the truth.[419] The term, *sensus fidei*, occurs only once in St. Thomas's writings, but the concept receives significant development in his thought.[420]

Thompson describes Thomas as "representative of the mature thought of this period."[421] Following Koster, he notes the topic was treated also by William of Auxerre, Alexander of Hales, Bonaventure, and Albert the Great, who variously referred to the subject of the religious "sense" as *sensus fidei* (or merely *sensus*), or as the *motus caritatis*.[422] Koster himself sees the theological importance of the idea as beginning in the work of these thinkers and that of Aquinas, with its current sense taking its roots in Spain in the Counter-Reformation.[423] This personal sense was not separated from the ecclesial sense of the faith, however. Thompson cites Étienne Ménard, who finds that Aquinas located infallibility in the whole Church. The *sensus fidelium* is thus a "concrete manner of realization of the judgment of the universal church."[424]

This judgment is found in the Church as a form of discernment; as a *habitus* or *virtus*, whose object is truth. There is here that "connaturality" by which the subject conforms to the object of faith.[425] Congar shows the influence of this focus in modern authors, and particularly of those of the stature of Moehler and Newman in their reflection on the personal aspects of the sense of the faith.[426] Moehler in particular saw a connection between the individual experience of this type of knowledge and the community that was the recipient of the common spirit of faith.[427] Koster describes the medieval understanding of the *sensus fidei* as an "illuminating of faith of the members of Christ through him as head."[428]

According to Thomas, it is certainly possible for the intellect to adhere to falsehood instead of truth. There is always the need for interrelation between the believer, the Church as recipient of revelation, and most of all the Spirit who gives knowledge of the truth.[429] In specific instances like the Arian crisis, believers fell into error, having a "perverse sense" of the truth. Thomas spoke also of the distortion of the sense of revealed matters as "spiritual adultery."[430]

Sancho claims that while the specific phrase *sensus fidei* does not occur widely in Aquinas, the concept it describes is found often in his work. Similarly, little explicit connection is made by him of the sense of the faith and the infallibility of the Church. Sancho observes that the link between the believer and the faith of the universal Church is significant in Aquinas's thought, however, and forms a foundation for later scholastic treatment of these issues.[431]

## THE REFORMATION

Events in the sixteenth century changed the face of the Western church dramatically, the most obvious effect being the breakup of Latin Christianity into several separate confessional bodies. If this breakup had cultural and political aspects, the ecclesial battles which caused it were fought in doctrinal terms. It is not surprising then, that the sense of the faithful, which was seen in the early Church in terms of the expression of the whole church community as the *consensus fidelium*, and which was studied in the Middle Ages in terms of the knowing subject as the *sensus fidei*, would be focused in the Reformation and Modern Eras in doctrinal terms as the *sensus fidelium*.

Yves Congar describes several key issues that became important at the time of the Reformation, and that introduced elements into theology that have had an impact both then and now. The turmoil of the sixteenth century was characterized by spiritual needs, by new critical approaches to texts and the consideration of their "historical sense," and a focus on cultural and anthropological concerns.[432] The political developments and intellectual challenges that followed the breakup of the Medieval world and world view placed particular stress on the question of tradition, which was appropriated in new ways to address theological problems and ecclesial corruption. Luther's impact on piety and doctrine through his insistence on justification by faith alone was connected to an influence no less important for the development of ecclesiology, as he insisted on the Scriptures as the sole theological norm. Congar finds that Luther "challenged (Catholic) theological science to its very foundations."[433] His impact contributed to "the creation of a defense and a critical methodology of those foundations: treatises on tradition, the theological sources and apologetic justification of the faith as well as the Church and its magisterium."[434] If the Patristic Church saw itself as responsible for handing on the *paradosis*, the sixteenth century Church found its responsibility in finding a new way for understanding this handing on.

Lowell Green points out that the modern expression of the problem of tradition is raised by asking how the Church might reconcile the old and new, without either abandoning the tradition or ignoring current issues. The sixteenth century discussion, as exemplified in Erasmus, Luther and Melancthon, was based on the commonly accepted view that "a doctrine had to be ancient to be authentic, and that any doctrinal or liturgical innovation was likely heretical."[435] Where reformers accused the Roman Church of straying from the apostolic faith, Roman Catholics accused the reformers of departing from genuine catholicity. Both turned to the greater consensus of belief exhibited in history and recognized by the Fathers as indicative of orthodoxy.[436] Green finds in Tertullian and Vincent of Lerins a difference in emphasis in which the sixteenth century adversaries rooted their own different views. In Tertullian, authority comes from God to the Church through the Scriptures. Any new expression must be consistent with the *regula fidei* of the Scriptures. Green sees Vincent as adding a criteria of *universitas* and *consensio* to that of the *antiquitas* of Tertullian, thus giving an emphasis to the Church as a locus of authority in its collective belief (the *consensus omnium*). Green points out that these different emphases in the early Church gave foundations to the approaches of the sixteenth century, with Luther and Melancthon following the emphasis of Tertullian and Erasmus following more closely that of Vincent.[437]

Erasmus developed his own view of the *magnus consensus* in reaction to Luther's challenge to reform in the Ninety-Five Theses, and particularly in response to pressure from other Roman Catholics who pushed him to criticize

Luther more strongly than he had originally done.[438] Three areas of consensus are discernible in Erasmus's approach: the church Fathers, the statements of councils, and the agreement of believers.[439] Luther accepted the importance of the Fathers, and had appealed to a church council to consider the issues in dispute between reformers and Rome. Yet, Green observes that Luther could not accept a consensus of the people that was based in the views of contemporary scholars, and was completely opposed to any criteria which would allow human reason consideration before the Scriptures.[440]

Green writes that Luther worried about the possibility that he had added any new doctrine to the Gospel. Certainly others asked him, "Do you think that you alone are right, and that all Christendom has erred these many years?"[441] Luther in fact asserted in his *Resolutions* of 1518, a commentary on his own Ninety-Five Theses, that he had never intended to stray from what had been taught in the Bible, the Fathers, or the Roman Church in its papal teachings.[442] He repeated a similar claim later that year to Cardinal Cajetan in Augsburg. Green writes that Luther's view of the papacy was mitigated only after he was left in a condemnable position after debating Johann Eck.[443] He notes that in opposing Eck, Luther appealed to the *magnus consensus* against the papacy. Luther claimed,

> That the Roman Church stands above all others can be proved (only) out of the coldest papal decrees of the past 400 years; as witnesses against this stand the attested history of 1100 years, the text of the Holy Scriptures, and the decree of the (first) Council of Nicaea, the holiest of all.[444]

When Luther found traditions in conflict with each other, he judged by two principles: the earlier view was to be given preference over the later, and all teachings were to be considered ultimately in relation to Scripture. Green attests that Luther was no Biblical reductionist; tradition was important, but it was subject to criticism in the light of Scripture. The *magnus consensus* thus had a legitimate place.[445] As he became more critical of the papacy, Luther continued to accept the importance of consensus, though understanding it as "unanimity in agreement with Scripture."[446]

Green describes Melancthon's view as similar to Luther's. With both Erasmus and Luther he shared a concern for a basis in antiquity for doctrine, and while he gave precedence to Scripture, he found tradition to be an important element in the Church.[447] In discussing the Trinity, Melancthon says that, "The churches among us teach, with the *magnus consensus*, the decree of the Council of Nicaea."[448] Green observes that, "Melancthon is not espousing a form of conciliarism but is pointing to truth revealed by God through one of the ecumenical gatherings of the ancient church."[449]

Green adds that on both the Protestant and Catholic sides, there was an acceptance of the notion that revelation had occurred both through Jesus Christ (known through the Scriptures) and through the Church's experiences in history (with results found in tradition). Although they differed in the way they understood these sources, both attempted to link their own views and practices "with the unanimous consensus of past ages."[450] Green thus sees in Erasmus to a large extent, as well as in Luther and Melancthon, important witnesses to this emerging modern appeal to consensus in the early Church.[451]

William Thompson sees the *sensus fidelium* as a "key concept" for the Reformation, inasmuch as concern for the laity was "reawakened" in the Church.[452] He cites Luther's teaching on the priesthood of believers, and Calvin's connection of Mt 28:20 and the Johannine texts on the Paraclete with the faithful as indicators of the importance of the laity's "sense."[453]

He finds in the Reformation a return of attention to the link between authority in the Church And the Word of God. The whole Church, and not only its leaders, receives the promises of Christ's presence and the gift of faith. He notes that Calvin found in these promises a "great certitude and firmness."[454] These promises are the foundation which the Church can trust, yet they are conditioned by limits; the Church must remain rooted in what God has revealed.[455] Following Congar, Thompson states that Luther and Calvin "equated the authority of the faithful with that of the ministry."[456] Specifically, Congar writes that Luther "transposes" the legitimate "exercise of inward anointing" by which the believer is "enabled to grasp the sense of true doctrine" onto an ecclesiological level.[457] He claims Luther uses this sense

> to replace the principle of apostolic function by an apostolicity of content which every man can judge for himself, and the community above all. Just as the Church's aspect as institution or order of the means of grace is set aside, so all hierarchical mediation is eliminated.[458]

Congar sees Luther's error as elevating the priesthood of believers to a "structural ecclesiological principle" where "private judgment," legitimate in its place, becomes a rule of faith.[459]

Thompson agrees that to the extent the reformers made this connection, they erred. Yet, he finds an important insight in their "reemphasis" on the limitations that characterize the Church's appropriation of Christ's promises or its exercise of authority.[460] Thompson finds in this focus that recognizes the role of the whole Church and not only its leaders, "a genuine aspect of tradition . . . which clearly needs to be kept in view for a balanced treatment of the *sensus fidelium*."[461] Importantly, the Church does not "regulate" revelation, either through its hierarchy or through the sense of the faithful. Rather, the Church is itself created and led by revelation.[462]

Thompson observes that this is nothing more than an appropriation of the insight of the early Church in its general councils, whose authority was seen as coming "from their faithfulness to the Spirit and his Word, rather than simply from a 'formal' authority."[463] Thompson recalls that this early understanding of the sense of the faithful was linked the Church's identification of itself as the living body of Christ.[464]

Yet, how the "regulating" of this body by the word of God is to occur is precisely the practical question that inspired the Reformation debates about authority. Identifications of the genuine tradition, the true community of believers and the trustworthy voice of authority were all tied together in this period.

The question of how the community of believers in particular was to be identified with Christ was posed in a new way in the Reformation. George Tavard cites the Augsburg Confession (1530) as the catalyst for the Roman Catholic Church's reflection on how tradition (*paradosis*) was legitimately expressed.[465] The relation of the individual to God and the consequent relationship to other believers in a visible community were issues that were faced in emerging ecclesiologies.

Concern for continuity and a rootedness in the genuine Christian tradition was the aim of both sides of the Reformation debates, even if there was not the sophisticated understanding of the way in which historical context shapes doctrinal expression that would characterize modern interpretations of tradition. Contemporary ecumenical discussions, which have included Roman Catholic participants since Vatican II, stress the importance of the role of consensus, in the ongoing reflections of individual ecclesial bodies and in the discussions between separated churches, as well as consideration of the related issue of reception.[466] The ecclesial structures and concepts that were the focus of the Church as it faced the task of handing on its tradition in early eras are being examined again in modern discussions.

George Tavard sees the return to the idea of *koinonia* as a central theme in ecclesiology, as a key theological emphasis since Vatican II.[467] It is founded not so much in an explicit discussion of the topic at Vatican II, as in the ecumenical awareness that found its Catholic impetus in the Council. In order to understand the relationship between tradition and *koinonia*, Tavard begins his study with an examination of the Reformation's approach to these themes.[468]

Tavard notes that ecumenical councils identified their own deliberations with the tradition expressed in earlier councils; Nicaea II (787) in particular made this link explicit. Yet, reflection on tradition was rare until the Reformation raised the issue by choosing and criticizing the choices that serve as foundations for the Church. Thus Tavard says, article 7 of the Augsburg Confession poses the Gospel as the criterion for judging what practices and traditions should be allowed or demanded in the community. The article affirms,

> The Church is an assembly of saints, in which the gospel is rightly preached and the sacraments are rightly administered. And for authentic Church unity it is sufficient for there to be agreement on the teaching of the gospel and the administration of the sacraments. It is not necessary for there to be the same human traditions in every place, nor humanly instituted rites and ceremonies.[469]

Tavard remarks that the Scriptures might themselves be seen as precisely this criterion. Yet the Augsburg Confession and other Lutheran texts do not themselves make this identification. It is in the Calvinist Second Helvetic Confession (1566, chapter 1) that the notion of *sola scriptura* first becomes officially expressed. It is included again in the Thirty-nine Articles of the Church of England and the Twenty-eight of Methodism.[470] In articles from these foundational collections, Tavard finds the exercise of the criterion of a connection to the Gospel, to be related to the church community. Article 34 in the Anglican collection reads,

> Whosoever, through his private judgement, willingly and purposely doth openly break the rites and ceremonies of the church to which he belongs, which are not repugnant to the Word of God,

and are ordained and approved by common authority, ought to be rebuked openly, that others may fear to do the like, as one that offendeth against the common order of the church, and woundeth the conscience of weak brethren. Every particular church may ordain, change, or abolish rites and ceremonies, so that all things may be done to edification.[471]

Here, individual insight is important enough to be corrected if a member of the body is in error. Such insight is to be sought for those who are weak. It is governed by the community's judgment of how well the Gospel is served. Such an approach "suggest[s] a 'communion-ecclesiology'" according to Tavard.[472]

The inclusion of the community with the laity forming its major part carried a renewed theological weight in the Reformation era.

## TRENT AND THE COUNTER-REFORMATION

The response of the Roman Church to the teachings of the reformers came in the Council of Trent. In its fourth session (1546) the Council took its lead from the "Calvinist approach."[473] It located the "truth and rule" of the Gospel in the "written books and in unwritten traditions that have reached down to us, whether received from the mouth of Christ himself or transmitted as though by hand by the apostles themselves at the dictate of the Holy Spirit."[474] Tavard observes that this view is not inconsistent with the Augsburg Confession. He notes, however, that the "Tradition" goes beyond the "traditions" of the apostles considered by Trent. It also includes the process of transmission, the administration of the sacraments and the passing on of the Scriptures. This transmission presupposes a community. It includes those who hand on traditions and those who receive them, and thus necessarily involves a community that links the past and future.[475]

Tavard writes that the nature of tradition requires not only acceptance of the fact of "binding traditions" but of some principle that can distinguish true ones and false ones as well.[476] The Reformers and the Council of Trent both found this "normative" principle or "central Tradition" in the Gospel. Tavard observes that in the "classical Catholic" position, the Church that passes on and accepts the tradition in succeeding generations is described as the *Ecclesia docens* and *Ecclesia discens*. The same body is, of course, described by both phrases.[477]

However, if the whole Church is involved in each activity, it is still clear that by the sixteenth century any critical examination of content in the tradition, and the explicit tasks of preaching and teaching the tradition were in the hands of experts—the magisterium. Avery Dulles observes that Trent (as well as the two later Vatican Councils) had some participants who were not bishops. He lists cardinals, abbots and general superiors of religious orders among those who attended and voted.[478] Robert McNally gives a striking description of the degree of intellectual and spiritual depth that could be exhibited by the Council Fathers in preaching and debate at the sessions, as well as the intolerance and charges of heresy that found there place there too.[479] Discussion and disagreement could make the exercise of magisterial responsibility a very active matter. Yet, important for the issues considered here, is the realization that such participants were clearly distinguished in their role as teachers from the general group of believers. The magisterium in the persons of the hierarchy or in other teachers prescinded from any active role for the laity, considered in terms of the priesthood of the faithful.[480]

In a discussion of the debates at Trent concerning the selection of bishops, Jean Bernhard describes how this practice was separated even farther from the ancient practice of election by the whole community.[481] When certain Gallican participants suggested that the ancient precedents made the participation of the people reasonable, other bishops spoke strongly against it. In May of 1563 during the Council's XXIIIrd session, the Cardinal of Lorraine cited Cyprian's 67th letter in support of the notion that the people were earlier involved in the selection of bishops, whereas in the current church practices, even other bishops in an effected area were now left unconsulted.[482] In the debate that followed, suggestions that the election process be widened to involve greater inclusion were strongly opposed. Bernhard quotes the Archbishop of Rossano saying,

> The people are hopelessly superficial and it can be taken for granted that they are more moved by rhetoric, kindness, favours, serious requests and sometimes by bribes than by a straightforward sense of responsibility (*prudentia*).[483]

The Archbishop cited the context of turmoil, where the faith of the people appeared "to be wavering from one extreme to another" to warn that their involvement in the selection of bishops would result in individuals of the same ilk.[484]

After his discussion of the complicated political aspects of the debates on the choice of bishops, Bernhard concludes that the policies finally chosen involved a strongly sacramentalized view of the ministry of the Church.[485] He observes that the conciliar statements that deal with the appointment of bishops "are part of a concept of the priesthood defined exclusively by its sacramental function seen as the power to consecrate the Eucharist and absolve sins."[486] He adds,

> It is obvious that with a ministry interpreted in this way the laity have only an extremely limited role to play in the choice of their own bishops. The Church's ministers, indeed, are not seen rising from the grassroots community but rather as descending to the community from on high.[487]

Following the trends of the Middle Ages the practical exercise of teaching and learning in the Roman Church became a matter of clearly distinguished groups. The time between Council of Florence (1439-45) and the end of the eighteenth century is described by Dulles as having "a growing emphasis on hierarchical authority and particularly on the papacy as the supreme instance of hierarchical authority."[488] In addition to the disputes with the reformers, Dulles cites the changed status of the universities and the need to resist "a variety of nationalistic and secularistic movements within the Catholic community" as factors contributing to this centralizing of authority.[489] At Trent, bishops and theologians met together to discuss doctrinal issues, with the bishops then voting on final statements in the Council's sessions. Dulles notes that many bishops, and particularly the Italians and Spaniards were proficient in theology and "could rightly boast that they had not turned over their teaching authority to the theologians."[490]

After Trent, the separation between the *Ecclesia docens* and the *Ecclesia discens* came to be taught explicitly. Dulles cites the Englishman, Thomas Stapleton (1535-98) as the first theologian to identify these with the hierarchy and laity. With this distinction comes the association of these roles with an "active infallibility" and a "passive infallibility" Dulles writes, that with these roles in place, "The duty of the faithful, therefore, is simply to accept what the hierarchy tells them."[491] He adds, "The 'sensus fidelium' in this theory ceases to function as a distinct theological source."[492]

The ecclesial structure of the Counter-Reformation period is described by Frederick Parrella in terms of its "pyramid" style of hierarchy, with the pope on top, the curia immediately under him and the people forming the wide base at the bottom.[493] Parrella contrasts this view with the early Church's understanding of itself as a community. He cites Congar's description, of this earlier view of the Church as "an organization where Christ intervened at its origin as the founder, and the Holy Spirit as the guarantee of its authority."[494] Parrella adds that many ecclesiologies in the period after Trent were either "vindications of the Church as a perfect society, or theological support for ecclesiastical authority and papal primacy."⁴⁹⁵

The confidence with which the "visible" Church was regarded is illustrated by a description of Robert Bellarmine (d. 1621):

> The one true Church is the community of men brought together by profession of the true faith and communion in the same sacraments, under the administration of recognized pastors and especially of the sole vicar of Christ on earth, the Roman Pontiff. . . . The Church is indeed a community (coetus) of men, as visible and palpable as the community of the Roman people, or the kingdom of France, or the republic of Venice.⁴⁹⁶

At the same time, the centralizing and organizing of authority begun at Trent had dramatic effects in achieving reform, and uniform systems in liturgical practice and church governance did eliminate abuse in many areas. Certainly such centralizing was not achieved without criticism. Giuseppe Alberigo describes how the bishops of Trent rejected the attempts of Rome to include in the canons of the Council, a statement declaring the Pope to be the supreme ruler of the Church.⁴⁹⁷ Alberigo sees the end of the fifteenth century as the period where the role of the papacy explicitly became a source of disunity in practical historical terms among Christians, that could prompt Paul VI's famous remark that "the papacy is without doubt the most serious obstacle on the path to ecumenism."⁴⁹⁸ The same Cardinal of Lorraine mentioned above saw that it was the "doctrinal and practical claims" made by Rome rather than the papacy itself that created greater division between Protestants and Catholics.⁴⁹⁹

Considerable debate on the primacy was included in the Council's deliberations before it promulgated the canons concerning the Sacrament of Orders. Yet despite the introduction of several different formulas describing such a role for the pope, none was included. The papacy is mentioned only in canon 8, which connects the "legitimacy" of bishops to the authority of the pope.[500]

Yet, after Trent, Pope Pius IV included in the 1564 Profession of Faith a phrase that left no doubt about primacy.[501] The Profession asserted,

> I acknowledge the Holy, Catholic and apostolic, Roman Church as the mother and the teacher of all the Churches, and I promise and swear true obedience to the Roman Pontiff, successor of Blessed Peter, chief of the apostles, and Vicar of Christ.[502]

Alberigo cites this claim as marking the start of a period where the papacy served the ironic role of symbolizing greater disunity among Christian groups in general, while playing an increasingly unifying role in the Roman Catholic communion.[503]

In the implementation of Trent in the years that followed, Rome achieved a powerful role in promoting real reform, and in eventually launching an effective missionary program. Alberigo also notes that the disputes instigated by Robert Bellarmine concerning the papacy resulted in a consolidation of authority for the pope in both "theory and practice." The activities of the papacy that are illustrated in the development of the offices of apostolic delegates and nuncios from the Counter-Reformation period on provided the Church with its credentials in European politics where the "common denominator" was "a monarchical ideology."[504]

Among the reforms achieved by Trent, the Council required bishops to live in the dioceses over which they held authority, and to preach in their churches.[505] Prusak notes that while such restrictions showed that the Council "rejected the notion of a diocese as a benefice for the personal advantage of a bishop," it retained the medieval view that the diocese was "a pastoral *administrative unit*."[506] Such an ecclesiology is also demonstrated in the emphasis given to questions about transubstantiation and the Eucharist as a sacrifice, which lacked any discussion of the role of the sacrament in the church as a whole.[507]

Prusak describes Rome as the "bulwark of a decimated Catholicism" which was more and more "identified with the universal Church."[508] He notes that at this time, the phrases "Apostolic Church" or "Holy See" were made synonymous with "Holy Church" or "Universal Church." He describes the period between Trent and Vatican I as being "greatly influenced" by a "fear of national churches," represented in the nineteenth century by Gallicanism and Febronianism.[509]

As the Church developed into a structured organization with strong central leadership, the lay role became less an active presence and more a theological construct. Jan Walgrave has examined the use of tradition by both sides in the Reformation, with an eye to the impact of the views developed in the period on the theology of doctrinal development. He sees the Vincentian Canon being appropriated by both Protestants and Catholics, though with different presuppositions and goals. Insisting on basing doctrine in the Bible alone, Protestants could maintain that doctrinal matters not found in the Scriptures had not been taught at all times. Catholics could claim that practices or beliefs that were current in the Church at large were believed everywhere and by all. Their antiquity was asserted by positing them in an alternative source of revelation, the tradition given orally by the apostles to the Church.[510]

Walgrave notes that this second source was claimed after Trent, even though the Council itself had refused to declare that there were "two distinct streams of revelation." Further, the content of oral traditions was left unspecified. Yet, some such oral deposit containing teachings on faith and morals was accepted as having been left in the hands of the hierarchy, and even those opposed to a two source schema "had to grant that both Scripture and tradition were to be treated with equal respect."[511]

The Council left the definition of the exact relationship of tradition and Scripture open, refusing to choose between the two source theory, or a theory that argued that there was one source, Scripture, which contained "all truths necessary for salvation."[512] In this latter view, the tradition continues not by the creation of anything new, but through refined interpretations of what has been received. Walgrave claims that Trent lacked a sufficient theory on doctrinal development, and thus wisely left the question open for discussion. Yet, with the absence of a theory, some theologians maintained the view of tradition as a sort of source for doctrine, and often claimed it as the warrant for specific teachings not found in the Bible.[513]

Walgrave points out that "first principles" of interpretation determined the results of both Protestant and Catholic appeals to the Vincentian Canon. If Protestants could dismiss doctrinal expressions not found explicitly in the Scriptures, Catholics could posit current doctrines as part of an original oral revelation. Walgrave quotes Arnauld (d. 1694) as an example of how this way of supporting doctrine bore fruit in later Jansenist views,

> All the dogmas of faith are as old as the Church: they were all explicitly (*distinctement*) believed by the Apostles and have been preserved by an uninterrupted succession of tradition in the consciousness of at least a part of the shepherds and the faithful.[514]

From within the theological lines drawn in the sixteenth century, presuppositions could determine the attitudes created concerning the way tradition operated, inasmuch as there was as yet no "recourse to a still non-existent theory of dynamic or evolutive tradition."[515]

The issues of doctrine and authority remained linked in the theologizing of the years following the Reformation, and greatly colored the treatment given to the operation of tradition in general, and the *sensus fidelium* in particular.

Melchior Cano (d. 1560) has been identified as the first author to refer to dogma in the "restricted sense" of revealed expressions which must be adhered to. In contrast to the medieval use of the word dogma as an equivalent to doctrine, this more precise use identifies those truths which are both apostolic and authoritatively defined, and whose denial constitutes not just the heresy of going against church authority, but the "pernicious opposition to revealed dogma." For Cano, the authority for expressing dogma could come from the pope, a council in union with the pope, or the faith of the people which was "constant and peacefully held."[516] His *De Locis Theologicis* (published in 1563) had an important impact on post-tridentine theology, as his "theological places" served both to support the expressions of the faith and to combat the reformers. Under his approach "dogma [became] a matter to be defined by the Church."[517]

Schrodt sees this view of dogma as the earliest expression of the view taken up later by the First Vatican Council.[518] Tavard sees it holding a dominant position in Catholic theology up until the Second Vatican Council's *Dei Verbum*. He criticizes the view that "a doctrine has the value of the authority that proclaimed it," as a "formal principle" that is "one-sided."[519] Tavard argues that the balance required by authority is found in the Church conceived as *koinonia*; a living community of believers that can give perspective to teachings that may be both true and yet so conditioned by their original historical contexts as to "no longer be understandable."[520]

Tavard notes that too narrow a dependence on authoritative pronouncements can bind the Church to statements that "become progressively obsolete." He cites Boniface VIII's *Unam sanctum* of 1300 as an example. Theology and ecclesial decisions that do not make sense in newer contexts can lead to

> a discrepancy between hierarchical decisions based on a formal principle of doctrinal authority, and the *sensus fidelium*, which, by

its very nature, is primarily sensitive to the needs of the present and pays closer attention to the content of Tradition than to the level of authority of its sources.[521]

Yet even with the centralization of authority in decisions made by the Church and the separation of laity from authoritative expressions of doctrine, and even when this separation could lead to a discrepancy between official Church expressions and the actual faith of the people, the tradition of the sense of the faithful was not rejected. Cano includes it as a testimony of the ancient faith along side of hierarchical authority. Bellarmine too teaches that, "What all the faithful hold as a matter of faith is necessarily true and of faith."[522] Gustave Thils notes that in arguing for magisterial infallibility, Bellarmine bases his argument in the accepted view that "the consensus of the universal Church . . . cannot be in error."[523]

In Cano and in Bellarmine we see instances where the sense of the faithful is accepted as an important theological source in the ecclesiology that grows out of the Counter-Reformation, and which influences ecclesiology well into the nineteenth century and even beyond.

Sancho writes that with the Counter-Reformation, the interpretation of the "sense" of Scripture was reserved to the authority of the Catholic Church. The *sensus fidei*, or instinct in the individual believer that was examined by the Scholastics was seen as too easily supporting the view of private interpretation considered to be the tool with which Luther objected to the Church's teaching. He notes that Trent referred to the "sense" in the Church as the *sensus Ecclesiae*, *universus Ecclesia sensus, unanimis consensus Ecclesiae*, or *consensus totius Ecclesiae*; "formulas that emphasize the role of solidarity of all the faithful."[524]

In Trent's treatment of sources of tradition, care was taken to connect the teaching of the Church to the *sensus Ecclesiae*.[525] Emphasis is on individual judgment being related to the whole. Sancho cites the decree from session IV which reads,

> Furthermore, to keep undisciplined minds under proper control, the council decrees that no one should dare to rely on his own judgment in matters of faith and morals affecting the structure of Christian doctrine and to distort Sacred Scripture to fit meanings of his own that are contrary to the meaning that holy Mother Church has held and now holds; for it is her office to judge about the true sense and interpretation of Sacred Scripture. Nor should anyone dare to interpret Sacred Scripture contrary to the unanimous agreement of the Fathers, even though such interpretations are never going to be published.[526]

Yet a relationship between the individual's sense of the faith and this sense seen as an attribute of the whole Church could not be easily severed. George Tavard describes two "heterogenous" views of Cano expressed in his *De locis theologicis*.[527] There is on the one hand, a spiritual view, that the Gospel is "written, not on stones, tablets, or paper, but in the hearts of the faithful."[528] Cano himself writes of the Bible, "We have received it from the Fathers; it is interior to and, as it were, sculptured in the souls of the faithful."[529] In this view, Scripture is seen as the primary "*locus*" for theology. The second view is of tradition, conceived as "an oral transmission of unwritten and even hidden doctrines" handed on from the apostles. It is with this second aspect that "Tradition becomes an institutional prerogative of Church authority, containing an extrascriptural part of revelation unknown to most of the faithful."[530]

If the two views were apt to be seen as conflicting, Tavard relates that both were maintained by Catholic proponents. Both Catholics and Protestants appealed to the "gospel in the hearts" that drew on the "subjective" knowledge of believers.[531] Tavard cites the remarks of the Catholic, John Driedo.

> What belongs to faith and salvation should not be learnt from another than the Spirit of faith, who teaches all the truth of faith and salvation which should be believed, proposing it either by Himself in an inward inspiration alone, or else through men, prophets like Christ, the apostles, the Church.[532]

Congar refers to Driedo and other "authors of the Augustinian tradition" as proponents of the importance of "the faith of the universal ecclesial community."[533] Here, Driedo clearly describes the faith in terms that link it to the *sensus fidei*. In regard to such treatment of this source Tavard says,

> The very fact that a key position of the Catholic polemicists was so similar to the central bulwark of their adversaries is eloquent. The Catholics would hardly have dared approach so near to Reformed positions unless this was a hinge of their own doctrine. In fact, they could not give up this point without renouncing a major part of their theological tradition. In their appeal to the "gospel of the hearts," they echoed the theology of medieval and patristic centuries.[534]

He sees a "partial collapse" of emphasis of this view in the two centuries before the Reformation.[535] Though developed in important ways by Aquinas and Bonaventure, it was not given significant treatment by later Scholastics.[536] Yet, Tavard observes that with Cano it "appears . . . to be a permanent acquisition of the Catholic understanding of God's dealings with men."[537]

Sancho describes the theological appropriation of the *sensus fidei* as a river that disappears underground only to reappear a few miles away.[538] Theologians after Trent sought to continue the use of this source that had been developed so richly in the theology of Thomas Aquinas, in order to oppose the Reformers. Rejecting the notion of the "individualist principle" attributed to Luther, and at the same time emphasizing the connection of the sense of the faith to the whole Church as "the dynamic characteristic of the gifts of the Spirit," as Aquinas had considered it, they moved away from the term *"sensus fidei,"* in favor of *"communis sensus fidelium"* or *"sensus fidelium."*[539]

Thus in his *De locis theologicis* Melchior Cano introduces the expression as he asks *"An ex fidelium communi sensu firma duci argumenta possint ad dogmata theologiae comprobanda."*[540] The faith of the people is seen here as a source in a passive sense. Yet it is possible to see that in this period when responsibility for assessment and expression of church teaching was taken up by theologians and the hierarchy, personal responsibility on the part of believers was not lost. Thils considers the position of the faith of the whole people of God to be enhanced by the stance that Cano takes with respect to the magisterium.[541] As a theological locus the sense of the faithful came to be expressed in terms of the view of ecclesial systems that grew out of the polemics and agendas of the Reformation, yet its actual exercise in the lives of believers was not necessarily limited by such descriptions.

## *EPIKEIA* AND RECEPTION

A clear indication of responsibility being alive on the part of ordinary believers can be seen in an issue that bore theological fruit in the post-Tridentine Church, though it took its roots in medieval reflection; the concept in moral theology of *epikeia*. Rooted in Aristotelian thought, it is an aspect of practical judgment used in the context of law. Specifically, it is a corrective which can allow a community or an individual to judge that a law does not apply in a particular context, due to the universal quality of the law. The first formal treatment of the topic among Scholastic thinkers is in the *Ethica* of Albert the Great (d. 1280).[542] Its most influential treatment comes, however, from Thomas Aquinas.

Thomas emphasized that *epikeia* is a judgment about a concrete case, and not about the law in question. Riley asserts that it "seems to be a logical inference from the teaching of St. Thomas," that for an individual to exercise this judgment and act contrary to the law there must be some aspect of the "public good" at stake. The intent of the lawmaker ought to guide the one who acts; if it would be certain that the lawmaker, seeing the circumstances, would not obligate the individual, the one acting is free to act without consulting another authority. If it is not clear what the lawmaker would do, "an authority with power to dispense" should be consulted if there is time to do so. If there is not sufficient time, the law should be obeyed. Where there are "cases of probability," authority must be consulted, but where this can not be done, the subject may exercise his or her own judgment.[543]

Riley describes how Thomas distinguishes *epikeia*, as "a purely private and moral institute," from *aequitas*, a similar act of judgment, but one exercised in a public context by a judge.[544] What is clear is that in the private realm, there is warrant in the concept of *epikeia* for individual responsibility, both for understanding the context of a legal or moral precept and for applying such a precept in the actual concrete context.

Franz Scholz points out that in Aquinas's teaching, even the duties prescribed in the "second table" of the decalogue could be exempted in certain conditions using *epikeia*.[545] Scholz thus emphasizes a wider scope for this aspect of judgment. He underlines the key issue for modern use of Thomas's teaching on *epikeia*, as its emphasis on clarifying the applicability of a particular formulation of law by the intent of the original giver. He argues that this clarifying, and the "authorization," might include appeal not only to human authority but to God as well.[546] Scholz admits his approach leaves important interpretive questions open. Yet he maintains that there are far-ranging possibilities for the notion as used by Thomas.[547]

In describing an act of responsibility in an individual believer, the concept of *epikeia* offers a correlative in the area of law and morals, to the medieval focus on the individual in the understanding of doctrinal truths. The Church's doctrinal expression might not have invited involvement of the subject's knowledge of the faith through the *sensus fidei* in an immediate way. Yet, if the common believer of the Counter-Reformation found a church centralized by authority and a highly juridical system, there was still an important aspect of freedom and responsibility to be exercised.

Riley points out that there was an "increased leniency" in the treatments of *epikeia* that followed Thomas and which culminated in the work of one of its most important students, Francisco de Suarez (d. 1617).[548] Among its liberal interpreters, the use of *epikeia* is even extended to situations where the common good is not at stake, and where consultation of an authority was not considered necessary when it was clear that in the case in question, the lawmaker did not intend to bind the one acting.[549]

At the same time, Riley points out that most commentators followed the stricter stance of Cardinal Cajetan (d. 1534), that *epikeia* should be used only where it would be sinful to obey the law. Riley adds that some authors disagreed with certain aspects of Cajetan's strict interpretation. Gabriel Vazquez (d. 1604) in particular, agreed in large part with Cajetan yet distinguished two mitigating cases. When it is not clear that a legislator had the authority to demand obedience to a law, the individual may judge whether such authority was present. Appeal to a different authority in the matter is not needed even when this could be obtained. Additionally, even where the authority behind a law is certain, ambiguity in the wording used may bring into question the intention of the lawgiver. Here "any prudent person may interpret the law," although this is not strictly *epikeia*, which applies to individual cases. In a case where the law is clear, but where the specific circumstances of an application were not anticipated by the lawgiver, the law should be followed. Thus Vazquez is only slightly less restrictive in his interpretation than Cajetan, yet Riley observes that his distinguishing of "power" and "intention" on the part of the lawgiver is a "starting point" for the view of later authors that *epikeia* may be used in situations where obeying the law "would not be sinful or unjust."[550]

Riley observes that among the authors from Suarez's time through the nineteenth century, there is no general agreement on this issue. In addition to those who either support or disagree with Suarez, some authors ignore the issue and still others simply remain unclear about it.[551] Another aspect of *epikeia* that is important in this period is discussion of the appropriateness of its use in cases of certainty, doubt or probability. Riley cites two areas of agreement. Where it is clear the legislator would not bind if he were aware of the context, *epikeia* is allowed. Most authors grant this even where a superior authority could be consulted. On the other hand, where the individual "cannot form even a probable judgment" that the lawgiver would not bind, the law must be followed. For other types of cases, a variety of views were developed.[552] Riley states, "as to the lawfulness of *epikeia* in relation to cases of probability, theologians in their teaching manifest more or less the tenets of the Moral System to which they adhere in general."[553]

What seems apparent is that the responsibility of the individual is admitted, though juridical science is not able to specify its use completely. Certainly *epikeia* is legitimately restricted to prevent abuse. Yet an exact and exhaustive description is lacking. The existence of *epikeia* in moral theology and the existence of wide array of debates on its nature indicate a respect for the judgment of individual believers. Such judgment is exercised on the basis of practical concrete understanding, and often without the assistance of authoritative expertise.

An important indicator of how the sense of the faithful may be seen to operate through the reception of official teaching by the wider group of believers is in the area of acceptance of law by the community. Geoffrey King writes that the question of whether civil and canon law should be validated in this way was for some time a question of great importance for canonists, and that many of them answered it positively.[554] King observes that although the question of acceptance was widely debated in the sixteenth, seventeenth and eighteenth centuries, little discussion of it occurred in the commentaries on the Code of Canon Law until recent times.[555]

The newly promulgated Code of 1983 has raised some counter examples to this trend. In the commentary commissioned by the Canon Law Society of America, the role of the *sensus fidelium* is raised in its early pages by Ladislas Orsy, though with a certain skepticism about the openness of the Code itself to such a role.[556] Orsy writes,

> The spirit that penetrates the whole Code is forcefully displayed in this first Book. It is clear that the modern Church intends to live by statutory laws and does not really want to give any serious role to customs. This, of course, raises the issue of how Catholic people can ever express their *sensus fidelium* in the practical life of the Church, if they are steadily impeded in expressing themselves in customs.[557]

He notes that Book I does not address the issue of reception, yet he adds his own observation that the law will not be "a vital force in the community unless it is received by the people."[558] He is careful to say that he does not propose a process of "validating ratification," but is giving "a statement of the absolute need for the intelligent appropriation of the norms." He adds that to truly receive a law, a community must understand its underlying value, and then embrace it in freedom and "internal conviction." Orsy asserts, "Christian people cannot act according to innate dignity unless they act with intelligence and freedom." The traditional statement, "custom is the best interpreter of laws," is restated by Orsy in human terms; "there is no better interpreter of the laws than the people of God, freely dedicated and well informed."[559]

Orsy discusses the "organic" nature of law in commenting on Canon 7, "A law comes into existence when it is promulgated." Four stages of its life are identified; law is "conceived" and "born." After it "lives," it "dies or fades away."[560] Promulgation is where the law that was conceived by a human author is actually born into the Church. Its life is then purposeful inasmuch as it is "adopted and used." These practical appropriations are distinct from promulgation. Interpretation occurs throughout the life of the law, and continues until the law has served its purpose. It then must die, or it will become a liability rather than an aid for the faithful. Orsy notes, "responsible interpretation must be more than the declaration of a meaning which was there, clear and certain, *in se certa*, at the time of its promulgation."[561]

Given this understanding of interpretation and reception, it may be fair to say that reception of law, though perhaps not the same as the operation of consensus in the area of doctrine, is a similar issue operating as a sort of cumulative effect of the judgment of believers. The theological treatments that have been offered historically show varying levels of weight given to this phenomenon.

King reviews the debates and controversies over reception in the period stretching from the end of the Middle Ages through the eighteenth century. He cites an early warrant in Gratian's *Decretum*, "*Leges instituuntur cum promulgantur; firmantur, cum moribus untentium approbantur*," noting that the official Code (1917) included Gratian's statement concerning promulgation while leaving out the portion on the importance of reception.[562] A clear historical shift in treatment of the question of reception occurred after Pope Alexander VII condemned a list of propositions including one that was seen to include supporters of the idea of reception. King thus examines the discussions of the topic that preceded and followed this condemnation in order to bring out the historical and legal context of the pope's action and the developments that came after it.[563]

King notes that following the Council of Florence, and Pius II's condemnation of appeals to a council to override papal authority, adherents to the idea of reception were scarce. Yet he cites in Felinus Sandeus (d. 1503) a supporter of reception who did not maintain a conciliarist stance. King summarizes Felinus's position, "for a human a law to have obligatory force (*vis obligandi*) it must be accepted by a majority of the community for which it is promulgated."[564] He adds that Felinus does not define key elements of the process; acceptance, obligatory force, and what constitutes a majority of the community are not adequately described.[565] King then offers a summary of the views of various proponents who attempt to specify particular aspects of the process of reception, and whose arguments draw on some of the same themes as those encountered in the treatment of *epikeia*.[566]

Several authors suggested that non-reception of a law may occur when the context (local circumstances or customs) of a community is not considered by a law's creator. King notes that authors proposing such a view "display a sense of local church and a sensitivity to local differences which is not usually associated with the Tridentine mind." These authors argued that bishops in such communities could appeal to the pope. At least one wrote that if no reply was received, the law could be ignored.[567]

King finds several authors at the end of the sixteenth century and beginning of the seventeenth century who assume the importance of reception without actually arguing to support it. He describes Molina, Lessius, and Covarrubias as "taking [the need for reception] for granted."[568] In this period, King finds those who are for reception outnumbering those who are against it. Yet a key opponent is found in Suarez. King cites Suarez's contention that few commentators would "deny the unqualified *potestas* of the papacy to impose law."[569] King notes that Suarez himself only cites one "conciliarist," John Major, but adds that Driedo, Medina, Valencia and perhaps others could be included as well. Suarez argues that legislators do intend to bind those addressed by the law.

King gives Suarez's view, "The wording of laws . . . is simply preceptive: there is expressed no condition to the effect that their validity depends on acceptance."[570]

Authors that follow Suarez add the argument that rulers may punish those who disobey them. Further, those who give laws must be stronger than those who obey them. Yet, King points out that those who argue against the need for reception discuss the circumstances under which either excess severity or lack of use can leave a law impotent. He notes that Suarez and others who follow his approach state that forty years of "contrary custom" is necessary to show "abrogation of laws by desuetude," if they have originally been received. Ten years of such custom suffices if the law was not received. King points out here the practical similarity between many opponents of reception and its supporters. Though not approving of non-reception, these authors set conditions for what to do when it occurs.[571]

It is with Alexander VII that an official statement is given that makes a dramatic impact on the theological discussion of reception. Among twenty-eight propositions condemned by the pope in 1665 was one which stated, "People do not sin even if without any reason they do not accept the law promulgated by the ruler." King observes that all of the statements on the list are characterized by the common theme of "Laxism."[572] King then recounts the developments that preceded the condemnations, that linked Laxism to the political and theological issues that were connected to Gallicanism, and which had become a concern of the papacy. King argues, in fact, that Proposition 28 was condemned precisely as a Gallican statement.[573] He adds too that the understanding of reception in the statement was of "an extreme form."[574]

King notes that Domenico Viva, "a leading opponent of reception," accepted that there were limitations in Proposition 28. In his *Damnatae Theses ab Alexandro VII, Innocentio XI, Alexandro VIII* (1727), Viva wrote,

> In this matter two questions must be distinguished—(1) Is a law valid independently of acceptance by the people, so that even when a community does not accept a law it remains bound by it? (2) Even if we admit that a non-received law is null, does a community sin when, without just cause, it fails to accept a law?[575]

King states that Viva answered both of these questions positively, while acknowledging that Alexander VII had not dealt with the first one. King argues that the authors who defended reception would admit that those who reject a law would sin, if their rejection is done "without just cause." The issue of proper cause was precisely the thing around which judgment turned in these cases. But he adds that

> the defenders of reception did not, strictly speaking, fall under the condemnation of proposition 28. If the interpretation offered here is correct, those who did fall under the condemnation were the Gallicans of the Sorbonne and of the Parliament of Paris.[576]

King points out that the condemnation stifled debate, having an impact that was greater than "a strict interpretation of its words" required.[577]

Authors after the condemnation of Alexander VII link their discussion not to the interpretation of the statement of the law, but to the intent of the lawgiver, and thus to the consideration of *epikeia*.[578] Finally, King argues that the difference between opponents and proponents of reception is really a difference between "rationalist" and "voluntarist" approaches to law. He maintains that if the issue is not couched in terms that pit the will of the lawgiver against the will of the people for whom the law is intended, many problems between the two sides lose their importance. What remains to be considered then is the actual quality of the law in question.[579] This quality must, according to King, still be understood with appropriate weight given to the role of authority. He states that,

No one would want to canonize a situation where laws are promulgated and then frequently "vetoed" by non-reception. That would, as Suarez and others saw, bring authority into contempt Rather, legislators should look to the receptivity of the community before passing a particular law or set of laws.[580]

He adds that non-reception may indicate that, if only with respect to "some groups of people," a law is "unreasonable" or has not adequately considered "local customs" or "particular social and cultural conditions."[581]

A specific doctrine that had carried considerable juridical impact may help illustrate the role that reception has played in the Roman Catholic Church. The practice of lending money at interest was once clearly designated by the Church as sinful. John Noonan's treatment of the topic in *The Scholastic Analysis of Usury* shows the scope of the Church's treatment of its moral implications in both theory and commercial life.[582] Interestingly, according to Noonan, the existence of usury as at important issue for society was directly due to the Church's initiative.[583]

Of interest to the present discussion, is the fact that the Church's teaching on usury was changed due to changed circumstances in Western culture and the ecclesial recognition of those changes. Noonan states that "the most striking aspect" of the scholastic treatment of exchange banking and usury was "the willingness of most of the authorities to consult merchants and to be guided by commercial custom."[584] In another work, Noonan describes the change in the prohibition of usury as a progress from the acceptance of medieval teaching in the post-tridentine era to a reversal of the teaching by the mid-eighteenth century.

> From improvisation of daring alternatives in the late fifteenth and early sixteenth century, the innovating moralists advanced by 1600 to positions that undermined the old rule altogether. Between 1600 and 1700 there was great debate on the theories involved in the new position, and as late as the early eighteenth century there were attempts to review strict medieval restrictions. By the time of

Liguori the battle was over, and the sixteenth century innovations appeared as commonplaces.[585]

He attributes success in changing the law, to some extent, on the existence of an "identifiable" voice, that of bankers, "who were willing to argue for revision of the law."[586]

In the nineteenth century, Curial officials handed down decisions in several concrete cases that sanctioned the lending of money at interest, while leaving aside the question of what theoretical foundation gave a warrant to such decisions. Noonan notes that these church officials neither condoned nor condemned the commercial practices in question as they made their judgments in particular cases, but appeared "to invite . . . theoretical development by the theologians."[587] Noonan contrasts the organized structure available to opponents of usury laws with the lack of representation for the laity on the topic of contraception.[588]

Involvement in or separation from practical input through the expressions of their experience and judgment seems to have played a major part in the laity's ability to affect the expression of church teaching.

The views of one particular Reformation figure, Thomas More (d. 1535), offer an interesting alternate perspective to the treatments of consensus in this era that typically wrestled with the relationship of believers to the authority of the magisterium, specifically in terms of the papacy or of general councils. More is notable for his personal stand in following conscience even to the point of death by beheading. He employed a great deal of subtlety in trying to avoid the charge of treason for not swearing the oath connected to Henry VIII's Act of Succession, and in attempting to remain loyal to both the Church and the King. Hans Hillerbrand quotes More saying,

I am the King's true faithful subject . . . and I pray for his highness, and all his, and all the realm. I do nobody no harm, I saw none harm, I think none harm, but wish everybody good. And if this be not enough to keep a man alive, in good faith I long not to live.[589]

More's dramatic personal integrity found an extension in his view of consensus in the Church that acknowledged the responsibility of each believer, but linked the faith of the individual to the unity of the larger body of Christ, with a notable lack of consideration of the role of the magisterium. Philip Sheldrake describes More's view of consensus in the context of the debates on conciliarism that were current in his day. He asserts that More was "reluctant to give any absolute authority to *any* human institution," and thus saw the roles of council and pope as qualified by their larger context.[590] Sheldrake describes More's view of consensus as based in "a fairly developed notion of the indwelling of the Holy Spirit in the Church as a whole, leading it into all truth."[591]

Sheldrake argues that More avoided entering the debate on papal primacy, even though he saw this office as important for preventing schism. Overall, he sees More as leaning to a conciliar rather than papal view of church governance. Yet, most importantly, both magisterial forms were seen by More as rooted in the consensus of the whole Church.[592]

Even though More was a lawyer, Sheldrake sees his view of consensus as based in a theological understanding rather than in a juridical one. He points out that the "legal or constitutional question" of consensus was raised in the debates about canon law and conciliar theory that preceded the Reformation.[593] Arguments focused on whether authority was to be found in a church's "head" or "members." The twelfth and thirteenth centuries saw the development of the notion of the Church as a "corporation." He notes that the *Decretals* of Pope Alexander III (d.1181) included issues that affected the rights of local churches in decision making.[594] David Knowles cites Alexander III as the first in a century of popes trained in law, who organized the discipline of the Church in its practical and spiritual life, giving canon law a place of prominence and respect, even while the role of Rome in local church matters increased.[595]

Ambiguity continued in debates over the role of the local church in its exercise of authority, and over the difference in the giving of "counsel" and "consent." In these notions the locus of responsibility in the Church was considered. Sheldrake cites the influential canonist Hostiensis as suggesting that "counsel" need not imply "actual consent," and yet that consent itself was needed "in any vital issue of the whole corporation." Later authors argued over whether it was enough to seek consent at some level even if it was not legally necessary to the exercise of authority that it be given.[596]

Sheldrake states that conciliar theory emerged as such issues were argued in relation to the Church as a whole and to the relationship between the pope, the cardinals and the councils. He notes that in the conciliar view, authority was seen not ultimately in the council itself, but in the people as a whole, in the "*congregatio fidelium*." He notes that although this view is similar to More's, it is a "legal-constitutional position" in contrast to More's theological approach.[597] Though there are "hints" of More's drawing on the terms of the conciliar theory, there is much clearer use of the view that the Church is a body distinct from the "secular society" that would be subject to a solely legal description of authority.[598] Sheldrake finds More's discussions to be oriented less toward juridical considerations and more toward the issue to spiritual discernment as underlying consensus.[599]

According to Sheldrake, it is unclear how familiar More was with the legal debates over *equitas* and *epikeia*.[600] Yet consent in his view is firmly rooted in the individuals responsible judgment, judgment which was understood as led by the Spirit. Sheldrake too, states that the tendency to subjectivism in More's view is offset by comparison of such judgment with the consensus of the group.[601] He is hesitant to attribute to More the view that this results in the stance that "whatever the Church teaches or does must necessarily be so," that is, the view that consensus would necessarily prevent a doctrine from developing.[602] What More is consistently concerned with is the setting up of an individuals judgment against that of the Church as a body. In speaking decisively against such a move, More leaves less clear the issues that do not directly concern him. Sheldrake finds a balance in More's view that the Church as a whole does experience change, though he does not exhibit a "sophisticated notion of development of doctrine."[603] His focus is on the unity of the community established by the presence of the Spirit. Under the influence of the Spirit, change may occur.[604] The tradition is not handed on as "a complete and unchanging deposit of faith."[605] Most importantly for More though, when development in a teaching is proposed, it is the consensus of the Church that attests to its truth.[606]

More's view of the unity of the community in the Spirit links his understanding of consensus to that of the Patristic period. Sheldrake notes that More "carefully avoids an over-institutional model of the Church and its authority" choosing instead "a model of a closely knit community."[607] Yet, he continually notes the lack of information available on More's explicit views of how the community might function in the light of the relationships of both the individual and the consensus of the believers to the leadership of the magisterium.[608]

More's lack of connection between a stress on the whole Christian community and the functioning of the magisterium, leaves room for the view that consensus among the people, in his view, could be set explicitly over against the magisterium. This is the concern of James Hitchcock who describes More's understanding of consensus as "perhaps the most extreme statement of the position in the entire history of the Church."[609] Hitchcock points out that in his polemics against the reformers, More did not argue for the authority of the hierarchy, although he was apparently willing "to defend all aspects of Catholicism, no matter how trivial or dubious," in debate.[610] Hitchcock too, notes that the legal considerations linked to the views of conciliarism that were developing at the time were not important in More's work.[611] Whether this was due to his "concern for the common people" or his interest to "meet the Protestants on their own grounds," More argued his case against them in terms of God's guarantee that the whole Church would not stray from the truth.[612]

Hitchcock identifies More as one of the first to use the term "living tradition," a phrase which came into use in the Reformation era, to refer to a view of oral tradition that saw the truth "implanted" in the hearts of believers, the "softest of materials" available to make its living on possible.[613] More wrote, "it was convenient for the law of life to be rather written in the lively minds of men than in the dead skins of beasts."[614] It was a "strong theory of consensus" that kept this view of tradition from supporting subjectivism. More's view, based in the Vincentian Canon, saw the large body of faithful as a sure guard against heresy in the few individuals or even leaders who might separate themselves from the truth held by all.[615]

According to Hitchcock, More anticipated Newman and his treatment of the Arian crisis of the fourth century, where the faithful laity kept the true tradition in the face of error among many of the bishops. He sees More as "unwittingly" giving the English laity a foundation for remaining in communion with the Roman Church, even while their bishops left it to follow the lead of Henry VIII.[616] He sees in More's notion of the sense of the faithful a source that could become distinguished and even separated from the authority of the magisterium.[617] The greater importance placed on the beliefs and customs of the faithful was not without cost; More found himself "virtually required . . . to defend almost every aspect of popular Catholicism."[618] Without using a source of

appeal in Scripture or the Church's hierarchy he had no means to critique "popular" views and practices.[619]

Hitchcock sees More's "extreme" view of the *sensus fidelium* as illustrating some key aspects of this theological source. He states that such a strong view of consensus comes from a "deeply intuitive and mystical sense of the Church, in contrast to a more functional concept." He observes that the sixteenth century separation of Scripture and tradition illustrates "a deeper and largely unperceived split in the European mind" between "mystical" and "sociological" images of the Church. Most importantly, consensus seen with this powerful role given to it by More is linked to the tradition of the past. Under the combination of this spiritual approach and dependence on apostolic tradition, Hitchcock cites More as "perhaps the first of those conservatives" to see consensus when associated with the "popular will," as "not by any means an agency of revolution but rather a force for preservation."[620]

Without a critical tension with ecclesial leaders and Scripture, More's view shows "the inadequacy of a theory of consensus unmodified by theories of superior authority."[621] Hitchcock argues that when the view embraced by consensus starts to change, the consensus itself is opposed to the change. A new development then cannot be supported by the consensus, but must appeal to a "superior principle of authority."[622]

If the extremity of More's position might give such weight to the role of magisterial authority when changes are proposed, it is interesting that Hitchcock argues to such a result by maintaining More's lack of dependence on authority in his own works during this very polemical era. Although such an approach may be argued on the basis of what More says about consensus, caution in regard to such an extrapolation seems appropriate. Pragmatic issues, as suggested by Sheldrake. may have kept More from expressing or even developing the connections that are necessary between the consensus of believers and the magisterium. More's concern was to give believers, effectively cut off in their own context from ecclesial leadership, a connection between their belief and the Christian tradition which they wanted to maintain.[623]

Just as More's personal stance eventually made it impossible for him remain at peace in the Church and live in his particular context, it is legitimate to conjecture how long the consensus of believers might survive if it were unsupported by an active, supportive church authority. Yet, More's concern was a focus on the role of the Spirit, the most foundational element of life in the community, which could itself be seen as a balancing influence against the "subjectivism" of the Reformers.[624] The role of authority within that community could not be clearly appealed to in the polemics of the time. The interrelationship of consensus and the functional authority of the Church was left to others to examine.

## THE HISTORICAL ROOTS OF A MODERN AGENDA

In the different periods of church history examined so far, an array of experiences, structures and insights have been identified as the material upon which the concept of the sense of the faithful has been based. Consensus within the community, inclusion of the laity in the process of selecting bishops, reception of law and doctrine by the faithful and the connaturality of the believer's mind in understanding and acting on the truths of the faith are among the resources that are recognized in history and that continue today to suggest foundations and models for understanding the continuing role of the *sensus fidelium* in the Church's reflections, actions, governance and mission.

With the Reformation, the Roman Catholic Church was called to consider in a more explicit manner the way in which its traditions informed its faith. After the challenges of the sixteenth century, the need to identify the sources for theology in the Church, to clarify the roles of authority and office and to consciously appropriate tradition in confronting challenges to the identity of the Church would remain matters of central importance. These issues also set the stage for a distinctively modern set of reflections on the sense of the faithful in the centuries that followed.

In the next chapter, the modern era in Roman Catholic thought will be examined with particular attention to the various ways that the *sensus fidelium* was seen to operate within an ecclesiological context where theologians both within and outside the magisterium more explicitly examined the nature and role of theological sources and method, and their relationship to authority, and where the impact of historical context would become a major issue in theological reflection.

# CHAPTER 3
# HISTORY OF THE CONCEPT: MODERN PERIOD TO VATICAN II

After the Reformation, Catholic apologists' appeals to consensus were intent on using the united belief of the larger body of believers to prove the Catholic Church was the genuine heir of the Christian tradition. William Thompson, following the treatment of Thils, sees post-Tridentine theologians as continuing the basic views of Cano and Bellarmine on the infallibility of the Church, as rooted in the *Ecclesia in credendo* though with some added developments.[1]

### THE SEVENTEENTH AND EIGHTEENTH CENTURIES

Thompson identifies an early shift in the era after Trent in Gregory of Valencia (d. 1603), who stressed the importance of the hierarchy. Thompson notes that the laity are recognized by some seventeenth and eighteenth century theologians as having an active role because of this infallibility *in credendo*. He cites J.-B. Gonet (1681) as maintaining that the whole Church does not itself actively teach only because of practical constraints. Yet, Thompson observes a move to "a decidedly 'hierarchical' emphasis" in Charles-René Billuart (d. 1757) and Gui Pichler (d. 1736), with an accompanying understanding of the believing church as passive.[2]

Thils makes it clear that in the case of Gonet, it is through a general council that the belief of the universal Church can be found. Consulting all of the faithful would be impossible.[3] Interestingly, Billuart links together the issue of the

Church *in credendo* and the responsibility for teaching of the bishops and doctors—the Church *in docendo*. If what the teachers offered were to be found as false, the faithful would believe falsely as well. But the believing Church cannot err. Thils states that it is on this basis that Billuart argues from the fact that the Church cannot err in its belief, to a confidence that it cannot err in its magisterium.[4] It is also on this same basis, that Billuart finds that a general council expresses the infallibility of the Church.[5]

According to Thils, Pichler emphasized the collective nature of the Church as the recipient of the Spirit, over against the view he attributed to the Lutherans, where each individual believer was guided by the Spirit.[6] Thils also points out that Pichler regarded the Church as a whole to be both the "active" participant and the "passive" receiver of infallibility through its source, Christ. The "active" nature of infallibility was present, however, only inasmuch as that ability was exercised by a subject who could form a judgment or definition of the faith. This is not likely to be a realistic function of the body as a whole.[7]

Henri Kilber (d. 1783) uses a similar criterion of formulation in the *Principia theologica* to describe the way a belief can be regarded as infallible.[8] This quality can be seen in the collective belief of all Christians, in the unified belief of bishops, either in council or teaching in their sees, or in the action of the pope. In each such expression the shared belief of the Church is recognized as given by the Spirit.[9]

A final eighteenth century example of the trend toward a focus on the magisterium is given by Thils in his description of Honoré Tournély (d. 1729), a representative of the teaching at the Sorbonne. An active participant in the debates over Jansenism and Gallicanism, he too stressed the role of hierarchy. Tournély accepted the testimony of the whole body of faithful *in credendo* as being valid, yet he did not dwell on this notion. The reformers accepted this idea too, and yet they did not give the hierarchy the importance that the Catholics did.

It was thus to a hierarchical focus that he turned. This points out the danger in such an approach; too much weight was given to the area in which Tournély spent his energies, even when he had also maintained the accepted place of the believing body of faithful in his theology. When discussing where the "rule of faith" was to be identified, he again pointed to the universal Church expressing itself through the bishops. This expression is particularly clear when it is given at a general council.[10]

During the seventeenth and eighteenth centuries, several trends can be identified. The Church as a whole is seen as infallible when all of its members are united in believing. Among those discussing what might be taught infallibly, there is a pragmatic interest in how clarity may be found. Infallibility may be recognized in the body as a whole, especially, it would seem, when a teaching has been sufficiently seasoned over time. Yet, clarity is also available, and perhaps more obviously, through the active functioning of those with authority to express the belief of the Church, the bishops acting together, or even the pope acting independently.

Avery Dulles sees the period after Trent as characterized by an emphasis on the hierarchy which treats the expression of doctrine in "highly juridical terms." Eighteenth century "pro-papal theologians" do not even speak of "magisterium;" the exercise of "infallible teaching" is itself seen as an "act of jurisdiction." Other teaching done by the hierarchy is likewise considered to be an aspect of ecclesial discipline.[11]

Dulles sees the theology concerning the hierarchy of this period as being one of two types: an episcopalian form that led to Gallicanism and Richerism in France, Febronianism in Germany, and Josephism in Austria, and a papalist form that was dominant in Spain and Italy, and which paralleled the monarchial emphases in civil governments. Infallibility, with its juridical guise, was readily accepted as another instance where a ruler had legitimate claim to the assent of those he ruled.[12] Dulles observes that during this time,

> The many instances of teaching authority recognized in the New Testament and in earlier church history are in effect reduced to one—the hierarchical, which is itself progressively reduced to the single voice of the papacy.[13]

He adds that though this reducing of church activity to a centralized, juridical function allowed the Church to meet the challenges of the period, such reducing "overlooks the necessary complexity of the believer's quest for truth," and neglects "the biblical, sacramental, charismatic and eschatological dimensions of the Church and Christian doctrine."[14]

During the post-Tridentine period, the traditional view that the whole Church cannot err continued to be maintained by theologians. This view stemming from Patristic times was used, in turn, to support a confidence that the whole body can have in those who officially give expression to the Church's faith. In this warrant for infallibility in a Church that is united *in credendo*, there is an anticipation of the statement of Vatican I concerning the pope who speaks with "the infallibility with which the divine Redeemer willed his Church to be endowed."[15] The early portion of Chapter Four of this document should also be noted, for its description of the "consultation" of the Church. Such consultation is considered normal in the Church's history.[16] The complexities of how the faith of the whole Church was seen as involved in magisterial expressions were key to the debates and actions of the First Vatican Council.

## GALLICANISM

Richard Costigan considers the impact of Gallicanism on the deliberations of Vatican I with particular attention to the role of consensus in "The Consensus of the Church: Differing Classical Views."[17] He sees the statement of Vatican I that the definitions of the pope are "irreformable 'ex sese, non autem ex consensu ecclesiae' (of themselves, and not from the consensus of the Church)," as a direct response to the Declaration of the Gallican Clergy of 1682 (Article 4), which states that "Although the Pope has the chief voice in questions of faith and his decrees apply to all churches and to each particular church, yet his decision is not unalterable unless the consent of the Church given."[18] Costigan finds the majority of bishops at Vatican I intent on preventing any diluting through Gallican notions of the conception of the papacy as a monarchy or of the infallible expressions of the pope. He notes that no references to the episcopate are included in the passage concerning the papal exercise of infallibility to avoid any opportunity for Gallican interpretations to be linked with it.[19]

Costigan chides modern authors for a lack of attention to original Gallican sources in their treatment of Gallicanism. He finds that seventeenth and eighteenth century thinkers were themselves quite aware of their historical precedents in "the more collegial and consensual ecclesiology of the early and medieval centuries."[20] In Honoré Tournély he finds a representative of classical Gallicanism who is both "moderate" and "learned."[21]

In his description of the Church, Tournély consistently maintains a vital role for the pope.[22] Costigan describes how he differs from some Gallican authors who give more authority to secular rulers. He states "only the Church is the supreme and infallible judge of controversies of faith."[23] In the term, "Church," however, Tournély does not include the whole body of believers. He refers rather to the hierarchy, "the supreme pontiff and the bishops, whom the Holy Spirit has placed as bishops to rule the Church of God. either in council or apart from a council."[24]

According to Costigan, Tournély places himself between an ultramontane position, where the pope is "an absolute monarch" and where the bishops derive what jurisdiction they have from him, and the opposite position represented by Edmund Richer, which would "effectively deny" to the pope any special primacy.[25] In Richer's view, the whole Church received the "keys of jurisdiction" given to Peter, with the bishops and the pope carrying an authority within the body that is merely "instrumental and executive." Costigan observes that although Tournély did not use the term "Gallican" for his own position, it does represent the "mainline episcopal or ecclesiastical Gallicanism as expressed in Articles 2, 3, and 4 of the Declaration of 1682."[26] In this position, the pope is responsible for leading all of the churches, and his decrees "in questions of faith and morals" are expected to elicit assent. His statements are not assumed to be infallible, however. Costigan summarizes Tournély's view,

> If there is a major and prolonged controversy, the Roman pontiff has the power to summon all the bishops to a council. It is *here*, at an assembly of the entire episcopate of the universal Church, that there is the "supreme and infallible authority" needed to settle definitively a question that has agitated the Church.[27]

Tournély thus describes the Church not as "purely monarchical," but as "tempered with aristocracy."[28] Further, in this view the rule of the Church here is not a matter of power, but of law. Tournély asserts that this notion is

> the very solid foundation of the Liberties of our Gallican Church, firm and constant adhesion to the sacred canons of the ancient and common law, which have been founded by the Spirit of God and consecrated by the reverence of the whole world.[29]

Thus, while the pope is recognized as having a real primacy and responsibility as head of the Church, his authority is not exercised in an absolute way. Costigan describes how in his specific discussion of infallibility, Tournély nuances the Gallican position to distinguish it from the ultramontane view that the pope can "define the faith singlehandedly."³⁰ The pope certainly leads the bishops within or outside of a council, and he may teach from his own see for the whole Church. His statements, in Tournély's view, are in fact binding on the faithful immediately, even if they are not irreformable.³¹ Yet, according to Tournély, his decrees are not irreformable unless they are supported by the consensus of the whole Church, as expressed by the bishops.³² Interestingly, this consensus may be "antecedent, concomitant, or subsequent, and it may be express or tacit."³³ Costigan adds, "What is necessary, in Tournély's view of the consensus of the Church, is recognition of the genuine role of the episcopate in teaching the faith."³⁴ This role of "teaching and clarifying doctrine" is one that is shared by all of the bishops, and is not only the responsibility of the pope.³⁵

The views of a second eighteenth century figure, Pietro Ballerini (d. 1769) are presented by Costigan as an example of that influence for a strong papal primacy which bore direct fruit in the majority opinion at Vatican I. Costigan sees a direct influence of Ballerini's systematic treatment of papal infallibility in the Council document *Pastor aeternus*.³⁶ Ballerini argues that the primacy of the pope, a reality admitted by the Gallicans themselves, leads by its very nature to the conclusion that the pope has power to impose his definitions of the faith on the faithful. As head of the Church, he is given by Christ the responsibility of maintaining its unity, and thus, is also logically given the means to achieve this end.³⁷ Ballerini asserts that Christ, "foresaw and provided everything that was necessary to guard and conserve his Church and its unity."³⁸ Any conditions placed on the full acceptance of papal prerogative would challenge that ecclesial unity that is meant to be the fruit of the pope's rule.³⁹

Ballerini confronts Article 4 of the Gallican Declaration specifically, saying that it would deny "All the coercive force for unity of faith" for which the pope is given responsibility.⁴⁰ He asserts that the Declaration does not acknowledge that the Pope's statements command a response of unity, "except after the *consensus ecclesiae* is added."[41] Costigan notes in regard to this point, however, that Article 4 "pointedly omits such a chronological term as 'after.'"[42] In addition to his argument that requiring a show of consensus offends the logic of unity in the responsibilities of the pope, Ballerini cites the difficulties of actually obtaining a consensus. In Ballerini's view, consensus is the result of the pope's expression of the faith, not its warrant.[43] The responsibility of obedience to him extends not just to the faithful, but to the bishops as well.[44]

Costigan notes that in a second work on infallibility, Ballerini repeats his argument for the logic of papal power in oven stronger terms.[45] In his *Appendix*, Ballerini quotes Irenaeus's *Adversus haerises* (3.3.2) where he states that "it is necessary for every church to concur with (Rome) because of its more potent principality."[46] Costigan observes,

> In Ballerini's treatment of it this is no longer simply a statement of a second-century author but a mighty near-divine proclamation of papal supremacy which seems almost to stand right beside the "Thou art Peter" of Matthew 16 and the "Feed my sheep" of John 21. It is a statement not only authoritative in the strictest sense in itself, but one from which one can deduce a whole array of corollaries about the sovereign papal power.[47]

Here it is the role of the Roman Primate to compel belief in his teachings from those in the other churches. Costigan notes that Ballerini sees the assertion of Irenaeus as a direct repudiation of the Gallican Declaration. Ballerini states that Irenaeus "attributes to the Roman faith and primacy a force *per se sufficiens* to oblige all."[48]

Costigan notes that while Ballerini argues his position in strong terms, he concedes that it is not a "dogma of faith." Ballerini admits that the issue "is controverted among Catholics and . . . has not been yet been expressly defined by the Church."[49] Costigan observes that Ballerini's understanding of the Church is not based on the notion of *communio*, but rather on "Christ's establishment of the primacy to ensure unity in the Church."[50]

Costigan observes that Ballerini's focus on "The Power" of the pope to maintain unity in the Church leaves little room for considering the involvement of other members of the body in ecclesial decisions, even in the case of bishops. The people in the Church should rather respond with respect and gratitude to God for the establishment of such a position of leadership.[51]

Tournély, though differing radically in his view of papal power, does not argue for a democracy, but maintains that the Church is a hierarchical body, with real primacy on the part of the pope. Yet, it is the entire hierarchy within the Church, and not its head acting alone, that can exercise infallible judgment. Following Congar, Costigan describes the view of several proponents of Gallicanism, that the jurisdiction of the Church's teaching is to be distributed between the episcopate and the papacy. The two "powers" are meant to operate together. He adds that "neither should be reduced to a merely nominal role."[52]

## THE SENSE OF THE FAITHFUL AND THE NINETEENTH CENTURY

It would be difficult to exaggerate the importance of the nineteenth century for the development of contemporary understandings of the *sensus fidelium*. Twentieth century issues in ecclesiology are directly influenced by the ecclesiological developments in this period. Vatican II itself, is obviously heir to the results and questions that come from this century. Such influences come from the work of theologians, but also directly from the magisterium, particularly during the pontificate of Pius IX. The promulgation of *Ineffabilis Deus* in 1854 following the encyclical *Ubi primum* of 1849, which sought the sense of clergy and laity on the Immaculate Conception, as well as the teaching of the First

Vatican Council (1869-70) on infallibility, introduced significant aspects of the use of authority and the interpretation of tradition.

Thils cites the *Institutiones theologicae* of J.-B. Bouvier (d. 1854) as an influential text in mid-nineteenth century France, which continued the trend seen in previous centuries of dependence on the "believing church" for an understanding of infallibility. In this work, Bouvier criticizes the Protestant view that denies infallibility to the teaching authority in the Church even while it accepts it on the part of the whole body. He sees the Catholic position as one that follows logically from the acceptance of an infallibility in the body *in credendo*. Because the people receive what they believe from their pastors, the faith *in docendo* must be rendered infallibly.[53]

A similar view is held by F.-X. Schouppe, with an eschatological focus. The Church *in credendo* may be expected to remain until the final age, if it is truly the Church of Christ. Thils remarks that it is after Schouppe, that the guarantee of truth in the Church was linked to an "inerrancy" associated with the magisterium.[54]

A highly political view of the sense of the faithful is expressed by Félicité Lamennais (d. 1854). Dulles notes that Lamennais drew on Rousseau and Scottish "common sense" philosophy to give "the argument from unanimity . . . a new lease on life," though his views were later condemned by Rome in 1834.[55] Early on, Lammenais argued that what society as a whole needed was the influence of a "dynamic Catholic faith."[56] He even suggested that Napolean Bonaparte could be a Christian leader who would restore the "Gallican Church in all its splendor."[57] He later embraced a "liberal ultramontanism" where he argued for a complete separation of influence of the Church and the state.[58] He looked, in fact, to Rome for help in freeing the Church from the hands of secular power.[59] He eventually repudiated this position too, and gave up any hope that the Church's hierarchy would lead in making the changes he sought.[60]

In his *Paroles d'un croyant* (1834) Lammenais distinguished between the obedience Catholics owed to the hierarchy in matters of doctrine, and the freedom they had in secular matters. This work brought his condemnation by Gregory XVI in *Singulari Nos* and his eventual estrangement from Catholicism.[61] His push for a "democratic style of Catholicism" was found wanting by the hierarchy.[62] Fundamentally, Lammenais's views lacked an ecclesiology that involved interaction of the laity and the hierarchy.

## TUEBINGEN

A significant amount of influence in nineteenth century theology came from the theological school at Tuebingen. Monika Hellwig writes that the shift from a focus on "unwritten traditions" and the "hierarchic Church as the trustee or custodian of these" to an interest in tradition as an ongoing process began when the Tuebingen theologians "began to discuss 'living tradition.'"[63] A central figure in this discussion was Johann Adam Moehler (d. 1838). Congar observes that Moehler, "rethought the old principle 'Quod ubique, quod semper, quod ab ominibus,' in a dynamic and mystical view of the ecclesial community, whose soul is the Holy Spirit."[64] Geiselmann notes that Moehler gave the theology of tradition a "Romantic stamp" in his younger work.[65]

In his *Einheit in der Kirche* (1825) Moehler describes the Church as an organic, living entity with the Holy Spirit filling it with life.[66] Owen Chadwick describes the way Moehler saw the Spirit working:

> Interior faith is the root of exterior faith, which is assent to dogmas. Though interior faith is communicated with the help of words, it precedes any external expression, any dogma. . . . The principle of life exists in Christians before they frame or comprehend the doctrine.[67]

Chadwick describes this stage of Moehler's thought as vague in regard to the way this faith might be expressed in concrete terms, and particularly in how such expressions might develop and deepen an understanding of the tradition. In reaction to criticisms of his thought as being excessively influenced by both Schleiermacher and Hegel, Moehler developed his view in a more "traditional direction" with his *Symbolik* (1832).[68]

Schrodt asserts that Moehler never adequately described the connection between the "inner life" of faith in the Church and its dogmatic expression. This, he adds, may be due to the polemical nature of *Symbolik*, where Moehler argues that "the beginning of dogma is occasioned by the appearance of heresy."[69] Geiselmann examines the psychological aspect of the impact of doctrine on the individual believer in regard to Moehler's treatment of the relationship of faith and reason with the conclusion that he placed belief prior to speculation in the mental life of the believer.[70] Both self-awareness and the life of faith are rooted in a person's "immersion" in relationships. Before the mind comes to any expression, it must first be "awakened, formed and matured." This process is "conditional on external instruction, authority, faith, in short, tradition."[71]

This relational quality is foundational in Moehler's view of the believer, and it is consistent with his organic view of the Church as a whole. This view, though tempered somewhat in its subjectivistic tendencies, is still very much a part of his later work.[72] The implications of his approach to ecclesiology for the issues considered here are illustrated in the treatment of infallibility given by Moehler in *Symbolik*. While contrasting his stance with the views of his Protestant antagonists, Moehler is clear that the claim to infallibility belongs to the whole, unified Church. He observes, "To no individual, considered as such, doth infallibility belong; for the Catholic, as is clear from the preceding observations, regards the individual only as member of the whole; as living and breathing in the Church."[73] The authority of the Church is also stressed. Because of the Church's visible nature, which is related directly to God's acting in the world through the Incarnation of Christ, the visible authority of the Church is of utmost importance. Moehler asserts that "Christ himself is only in so far an authority, as the Church is an authority."[74] In a section on the hierarchy, he describes how visible authority operates. Within the Church, authoritative leadership is needed; "In a visible Church, a visible head is necessarily included."[75]

Moehler describes a strong role for the papacy within the episcopate, unifying, correcting and maintaining the faith of the universal Church.[76] Citing the Councils of Constance (1414) and Basel (1431) he describes some attempts "to draw authority more particularly toward the circumference" instead of the center.[77] He considers the view that "the Pope is *subject* to a general Council lawfully convoked" as a "one-sided principle which, when carried out to its legitimate consequences, threatened the Church with annihilation." This view, he adds, "may now be considered as obsolete."[78] Interestingly, he finds a sense of balance between the pope and the bishops in the historical interplay of "episcopal" and "papal" systems:

> As each system acknowledged the essence of the other to be divine, they constituted an opposition very beneficial to ecclesiastical life; so that, by their counteraction, the peculiar free development of the several parts was, on the one hand, preserved, and the union of these in one living, indivisible whole, was, on the others maintained.[79]

He adds that the "dogmatic decrees of the episcopate (united with the general head and center), are infallible."[80]

An explicit understanding of the sense of the faithful as an active element in the Church is identified in Moehler by Wolfgang Beinert.[81] In the section of *Symbolik* cited by Beinert, Moehler describes the Church as the "body of the

Lord," his visible, ongoing revelation.[82] Moehler describes the "sense" of believers, saying,

> What then is tradition? The peculiar Christian sense existing in the Church, and transmitted by ecclesiastical education; yet this sense is not to be conceived as detached from its subject matter—nay, it is formed in, and by this matter, so it may be called a full sense. Tradition is the living word, perpetuated in the hearts of believers.[83]

Moehler adds in a line not quoted by Beinert, "To this sense, as the general sense, the interpretation of Holy Writ is entrusted."[84]

As he becomes more concerned in his later work for the actual expression of tradition through the magisterium, Moehler describes the functioning of authority in the hierarchy in a way that is itself consistent with an interactive, organic functioning. His understanding of the faithful in the Church certainly is part of a dynamic ecclesiology. At the end of the section cited, where Moehler considers the Church as judge of the faith, he explicitly points to the Spirit as the life of the Church. He connects the "movements of the whole community" in the Spirit, and the Church's infallibility.[85]

The discussion of infallibility among other nineteenth century figures, and particularly those linked to the hierarchy itself, continued to take a more centralized approach to the topic. which culminated in the views of the infallibilists at Vatican I.[86] Moehler and others of the Tuebingen School remained among the few strong influences in ecclesiology outside of Rome during this period.[87]

Some question has been raised as to Moehler's direct influence on another key voice in the theology of development of doctrine, John Henry Newman. Chadwick argues that Newman did not read Moehler, and that his influence on Newman was at best indirect.[88] Ideas of development fostered by the work of

Moehler were "in the atmosphere which surrounded Newman" but no direct contribution was made.[89] Chadwick does admit that Lord Acton saw the influence of Moehler in Newman's work, and that Acton had been a close friend of Doellinger, who was quite familiar with Moehler's ideas.[90] Congar describes briefly the influence of Moehler on Doellinger but notes that Doellinger later came under the influence of a "critical classicism" like that of the theorists of the 17th century.[91] Hellwig notes that it was after Doellinger presented his ideas in the *Rambler* that Newman himself entered the controversy over "consulting the faithful."[92]

Congar notes the view of the Tuebingen theologians based in "patristic ecclesiological themes" that the Church as a whole was the "organ of Tradition." This view was maintained, "Sometimes not without a certain exclusivism to the detriment of the hierarchical magisterium." He characterizes this view, presented also by Newman, as one that was received well by Perrone, who was seemingly not interested in the role the people as a whole might play in expressing the Church's faith until the *sensus fidelium* proved useful in supporting the definition of the Immaculate Conception. Congar states, however, that "Perrone did not fully grasp the patristic concept of the *ecclesia*," and found only a passive role for the faithful.[93]

Another theologian who exerted considerable influence in the nineteenth century through his professorship at the Gregorian University in Rome and his preparatory work for the First Vatican Council, was Johann Baptist Franzelin (d. 1886).[94] Thils shows the scholastic nature of Franzelin's approach to the *Ecclesiae in credendo*, in describing the faith of the people as placed in God as its "formal object," while it is engendered in them through the efforts of the magisterium, who claim infallibility *in docendo*. It is through their *obedientia fidei* that the believing faithful then have a passive infallibility *in credendo*.[95]

J. P. Mackey has asserted that "The modern Catholic theology of Tradition begins with Franzelin."[96] Congar asserts that Franzelin gave the peoples' role "special attention," yet he "whittles down the meaning of the scriptural and patristic texts that speak of it and reduces this role to one of passive infallibility *in credendo* and of testimony rendered to the hierarchy concerning teachings received from it."[97] Mackey characterizes Franzelin's *De Divina Traditione et Scriptura* (1870) as the classic work on the view of tradition that developed in the Vatican I era.[98] He sees Franzelin's contribution in direct relationship to the rising focus on infallibility in the hierarchy:

> It has been said, and it is probably true, that [Franzelin] gave the theology of Tradition a bent which it never had up to then: it was Franzelin who first related the concept of Tradition so closely to the infallible teaching of the Magisterium as to derive his definition of Tradition from that relationship.[99]

Mackey notes that Franzelin consciously worked to refute nineteenth century heirs of the Reformation principle, *sola scriptura*.[100] Maintaining the importance of a larger source of tradition, he searches for and identifies the "organ" that transmits this tradition.[101] In the Council of Trent he finds the warrant for asserting that the Catholic Church is that organ.[102] The magisterium in particular is the authority through which the tradition is transmitted. According to Mackey, Franzelin specifically claims that the authority for tradition derives from the authority of the magisterium. Mackey himself adds that "a simple verbal analysis" of the text of Trent cited by Franzelin links the authority of the tradition to its source in Christ and the Spirit.[103] Mackey remarks that it is likely that in placing the active element in the handing on of tradition in the magisterium, Franzelin was influenced by the "growing emphasis on the official Church Magisterium by the Magisterium itself—and particularly an emphasis on the Papacy."[104] Contributing to this context were the 1854 definition on the

Immaculate Conception and the definition of papal infallibility promulgated at Vatican I, which as Mackey points out, was meeting as Franzelin produced his own influential text in 1870.[105]

Mackey summarizes Franzelin's theology of tradition and the authority that is responsible for it, saying,

> [Authority] belongs to objective tradition because of the organ which hands it on. It belongs to the truth in virtue of the divinely appointed mission of the organ which teaches it and in virtue of the infallibility of that organ in teaching it.[106]

A somewhat different approach is found in Matthias Joseph Scheeben (d. 1888), who Congar characterizes as placing "the subject of the *transmission* of Tradition within the *ecclesia* as a whole, laity included."[107] Both Thils and Thompson comment on lack of clarity in Scheeben's treatment of the infallibility of the believing Church.[108] Beinert describes Scheeben's treatment as "cautious."[109] Yet, describing his contribution, Thompson says Scheeben "systematically summed up the best in sixteenth to nineteenth century classical theological thought on the *sensus fidelium*."[110] In his *Handbuch der katholischen Dogmatik* (1873-1887), Scheeben considers the contribution of the whole Church in handing on revelation. Thompson claims that this focus "leads him to assert an 'intimate and organic union' between the *Ecclesia docens* and the *Ecclesia discens*."[111] Scheeben states that the faithful are prevented from falling into error by the presence and direct action of the Spirit.[112] Yet, Thompson notes the ambiguity created in Scheeben's view that believers exercise a "*private* profession and act of faith, 'echoing' the *Ecclesia docens*."[113] Thompson concludes that Scheeben was being careful to avoid emphasizing the direct involvement of the Spirit among the people at the expense of the proper role of the hierarchy.[114] At the same time, he adds that Scheeben maintained that the faithful "should normally be consulted before any doctrinal declarations."[115] The issue of consultation was to take on practical importance in the understanding of the *sensus fidelium* in the mid-nineteenth century.

If the nineteenth century theological climate was effected by Gallicanism (and its German speaking analogues of Josephism and Febronianism) and the theological views that were developing in Tuebingen, these were in strong contrast to the Scholasticism of the Roman schools. The latter had a considerable impact on the hierarchical approach to the sense of the faithful, and the consequent impact on Catholicism as it was popularly conceived. This is illustrated particularly by the definition of the Immaculate Conception of Mary.

J. M. R. Tillard has observed that, in drawing on the *sensus fidelium* to help authenticate the solemn definition of an element of its faith, the Roman Catholic magisterium distinguished its understanding from those of the Reformation churches. At the same time, it also

> indicates that the *sensus fidelium* implies infinitely more, at least in the eyes of Roman Catholic tradition, than just a force of balance or positive criticism towards hierarchical decisions as is imagined in certain Anglican circles.[116]

He adds, claiming "the vocabulary of Max Weber," that the sense of the faithful is "the bearer of a conviction on which the Magisterium itself must draw when it feels the need to affirm the content of the faith in the most authoritative manner at its disposal."[117] If later commentators see such importance placed on the faithful by the definition of the two Marian dogmas, a strong statement was certainly made by Pope Pius IX in his request in *Ubi Primum* (1849) for bishops to report on the faith of those under their charge.[118] Tillard notes that in *Ineffabilis Deus*, argument from the *perpetuus Ecclesiae sensus* is "found in the forefront."[119]

Eamon Carroll notes that the antiquity of the belief defined was hardly accepted without reservation throughout its history.[120] He observes that René Laurentin, writing on the role of the magisterium in the development of the doctrine in question, noted the lack of support of the defined view by Thomas Aquinas, the late acceptance of the feast day in Rome itself, and seventeenth century controversies in Roman congregations.[121] Gerard Owens maintains that the opposition of some medieval theologians to the doctrine concerning the Immaculate Conception was omitted from *Ineffabilis Deus*, because it was not clear if the doctrine as specifically formulated by Pius IX actually conflicted with the earlier views.[122] Carroll observes that in *Ubi Primum* itself, Pius IX avoids the phrase "Immaculate Conception," writing,

> It is Our earnest wish that you make known to Us as soon as possible what devotion your clergy and faithful people entertain towards the Conception of the Immaculate Virgin, and what may be their disposition to see this matter defined by the Holy See.[123]

Carroll argues that the proclamation of *Ineffabilis Deus* was connected not only to the current faith of the Church, but to the views of hierarchical authority and its practical exercise that were current among bishops.[124] In the discussions and clarifications of the document that preceded the 1854 bull, there were questions as to the role the bishops involved wore asked to play. He notes that in four meetings in November of that year, the bishops raised a variety of questions that postponed the final draft of the statement, and yet it "was made clear to them they were being questioned not about the substance of the definition, but on forms of expression."[125]

Several bishops suggested that the document should include a statement that the definition had received the explicit approval of the bishops. Bishop Malou of Bruges, on the other hand, argued that such an approach would shift attention away from the pope's authority, and might lessen the importance given to papal infallibility.[126] The bull was issued without such a statement about the role of the bishops, though as Carroll asserts, "[their] consent had in fact preceded the papal act, and the pope had sought it." Carroll adds,

> At the time Msgr. Talbot, the constant Roman adversary of Newman, had said, "You will see that the most important thing is not the new dogma in itself but the way in which it is proclaimed." Or, as the Doellinger correspondence puts it, "The pope could not directly declare his own infallibility, he did so equivalently through the Immaculate Conception."[127]

Carroll adds, however, that while *Ineffabilis Deus* was perceived as "a triumphant affirmation of papal infallibility," those supporting the Marian definition did not necessarily see it as linked to a later declaration on infallibility. Carroll notes too that some motivation for the definition can be found in the significant place held by Mary in the personal piety of Pius IX.[128]

There were bishops who in response to *Ubi Primum* stated that the definition was either inopportune or unnecessary in the light of current belief.[129] Interestingly, bishops in Germany found "mostly negative" response when they asked for the views of the theologians in their sees before the definition.[130] Yet few of these saw any indication that it would have a role as a "harbinger of a definition of papal infallibility."[131] Many commentators in Germany, in fact, saw the definition as "a great public proof of unity in faith between pope and bishops and between bishops and people."[132] However clearly its later influence might have been anticipated, Carroll states that among papal partisans among the bishops at Vatican I. the solemn papal proclamation of this doctrine had the effect of serving as "a precedent of the pope speaking on his own authority, without explicit reference to the consent of the bishops."[133]

Some indications that the definition did not indicate a simple expression of the prevailing faith of the people, but was an exercise of magisterial authority which defined authority as much as doctrine remained long after the bull. In his retrospective and apologetic study in 1954, Gerard Owens examines its promulgation with attention to the theories of tradition that were current. He notes that the theologians consulted in the preparation of *Ineffabilis Deus* rejected the idea that belief in the Immaculate Conception had been received through a "primitive formal oral tradition." He adds that the statement that the doctrine "*constantem fuisse et esse Catholicae Ecclesiae doctrinum*" was removed from the second to the last draft of the document. Owens asserts that the power of the definition came in its affirming the role of Mary "in the economy of salvation" which was then used as a basis to interpret the doctrine's presence in historic events.[134]

In describing the way the bull drew on Scripture for support, Owens stated,

> The Church's role is to preserve and explain the whole deposit of Revelation and to set forth the truths therein contained. That is her first responsibility. Only secondarily is she interested in establishing the particular passages in which particular beliefs are contained. That she usually leaves to the work of theologians. Hence in the Bull of definition, she did not settle the question whether the Immaculate Conception is to be found explicitly in Scripture or in Tradition, taken as a source and forming with Scripture the deposit of revelation. Neither has she decided whether it is contained formally implicitly or virtually.[135]

This passage exhibits a certain doctrinal positivism, a stance which did not completely characterize the view of magisterial authority in the pre-Vatican I Church, yet a stance which did have sufficient impetus to appear a hundred years later in the theological views of authority that preceded Vatican II.

It is important to recognize that if belief in the Immaculate Conception did not have the unanimity of history behind it, it did have, as indicated by a significant consultation of the Church in the nineteenth century, a widespread acceptance in the Roman Catholic world. It is also evident, however, that if the definition of this Marian dogma might be offered in support of papal authority, the fact of the pope's use of explicit support from the faith of the Church also includes a question within the exercise of papal authority. It is not trivial to ask what type of interrelation with the faithful is necessarily involved in the expression of such authority.

## JOHN HENRY NEWMAN AND THE "*RAMBLER* AFFAIR"

There has, in fact, been debate about the level of direct inclusion of the laity and the bishops themselves in the definition of the Immaculate Conception. In discussion about the promulgation of the dogma questions have been raised as to what elements that contribute to its definition are due to doctrinal concern and what elements are motivated by ecclesial politics. The two are mixed together, and they are difficult to separate at a short historical distance.[136]

The fact that the faith of the Church at large was considered by the magisterium as an immediate preliminary step to defining the dogma of the Immaculate Conception contributed to a controversy that erupted quite quickly, just five years after *Ineffabilis Deus*. In his article in the *Rambler* of July, 1859, "On Consulting the Faithful on Matters of Doctrine," John Henry Newman cited *Ubi Primum* where the bishops were asked to describe the faith of the common people. Newman's article elicited responses on several key issues. It created an animated discussion over the meaning of "consulting," cast his own orthodoxy in doubt, and opened the modern discussion of the *sensus fidelium* that continues today.

Newman's *Rambler* article and portions of his other work have given him the role of champion of the laity in the eyes of many contemporary authors. During his own time the state of the laity in England and elsewhere, was characterized by a split between clergy and laity. Even the educated lay people were left out of any relationship to the Church that acknowledged or drew upon their talents. Thus Newman himself observed "that the Clergy do treat the gentry with great inconsiderateness, or plainly do ignore them."[137] In another personal letter where he discussed the need for higher education for Catholics, following his return from Ireland and his work to develop a Catholic university there, Newman wrote,

> So far as I can see, there are ecclesiastics all over Europe whose policy is to keep the laity at arms-length, and hence the laity have been disgusted and become infidel, and only two parties exist, both ultras in opposite directions. I came away from Ireland with the distressing fear, that in that Catholic country in like manner, there was to be antagonism as time went on between the hierarchy and the educated classes.[138]

Contemporary authors who describe deficits in the ecclesial resources or responsibilities of lay people in the post-Vatican II Church thus find in Newman an advocate for lay involvement in a very similar context.

A thorough treatment of Newman's theology of the laity would require an analysis of his writing over a period extending from his Anglican days through his later works, and is beyond the focus of the current work. Such a study has been done by Richard Penaskovic, whose intent is to examine the development of Newman's ideas on the laity.[139] Penaskovic's aim is to fill the gaps left by other key studies that have addressed Newman's theology of the laity. He examines Jean Guitton's *L'eglise et les laics*, Samuel Femiano's *Infallibility of the Laity* and Webster Patterson's *Newman: Pioneer for the Layman*.[140] He finds that Guitton and Femiano have overlooked or paid insufficient attention to such works as *The Idea of the University*, the "*Newman-Perrone Paper*" and the *Preface to the 3rd edition of the Via Media*, and have isolated the *Rambler* article in their treatments, though he notes Guitton's stated intent to focus more narrowly.[141] Penaskovic faults Patterson for using Newman's writings without regard for their chronological context.[142] His own work then, aims to focus on the totality of Newman's deliberations about the laity with regard to their role in doctrinal development. He is also concerned to point out the importance, recognized by Newman, of the work of the Holy Spirit in the role played by lay people in the Church.[143]

No attempt is made in the present study to be comprehensive in recounting either the historical or the theological contexts that informed Newman's mature views on the laity. Rather, those texts of Newman's will be considered that are employed by contemporary authors as they make a case for the importance of the *sensus fidelium*. Penaskovic indicates the hermeneutical foundation for his own approach to Newman's texts. Citing Gadamer, Penaskovic describes his own interest in finding Newman's "effect in history" (*Wirkungsgeschichte*).[144] With such a hermeneutical "frame of reference" Penaskovic considers the matrix of key authors from which he extends the study of Newman's theology of the laity in a wholistic way, particularly, by emphasizing Newman's view of the theological impact of the Holy Spirit on the role of the laity.[145] The present study on the other hand, is focused on the effect Newman has had in the understanding of the *sensus fidelium* in the Second Vatican Council and its pluralistic aftermath. In this context Newman's *Rambler* article has proven to be a rallying point for discussion of the role of the faithful in regard to doctrinal development. Certainly his *Essay on the Development of Doctrine* is often examined to give this article context, as are the *Newman-Perrone Papers*.[146]

In evaluating the impact of Newman we see vividly how a plurality of interpretations can characterize the study of texts and ideas when they are examined at close historical range. This is certainly true of other authors considered here. Yet because of Newman's unique, ongoing role in the modern discussion of the sense of the faithful, it may be pertinent to consider how his historical and theological influences are intertwined with interpretation. The large amount of documentation available on Newman itself creates problems in interpretation that earlier historical events may escape. In events that are more distant, the impact of human agents or texts has had a longer time to come into focus. Newman's own views on Arianism, for instance, could draw on historical conclusions of the import of key figures and movements that were very much a matter of debate during the fourth century. When hermeneutical distance is short, the array of effects that a text can produce are subject to less sifting out. The assessment of the influence of a text and the understanding of it in its own context are apt to be intermingled as they are subject to the same or similar questions or pressures. Any judgment of the significance of Newman's work for the contemporary understanding of the laity is thus tied to the judgment of the interpretations given to Newman's own views by those who use his texts in the current discussion. The interpretations of the *sensus fidelium* that come from those drawing, for instance, on *On Consulting the Faithful in Matters of Doctrine* do vary, often in important ways. Inasmuch as Newman's period and the current one share some common issues, Newman is a valuable ally in facing the questions concerning the roles of the laity. At the same time, when Newman or the Second Vatican Council have spoken, the implications of their statements for practical action have not received their final word.[147]

The background and events surrounding Newman's editorship of the *Rambler* and the publication of his article have been detailed by several authors whose work will be drawn on for the summary here. John Coulson gives a useful introduction in his edition of Newman's article.[148] A printing of the same article with a discussion that places it in the context of the questions that concern a theology of the laity is available in Jean Guitton's *The Church and the Laity*. An expanded analysis of the context of the original *Rambler* incident and the expression of Newman's ideas on the laity, focused by but not limited to his article, are discussed by Webster Patterson in his *Newman: Pioneer for the Laity*.

Previously the *Rambler* had lived in the midst of controversy and criticism from the local hierarchy. Patterson describes the journal immediately prior to Newman's involvement as a vehicle adopted by Sir John Acton, A student of Doellinger, for promoting a critical form of scholarship in regard to Catholicism in England as well as a sense of historical perspective like that which had influenced him in the "Catholic intellectual revival" of Tuebingen.[149]

The *Rambler's* founders had already developed it as a source for criticism of church authorities. Any notion that was not specifically protected as dogma was open to attack. Patterson observes that, "By their attitude, they seemed to deny that ecclesiastical authority had any claim to the laity's obedience outside of matters of strict faith and morals."[150] The style of approach as well as the content of the journal brought it into conflict with Cardinal Wiseman, and Newman himself had attempted early on to moderate informally the efforts of its leaders, so that it might avoid its own excesses and be more effective in providing a counterpoint to the hierarchical focus of Catholicism that was dominant in England and elsewhere.[151] His efforts to mediate between the authors of the *Rambler* and the bishops who were considering censuring them became explicit when Newman was asked to take over the editorship of the journal in 1859.[152]

In the August edition of the *Rambler*, Lord Acton had remarked that St. Augustine, though he was "the greatest doctor of the West," could also be called the "father of Jansenism."[153] This touched off a controversy that warranted a response by Doellinger in the December issue.[154] Acton's fellow editor Richard

Simpson was faced with the brunt of the criticism when Acton left the country.[155] Coulson notes that Newman's decision to take on the editorship, one over which he suffered considerable anguish, may have been made to avoid any damage Simpson might cause if he were forced to resign. Simpson warned that he might make the controversy between the *Rambler*'s editors and the bishops public, or even sue the bishops for financial damages.[156]

At the request of Bishop Ullathorne and Cardinal Wiseman, Newman agreed to take the publication, hoping to lead it to a less controversial position. Newman saw three problems in the *Rambler*'s approach as summarized by Coulson: "It had treated of theology proper, it had done so in magazine fashion, and it had allowed laymen to do so."[157] Coulson describes Newman's efforts to return to an "innocuous" agenda in the May edition.[158] Yet, critics who were intent on finding offending material were successful in regard to two items. One came in a letter that asked the question, "How far is it allowable, or desirable, for laymen to study theology?"[159] The other was a collection of remarks that occurred in an editorial section on "Contemporary Events," where in an unsigned article Newman discussed the decision of the bishops in regard to a Royal Commission that had been suggested for the study of elementary education.[160] Newman wrote,

> We do unfeignedly believe . . . that their Lordships really desire to know the opinion of the laity on subjects in which the laity are especially concerned. If even in the preparation of a dogmatic definition the faithful are consulted, as lately in the instance of the Immaculate Conception, it is at least as natural to anticipate such an act of kind feeling and sympathy in great practical questions.[161]

The *Rambler* had discussed the issue of education as an open question in its January and February editions the same year. The education issue was a controversial one, involving the question of how church schools were to remain free from public control, even while they were subsidized by public money. The

*Rambler* was published under the assumption that the bishops had not yet spoken officially to the issue, though Coulson describes them as having been "extremely sensitive" to it.[162] It was unknown to the *Rambler*'s editors at the time of their February publication, that the bishops had, in fact, decided on the matter. Coulson summarizes Bishop Ullathorne's warning that the proposed Commission would give students "an impression of the state's exercising authority in matters religious."[163] He adds that some detractors had earlier "used the public press as a weapon against the conduct of the episcopacy, and might have separated the faithful from its pastors in a matter involving ecclesiastical freedom, episcopal prudence and religious discipline."[164]

In is own remarks cited above Newman apologized strongly for any disrespect of ecclesial authority that might have been seen in the *Rambler*. He was especially intent on maintaining good relationships between the bishops and the people. He writes further,

> We are too fully convinced of the misery of any division between rulers of the Church and the educated laity,—we grieve too deeply, too bitterly, over such instances as are found, either in the present day or in the history of the past, of such mutual alienations,—to commit ourselves consciously to any act which may tend to so dire a calamity. It is our fervent prayer that their Lordships may live in the hearts of their people; of the poor as well as of the rich, of the rich as well as of the poor; of the clergy as well as of the laity, of the laity as well as of the clergy: but whatever be our own anxious desire on the subject, we know that the desire of the Bishops is far more intense, more generous, more heart-consuming, than can be the desire of any persons, however loyal to them, who are committed to their charge.[165]

Newman's critics were led by Dr. John Gillow, a theology professor at Ushaw Seminary. Gillow had also drawn the bishop's attention to the earlier remarks on St. Augustine by Doellinger.[166]

In his effort to settle the problems caused by the most recent *Rambler* issue, Newman entered into a correspondence with Gillow, where their attention focused specifically on Newman's use of the word "consult." Gillow had written to Newman claiming that the notion that the laity had been consulted in the case of the Immaculate Conception "would certainly be characterized as *falsa* as a matter of fact."[167] Such a view would imply that the hierarchy lacked some necessary element in coming to an infallible decision, that "the infallibility of the Church resides in the Communitate fidelium, and not exclusively in the Ecclesia docente." Gillow claimed that Newman's view could be construed "as at least *haeresi proxima*."[168]

In his response, Newman distinguished consulting the laity as to their feelings or opinions from consulting them on the fact of their belief. He maintained that this fact of their belief is what his reference to "consulting" meant. At the same time, Newman notes that a stronger meaning, one closer to "feeling" was included in the bishops' interest in the beliefs of the faithful prior to the promulgation of *Ineffabilis Deus*. He quotes to Gillow a section from Perrone's own work that preceded the definition.[169] Referring to a phrase of Perrone's, Newman asserts, "'asking an opinion,' still I conceive, is very like 'consulting,' in the popular sense of the word."[170] Newman also recalls a discussion he had with Perrone in Rome in 1847, noting, "As I understood him, it was *the* method he took to meet deficiencies of historical evidence on particular points of dogma."[171] Newman summarized his view in saying that, following Perrone, infallibility "resides *per modum unis* in both, as a figure is contained both on the seal and on the wax, and primarily in the mind of the engraver."[172]

Their correspondence satisfied both Gillow and Newman that the latter's "unscientific" use of the word "consult" was not intended to discount the authority of the magisterium by requiring a juridical consultation.[173] As he closed the correspondence, Newman distinguishes the "power and prerogative of definition" that belongs to the hierarchy from the infallibility that is the Church's.[174]

Patterson remarks that "prudence might have suggested leaving the question where it was, buried in private correspondence." He adds that if Newman had realized what was ahead, "he most likely would have left it so."[175] Yet, Newman contacted Bishop Ullathorne about the correspondence with Gillow, and asked that he select a "theological censor" to work with the *Rambler*. Ullathorne responded by asking for a meeting with Newman. Patterson conjectures that the bishop was then being influenced by an article in the May 21st edition of *The Tablet*, where the situation of the *Rambler* was discussed.[176] The issue described there was

> How to reconcile the largest amount of free discussion with a due homage to Catholic truth and Catholic principle, including . . . a recognition of the just rights of ecclesiastical authority, either soluble by Dr. Newman or not soluble at all, but probably, circumstances being what they were, wholly insoluble.[177]

Patterson records that in his meeting with Newman, Ullathorne expressed affinity with *The Tablet*, and observed that he saw the "old spirit" of the troubled journal as still being present. He also declined to take on the official supervision of the journal, inasmuch as it was not produced in his own diocese and because the theological views it expressed were combined with other material rather than being located in one area. He expressed concern as well for the laity, "a peaceable set," who did not want their faith disturbed by the doubts of others. Newman responded that Ullathorne and he saw the matter quite differently, and that those in the episcopate generally did not appreciate the lay situation. He referred in particular to his own recent experience of the Irish people as "unsettled" yet "docile."[178] Patterson writes,

To this, Bishop Ullathorne replied in words to the effect: "Who are the laity?" Newman answered, though not in these words (as he noted in his memo), "that the Church would look foolish without them."[179]

Though the meeting ended in a cordial way, Patterson observes that the negative remarks of the Ullathorne probably "had some influence" on the July *Rambler* article. At the meeting, Newman agreed to stop editing the journal after the July issue.[180] Femiano considers it a mark of Newman's character that he "refused to let controversy subside" unless he had done whatever he could to resolve it.[181] He also states that if the printing of the July article had not come into a context marked by such controversy, "it might have been accepted with little comment."[182]

Newman begins "On Consulting the Faithful in Matters of Doctrine" by discussing the use of "consult," again distinguishing between the fact of belief among the faithful and their views or opinions. The problem, he states, is in linking the English word too closely to the Latin, technical term.[183] Patterson remarks that Newman's defense, though plausible, is not completely convincing, even in hindsight.[184] Femiano notes that soon after the article was published, Bishop Ullathorne observed that he had not found Newman's arguments on the use of "consult" to be successful.[185] Patterson finds Newman's claim that his intended meaning was obvious, when another meaning was quite as likely to have been understood, to be "a case of over-emphasis and over-refinement."[186] Yet, he adds that whatever interpretation was given to this word, Newman's case was not based on this point. His intent was to show that the magisterium had indeed drawn on the faith of the Church. He describes Newman's view "that the laity are looked upon by the magisterium as having a witness to beat regarding a state of belief in the Church, a function which is not to be identified with that of the hierarchy."[187]

In his second section, Newman treats the "matter" of the problem raised by the May *Rambler*, "putting aside the question of the wording."[188] He adds that however the word "consult" is to be judged, he had "implied, from the very force of the term, that [the faithful] are treated by the Holy See, on occasions such as that specified, with attention and consideration."[189] In answer to the question, of why they should be treated in this way, he links his view directly to the infallibility of the Church, claiming,

> the answer is plain, viz. because the body of the faithful is one of the witnesses to the fact of the tradition of revealed doctrine, and because their *consensus* through Christendom is the voice of the Infallible Church.[190]

He describes the way the Church reaches expression through history, continuing,

> I think I am right in saying that the tradition of the Apostles, committed to the whole Church in its various constituents and functions *per modum unius*, manifests itself variously at various times: sometimes by the mouth of the episcopacy, sometimes by the doctors, sometimes by the people, sometimes by liturgies, rites, ceremonies, and customs, by events, disputes, movements, and all those other phenomena which are comprised under the name of history. It follows that none of these channels of tradition may be treated with disrespect; granting at the same time fully, that the gift of discerning, discriminating, defining, promulgating, and enforcing any portion of that tradition resides solely in the *Ecclesia docens*.[191]

Newman observes that each person may emphasize one of the elements of doctrine over another. He then adds that his own interest in the *consensus fidelium* comes from a specific source.[192]

Newman recounts how in 1847 he had discussed with Perrone and Passaglia different doctrines which before their definitions had not been sufficiently attested in the "Bishops, doctors or theologians" in history. He relates that Passaglia had "seemed to maintain that the Ante-Nicene writers were clear in their testimonies in behalf (e.g.) of the doctrines of the Holy Trinity and Justification."[193] Perrone, however, while alluding to a different context

> seemed to me to say *"transeat"* to the alleged fact which constituted the difficulty, and to lay a great stress on what he considered to be the *sensus* and *consensus fidelium*, as compensation for whatever deficiency there might be of patristic testimony in behalf of various points of the Catholic dogma.[194]

Newman notes that he might have thought that Perrone was speaking in terms that were meant only for Newman's own reflection, if Perrone had not been so recently involved in the groundwork for understanding the definition of the Immaculate Conception. Newman then gives an account of the content of Perrone's book and the influence it exerted before the 1854 definition.[195] Perrone's work encompasses five focuses in regard to the *sensus fidelium*, summarized here by Patterson:

> 1. the *fact* of such *sensus*; 2. the relation of the *sensus fidelium* to the *sensus Ecclesiae*; 3. the *sensus fidelium* as an *instrumentum traditionis*; 4. the force of the *sensus fidelium* as distinct (not separate) from the teaching of their pastors; 5. instances in which the definition of doctrine was made in consequence of nothing else but the *sensus fidelium*.[196]

In the fourth point, Perrone illustrates the notion that the sense of the faithful is a distinct voice of the infallibility of the Church even (as Newman points out) if this infallibility is not identified as being "*in* the 'consensus fidelium.'"[197]

As he closes his discussion of Perrone, Newman cites the work of Bishop Ullathorne, who describes the sense of the faithful as "the *faithful reflection* of the pastoral teaching." Newman notes that Perrone's own view can be reconciled with the idea invoked by this image, that "a person may *consult* his glass, and in that way may know things about himself which he can learn in no other way."[198] Newman adds what Ullathorne himself writes about the faithful's role in the development of the Church's understanding of the Immaculate Conception.

> The more devout the faithful grew, the more devoted they showed themselves towards this mystery. And it is the devout who have the surest instinct in discerning the mysteries of which the Holy Spirit breathes the grace through the Church, and who, with as sure a tact, reject what is alien from her teaching. The common accord of the faithful has weight much as an argument even with the most learned divines. St. Augustine says, that amongst many things which most justly held him in the bosom of the Catholic Church, was the "accord of populations and of nations." Elsewhere he says: "In matters whereupon the Scripture has not spoken clearly, the custom of the people of God, or the institutions of our predecessors, are to be held as law." In the same spirit St. Jerome argues, whilst defending the use of relics against Vigilantius: "So the people of all the Churches who have gone out to meet holy relics, and have received them with so much joy, are to be accounted foolish."[199]

Although Ullathorne favors the notion that the faithful reflect the teaching of the Church's magisterium, in the same section of his treatise, Ullathorne elaborates on the faithful's role in the development of the Marian doctrine, and he does so in a way that shows a more nuanced and involved role. He writes,

> What has wrought this universal conviction but that a sense of it was always living in the hearts of the faithful, those hearts in which the most pure image of Mary dwelt? The faith of it moved through the living frame of the Church before it was spoken clearly with her lips. She meditated on the mystery, and its light shone on her features, long, very long, before she reduced it into solemn sentences, and imprinted on them the seal of her infallible authority.[200]

Thus having contextualized his treatment in the immediate backdrop of magisterial use of the *sensus fidelium* a few years earlier, and in the theological approaches that had clearly had an official impact in Rome and England, Newman then described a collection of theological views on how consensus was

> to be regarded: 1. as a testimony to the fact of apostolic dogma; 2. as a sort of instinct, or *phronema*, deep in the bosom of the mystical body of Christ; 3. as a direction of the Holy Ghost; 4. as an answer to its prayer; 5. as a jealousy of error, which it at once feels as a scandal.[201]

Each of these aspects he links to specific theologians; Perrone (1), Moehler (2), Cardinal Fischer (3), Petavius, quoting Augustine (4), and his own views as expressed in his second *Lecture on Anglican Difficulties* (5).[202] This last case of the Arian crisis is elaborated then in detail, to establish that the orthodox belief was carried in the fourth century, "not by the unswerving firmness of the Holy See, Councils, or Bishops, but . . . by the 'consensus fidelium.'"[203]

This synthesis of characteristics have served the modern discussion as a focus for ongoing discussion. Walgrave identifies an anticipation in the selection of Newman's later "famous distinction" in the *Grammar of Assent* between "real" and "notional" assent.[204] In Newman's view, faith in the individual is the practice of real assent, with theology being the work of notional assent. Walgrave describes the character of active faith in Newman,

> Real or "imaginative" apprehension, leading to real assent, is a growing process of "realising," penetrating into reality itself as if experienced and growing in depth and firmness of grasp, stirring the emotions, leading to action and, if it is concentrated upon one comprehensive object, unifying the whole of a man's life and forming in him one consistent character.[205]

This theological view of the "instinct" for the truth that operates in the faithful serves as a support for Newman's view of how ecclesial insight grows and expresses deeper insight into doctrinal truth. Owen Chadwick has described how Newman saw three "organs of expression" in the Church. The pope and the bishops, especially when gathered in council, have the responsibility "to declare and express the mind of the Church." The theologians have the task of discerning the meaning of doctrine, and of determining the effect of new scientific or philosophical developments on theological thought and language. The people's role is to be "the repository of that profound understanding, hardly expressed in words, which is the Church's immediate apprehension of the Christian way of life."[206]

In describing the interaction of these three organs, Newman prescribed that those responsible for teaching "the mind of the Church" should examine the ordinary faith and understanding of its members. Even though there are often cases of error and superstition among the laity, there remains in them a genuine intuition into the Church's message. Chadwick points out that Newman understood the pastors' responsibility to "consult" as including two aspects. In one sense it is passive. The behavior of the faithful is observed, and the implications of their actions and worship are inferred. Still, additionally, the "opinions" of the people are to be actively sought; not in the style of an opinion poll, but in a way that attends to the "instinct" of the people which is rooted in the "experience of truth" and which is accessible to the whole Church.[207]

Kevin Bucher states that Newman had become convinced that the "equilibrium of the Church's functions" was seriously out of balance.[208] He found that too great a stress on the power of the hierarchy and "a corresponding lack of freedom and diversity" characterized the nineteenth century Church.[209] A "dialectical tension" between "authority and individual judgment," exercised in a genuine context of freedom was seen by Newman as essential to the health of the

Church.[210] In this regard, Bucher cites the views that Newman later expressed in his *Apologia Pro Vita Sua*

> It is the vast Catholic body itself, and it only, which affords an area for both combatants in that awful never-dying duel. It is necessary for the very life of religion, viewed in its large operations and its history, that the warfare should be incessantly carried on.[211]

If Newman's idea of development of doctrine was based in his reading of church history, his view of the consensus of the faithful was of an active process that continued to operate in a specifically historical manner. The people are the receivers of the Gospel and their lives are evidence for its truth. It is precisely the life, teaching and worship of the Church, confirmed in the experience of the laity that is the Church's tradition. Coulson points out that in "On Consulting the Faithful," Newman saw great importance in the interaction of the faithful and the clergy. He identifies the same element that Newman saw in the Church's struggle with Arianism in the fourth century, and in his own experience with the "unhappy controversies which had arisen as a result of his frustrated efforts to educate the laity and to see them established in the economy of the Church of his time."[212]

Coulson describes the "cardinal theological principle" identified by Newman concerning the relationship of clergy and laity: "Though the laity be but the reflection or echo of the clergy in matters of faith, yet there is something in the 'pastorum and fidelium *conspiratio*,' which is not in the pastors alone."[213] Following this statement Newman immediately cites the process that led to the definition of the Immaculate Conception as an example of the working of this *conspiratio*. He looks to future inclusion of the faithful in expressing the *sensus fidelium* when he then refers to both celestial and earthly warrants for claiming a distinct role for the laity.

> It will be one among the blessings which the Holy Mother, who is the subject of it, will gain for us, in repayment of the definition, that by that very definition we are all reminded of the part which the laity have had in the preliminaries of its promulgation. Pope Pius has given us a pattern in his manner of defining, of the duty of considering the sentiments of the laity upon a point of tradition, in spite of whatever fullness of evidence the Bishops had already thrown upon it.[214]

Newman goes on to say that if consulted, the laity would have a contribution to make on most definitions that might be considered, but especially on those that relate to devotion. He notes as examples of topics close to the heart of the faithful, the ninth century expressions concerning the Real Presence and the fourteenth century response to John XXII on the beatific vision.[215]

Newman ends his essay with the long description of Dalgairns's *The Devotion to the Sacred Heart of Jesus* (1853), of the popular response that greeted the fifth century definition of Mary as *theotokos* at Ephesus. Here intricate disagreements in the church finally culminated in a response among the faithful that could be not inaccurately described as dancing in the streets. Newman quotes Dalgairns, saying, "There was but little sleep in Ephesus that night; for the very joy they remained awake; the whole town was one blaze of light, for each window was illuminated."[216]

Newman describes his own focus, different from Dalgairns's, as rooted in the same argument. There is an unmistakable contrast in Newman's own sense of how the laity may respond to current ecclesial attitudes toward the faithful as he describes how the magisterium might regard the faithful and the repercussions possible if they are disregarded:

> I think certainly that the *Ecclesia docens* is more happy when she has such enthusiastic partisans about her as are here represented, than when she cuts off the faithful from the study of here divine doctrines and the sympathy of her divine contemplations, and

requires from them a *fides implicita* in her word, which in the educated classes will terminate in indifference, and in the poorer in superstition.[217]

Newman saw the definition of the Immaculate Conception as a modern stage in an ongoing historical dependence on the sense of the faithful. It was both an important distinct source for the Church's ongoing development of doctrine, and one which needed the recognition and appropriation of the hierarchy to function with any sort of vitality. Coulson identifies the significance of Newman's *Rambler* article in its taking the question of "consulting" the laity out of the "realm of policy and discipline" and making it a theological issue. Coulson asserts that because of Newman's work the issue became "an argument about the laity's place in the very heart, mind and structure of the Church."[218]

If his arguments later held a key place in the Church's reflection at Vatican II on the role of the laity, the immediate response was negative and devastating for Newman. Coulson describes Newman's surprise at the strong criticisms he received after the July article, and notes the difference in mindsets between Newman and his detractors.[219] The question of consulting was taken up again by Bishop Ullathorne, who wrote to Newman saying that "the defender of the word 'consult' has not succeeded."[220] Gillow too wrote, withdrawing his earlier claim to agree with Newman, at least in principle, on the meaning of infallibility in the Church. In particular he disagreed with Newman's statement that during the Arian crisis there had been a "temporary suspension" of the *Ecclesia docens*.[221] Again the meaning to be attached to a word led to disagreement, with Gillow understanding "suspension" of the bishops' normal teaching in the sense of a "failure," and Newman understanding it to be a "clouding" over of the light that ordinarily came from the magisterium.[222]

In his criticism of Newman, Gillow was aided by Bishop Brown of Newport, who contacted the Secretary of the Propoganda in Rome about the

Newman.²²³ Newman remained under suspicion for some time, suffering from poor communication between himself and Rome. In fact, he wrote nothing for five years because of the trouble caused by the *Rambler* incident.²²⁴ In 1867 two priests of Newman's own Oratory went to Rome and were able to address the array of problems that had been linked to Newman's activities and ideas. Perrone suggested that at some point Newman ought to respond to the criticisms of his article, a suggestion which Newman followed in 1871 when he included a shortened form of it as an appendix to his third edition of *The Arians of the Fourth Century*. In addition he responded to specific points that had subsequently been identified in a lecture of Franzelin who was teaching theology at the Roman College. Several controversial elements were changed by Newman in the new edition, including portions that referred to the "temporary suspense of the functions of the Ecclesia docens."²²⁵

Though Newman was "rehabilitated" in 1867 through the efforts of his fellow Oratorians, Coulson points out how the difference in approaches that characterized Newman and his Roman counterparts continued to be a factor even after the suspicions about him abated.²²⁶ Coulson describes Newman's view of the Roman approach, citing Newman's own remarks from 1863.

> Matters requiring a theological attention were evaluated diplomatically, in terms of their power to cause good or bad "impressions", pain or pleasure; and the penalty of defeat was no longer the precision of formal condemnation, but the unending frustration of "life under a cloud."²²⁷

Newman retained a historical-theological approach which was to remain foreign to the scholastic-diplomatic perspective in Rome. This difference is consistent with the difference between Newman and Perrone that was clear in their views of doctrinal development when the two met in the mid 1840's.²²⁸ Chadwick describes Perrone's view:

> When heresy appears, the local bishops resort to Rome and Rome declares a sentence which makes clear the mind of the Church upon the question. Definition is therefore but a seal of truth, and nothing is new except the sealing. The Church declares its mind, of which it was fully aware before the heresy arose.[229]

Newman, on the other hand, held that,

> when heresy appears, the mind of the Church has to be *discovered* by meditation, discussion, dialectic, until a definition in accordance with it can be made: and so "after a difficult childbed, a new dogma is born." The Church has to reach a recognition of its mind before it can pronounce on the heresy.[230]

Chadwick adds that Perrone did not realize the problems caused for his view of doctrine by the new approaches to history, approaches that were central to Newman's understanding of Catholicism itself.[231]

The interrelatedness of the Church's various components and the wholistic overview that governed Newman's understanding of it, fed, as it was, by a profound sense of its history, is illustrated in the way Newman wrote about the Church's infallibility. One place where he does this, can be found in a letter to John Stanislas Flanagan, a priest and friend of Newman who was concerned that Newman clarify his own views of infallibility in the light of a dispute between one of Newman's students, Ignatius Ryder, and the avid infalliblist, W. G. Ward.[232]

Newman's view is contrasted with one that sees the *depositum* of faith as a "collection of barren propositions," with development coming from "logical conclusions" based on these propositions. In this view, infallibility would protect these truths and not allow anything to be added that is not already present.[233] Newman, on the other hand, maintains a living, organic model of the Church. He speaks in particular of the "mind" of the Church as the focus of this living reality.

Newman illustrates his point by describing how a student of Aristotle might respond to questions by drawing on a sense of the philosopher's own mind. A disciple of the philosopher who had received the master's teaching could respond from Aristotle's thought, in ways consistent with what Aristotle himself might have said. The disciple could do this even with questions that were not or could not have been raised in Aristotle's own time.[234] Similarly the mind of the Church given by Christ could respond to new questions and challenges, and do so in a way that was free from error.[235]

One of the ways in which a disciple would retain and apply the wisdom of the master is in absorbing the system of his thought, the "technology" that has grown from the original thought. Aided in this way, the follower can have his own intellect supported, allowing him to see the received teaching "as a whole, per modum unius."[236] Newman also cites disadvantages in such a "scientific apparatus." He sees danger because "common minds, instead of throwing themselves into the genius and animus of the philosophy, will make the technology the beginning and end of their study; and will be formalists, pedants, bigots."[237] Using the system is not a substitute for embracing the truths given to the Apostles and maintained through the Church which Newman calls "a living, present treasury of the Mind of the Spirit of Christ."[238] The *depositum* is not a "list" of truths, but "a large philosophy; all parts of which are connected together, & in a certain sense correlative together, so that he who really knows one part, may be said to know all."[239] Such doctrines that are recognized in the Church's later history are not then

> deductions from a creed or formularized deposit, but in truth they are original parts of it, communicated *per modum unius* to the Apostles' minds, & brought to light to the minds of the Fathers of the Council, under the temporary illumination of Divine Grace.[240]

Avery Dulles has given a systematic overview of Newman's thoughts on infallibility in an article marking the centenary of his death.[241] Dulles describes how Newman "ran the gamut of practically all the positions on infallibility that are compatible with a sincere acceptance of a once-for-all revelation of God in Christ."[242] He adds that during Newman's long ecclesial journey, he never wavered in his view that infallibility was the "fundamental dogma" of the Roman Catholic system.[243] His interpretation of its proper exercise changed somewhat, however.[244] Dulles notes that Newman had doubts about the appropriateness of a definition concerning infallibility before and even after Vatican I, although he eventually became "a leading apologist" for it.[245]

The key to Newman's understanding of infallibility throughout his life was that he saw infallibility as something that characterized the Church as a whole.[246] Dulles observes that the moderate definition of Vatican I concerning the papal exercise of infallibility was one that Newman was pleased with.[247] This definition allowed a nuanced interpretation of the teaching even in the highly charged climate of Newman's time.

Newman's own view of infallibility obviously changed from the days of his early attacks on the Roman Church. He also changed his argument for a "via media" between a Protestant stance of *sola scriptura*, a view that "believed too little," and the Roman tendency to continue adding to the creed, an approach that "believed too much."[248] The Anglican "rule of antiquity" was founded in a united Church. The ancient Church could see clearly the truth of the doctrines that were still shared by the churches of both the East and West, and this early Church could properly be said to be infallible. With a divided Christianity, such unanimity and the infallibility consistent with it was no longer possible, although an "indefectibility in the essentials of the faith," was still maintained in the main "branches" of the Church.[249]

Dulles calls the via media of Newman "an unstable compromise." His adherence to it wavered when he began to examine Monophysitism.[250] In this fifth century controversy, Newman saw an analogy to the sixteenth century, in terms of the roles played by the overall ecclesial context, the Council of Chalcedon, and Pope Leo. Newman began to question how he could argue against the Council of Trent without applying the same arguments to Chalcedon. He thus came to see not the ancient Church, but the presently existing Church as the seat of judgment concerning doctrinal truth. The infallibility that attended the judgment of this contemporary Church, he finally identified in the Roman Catholic Church.[251]

Dulles describes Newman's view of infallibility throughout his life as always being cautious. It was not a teaching contained in Scripture, but was tied to a larger interpretive context for revelation and tradition.[252] Dulles observes that Newman based his view of infallibility, as Rahner has done more recently, on "antecedent probabilities."[253] He describes Newman's understanding as follows,

> Infallibility, as distinct from revelation or inspiration, was a mere assistance, and at that a primarily negative assistance. It served to prevent the Church, in certain of its acts, from falling into error.[254]

Dulles writes that Newman described the "seat of infallibility" (in his *Rambler* article, but elsewhere as well) as the whole Church.[255] Yet, he did not minimize the role of the hierarchy. Dulles attributes the criticism that Newman received in Bishop Brown's delation of him to Rome to a misunderstanding of his views. Newman did not intend to set up the laity as an "infallible witness" separate from the hierarchy, but insisted only that they were "a constituent part of the total Church, which was infallible."[256] Dulles notes that Newman even used the distinction of "certain Continental theologians" of an "active" infallibility on the part on the hierarchy and a "passive" infallibility in the response of the faithful.[257] He adds,

These terms, however, do not do justice to Newman's real thought on the matter. The laity, in deciding what they are bound to accept or reject, are in some sort active. Their instinct of faith is in its way an authentic expression of the infallibility of the Church as a whole. In certain cases in which the pope or the bishops failed to teach, or taught wrongly, the sense of the faithful could serve as a corrective.[258]

Reception by the larger body of believers was for Newman, an important element in resolving questions of whether the definition of a belief had met the criteria for infallibility. Additionally, he saw an important role for theologians in discussing and interpreting the meaning and implications of such decrees. Dulles writes, "In the jargon of our day we would say that Newman was keenly aware of the hermeneutical problem and of the role of the theologians as a kind of 'second magisterium.'"[259]

Dulles points out that the teaching of Vatican I on infallibility and the practical complications that were connected to its general acceptance gave Newman a basis for retaining his view that infallibility belonged to the whole Church.[260] Some eighty to ninety bishops had left the Council rather than vote on the definition. The subsequent reception of the teaching by an overwhelming number of them was instrumental in Newman's own acceptance of the teaching.[261] Dulles adds that even with this acceptance, Newman saw the Vatican I definition as describing only one side of the Church's exercise of infallibility. In the letter to Alfred Plummer cited above, Newman even "predicted" that another council would be needed to balance the teaching of Vatican I.[262]

Dulles finds Newman's understanding of infallibility to be quite compatible with Vatican II.[263] Though he finds perhaps too strong a case made in Newman for the part to be played by theologians in preparing and interpreting doctrine, he sees him anticipating the important role of reception emphasized by later thinkers like Congar.[264] He comments that "Newman is rightly praised for his recognition of the importance of the assent of the faithful."[265] Specifically in regard to the sense of the faithful Dulles writes:

> He used the *sensus fidelium* not to offset the infallibility of the magisterium in teaching and defining, but rather to confirm the teaching of the magisterium when the latter is not uncontestably infallible. Newman might have admitted that in certain cases the lack of acceptance on the part of the faithful could raise a question as to whether a given pronouncement of the hierarchy was in fact infallible, but he never suggested that the views of the faithful had infallible normative value apart from, or in opposition to, the teaching of the hierarchy.[266]

The interest that Newman showed in the nature of reception of doctrine, and in particular the doctrine of infallibility, illustrates from another angle the view of the faithful he expressed when discussing how they should be "consulted." The issues that the First Vatican Council raised for the understanding and exercise of infallibility, and the role of the whole Church, have continued to have an impact that is intertwined with Newman's own influence.

## THE CONTEXT OF VATICAN I

The differences of approach or "mind-set" that could cause a lack of understanding between Newman and his contemporaries in Rome are further illustrated by the response given to the views of Ignaz von Doellinger. Joseph Hoffmann has described how the theological and political contexts in the mid-nineteenth century contributed to conflict between Rome and a developing German perspective on ecclesiology, a conflict that become apparent in an address given by Doellinger to the Congress of Catholic Scholars, in 1863.[267] Hoffmann describes the tendency in German speaking countries to reject the scholastic theology of the Latin speaking schools, in favor of a "practical theology" that could be said to employ "the two eyes of theology: philosophy and history."[268]

In his speech before the Congress, Doellinger argued that theology has the role of helping to build "just and sane public opinion in matters religious and ecclesial, and before this opinion all, in the end, yields, even the heads of the Church and the holders of power."[269] He adds that even when "the thoughtless mass does the opposite" of what theology calls forth, any genuine progress will be based in what "the whole institution and whole action of the Church is invested in, in correspondence with its idea." Theology has a key role in any movements of reform in the Church.[270]

Hoffmann observes that Doellinger's remarks created strong reactions, not the least of which was a letter from Rome to the bishop of Munich, which Hoffmann describes as "criticizing the attacks against scholasticism and deploring that an assembly of theologians themselves would thus convene without a mandate from the hierarchy, 'to which it belongs to direct and oversee theology.'"[271] Hoffmann notes that the letter further asserts in direct response to Doellinger, that although Catholic theology is not a matter of merely repeating solemnly defined propositions, it should respect the official teachings of the Church.[272] Hoffmann cautions against reading Doellinger's program for theology expressed in this speech in the light of his later stances and subsequent excommunication in 1871. In 1863, Doellinger was interested in promoting a form of theological study well within the context of obedience and service to the Church and its authority.[273] His views on the "prophetic" role of theology and the role of "public opinion" in the Church lie well within "the classical tradition of theology," and are not greatly different than the views expressed by Newman in his *Rambler* article.[274]

Hoffmann cites M. Seckler's view that Doellinger stressed the "charismatic and prophetic function" of theology as "an extraordinary authority" specifically to show theology's importance in assisting the "ordinary doctrinal authority" of the Church. As theology seeks to form opinion at large in the

Church, it is "understood as being rigorously scientific in its method of operation, but political in its operative design: it sets itself in public opinion as a 'megaphone' and a 'level.'"[275] Doellinger saw the force of public opinion as playing a key role in society, and he saw theology as having the responsibility of developing a "sane" version of it.[276] Hoffmann describes the logical result of Doellinger's stance as creating not a simple juxtaposition of power between theologians and Church authorities, but a vying for influence where public opinion is both the content and the medium of concern, or "at once the place and the thing at stake."[277]

Hoffmann emphasizes the importance Doellinger saw in keeping the Church free of the influence of the state.[278] Christianity's contribution to the benefit of the German nation would be made through influencing society and its values through its normal structures.[279] He argues for a "national" church, which could focus the efforts of Christian influence in Germany, while at the same time explicitly avoiding the notion of a Church that would be "autonomous" or Gallican.[280] Hoffmann quotes Doellinger as arguing for a form of Christianity in his own country that allows its own nature and qualities to find expression, and that will avoid the tendency to force into the German context a "religious particularity that another nation has developed according to its proper nature."[281] Hoffmann observes,

> From this point of view the conflict evoked in the Discourse of 1863 is altogether between scholastic theology and historic theology, and between "Latin" theology and "German" theology. It is not, in any case, a conflict between "liberalism" and "orthodoxy."[282]

Hoffmann ruefully notes that Doellinger's efforts to find a "reasonable Catholicism" in the context of Europe in the age of political upheaval, suffered the fate of "cleavages and oppositions" that such liberal attempts generally engendered in the second half of the century.[283] He concludes that the theological issues embedded in Doellinger's appeal to public opinion did not receive a sympathetic pastoral hearing in his time because of the dominant view of the world and especially authority among those in the magisterium. He adds his own observation, that then, as now, the issue of public opinion is significant inasmuch as it is tied to the "historical and social form of Catholicism that one intends to promote or defend." Defining public opinion is both a matter of the content and the form of the debate.[284]

The scholastic perspective of Rome is readily identifiable with the "Roman School" represented at Vatican I by Franzelin who systematized the work done earlier by Perrone, Passaglia, and Schrader. These three were influential professors in the Roman College after its was returned to the Jesuits by Leo XIII.[285] Perrone was influenced by Moehler in seeing the Church as a further expression of the Incarnation and as the "Mystical Body."[286] Perrone reasoned, that as Christ was "indefectable," so was the Church. Extending the analogy further, he saw the will of Christ as directly expressed in the actions of the Church's leaders.[287] As Sanks describes Perrone's understanding,

> The church is not only a mediator of the Word of God to men, but is the immediate direct witness of the Word of God. The doctrine and practice of the church is the immediate, direct, representation of divine tradition.[288]

Sanks goes on to describe the "foundation of this teaching authority" in Perrone's view, as being the placing of the deposit of faith in the care of the apostles and their successors. This deposit was partly given in written form, but partly in an oral tradition which "determines the sense of what was written down and completes it."[289] Those with authority to teach exercise three responsibilities:

1) that of witness, to propose the truths of faith, 2) that of judge, to settle controversies that may arise in the understanding of the faith, and 3) that of teacher, in the daily ministry of instructing the faithful in all things pertaining to doctrine and morals.[290]

The highest authority in teaching resides in the pope who ranks over other bishops and even synods, although Perrone assumes the pope and these others will work together.[291]

Sanks describes the influence of Passaglia and Schrader as coming in a single, shared theological perspective.[292] Sanks writes, "The dominating result of [their] analysis of the metaphors, similes and analogies for the church in the New Testament and the Fathers is *the unity of Christ and the church.*"[293] From this emphasis on unity there results a view of the magisterium as a "divine-human" organ; Christ is identified with the Church and thus with the apostles and the magisterium that succeeds them in a way that is "more than analogous."[294] Passaglia and Schrader call this "divine-human magisterium" the "objective norm of faith."[295] This "norm" is then described as "unified," "consistent," "universal" and "perpetual."[296] Sanks adds,

> This objective norm of faith can neither be added to nor diminished, and is completely immutable because it is divine and perpetual. This objective norm is not subject to any ontological growth or progress nor can it undergo any change the way philosophy or human culture can.[297]

Sanks notes that the authors did not distinguish "between the *content* and the *activity* of the magisterium which was customary in later treatments of the matter." Similarly, Schrader did not distinguish the "active" from the "passive" aspect of tradition.[298] According to Sanks, Passaglia and Schrader expected the "objective norm" which was "unified, consistent, universal, perpetual and immutable" to elicit a "subjective faith" in the believer with the same characteristics. Sanks remarks that they did not deny the developmental quality of faith, which might even include some periods of confusion, but they expected the more positive response in the "public profession of faith." To assure this in the public dimension, the Church needs a strong magisterium.[299]

Within this magisterium the bishops exercise three aspects of "teaching," "pastoring," and "witnessing" that were given to the apostles, and maintained in the early Church.[300] Sanks notes that Passaglia and Schrader saw the magisterium as residing in the apostles and their successors, and not only in the pope, although the unique place of papal office was recognized.[301] Schrader in particular emphasized this place in his later life, becoming a staunch supporter of infallibility while serving on the commission that preceded the First Vatican Council.[302]

Sanks notes that the three "founders of the Roman School" saw a rich image in the Incarnation for maintaining the "divine-human character" of the magisterium.[303] From this base, they developed an ecclesiology with an "emphasis on authority as the source of unity and order that was characteristic of the Restoration period in which they lived."[304]

From such a foundation, the systematic understanding of the magisterium that was developed by Franzelin finds a focus and impetus.[305] A key role for the magisterium was assured from his view that although God has communicated with humankind, this does not imply a divine contact with every person.[306] God's self-revelation in Christ was handed on for the salvation of all through the Church, and this handing on is protected in a flawless way by the "infallible authority of God."[307] Franzelin distinguished tradition in the "objective sense," "*that which is handed on,*—doctrines or instructions," and tradition in the "active sense," "*the acts and means by which* the doctrines and practices" are passed along.[308] The two aspects are not to be severed from each other.[309] Yet, the active sense takes a certain logical priority. The certainty of the "content" of tradition would not be assured with out a prior certainty concerning the "mode" of its transmission.[310] Sanks quotes Franzelin as saying the "principal instrument for the original promulgation of the Christian faith was not only Scripture but the personal authentic magisterium" to which he adds that the "living authentic magisterium remains the organ of perpetual preservation."[311]

In regard to the actual active functioning of tradition, Sanks quotes, with approval, Mackey's view that, although Franzelin does not explicitly equate this functioning with the magisterium, on the other hand, "it is hard to see how he could have more definitively proposed the same idea."[312] The implications of this emphasis on the magisterium come out in Franzelin's description of who receives "the charism of infallibility."[313] Sanks describes his view, writing, "The charism given to the apostles refers immediately to them and their successors as its subject, but to the whole church for its use and growth."[314] The two aspects of infallibility *in credendo* and *in docendo* can be "distinguished but not separated since the profession of the faith of the believing church is the end and purpose toward which the office of preaching and teaching is ordered."[315] Sanks also describes Franzelin's understanding that the magisterium's actions are "external" while "internal" activity is the work of the Holy Spirit.[316]

The exercise of authority is given to the bishops as a "corporate body," although Sanks emphasizes that this is not to be understood from the point of view of collegiality that comes from Vatican II. Each bishop is subordinate to the Church as a whole. Sanks notes that this does not apply, however, to the pope, who can act on behalf of all with the charism given to the Church.[317] Franzelin asserts, "it is both the visible head of the church *per se spectatum*, and this visible head insofar as it so constituted (as head and body) that is infallible with the assistance of the Spirit of truth."[318] Sanks describes the bishops in this understanding as distinguished within the magisterium, yet as "*inadequately* distinct." As a body they are not to be considered as infallible apart from their head. Sanks observes that though their authority is not distinguished completely from his, they are certainly seen as subject to the pope. He notes too, that Franzelin continued the approach that placed the "prerogatives" of the pope "in opposition to the Gallican or Febronian position which he seems to find lurking behind every mention of episcopal consensus."[319]

Consensus of the faithful, accordingly, has only a passive role as well. Its meaning is derived in relation to the magisterium. Sanks describes Franzelin's view:

> The faith is preserved in its integrity in the community of the faithful, not by the immediate operation of the Holy Spirit or without a visible ministry, but through the authentic magisterium of the apostolic succession.[320]

This infallibility *in credendo* is described also as being *in fidei obedentia*. The relationship of the people to their pastors "is one of subordination, of obedience."[321] Acknowledging that the pope had considered the consensus of the faithful before defining the recent Marian dogma, Franzelin saw it as "only one of several possible means" of testing the definability of a doctrine.[322] Sanks sees here another indicator of Franzelin's watchfulness for "anything that smacks of Gallicanism."[323] He notes that in the preparation of Vatican I's *Pastor aeternus*, Franzelin was against the suggested inclusion of a stipulation that prior to defining a doctrine the pope had to see if the Church was in consensus on the matter.[324]

Sanks writes that the overriding concept of Franzelin's ecclesiology was that of "Kingdom," even with the dependence he also shows on the notions of "the Bridegroom and the Bride" and that of "the *Corpus Christi mysticum*." He notes that Franzelin viewed the monarchical nature of the Church as instituted by Christ, and therefore unchangeable. Sanks adds too the "amazing" fact that in

Franzelin's main ecclesiological work, "there is little or no mention of the functions of councils (ecumenical or local) as part of the magisterium at all," even though the work was published while the Council was meeting, and while Franzelin himself served as the pope's advisor.[325]

Sanks summarizes the key theological points of the Roman School with respect to the magisterium, which were to be maintained by those who followed Franzelin;

> the close identification of the magisterium with Christ and the consequent elevation of its authority to the more-than-human level, the assumption that all truth necessary for salvation is already contained in the "deposit," that there is some semi-magical device, the "charism of truth," given by God to the apostles and their successors in office, that the main function is to protect something already possessed.[326]

The Roman School contributed significantly to the mindset that dominated Catholic theological treatment of doctrine, the papacy, and infallibility, before and after the Council.[327] Sanks is concerned in the work cited to show that the issues introduced in different ways by Newman and the modernist controversy, and the emphases brought into official ecclesiological reflection with Vatican II, represent changes of the order described by Thomas S. Kuhn in the area of science, under the image of "paradigm shifts."[328]

Sanks sees the major model of ecclesiology as being one of monarchy or kingdom.[329] Important implications for how doctrine and more importantly, doctrinal development, could be understood are tied to such models. He notes, for instance, that

> the only possible way for the Roman School to understand progress or development was in terms of growth in clarity or explicitness. There was no way for them to understand how

something could be true in a certain context or framework but not in another.[330]

The "shift" toward a new sort of paradigm, and a richer understanding of authority is connected by Sanks to a deeper realization of the role of "historical awareness" and to the influence of pluralism. He observes that the latter was not recognized as an important factor until just prior to Vatican II.[331]

The possibility of seeing the truths of the faith in different terms as they become expressed in different contexts, while at the same time not falling into a relativistic approach, was expressed by John XXIII at the opening of the Second Vatican Council, where he made the often quoted statement, "The substance of the ancient doctrine of the deposit of faith is one thing, and the way in which it is presented is another."[332] Such insight, nuanced and hammered out in the Church's experience of the excesses of Modernism on the one hand and a "creeping" infallibilism on the other, was not yet expressed at the time of the First Vatican Council.

At the same time, even in a climate that was characterized by a static, centralized view of the magisterium and doctrine, and in which a strong definition of infallibility was favored by many, the Council still produced a nuanced official teaching.[333]

## THE FIRST VATICAN COUNCIL

The most "famous" aspect of the work of Vatican I is its teaching in *Pastor aeternus* concerning infallibility. Andreas Lindt has described how, as Pius IX closed the fourth session of the Council on July 18, 1870, a storm, complete with thunder and lightning broke out in Rome, which was seen variously as "heavenly applause" and "a manifestation of God's anger."[334] A political storm brought the Council to an abrupt end the next day as the eruption of war between

France and Prussia left the Council's work to stand as complete in the form it had taken. The Council was officially suspended by Pius IX on October 20, 1870.[335]

Although considerable controversy had attended debate over infallibility at the Council, eventually all of the bishops who had represented the "minority" view expressed acceptance of the teaching in *Pastor aeternus*.[336] Disagreement over its meaning did not end with such acceptance, however. John T. Ford has observed that responses to Vatican I "ranged on a spectrum from hyperbolic ultramontanism to obediential minimalism."[337] Ford states that theological differences like those between Newman and Manning were "sharpened rather than lessened" by the Council.[338]

Examples from the bishops themselves illustrate that acceptance of the Council's teaching should not be viewed simplistically. Archbishop Peter Richard Kenrick of St. Louis submitted after being decidedly against the definition of papal infallibility.[339] Paul Hennessy has pointed out that this submission was made through Kenrick's recognition of the authority of the Church rather than through his being convinced of the appropriateness of the definition. Hennessy notes that in a letter to Acton of March 29, 1871, Kenrick wrote that his decision was motivated by his recognition of the acceptance on the part of the other bishops, including those who had been of the minority view.[340] Kenrick struggled during the Council with those who wanted a strong definition of infallibility. He and his fellow bishops in the "minority" camp served an important role in nuancing the final wording and content of the definition. Hennessy also points out, that after the Council both Kenrick and a strong infallibilist like manning did not grasp all of the implications of the definition.[341] Though carefully worked out at the Council, and placed in a practical, ecclesial context by several speeches on the Council floor (particularly by the official relatio of Bishop Vincent Gasser) the definition did not close debate on infallibility.[342]

In a study marking a century of interpretation of the teaching on infallibility since Vatican I, Ford has observed that the very bishops who wrote the documents of the Council did not understand them in the same way.[343] He sees controversy over the meaning of infallibility after the Council as following similar lines to those that preceded it. Ford comments that the "anti-infallibilist contention that infallibility was incapable of precise theological definition, a problem adroitly by-passed at Vatican I, has become an even more crucial question than ever before."[344] He notes too, that a "commonplace view" of Vatican I has pitted infallibilists and anti-infallibilists against each other in a simplistic fashion, when in fact, disagreements over the meaning, "opportuneness" and juridical scope of infallibility were much more complex.[345] To analyze the interpretations of the Council teaching on infallibility, Ford suggests and employs a three-leveled approach similar to that used in biblical criticism, that would distinguish

> 1) the meaning of the council and its documents to its participants and contemporaries; 2) the meaning of the council and its teaching in subsequent presentations; 3) the meaning of Vatican I a century later.[346]

He observes that the controversy that surrounded the Council "probably necessitated some kind of definition."[347] Some resolution was needed of what had become a serious, complex issue. Ford notes that many agreed with Newman, an "inopportunist," who "thought the way in which it was passed was a scandal."[348] Kenrick and fifty-four fellow bishops left before the deciding vote, after first writing to Pius IX to state their disapproval of the Council's proceedings.[349] Ford observes that, "The ink was hardly dry on *Pastor aeternus* before there was a spectrum of interpretation, ranging from 'maximalist' to 'minimalist.'"[350]

He notes that the maximalist view was most often the one that was "proposed as the acceptable pattern for Catholic belief in England, Ireland and the United States," with "theological-ecclesiastical maximalism [finding] a compatible partner in the Anglo-Saxon attitude towards law, which has generally been much more rigid than its Mediterranean counterpart."[351]

Vatican I was very careful in speaking of infallibility. Ford observes that the Council itself found it "misleading to speak of 'papal infallibility.'"[352] The definition clearly speaks of the infallibility of the Church as being exercised by the pope under certain carefully described conditions. Yet, in the century following Vatican I, popular attitudes among many Roman Catholics have given the pope's prerogative an aura that was not part of the actual definition Ford quotes the view of G. Wilson on the development of such attitudes,

> The opponents of the definition had, as we know, predicted what would happen: if you define, even with all sorts of qualifications, that the pope can *sometimes* teach in an infallible manner, then it will be but a short time before people are saying that he *always* teaches infallibly, and indeed that this is because he *is* infallible.[353]

These maximizing perceptions were not without support in the actions of the magisterium at the time of the Council and in the years that followed. Giuseppe Alberigo has described how the Roman, scholastic approach to theology and the Roman hierarchy became wedded in a combining of doctrinal teaching authority and juridical authority, as well as a growing centralization of both during the pontificates of Gregory XVI and Pius IX.[354]

The widespread perception of infallibility that maximizes hierarchical authority is detrimental particularly to ecumenical relations.[355] Lindt has illustrated that the impact of Vatican I's definition was still a problem for ecumenical relations, even after the attempts at restoring balance to the understanding of infallibility that were undertaken at Vatican II and the renewed reflections that followed the Council.[356]

The criticisms raised by bishops at the First Vatican Council and by interpreters since have been focused on the maximalist interpretation of infallibility of the Pope, which is understood as claiming authority for him at the expense of the Church as a whole. At the time of the Council, such criticism was expressed by bishops in the minority, who wanted a direct statement of the role of the Church included in the definition.

The passage of *Pastor aeternus* which speaks most directly to the role of the Church in the exercise of infallibility would appear, on the fade of it, to deny any role except passive acceptance The document proclaims:

> It is a divinely revealed dogma that the Roman Pontiff, when he speaks *ex cathedra*, that is, when acting in the office of shepherd and teacher of all Christians, he defines, by virtue of his supreme apostolic authority, a doctrine concerning faith or morals to be held by the universal Church, possesses through the divine assistance promised to him in the person of Blessed Peter, the infallibility with which the divine Redeemer willed His Church to be endowed in defining the doctrine concerning faith or morals; and that such definitions of the Roman Pontiff are therefore irreformable of themselves, not because of the consent of the Church [*ex sese, non autern ex consensu ecclesiae*].[357]

Little room seems to be allowed for discussion of such definitions. Yet, many commentators observe that in the context of the Council, exclusion of "consent" is aimed explicitly at a sort of juridical consent required by a Gallican view of authority. The definition need not imply a power in papal infallibility that is set against the Church as a whole.

The sort of Gallican views that were present at the Council have been illustrated by Margaret O'Gara in her discussion of the French minority bishops at the Council.[358] These twenty-two bishops were the largest regional element among the Council's seventy-three minority voices.³⁵⁹ O'Gara asserts that their view of papal authority was directly influenced by the position taken in the Declaration of 1682 which claimed that the decisions of the pope concerning the faith were not irreformable without the subsequent agreement of the Church. This stance, even though it was held in a "moderate version" by the "Gallican" bishops at the Council, was the target of the "troublesome phrase, 'and not from the consent of the church,'" that was included in *Pastor aeternus*.³⁶⁰

O'Gara observes that the French minority participants at Vatican I "formed their opposition to the definition in an atmosphere of exaggerated personal devotion to the pope and alarming rumors about the Council's purpose."³⁶¹ They perceived this purpose as being the declaration of the "separate, personal, absolute infallibility of the pope."³⁶² With this expectation, they were intent on maintaining the distinct role of the bishops as judges of the faith, both in their sees and gathered together in councils.³⁶³ According to O'Gara, their objections to the definition of infallibility that was put before the bishops at Vatican I was expressed in three categories.

> Three questions synthesize the general concerns to which their arguments responded: (1) Is the proposed teaching true? If yes, (2) Is the proposed teaching definable? if yes, (3) Should the proposed teaching be defined?³⁶⁴

O'Gara observes that answers to the last question concerned the timing of such a definition. Many bishops, recognizing the intent of the pro-infallibilists to stem the tide of a rising crisis of authority in the secular context yet argued against the effectiveness of such a move. They noted too, that the definition could seriously damage the already strained relations between Roman Catholics and the other Christian churches.³⁶⁵

In regard to the second question, O'Gara observes that some in the minority group criticized papal infallibility as an innovation. They maintained that a *de fide* statement was not definable where the agreement of the whole Church could not be demonstrated.[366] Others argued that the conditions at the Council itself were so unacceptable, as to invalidate any definition. Excessive heat in the Council sessions and at inability to hear did not allow for proper deliberations.[367] O'Gara comments,

> More seriously, arbitrary decisions about the Council procedures kept minority viewpoints virtually unrepresented on the drafting deputation, and allowed closure of discussion and majority voting to settle a matter that French minority bishops felt could be defined only by virtual unanimity.[368]

O'Gara sees the "need for consensus" as being the primary sticking point in the bishops' criticism of definability. Even where the infallibility of the pope was considered as "the most probable opinion," it could not be shown to be "a part of the ancient and universal faith."[369] O'Gara states, "Many objected that to define papal infallibility as a dogma of faith would be to make the opinion of one theological school into an article of faith."[370] Some bishops insisted that to teach infallibly, the pope needed the backing not only of the bishops but of the whole Church.[371] Some bishops pushed this last point to give a negative answer to the remaining question of the truth of the teaching. They viewed the definition as leaving out the "ecclesial character" of infallibility.[372]

O'Gara notes that in later accepting the definition, each bishop agreed that *Pastor aeternus* held either "formal" or "material" authority.[373] As in the case of Kenrick and others, the fact of a decision by the Council was respected by some to such an extent that it caused them to attempt an understanding of the content of the Council's teaching that put it in the best possible light. Some stated explicitly, that while during the Council they considered it important to challenge the teaching, afterwards they had to switch their stance and support it.[374] O'Gara cites Bishop Ginoulhiac as stating that his leaving before the final vote facilitated his later support of the definition. An actual vote against the definition, which would have been consistent with his views at the Council, would have compromised his ability to give such support.[375] Some bishops supported the definition by employing careful distinctions. O'Gara writes,

> Their arguments for the material authority of *Pastor aeternus* were guarded. Rather than finding *Pastor aeternus* compelling, they found it acceptable when interpreted in certain ways. They struggled to find such interpretations, and for the most part their struggle was given impetus by their *a priori* assumption of the decree's formal authority.[376]

O'Gara notes that, importantly, some French bishops explicitly claimed that the definition did not define "the separate, personal, absolute infallibility of the pope," over which they had been so concerned, but had, in fact, linked the pope's action to the Church as a whole, whose consent was ruled out only as an action to be taken after his exercise of his authoritative role.[377]

O'Gara sees in the continued nuanced response of some of the French bishops after the Council, a warrant for a current, critical understanding of Vatican I's definition, that places it in a wider ecclesial context. In relation to the contemporary understanding of the Council she states, "Today their interpretive work seems not only legitimate but prophetic."[378]

O'Gara interprets the French minority bishops as insisting on "evidence" that infallibility had been validly invoked in papal decrees. She observes,

> Consensus of the churches, or reception by the whole church, or moral unanimity of the bishops after free and lengthy discussion: these were signs that indicated to them an exercise of infallibility. They emphasized that knowledge, even divinely assisted

knowledge, had to include the step of judgment as to whether or not a teaching was in fact an exercise of infallibility.[379]

This judgment was the task of the whole Church. God insured that within the community the mistakes from one quarter would be offset by efforts from others. The pope could err too, and thus he depended on the Church. Interestingly, O'Gara sees the "use of the human mind in a self-correcting communal setting" as an "accurate epistemology, one that avoids intuitive cognitional theories, as a foundation for the work of transposing the concept of infallibility from a 'classicist' form into 'historical-mindedness.'"[380]

It may be important to ask why such cognitional theories (theories, that by implication, are less accurate?) should be avoided. In a contrasting approach, Francis Schuessler Fiorenza has argued convincingly, that the implications of the "transcendental and linguistic turn" are central to the understanding of differences in the approaches to truth of the Roman School in the nineteenth century and the secular counterparts that this school attempted to confront. The scholastic approach of Franzelin in particular affects the theological formulations in Vatican I's Constitution, *Dei Filius*.[381] Fiorenza writes,

> Franzelin's theology was caught up within the framework of the very modern rationality which he criticized. In sketching a raster of heresies he points to an absolute opposition between the autonomy of reason, on the one hand, and the belief in the authority of revelation, on the other hand. In his conception, Christian theology has its foundation exclusively from the standpoint of the formal authority of God. Philosophy and science rest on the standpoint of an autonomous rationality. Therefore the autonomous rationality of reason and a Christian faith based on authority are contrasted.[382]

Fiorenza sees Vatican I's approach to authority as bound up in a "false alternative" between the "authority of faith" and the "autonomy of reason."[383]

O'Gara's intent is to hold up the French bishops as examples of the interpretations that occurred in the nineteenth century which may inform the understanding of the twentieth. Yet, if contemporary disagreements are not to be simply re-formed in the categories of the original debates, a view like Fiorenza's must at least be examined as suggestive of an overview that can offer new insight. Recalling Hoffmann's three-leveled approach to investigating events that are both historical and theological, the issues may be clearer when it is accepted that history and interpretation are bound together in each level.

Fiorenza follows Wilfred Sellars in calling the tendency to separate "what is given and what is interpreted," the "Myth of the Given." This approach sees history as a place that can be mined for "facts" that can then be reinserted in the reflections of another epoch. A more adequate hermeneutical approach must recognize the interpretive framework in which all "facts" arrive for any historical examination.[384]

A useful study of Vatican I's teaching on infallibility that attempts to relate the interpretations given by the Council Fathers themselves is that of George Dejaifve.[385] Dejaifve examines the actual debates at the Council to show what meanings were given by the bishops themselves to the definition of infallibility. Writing even before the explosion of literature that marked the centennial of the definition, led by Hans Kueng's *Infallible? An Inquiry*, he asserts that the bishops' own views have been "obscured by the controversies which have now for nearly a century been kept going equally by the prejudices of its opponents and by the excessive interpretations of its well meaning defenders."[386]

Dejaifve cites "two extreme positions" as being evident at the start of the Council's debate on the inclusion of a chapter on infallibility on March 6, 1870. Supporters of a strong stance on the "personal infallibility" of the pope included three Italian bishops who wanted to include the view that "the definitions of the

Pope are irreformable in themselves, without any consent of the Church, either antecedent or consequent."[387]

The other position stressed the necessity of agreement of the whole body of bishops. Dejaifve cites the reason given by Bishop Vaughan:

> One could easily imagine that the Supreme Pontiff might claim the right to define anything he saw fit, *opportune importune*, without any consent of the bishops. We must take care not to give cause for any suspicion to arise of any sort of schism between the head and the members of the Church.[388]

Such concerns were taken seriously as the Deputation of the Faith brought the matter to the Council for debate. The struggle of the Council Fathers was more subtle than that of the two extremes. Dejaifve describes the efforts of the participants to critique the definition of infallibility in the light of its connection with historical understandings or with the conciliar responsibility of the bishops. He also notes that some bishops claimed that papal infallibility was an innovation, especially when considered in the light of the Vincentian Canon.[389]

To objections that the definition should mention the role of the bishops, a representative of the Deputation of the Faith, Bishop d'Avanzo, countered that their assent was "always understood" by the fact of Christ's institution of the episcopate, with the pope serving as its head. Yet, he added, the definition itself should not include the role of the bishops, inasmuch as it would introduce a condition that would have to be checked to determine whether a given exercise of infallibility had been valid.[390]

Dejaifve sees d'Avanzo's argument as key to the focus taken by the Council's debates and definition. Making reference to an earlier critical speech by a Bishop Guidi, Dejaifve asserts,

> Notwithstanding the severity of [d'Avanzo's] strictures on the speech of Mgr Guidi, the fact remains that in reality he admitted,

and that in the name of the Deputation of the Faith, that a good number of the latter's observations were wellfounded, and in particular that concerning the necessity of there being an enquiry previous to any papal definition. Mgr d'Avanzo's concern was simply to discuss the modalities of such an enquiry; the fact of its necessity he simply recognized.[391]

Dejaifve adds that a major reason that the Deputation did not include a reference to the bishops in the definition, was "the fear of seeming to allow an appeal from the judgment of the Pope to that of a Council." He sees this omission as unfortunate, inasmuch as it prevented "any serene quest for a formula of conciliation" from developing, that could have brought unity to the Council.[392]

In early July, as the minority group was growing "increasingly hostile," Bishop Freppel of Angers addressed the Fathers on the reasons that the definition ought not include the modifying description of context for the exercise of infallibility by the pope. Dejaifve describes Freppel's efforts:

> The previous enquiry among the bishops, the invocation of the Holy Spirit, the human diligence to be employed as far as possible in the enquiry—"all this," he said, "belongs to the moral order, and refers to the moral obligations which are incumbent upon the Supreme Pontiff, not to the authority itself which he possesses to define these truths."[393]

On July 11 Bishop Vincent Gasser presented the proposed definition to the Council on behalf of the Deputation of the Faith. Gasser again insisted that the juridical condition of consulting the bishops should not be included, even while admitting that such consultation would be a normal part of the process of the Pope.[394] Dejaifve notes that throughout, the Deputation sought to avoid any phrase that could possibly be construed as requiring a legally binding procedure.[395] When the definition was finally written to include the statement, "*irreformabiles ex sese, non autem ex consensu Ecclesiae*," Gasser

> made it clear that the negative part of the formula was simply an explanation of the "*ex sese*," and that its sole object was to show more clearly that the irreformability of the pontifical definitions did not depend upon the fulfillment of some external condition, such as the consent of the bishops or of the Church, but from the simple fact of the Supreme Pontiff's act in speaking "ex cathedra."[396]

Dejaifve notes that the word "consensus" in this formula was used differently than had been the case throughout the Council debates. Where those debates had used it in a traditional, wholistic sense, in the formula "it is used in the sense of 'juridical assent.'" Dejaifve adds that critics and even infallibilist bishops at the Council were quick to recognize that the formula could easily be construed as separating the Pope from the rest of the Church, placing him above it.[397]

That this has in fact occurred is obvious from the maximizing tendencies that followed the Council.[398] That this was not the Council's intent is clear from the context in which the definition was received and approved, and it is evident in the official relatio of Bishop Gasser of July 11, where he speaks of the pope's moral duty to consult with and to speak in union with the Church. The contextualization of papal infallibility within that of the Church as a whole is clear in Gasser's official statement. An extended citation of his speech may be helpful to illustrate this point. In the relatio, Gasser asserts,

> The purpose of this Prerogative is the preservation of truth in the Church. The special exercise of this prerogative occurs when there arise somewhere in the Church scandals against the faith, i.e., dissensions and heresies which the bishops of the individual churches or even gathered together in provincial council are unable to repress so that they are forced to appeal to the Apostolic See regarding the case, or when the bishops themselves are infected by the sad stain of error. And thereby we do not exclude the cooperation of the Church because the infallibility of the Roman Pontiff does not come to him in the manner of inspiration or of revelation but through a divine assistance

> Therefore the Pope, by reason of his office and the gravity of the matter, is held to use the means suitable for properly discerning and aptly enunciating the truth. These means are councils, or the advice of the bishops, cardinals, theologians, etc. Indeed, the means are diverse according to the diversity of situations, and we should piously believe that, in the divine assistance promised to Peter and his successors by Christ, there is simultaneously contained a promise about the means which are necessary and suitable to make an infallible pontifical judgment.
>
> Finally, we do not separate the Pope, even minimally, from the consent of the Church, as long as that consent is not laid down as a condition which is either antecedent or consequent. We are not able to separate the Pope from the consent of the Church because this consent is never able to be lacking to him. Indeed, since we believe that the Pope is infallible through the divine assistance, by that very fact we also believe that the assent of the Church will not be lacking to his definitions since it is not able to happen that the body of bishops be separated from its head, and since the Church universal is not able to fail.[399]

The "papal infallibility" that the Council Fathers approved in July, and which the dissenting bishops received in later months, was received with a clear understanding of the pope's moral responsibility and intrinsic connection with the Church, even if his juridical role was clarified and recognized as unique among bishops.[400]

Nevertheless, the complicated mix of interpretations that followed the definition does not allow an easy acceptance of the view that the pope's prerogative has been understood wholistically in the past or is understood in such a way now. The combination of historical and dogmatic issues that have fed this mix are described under the heading of a "Dilemma Between History and Dogma" in an article by Georg Denzler. He argues that, "knowledge of the historicity of dogma includes, in my view, admitting the possibility of error in definitions of faith."[401] Writing of the need for revising the popularly received maximalist interpretation of infallibility, he observes,

So it would be right to say today that when the infallibilists, with Pius IX as their leader, they ascribed absolute infallibility to the papal *magisterium*, i.e., in disconnecting the pope from the Bible and tradition and also the Church's sense of faith (*sensus fidelium*), they proclaimed a very historically determined view, which we are now slowly, although not completely discarding in favour of a synodical and collegial primacy such as was practised in the early Church.[402]

If it is clear that Vatican I's definition of infallibility is historically determined it is not so clear that Denzler's optimism concerning a contemporary collegial primacy is warranted. An easy theological solution is no more likely than an easy historical one.

## THE *SENSUS FIDELIUM* AND VATICAN I

If the First Vatican Council is a watershed in the Catholic understanding of infallibility, it is no less an "incisive event" for the understanding of the sense of the faithful.[403] The issues of the magisterium and the *sensus Ecclesiae* are certainly related, as is obvious from the historical developments examined in the present study. William Thompson, following his own historical survey, observes that both the early Fathers and subsequent theologians have recognized an important connection between the sense of the faithful and the hierarchy. He then examines the question of "whether the hierarchy itself has been equally aware of this close connection." He notes that they have not taught much specifically on the topic. This "sense" must then be explored as an "underlying reality manifested in the authentic tradition."[404]

Thompson, following Thils, has pointed out that the first draft of the document on ecclesiology that was prepared before Vatican I retained the influence of the approach that followed Trent and acknowledged the role played by the *sensus fidelium*.[405] He then describes a change of focus,

> However, the council quickly turned its attention to the question of magisterial infallibility, and on March 12, 1868, the special deputation made a very important change with respect to the subject of infallibility: from *universae ecclesiae competit* to *ad universalem ecclesiam spectat*, thus separating the faithful from the subject of infallibility. Instead, they become its object, the people being taught by an infallible subject.[406]

Thompson sees this change as indicating that "the deputation had no intention of orienting the Council Fathers toward a discussion of the *Ecclesia in credendo*, and thus its discussion is quite rare."[407] He notes that the minority bishops were themselves too occupied with establishing the role of "episcopal prerogatives" to bring up the matter. In Kleutgen's second draft of the proposed document, the *sensus fidelium* was again included, though the bishops on the floor of the Council never saw it. Thompson points out though, that the sense of the faithful was certainly understood as part of the overall context of the Church, and was specifically connected to the pope's exercise of infallibility as it was described in Gasser's relatio.[408] Yet, it is also clear that the role of the faithful was not considered to be an active one.

Alberigo offers a graphic description of the predominant view:

> The dominant ecclesiology in the council presupposed a subordinate and passive role for the faithful and granted authorities the right to intervene all the more incisively in the fluid domain of doctrine.[409]

He sees this view of the faithful as part of the focusing of the teaching authority of the Church within a hierarchy whose theology was devoid of a sense of historical context, and who had taken on "the task of ascertaining and condemning error as well as that of finding effective juridical sanctions."[410]

## MODERNISM

The exercise of centralized authority, in active pursuit of doctrinal error is illustrated vividly in the papal responses to Modernism in the early twentieth century. Alberigo observes that although Leo XIII understood the impact being made by "historical consciousness," he did not see as clearly the value of historical-critical method in Biblical and theological studies.[411] Yet, a negative position against the new intellectual developments found expression in his successor, Pius X's *Lamentabili* (1907), where sixty-five propositions proported to be held by the Modernists were condemned. A defensive stance is readily seen in proposition six, which reads, "The 'Church learning' and the 'Church teaching' collaborate in such a way in defining truths that it only remains for the 'Church teaching' to sanction the opinions of the 'Church learning.'"[412] Alberigo observes that the subsequent encyclical, *Pascendi*, "turned the Modernist concerns into a compact doctrinal system in order to reject them more effectively as a whole."[413]

John Thiel cites this encyclical as the most vivid example of a development that occurred between Vatican I and Vatican II, which he describes as "the magisterium's outright rejection of the Romantic paradigm of theological responsibility." Thiel sees in the work of the Modernists an effort to seek "the same Romantic reconciliation of truth and history" that characterized the Catholic theologians at Tuebingen in the previous century.[414] *Pascendi* condemned the view that there is a dialectical development in expressions of the faith, with those in authority needing the active, progressive insights of the faithful.[415] *Pascendi* condemns the view it perceives in Modernists:

> The conserving force in the Church is tradition, and tradition is represented by religious authority, and this both by right and in fact; for by right it is in the very nature of authority to protect tradition, and in fact, for authority, raised as it is above the contingencies of life, feels hardly, or not at all, the spurs of progress. The progressive forces on the contrary, which responds

to the inner needs lies in the individual consciences and ferments there—especially in such of them as are in most intimate contact with life.[416]

Thiel understands this view to have been "condemnable not only because of its deficient notion of truth and populist understanding of authority but also because of the direct power it accords to theological sensibility."[417] Thiel sees genuine theological responsibility as the casualty in the rejection of the Romantic paradigm, particularly as such responsibility and even authority are found in "the developing experience of the ecclesiastical community, especially in the personal sensitivity and constructive abilities of the community's theologically talented members."[418] He finds this responsibility and "theological creativity" vindicated in Vatican II's "positive regard for historical development, especially the development of doctrine, and the consideration of the magisterium's infallibility in the broader context of its relationship to the *sensus fidelium* of the entire Church."[419]

The movement toward an acceptance of historical consciousness in theology was obviously not a smooth one. In his study considered earlier Sanks sees the pattern of reactions to challenges from both historical consciousness and pluralism as consistent with a "paradigm shift" in Roman Catholic theology, in a way analogous to the shifts T. S. Kuhn has described in the history of science.[420] In Kuhn's theory, such a shift begins with an "anomaly," an alternative view, that gives "rise to a sense of 'crisis'" in the group concerned.[421] Sanks sees the Roman response to the ideas of both Newman and the Modernists as a "retreat to a non-historical approach" and refortification of Neo-Scholastic ideas. Here the prevailing group attempted to reject the new view.[422]

Avery Dulles has noted a common criticism of the Neo-Scholastic period, that in focusing power in the pope, it lessened the legitimate authority of the episcopate. He observes that at Vatican I, "the dogmatic decrees were issued, significantly, not by the council itself but by the pope 'with the approval of the sacred council.'"[423] He agrees with Sanks, that the expressions of popes at this time were not devoid of theological input; rather they were steeped in the activity of theologians from the Roman School, "who thus gave official status to their own opinions."[424] Dulles thus adds, "What appeared on the surface as a conflict between certain theologians and the papal magisterium was at a deeper level a clash between different theological schools."[425] He notes that though it is acceptable for popes to draw on theological experts for the preparation of their official statements, such a practice "calls into question the Neo-Scholastic contention that the theologians are mere disciples of the pope and his fellow-bishops."[426] The significance of the use of the theology of the Roman School on the possibility of developing a wholistic faith on the part of believers is indicated in the description Dulles gives of how the magisterium focused more and more on juridical matters:

> Little attention was given to the sacramental aspect of the Church, to worship as context for credal utterances, to the unpredictable initiatives of the Holy Spirit, and to the eschatological dimension of revelation. . . . They spoke as though faith terminates in words of the hierarchical teachers. In a deeper theology it becomes apparent that ecclesiastical teaching, however authoritative, is at best a sign permitting the believer to receive or recognize the word of God, to which alone the assent of faith is due.[427]

The appropriateness of characterizing the approach of the magisterium as a "paradigm" is further illustrated by Gabriel Daly.[428] He asserts that the "pastiche of ideas" from Loisy and Sabatier that made up *Pascendi* would have been unrecognizable as a system to anyone not familiar with the original writers.[429] He claims that the encyclical "not merely condemned modernism; it defined it," taking a "scattering" of unconnected thinkers and combining their views into a movement.[430] Daly adds,

> The only movement afoot in the Church at that time was the movement which crushed all dissent from Ultramontane scholasticism. It is precisely because modernism was *not* a movement that Rome was able to destroy, as "modernist," all manifestation of liberal thought so easily.[431]

Daly's analysis supports his point well, even though his passion approaches the zeal of the anti-modernists he criticizes. In his discussion of "Integralism" he provides a clue as to why the supporters of an understanding of the Catholic faith as a "logically organized system of inter-connected doctrines each of which goes to make up a divinely guaranteed whole," might see any challenges to those doctrines as the attempts of a competing inter-connected system.[432] *Pascendi* certainly exhibited a siege mentality, even if the sometimes ornate wording of papal encyclicals is taken into account.[433]

In considering the use of authority in the Church on an international scale, Alberigo admits the reality of both positive and negative aspects to centralizing authority in the papacy.[434] Yet he cites too, the theological problems that such authority has given Rome in its relationship to other Christian bodies. He notes that ecumenism found a sympathetic papal participant only with John XXIII.[435]

If ecumenical rapprochement was a long time in coming in Rome, other shifts in the Roman approach to theological issues are still in question. Citing Kuhn's own research, Sanks notes that scientific "revolutions" can take between sixty and one hundred years, and he observes that "a less exact discipline" may take longer.[436] In addition to the rise of an "anomalous" minority and a consequent crisis among those involved in a confrontation, already considered above, Sanks describes other characteristics of a paradigm shift that can be identified in the theological events of the last century. When an anomalous view is identified, research is usually focused in the topical area. Sanks notes that such research, with a focus on historicity, occurred in Rome with Perrone, Passaglia and Schrader as well as in Tuebingen.[437] Interestingly, Sanks's approach recalls the discussion of paradigms done more recently by Thiel, when he cites T. M. Schoof's description of these examples as indicative of a "creative theological impulse."[438]

Sanks identifies two more indicators of a paradigm shift as described in Kuhn's theory, among Catholic theologians active since the era of Pius IX. Kuhn's theory predicts both the growth of the initially small group holding the anomalous view, and an ensuing period of "professional insecurity."[439] Sanks sees the "increased preoccupation with the question of 'development of doctrine'" as indicative of the first characteristic.[440] Professional insecurity is illustrated in "the atmosphere created by the fusillade of condemnations issuing from the Vatican since the time of Pius IX."[441]

Sanks describes "perhaps the most striking parallel" of the modern theological events in Roman Catholicism and the scientific paradigm shifts in Kuhn's theory, as "the proliferation of theories or of versions of a theory which follows the awareness of anomaly and is 'a very usual symptom of crisis.'"[442] Sanks then describes in detail how the events of Newman and the *Rambler*, and Modernism, in the specific cases of Tyrrell and Loisy, illustrate the differences between the paradigms of the innovators and of the Roman School.[443] If Sanks's appropriation of Kuhn's model is of value in interpreting the events in recent Roman Catholic history, it is important to recall another facet of the theory. Sanks writes,

> "The transfer of allegiance from paradigm to paradigm is a conversion experience that cannot be forced." Even if we understand the process, the outcome cannot be induced by coercion. To realize this may help with the crisis a bit better.[444]

If some theological creativity remained active to challenge the growingly centralized control of doctrine and its interpretation, the majority of the faithful were cast more and more in a passive role in the early twentieth century. Congar observes that in the reediting of standard texts which described tradition in the decade from 1910 to 1920, there was an "evolution" toward identifying the "active tradition" of the Church solely with the hierarchy, which he notes is "something Franzelin, Scheeben and even Perrone did not do."[445] At the same time the "rule of faith" is focused less on the "remote rule" associated with Scripture and other "monuments of tradition," and toward the rule as identified in the active magisterium. Congar suggests that such moves make the magisterium into a sole *locus theologicus* for finding revealed truth.[446]

## THE *SENSUS FIDELIUM* BEFORE VATICAN II

Following the condemnation of Modernism, there was both a tightening of magisterial authority and a continued interest in some theological circles in exploring the historical rootedness of the faith.

Alberigo writes that in the wake of the Modernist crisis the magisterium operated more and more consistently as a government, using its authority "to determine conformity to the doctrinal content of the Gospel as an everyday instrument of regulating the life of the ecclesial community.'"[447] It faced the "age of 'ideology'" with a centralized system for combating error, Alberigo asks, "Was this an enviable anticipation of the ideological states or a tragic step toward the radical reduction of pluralism and all minority opinion under the pretext of error?" He comments that such centralization, in fact, removed responsibility from "the Church as *universitas fidelium*, the hierarchy itself as well as theologians." Alberigo identifies the height of Roman power, as occurring in the 1930's and 1940's, especially as it was entrusted to the Congregation of the Holy Office.[448]

The 1950 encyclical, *Humani generis*, which rejected the "*theologie nouvelle*," is described by Alberigo as the "apex" of the move to control doctrine. He notes that its "joint denunciation of '*discordia et aberratio a veritate*' is a formula which blurs the distinction between dissent and error."[449] After this encyclical, theologians could no longer openly discuss an issue once the pope had decided it. They were left with the role of showing how the magisterium's teaching was consistent with the sources of tradition.[450] The faithful were to respond to the hierarchy with obedience.

Yet during the same period, theologians had turned to history and to the notion of development in doctrine. Jesús Sancho Bielsa finds in this period a return to theological discussion of the *sensus fidei*.[451] Following *Lamentabili* and *Pascendi*, the roots of modernism's errors were examined in works like those of Garrigou-Lagrange (*Le sens commun, la philosophie de l'être et les formules dogmatiques*, 1909), De Grandmaison (*Qu'est-ce qu'un dogme?*, 1905 and *Le développement du dogme chrétien*, 1907-1908), and Gardeil (*Le Donné révélé et la theologie*, 1910).[452] Sancho identifies the work of Gardeil, as indicative of the sort of response the modernist debate drew, and observes in it a return to an appropriation of the sense of the faithful.[453] What he sees as most significant is the impact of the work of Gardeil on F. Marín-Sola's *La evolución homogénea del dogma católico* (1923), where the sense of the faith played an important role.[454] Sancho observes that while Marín-Sola defended the view expressed at Vatican I and in *Lamentabili* that the pope does not require approval or consent from the faithful to express a teaching infallibly, he also found that the meaning of the *sensus fidei* had not been adequately treated.[455]

Sancho cites Marín-Sola as key to the re-establishment of the phrase "*sensus fidei*" in modern theology, which culminated in its eventual appropriation by Vatican II. He acknowledges, too, the work of several other authors before the

Council, such as Koster, Beumer, Balic, Dillenschneider, García Extremeño, Congar, Bartolomei and others.[456]

Congar sees the return to the term "*sensus fidei*" as a move away from understanding of the work of the Holy Spirit as a "hierarchic charism" and a refocusing on the "mystical life of faithful souls, including pastors."[457] He too, cites Koster, Beumer, Balic and Dillenschneider as leaders in the retrieval of this insight.[458] He also sees a need for better balance in the use of this source. He sees the *sensus fidei* as being given "something like an autonomous value" with too little attention being given to the objective quality of what is revealed. He adds, however, that the same objective norm must be seen as prior to the magisterium. Though the hierarchy has an active authority in the Church, it is itself "secondary and dependent in relation to the *revelationis fontes*, Scripture and tradition."[459]

The theology of the sense of the faithful received a new impetus in the mid-twentieth century that was not unlike that of the mid-nineteenth, when Pius XII solemnly defined the Assumption of Mary into heaven. As in the case of *Ineffabilis Deus* a letter was sent by the Pope to determine the faith of the people in regard to the Assumption before the issuing of his own encyclical.[460] The responses to this letter made it possible for Pius XII to claim "an almost unanimous affirmative response" in favor of the definition.[461] The encyclical asserted,

> This "outstanding agreement of the Catholic prelates and the faithful," affirming that the bodily Assumption of God's Mother into heaven can be defined as dogma of faith, since it shows us the concordant teaching of the Church's ordinary doctrinal authority and the concordant faith of the Christian people which the same doctrinal authority sustains and directs, thus by itself and in an entirely certain and infallible way, manifests this privilege as a truth revealed by God and contained in that divine deposit which Christ has delivered to His Spouse to be guarded faithfully and to be taught infallibly.[462]

Carroll writes that the magisterium "based itself on the *sensus fidelium*" in defining the Immaculate Conception and the Assumption, adding that in both cases "the infallible pontifical teaching authority was invoked to clarify and fix by an official expression a belief recognized as already living in the consciousness of the people of God." He goes on to say "two great forces converged in the *conspiratio antistitum ad fidelium*."[463] Carroll quotes J. M. R. Tillard's description of these elements as "on [the one hand] the spontaneous attitude and instinctive perception of the faithful, and on the other hand the more and more explicit accord of the various leaders of the local churches."[464]

The encyclical itself appears to favor an understanding of the *sensus fidelium* that corresponds more to the notion of the faithful as a "mirror" for the magisterium, rather than a "great force."[465] If an organic understanding of the relationship between the faithful and the magisterium was held by some who wrote about the *sensus fidei* at the time of the encyclical, there was certainly more focus on the role of the pope himself in the way it was understood by both its supporters and detractors.[466]

Juniper Carol illustrates this focus on magisterial prerogative in his "The Definability of Mary's Assumption," written before the solemn definition of the pope.[467] He describes how *Deiparae Virginis* and the pope's anticipated definition was met with "reserve, hesitation and even open hostility."[468] Such responses had spawned a host of articles and dissertations opposing or defending the definability of the doctrine. Carol refutes the view of J. Coppens of Louvain, in particular, who used a historical approach to show a lack of support for the proposed doctrine, and who supported the notion that the teaching of the bishops "must reflect the belief of the faithful."[469] Carol affirms,

> The *consensus fidelium* has always been considered a most cogent argument in doctrinal matters *because* it reflects the teaching of the bishops. Let us not forget that the faithful (and that includes the

most learned theologians and historians!) belong to the *Ecclesia discens*, while the bishops and only the bishops, however unlearned, constitute the *Ecclesia docens*.[470]

In his conclusion, Carol reiterates his own intent to argue in support of the definability of the Assumption on the basis of the authority of the magisterium in contrast to a "*purely historical* method which would lead to rather disappointing results."[471] He chides an unnamed colleague who sees such an appeal to the magisterium as "a handy life-belt to those who have suffered shipwreck in the science of theology."[472] Carol asserts,

> This attitude, besides being incredible in a Catholic, can only lead to disastrous results in the field of theology. It is the firm conviction of the present writer that, in doctrinal matters, the *Magisterium Ordinarium* is *always* right. He will continue to stand fast by that authority.[473]

An article that takes a more nuanced approach is that of Walter Burghardt, "The Catholic Concept of Tradition in the Light of Modern Theological Thought," which followed the definition.[474] Where Carol appealed to hierarchical teaching in the nineteenth and twentieth centuries, Burghardt traces the historical views of the magisterium from the Council of Trent. He thus considers the hierarchy's magisterial role in the light of the Church's growing focus on doctrinal expression as the vehicle of tradition.[475]

What is taught and believed in the contemporary Church is seen as an acceptable theological tool for interpreting historical evidence that is in itself inconclusive.[476] He sees present consensus in belief as an outgrowth of tradition and thus as a legitimate interpreter of previous "evidence." The legitimate judge of the faith of the Church is the magisterium. When the pope defined the Assumption, he recognized the consensus of the present belief, as being part of the tradition. This decision thus legitimized the belief that as part of the tradition, the truth of the Assumption was taught throughout the Church's history, albeit implicitly.[477] Though the result is the same, Burghardt's argument involves a theological interpretation where Carol appeals directly to magisterial authority. Obviously, at the time of the definition, views of magisterial judgment, even where this judgment was accepted as legitimate and vital, could differ in the stress they accorded to the role of pope (and the bishops) in their relationship to the faithful.

In the period just prior to Vatican II, the faithful were often seen as having a passive role. Mackey has described how the view expressed by Franzelin continued to be accepted in standard treatments of authors like Burghardt in his 1951 address to the Catholic Theological Society of America (cited above) and in A. Michel's article on "Tradition" in *Dictionnaire de Théologie Catholique* in 1946.[478]

Some authors insisted that the working of the Holy Spirit made the sense of the faithful a valid source of the truth, even though the magisterium held the role of judging and expressing doctrine. In an article in 1958 Michel moved to such a view after reflecting on the definition of the Assumption.[479] Dillenschneider developed a sophisticated argument maintaining both the authority of the magisterium and an infallibility of the faith given directly by the Holy Spirit.[480] Balic describes the work of the Spirit in both the internal and external aspects of faith and in the interaction of the faithful with each other within the Body of Christ.[481] Koster sees the Spirit as giving particular gifts to several distinct groups; the magisterium, theologians, or the faithful.[482]

Mackey himself, writing in 1963, argues that the Church's teaching is "carried forward" by a "continual interplay . . . between the Magisterium and the other organs of Tradition."[483] He adds:

> It is that interplay which explains at once the development that is essential to Tradition, and, together with the direct influence of the

Holy Spirit upon them, guarantees its integrity in the organs that are without a special charism.[484]

Such theological reflections notwithstanding, an active role for the laity was not generally understood or expressed in descriptions of the sense of the faithful prior to Vatican II. It would take the Council's acceptance of the historical development of tradition, and a more contextualized view of the magisterium, with the pope being linked to the bishops and the bishops to the whole Church, to allow for the emergence of a perspective like that of Tillard twenty-five years after *Munificentissimus Deus*.

> The 1950 declaration is the fruit of what appears (to anyone who has the patience to read the main parts of the dossier) like a slow conquest by the *sensus fidelium*. The decision coming from above seems to have been called for from below rather than to have been imposed.[485]

## THE MODERN AGENDA FOR UNDERSTANDING THE *SENSUS FIDELIUM*

The particular theological issues raised in the modern era by the study of history, the recognition of the role of historical consciousness and the challenges of new frameworks for considering the development and interpretation of doctrine resulted in strong contrasts among the views of theologians both within and outside of the magisterium. Authority itself grew increasingly centralized and the content of doctrinal teaching was linked to the exercise of authority in ways not anticipated by earlier eras in the Church's history.

An important result of the historical factors that influenced ecclesiology in the modern period was the official establishment of "active" and "passive" roles for the *Ecclesia docens* and *Ecclesia discens*. This occurred even while significant theological reflection continued to understand the *sensus fidelium* in richer, more traditional ways.

Both practical and theological developments in the Church in the modern period, especially after the First Vatican Council, set the stage for the dramatic impact of Vatican II especially in the understanding of theology and authority. In the next chapter, the Council's teaching and its influences on the conditions for further developing the theology of the *sensus fidelium* will be examined.

# CHAPTER 4
# INTERPRETATION OF THE *SENSUS FIDELIUM* WITHIN THE CONTEXT OF VATICAN II

The preceding discussion of events and theological interpretations that make up the history of the sense of the faithful will serve here as a foundation for examining how this concept is used in the post-Vatican II Church. To complete the groundwork necessary for such an examination, the Council's own treatment of the sense of the faithful will first be discussed and several key characteristics will be identified in an attempt to summarize the tradition of the *sensus fidelium* in the light of Vatican II.

### VATICAN II AND THE SENSE OF THE FAITHFUL

As discussed in Chapter One, a key passage on the *sensus fidei* occurs in *Lumen Gentium* (# 12), where the infallibility of the Church is described as residing in the "People as a whole," when agreement is shown "from the bishops down to the last member of the laity."[1] This statement invites reflection on the relationship of the sense of the faithful to the role of the hierarchy. The section begins with the statement that "the holy People of God shares also in Christ's prophetic office," and identifies the charism given to the faithful with that described in 1 John 2: 20 and 27. The same section includes a reminder that the operation of this charism is done "under the lead of a sacred teaching authority to which it loyally defers."[2]

Not long after the close of the Council, Gérard Philips hailed the ideas expressed in section 12 as being of "principal importance for the renewal of the Church desired by Pope John."[3] He adds that here a deeper understanding of the work of the Holy Spirit is made possible even while the role of the faithful and the exercise of their unique charisms within the Church is further enhanced.[4]

The role of prophetic living and evangelization on the part of the laity is reiterated in a later passage (# 35), where their witness through marriage is singled out for special mention, and where their possible modes of involvement are described as including those which are "preoccupied with temporal cares" and those who "devote themselves entirely to apostolic work."[5]

An important aspect of Vatican II's teaching on the laity is its encouragement of an explicit initiative on their part. *Gaudium et Spes* asserts,

> Laymen should also know that it is generally the function of their well-formed Christian conscience to see that the divine law is inscribed in the life of the earthly city. From priests they may look for spiritual light and nourishment. Let the layman not imagine that his pastors are always such experts, that to every problem which arises, however complicated, they can readily give him a concrete solution, or even that such is their mission. Rather, enlightened by Christian wisdom and giving close attention to the teaching authority of the Church, let the laymen take on his own distinctive role.[6]

The active involvement of the laity is a major theme in this document on the Church's role in the modern world. The passage cited here illustrates that while certainly this involvement is guided by the tradition as protected by the hierarchy, it is not limited to the insight or practical expressions available from its leaders. Complicated problems call for the combined, interactive attention of all the "levels" of faithful, including both clergy and laity.

The link of the *sensus fidelium* to the appropriation of tradition, rooted in Scripture itself, has been noted above, in remarks on the Dogmatic Constitution, *Dei Verbum*.[7] Significantly, this passage includes a recognition of the need for continual study and the development of new ways of understanding apostolic teaching. The document states, "For, as the centuries succeed one another, the Church constantly moves forward toward the fullness of divine truth until the words of God reach their complete fulfillment in her."[8]

If the understanding of divine truth is itself growing toward completion, with the implication being clear that current insight is not yet complete, the same may be said in regard to the tools that serve the understanding of tradition, with the sense of the faithful certainly being among them. The Council only haltingly reappropriated this element of the Church's ongoing reflection.[9] Beginning with the received view of a passive role for the faithful, it did eventually ascribe an active involvement for that most obvious portion of the faithful, the laity. Yet, as many commentators have pointed out, passages focusing on the Church as a whole under the image of the People of God and those describing an active laity are included in the Council documents with those that reiterate views that maintain that the Church's responsibilities remain in the hands of the hierarchy. Such passages are often placed in the same document without any reconciliation, as in the case of *Lumen Gentium* with its chapter on the Church as the People of God coming before the chapter on the hierarchy.[10]

It is important to point out that this ambiguity was not created at a superficial level by some newly found desire to include the laity. The view that there is an active role for the *sensus fidelium* in particular, and thus by inclusion for all believers, was argued immediately before the Council by Gustave Thils. Thils claims that the "essential elements" for understanding the whole Christian people as infallible *in credendo* "have been transmitted from generation to generation." He adds that these elements made an impact among mid-twentieth century theologians especially through their work in Biblical and Patristic studies.[11]

Herwi Rikhof has attributed ambiguity at Vatican II to a mixture of "metaphors" for the Church, as seen in the attempt of *Lumen Gentium* to combine the juridical and hierarchical approach to ecclesiology typical of the Roman school and the "more theological approach" that is heir to nineteenth century figures like Moehler and Newman.[12] He states that the document "is an attempt to integrate what cannot and should not be integrated, and consequently it does not present a coherent and consistent view of the church."[13]

William Frost asserts that the role of the laity is almost completely limited to the secular sphere by the Council. Asking if the *phronema* described by Newman is sanctioned in the documents of Vatican II, he answers negatively.[14] Following Femiano, he remarks that Newman's view "colored a mentality which surfaced in discussions about certain formulations." He cites *Infallibility of the Laity* (discussed elsewhere in the present work) where Femiano notes the Council Fathers' clear intent in chapter four of *Lumen Gentium* to speak of infallibility as an attribute of the whole Church, with laity and bishops united. Yet Frost sees it as the work of a future council to appropriate the people's *phronema* as an active resource in maintaining the Catholic faith. This is to be done not just through work in the secular areas, but in the laity's development of a "greater understanding of their faith in their historical struggles for social justice, liberty, and human love."[15]

A more positive assessment is given by Eduardo Molano, who asserts that while the Council focused on the laity's role in the secular domain, this "secular" role does not adequately describe their mission. He observes that it is difficult to distinguish the roles of the laity in the world and in the Church itself. The mission which the laity exercise in the world is an ecclesial one. Thus, as they live out their charism to transform the world, they play an ecclesial role.[16] Molano adds that this role and the spiritual preparation that supports it still require more development.[17]

Webster Patterson notes that Vatican II affirmed Newman's view that the laity should express themselves freely to the Church's leaders.[18] He quotes *Lumen Gentium*'s observation, that people are "permitted and even sometimes obliged" to give their views. He notes that the document adds, "when occasions arise, let this be done through organs erected in the Church for this purpose." Yet, as he anticipates (writing in 1968) the reforming of Canon Law, he looks for "much needed formal and structural channels of communication between laity and hierarchy," but adds ruefully, "at the present time, we must simply admit that neither the Council (nor Newman) have anything specific and practical to offer on the subject."[19]

Joseph Komonchak has noted that in *Lumen Gentium* and *Apostolicam Actuositatem*, the Decree on the Apostolate of the Laity, the Council had three goals: to "vindicate the laity's right" to take part in the mission of the Church, where they would "be more than the passive objects of the clergy's ministrations"; "to clarify the nature and basis of the lay apostolate" (particularly as rooted in the "sacramental and charismatic" foundation given by baptism); and "to affirm the truly Christian and ecclesial character of the laity's daily secular activity."[20] He notes too, that in giving a "typological" rather than "ontological" description of the lay person, the Council avoided settling theological disputes over the nature of the lay state.[21] Thus, "the description need not necessarily apply to every previous age of the Church nor be considered to preclude future developments which might alter the customary typical differentiations of roles."[22] In its discussion of the laity and its mission in the Church, the Fathers were seemingly interested in opening discussion of the laity rather than limiting it to previous theological understandings. Their "typological" description of the laity thus takes on a certain heuristic function.[23] Komonchak goes on to argue that the specific roles of laity, clergy and religious are all given to work as a whole in challenging the world especially in specific, political ways.[24]

Such evidences of "unfinished business" from the Council illustrate the plurality of influences that met for the first time in any official debate during its sessions. Alberigo has described the preliminary documents prepared before Vatican II to focus the Council's deliberations on the Church. He observes that these preliminary papers continued to see the solution of any "crisis of authority" as being the response of obedience.[25] He notes that several anathemas were included against "any vindication of the value of consensus," and that there was specifically "an attempt to distinguish clearly between the *sensus fidei* of the People of God and the concept of public opinion."[26] He adds that in the same document, it was asserted that the *sensus fidei* is the "consensus of the faithful and pastors in matters of faith and morals, governed by the authentic magisterium."[27] Yet, Alberigo goes on to discuss the impact of the inaugural speech of John XXIII on October 11, 1962, which clarified the intention of the Council, and set the tone for its work.[28]

Peter Hebblethwaite has described the Pope's address as being in both content and style, a repudiation of the Roman approach expressed since Gregory XVI's *Mirari Vos*, and operative throughout the pope's own experience.[29] In his opening remarks, John urged a turning to the possibilities of the historical moment, as well as the acknowledgment of value in a historical understanding of tradition.[30] Alberigo summarizes the Pope's challenge to the Council Fathers' view of doctrine, as the need to

> (1) overcome the static repetition of the essence of the *depositum fidei*; (2) take account of the new cultural demands of humanity, among which the inductive method and attention to historical evolution are prominent: and (3) reformulate doctrine in a way that respects—more than in the past—the pastoral and not the theological or philosophical character of the magisterium, and

hence remove it from a disturbing spiral of competition with theology.[31]

Alberigo applauds the discussion of the *sensus fidelium* in *Lumen Gentium* (# 12) that "saved this concept from an oblivion which held grave consequences." Yet, he sees the later assertion that "the assent of the Church can never be lacking because of the action of the Holy Spirit" (# 25) as a "vague allusion without further concrete specifications" which was seen by the Council's doctrinal commission to be "destined to negate the importance of consensus by contradicting that which was affirmed in n. 12." Alberigo adds that this made the reference to the Holy Spirit appear to be "primarily ornamental."[32] With this observation, Alberigo joins other authors who find the Council, and *Lumen Gentium* in particular, ambiguous about the laity. Thus he asserts, that while the Council "appreciably corrected the hierarchical and authoritarian perspective" of the Church, and replaced it with one based in a view of the Church as communion, an "undeniable difference" remained between its results and the intent of John XXIII.[33]

Some authors, while acknowledging the work that remains ahead, still see clear indicators in the Council of new ground that has opened up. The tasks that remain have legitimate warrant. Patrick Granfield has observed that in their early debates, the Council Fathers began with a juridical view of the indefectibility in the Church and a passive understanding of the role of the laity. Cardinal Ruffino spoke specifically of the *sensus fidelium* as "an echo" of the magisterium.[34] He notes that Cardinals Paul Emile Léger and Franziskus Koenig, on the other hand, described the role of the faithful as active.[35] Yet, Granfield stresses that the Council linked the *sensus fidelium* to the infallibility and mission of the Church, through its quality of catholicity which expresses "not a spatial or temporal universality but a consistent relationship to apostolic tradition."[36]

Granfield adds that not everything that is believed by the Church can be verified as being "explicitly believed always, everywhere, and by all." For some insights in the developing understanding of the tradition, the living Church must make up for the lack of historical support. He cites section eight of *Dei Verbum* to argue for the inclusion of the faithful in the "dynamic and creative" development of understanding. The "contemplation and study" of believers is an important part of the Church's resources. Granfield describes the active nature of the whole process in saying, "Apostolic tradition remains a constant rule of faith; it is not an archaic remnant of the past but a vital energy within the present People of God."[37]

Vatican II's vision of an interconnected body of faithful, with the laity serving in real capacities to spread the Gospel is certainly in stark contrast to the view of the laity that preceded the Council. Jan Grootaers describes the passive role of lay people, saying, that they were "practically-speaking, excluded from the 'communio.'"[38] This was evidenced in their distance from a "valid spirituality." Their status was contrasted with that of religious or clergy. They were kept from an active liturgical life and from the reading of Scripture. Grootaers asserts too, that the laity were "excluded from the theology concerning the Church" and that "the common priesthood of the faithful and the *sensus fidelium* were relegated to the background."[39] He goes on to examine several models for understanding a "theology of the laity" in the light of both the successes and failures since Vatican II.[40] Especially important to the focus of the present work, is his arguing for an "integral ecclesiology."[41] He notes, as did Komonchak, that the Council Fathers specifically claimed to give a "typological" rather than "ontological" definition in dealing with the laity in the fourth chapter of *Lumen Gentium*.[42] Grootaers goes on to say that in his opinion, the focus of Vatican II on the Church as the "People of God" makes the issue of a theology of the laity a "false problem."[43] He finds the importance of a theology of the laity to be in its short term usefulness in focusing ecclesiology on developing a more integrated understanding of the "Church-communion."[44]

It has been observed by George Tavard that although a focus on the People of God "counterbalances the hierarchic conception of the Counter-Reformation and of Vatican I," such ecclesiologies based on "peoplehood" remain "profoundly ambiguous."[45]

Frederick Parrella describes the affirming of unity within the diversity of roles in the Church, "each with their own place and responsibility," as "the great achievement of *Lumen Gentium*."[46] This newly acknowledged responsibility of the laity would not be brought to full expression easily. William Thompson has observed that an overly hierarchical approach had long taken its toll. The Council itself realized that development of an active laity would take time. In an article on the exercise of the magisterium Thompson wrote:

> [Magisterial] authority has been too exclusively patterned after an undifferentiated "paternal" model of authority, for by not allowing any effective participation by others in this teaching authority, it practically presupposes and fosters a basic deficiency in all but the hierarchy. As we have already indicated, paternal authority should really aim at the maturation of those who are governed, and this is precisely what is not given expression to by the Roman view. The tradition itself is quite aware of a real participation by the entire Church in its teaching, and Vatican II has recalled this to mind by it stress on the "people of God" and the "sense of the faithful." It especially refers to the hierarchy's members as "bearing with themselves and expressing the consent of the entire community" (*Relatio* to n. 25 of Lumen Gentium).[47]

Following the Council, hopes for an integration of the various levels of the Church were discussed under the theme of coresponsibility. Cardinal Léon-Joseph Suenens described it as "the central idea of Vatican II."[48] He discusses in detail the issues of coresponsibility that pertain to the pope, bishops, priests, theologians, deacons, religious and laity and asserts, "At every one of these levels, Vatican II desires more organic collaboration."[49] He clarifies this point by saying that an "organized collaboration for mere practical pastoral efficiency" is not enough. What is sought is "a cooperation which is the corollary and manifestation of the church's deepest nature."[50] In discussing the laity, Suenens reaffirms the role of the sense of the faithful, acknowledging that it "is a reality which finds its place in the hierarchical communion and bears its stamp."[51] Yet he affirms too the active role of this source.

> It even happens that this sense of the faithful, of which the pope [Paul VI, in a previous citation] makes so much, can precede theological work and provide it with a fundamental intuition. It suffices to think here of the long history of the proclamation of the dogma of the immaculate conception in which the sense of the faithful was finally joined, after laborious discussion, by the assent of theologians and the ratification of the magisterium.[52]

Here, the *sensus fidelium* is recognized as having not just an active role, but one that at times provides the "fundamental intuition" for theological work. Significantly, this is made explicit specifically in Cardinal Suenens's interpretation of the definition of the Immaculate Conception, where the faithful are not described as mirrors of the magisterium but as originators of the process of reflection.

Suenens cautions that "the sense of the faithful is not a sort of human public opinion, dominated by the ebb and flow and fashions of the day," but is the work of the Holy Spirit.[53] Yet he accents the very practical role of this source. Suenens recalls that recognition of the "pneumatic aspect of Christian life" is vital to ecumenical efforts with both Orthodox and Reformed traditions. He closes the section saying, "The church, in asking the faithful to accept their full and prophetic coresponsibility in the world, knows well that the Holy Spirit is at work to accomplish in and through them his great designs."[54]

In the view of some Council Fathers, Vatican II gave the understanding of the laity and their role in the mission and theology of the Church a boost. Yet it is evident that in the time since the Council no clear understanding has arisen to show how practical appropriation of this source is to be made.[55] It is not obvious how the laity should be integrated, and there are many who see the Church backing away from an acceptance of this source. Lack of clarity about the role of the laity contributes to the ambiguity that continues concerning the role of the *sensus fidelium* which is associated with all the faithful, but which in a particular way, is linked to the laity.

The result of this ambiguity in regard to authority and involvement of the many facets of the Church in its ongoing expression of the *sensus Ecclesiae* is aptly described by Avery Dulles.

> Vatican II, largely through its skillful resuscitation of the Patristic model of representation and consensus, supplied a helpful corrective to the juridicism and papalism of the post-Tridentine and Neo-Scholastic periods. But it did not provide a new or thoroughly consistent paradigm, and thus left to the post-conciliar church the task of completing its own program.[56]

The need for renewed reflection on the nature of the sense of the faithful after Vatican II is obvious. Since the Council, there has in fact been a great deal of interest in the concept. The plurality of views that are expressed demonstrates itself the need for more work. Yet even with the difficulties that have been found to be part of the interpretation of the *sensus fidelium* in the wake of Vatican II, it is possible to identify several central elements that illustrate its function in the Church.

## Key Characteristics of the Sense of the Faithful

The historical treatment offered above draws on a wide range of events and theological assessments that have been associated with the sense of the faithful and which continue to be offered as evidence of its role as a *fons theologiae*. The following characteristics can be summarized from the historical sources we have been studying, considered in the light of Vatican II.

1) The sense of the faithful is an ecclesial quality that involves the whole Church.

2) The sense of the faithful is a multidimensional source for theology.

3) The sense of the faithful requires an interrelationship between the Church considered as a whole and the magisterium.

4) The sense of the faithful as it was described at Vatican II has a foundational role in the Church's inner life and in its task of bringing the Gospel to the world.

5) The *sensus fidelium*, particularly as it is located in the laity, cannot be adequately described as a solely passive element in the Church.

6) The *sensus fidelium* has implications for each believing person.

Two other characteristics emerge that can shed light on the contemporary discussion, but which are not strictly criteria for identifying the sense of the faithful.

7) The presence of conflict does not necessarily indicate the absence of the sense of the faithful.

8) Any contemporary assessment of the sense of the faithful is linked to a hermeneutic of doctrine.

These characteristics will now be considered in detail with reference to the preceding historical discussion.

**1) *The sense of the faithful is an ecclesial quality that involves the whole Church.***

This characteristic, reaffirmed at Vatican II (*Lumen Gentium*, # 12), is foundational for the others. The sense of the faithful is the insight and expression of faith that grows in individuals and in the Church as a body from the roots of the Gospel and the tradition first preached by the apostles. In the earliest Christian era the *communio* was the focus for understanding the carrying on of this tradition. Each believer participating in the community was joined to Christ himself, the source of true unity. The charisms of each person were recognized as given by the Spirit for the good of all. A living unity in Christ was sought within the life, teaching and worship of the community.

It is significant that explicit discussion of the sense of the faithful is not found in the earliest communities. Monika Hellwig has observed that there was a lack of attention to the process of the developing tradition in the early centuries.[57] However, rather than indicating an absence of development or the *sensus fidelium* in the Church's life, this lack of attention is consistent with the unreflective acceptance of the whole body's responsibility for the tradition that characterized the first centuries. The treatments of authority in the New Testament itself indicate the operation of Church leadership in a context of shared responsibility.

In response to challenges to the identity and unity of the early Church, there was an emergent realization in these communities of the explicit task of preserving the tradition. Bishops were recognized as playing special roles in protecting the *paradosis* given by the apostles. These leaders became the focus of the Church's response to challenges to the life or faith of the Church at the same time that the canon of Scripture was identified as the foundation for the tradition.

The ability to identify both sources for the tradition with the consensus of the faithful was vitally important.

The practical, concrete responsibility exercised by the whole community is seen in the ways that bishops were selected and accepted by their communities. Documents as early as the *Didache* show the role of community involvement in the selection of bishops. In the third and fourth centuries, there is clearly active involvement of the church communities, even where the actual method of election is unclear. Throughout the churches a variety of methods were employed. Variations in the structures of leadership itself could exist, as shown by the *seniori laici* in Africa. Eventually the assent of the whole community became a formality, notably after the fifth century, although lay involvement by secular princes was significant by the beginning of the seventh century. This "lay involvement," however, was to pose long lasting problems and to contribute to the eventual increase of authority in ecclesial office at the expense of lay influence.

The reception of bishops by the community had retained an important role even after candidates for bishop began to be selected from outside of the local community. Reputation was an important factor in determining the qualifications of a candidate; the choice was dependent on the people's practical judgment of who would make a good leader.

The early involvement of the people, seen in the processes of debate and the selection of candidates, was reflected also in liturgical action. It was in the liturgy in particular that the action of people and bishops were seen as evidence of the work of the Holy Spirit.

The well-documented views and practices of Cyprian are an important example of balance in the use of authority in the early Church, offering the contemporary Church an example of a "coresponsibility" that was exercised in practical ways during a period of great turmoil. Even where Cyprian clearly affirms the importance of the episcopate as the center of authority in the Church, he does not stress authority at the expense of lay involvement and responsibility. Rather, he encouraged and sought the interaction of his church's members.

If active lay involvement waned after the fifth century, it is instructive to recall the reasons for this decline as summarized by Granfield. The lack of education among the laity, misuse of the election process and the interference of civil authorities all contributed to the change.[58] The goals that originally focused the bishops within their communities in the exercise of responsibility now motivated them to extend that responsibility even further. Their authority was needed to overcome the violence and factionalism that threatened the integrity and unity of the church bodies.

Responsibility for expressing the mind of the Church developed along the same path as responsibility for meetings its structural and practical challenges. The bishops became the focus for preserving and teaching the Church. In the third century, emphasis shifted from viewing the bishops mainly as the successors of the apostles, to regarding them as heads of churches. At the same time the consensus of the whole Church was recognized as a tool to serve the *depositium fidei*, with Church members developing their understanding of the faith both by living it out and by listening to and probing disputed questions.

Eno has identified three views of consensus that illustrate a development in the early models used to understand the preservation of the tradition. In Vincent of Lerins he sees a focus on the consensus of the past, in Augustine he notes the importance of the consensus of the present, and in the papal letters of the Patristic period he sees the development of a consensus that is dependent on the influence and authority of Roman tradition.[59]

A significant shift occurred as orthodoxy was seen to be established no longer by merely identifying what was in apostolic teaching, but by looking to the unanimous belief of the churches, thus making it possible to confront new issues. The roles of the bishop evolved with the changing needs of the Church. The council became an ecclesial tool where the bishops gathered together as a single body. Here the whole Church was represented, extending the earlier insight of the Church as *communio* with everyone involved. At the same time, conciliar history illustrates that it was hardly clear in many instances what view in the Church should be regarded as orthodox. Unity was created in contexts of great diversity and debate, and often final decisions caused the negative result of factions being left outside the body of unity. Lay involvement was eventually left behind as the councils began to conform to the models of Roman government.

The active responsibility of the all elements in the Church in the creation the *consensus fidelium* was dramatically shown when the laity maintained orthodox belief during the Arian crisis. Other examples have been discussed by Newman and others. Nevertheless, lack of general lay involvement in giving expression to doctrine became the norm in the Middle Ages, as the common believer lacked the resources or access needed to be involved in decision making in the Church. Even in this situation, the common response could impact church expression in the area of law. Believers' judgment and decisions remained important in the moral realm, and by extension, in the theological understanding of moral matters.

With a growth in size and complexity, the *sensus Ecclesiae* came to be expressed by representative "specialists." A clearly delineated clergy and laity and an ongoing centralization of authority characterized the Western Church after the Patristic age. Though it is accurate to speak of the whole Church as contributing to the *sensus Ecclesiae* even during this developing centralization, a clear "division of labor" had occurred and had become firmly established. That the faith of the whole Church was involved was not disputed. How the mind of the Church was to be expressed was to become the issue. The ways in which the *sensus fidelium* operated after the Patristic age will be considered under a later criterion, concerned with the interrelation of the Church as a whole and the magisterium.

**2) *The sense of the faithful is a multi-dimensional source for theology.***

As illustrated by Congar and others, the sense of the faithful has been described by a variety of names.[60] Three of these names are particularly helpful in highlighting its major elements. The *sensus fidei* describes the subjective focus or "instinct" for the truths of the faith that is given to believers. The *sensus fidelium* is usually seen as the objective or theological expression of what is believed. The *consensus fidelium* describes the unanimous agreement of believers about a particular matter of faith.[61]

The Scriptural references that are often used to support the importance of the sense of the faithful illustrate the diverse aspects that have contributed to the *sensus Ecclesiae* since the earliest times. Further, Thompson has identified different eras that have focused on particular aspects of this part of the Church's life, with authors in the Patristic period depending on the *consensus fidelium*, Medieval thinkers developing the notion of the *sensus fidei*, and theologians since the Counter-Reformation discussing the *sensus fidelium*. As different questions or agendas are brought to the "supernatural sense of the faith," different characteristics are illuminated.

In the past, where one aspect of the sense of the faithful was the focus of interest, other aspects were assumed to be operating as well. Consensus in the early Church was always developed from the experiences and insights into the faith of actual believers. Consensus in any era is possible because of the theological expression given in the *sensus fidelium*. The *consensus fidelium* is based on the expressions of the *sensus fidelium* and rooted in the *sensus fidei*. On the other hand, the *sensus fidei* that is found in an individual believer is impossible without the testimony of the Gospel mediated by the Church.

Viewing the sense of the faithful from the perspective of one of its aspects, without the balancing effects of the others, can lead to conflict and misunderstanding. Emphasis on the individual's instinct or charism without recognition of the need of correlating with other believers can lead to subjectivism. Thus Congar has criticized some Reformation authors for promoting the autonomy of private judgment. A stress on objective expression without regard for ongoing insight can stifle the deepening of understanding of the tradition and ignore what may be the promptings of the Spirit. Modern discussions of development of doctrine that include the role of the *sensus fidelium*, especially since Newman, have emphasized this.

The formation of consensus is itself a complex matter. A focus on unity without regard for individual charisms or theological discussion may seek a uniformity that prematurely settles a question. The magisterial response to modernism and its aftermath illustrates how an authoritative establishment of conformity, even while it carries an objective doctrinal weight, can fail to treat the important theological insights and issues in question and require an eventual return to the questions and processes of debate that are needed to bring out precisely those elements that can contribute to further development.

By the same token, consensus founded on reflection, debate and a majority point of view has not guaranteed the "final word" in the past. Doctrinal history offers important examples where the opinion held by the majority later proved to be inadequate or in error. The views of St. Thomas More may further illustrate that consensus which is formed without the benefit of interaction with the magisterium cannot contribute to the development of new understanding, and may serve only a role of conserving past expressions.

A wholistic understanding of the sense of the faithful is necessary to allow recognition of the impact of a variety of elements in the Church. The involvement of common believers, individual prophetic voices, theologians and the magisterium have all been needed at different times to balance and correct the Church's understanding and expression of its faith. Different elements have spoken more clearly at different times. Often the *sensus fidelium* and *consensus fidelium* have been formed by a process that is recognizable in retrospect, but which may not be obvious when it is sought in a limited time period or in one source. The *sensus fidelium* is sometimes recognized after viewing the movement of the Church through a considerable process of facing obstacles and making several different attempts at clarification.

**3) *The sense of the faithful requires an interrelationship between the Church considered as a whole and the magisterium.***

Although the interrelationship between the Church's communities and its leaders has always been important, the ways that involvement has actually occurred have varied. As the distinct loci of *sensus fidelium* and magisterium have been identified and developed so have the factors that have defined their relationship to each other.

A vital interaction of the various members and charisms is seen in the New Testament churches. Inclusion is obvious in several practical ways in the first five centuries. As has been described, the central importance of both bishops and the canon of Scripture was linked to consensus in the whole Church. Later as consensus of belief was itself identified as an indication of the guidance of the Holy Spirit, explicit attention was given to the ways that this consensus might be formed.

The interaction of those who spoke for the tradition and those whose role it was to live it out found an important expression in the early councils. Both bishops and lay people exercised an active influence. Certainly the bishops' responsibility for expressing the tradition was distinctive yet at the same time it was conceived as a form of service for the unity and faith of the whole Church.

Episcopal ministry continued to be a focus for the unity of the community. It is significant in this regard, to recall the observation of one Orthodox writer, that the bishops themselves acted as a body, and did not operate as "episcopal monads."[62] It is worth remembering the observation of R. A. Markus also, however, that as the sole major see in the West, Rome took on responsibility in a manner that was different from that of the East, where multiple authorities made a collective perspective more natural.[63] Episcopal authorities responded to a common goal with different strategies. Structure depended on the needs and possibilities in particular contexts.

During the Middle Ages and for some time afterwards, both bishops and theologians exercised responsibility for expressing the tradition. The majority of believers were not equipped to engage in theological reflection. Yet in those areas where lay people retained a practical level of expertise, lay involvement remained an important factor. The reception of law, for instance, shows the corrective power of custom and the influence of practical moral decision making among the laity. If the laity were for the most part not sophisticated enough to contribute to theological reflection, their insights into their own situations and their struggles with moral issues in living the faith had an impact on the laws or doctrinal expressions that evolved.

Several authors have noted that the form in which church teaching was presented often limited the sort of response available from the laity. In the early centuries, when leaders, laws or doctrinal expressions were accepted in the community, the process was often attended by conflict. Authority was exercised with the recognition that an affirmative response was to be won. In cases where this did not occur, other alternatives had to be pursued. Both reception and non-reception contributed to the creation of structures for aiding the faith.

Shifts to more limiting forms of ecclesial expression also limited the faithful's interaction. Walgrave has described the Church after the fifth century as living on formulas instead of creative thought.[64] In the examples given by Newman from the Middle Ages, only "reactive" responses were possible to official statements concerning the real presence and the beatific vision.

As Kilmartin has observed, when reception itself was couched in juridical terms and combined with a strong distinction between the *Ecclesia docens* and *Ecclesia discens*, the active dimension of reception was disregarded.[65] When the debates of the Reformation were carried on in doctrinal terms and focused on the use of authority and the identification of proper theological sources, the *sensus fidelium* became a source to be pointed to rather than drawn upon.

With the Counter-Reformation, the Roman Church stressed centralized authority and teaching, and became to a greater extent a more ordered, hierarchical structure. This ordering was at the expense of an understanding of the Church as a community. In this context, when the *sensus fidelium* was explicitly included for the first time as an ecclesiological source by Cano, it was as a passive entity. In the polemics of the Reformation, doctrinal clarity and unity within the Roman Church was defined in terms of uniform practice and belief. These were attained not just at the expense of the ecclesial bodies that left communion with Rome, but at the expense of a theological recognition of the active responsibility of the whole Church.

Yet in the face of this growing view of a passive laity the actual interdependence of the people and the Church's magisterial including both its ecclesial officers and its theologians, did not disappear. As an example, the official teaching on usury was changed even after being given strong magisterial emphasis because of changing views on the nature of interest and, most importantly, because of the practical knowledge and arguments brought to the Church's teachers by lay people.

On a larger scale, the exercise and theological critique of both *epikeia* and reception continued during this time. *Epikeia*, with its link to practical judgment and the *sensus fidei* was debated and regulated to avoid abuse, but it could not be defined. Debates on the place to be given to reception in the area of law illustrates well how a larger issue of common responsibility could be defined in a restrictive way at one level, while in a larger context it retained a more wholistic meaning. When seen in juridical terms, the enactment of a law was regarded as imposing the presumption of acceptance on the group for whom it was intended. At the same time, the lawgiver was seen as having a responsibility to understand the community over which authority was exercised.

The continued importance of interaction between the magisterium and the Church is further supported when viewed in the context of developing insights into the nature of doctrine. Although both Protestant and Catholic thinkers maintained that their authority was built from the tradition of the apostles and that it reflected what was taught *quod semper, quod ubique, quod ab omnibus*, their views of how the tradition actually operated were different. The Roman Catholic side linked its understanding of tradition to the authority of office. Yet Walgrave notes that while Trent recognized the reality of both Scripture and "oral tradition," with the latter being connected to office, it also left their relationship undefined. He suggests that the reason for this was the lack of an adequate theory on doctrinal development.[66] The "meta-issue" of how the tradition was actually carried and developed in its historical expressions was left open for discussion. The fact that an active role for the Church as a whole continued to be seen as important in post-Reformation theology is apparent in the many examples offered by Thils, who demonstrates that theologians continually argued for the "infallibility of the people *in credendo*."

Nineteenth century discussion of the sense of the faithful continued to be characterized both by a juridical perspective which defined the role of the people narrowly and passively, and by a practical perspective that acknowledged the importance of the faith of the whole Church by drawing on it in doctrinal definitions.

An explicit role of reception, exercised by local bodies of bishops, was rejected in its Gallican form in the nineteenth century. Attempts to link the expression of infallibility with a "democratic" structure were likewise rejected. At the same time, the emphasis on viewing the Church in terms of its visible, hierarchical structure was confronted with an alternative view. Moehler attempted to restore a balance to this structural emphasis with a more organic model for the Church. In his attempt to shift from the "unwritten traditions" to the "living tradition" of the Church, Moehler stressed that the whole Church was infallible.

The faith of the people in the Immaculate Conception of Mary was used by Pius IX to support a solemn definition of the dogma when scriptural and historical evidence were limited at best. Newman's recognition that this "consultation" gave the *sensus fidelium* and the laity in particular an important role was received with criticism and a lack of understanding not only within his own local context, but in Rome as well. His relationship with Perrone and the Roman theologians demonstrated the wide gap between the dominant scholastic ecclesiology and a historical perspective on doctrine.

Dissonance between the centralized, hierarchical view of power in the Roman Church and an ecclesiological perspective that sought a wider base were vividly illustrated in the treatment of infallibility at the First Vatican Council. The variety of views represented by the Council Fathers themselves resulted in a somewhat tempered definition, even if the role of the pope was given central importance. If Vatican I's definition supported an overemphasis on the "pope's" infallibility, especially in certain segments of the Church, it was recognized by many bishops and by the official *relatio* at the Council itself as being much more nuanced. Even the famous "*ex sese, non autem ex consensu Ecclesiae*" statement was recognized as a serving a specific function. No requirement for further appeal to any other source was recognized. Yet the pope was seen as having the moral responsibility to draw on the faith of the whole Church and the teaching of the body of bishops in the exercise of his own special role.

As in earlier treatments of individual responsibility in the case of the notion of *epikeia*, or of collective responsibility and the operation of reception, a larger meaning served as a foundation for a specific definition in the case of "infallible expressions" by the pope. The definition from Vatican I describes the pope as speaking with that infallibility which Christ intended for the Church. Juridical concerns led to a limiting nature in the definition. The specific role of the pope could not be eliminated by the need for a specific ratification of his statements by others in the magisterium or in the Church at large. At the same time, the richness of the theological reality that was involved in his exercise of a unique responsibility was recognized at the Council.

The decades after Vatican I saw a continued increase of centralization and the focus of ecclesial power in the magisterium. The official reaction to Modernism in *Lamentabili* and its aftermath gave definite weight to a juridical paradigm for Church governance and expected lay response. Yet during the same period renewed theological interest focused on the *sensus fidei* as a spiritual source in the Church, returning as Moehler and Newman had to historical treatments, and to a link between the sense of the faithful and the development of doctrine.

When Pius XII cited the *sensus fidelium* in solemnly defining the Assumption of Mary, the faithful were regarded as a "mirror" for the teaching of the magisterium. However, before and after the definition, the "definability" of the doctrine was the subject of significant discussion attempting to understand the relationship of the magisterium and the faith of the people.

Vatican II described the interactive quality of the Church's many levels, making such interrelatedness a major focus with its treatment of coresponsibility, subsidiarity, and the sense of the faithful. Before the Council too though, there was recognition that there was something in the *conspiratio* of laity and clergy that was irreducible to either group alone, even if a clear articulation of what was meant through this interrelationship was lacking. Vatican II recognized the importance of the interaction of the people and their leaders, using the *sensus fidelium* as a foundation that they share in common.

**4) *Vatican II placed the sense of the faithful in, a foundational role in the Church's inner life and in its task of bringing the Gospel to the world.***

It is clear that Vatican II recognized that the whole Church and the laity in particular share with the magisterium the responsibility for bringing the message of the Gospel to the world. Through their secular vocations and even in direct ecclesial ways, lay people are to play vital roles. The Council Fathers drew directly on the sense of the faithful as a warrant for this active participation of the laity. Most importantly, it is a theological foundation for a unified commitment of laity and clergy working together.

It is also evident that Vatican II was more successful in opening the door for coresponsibility and new paths for lay involvement than it was in indicating how a mature interactive model for the Church would look. The practical ways in which the sense of the faithful can help integrate the Church's inner life and self-understanding, and the ways in which its own inner sense can challenge and enlighten the modern world, are not yet clear. However, even prescinding from the question of how a complete "Vatican II ecclesiology" might be defined, it is clear that it must include an active laity, and that the *sensus fidei* must underly any effective work in the world for the Gospel.

**5) *The sensus fidelium, particularly as it is located in the laity, cannot be adequately described as a solely passive element in the Church.***

This assertion is made in direct reference to the theology, practice and attitude that came increasingly to characterize much of the treatment of the sense of the faithful in the Church in more recent times. Some support for a more passive view can still be found in the Church after Vatican II.

This criterion attempts to reclaim the fuller view of the sense of the faithful, drawing on the historical tradition that includes the New Testament communities, the ecclesial practices of the Patristic period and the early councils. It relies too on the observation that even where later theological approaches to the *sensus fidelium* defined it as a passive element in the Church, its *de facto* role included active responsibilities.

At the height of the hierarchical insistence on a passive role for the *Ecclesia discens* after Vatican I, opposition remained since some theologians saw an essential role for the infallibility of the people *in credendo*. Prior to Vatican II several authors again studied the historical roots of the sense of the faithful, recognizing in it the movement of the Holy Spirit, and, following in the footsteps of Moehler and Newman, by drawing on Patristic and Medieval insights.

Vatican II did not resolve the theological tension between the passive and active views of the *sensus fidelium*. Yet the Council gave "official" status to the view of the Church as actively addressing the modern world while employing an active laity. The tension between the active and passive approaches is now embedded in the Church's official documents. Substantial work remains after the Council in the task of developing an adequate ecclesiological paradigm that incorporates the roles of both magisterium and the people of God in the work that faces the Church.

If lay people have been given a mandate to work actively in the world, they have not left behind the role of *Ecclesia discens*. A great deal of learning must precede the use of the tradition in the tasks that face them. Yet a new element for the modern Church, reintroduced by Vatican II, is the realization that their responsibility cannot be reduced to simple reception. The encouragement given to lay people in *Gaudium et Spes* to engage the secular world with the values and message of the Gospel draws on those strengths that have long been exhibited by the faithful in the practical living of the faith. Such practical living of the faith has continued among the faithful even when they lacked theological sophistication. The sort of practical knowledge called for is the same quality that is identified from Thomas Aquinas to Newman, in descriptions of the instinct for the faith that realizes proper judgment in practical contexts.

With the added realization that through practical work, the fruits of Christian faith are to be realized in the world, the laity can work with the magisterium to address both the practical tasks and the theological understanding that places these tasks in their wider ecclesial context. From the foundation of common faith, they can together give expression to the *sensus fidelium*. No adequate understanding can be reached if the laity are regarded solely as a passive element in reflection on these matters.

Thus, in the more active role of the laity in the apostolate, the *sensus fidelium* is also necessarily active. At another level too, if the Church is to develop a deeper understanding of the active role of the laity, the task of reflection must itself be taken up by the laity.

**6) *The sensus fidelium has implications for each believing person.***

In *Lumen Gentium* the *sensus fidei* is said to characterize the faithful "from the bishops down to the last member of the laity (# 12)." Each member of the Church has a responsibility to the faith and for the faith.

The dynamic by which this *sensus fidei* operates was the special focus of Medieval theologians. Thomas Aquinas, drawing on Aristotle, probed the nature of this type of knowing that is rooted in the action of the believer and that is above all a practical knowledge. Issues of moral decision making, *epikeia* and conscience are related to this "connatural knowledge" of the object of faith. A direct connection was made by Medieval thinkers between the *motus caritatis* of believers and the ecclesial sense of the faith. This spiritual aspect was to hold an important place in later reflection, in the work of Moehler and Newman and in the twentieth century authors who drew on their work.

Newman's description of the *sensus fidelium* is especially instructive for the understanding of the sense of the faith in the individual believer. He described the "instinct" or *phronema* of each believer as the work of the Holy Spirit, an answer to prayer, a "jealousy" of error and a commitment to apostolic faith. All of these elements characterize the Church as a whole, but they are rooted in the faith of individual believers who respond with this "instinct."

**7) *The presence of conflict does not necessarily indicate the absence of the sense of the faithful.***

Obviously, the negative quality of this statement prevents it from being a criterion for identifying the *sensus fidelium*. It is important to include this assertion among the other criteria, however, since its opposite might conceivably be assumed to be true. Because of the link between the sense of the faithful and the establishment of consensus, conflict might be offered as an indicator that the *sensus fidelium* is absent in a given situation. Yet many of the historical examples given already indicate that ambiguity, disagreement and debate are compatible with the process of development that results in new doctrinal statements. Conflict and dissent do not of themselves indicate sin, heresy, or "bad faith." Especially in hindsight, the *sensus fidelium* has been recognized as operating through conflict to clarify doctrinal expression. The cases cited by Newman are widely accepted examples where conflict was an integral part of the process by which the Church deepened its insight and moved to consensus.

On the other hand, conflict or dissent even on a large scale do not of themselves indicate the presence of a prophetic voice. Both potential prophets and majority groups have been wrong. Because the results of specific conflicts have often become clear only after a significant period of time has passed, issues that are raised in turbulent times must be treated in terms of their content. Conflicting arguments must be evaluated in terms of their merit and connection with the apostolic tradition, and this must be done in the context of ongoing theological reflection and the work of the magisterium.

Congar has pointed out that, "too much must not be attributed to the *sensus fidelium*, not only in view of the hierarchy's prerogatives . . . but in itself." He offers historical examples where "widespread failure of the faith" occurred among the people.[67] The presence of conflict cannot be immediately assumed to be a prelude to progress or development.

Yet in a period where a plurality of viewpoints exists on important issues and where "paradigm shifts" may be occurring, conflict may well be an indicator that the Church is confronting new challenges and developing new insights. The advantage of conflict may be in the response it elicits of a desire for resolution. The history of previous conflicts may remind those in contemporary confrontations that genuine resolution can come from acknowledging honest questions and challenges.

Involving many levels in the Church in the process of discernment may be expected to create more work, confusion and tension. Yet a deeper unity can be created within diversity if the relative merits of different positions are understood and allowed to contribute to a final consensus.

8) *Any contemporary assessment of the sense of the faithful is linked to a hermeneutic of doctrine.*

Any contemporary attempt to understand the sense of the faithful which does justice both to its long history and to its treatment at Vatican II must interpret it in the light of the issue of development of doctrine as well as the question of how to locate the *sensus fidelium* as a source in theological controversies. Such attempts to understand are made more complicated by the plurality of ecclesiological paradigms that exist in the post-conciliar Church.[68] These paradigms all purport to represent the history and tradition of the Church, yet they differ from each other in significant ways. The plurality in this area illustrates vividly that the interpretation of doctrine in the modern Church is complicated by the additional task of interpreting the sources of doctrine.

A thorough treatment of the hermeneutical issues involved in understanding the *sensus fidelium* in the light of both the different ecclesiologies and different views on the development of doctrine that claim warrants in Vatican II is beyond the scope of the present study. What will be indicated here are some of the ways in which current issues of ecclesiology are related to the history of the *sensus fidelium*.

A helpful discussion of how Catholic theology might employ the insights of modern theological hermeneutics is given by Edward Schillebeeckx in his often cited article, "Towards a Catholic Use of Hermeneutics."[69] Schillebeeckx stresses the wholistic character of a Catholic hermeneutic and illustrates a role for the sense of the faithful that is consistent with the elements that have been summarized in the present study:

> It is only the unanimity of the whole community of the Church, guided and accompanied by the world episcopate in its unanimous interpretation of faith, together with the office of Peter as the keystone of the vault of the great *koinōnia* of the same faith,

hope and love, that any new theological interpretation is authenticated as contemporary understanding in faith by the hallmark of the Holy Spirit.[70]

The issue of hermeneutics is included as a "criterion" here to make explicit a point that is indicated especially in the more recent history of the *sensus fidelium*. Any definition of this source includes in itself an interpretative stance toward the tradition and the role of the magisterium. The systems that have been developed and taught by both the magisterium and by theologians are bound up with specific understandings of authority and doctrine. In the light of the identifying characteristics already discussed above, the goal of the present point is to argue for an understanding of the *sensus fidelium* that does not restrict its scope to only some of its elements.

Such a restriction has occurred in the approach to the sense of the faithful that characterized both the magisterium and the laity in the period between Vatican I and Vatican II. In this period the dominant ecclesiology was one that emphasized authority to such an extent that the sense of responsibility among the faithful was not developed. To the extent that teaching authority was reduced to juridical terms, response among the faithful was reduced to obedience. The inclusion of the style of ecclesiology that preceded Vatican II along with the perspectives promoted by the Council itself contributes a great deal to the current dissonant context of ecclesiology. The various historical uses of the *sensus fidelium* that have been described above illustrate an appropriation of this source that implies a much richer understanding of its function in the Church than that which preceded the Council. The renewed interest of Vatican II in coresponsibility within the hierarchy itself, and of interaction between clergy and laity, has encouraged a return to a more enriched understanding of the *sensus fidelium*. The Council has created the need for richer ecclesiology that does not exclude a strong magisterium but which embraces an active laity.

The connection between ecclesiology and the interpretation of the sense of the faithful has been examined with particular attention to the period between Vatican I and Vatican II in a recent work by René Camilleri.[71] He argues for the importance of understanding the sense of the faithful as an active element in the Church and observes,

> Whenever an adequate ecclesiological context and perspective came to be lacking, only the hierarchy was held competent to solve any questions of faith whatsoever; the simple faithful were left with a faith almost exclusively founded upon this authority of the magisterium.[72]

Camilleri notes that it was in response to such an absence of "context and perspective" that Newman initiated his own discussion in the *Rambler*.[73]

It has been especially in the last century and a half that a different approach to the *sensus fidelium* has been one indicator of the hierarchy's more narrow understanding of the Church and its own role within it. Yet as has been indicated earlier, the roots of the tendency toward centralization in the West go back well into the first millennium. The specific connection between this centralization of authority and a centralization of doctrinal expression finds its interpretive foundation in the Counter-Reformation. A view of the evolution of this connection is instructive for understanding why the *sensus fidelium* came to be seen as a passive response to the magisterium, and how a richer and more historical understanding of it might be reclaimed.

John O'Malley has described how the desire for moral reform within the Church motivated the Fathers at the Council of Trent.[74] He notes the main tool for reform was to be an increase in discipline. The different approach to tradition that occurred at the Council is described by O'Malley.

> Before Trent the text from John's Gospel concerning the Spirit's ongoing teaching mission (14:26) was used on occasion to explain

growth or increase of understanding of truth in the Church; Trent quotes it in favor of the Church's faithful conservation of apostolic teaching.[75]

Trent's response to the Reformation crisis was to create a centralized ecclesial system. The combination of doctrinal interpretation and ecclesial authority became explicit when the authority of church leaders was questioned in the sixteenth century. At the time of the Reformation, the foundations of tradition were challenged as the focus shifted from the issue of taking responsibility for handing on the tradition to developing an understanding of how it was handed on. In place of the centrality of Roman authority the Reformers argued for the central role of Scripture. In the Roman Catholic response the claims for authority were made even more strongly and, under the influence of Melchior Cano, authority and doctrine were connected to the exercise of the magisterium. Dogma came to be understood in a restricted way as doctrinal expressions to which believers were to adhere.[76]

Tavard points out that largely due to Cano, the value of doctrine came to be considered in reference to its source rather than its content. He observes that such a "formal" criterion "is not entirely false, but it is onesided."[77] In arguing for a more balanced understanding Tavard proposes three necessary elements; a "material principle" that considers content, attention to "historical continuity," and a testing of the "formal principle of authority" that has remained since the Counter-Reformation through "the ongoing experience of *Christus praesens* in the community of the Holy Spirit."[78] Tavard discusses Newman's criteria, expressed in *An Essay on the Development of Christian Doctrine* as "neither formal nor material," but focused on the form that doctrines have taken in their historical development and on their impact on the *koinonia*. He does not find Newman's criteria to be useful in gauging the expression of tradition in the Church. He asserts that they are too complex for the use of anyone other than scholars.[79]

In his study of the sense of the faithful in the theologies that immediately preceded and also included the Second Vatican Council, Trocóniz y Sasigain has recommended these same criteria of Newman's as a way to observe how the *sensus fidei* becomes expressed in the concrete life and worship of the Church (in what he calls the *consensus fidei*).[80] Yet even here it is clear that they are meant to be used to assess the faith of the community by those with a theological vantage point. The concrete life of the Church is still interpreted most effectively when theological reflection can benefit from the passage of time.

The difficulty of identifying consensus in the community of the faithful is described by Heaney:

> The traditional norms for the verification of such a consensus are: that the agreement be morally universal; that the teaching be presented precisely as revealed; that the consensus prevail for a good length of time. There is no agreement as to how long this consensus must last. There is no doubt that it is extremely difficult to verify in the concrete when even the first two of these conditions are established.[81]

In each era, the prospects of expressing the belief of the whole Church have proven to be difficult. Piet Fransen has pointed out that the expressions of the Church's faith are always subject to the characteristics of human language and sociological realities.[82] Yet the movement of the community to express itself in confessional statements as a way to greater unity in the Spirit is ancient. Fransen sees the function of expressions of faith as part of a movement of the Spirit.

> This same movement towards self-legitimation in doctrine and practice was supported by a deeper inner attraction and impulse of the heart through the power of God's Spirit, which was keeping the Church as a whole faithful and true to the divine reality *from which* she was born and *towards which* she was being driven, two dialectical terms, remembrance and expectation, structuring the life of the Church.[83]

It is because of the nature of doctrinal expression itself that a process of development is needed to clarify the faith. In this process, the *sensus fidei* is the "source of truth" from the Spirit that "irrigates" the efforts of theologians, pastors and bishops, keeping them open to the Spirit.[84] Fransen sees the process of clarifying doctrinal expression in the early *koinonia* and in the early councils as bound up with the community's struggle to express its "spontaneous need for unity and communion." He sees the focus of Vatican II on collegiality as a return to an "inner law" in the Church that seeks a "living communion."[85]

In the critical context of the Reformation, the struggle for unity was being undertaken at a level that questioned ecclesial structures themselves. Concrete authority to speak for the tradition was both the issue in question and, as it appeared from the Roman Catholic point of view, the area in need of strengthening if the crisis was to be resolved. As officials within the Church took on a heightened responsibility for doctrine, the sources of the tradition were seen in a new way.

Tavard has described how the Catholic reaction to the Reformers' *sola scriptura* left the Church with an uncritical, unofficial view of "two partial 'sources'" for the faith.[86] The focus was taken away from an organic understanding of tradition, where Scripture and tradition operate in unity through a living community. If the Protestant stance was "one-sided," the reaction to it was also unbalanced. In locating responsibility for the tradition in one portion of the hierarchical structure, the Roman Catholic response could not maintain the fullness of the Catholic understanding.[87]

The Reformation conflicts over authority had a major impact on the ways in which the *sensus fidelium* could be understood. Within the structure of the Church, the laity were left with a passive role. The main response that remained possible for them was obedience to magisterial teaching.

As the influence of Counter-Reformation ecclesiology grew in the seventeenth and eighteenth centuries, the teaching of the hierarchy was conceived in increasingly juridical terms, and was located more and more centrally in the papacy. As Dulles has observed, this approach helped the Church to successfully meet the challenges of the modern era, but it did so at the expense of the richer view of the Church that included its "biblical, sacramental, charismatic and eschatological dimensions."[88] Costigan gives further support to this point when he describes the nineteenth century rejection of Gallicanism as an occurrence where power was more important than community.[89]

In the nineteenth century, a static model for governance in the Church coincided with a systematic understanding of doctrine that was mediated through the scholasticism of the Roman School. Although interest in Patristic insights into the consensus of the faithful were revived by Moehler and Newman and were somewhat influential even with Perrone, ecclesiology in the style of the Roman School dominated any historically focused alternatives. With Franzelin the Church's responsibility for tradition was joined to the infallibility of the magisterium as a further response to the Protestant foundation of *sola scriptura*. Scheeben argued that the laity should be consulted in doctrinal expression, since the Church as a whole transmitted the tradition, with an organic relationship between the Church teaching and Church learning. Yet his ambiguity over how the sense of the faithful was to be expressed typifies the problems that such a theological approach faced. By contrast, when official ecclesiology stressed the role of the magisterium as central, a clear source for the Church's position overcame any questions concerning the expressions of the faith.

When the *sensus fidelium* was employed in the 1854 Marian definition to overcome ambiguities in other theological sources, Newman suggested that Pius IX's "consultation" of the laity offered evidence of the use of the sense of the faithful as an integral source for doctrine. His historical approach was rejected however. As Sanks has observed, Franzelin's view of an infallible magisterium, embodied in those who act as successors of the apostles, left only a passive role to the consensus of the faithful.[90]

Vatican I firmly established the centralized authority of the Church in strongly juridical terms, linking doctrinal definition to "papal" infallibility. Although many Council Fathers saw the definition of infallibility in a wider context, much popular understanding and many expectations of doctrinal expression were reduced to viewing the magisterium as solely responsible for the content of truth. Obedience was the proper response among the faithful. As Thompson has observed, the *sensus fidelium* became an "object" which was "taught by an infallible subject."[91] Though many of the bishops at the First Vatican Council had understood the pope to have a moral responsibility to consult the Church in defining dogma, the operative ecclesiology that followed the Council contained little that might develop either the expectations or expertise in the faithful that would have given such consultation any practical theological meaning.

When the post-Vatican II context is viewed as a struggle for an ecclesiology, the current plurality of views on the sense of the faithful is not surprising. The renewed interest in an active *sensus fidelium* that began before the Council and which the Council embraced, is part of a larger challenge to the previous static view of the Church. No consensus is present on how an active sense of the faithful can serve the Church by interaction with the magisterium. What is clear is that the definition of the sense of the faithful cannot be made in isolation from an understanding of the magisterium. Further, it is unlikely that the relationship between the sense of the faithful and the magisterium will be clarified without a prior deepened understanding of how doctrinal expression develops through history. As Camilleri observes, from the complex evolution itself of the two notions [the magisterium and the *sensus fidei*] one can see how effectively they both and together constitute one vital question that can have many facets in the many problems that concern the Church in the manner God's revelation continues to be transmitted to the Christian people.[92]

Camilleri sees Vatican I's teaching on the magisterium and Vatican II's regard for the whole body of believers in the Church as "inseparable and complementary."[93]

In the period between the two Vatican Councils, the uneasy competition between a centralized authority that operated in juridical terms and the rekindling in theology of a historically minded approach to doctrine generated both ecclesial turmoil and theological development. Sanks and others have recognized the signs of a "paradigm shift" in the struggles with the centralized ecclesiology that developed in the wake of Vatican I and in the pluriferation of ecclesiologies that has come to characterize the response to Vatican II. The theory of paradigm shifts developed by T. S. Kuhn indicates that any shift from one paradigm to another— any "conversion"—cannot be forced. The genuine acceptance of either one main model or an interdependent set of models for the Church will take time. Sanks suggests that in addition to understanding the particular ecclesiological paradigms in the Church, a "theology of change" should be developed, based in historical and sociocultural research.[94]

A challenge is embedded in Vatican II as to how the Church as a whole should function in the expression of doctrine. Any post-conciliar understanding of the Church must incorporate a role for the sense of the faithful. John E. Thiel has argued that the view of the Church at Vatican II already represents a move away from the "classical paradigm." He observes,

> the Council's ground-breaking recognition of theological creativity was related to two conciliar positions that pressed beyond the heritage of Trent and Vatican I: a positive regard for historical

development, especially the development of doctrine, and the consideration of the magisterium's infallibility in the broader context of its relationship to the *sensus fidelium* of the entire Church.[95]

At the same time, it is important to see the sense of the faithful as one source within the Church's reflection on tradition, and to avoid the different sort of imbalance of giving it a role it cannot fulfill. Nicholas Lash has asserted, "as a criteriological principle, an appeal to the *consensus fidelium* is notoriously fragile, especially when such an appeal is made only when more favoured sources of verification—exegetical and historical—have failed."[96] Acknowledging that the use of the sense of the faithful, as in the 1950 Marian definition, "marked an escape from the excessively intellectualist straitjacket into which 'logical' theories had enclosed the problem," he notes that there is danger of accepting the influence of the contemporary age at the expense of the tradition, inasmuch as the "religious sense" of the people is subject to many influences in the culture other than the Gospel.[97]

The development of a better understanding of the *sensus fidelium* must be part of an overall rethinking of ecclesiology. Yet as this ecclesiology develops, the present discussion of the sense of the faithful may serve as a guide to recognizing when an inadequate treatment is being offered. Though a complete understanding of tradition cannot be based on the sense of the faithful no matter how thoroughly it is understood, an ecclesiology that fails to include it as an active contributor can be recognized as inadequate to the tradition. The faith of the Church considered as a living community is a foundational element in the carrying of the tradition.

O'Malley insists that for Christian theology, "a total shift of paradigm is by definition impossible."[98] Continuity must be maintained with the tradition. He observes, however, that although Vatican II gave only an ambiguous indication of what a richer paradigm would entail, it did in fact create a fundamentally new model for church order from what preceded it by its very focus on *aggiornamento*.[99] He suggests that the ambiguity and crisis created by the Council can themselves contribute to a new ecclesiology, inasmuch as they are related to the Church's new interaction with the world. O'Malley thus sees "the central point of contact" with contemporary culture as historical consciousness.[100] He observes that in facing this reality, "the Council admitted the inevitability of ongoing change, admitted the impossibility of being immune to such change."[101]

The questions raised by Vatican II, the resources it reclaimed from the Church's long history, and the acceptance of the importance of understanding historical context in evaluating doctrinal development all strongly influence current reflections on ecclesiology and the *sensus fidelium*.

The "criterion" that is presented here asserts that any interpretation of the *sensus fidelium* necessarily entails a stance on the way doctrine develops. This complex topic will not be resolved by focusing on the *sensus fidelium* itself, but must be more broadly based. At the same time, as different views of the sense of the faithful are examined, it will be useful to see if the ecclesiologies that are implied or stated include an interpretation of the *sensus fidelium* that deals adequately not only with its rich history of expression, but with the related interpretive issues as well.

It is possible to eliminate the conflict of ecclesiologies embedded in Vatican II by choosing only one focus from among the competing issues. Returning to a passive view of the faith based in a neo-Scholastic view of theology or a view of the magisterium that lacks a real interaction with the sense of the faithful disregards its rich history and begs the question of ecclesiology set forth by the Council. It is, of course, possible too, to so closely identify this source with public opinion that secular values are given too strong a voice.

Accepting the rich history of the *sensus fidelium* means embracing a very difficult task. The history of this source presents elements which are necessary for its inclusion in the Church's expression of its faith. Yet these are not sufficient to identify it clearly in specific doctrinal expressions. The question of the role of the *sensus fidelium* in the contemporary context thus necessarily requires a complex hermeneutical approach.

## USE OF THE CRITERIA

The characteristics that have been identified and described here are wide in scope. much of the ambiguity and diversity in contemporary theological treatments of the sense of the faithful may be linked to the many starting points that are possible from within a rich tradition. It is certainly legitimate, as has been illustrated historically, to probe one aspect of this theological source while giving less emphasis to others. At the same time, if one aspect of the sense of the faithful is stressed at the expense of another, an inaccurate picture is developed. It is the view of the present study that some contemporary authors use the tradition selectively, and thus collapse a complex source for understanding the faith into a partial view.

The criteria given here attempt to capture the wholistic nature of the *sensus fidelium*. There are disadvantages to criteria with such a wide scope and heuristic nature. Modern authors agree that identifying the sense of the faithful in a specific setting is difficult. The characteristics described here may be more useful in identifying when the sense of the faithful is not being considered wholistically.

The active use of the sense of the faithful in history is most often done as part of a process of discernment and expression. The *sensus fidelium* can be characterized as a dynamic for unity and wholeness in an ongoing community. It integrates the individual believer, the church community and the universal Church, The expressions of the *sensus fidelium* are best served when all of the charisms in the Church are allowed some impact on their creation. Part of the dissonance of the modern discussion may come from the lack of information or clarity in a particular area that is still in the process of development. Part of the differences may be due to certain authors focusing on only one part of the process at the expense of others.

After a consideration of the main treatments of the sense of the faithful in the period following Vatican II, an assessment of the key authors will be made using the criteria offered here. These authors will thus be examined next, with particular attention being given to their use of the history of the concept, to the relationship they describe between the *sensus fidelium* and the magisterium, and to the role they see for the laity. Additionally, any methods that they suggest for identifying the source in the Church will be noted as well as any issues concerning the concept that they see as being unresolved.

# CHAPTER 5

# THEOLOGICAL TREATMENTS OF THE *SENSUS FIDELIUM* SINCE VATICAN II

The authors who are examined here will be treated in two main divisions. Those who have written specifically about the sense of the faithful will first be considered. A roughly chronological ordering will be used, with those authors whose important work influenced the discussion nearer the time of the Council being considered first. No claim is made here to a complete treatment of relevant texts on the topic. Yet, the main lines of the post-conciliar discussion will be made clear from the authors whose views are summarized here.

Following this treatment of key authors, some representative examples of viewpoints on "practical" issues related to the sense of the faithful will be considered. Some attention will finally be given to the practical context for theological discussion that has been created by post-conciliar statements from the magisterium.

### THEOLOGICAL PERSPECTIVES ON THE *SENSUS FIDELIUM*

#### *Yves Congar*

Yves Congar is an author whose influence on reflection on the nature of the *sensus fidelium* has bridged the pre- and post-Vatican II periods. His work has been foundational for many aspects of the topic. Congar's *Lay People in the Church* (originally published in French in 1957, and revised in 1964) included reflections on the role of the faithful that have been cited earlier, as well as an often cited appendix that offers key texts from the Fathers to support the antiquity of acceptance of the *sensus fidelium* as an important source in the tradition. His major work, *Tradition and Traditions* (originally two volumes in French, 1960 and 1963), presented his historical-theological treatment of tradition as an organic, living work in the Church, and included a section specifically on the sense of the faithful entitled, "The 'Ecclesia' as the Subject of Tradition."[1] Throughout this book, Congar offers extensive historical and theological illustrations of his view that the sense of the faithful is a vital element in that "organic reality" that is the Church.[2]

Congar finds no warrant in the early history of the concept for separating the "subjective sense" or "instinct," normally referred to as the *sensus fidelium* or *sensus fidei*, from the "objective content" of the tradition.[3] He draws on the more modern insights of Moehler and Newman, but considers the approach of Thomas Aquinas as well, to develop an active view of the subjective element. Congar stresses that combined insight in the Church is a function not of "fusion" but "communion." Common faith is not some higher synthesis of personal views, but a sharing in the faith that comes from the apostles. Each believer participates since all receive the *sensus fidei*.[4]

In contrast to a view of the faithful at passive recipients of the Church's public teaching, a perspective he says "seems excessively dominated by the idea of 'infallibility,'" Congar sees the faithful as making a real contribution. He sees the passive view as restricting the New Testament texts themselves to a limited framework of interpretation.[5] Drawing on Newman and Scheeben, he asserts that the *sensus fidelium* adds "its own value as testimony, and, possibly, an element of development."[6] For the most part the faithful assist in "preservation and transmission" of the tradition. The magisterium is, of course, responsible for the "final ratification" of the *sensus fidei* in its "objective sense."[7]

A later work that has had a major impact on post-Vatican II reflection on the sense of the faithful as well as on other issues, is Congar's "La 'réception' comme réalité ecclésiologique."[8] In this article, Congar extends his previous insights on the interactive roles of the faithful and the magisterium to make explicit the role of response of the faithful to the official public teaching of the Church's hierarchy. With an eye to ecumenical discussions, he clarifies his own use of "reception" as the "process by means of which a church (body) truly takes over as its own a resolution that it did not originate in regard to its self," but whose authority it recognizes in its own context. This process is more than the Scholastics' understanding of "obedience."[9] He asserts that

> reception is not a mere realization of the relation "secundum sub et supra": it includes a degree of consent, and possibly of judgment, in which the life of a body is expressed which brings into play its own, original spiritual resources.[10]

Congar finds a warrant for the validity of reception in the recognition made by Vatican II of the "collegial initiative emanating from the bishops."[11] He goes on to review the historical reception of various councils historically.[12] He introduces a dynamic view of magisterial hermeneutics when he discusses the notion of a later council giving a "renewed reading" of a previous one. Specifically, he writes of a "'re-reception' of Vatican I by Vatican II."[13]

After considering the historical development of tradition through the reception of councils, where even lesser gatherings took on universal importance in the Church due to a wide reception, Congar stresses the need to seek the "greatest possible unanimity, agreement and consensus as an indicator of the work of the Spirit.[14] In discussing the acceptance of the canon of Scripture, the reception of synodal letters, the spread of liturgical reforms, canonization of saints, and church law, Congar illustrates the active role exercised through history by the Church as a whole.[15]

Congar's appeal is to a wholistic view of reception. He rejects historical attempts to limit the process as in the overly juridical use of authority in the acceptance of law.[16] He criticizes too, the shift "from a primacy of truthful content" to a "primacy of an authority" in recent ecclesiology.[17] He argues that where authority is the primary focus, a juridical mode is chosen where obedience is the only possible response. If rather, content is to be the focus, "the faithful and, better, the *ecclesia*, may be allowed a certain activity of discernment and 'reception.'"[18] Congar sees the latter approach as operative in the first millennium of Christian history, with a focus on authority being stressed in the West from the eleventh century until Vatican II.[19]

Congar insists again, that reception is not a "sum of individual ways" but rather "a totality such as that of the memory of the Church."[20] The "legitimacy" and "obligatory value" lies in the authority of the source that originally proposed the decision received.[21] Congar affirms that reception "has no bearing on the formal aspect of the action, but on its content." It asserts that the decision about doctrines, laws or ethics was right from the start. Non-reception does not indicate that a teaching is false. Congar asserts, "It means that this decision does not call forth any living power and therefore does not contribute to edification."[22] Reception in the Church gives a teaching "credence" or "credibility."[23]

In his article, "Toward a Catholic Synthesis," (1981) written to draw together the ideas of several contemporary theologians, Congar has summed up some of his own views on the sense of the faithful.[24] In regard to the Church learning and teaching he again appeals for balance, stating, "It is the whole Church that learns, it is the whole Church that teaches, but in different ways."[25] Calling the views he expressed in *Lay People in the Church* outdated, he stresses the active responsibilities of the laity to "speak freely" and to make "the expression of their prayer coincide with what they really are and do."[26] In regard to the impact that should be accorded the expressions of public opinion, he notes the difficulties of realizing accurate information and communication.[27] He warns that the sense of the faith of individuals or groups may be unreliable inasmuch as social and psychological conditions may skew their perspectives. He writes, "Fervent but directionless communities can deviate or slip into syncretism."[28]

In another place, Congar has elaborated on the tenuous nature of input from public opinion.[29] He sees in the Church the new "freedom, if not always the competence, with which laypeople express themselves."[30] He continues to assert that public opinion which shows an acceptance of teaching is important, as has beet shown historically. Congar warns, however, of the danger of "pressure groups" that are being created by political or cultural factions in the Church, saying, "no particular group can claim to express the faith of the Church." He observes that "the value of public opinion in controlling the faith is greatly lessened by this tendency."[31] Another warning is directed at theologians who stress their own agendas at the expense of the integrity of the faith of the people. Congar cites John Paul II's remark (made in Washington in 1979) that

> the faithful have the right not to be upset by theories or hypotheses which they are not able to judge, for want of proper training, or which are easily over-simplified by public opinion and understood in a way quite removed from the truth.[32]

Congar sees the pope's remark as a reminder that the work of theologians, though important, "is far less significant than the grandeur and depth of the life of faith of the people of God."[33]

At the close of "Toward a Catholic Synthesis," Congar notes too, that the particular eloquence and power that comes in the actions of Christians is even greater than that of their words. He acknowledges too, the importance of this issue with its links to apostolic roots and the work of the Holy Spirit, for ecumenical progress. He finally suggests "the major ecumenical question" to be "how much diversity is compatible with communion."[34]

### HISTORICAL FOCUSES

As is illustrated in the case of Congar, a renewed understanding and appreciation of the sense of the faithful as a source of Christian belief after Vatican II owes a great deal to the study of the historical events and expressions associated with the concept. Two previous chapters in the present study have drawn heavily on contemporary authors whose historical work contributes to the current understanding of the *sensus fidelium*. It is worthwhile to also consider here those authors who specifically use a historical focus to argue for an important place for the *sensus fidelium* in current theological reflection.

*John Coulson*

The most obvious influence in the era of Vatican II on including historical and particularly Patristic study in relation to the sense of the faithful has been John Henry Newman. John Coulson's edition of *On Consulting the Faithful in Matters of Doctrine*, published a century after Newman's original *Rambler* article, was reprinted again as the centary of Newman's death was marked in 1990. In his introduction, Coulson offered Newman's "abiding vision" that "the fullness of the Catholic idea demanded that the intellectual layman become religious and the devout ecclesiastic intellectual."[35] He sees this vision as one that Newman held with a heavy heart, anticipating "dark days" that arrived in the present century, even though a renewed interest in striving for "a conspiratio of priests and faithful people" was to vindicate Newman's struggles and hope.[36]

In an assessment of the ecumenical discussions on authority of the Anglican-Roman Catholic International Commission, Coulson notes the irony of Newman's influence in its statement that "the community, for its part, must respond to and *assess* the insights and teachings of the ordained ministers."[37] Coulson observes elsewhere that although Newman's theological confrontation with the prevailing view during the *Rambler* affair was certainly courageous, it was just as much a condition of his own survival in the Roman Catholic Church, which he had come to understand in broad terms.[38]

## Jean Guitton

A presentation of the *Rambler* article that is similar to Coulson's including both Newman's own essay and an extended commentary was published for French readership at the time of Vatican II by Jean Guitton, the only layperson to be invited by Pope John XXIII to attend the Council's first session.[39] Recounting the misunderstandings Newman encountered with his use of the word "consult," Guitton argues for Newman's orthodoxy in regard to the authority of the *Ecclesia docens*, even while he maintained "his right, even his duty, to write in the common language when he addressed himself to the laity."[40] Guitton identifies the principle that was argued consistently by Newman:

> It consisted in making a distinction between the unanimous faith of the Church, which belongs to it as a community, and the power of defining that faith, which power is the province of the Hierarchy and of the teaching Church.[41]

Although the hierarchy has the responsibility to "control, if necessary to authenticate" the "instinct" of the believers, the faithful held an important position as carriers of the tradition.[42] Guitton sees Newman's contribution as focusing on

260                                  *Chapter Five*

all of the baptized as those responsible for "the *development* of revelation" even if defining the faith is the role of the magisterium.[43]

*Guenter Biemer*

Newman's views on the development of doctrine were the focus of a study by Guenter Biemer during this same Conciliar period.[44] Though not dealing directly with the sense of the faithful, Biemer cites Newman's discussion of the faithful in his *Rambler* article and in *The Arians of the Fourth Century*, observing that Newman saw the "instinctive faith of the people, the accord of the faithful on a matter of revealed truth," as "one of the organs of tradition," although this was seen "in a passive sense."[45] He adds that Newman emphasized that the faith of the people was still something sought after by the magisterium when it made key definitions.[46] Interesting too, is Biemer's treatment of Newman's views on infallibility, where he again characterizes the role of the laity as being "the function of service and the attitude of watchfulness."[47] Biemer notes, however, that in a key manuscript where he discusses infallibility, Newman does not distinguish between the active and passive elements of tradition.[48] Biemer remarks, "One may take it that he thought of the passive testimony to the faith on the part of the laity as an extremely vigorous activity."[49]

Newman saw the people as a whole providing an important testimony to the tradition in history. Biemer identifies this testimony in Newman particularly with the "heart," the element of each believer that as a "miniature" of the Church, responds to the Spirit and makes real the tradition in a life of faith.[50]

*Samuel D. Femiano*

A historical and theological examination of Newman's thought on the laity's role that recognized in Newman an active role for the faithful in the development of tradition was done in the period immediately following Vatican II, by Samuel D. Femiano.⁵¹ He identifies in article 12 of *Lumen Gentium* the influence of Newman's understanding of the infallibility of the laity, noting that the paragraph specifically describing the sense of the faithful was placed in the present location instead of the fourth chapter on the laity where it had been originally located, in order to emphasize the unity of hierarchy and laity.⁵² Femiano finds an "echo" of Newman in the Council's emphasis on the whole Church rather than on the hierarchy alone as the recipient of the *sensus fidei*, and on its interest in seeing the different roles of the laity and bishops as operating in a "*conspiratio*."⁵³

Femiano relates this recognition of the importance of such a *conspiratio* specifically to the development of doctrine. Quoting Newman, he notes that if the laity are to be included in the definition of doctrine, as in the case of the Immaculate Conception, they should be included in other "great practical questions."⁵⁴ He sees the study of Newman's theology as an opportunity to enhance the effectiveness of the laity's witness in a world that has less use for "official" representatives of the Church; it is particularly in the *conspiratio* of laity and hierarchy, that the Church can witness to the Gospel.⁵⁵

## Webster Patterson

A focus on the lay apostolate draws the attention of Webster Patterson as he also recounts the views of Newman in general and in particular during the *Rambler* affair.⁵⁶ Patterson describes Newman's view of the *sensus fidelium* as a "theological font" that has served among others in the tradition, but which is always "clearly subordinate" to the "living mind" of the Church which resides in the magisterium, and which is the "ultimate norm and measure" of the deposit of faith.⁵⁷ Newman saw in history, as in the activity of the magisterium current in his day, that the *sensus fidelium* was viewed as a source that "fills in" when other sources were "scanty or defective."[58] Regarding the nature of this source, Patterson distinguishes the theoretical or speculative theological aspects of the faith from those proper to the "ordinary Christian"; that is, those of a practical nature.[59]

Patterson describes the simple Christian's ability to judge truly and consistently in matters that such a person cannot analyze theologically. Since the nature of faith is itself not subject to pure analysis, Patterson sees an apt connection to the supernatural ability of the faithful to approach it with the instinct described by Newman.[60] He sees, in fact, a similarity between the *sensus fidelium* and the "pre-theological sense" of tradition described by Karl Rahner, the "habit of opinion" of John Whalen, and the "dynamic life" of believers seen in relation to those in authority as described by Gabriel Moran.[61] Patterson thus begins making connections between the element of "instinct" or practical wisdom in Newman and the systematic thinkers that were important in the years following the Council.

Patterson emphasizes the connection Newman made between the *sensus fidelium* and the faith seen as a whole. Here in particular the work of the Holy Spirit was to be recognized in the Church, seen as a community.[62] Patterson finds that Newman's approach leaves unresolved problems among the tasks left to the Church by the Council, particularly in regard to ecumenical relations.[63] He adds that as Newman expressed his insight within the practical circumstances of his own day, his influence must be renewed in the practical terms of new issues and possibilities of a different age.[64]

In the work ahead, the laity have been recognized as having a unique apostolate given not as an offshoot of the activity of the hierarchy, but as a mandate from Christ.[65] Patterson ends this particular study with a discussion of consensus as a lasting ecclesial agenda item from Newman. The whole Church is responsible for the witness to the Gospel, and from this responsibility comes the importance of greater freedom, involvement and opportunity for education of the laity.[66] Better communication is seen as essential for the cooperative work ahead. It is noteworthy that in this early post-conciliar period, even with the optimism and challenge that are included in Patterson's writing, he describes consensus as "that rather illusive word."[67] Particularly in the important area of communication, Patterson observes that "no practical working channels . . . have been established."[68]

Yet, Patterson returns to the topic of the sense of the faithful again, with a renewed reflection on the practical influence that the Church should seek in the opinions of lay people. In "Apologetics, Newman and the Teaching Church," he takes up the question of how consensus, lay expression and the interaction of the faithful, theologians and the hierarchy should occur.[69] He bases his argument for active lay involvement on the fresh views of Vatican II and on Newman's own understanding of the tradition and the consensus of faith, as dynamic rather than static realities.[70]

Patterson argues that if Newman were speaking to the present context, he would stress the importance of individual opinion and its active contribution to an active, living consensus of the whole community. The nature of such opinion is of a specific type; responsibility must be accepted by church members. It is of course possible for public opinion to be formed among a group of people who each fail to accept personal responsibility.[71] Thus in Newman's own terms, judgment in matters of faith must be a function of real and not merely notional assent.[72]

The concrete responsible judgment found in the many elements in the Church joined together through "interaction and confrontation" is then focused and expressed by those who have the role of official judgment and expression, the magisterium.[73] Patterson describes Newman's view of the teaching office as "the *focus*, rather than the exclusive *locus* of the action of the Spirit who brings the Church to discover and express the truth.[74] He sees Newman's vision as a preview of the task set before the Church by Pope John XXIII and the Council: "The whole community of faithful must be subjected to the pains of growth and development, the chief characteristic of any truly vital body."[75]

If the community is to be actively involved in deliberation and judgment the one who leads this body, the bishop, is not a mere spokesman for the group. His role is to be a witness of the consensus, but in a distinct sense, a judge, as well, who follows the direction of the Spirit.[76] The problem recognized by Newman and by contemporary authors is that the hierarchy has at times construed its task solely in juridical terms and has neglected the theological and communal dimensions of its decisions, as well as the practical aspect of consulting the faithful.[77]

Patterson's argument is for such involvement. He describes the practical dimension, but does not dwell on actual examples or actions that could be implemented. His promise of a description of how change should take place remains more an argument for change. He closes with an application of Newman to the post-Vatican II context, offering him as one who suffered in his own situation rather than rebelling against the ill treatment he received from the Church authorities of his own time, and whose ideas have since been vindicated.[78]

### *Richard Penaskovic*

Richard Penaskovic has sought to draw on historical study to bring understanding of Newman's view of the laity "back to a more profound level." By this he means seeing in the work of the *sensus fidelium* and the development of doctrine the action of the Holy Spirit in the Church.[79] As noted earlier, Penaskovic sets the study of Newman's approach to the laity in a wider context of Newman's work than those like Patterson and Femiano whom he criticizes to some extent. He considers the *Rambler* article in the light of the texts by Newman that preceded it when he wrote as an Anglican and those he wrote later as a Roman Catholic. He also examines a letter written by Newman to Pusey in 1865, in which Newman gives his views on Marian devotions and elaborates on the difference between faith and devotion. The latter are seen as the concrete, dynamic aspects in the expressions of the faith.[80]

Newman saw that devotion can at times run beyond the intellectual precepts of faith, yet this is an advantage even if it is only a part of the larger operation of faith. Devotion requires the wholistic context of the Church, including doctrinal understanding.[81] The role and dignity of Mary have been expressed since ancient times in works of art, however. Penaskovic writes that "the sense of the faithful points to realities in the Church which are to be found at a more profound level than that of theological reflection."[82] He adds, "This is tantamount to saying that the life and devotion of the faithful possesses an ontological priority over the reflection of theologians."[83]

Penaskovic expresses a hesitancy to claim too much for the *sensus fidei* or the *consensus fidelium*, commenting approvingly on those who take a conservative approach. He observes that "theology is only beginning to investigate" the concept's nature.[84] He adds that the *sensus fidei* is "only indirectly available" in the creeds, where it finds expression but where it cannot be fully represented. Finally, he sees the "complexity" of the issue as most telling in situations where neither consensus nor magisterial direction exist on a specific problem. He sees a need when confronting particular issues, for "a critical interpretation of the whole questions . . . in reference to Scripture as the *norma non normata*."[85]

In summarizing Newman's thought, Penaskovic emphasizes "an intimate connection between the illative sense, the laity and the Holy Spirit."[86] He sees in Newman's lifelong treatment of the laity an emphasis on the need for lay people "to strive after holiness."[87] In this striving they witness on behalf of the Church to the work of the Holy Spirit, and serve as "signposts, which show the world the true meaning of Christianity."[88] In the area of worship and devotion, the laity have a particularly active role.[89] The hierarchy for their part should look for a relationship marked by "mutual trust, confidence, respect and cooperation."[90] A respect for the laity's freedom should be joined with a realization of their responsibility.[91]

Within this sort of framework, the laity should be consulted as recipients of the Spirit who works through the illative sense, directing the hearts of believers to accept true doctrine.[92] Penaskovic describes the infallible judgment of the Church as an element that "serves to ease the minds of the laity by pointing out whether individual writers and theologians are on the right track or not."[93] He does not ascribe to Newman the view that the laity should be simple respondents to the magisterium, but urges instead an appreciation of Newman's view of the Church that is wholistic, and ultimately mysterious.[94] He advises that Newman's "On Consulting the Faithful" be "demythologized."[95] Where it is not seen in the context of Newman's long treatment of the laity, the central role of the Holy Spirit will be missed. Penaskovic sees the "highpoint" of Newman's thought on the laity and on the Church in the Preface to the third edition of the *Via Media* (1877), where Newman links a sacramental view of the Church to its "ineffable mystery" and the action of the Spirit.[96]

From this theological and spiritual approach to the sense of the faithful there is a clearly practical shift in a later article where Penaskovic proposes an active role for the laity in leading a Church that should be more "democratic" than "institutional."[97] He argues that such leadership can resolve the growing tensions between the magisterium and theologians. He finds in *Lumen Gentium* warrant for an ecclesiology that contextualizes the magisterium in "the teaching authority of all believers," a source that has been undervalued, but which is gaining expression particularly in the Latin American context, and in the "rise of nonacademic theologies."[98]

At the same time, this authority of believers is of a different sort than the doctrinal expression proper to the official leaders.[99] The *sensus fidei* "is much richer, more differentiated, and more active than the statements of the magisterium by themselves."[100] This source must contribute to theological reflection by way of two areas: public opinion and reception. Penaskovic draws on Newman and Rahner to support the importance of lay voices in the public context. Rahner in particular has observed that while the magisterium bears responsibility for determining the limits of public expression, it has exercised this responsibility in too confining a way historically. It may in fact be the work of the Spirit when expressions go beyond the officially determined parameters.[101]

Penaskovic describes reception as "a never-ending process of reflection about the faith carried on in faith by the entire community of believers." The process includes "Church authorities, academic theologians, and the people of simple faith." He notes that in the early sixteenth century, the Fifth Lateran Council offered a program of reforms quite similar to Trent's, but found no significant response. Referring to the work of Vatican I, he writes, "Instead of bringing about a living faith, the definition of papal infallibility in 1870 created more problems than it solved."[102]

He describes current interest in reception as "a new theological category." The newness appears to be in its application to contemporary contexts. Penaskovic cites the response of Catholics to *Humanae Vitae* to raise the question of whether it represents a case of "nonreception."[103] Following Rahner again, he is interested in showing the importance of accepting certain questions as open in the ongoing reflection of the Church.[104] He describes the role of the theologian in this process as being "like the artist whose innovations are misunderstood by contemporaries and only appreciated in the history of art from a vantage-point of temporal distance."[105] The interaction of theologians and the magisterium is made more complex by a shortened time framework. The teaching, criticism and response that once might take decades can occur in the current technological culture in a few days.[106]

To improve the process by which doctrinal understanding and expression occurs, Penaskovic recommends greater subsidiarity, so that decisions are made with the greatest possible involvement of different elements in the Church, and reflection is done in a more regionalized manner.[107] Additionally, those responsible for authentic teaching might consider acknowledging the provisional character of some of their teaching, developed as part of an ongoing process, in a manner similar to that of the United States' Bishops in the preparation of their pastoral letters on war and peace and on economics.[108] In actual disciplinary cases, he suggests the Congregation for the Doctrine of the Faith might consider consultation with the International Theological Commission.[109]

## *Denis Read*

An emphasis similar to Penaskovic's early spiritual focus on the *sensus fidei* in the individual believer is shown by a study of Denis Read completed shortly after the Second Vatican Council.[110] Read's historical treatment does not have the scope of Penaskovic's, but his study is noteworthy for the interest it shows, following Vatican II, in appropriating the sense of the faithful in the "practical" faith life of believers. Read draws on Newman's treatment of the illative sense and the active development of insight described by Lonergan to pose a challenge to the modern Catholic to develop a moral conscience in the light of both apostolic tradition and empirical sciences. It is worth noting too, that after describing the importance of a synthetic approach to conscience, Read describes the actual development of such a program in fundamental theology that would apply these insights as "the matter of another much more difficult investigation," which he hopes to find in the "collaboration between dogmatic and moral theologians."[111]

### *Luis M. Fz. de Trocóniz y Sasigain*

It is appropriate to include among those authors who extend the thought of Newman into the post-conciliar discussion, the study of Luis M. Fz. de Trocóniz y Sasigain.[112] In this doctoral dissertation, the author reviewed the insights of key authors from the 1950's and 60's, after first examining the topic in Thomas Aquinas, Moehler, the Roman School, Newman, Scheeben, Blondel, and Marín-Sola. The published portion of his study contains the third and final portion of the dissertation. Here he argues for an integrated, wholistic view of the sense of the faithful as an intuition into the tradition and vehicle for development of doctrine.[113] The sense of the faithful is a source for the "spontaneous" entrance of the Spirit in the life of the Church, and when it bears fruit in the *consensus fidelium*, it allows all of the faithful to participate in the expression of the tradition.[114] It can challenge and say more than the official magisterium, but in its full authentic expression it will not reject the Church as a structure.[115] In seeking criteria for assessing the working of the sense of the faithful, he finds the criteria of Newman as expressed in his *Essay on the Development of Doctrine* to be both pertinent and underrated.[116] He thus ends his study with a review of these principles and expresses the hope that they will be a source of reflection for others.[117]

## John T. Ford

The importance of the two modern Marian definitions and the work of Newman for the contemporary discussion of the sense of the faithful are obvious. An explicit connection between Newman's view of the *sensus fidelium* and his own Mariology has been examined by John T. Ford. Ford describes the link between these issues as "personally forged" by Newman.[118] In *On Consulting the Faithful in Matters of Doctrine*, the definition of Pius IX is, of course, a key case in Newman's argument. Ford sees a central basis for linking the two issues not in the "convenience" of a contemporary example, however, but in the Patristic roots of both topics.[119] He adds that as his Anglican period ended, Newman came to believe that "devotion to Mary as *Theotokos* is a necessary safeguard for preserving an authentically patristic Christology."[120]

Ford reviews the events of the *Rambler* affair and describes Newman's article as "fascinatingly heuristic." In it, he sees Newman arguing "simultaneously at a number of different levels" which included attempts to address historical, abstract and personal issues raised by his critics.[121] He sees this strategy as indicative of a wholistic, "organic" view in Newman, where the laity are seen as one "channel" in the process of tradition that must be given consideration, although this is always to be done in relation to the magisterium which has the final responsibility for expressing it.[122]

Ford observes that some aspects of this process are not settled by Newman, asserting, "while Newman's vision of *consensus* is quite attractive, the critical question, the existence of such a *consensus*, is apparently assumed."[123] He characterizes Newman's argument as rhetorical in its claim to follow the views of Perrone (and thus avoid the possibility of any taint of Protestant influence).[124] Ford cites Nicholas Lash in saying that Newman's use of the sense of the faithful is not merely "an appeal to the 'facts,'" but an appropriation of them that already incorporates a preferred interpretation.[125] Ford also sees Newman's description of the *sensus fidelium* as indicative of a "quasi-Platonic view" he finds in the *Essay on Development*, where Christianity is a "living idea" moving in history. The tradition may be seen as concretized through the bishops or through recognition of the views of the faithful, depending on the particular definition.[126] Yet, Ford observes, "However congenial this vision of Christianity as an Idea progressing through history may be, critically speaking, it also must be recognized as 'an hypothesis to account for a difficulty.'"[127] In a similar way, each of Newman's other supporting "witnesses" in *On Consulting the Faithful* are seen by Ford as indicating the heuristic nature of his view of the *sensus fidelium*.[128]

In a later treatment of Newman's ideas, Ford elaborates on the elements that are important to the "heuristic" role of the faithful. He writes that "Newman emphasized that the faithful realistically needed time to 'receive' a new doctrine, rather than have its acceptance forced upon them." Additionally, the laity "had a right to know and to choose among different legitimate interpretations of doctrine, rather than be forced to accept the particular interpretation of a particular school."[129] Dogma itself is seen to have "a heuristic quality insofar as it admits of further development, sometimes by addition or enrichment, sometimes by minimizing or trimming."[130] Ford finds in Newman's interpretative approach, important balances to an ultramontane view of the magisterium. In the process of development theologians perform key tasks. Newman also acknowledges that even where there is a presumption of normal acceptance of church teaching, an individual believer may find it necessary in conscience to reject a specific doctrine, though perhaps temporarily.[131]

As he considers the relationship between Mariology and *sensus fidelium* in Newman, Ford sees Newman's approach as connecting historical facts and an interpretation of these facts through his theory of development. He sees this connection as "the most problematic aspect" of Newman's view as well, inasmuch as it involves a circularity.[132] Ford writes,

> A number of historical incidents are interpreted as projecting [the *sensus fidelium*'s] existence, which once presumed, is in turn used to explain these historical incidents. Perhaps this hermeneutical circle is inescapable; nonetheless, it might be more helpful to approach *sensus fidelium* through a functional analysis of the tradition-process.[133]

He adds that the sense of the faithful "is seemingly most intelligible when viewed as an aspect of an homogeneous theory of development."[134] Though he questions whether Newman's approach should be characterized as such a "homogeneous" view, he also calls into doubt the use of his platonic approach in the light of "modern historiographical critique."[135] Even if it has diminished critical value, however, Ford sees Newman's contribution and challenge as vital to contemporary discussion.[136]

## *Robert Eno*

Though much of the historical interest in the sense of the faithful since Vatican II was motivated by Newman's influence, such studies have not been limited to the areas Newman addressed. A significant contribution to reflection on the active role of the laity in the area of shared authority and responsibility in the early Church has been made by Robert Eno.

In his "Consensus and Doctrine: Three Ancient Views," considered earlier, he examines three different approaches or emphases in the early Church regarding the consensus within the community that bore the responsibility for transmitting the *depositum fidei*.[137] He stresses that the focus of Augustine on the consensus of the past, of Vincent of Lerins on a contemporary consensus, and the growing focus in papal letters on the Roman tradition as primary, represent not opposing views but complementary aspects of a developing strategy.[138]

Eno does add that with the modern development of a teaching office focused in the hierarchy, the emphasis on the magisterium as "the proximate rule of faith" has rendered the other approaches to consensus subservient to the hierarchy. The present magisterium is seen as the deciding voice for the Church. Eno observes, however, that the hierarchy has at times interpreted consensus selectively. The present consensus among bishops is stressed and carefully monitored. At the same time, the repetition of previous doctrinal stances in *Humanae Vitae* was justified by Paul VI when he claimed he could not change the teaching of his papal predecessors.[139]

Eno sees consensus as a key theme in the work of promoting greater Christian unity. In response to critics who question the existence of any true consensus in the past, Eno maintains the reality of a "central stream of Christian doctrine in history." The early creeds and the *regulae fidei* provide evidence of consensus in "propositional form." He advises a re-examination and possible discarding of certain doctrines "that have come to characterize a community over the more recent centuries," in order to achieve unity, and suggests, "Perhaps the willingness to leave them behind will spell the difference between a Church and a sect."[140] Eno finds evidence in history that the tradition can be embraced in a unified community even while differences remain.

An important contribution of Eno is in his historical description of the conflicts and plurality of strategies for unity in the early Church. Although the present centralization of structural authority produces issues for the contemporary Church that are different from those of the first centuries, the reality of early consensus of community life and faith amid significant differences can offer the present Church hope and even some practical precedents for finding greater unity in the midst of different gifts. In his article on "authority and conflict" cited earlier, Eno writes, "The conflict between institutional and charismatic authority is always with us."[141]

Eno has also observed that if such elements found among both laity and clergy were melded in different ways in the early Church, a similar use of them should be possible in the current Church. Both prophetic and structural aspects of the Church must still be included in some fashion. He argues specifically for the rekindling of those strategies for the transmitting of the tradition that have been neglected in more recent times.[142] Shared responsibility is still important for the contemporary community. He sees the ancient Church as a witness to the possibilities of an ecclesiology that is "not bound by the chains of historical and sociological inevitability," but rather one that can use proven structures from its own history.[143] Eno holds out the hope that the present Church can draw on a past model where in a structured community the laity could be included in doctrinal decisions even in councils. With such an inclusion collegiality can balance centralization. The selection of bishops could itself be done through shared responsibility in the community.[144]

## *Geoffrey King*

The research of Geoffrey King has been considered above in connection with an examination of the historical evidences supporting the importance of reception in the establishment of law in the post-Tridentine Church.[145] It is only important to recall here King's view that the difference in approaches to reception of law in that period was based in the difference between "voluntarist" and "rationalist" understandings of law.[146] In the rationalist perspective, reception is seen as an "intrinsic necessity" where the "will of the people [would necessarily] prevail over that of the legislator or would cast doubt on the effectiveness of the will of the successor of Peter."[147] King claims that if the voluntarist focus on will is not seen as the central issue, "the difficulties disappear." The rationalist perspective finds that something of the "intrinsic quality" of a law that has been promulgated can be shown by its reception or non-reception. King observes too, that it was the voluntarist approach that became established in the modern Church.[148]

King asserts that proponents of the rationalist view do not advocate "a situation where laws are promulgated and then frequently 'vetoed' by non-reception.'"[149] However, he would encourage an approach where the law makers would consider the "receptivity of the community" prior to their own action.[150] Non-reception might still occur where such involvement existed, but this sort of response might indicate the unreasonableness of a law, if only in a specific context, and it could thus add to the overall process of legislating.[151] King thus argues for an approach to jurisprudence that places law making in a wider context of ecclesial judgment.

## SYSTEMATIC TREATMENTS

### M. D. Koster

The views of M. D. Koster have made a significant contribution to the understanding of the sense of the faithful both before and after Vatican II, though his interpretations have not always been without criticism.[152] Koster's key insights into the *sensus fidei* are included in the article "Der Glaubenssinn der Hirten und Glaeubigen," which was printed originally in 1949, and included in *Volk Gottes im wachstum des Glaubes* a year later. It is included in the present study, inasmuch as it was part of a collection of Koster's work published after the Council, which has continued to inform the post-conciliar discussion of the *sensus fidei*.[153]

Koster compares the "sense" spoken of in the *sensus fidei* to its uses in other common phrases such as "sense of justice," "sense of truth" or "sense of business." This tool of perception is distinguished as unique to an individual. It involves and motivates a person in the thing attended to.[154] When applied to "the faith," this "sense" includes the movement of the Spirit, who brings the one involved toward understanding and salvation.[155] The sense of the faith contains as the foundation for its very existence, the operation of the Spirit. Following Thomas Aquinas, Koster describes this sense as bound up with the object of faith, seeking to embrace in a direct way what is revealed and in an indirect way those elements that support the objects of faith.[156]

The richness of the gift of faith, which is amenable to theological discussion but not subject to a full description by it, is described by Koster as he distinguishes "the gift of supernatural understanding of faith" (*die Gabe des Glaubensverstandnisses*), "the knowledge of faith" (*der Glaubenskenntnis*) and "the wisdom of faith" (*der Glaubensweisheit*).[157] Koster finds these elements in Aquinas and in later statements of the magisterium. Koster sees these three gifts as essential; any progress in knowledge, maturity or dogma are founded in these gifts, both for individuals and for the Church as a whole.[158]

Koster draws on both Scripture and the Fathers to show the long-standing acceptance of the sense of the faith by theologians and the magisterium. He sees, however, an absence of a consistent definition in these various sources, and he faults its more recent (nineteenth and twentieth century) proponents for reducing the "sense of the faith" to the "obedience of faith."[159] A consistent, full understanding of the sense of the faith is not possible from an overly rationalistic approach, but lies in the realization that the faith is given in the Church by the Spirit, in a way that is prior to any theologizing about it.[160]

The unified nature of the sense of the faithful as it is experienced in pastors and in the faithful is stressed by Koster, even while he recognizes the distinct roles and forms of expression that are proper to the two groups. He does affirm that among the faithful, this charism is an active one. The faithful share in the gifts of the Spirit through Baptism, and their role in actively living them out is also expressed in the prayers at Confirmation. There is thus an "inner coherence" between the work of the magisterium and the life of believers in general as they both take part in the "growth and progress" of the faith. Similarly, believers share in the infallibility of the whole Church, and, through the action of the Spirit, they share in the responsibility for "the making conscious and proving of a revealed truth." The people and their pastors are not to be seen as having conflicting "senses"; the errors of modernism and an excessive emphasis on the teaching office should both be avoided.[161]

The difference in the infallibility that is exercised by the pastors and that which resides in the whole Church, including that in the laity, is understood by considering the "power of faith" (*Glaubenskraft*).[162] Koster identifies this as the ability to embrace the faith when it is expressed through symbols and creeds. It does not itself make distinctions at the level of the content of the faith, but rather moves the believer to embrace the faith as it is presented. The three gifts of the Spirit that Koster has earlier described are needed to complete and enlighten faith in its particular expressions.[163]

Clarification of such expressions is the specific role of the magisterium. In itself, the power of faith in a believer is "secure and correct," but not infallible without the gift of knowledge (*Glaubenskenntnis*).[164] Koster states, however, that this gift, necessary also for the magisterium, may be expressed through its infallible office, or it may be given directly from God. Theologians, in stressing only the statements of the magisterium, have neglected this second source. The need for theological discussion and even proof of the expressions of faith were brought out at the First Vatican Council, where opponents of the definition of papal infallibility claimed to also have the capacity to correctly judge the faith.

This same gift of knowledge of the faith is found in the faithful who in a "secure and correct" way also "judge" the faith. It is from this commonly held charism that the pastors draw in the act of defining, and they do so in a way particular to their office, so that the faith is taught officially.[165]

The movement of the sense of the faith from instinct to definition has been seen in actual historical cases. The expression of doctrine was preceded by a prior insight and belief in the cases of the doctrine of the real presence or in the beatific vision, for instance. Aquinas observed that a deeper understanding of the faith (*Glaubensverstaendnisses*) served a subsequent knowledge (*Kenntnis*) as the believer penetrated the truths revealed by God.[166] This deep understanding is what allows the believer to recognize truth and reject error in the various expressions which attempt to give voice to the faith. This sense is what allows the believer to grasp the faith as it is met in the Scripture itself. It is thus also essential that this gift should operate in the magisterium, as it recognizes and expresses the faith publicly in the genuine, unified sense of believers in the Church. All depend on it to clarify views that purport to belong to the tradition.[167] Koster expresses confidence in the ability of the sense of the faith to clarify and express the teaching of the Church, but he is just as certain that the proper functioning of insight in the Church's pronouncements must draw on the sense of the faithful.[168]

The response of the faithful is not an autonomous source. It needs the official expressions of the Church, and its own response confirms those of the magisterium. It expresses a genuine function in this confirmation, however, as seen in cases like that of the Immaculate Conception or Assumption, where differing theological views were expressed, and genuine conflict occurred. The people's responses contributed significantly to the view that eventually prevailed.[169]

In the "wisdom of faith" (*Glaubensweisheit*), the work of the Spirit completes what is rendered by the other gifts. Obedience is possible; worship and praise of God are found as understanding finds its proper goal. Insight and knowledge are completed by wisdom, which makes it possible for the Church to witness to the truth in its liturgical life. It is in the Church, led by its pastors and moved to action, that the Holy Spirit is found.[170] In describing this unified action and expression of the truth, Koster again adds that the magisterium in its particular role cannot act in an ad hoc manner; it must consider the genuine faith of the Church when it prepares to define a dogma.[171] If conflict comes as expressions are sought, this is not to be seen as evidence that the sense of the faith is divided in the pastors and people. Rather, it is an indicator that the pastors must work all the more to serve the people, and find a better way to express the apostolic truth. The "wisdom of faith" which is not as "visible" as the instinct or knowledge of the faith in the process of bringing faith to expression, here shows its priority as it calls the pastors and faithful to work. The presence of this wisdom indicates the unified quality of the sense of the faithful, rooted in the action of the Holy Spirit.[172]

The immediacy of this undivided sense finds its end in the love of God that is founded in the saving grace of God.[173] This link to God is not the same as the "objective" understanding or knowledge of matters of faith. It is also not achieved at their expense. Koster asserts that the God who is immediately present to those in heaven is found only in an intermediate way by those who are pilgrims on earth. At the same time the sense given to them by God leads them in probing and following their path. They are led by the Holy Spirit in expressing the faith through different roles, but with the same foundation.[174]

## *Michael Schmaus*

The influence of Koster's ideas was extended in the periods both preceding and following the Council through the influential work of Michael

Schmaus in his multi-volumed *Katholische Dogmatik*.[175] After some brief historical remarks highlighting the influence of Vincent of Lerins and Melchior Cano, Schmaus describes the nineteenth century background of the sense of the faithful, noting the importance of Franzelin, Scheeben and Newman, as well as the influence of Moehler and Perrone. He then cites Koster as fixing the new direction for understanding the tradition.[176] He draws on Koster's differentiation between the active and objective views of tradition and his description of the three levels of understanding given by the Spirit in the sense of the faithful.[177] He notes with approval, the notion that while the magisterium draws on the sense of the faithful when it teaches, this does not detract from the authority of the teaching office in some forced or simplistic way. Examining the sense of the faithful illuminates the work of the Spirit who brings the Church to a better understanding of its tradition.[178]

Schmaus later considers these same issues in their sociological and ecclesial contexts in reference to the issue of "democratization" in the Church.[179] Here again, he stresses the reality of both a tension and balance between the role of the laity and the magisterium. Though he insists on the genuine importance of the hierarchy, he describes the dynamic action that must include the whole Church in its deepening understanding and expression of the faith over time.[180]

In a different extended work on dogma a decade and a half after his original effort, Schmaus described an active role for the laity, following the teaching of Vatican II and drawing on both earlier historical witnesses like Clement, Origen, and Augustine, and the theology of Congar in his *Lay People in the Church*.[181] He describes the need for balance in including the prophetic gifts of all believers and stresses the need for cooperation between clergy and laity.[182] Later, in discussing infallibility, particularly as taught by Vatican I, Schmaus asserts that the Council's definition of papal prerogative "appears to put unusual stress on the isolation of the pope over against the entire Church" which could lead to the mistaken view that "the pope could define a dogma contrary to the faith of the Church, and impose it against the Church's will."[183] In contrast to this view, however, he cites Vatican II's corrective emphasis on the pope's expression of the infallibility of the whole Church. In this infallibility, all are active and all are passive.[184] Schmaus notes the difficulty of examining particular teachings of the pope and reactions to them in the light of this shared responsibility, citing the Galileo case and *Humanae Vitae*.[185] Schmaus tries to strike a balance between the real authority of the pope within the community and the context into which he speaks, where its reception through human characteristics of language and knowledge bring the possibility of nuance and further development.[186]

## Magnus Loehrer

The richness and perplexities of the sense of the faithful, seen as a source for theology in the wake of Vatican II, are seen in the brief but often cited treatment given to the topic by Magnus Loehrer in the multi-authored *Mysterium Salutis: Grundriss Heilsgeschichtlicher Dogmatik* published immediately after the Council.[187] The sense of the faithful is seen as a gift to all believers, and at the same time it refers to the Church as a "collective subject."[188] The intimate connection of the sense of the faithful and the *consensus fidelium* is maintained even while the difficulties of finding an adequate "objectivisation" of this consensus is recognized.[189] The importance of critical assessment of the beliefs of the faithful by the magisterium is stated, and yet again, the distinct role of the whole Church in understanding and finding expressions for the received faith is seen as key to the development of doctrine. Loehrer sees interaction of the people and their pastors in the liturgy as especially important to understanding the relationship of the *sensus fidelium* and the magisterium.[190]

Loehrer sees an important problem in identifying the expressions of the *sensus fidelium* in the question of which areas are those in which the laity hold genuine theological competence.[191] Following Vatican II he finds a central role for the laity in their tasks in the world. Particularly as they achieve a level of sanctity through the successful exercise of their faith in the practical decisions they make in the world, they witness to the truth in a vital way.[192]

## *Wolfgang Beinert*

The sense of the faithful has been given a thorough treatment from the perspective of systematic theology by Wolfgang Beinert, in an article published not long after Vatican II.[193] He includes the *sensus fidei* along with the testimony of the Fathers, magisterial statements, and theological reasoning as a source for theology. Such sources have been used in different ways in the Church's history. Beinert points out that as recent theology has tried to distinguish its task from that of merely implementing the statements of the magisterium, it has found it useful to draw on the *sensus fidei* as a distinct resource.[194] As has been made clear, particularly in the work of Karl Rahner, the nature of subjective, reflective understanding and an acknowledgment of the importance of historical context for the faith on the part of the believing community, have made theologians aware of a "totality" in the experience of faith that is prior to any analysis of it into parts.[195]

Renewed interest in the sense of the faithful on the part of theologians is warranted by increased references to it. Beinert warns, however, against identifying it too quickly with surveys, or too simply with the reception of magisterial teaching. It is not to be equated with church discipline.[196]

Beinert surveys the key authors that have figured prominently in the history of the sense of the faithful.[197] Key figures from the Patristic, Medieval, and Counter-Reformation eras are cited with their main ideas. The impact of nineteenth and twentieth century thinkers on the teachings of the two Vatican Councils are examined as well. Vatican II, he notes, corrected the "Pian monolithism" (*pianische Monolithismus*) that preceded it. Before the Council, a "magisterial positivism" (*Lehramtspositivismus*) left no room for any genuine role for the *sensus fidei*.[198] Vatican II also clarified the intended meaning of the phrase "*ex sese, non ex consensu ecclesiae*" in the teaching on infallibility from Vatican I.[199]

The period after Vatican II saw a continued interest in theological and structural elements of ecclesial understanding that led to the "so-called democratization debate."[200] This debate increasingly saw a consensus forming that accepted the *sensus fidei* as a key resource in such democratization. Beinert asserts that the interaction of different segments of the Church is not to be seen as a usurping of the hierarchy's proper role or as a "concession" to growing problems from both outside and within Church, but as the refocusing on an element in the life of the Church that has not been given sufficient attention.[201]

After his historical review, Beinert turns to the theological meaning of the *sensus fidei*, which he sees as bound up directly with its historical-theological meaning.[202] Inasmuch as the sense of the faithful has served as a criterion for identifying and clarifying dogma, it operates in the more recently recognized realm of the development of dogma. This role, performed implicitly until modern times, was legitimized in the definitions of 1854 and 1950 in a more explicit way. Its active role in theological reflection was given considerable impetus with Newman.[203] By introducing the role of the believing subjects into the expression of infallibility, Beinert finds that this newer focus has balanced the tendency seen in Vatican I to narrow the focus on the magisterium, and has returned the matter to theological discussion. Thus the balancing role of the sense of the faithful shows that the Church's understanding of the faith cannot be resolved through political or "theological-political" approaches.[204] When the faith community responds with a consensus around or a reception of official teachings, a "greater Catholicity and better clarity" is shown. Such a response is especially important in ecumenical contexts. Greater involvement of the role of the believing community similarly moves theological reflection from the theoretical to the practical arena.[205]

This influence is brought out again as Beinert describes the relationship of the *sensus fidei* to the *consensus fidelium*. Citing several standard treatments (e.g., Beumer, Congar, Seckler, Balic, Grillmeier, Philips) he asserts that all authors agree that the consensus of believers in the Church indicates the action of the Holy Spirit.[206] However, as indicated, Vatican II has reiterated that this work is not confined to doctrinal formulas and the work of theologians or the magisterium, but is expressed in the worship and action of the Church. The tradition is thus carried in a dynamic way. By the same token, the sense of the faithful is not to be elevated to the status of some sort of "super criterion"; the Church must remain aware of all the criteria at its disposal for understanding the faith, and must use them in a balanced way.[207]

Beinert also observes that in the host of authors he has considered there is no unanimity in regard to a definition of the sense of the faithful. Though this source is recognized as foundational for all structures in the Church, with a genuine if unofficial role for the laity, there are differences in the way it is seen in relationship to Church leadership, the work of theologians, and the laity.[208]

Beinert distinguishes several aspects that may be recognized in the various approaches to the sense of the faith. There is an ecclesial sense (*kirchlichen Sinn*) or *sentire cum ecclesia* by which a believer is willing to accept the "mind" of the Church; an *instinctus fidei* or "aptitude" out of which belief can emerge; an "enrapt enthusiasm" (*den schwaermerischen Enthusiasmus*), the emotional aspect or "religious sentiment" that must be balanced with objective criteria; a "magisterial positivism" (*Lehramtspostivismus*) which repeats official formulas without consideration for their interpretation or subjective responses; and a "sociologistic" (*sociologismus*) approach that stresses objective statistical measures at the expense of spiritual experience. In contrast to such partial views, Beinert sees the proper understanding of the sense of the faith as a "free charism" by which the believer embraces the "object of faith" and by which the whole Church moves to consensus in the faith, which is recognized and confessed by the faithful in union with the teaching office.[209]

Beinert's specifically theological understanding of the sense of the faith is rooted in the statement "God is love." The truth of salvation is intended to unite believers with God.[210] He observes that this certainly means drawing them into deeper knowledge of God. Following Aquinas though, Beinert stresses that such knowledge is not merely *scientia*, but *sapientia*. The wisdom of faith can draw a person to God even without express formulas or definitions, though these are certainly of value. The message of the Logos in the world is foundational to Christian understanding, but it must always be recognized as ultimately "inexhaustable and unfathomable" at its core.[211] It is in this vein that Beinert writes that "the *sensus fidelium* is therefore not determined nor eliminated, when the magisterium has formulated a dogmatic statement."[212] He thus finds it appropriate that the ones making dogmatic statements must themselves look to the consensus of the Church.[213]

Beinert asserts that the "concrete image of salvation" has a social nature. Individuals find this image in the whole community. In a gathering of human beings errors are to be expected. Yet the Church as a whole is given freedom from error by the power of God present in it. As members of the body, each person remains in the truth by remaining in the body. Conversely, faith in the body is an activity that draws on all of the members. Beinert thus finds it inappropriate to speak of "active" and "passive" infallibility in the magisterium and the faithful; the personal nature of faith involves an active confession and living out of the truth throughout the Church as a whole.[214]

He extends the influence of the "sense of the Church" to include its role as a sacrament in the world.[215] Here the key role of the *sensus fidei* of the believers is recognized. Through it, God's revelation is brought into focus. In this foundational role the responsibility of the Apostles is rooted, as is that of their successors and in particular the Bishop of Rome. The sense of the faith is found in a three-fold source: the faithful, the bishops, and the pope.[216] Different levels and tasks are then distinguished in a "multifunctional community" that recognizes and responds to the received faith. The bishops specifically have a dual role of teaching and witnessing to the tradition.[217]

Beinert has treated the role of the whole community in the mandate to bring the Gospel to the world as a structured, organized entity in a different article that addresses the "value" of the laity.[218] Here he recalls again that "the distinction of clergy and laity is essential," while reiterating that the different roles are interdependent and are given to serve the overall task of evangelization and love.[219] He claims that the task of being a sacrament in the world can only be achieved "if the church is experienced as a living, witnessing, community of members with differing charisms and a vital faith conviction."[220]

Beinert closes his systematic treatment with some summary observations. The ongoing life of tradition in statements and actions is the work of the Church as a whole. Following Rahner, he asserts that as the magisterium roots its authority in Christ it roots it in the Church.[221]

In regard to the expressed knowledge of tradition in the Church, the action of both the magisterium and the faithful are criteria for recognizing dogma. Neither can take precedence over the other, although in practice, the hierarchy is favored "*in ordine executionis*," and has a distinct representative and interpretative role. At the same time, the *sensus fidei* takes priority "*in ordine intentionis.*" Beinert recalls that the truth of the faith is realized most fully in the way all of the members of the Church live, and is not limited to a rational, logical form. The sense of the faith that exists in the lives of the large body of the faithful is thus a more effective place to examine the living out of the tradition and official church teaching.[222]

Referring to official ecclesial expressions, Beinert states that where a stronger binding force is involved, a wider scope of representation is connected to the person or persons doing the teaching. Hence when the pope is fulfilling the conditions for the definition of a expression that represents the belief of the whole Church, this expression is free from error "*ex sese.*" He exercises a unique role as he represents the whole. The bishops as a college likewise are protected from error when they teach together, representing all of their sees and thus the faith of the whole Church. The faithful themselves are seen to be without error only when they are in consensus.[223]

Expressions of the sense of the faithful remain a key criterion for the Church's own expression of its truth, however. Citing the influence of Justin, Tertullian, Clement of Alexandria and others, Beinert asserts that while the issue of who has expressed the Church's tradition is important, even more important is what has been expressed. The truths that are expressed have their real source in the Holy Spirit.[224]

Beinert admits that his discussion leaves the question of concretely determining the *sensus fidelium* unanswered. Human expressions are always subject to error, but he adds that this is true of those that come from officials in the Church as well as the people. Examples from history clearly indicate that magisterial statements have fallen into disuse, and in those which remain important, it is clear that theological reflection must continually reexamine the forms of statements to find their renewed meaning. Beinert recalls that underlying all such attempts at understanding the faith is the source described by St. Paul's words in 1 Corinthians 2: 14-16, the "mind of Christ."[225]

Beinert augmented his views on the sense of the faithful in a later article written in an ecumenical context that addressed the relationship between theology and the magisterium.[226] He argues for the appropriateness of a "conviction of the infallibility of the Church's teaching office" held within the Church, which affirms that the message of revelation has been brought genuinely into expression.[227] He adds, however, that this same magisterium draws in a primary way on the members of the Church. Its appropriation of this source is neither through an antagonistic, grudging use nor through a simple acceptance, but in a foundational "being-in" (*In-Sein*). The pastors too "are first of all believers."[228]

The successful proclamation of belief requires both the expression of consensus by the bishops and the recognition of the expression by the faithful. Beinert writes, "Where no one is prepared to hear, no one can teach. Where no competence is recognized, similarly no message can be received."[229] Lack of reception has been seen historically in examples like the response to the Council of Florence, and more recently in the reaction to *Humanae Vitae*.[230] Beinert finds that the people are able to judge such issues concerning the faith, and are, in fact, given a mandate to do so by their baptism and confirmation where they receive the help of the Holy Spirit. He notes that the involvement of the people was reaffirmed at Vatican II. Important too, is the special "competence" of theologians, whose contributions have also long been recognized in the Greek Church.[231]

Particularly in the pluralistic and complex context that the Church now inhabits, the bishops must draw on the resource of the people of God and their insights. Beinert notes that the extended use of consultation by German bishops and those of the United States in their writing of the peace pastoral exhibit a new approach to the mediating role of the pastoral office.[232] Beinert links the connection of teaching and the living faith of the people to the earliest Christian times. The fundamental image of the sense of the faithful is in the *regula fidei* which "is not a rule *for* the faith, issued by some authority, but rather the rule that *the faith itself* is, because of its conformity with apostolicity, the long-standing message adhered to in the Scriptures and the Tradition."[233] The rule of faith remained an active criterion throughout the centuries, focusing the community's faith, particularly through the work of councils, and involving the community through its response to teachings. Beinert recalls that in the break between East and West at the beginning of the second millennium, the East retained its "communal" view of Church involvement, whereas in the West, the practical mediation of the truth rather than the content of the truth became the focus.[234] Beinert observes that here the question of interest in the West became one of who expresses the truth, and how this authority is established. The answer given was the magisterium.[235]

The magisterium today has retained the central focus that it received historically. Beinert notes that it has also received an inherent tension between its task of unifying the community with a clear teaching of the tradition and the ongoing challenge of developing that tradition in each era.[236] Beinert sees the central role of communication held by the bishops as one that must be exercised pastorally, informed by theological reflection, and protective of Christian freedom.[237] The interaction of various elements in the Church are finally delineated in practical terms by Beinert. If reception of magisterial statements is lacking, the tradition itself is lost. If theology is neglected, these statements "remain empty." He adds, however, that "disconnected from the magisterium, theology is incapable of communication." He closes by saying that "further reflection" on these matters is needed by all concerned.[238]

## *Patrick Granfield*

Patrick Granfield is one of the most important contributors to the understanding of the *sensus fidelium* in the period following Vatican II. He is also perhaps the most eclectic, as he has offered his insights on the sense of the faithful through articles and books in the areas of history, systematic reflection and practical ecclesial issues in regard to the topic.

In an early work on the *sensus fidelium*, Granfield drew on the developing field of cybernetics, to offer a practical, but scientifically sound model for improved communications in the Church.[239] Key to the use of this model was the acceptance of communication in the Church as an "open system."[240] Writing just after the close of the Vatican II, Granfield found warrants in the Council documents and in theology that followed the Council for viewing the interaction of authority and the Church as such an open system.[241] He addresses the teaching of Vatican I on the Pope's prerogative of defining dogma without juridical approval, but goes on to discuss the importance of consensus in the Church. He stresses the connection of the magisterium and the whole body of the faithful. Granfield draws on *Lumen Gentium*'s recognition of the *sensus fidei* as the theological warrant for lay involvement.[242]

In some practical reflections, Granfield suggests avenues for an ongoing expression of the views and reactions of the faithful. These include lay participation in conferences and councils, the use of the media, public protests, elections, and computer questionnaires. The latter he suggests may present new opportunities for determining the *consensus fidelium*.[243] In this work, Granfield is very much in favor of encouraging an active laity. Such tools of feedback could enhance Church unity, and aid in the development of doctrine. He sees an improved system of communication as a way of helping the Church to be "more sensitive to the growing edge of truth."[244]

Much of Granfield's detailed analysis of historical expression of the sense of the faithful has centered on Cyprian.[245] In "Concilium and Consensus: Decision Making in Cyprian" cited above, Granfield examines letters of Cyprian for evidence of the manner in which the laity might have been consulted in early councils, while remaining careful to avoid claiming more than they reveal.[246] He shows that conciliar involvement was important in Cyprian's see.[247] He adds, however, that it is not possible, on the basis of the same texts, to conclude that members of the laity participated in the councils.[248] He also considers four letters where Cyprian is concerned with the *lapsi*.[249] He shows Cyprian's concern for "broad consultation," and concludes, "It would be reasonable to suppose that at the councils that discussed the *lapsi* the clergy and laity did have a voice in the deliberations."[250]

Granfield observes that throughout Cyprian's tenure as bishop, even when he was exiled from the community because of persecutions, he continued to keep his church informed. When the climate was calm, he encouraged input from those under his charge.[251] Granfield notes that even though he had a highly developed concept of his own responsibilities as bishop, and the importance of obedience on the part of the faithful, "Cyprian was, nevertheless, in practice a man of the people who fostered their faith and devotion and welcomed their advice."[252] Above all, Cyprian sought the unity of the Church; and both strong government in the Church and the consultation of its members were established to achieve this goal.[253]

In an article on the structure of episcopal elections, Granfield shows how Cyprian's concern was expressed in the case of a particular ecclesial responsibility.[254] Details of the election process have been discussed above. Important to recall here is the theological meaning recognized by Granfield in this practice of Cyprian's time. He notes that Cyprian's view on elections was rooted in "apostolic tradition and divine authority," and although he did not insist on involvement of the whole community as essential to elections "under pain of invalidity," he saw it as an ideal to be sought.[255] Granfield attributes the failure of the ideal to "the lack of an educated laity, abuses in the traditional electoral process, and interference by secular authorities."[256] Finally, Granfield sees the participation of laity and clergy in the present Church as a "functional goal." He suggests such inclusion would affirm Vatican II's insight into "the fundamental equality of the People of God as well as collegiality and subsidiarity."[257] Granfield sees difficulties in implementing procedures that can avoid "the twin dangers of exaggerated idealism and biased immobilism," but sees in Cyprian's church, an important precedent for "a balanced theology of shared responsibility."[258]

Such a theology is explicitly developed by Granfield in his later writing. In "The *Sensus Fidelium* in Episcopal Selection," he stresses that the *sensus fidelium* serves as a legitimate warrant for active involvement of the laity in episcopal selection because of this sense's "sacramental and pneumatic dimensions."[259] He draws on the classic expression of Newman, describing the sense of the faithful as a *phronema*, and notes the approval Vatican II gave to this source as something within all the people of God.[260] Most importantly, the *sensus fidelium* is to be seen as a "spiritual quality." It is the work of the Holy Spirit, and this foundation is the key to keeping its use in selecting bishops from being "excessively juridical."[261] Granfield claims that in describing the gift of the Spirit working through the sense of the faithful, and in employing the "predominant theme" of co-responsibility, Vatican II "laid the foundation for ecclesial democratisation and made lay participation in the election of bishops a natural consequence."[262]

Looking for evidence of the active participation of the laity in the Church since the Council, Granfield finds it in liturgical reform, active elements like the charismatic movement pastoral teams, groups working for social justice and base communities, as well as "non-hierarchical decision-making bodies" like the senates of priests and sisters, and various other councils and synods.[263]

He offers cautions too, in arguing for greater involvement in selecting bishops. A nostalgic or utopian desire to "return to the past" is to be avoided. Rather the richness of tradition of the *communio* is to be sought. Popular involvement ended in the early Church because of cultural reasons (and especially abuses), and not because such involvement was found wanting theologically.[264] He cautions that a democratic process would not necessarily choose the best candidate but adds that the same is true of the current system. He argues that involvement of the whole *communio* would add "a much needed element of accountability" bringing the bishop in closer touch with the people.[265] Finally Granfield warns against seeing the Church as a democracy. Democratisation in some form could help to draw the Church's resources specifically the sense of the faithful, into the choice of its bishops. Such leaders are not mere legal representatives, however, but shepherds who have both the responsibility and authority to lead.[266]

Concern for practical involvement at a grassroot level that still serves a larger, structured ecclesial framework is described by Granfield in "The Local Church as a Center of Communication and Control."[267] Here he again applies the cybernetic model to communication in the Church, as he argues for the local church as the place where effective work can be done on the tasks of resolving conflict, adapting to different cultures, developing doctrine and improving ecumenical efforts, as well as in those areas he has previously stressed of conciliar involvement and the selection of bishops.[268]

In more recent writing though, Granfield has been more circumspect in his expectations of ecclesial dynamics. He has acknowledged practical problems and an ambiguity in the theology of the Church in the aftermath of Vatican II.[269] In regard to collegiality in particular, he offers three principles which must be considered for an effective future. Collegiality must be recognized as a "theological reality," with an apostolic foundation and ties to the local church, and with an understanding of the role of subsidiarity.[270] He stresses that success depends on the Pope. Theologically, collegiality among the bishops is bound up with their head. Practically, the pope must draw on collegiality if it is to survive.[271] Finally, he maintains that "collegiality is essentially dialogic."[272] The pope and the bishops must interact with each other and with the whole Church in order to lead properly, as difficult as such processes might be.[273]

Granfield combines his insights into the interrelationship of tasks and responsibilities within the magisterium and of the magisterium within the Church and the world, in *The Limits of the Papacy*. In a chapter devoted to the sense of the faithful, he draws on the historical and systematic work he has done earlier, and uses these in conjunction with the work of other key authors to show the possibilities for the *sensus fidelium* twenty-five years after the opening of Vatican II.[274] Regarding the *sensus fidelium* as "an essential element in the life of the Church," he sees it as important for the pope, "himself one of the *fideles*," to operate within the context of the faith of the whole body of believers.[275]

He offers several notions that might inform this context. The positions held by the faithful may not be actual expressions of the *sensus fidelium*. Granfield again observes that it is a "spiritual reality," not a matter of sociology or of "counting heads."[276] Here, interestingly, he has shifted away from an earlier willingness to attempt a practical assessment of consensus, toward a position that sees the source in a more complex light. He stresses that "the *sensus fidelium* is not self-sufficient," but rather is "necessarily related" to the Church's pastors, who have the responsibility to determine its legitimate expressions.[277] At the same time. he sees the sense of the faithful and the magisterium as interdependent.[278] He asserts, "broad consultation should be part of the process by which the Church teaches, even when it teaches infallibly."[279] He notes the responsibility that was considered to be attached to the Pope's exercise of infallibility even by the Fathers of Vatican I who would not impose a juridical demand.[280]

Addressing himself to the issue of what limits to the papacy the sense of the faithful may involve, Granfield writes,

> The Pope, then, is limited by the *sensus fidelium* in that he cannot neglect the faith of his fellow believers and should recognize it as one among many channels by which God's self-communication is transmitted.[281]

Granfield elaborates a view of how such "moral" limits might operate, by discussing the reception of Church teaching.[282] Here he makes clear that the complete exercise of teaching is a process. In the "intriguing theoretical case" where reception would be lacking in "a significant group of committed Catholics" Granfield cites both Avery Dulles and Joseph Ratzinger as saying that such a response would indicate that an infallible definition had not occurred.[283] In reception Granfield sees the movement of a teaching that is guided by the Spirit in the community's "sense." By its nature, reception occurs over time.[284] Within the process, the Pope "can expect opposition, criticism, and at times disloyalty, even though objectively his actions may be for the good of the Church."[285]

Granfield notes that non-reception need not be an example of "disobedience or recalcitrance," but may indicate that a law is "unreasonable" or "unworkable" in a given context. Reception might still occur after a process of clarification.[286] He further observes that such negative reactions imply the possibility of actual dissent from official teachings. Distinguishing private and public forms, Granfield accepts a legitimacy in each, discussing the varying realizations of seriousness that pertain to them, and maintaining throughout the necessarily interactive quality of the decisions and responsibilities of those among the magisterium, the theologians, and the general faithful.[287]

As Granfield discusses the significant factors involved in the inclusion of the *sensus fidelium* with other elements in the Church, he adds a depth to the understanding of each aspect, especially as it is interwoven with others. As his views have developed, they have gained complexity and he has become more and more hesitant to claim final judgment on the expressions of the sense of the faithful. In *The Limits of the Papacy* in particular, this tentativeness or ambiguity in regard to practical, contemporary assessment of the voice of the *sensus fidelium* in specific matters is not the result of specific practical problems, nor the failure of any particular participants in the process. Rather Granfield's thorough systematic description of responsibilities among all the faithful, with members of the hierarchy included, illustrates the inherent tentativeness in the steps of the process of the teaching and reception of doctrine in time. Such hesitancy acknowledges the working of the Spirit in the interaction of the several pertinent elements in the Church, each with its own charisms and tasks. "Final" judgment is approached only when sufficient time has lapsed to let the interactions, false starts and clarifications include the contributions of all.

## *Bernard Sesboüé*

In an important article, Bernard Sesboüé examines the magisterium and dogmatic teachings in the practical light of how they are understood and received by the faithful.[288] Concerned over whether dogma has a vital role in the Church, he finds that the modern Christian sees it as something extrinsic; an abstract thing which when it is presented without reasonable argument "does violence to liberty and to life."[289] He thus tries to understand and overcome a "dogmatic mentality" with the strength of the tradition, rooted in an ancient sense of community.[290]

Sesboüé identifies this mentality as the product of recent (post-Tridentine) times.[291] Although he notes that the modern era presented "an extremely difficult historical situation" for the Catholic understanding of the Church, he faults a move to "formalization" for reducing the understanding of doctrinal authority to an "ecclesial 'monophysism'" where "the voice of the Church is no longer at all considered in its density and its inevitable relativity of language, but it is conceived as immediately divine word."[292] The continually more restrictive approach to doctrine that culminated in *Humanae Generis* resulted in the mindset of believers undergoing "a ruinous split between the objective side of faith, its continuous profession, and its subjective side, the act of confessing and of giving witness."[293]

Sesboüé traces the historical development of the dogmatic mentality, from the eighteenth century.[294] He identifies several "ruptures and disconnections." With the loss of a sense of *koinonia*, "the word of authority in the Church becomes an estranged voice: that which it affirms has lost the original clarity which permits the good Christians and their communities to spontaneously recognize it."[295] There is a cultural rupture where the ability of the Church to present the Gospel in the world is made harder.[296] A "crisis of confidence in words" results, where the institution is no longer criticized, but dismissed completely.[297]

Sesboüé suggests that returning to the lessons of the early Church can provide a key to the dogmatic problem. In the first four ecumenical councils, he sees evidence of dogma operating for the good of the living community, which was aided by the clarifications produced in the practice and confession of the faith.[298] Unity was directly tied to doctrine. He observes that "the refusal to consent to a new language expressed in fact the loss of communion in the faith."[299] Sesboüé further describes the living nature of such definitions, saying they were "inserted in the continued movement of ecclesial life" as both *"a result and a point of departure* in the experience formed by the Church from the sense of its faith."[300] He sees too, in the actual, conflictual process of reception of the councils, a key connection between meaning and the community's action, noting, "the definition is not separable with regard to its meaning, from the *act of reception* that the Church makes."[301] It is precisely in the difficulties experienced in the process of reception that the "extraordinarily vigorous investment of the act of faith of the whole body of the Church" is realized.[302]

As a second illustration, Sesboüé describes the shift in understanding of the definitions of faith produced by Trent. Where early councils intended authoritative teaching and the drawing together of the community in faith, the canons of Trent have come to be seen as "articles of faith" in a different sense. In the context of the Reformation, it was necessary to define and distinguish the elements of belief "necessary for salvation," yet Trent itself left open the possibility of later theological contextualizing and interpretation. Even with the inclusion of anathemas in its canons, it did not intend to identify "formally revealed" propositions that could be held in a nonhistorical manner. Following Trent, however, and especially with Vatican I, dogmatic teaching came to be understood in a more limiting, a-historical way.[303]

In the light of these historical observations, Sesboüé offers three reflections. A dogma is "relative" in that it is historically conditioned and cannot be deduced through abstract analysis alone. It is definitive in that a true understanding of the faith is distinguished from alternative, incompatible meanings. At the same time a dogma does not exhaust the meaning of what it discloses. Any new expressions must contain the truth already given, but such an expression may say more. Secondly, the "hierarchy of dogmas" concerns both the relative authority given to statements by the magisterium and the relation particular statements bear to the core of the faith. Finally, the strength or "definitiveness" of a statement is relative to the duration of time it exists. In its original period, it carries a great deal of weight and may well be essential to the resolution of a crisis. As new eras are entered, however, the importance of the statement for meeting issues that confront the community may lessen or shift.[304]

With these reflections on history and interpretation, Sesboüé outlines key aspects for understanding the role of the magisterium. Revelation is not a matter of passing on propositions, but of realizing an interpersonal, covenantal relationship with God.[305] Rather than accepting the dogmatic mentality which is settled and "riveted to the past," the community should realize its eschatological, "not yet," relationship to the truth which cannot claim a complete understanding of it.[306]

Central to the process is the realization that the entire *"catholica"* is involved in the covenant. Infallibility and indefectability in the faith are aspects of the whole Church, and the "hierarchical organs ought to be considered in their ministerial relation to this fundamental infallibility." The People of God is the locus of the witness given to revelation. Sesboüé sees the renewing of a focus on consensus in the community as a slow process. The "spontaneous communication" of the faith in the "fraternal and hierarchical communion" is no longer facilitated by a shared language, because of the way authority has been used especially since the narrowing view of dogma seen with Vatican I.[307]

Sesboüé describes the responsibility of the magisterium as the task of building up the communion: "a *diakonia* at the service of the *koinônia*." As it fulfills its teaching function, it would do well to remember the limited nature of its own words. These carry authority to bring unity of faith in the Church, but this unity "is a creation always to be remade."[308] To do it well, the magisterium must engage the whole Church in the process of communication, using its expressions to draw the community closer together.[309]

In an appendix to his article, Sesboüé notes that it was originally delivered as a lecture, and he addresses a question that was raised concerning the reception of the encyclical, *Humanae Vitae*.[310] He remarks first, that in taking responsibility for the decision after the Council, instead of presenting it for consideration among the bishops where its issuance would have had authority that was "infinitely greater," the pope chose to take a "prophetic" stance. He declines to judge whether this strategy was the best that could have been used.[311]

Interestingly, he says it is too early to say whether the teaching of *Humanae Vitae* has been received. He notes that a lack of any response would have made the question easier to settle. The strong response has indicated that an important matter is being confronted.[312] He adds that the debates engendered "express [the] genesis of meaning," by which the teaching will be understood. He adds that

> this meaning is not itself situated in the terms of a dialectic of yes or no, but that it will be found very likely beyond the present perspective. The meaning is not brought to maturity by these deductions, but by an integration of the point of view of the encyclical in a perspective more vast than will be brought by a certain correction by discussion of its unilateral aspect.[313]

He sees this process as beginning in episcopal letters. Since the input of the bishops was not included prior to the encyclical, it "has been practically demanded" afterwards.[314]

Sesboüé notes that in the immediate response to the encyclical, its non-infallible nature was often presented as evidence that "there is a great chance that it is mistaken."[315] He sees this approach as further evidence of the entrenchment of the dogmatic mentality in this situation harming the exercise of normal papal authority. The gravity of the issue raised is missed because of a rejection of the encyclical that is based in an "all or nothing" approach to magisterial teaching.[316]

## William M. Thompson

Throughout the present study, reference has been made to an important article by William M. Thompson, "Sensus Fidelium and Infallibility." Thompson examines the topic historically, and describes the particular aspect of the sense of the faithful that is characteristic of each era. He sees the Patristic period as focused on the *consensus omnium*, with the members of the community understood as united with Christ. In the Middle Ages, the internal aspect of *sensus fidei* was studied. The Reformation stressed the priesthood of believers who live in obedience to God's word. With the Counter-Reformation, the emphasis is on the *Ecclesia in credendo*. The Patristic insight is retained, while the hierarchy grows in importance. Thompson observes that Franzelin and Scheeben "obliquely accepted" the Patristic view. The difference between the hierarchy and laity is stressed, however, and "the ground is well prepared" for with the sense of the faithful being eventually seen as a passive element of the Church. With Newman, there is a return to a historical under" standing of the *sensus fidelium*, an emphasis on the Patristic view, and a concern that the laity be educated and involved.[317]

Thompson examines the relationship of the magisterium to the issue of the *sensus fidelium*, by reviewing the official views expressed since the Council of Trent.[318] These sources exhibit "the traditional emphasis on the faithful as both a source of church doctrine . . . and as infallible."[319] He sees "the seemingly 'hierarchical' mentality of a Scheeben and Vatican I" brought into balance by an active view at Vatican II, which regained the insights of the Patristic era.[320]

In his later "systematic observation" Thompson reviews key scriptural warrants and links his understanding of the *phronema* expressed by Newman to the understanding of knowing developed by Rahner, thus drawing on a Thomistic approach to "connatural" knowledge that is attuned to issues in modern fundamental theology.³²¹ He argues for balance in understanding the ecclesial importance of the sense of the faithful, and follows Congar's lead in warning against two opposite "poles"; that of seeing the magisterium's role as merely approving the views of the faithful, or that of seeing the faithful's role as merely listening to the magisterium.³²² He desires to go beyond the view of Congar in asserting that the *sensus fidelium* is a *regula fidei* when it is "properly understood and interpreted by the magisterium."³²³ Following Gregory Baum, he claims that a proper understanding of the *sensus fidelium* teaches that infallibility is not solely the province of the magisterium, and in fact, allows "a certain 'demythologization' of the hierarchy, by which we can understand the latter in its proper proportions."³²⁴

Thompson finally suggests that the *sensus fidelium* may enhance ecumenical discussion with the Russian Orthodox Church, as it provides a link with the insight expressed there by the notion of *Sobornost*.³²⁵ He suggests too, that the *sensus fidelium* may help in developing an understanding of reception of official teaching by the faithful. Thompson offers the view, that if it is seen "not in a purely positivistic and juridical sense, but in a personal, human and spiritual sense," the process of reception has existed in the Church since the earliest times.³²⁶ He sees "good evidence" that through the fourth century conciliar authority came "not so much from a formal or juridical power, but precisely from the importance *for the life of the whole Church* their teaching had, as further clarifications of the scriptural faith."³²⁷ Thompson's intent is to show that properly understood in relation to each other, both the *sensus fidelium* and the magisterium are "essential to the *full* life of the Church."³²⁸

Thompson does not offer any advice on identifying the sense of the faithful in action, but rather argues for its importance, with implications especially, for how the relationship of the hierarchy and an active faithful should be regarded. In a later work he presents a creative theological approach to fostering the practical appropriation of the tradition in contemporary theology, where he consciously links the Church's "saints" to the suggestion of Newman that the Church "consult" the faithful.[329]

## Jean-Marie R. Tillard

The *sensus fidelium* has remained a central focus in the theology of Jean-Marie R. Tillard.[330] Several important historical and systematic aspects of the sense of the faithful are included in Tillard's work, and are drawn together in an address he gave to a conference in 1974 at the Dominican College in Ottawa, commemorating the seven hundredth anniversary of the death of Thomas Aquinas.[331] His paper also demonstrates the polemical possibilities and controversial issues that mark the contemporary discussion. He introduces the topic by saying that it is as important in the midst of controversy following *Humanae Vitae* as it was at the time of the *Rambler* affair. He sees the *sensus fidelium* as important for understanding the "very nature of the Church" and the "concrete relationships" of its internal structure, but notes that this source has many aspects which have not been studied sufficiently.[332]

Tillard cites examples where the faithful and the hierarchy have not been in "full concordance" and asks whether the stress in the Church should be on "popular faith" or "educated faith."[333] He speaks of the dissonance that exists as being "between official attitudes and the spontaneous awareness of the faithful."[334] Tillard claims that one can "grasp the *sensus fidelium*, in its most usual daily exercise, even before any attempt has been made to define it."[335]

Tillard believes that the emphasis of the Roman Catholic Church on the *sensus fidelium* when considered with the "unanimous *consensus* of the Fathers and Doctors" is "one of the major threads making up the fabric of Tradition," setting it apart from other Christian communions. For the Roman Church it is "infinitely more" than a balancing agent for the hierarchy. Acknowledging an influence from Max Weber, he calls it "the bearer of a conviction on which the Magisterium itself must draw when it feels the need to affirm the content in the most authoritative manner at its disposal."[336] The immediacy that Tillard claims for the contemporary action of the *sensus fidelium*, as a link to the tradition even when it gives rise to dissonance, is apparent when he writes,

> For this same *sensus fidelium*, which often expresses a certain dissatisfaction towards the attitudes or declarations of the hierarchical authorities (as in the case of the Arian crisis studied by Newman, or in the upheavals caused by *Humanae Vitae*), is also the element upon which the Roman Magisterium, subsequently appealing to pontifical infallibility, based itself in the only two dogmatic definitions that it has made.[337]

Tillard reviews the history of the two Marian promulgations, and claims that it is the sense of the Church's faith "already living in the consciousness of the people" that is seen as primary, with the Pope's action itself operating secondarily. His expressions are "conditioned by the *lived* content of ecclesial faith."[338] Tillard asserts that even though these definitions are given with various "nuances and emphases," they

> imply the linking, the convergence of two great forces, on the one hand the spontaneous attitude and instinctive perception of the faithful, and on the other hand the more and more explicit accord of the various leaders of the local churches.[339]

He adds that his identification of the *sensus fidelium* with "the ordinary faithful" is consistent with the views of Newman and Perrone, and follows the lead of Melchior Cano.[340]

Tillard sees in the preparatory papers for *Ineffabilis Deus* "the slow conquest by the *sensus fidelium*."[341] He recognizes that in this definition, other motives may have been involved, "in particular the desire to assert papal power."[342] Yet, he sees the leadership of the magisterium and the "action" of the people's faith as "complementary principles." Tillard asserts,

> Cut off from this essential reference to a "lived truth" which in a certain way precedes and conditions it, the act of the Roman Magisterium involved in what is called "dogmatic definition" has no meaning any more: it is a decision without an object.[343]

Tillard claims that when the Roman Catholic Church acts in what others see as its "most autocratic" way, it is actually "strictly dependent upon the body of the faithful."[344]

Tillard next examines the Scriptural texts that support the reality of the work of the Holy Spirit through all the baptized.[345] He connects the aspect of faith described there, which he characterizes as "often more intuitive than reasoned, and coming from the Holy Spirit," with the *phronema* described by Newman and the instinct for truth described by Aquinas.[346] He warns against an overly "optimistic" approach that would identify the *sensus fidelium* with "every widespread opinion" or see it as "purely and simply identical with what the faithful think, say and do."[347] To approach the topic in these ways "would be to confuse the *sensus fidelium* with a simplistic subjectivism."[348] Errors are possible, and Tillard relates examples from history where important individual teachers and even whole groups of believers have erred.[349] He stresses that the objective expression of the faith must be the guide in judging such cases. Tillard asserts, "The *sensus fidelium* implies, at every level, submission to the objective data of faith." The "primary norm" for this data is Scripture.[350]

Nonetheless, while revelation is given to the whole Church to live and understand, theologians, those specializing in "educated faith," play a key role. Those trained in scientific techniques must help others in the Church grow in understanding, raise questions and keep it from a "slow suffocation" which would result if a fundamentalist approach were employed.[351] Tillard sees the task of the magisterium as fostering the growth of the faithful, and not merely a matter of repeating definitions. He adds, however, that a stress on "educated faith" need not detract from the importance of "popular faith," inasmuch as Scripture itself and the devotions that have long been part of the tradition contain elements of popular expression.[352] The faith of all believers is incarnational at its roots, and is lived out in human terms. To interact in a living way in human cultures, the expressions of popular faith must be understood as linked to "popular religion" and accepted even though they are recognized as having a temporary nature.[353] It is because such expressions change, that the movement of the faithful through history requires new expressions of their tradition.[354]

Tillard argues that the tradition is based in the "acts and attitudes" of the early Christians that were prior even to sacred writings. In addition to the influence of worship, he suggests that believers gain the "transmission of [the] mysterious knowledge of God" by an "osmosis" with the "Christian background." Their knowledge is thus not merely from "conceptual teaching."[355] According to Tillard,

> The *sensus fidelium* does far more here than merely give a keen feeling for doctrine it creates a climate, a collective instinct, which will be as it were the lived data to which each believer will feel himself more or less consciously linked from the very fact that he means to avoid any breach with his original background.[356]

The Church community is not "merely a school of thought," and when doctrines are defined within it, especially as in the case of the Marian dogmas with their roots in piety, the finished doctrines cannot separate themselves from the sort of beginnings that originally bore them.[357] Theologians—those of the "educated faith" who study the *sensus fidelium*—must consider the nature of such "truth-ingestation" to understand the "instinctive conduct" that is connected with "popular faith."[358] In addition, those concerned with the area of morals in particular must include the perspectives of philosophy and the sciences.[359] Tillard claims that with the sense of the faithful, "Here an affirmation made in the name of Christian allegiance bears upon a matter the knowledge of which in depth does not depend solely upon the outlook of faith."[360] He suggests in particular, that those who consider moral questions of sexuality may "risk a new trial of Galileo" if they use only "classical" perspectives, "which [are] contradicted by the daily experiences of *simplices* and researchers."[361]

Citing the changes made in the past fifty years, in magisterial teaching on "collective justice and questions relating to property," Tillard suggests that new developments need not be seen as "a relativization of truth," but may be "an evolution in conformity with the nature of this truth." Where Scripture is silent on modern questions, it is vital not to "simply . . . repeat the 'traditional' themes which precisely constitute the problem." At the same time, the consensus of scientists is not to be accepted uncritically, without consideration of the human image that is taught in Scripture. Tillard asserts confidently, "The intimate interaction between the practical intuition of the *sensus fidelium* and theology's efforts to scrutinize and assess this *praxis* thus ensures the progress of the people of God in truth."[362] Drawing on the image of *conspiratio* offered by Newman, Tillard adds,

> *Sensus fidelium* and Magisterium, popular faith and educated faith: it is through the *conspiratio* of these two forms of the action of the Spirit in the people of God that the latter can live in a fidelity to the Word of God that remains distinct from a sterile fundamentalism.[363]

In Tillard's view, the magisterium finds its role in a "service of discernment," not in an "authority added on to that of the Word of God."[364] *Conspiratio* works through a process of "osmosis," where different parts of the Church, while pursuing "one same goal through one same fidelity," interact with each other and the world, "to manifest that faith in communion with the progress of mankind."[365]

In another place, Tillard has described the active work of the Church, especially during times of change as a "symbiosis." The hierarchy and the faithful as they emphasize praxis as an expression of the faith draw on a combination of the *sensus fidelium* and "remembrance." The community's very identity is guaranteed by this active living of tradition.[366] As the institutionalized offices in particular serve this "remembrance" and the *sensus fidelium* expresses the charismatic instinct in immediate ways, there is a creative tension that engenders progress even while drawing on the authoritative foundation of the tradition.[367]

Ecumenical considerations have been an important aspect of Tillard's theology and his treatment of the *sensus fidelium*. He closed his Ottawa address with the hope that other Christians might no longer find "an insurmountable contradiction" between their dependence on revelation and the Roman magisterium seen in the light of a proper understanding of the sense of the faithful.[368] In discussing the role of "reception" in ecumenical dialogue, he has stressed the importance of a critical "re-evaluating and re-confessing of the apostolic faith itself," arguing that even though painstaking work is required, Christian unity is not to be obtained at the expense of the tradition.[369] He asserts that "mutual understanding" is not enough. There must be "mutual understanding based on the apostolic faith."[370]

While considering reception within the Roman Church, Tillard has stressed that the *sensus fidelium* "does not create the truth," but recognizes it. Expression is the task of the hierarchy. Reception of teaching by the faithful shows the completion of a process of "profound harmony" that is a characteristic of the "corporate personality" of the Church.[371] He adds that "'reception' sets in motion a process of clarification by critical reflection which furthers the knowledge of the faith."[372]

Tillard's insistence on the proper foundation for any unity is illustrated again in his treatment of pluralism in the Church, where at the same time, he exhibits a rigor in drawing out the tradition as an active player in the real attempts to achieve unity among those with differing ecclesiologies.[373] Tillard sees the "challenge of the Gospel" as being "precisely in making it possible to achieve a unity of communion (*koinonia*) within which diversity and pluralism are seen as riches and not as dangers."[374] Tillard cites several historical conflicts that illustrate that the Church "has always been pluriform, even during the most striking periods of unity."[375] These conflicts included issues in liturgical practice, piety, and understanding of the sacraments.[376] He notes that after the separation of Eastern and Western Churches, the West "became gradually more uniform." Tillard asserts that the Eastern Churches have maintained a better type of unity precisely because they have allowed a diversity of expression in different cultural settings.[377] He sees many of the problems in the West during the Reformation as due to the "clumsiness" of Rome, in demanding uniformity as a mistaken strategy to achieve unity.[378]

He sees the current pluralism in theology as the effect of "a more fundamental level of pluralism of cultures, contexts and practical options in the Catholicity of the Church." He sees the role of theology both in the past and now, as being the "faithful translation—into the fabric of a community of men and women who are proud of their own characteristics." Most importantly, this task is not solely an intellectual one. It is precisely here that the role of the *sensus fidelium* is seen, in "the whole network of attitudes, signs, reactions and intuitions inherent in [it]."[379]

At stake in Tillard's view, is nothing less than the embodiment of the Gospel in human terms. thus, he cites the importance of cultural context in the witness of Francis of Assisi, Dietrich Bonhoeffer, Martin Luther King, and Oscar Romero, as well as that which "in the power of the spirit, the African, the Peruvian peasant, the Indian woman, the oppressed labourer and the sinner (whether he is rich or poor) who is imprisoned within his wrong attitude, 'feels' in his heart or her heart about the Gospel."[380] In such contexts, "the objective sense or meaning of Scripture" can be understood as expressing diverge yet unified ways. The magisterium retains the key role of seeing that it is the full tradition of this revelation that is presented.[381] In addition Tillard notes the role to be played by reason, observing,

> It will distill a coherent and articulate expression from the common faith, whilst taking into account the authenticity of its translation, in communion with the faith of every community of believers, into the soul of this particular people or this group of human beings.[382]

The magisterium thus guards the ancient tradition, but it does so as this tradition is given to the community to live out. Tillard observes that it is possible that in particular societies there is a risk that communities will serve political ends rather than the Gospel. To retain the right sense of purpose, ecclesial communities must maintain their connection with the wider communion of believers.[383]

In this process, theology has the active role of translating the Gospel and the community's understanding of it.[384] As theology does this in a Church characterized by pluralism that is rooted in "a praxis of communion and unity," it will attend to the expressions of both the magisterium and the *sensus fidelium*.[385]

## *Emilien Lamirande*

Some of the papers given at the 1974 Ottawa conference and published in the text *Foi populaire, foi savante* edited by Tillard, give added insights which though addressed to particular points, contribute to an overall understanding of the sense of the faithful.

The problem of evaluating the quality of information obtained by public opinion is considered from the side of the historian by Emilien Lamirande.[386] He asserts that in cases such as the definition of the Assumption, the historian must ask if genuine information is available to support the meaning given, and particularly whether the people's "spontaneous" instincts were moved by such issues in the same way that they are then appropriated. He poses the question of whether public opinion is engaged in a vital way by such matters, or whether the views attributed to them have somehow been prompted or even manipulated.[387] He asks further how an assessment of public opinion could discover the "sentiments" of those who remain silent in their faith and piety.[388]

Lamirande describes the ease with which the historian can find examples where consensus has not helped in the support of doctrines. The people were involved in divisive errors in fourth century Africa as well as sixteenth century Europe. He points out that they followed false trails in regard to issues that include the pope, the sacraments, the cult of saints, and the relations between East and West. Lamirande asks how the response of many of the faithful and even some of the saints has been on the side of error, and questions whether the legitimacy of their "instinct" is supported sufficiently by saying that they have remained in relationship with the magisterium.[389]

Lamirande concludes that it is precisely in the interaction between the faithful and the magisterium that one finds the validity of the *sensus fidelium*.[390] It is possible to reduce the result of this interaction to the judgment of the magisterium, yet to do so seems to take away any role it might have as a genuine "criterion." He asks, however, if the alternative would not give it a purely interior meaning that is independent of that given by the official teachers. Such a view would make it something very different from the source it has been recognized to be.[391]

## Fernand Dumont

The views expressed by Tillard in the 1974 colloquium were discussed at the same conference by Fernand Dumont in "Remarques critiques pour une theologie du 'consensus fidelium.'"[392] Dumont takes up two main points; the epistemological difficulty in understanding the notions of consensus in the faith and "popular religion," and the phenomenological problem of seeing how popular religion is to be understood in relation to tradition, while maintaining a sufficient respect for history and sociology.[393]

The epistemology of the *consensus fidelium* is complicated by the number of terms which may be connected with it, as evidenced in Tillard's treatment. Concepts such as "perception," "spontaneity," "lived truth," "intuition," "fundamental inclination" and others represent different elements in the sense of the faithful. According to Dumont, the meanings of these phrases are not made clear enough by Tillard.[394] Additionally, terms like "explication" and "incarnation" of lived religion are connected to popular religion among the faithful, but this is done without due attention to the way such religion is understood in the "systems of interpretation," as well as the "theories" and "doctrines" that characterize not only religion but "popular culture."[395]

To clarify how the many faceted sense of the faithful may be understood, Dumont suggests that a distinction be made between "faith," "expression," and "norm."[396] "Faith" is what refers the believer to Jesus Christ, who is at the core of the "Christian drama." This drama is itself, the "content of faith."[397] "Expression" refers to the cultural form taken by the drama. This expression is not contained completely in language, but also includes the "historical universe of signs and those practices by which the human person discovers and establishes his/her rapport with the world."[398] The discernment that is established in these terms may be scholarly or popular in nature, but in either case it is of a fundamental type like that employed by the first believers when they came face to face with the one "who called himself the Son of the Father."[399]

"Norms" then are the criteria that provide guides by which expressions are examined. These fruits of theology and the magisterium are not to be seen as though they "constitute the *objective* content of the religious *sentiment*" which can somehow be separated out and examined. The definitions of the magisterium and the reflections of theologians are not to be equated with the experience of faith itself. At the same time it is understood that these criteria grow out of this faith and its expressions.[400]

The *consensus fidelium* is certainly present in both the levels of "faith" and its "expressions." Dumont observes further though, that it is in the historical relationship between the lived faith and the "norms" which are found in doctrinal expression, that ambiguity is found.[401] He asks in what sense or senses the Marian definitions or the early Christological debates were "required." Specifically, he asks whether the one resulted from popular religion and the other from the threat of heresy.[402] He acknowledges that, following Newman, it is possible to describe criteria by which development can be understood. Yet he finds that questions still remain as to how consensus is to be determined in regard to modern issues. Dumont asks, for instance, why there was consultation in regard to the Assumption and not for the teaching of *Humanae Vitae*. He opts for an ongoing image for the working out of consensus, maintaining, "The dialectic of the faith, of the expression and the norm, by presenting itself first under the guise of epistemology, is a living dialectic."[403] All of its levels must be considered in order to understand it fully.

When Dumont turns to the "phenomenological" problem of consensus, he first notes the tendency to polarize the components of faith and norms. The way that faith is found in the heart and the way it is expressed in theological definitions have been set against each other.[404] Doctrinal norms have been given the lead role in modern times. The movement to standardized definitions is clear since Trent, in the catechisms, polemics with the Reformers and the efforts specifically in opposition to "popular" religious forms. A misleading sense of unity has also been found in actions where definitions have been presented by a centralized source.[405] Dumont notes too in modern Catholicism a form of theologizing that goes beyond its appropriate role in relation to the norms for faith, to exhibit a "troubling tendency to autonomy."[406]

Dumont finds particularly important the fact that "the double polarization of *faith* and *norm* have impoverished the dialectical moment of *expression*."[407] Because faith lacks suitable contemporary expressions, it is left to either "an abstract transcendence or a cacophony of voices." It is not found in "the drama of contemporary culture."[408] In this context, teachings ("norms") are presented without regard for the experience of the faithful. Dumont observes that the response to *Humanae Vitae*, the decrease in practice of Confession, and other indicators show that the usefulness of the tridentine approach to theology is over.[409] He adds that in the broken down state of theology and its relations with the life of the faithful, "expression" of the sort needed for the *consensus fidelium* is suffering the effects of a prolonged state of "anemia."[410] Dumont asserts, "The crisis of *consensus fidelium* is first a crisis of expression. Cultural phenomenon is by definition phenomenon of community."[411]

Dumont advises that if creating consensus among the faithful in a cultural context that is undernourished and fragmented is problematic, it is important not to try to add more uses of it in the form of definitions, but to rekindle "the modes of expression of the faith," such as liturgy, that can develop the common faith.

and also overcome the hold of the "dialectic of law" that continues to deny genuine "expression."[412]

Dumont stresses that *sensus* and *consensus* are not only elements of "religious experience," but characteristics of the interactive internal life of a community. The *conspiratio* that occurs in the Church is formed by the movement of the Spirit in the "convergences and conflicts" of the different elements in the whole. In Tillard, Dumont does not find disagreement on this point, but the need for more emphasis. Without a focus on the need for such interaction, disagreements can lead to setting different groups in the Church—the faithful, theologians or the hierarchy—against each other.[413]

Dumont considers Tillard's description of the magisterium's role as "a service of discernment" to be an apt one but is more critical of his placement of responsibility for determining the "evangelical authenticity" of new developments. Dumont finds this task to be "ambiguous" or "even dangerous" if it is not understood properly.[414]

Dumont closes by drawing attention to what he deems to be the most important challenges in the contemporary context. The magisterium must leave behind the theological "yoke" it has had since the sixteenth century. Theologians should admit that they are in a "state of diaspora" that mirrors that of the Church itself. Dumont suggests that if both groups can open themselves to different ways of understanding their roles, the seeking of *consensus fidelium* can be not just a theological issue but the effort of the whole community.[415]

## *James Hitchcock*

In the earlier discussion of the views of St. Thomas More, the article, "Thomas More and the Sensus Fidelium," by James Hitchcock was introduced. The historical information already described will not be repeated here. What is interesting for the current discussion are Hitchcock's own views that are expressed in his critique of More. He views More's understanding of consensus, cut off to a large extent from magisterial interaction, as important in its demonstration of the need for another authority. Such an isolated expression of consensus can become stuck in a logic of conservatism. According to Hitchcock, More found in the "popular will," not "an agency of revolution but rather a force for preservation."[416] At the same time, a consensus of the faithful that is developed in isolation has no other reference point which can balance or challenge popular views.[417]

Hitchcock suggests that "the very consistency of More's position" shows that consensus cannot serve as a sole carrier of tradition.[418] He argues further that it must necessarily be an agent for preservation. Any innovation in the views of the majority must begin as minority opinions, and must thus be rejected by the mass of believers or gain acceptance because of the action of a higher authority.[419] Hitchcock closes his reflections with the statement, "In the Church of today as in the Church of More's time, the *sensus fidelium* will, if properly understood, serve as a principle of conservation."[420]

### Jose Morales

A view similar to Hitchcock's has been expressed in a slightly different way by Jose Morales, in an attempt not long after Vatican II to place the magisterium, theology and the sense of faith in some sort of balance.[421] Morales identifies the sense of the faithful with a "simple faith" that is realized in instinct and the holy living of a Christian life, in contrast to any analytical, theological activities.[422] He distinguishes the roles of the hierarchy, theologians and the laity, seeing in theologians a responsibility for analyzing and understanding the deposit of faith and in the hierarchy the responsibility of authoritatively expressing and unifying the faith that is given to the Church as a whole.[423]

Morales finds in the conserving quality of the simple faithful, a need for balance and challenge to develop, that must be elicited by the magisterium and a solid life of worship.[424] The overriding point made by Morales is that the various levels in the Church, each distinct in their contribution and gifts, are meant to interact for the good of the whole.[425] Balance and "equilibrium" are essential. He cites the Arian crisis as an example from the Church's experience where this equilibrium was broken. Morales observes that in specific, temporary circumstances it may fall to one voice among the several needed to "speak for all the Church." The *sensus fidelium* fulfilled this task for a while during the fourth century. The Church as a whole struggled then, as it must throughout history, to restore a proper balance within itself.[426] Tensions may exist within the Church when the different levels function. Yet when each truly listens to the others according to its proper place, they work together to create the *sensus Ecclesiae*.[427]

## *Jesús Sancho Bielsa*

Jesús Sancho Bielsa has examined the meaning of the *sensus fidei* in several contexts with particular attention to its relationship with the doctrine of infallibility. His *Infallibilidad del Pueblo de Dios* (cited above) appeared in 1979 as an extended version of his original doctoral thesis which examined the sense of the faithful in *Lumen Gentium*. Noting that Vatican I clearly taught that this infallibility may be expressed by the pope, and that Vatican II contextualized this same element in the bishops and the people of God themselves, Sancho asserts his goal as an attempt to show the organic relationship of the different aspects of the Church that express a single infallibility. He is, however, clear in his insistence that no unified understanding of this aspect of the Church's teaching is possible without the central role of the magisterium.[428]

Sancho argues that the infallibility of the Church, and thus the magisterium, is given through a participation in Christ's own freedom from error precisely to overcome the effects of sin in fallible human beings.[429] In Thomas Aquinas in particular he finds the notion that infallibility is only attributable to God. All humans are fallible, including those who make up the hierarchy as they pursue their normal tasks. Yet these pastors perform a special role within the Church, and when they act in their capacity as protectors of the Church's faith, they are given the gift of being kept from error.[430] Drawing on the work of Aquinas, Torquemada, Cano, and Mancio (a less well known professor of theology in sixteenth century Salamanca), Sancho argues that even in divergent contexts and with divergent interests the teachings of these authors "converge" to support the truth of the infallibility of the Church. He notes that following the lead of these figures, the topic has been taken up in the work of many others.[431]

When he discusses Vatican I's treatment of infallibility, Sancho acknowledges the organic relationship of the charism as expressed by the pope and as given to the whole Church. However, Sancho clearly sees in the pope's unique role a focusing agent for any expressions of the infallibility in the Church, and by extension, a limiting agent on the expression or understanding of the sense of the faithful.[432]

He later argues that the key to clarifying Vatican II's understanding of the sense of the faithful lies in understanding the distinction between the infallibility and indefectibility of the Church. The Church as indefectible is protected in its life; it will not fall away from its goal through the human frailties that plague other endeavors. Sancho notes that infallibility is a special aspect of indefectibility by which the Church is kept from erring in doctrinal matters.[433] This area is the province of the magisterium, who are given the specific job of discerning and protecting the expressions of the tradition. They thus exercise the Church's infallibility *in docendo*. Sancho connects the infallibility of the people of God as a whole to the notion of their infallibility *in credendo*. He observes that the Council did not describe this role of the faithful as a merely passive function.[434] At the same time, he sees the expression of their active role in the practical living out of the faith. He writes,

> The function of the people of God in the infallibility *in credendo* is exercised in the life of faith, without any public actualization [*actuación*] in the name of Christ. This belongs to the infallible magisterium of the hierarchy, and is done in two ways: one extraordinary and solemn, the other ordinary.[435]

The importance of understanding the expression of the sense of the faithful predominantly in relation to the exercise of the magisterium is evident again when Sancho describes the "social connotation" of the *sensus fidei*.[436] Noting the lack of agreement that attends expressions of a "communal sense" (*sentido común*), he attributes such limitations to "risk of fallibility inherent in the human condition" and to the effects of sin.[437] The genuine sense of the faithful (*sensus fidei*) as described at Vatican II is a gift granted to the Body of Christ. When the people are united in expressing their faith this is evidence of the work of God. The "communal sense," sociologically considered, is in fact "no more than an analogy." The sense of the faithful as a supernatural gift is inherently different. In creating consensus through it the Spirit acts and assures that the Church as a whole believes infallibly.[438] Sancho notes that infallibility is attributed to Church, not to the *sensus fidei*.[439] This sense is a "supernatural faculty" given to all believers so the Church can "conserve, defend and develop" the tradition "under the direction of the sacred magisterium instituted by Christ as a supreme guarantee."[440]

The eclipse of an active faithful in Sancho's understanding of the *sensus fidei* is made quite clear in his section concerning the "Relation of the 'sensus fidei' with the Magisterium."[441] Here Sancho notes that there is some "suspicion" that the sense of the faithful might provide a "legal avenue for action that is independent, anarchic or oppositional to the magisterium."[442] In resolving such attempts, "the intervention of the magisterium is unavoidable," as it exercises its function of protecting the faith. He adds that in the genuine expression of the *sensus fidei*, ultimately "it is not possible to have friction with the magisterium": both elements in the Church "move in the same direction."[443]

While speaking of the organic relationship within the various members of the body, Sancho focuses solely on the clarifying role of the magisterium within the Church, leaving behind any movements within the faithful that might cause dissonance.[444] Obvious by their omission are any references to historical cases where the faithful served the Church in a unique way by retaining orthodox belief, as in the examples of Newman.[445]

Sancho considers the *sensus fidei* solely in its relation to the Church's infallibility. Because of this focus, the view he gives of the role of the faithful is reduced to that which is left by a magisterium that has a unique role in actively defining the faith of the Church. He himself concludes,

> In the final analysis, the doctrine of the sense of the faith comes to be the culmination of the long itinerary of infallibility, by completing the prior teaching on the infallible Magisterium.[446]

In 1980 Sancho published a short article in which he described the sense of the faith as a topic treated at Vatican II which had not been developed afterward with "sufficient dilligence."[447] Citing his early book, he here describes the *sensus fidei* as the "technical formula" used by Vatican II to refer to the infallibility which Vatican I taught was expressed by the pope, but which is to be understood within the context of the whole Church. Sancho stresses here too, that the sense of the faith is not to be identified with infallibility; it is "the channel by which infallibility is manifested."[448] Insisting again on the link between the *sensus fidei* and the exercise of the magisterium, Sancho claims the concept is "confused by a general ambiguous interpretation of the Council."[449]

Sancho sees a "typical case" of misuse of the concept in the attempt to draw on the sense of the faithful instead of "the intervention of the infallible magisterium" in interpreting "immutable moral norms."[450] Drawing on Aquinas and Torquemada he describes how the magisterium cannot dispense the faithful from adherence to the teaching of the natural law, but how it does have the role of interpreting it.[451] He warns that anyone who would attempt "to interpret the natural law or concrete applications of the natural law" with reference to the views "one believer in particular, a group of believers, or even—in theory impossible—the universal Church," in a way that would "[force] an interpretation or application contrary to the magisterium" would demonstrate in such action that he or she was not expressing the sense of the faithful.[452] Sancho insists again that in this source the Spirit moves the faithful to respond in concert with the Church's official teachers.[453]

In a later article, Sancho focuses on the role of the laity in more detail.[454] He describes the active responsibilities that the laity have through "their ordinary and concrete life" for carrying the mission of the Church into the world.[455] He notes that the laity may be distinguished as a group within the broader collection of the faithful that also includes clergy and religious, bishops and pope.[456] He cautions, however, that it is not possible to define the sense of the faithful as a property of the laity alone, in a way that positions them against the rest of the People of God or their pastors.[457] Sancho stresses here again, that it is in consensus that the Church exhibits the work of the Spirit. In regard to the sense of the faith, the laity are to be regarded not as laity, but as faithful, bound together in organic unity with those in the hierarchy who have the special functions of teachers and judges of the faith.[458]

Sancho argues (as he did in his earlier book) that as the Fathers at Vatican II considered the early versions of *Lumen Gentium*, their understanding of the sense of the faithful developed and clarified. The "opinions" that might be found among the faithful were distinguished from their actions in the world. It was in practical living that the sense of the faith expressed through the laity was seen to function.[459]

Sancho notes the particular attention given in both *Lumen Gentium* and *Gaudium et Spes* to the role of Christian marriage and family life.[460] He expresses finally his own wish that the Synod on the Laity that was approaching as he wrote would rekindle the focus on this role for the laity that he found in Vatican II.[461]

## Luigi Sartori

The problem of identifying the *sensus fidelium* is taken up by Luigi Sartori in "What is the Criterion for the *Sensus Fidelium*?" He notes that *Lumen Gentium* (# 12) recognizes in the work of Holy Spirit alone "a direct causality ('excitatur et sustenatur') in the arousal of the sense of the faith while acknowledging to the *magisterium* merely a guiding function ('sub dictu')." He sees this as removing the earlier separation of the *Ecclesia docens* and *Ecclesia discens*, and creating the need for a new way to recognize this sense.[462]

The immediate task in discussions of such tools for recognition is "to bear on concrete living conditions in order to create a Church capable of producing a valid *sensus fidei*."[463] Sartori sees the foundational "criterion" for this sense in the "discernment of prophecy."[464] To describe the ecclesial context that can "give scope to the '*sensus fidelium*,'" he lists characteristics of "fidelity to the divine" and "fidelity to the human." Under criteria for "relating to the divine," he lists the primacy of faith, the giving of the Spirit to all members, the dynamic nature of the Spirit's gifts, and consensus as the goal of the process. He describes the "consensus of teachers" as a functional, temporary criterion on the way to the ultimate goal of the "consensus of believers."[465]

Under "criteria relating to the 'human,'" Sartori stresses that anthropology teaches that communication is prior to communion. Freedom, not "mechanical repetition" must characterize the exercise of the *sensus fidei*.[466] The responses of the faithful to teaching may come in either expressions of consent or dissent.[467] A "realistic" view of communication will acknowledge that conflict is "a quite normal" aspect of response in concrete cases. Sartori notes that ambiguity now characterizes both consent and dissent, and thus a rapid response of the "sense of the believers" may be less desirable than it was in previous eras, where more direct responses were more common. He advises that consensus should be sought in the "quality" of response not in its quantity. Even where majorities are found on issues, these must be considered as part of a dialectical process, where new insights or emphases will change the results found. Sartori adds that such dynamics of conflict will especially be found when consensus is sought in ecumenical contexts.[468]

Sartori sees these criteria as "remote" characteristics of the *sensus fidelium*, ones that describe a Church that can give rise to a healthy *sensus fidei*.[469] He also proposes more concrete practical observations, giving attention to the "limits" that are sometimes prescribed for the *sensus fidelium*. There are certain "objective" limits on the *sensus fidelium* due to the "competence" of the faithful, though he sees a more educated laity becoming better able to exercise a "critical capacity" even in theological areas. He adds that the laity are seen as more likely to have insights in the area of practice however, he observes that

> "practice" is never without incidence on "theory"; verification is itself one path of exploration and investigation of truth (and not of

one application only), especially if the ideological character which accompanies a large part of our theological activities is taken into account.[470]

Sartori cautions finally, that if a representative structure is considered, it must be remembered that appeals to a "silent majority" of the faithful may merely continue to retain the established view at the expense of new, prophetic voices, and may ignore the "evangelical criterion of *solidarity with the last*, and above all with sinners and outlaws, on the model of Jesus, who identified himself above all with outcasts."[471]

Sartori ends by acknowledging the more important and yet more complicated place of the *sensus fidelium* in the Church since the Council. He describes it as "more complex and easily manipulable" but warns too against looking for "greater securities" in tools that are more "juridically authentic" but that also may be legitimized "by citing the 'juridical incompetence' of the people." Sartori appeals instead for an active expression of prophesy among all the faithful.[472]

### *Leonard Swidler*

One of the most staunch advocates for viewing the Church as a democracy, and for basing such a view in the sense of the faithful is Leonard Swidler. His most direct treatment of the topic is in "*Dēmo -kratía*, The Rule of the People of God, or *Consensus Fidelium*," cited above. Against critics of this notion, Swidler maintains that there is more support "rationally, scripturally, historically, and from experience" for the idea "that the Church *ought* to be a democracy," than there is against it.[473]

In support of this claim, Swidler first argues that the fullest form of human living is found in persons who are active in "thinking and deciding." He thus reasons,

> If the main purpose of the Church is to lead human beings to be followers of the Way to Salvation i.e., *salus*, healthy life, a fully human life (Yeshua said: "I have come that they may have life and have it more abundantly"-Jn. 10:10), then an analytic argument pointing toward a democratic Church—and world—would seem imbedded in the very notion of the Church.[474]

Though acknowledging that there are forms of government where only some of the people are given responsibility for making decisions, Swidler maintains that problems are best addressed by "the maximal involvement of the maximum number of persons possible."[475] He concludes, "The greater the democracy employed, the more fully human the life of that society."[476]

Turning to Scripture, Swidler argues against basing any developed hierarchical views on the direct actions of Jesus.[477] Current studies do not show that Jesus set out "to found a Church," simplistically understood.[478] He asserts that the Twelve who were selected by Jesus were intended to symbolize the patriarchs and the tribes of Israel. Their gender thus cannot prove that Jesus intended an all-male leadership.[479] Swidler sees it as important that when a replacement for Judas was needed, the new apostle was not given "from the top down," but was found by casting lots. He notes that the selection of the first deacons "was even more democratic," as Stephen was chosen by all the people. When Paul and Barnabas went to Antioch, "the whole Church" took part in selecting companions for them (Acts 11:22). Swidler comments that such inclusion occurred not only in "the later, more freewheeling, charismatic, Pauline churches," but in the "earlier more structured churches stemming from the pattern found in Jerusalem" as well.[480] Swidler is most emphatic that Scripture does not warrant "the supreme monarchic governance over the entire Church by Peter, and therefore Rome." He recalls that support for Peter's even having been to Rome "is all post-Biblical."[481]

In a brief overview of the early period in the Church, Swidler stresses the diversity of structures in the churches, and the slow development of "monepiscopacy." Even when this form of leadership was in place it was "more like a limited monarchy or, just as accurately said, a limited democracy."[482] An important expression of the shared responsibility of the early churches was the election of bishops, priests, and deacons.[483] Swidler cites the familiar examples, and then notes especially that "early Christians saw no contradiction" in the fact that their leaders received their authority from both God and the congregation.[484] Further, through involvement in both election and removal of church leaders, large local synods (e.g. Carthage and Elvira), and in ecumenical councils, there is evidence of universal involvement of lay people in decision making in the Church.[485] Swidler describes lay involvement as significant up until Vatican I which saw it "shrivel to almost nothing."[486]

Swidler sees the viewing of the *consensus fidelium* as a passive criterion as "a perversion of the ancient tradition." He adds that in its mission to the modern world, the Church "will find itself less and less credible" if it does not restore its more ancient democratic ways.[487] Swidler quotes Norbert Greinacher:

> One thing must be clear: one cannot speak of the co-responsibility of the laity if participation in *decision-making* is not granted . . . Only under this condition of genuine participation in decision-making will it be possible in the long run to integrate the laity into the Church in some authentic way.[488]

After looking at the historical dimensions of the *consensus fidelium*, Swidler considers some practical issues. He criticizes official use of the consensus of the faithful in history and particularly in recent times, stating that it has been introduced selectively to support predetermined stances. He questions why the *consensus fidelium* should be identified in the definition of the Assumption of Mary and not in the response to *Humanae Vitae*.[489]

Swidler notes that even "careful empirical analyses" have found "a substantial pluralism in the *consensus fidelium*." Within this range of views, there are "minimal" and "maximal" levels of agreement.[490] Dissent is a major effect of differences in the Church. Swidler argues that pluralism and dissent should not be considered merely as "necessary evils," but should be encouraged, and "even celebrated" as indicators that cultural and historical contextualizing engenders a rich diversity of responses on given issues.[491]

Swidler sees an important task for the social sciences, in the need to develop techniques to find not just the content of faith, the "*fides quae*," but the "*fides quo*," as well, and the way in which these two aspects of faith work together. He sees the practical growth of faith as accomplished through symbols, education, and worship, and by "putting beliefs into actions, into life, and having their feedback to shape the understanding of the belief." Growth also happens "through dialogue on a whole range of levels."[492]

Swidler next turns his attention to the importance of dialogue. Foundational for the development of *fides* is a "healthily critical" inner-dialogue. Swidler suggests that a trust in the inner-self must be balanced against a self-centeredness, as each believer engages in a personal dialogue with God. Dialogue within both secular and ecclesial communities must be developed, as well as a dialogue with the past. The living reality of God's actions described in the Scriptures, and especially of Jesus' actions in the New Testament, must be the source for the Christian's development.[493]

In relation to the Roman Catholic Church, Swidler comments, "There can be no complete disjuncture between the Church as magisterium and *fideles*, between the *ecclesia docens et ecclesia discens*." He calls for recognition of the "primordial and ancient Christian tradition" that the Church is "the *ecclesia in dialogo*."[494] To make this sort of dialogue possible, Swidler insists that the tradition be rooted in its proper source.

> I would argue that it is not the decisions of the present magisterium, nor of the past magisterium—that is, the past authoritative statements of the Church, Tradition with a capital "T"—nor even the New Testament. Rather, the ultimate Christian measure must be the Jesus of history.[495]

Swidler acknowledges that there are "grave difficulties in penetrating" this Jesus of history. He stresses, however, that other elements, "the magisterium, the Tradition, the Scriptures, are all simply means" for understanding him.[496]

Swidler cites a variety of modern Church statements calling for greater dialogue within and outside of the Church. These acknowledge that doctrinal as well as practical matters are to be engaged, and that the risk of reevaluating accepted positions will be a part of the process.[497] He observes that "there was an extraordinary return to the pre-Vatican II defensive model by the Congregation of the Doctrine of the Faith in 1979," but adds that John Paul II has continued to speak publicly of a dedication to "intellectual freedom of inquiry, which is the foundation of the dialogic model."[498]

Swidler suggests that the primary focus of leaders in the Church should be positive; in particular, "the Congregation of the Doctrine of the Faith, should . . . promote dialogue among theologians of varying methodologies." He advises that the Congregation be urged to pursue such an end, and offers an example of the sort of proposal that could be sent.[499]

In outlining another specific strategy for improving dialogue, Swidler argues that its genuine practice can only happen between equals. He notes that many Roman Catholics do not know what rights they have in the Church, and he encourages those who recognize the importance of dialogue to help in "spelling out and securing" those rights. He notes there are a number of groups designed to promote such work, and comments that "it is vital that not only the theologians and canon lawyers but also the base communities and all Catholics 'in between' throw themselves into this project of a *Magna Carta Catholica*."[500] He adds,

> In this way we all would be taking a practical step to bring about the *kratía* of the *demos theou*, the *consensus fidelium*, and thereby promote true authority in the Church, the *ecclesia in dialogo*.[501]

## Heinrich Fries

In his treatment of the *sensus fidelium*, Heinrich Fries has focused specifically on its relationship with the magisterium. In an article written immediately after Vatican II, he described the view of infallibility coming from the Council as richer in scope than that which was held prior to it.[502] He expected it to bear fruit in ecumenical dialogue. He also offered the view that all of the faithful, in the *sensus fidelium*, participate in the Church's infallibility even though it is most expressly communicated by the bishops as a whole and by the pope.[503]

A developed expression of Fries's views is given more recently in his response to the question of whether the faithful have an actual teaching role in the Church.[504] Here Fries reviews the teachings of *Lumen Gentium* on the *sensus fidei*, and describes the *consensus fidelium* as its outgrowth, stressing that these concepts do not describe "a critically derived or systematically presented product but a living testimony of faith."[505] Vatican II's treatment of the sense of the faithful is very important for an understanding of infallibility. Vatican I had "enlivened and reinforced" the difference seen between the *Ecclesia docens* and *Ecclesia discens*, and had emphasized the passive role of the laity.[506] Fries adds that this was consistent with a view of the faith that identified it with the official expressions of the magisterium.[507] Citing *Dei Verbum* (# 1), Fries notes that Vatican II viewed the faith of the People of God as wider than merely statements of doctrine. At the same time, the Council did not reconcile the two ways of viewing infallibility that it had acknowledged.[508]

To aid in understanding the distinction, Fries considers the views of Scheeben. Distinguishing the "body of faith" and "the body of doctrine," Scheeben teaches that the Church accepts both, and that both are the work of the Holy Spirit. Fries notes that a key point of Scheeben's is his view that "the body of faith is not merely derived from the body of doctrine; rather it is directly and inwardly established by the grace of baptism." Further, Scheeben regards the work of the Spirit as more obvious in the living faith of the body than in the magisterium's pronouncements. The faith then is infallibly manifested in both aspects of the one Church, but it is clearly found as the direct work of the Holy Spirit in the "autonomous activity and subjective nature of the faithful—the body of faith." Fries summarizes: "The activity and function of the *magisterium* is only possible in the form of *communio* in the *consensus ecclesiae* as properly understood."[509]

Fries cites the historical consideration of the sense of the faithful given by Luther with regard to Scripture, Newman's classical treatment, the views of Perrone and Doellinger, and the 1950 Marian definition.[510] These support the importance of consulting the faith of the Church. Fries raises the question about whether Pius XII's actions satisfied the necessary conditions "to obtain a consensus in a wholly unobjectionable way." He wonders too if the teaching was "necessary or opportune." He sees this last example of explicit use of the sense of the faithful by the magisterium as being in sharp contrast to the reactions to *Humanae Vitae*, whose teaching was given "without sufficient consideration of what [was] living in the faith of the faithful." Fries stresses that "the active witness of the laity" to such teachings is a crucial element of the reception to be expected for them.[511]

It is in the light of these prior considerations that Fries attempts to answer his initial question, "Is there a *magisterium* of the faithful?" Inasmuch as the faithful are responsible for "specific services and functions" that include explicit recognition on behalf of the community, he answers affirmatively. They have the task of "discovering and bearing witness to the truth" in a way that cannot be reduced to dependence on the hierarchy. Fries describes the people as "co-authors" of the Church's history, since their "sense or sensibility of faith is the subjective presupposition for a more profound knowledge of the *Depositum fidei* and a function of the living understanding of faith." Insight can come "from below."[512] The official magisterium retains a distinct role, but it is in relation to the faith received by the whole Church. This magisterium has "the function of authentically critical interpretation and an ultimate necessary decision."[513] Fries recalls here the teaching of *Lumen Gentium* "that pastors should 'recognize and promote the dignity as well as the responsibility of the layman in the Church. Let them willingly make use of his prudent advice.'"[514] Fries suggests that it might be better to think of the Church as a democracy, to contrast its structure with the "totalitarian State," and to emphasize the way the diverse charisms within it are to be guided by those in office. Central to the process is the encouragement of genuine dialogue.[515]

An expanded treatment of the same material was published three years later as "Sensus Fidelium. Der Theologe Zwischen dem Lehramt der Hierarchie und dem Lehramt der Glaeubigen."[516] Fries here focuses on the role of the theologian who has the responsibility of drawing on all the Church's resources, among them, the *sensus fidelium*. Reflecting again on the Church's history and noting where the laity was regarded as having a passive role before the ecclesiological perspective of Vatican II was introduced, he observes that the sense of the faithful was considered a "valid and efficacious" witness to the faith, specifically as a reflection of the teaching of the hierarchy.[517]

Fries notes that theologians were given an important description of their own mandate in the remarks made by John Paul II to a gathering of German theologians in 1980. The pope described the importance of freedom in theology to do its work properly, "correcting and expanding" the understanding of the faith for the benefit of the faithful. The magisterium itself is not devoted merely to "censoring" or "regulating" new expressions.[518] He described the task of theology as a "service to the community of faithful," adding that "the magisterium and theology both have a distinct task."[519] The pope stressed that cooperation is to characterize their relationship.[520] Fries observes however, that such a clear description only serves to underline the lack of success the Church has had in developing such an "integrated" relationship of authority and theology. He notes, in fact, a return to a pre-Vatican II approach to authority.[521]

Fries sees a "stark *centralism*" in the magisterium's use of power.[522] He sees the climate as a dubious one in which to expect an emphasis on the *sensus fidelium*.[523] Instead of being the focus for communication he had described earlier, he sees the magisterium as "an independent authority for teaching and direction." As in the case of Paul VI's teaching on birth control without consideration of his commission of experts, current decisions on matters of faith and morals are made throughout the world by the centralized authority that seeks unity through uniformity.[524] The 1987 Synod on the Laity reflected this centralizing tendency as well. It included only a minority of lay people in its meetings, and these were merely observers. Fries sees it as "treacherous, that this Synod directed a message to the People of God, as though they themselves did not belong to it."[525] In its style and its reiteration of old positions (in particular those concerning the possible ministry of women) the Synod appeared far removed from Vatican II.

Fries maintains, however, that the Church must continue to pursue the agenda set forth by the Council.⁵²⁶

Fries asserts that in this context, "The witness of the faithful is as urgent today as ever." He insists that the people's faith has to be more than the orthodoxy found in a ratification of the statements made by the magisterium; it must include the living quality of orthopraxis. In both society at large and in their private lives, the laity have an expertise that must be sought through genuine dialogue if the Church's leaders are to have either credibility or actual reception of their teaching.⁵²⁷ The "concrete" nature of the Gospel and the foundation of its interpretation is brought out strikingly in Latin America, both in the plight of the people and in the recognition that the Church must preach the preferential option for the poor. Fries notes that the exercise of the Church's ministry is directly affected by this focus on the people's experience.⁵²⁸

From his own context in Germany, Fries describes the hopeful work that was done in the Wuerzburg Synod, which combined the efforts of laity, priests and bishops to deal with the problems created by the promulgation of *Humanae Vitae*.⁵²⁹ He adds, however, that lasting results from the Synod are questionable, and that more recent synods "have other foundations and presuppositions."⁵³⁰

Returning finally to the question of whether it is possible to speak of the "magisterium of the faithful," Fries repeats his previous remarks concerning a legitimate, distinct role for the laity in relation to the official teaching office, and the need to honor the variety of gifts in the Church.⁵³¹ He then adds some summary conclusions:

    a. *The whole Church as community of the faithful is the learning and hearing Church.*

    b. *The whole Church is also the teaching Church.* It has a share in the prophetic mission of Christ.

    c. *Learning and teaching are two tasks of the whole Church,* not of different groups in the Church.

> d. *An understanding of Church, that would split it into a teaching and learning Church, betrays a false and unhealthy view of the reality of the Church.* This does not exclude a difference of services, charisms and functions, but these have their places of value in the Church as Communio.[532]

Fries ends his discussion with some reflections on the role of the theologian in relation to both the hierarchy and the faithful. This role is not one of being an "alternative" source, but of drawing on both, while giving special consideration to the "magisterium of the faithful." Fries asserts again, that this is because the faith is not identical with the acceptance of doctrinal statements. Faith is found in practical living or in Newman's words, "the 'realizing' of truth." He draws for support on the teaching of Vatican I and Vatican II that the hierarchical expression of infallibility itself is based in the infallibility of the whole Church.[533]

Fries sees an emphasis on the *sensus fidelium* as a valuable source for giving magisterial statements greater impact in such areas as ecumenical relations, theology of marriage and questions concerning reception of the Eucharist.[534] He stresses that the theologian does not have the role of determining doctrine that is given to the hierarchy. The theologian does, however, have the responsibility of arguing for the credibility of the official statements made.[535] He observes that definitions that are offered without a reasonable basis "are simply regarded as a demonstration of power," and thus they lose their usefulness.[536]

Fries advises that the theologian should express the faith of the people and make it understandable to them. Such work can serve the *conspiratio fidelium et pastorum* described by Newman, by increasing the power of a united witness to the truth. When there are problems between the magisterium and the people, the tools of theologians can help create resolutions. Fries observes that disciplinary actions in such cases do not resolve the disputed issues, but merely push them aside until they return at a later date. In such circumstances, the work of theology can serve the interaction of the two "magisteriums" as a "self-purifying stream" clarifying the issues.[537]

Fries sees the goal of such work in an expression of P. Neuner, with which he closes his own article. A true "theology of the laity" is found in having no theology of the laity; it is in understanding the People of God well that the role of the laity should be discovered.[538]

## Herbert Vorgrimler

A systematic reflection on the nature of the sense of the faithful is offered by Herbert Vorgrimler, where he distinguishes between the *sensus fidei*, as the "'feeling' for faith's basic themes" in individual believers, and the *consensus fidelium*, where agreement of such believers is reached and finds expression in specific areas.[539] Vorgrimler notes that challenges occurred in the early Church (evident even in some New Testament texts) which put the Gospel message "into the hands of educated 'experts,' theologians and bishops (mostly bishops who, at the time, were also theologians), who reformulated it to respond to particular situations." Such responses included the forming of "dogmatic propositions" that were intended to resolve conflicts. He adds that during this process there remained an acknowledgment that consensus among the Church's members "was a criterion of the genuineness and truth of a tenet of faith."[540]

Vorgrimler notes the shift to an active hierarchical role and passive lay role after Trent, and to an especially juridical understanding of consensus with Vatican I.[541] In Vatican II he identifies a recognition that infallibility should be contextualized in the faith and life of the whole Church and "a start . . . in overcoming the one-sided preoccupation with theoretical truths."[542] He finds the

Council's treatment to be inadequate, both in a lack of consistency and concreteness. [543] He addresses two key issues that are left unresolved:

> (a) Are all believers, on the basis of their sense of the faith, in some way competent to express and teach the faith, even in matters of theoretical truth, i.e., in doctrine? (b) How and where can we discover that consensus regarding particular items of faith which results from the sense of faith?[544]

Vorgrimler at first gives a negative answer to the first question. In the contemporary Church the magisterium retains its authority to determine doctrinal issues. Theologians offer their views, at times in competition with the magisterium, on the basis of "professional expertise." At times, these two groups seem to be vying for recognition that they are protecting the interests and faith of the people.[545] Vorgrimler observes that, "Neither parties have yet proved that 'ordinary' believers want to be represented by them."[546]

Vorgrimler notes that some theologians have worked to return a focus to the faithful. Johann Baptist Metz has argued for the dignity of each person, and against "the elitist way of thinking which condemns the great majority to inarticulate acceptance."[547] Metz's mentor, Karl Rahner, has described the individuals "faith-awareness" as a "'concrete catechism' which is more than simply the repetition of the Church's total self-awareness."[548] The individual may legitimately weigh the relative worth of elements within the "hierarchy of truths." Most importantly, Rahner has emphasized that divine revelation is truly received when it is "experienced and accepted, not as a theory, but, far more radically, in the existential mode of human life."[549] Vorgrimler notes that Rahner has not described how the faithful might be expected to express their experience of faith. He suggests that their approaches will not be that of "intellectualized theology," but will be similar to the "narrative" or "oral" histories that have begun to come from feminist authors and from those writing in Latin America and Africa.[550]

Addressing the issue of how consensus can be identified, Vorgrimler first cites the need for the faithful to express their own views. He sees in their repetition of the Creed and adherence to doctrinal definitions not so much the expression of understanding or agreement, as the expression of the will to agree.[551] Actual consensus will be found in an active process, and will always be in need of renewal. Consensus is more recognizable when it is achieved through praxis. When practical issues of faith are addressed, agreement can be seen not only by those seeking to serve God, but by those outside the Church as well.[552]

Vorgrimler sees such "simple, practical proclamation of Jesus of Nazareth" as accessible to believers without the mediation of theological experts. He sees Christian involvement in "the worldwide movement for peace and liberation" as an indication of a commitment to a "fundamental Christology" which also gives voice to the concerns and insights of the people. Vorgrimler contrasts these grassroots manifestations of the sense of the faithful with teachings that come from "the top." He thus identifies the cause for rejection of official teaching on birth control in a view of natural law that does not elicit consensus among the faithful.[553] He summarizes his own view of the movement from insight to consensus:

> The more a particular praxis of faith responds to the actual situation of need and is rooted in the proclamation of Jesus, the more it grows beyond individual prophetic subjects and limited social groups and tends to become a faith-witness common to all believers.[554]

## Jan Walgrave

The insights of Jan Walgrave on the sense of the faithful have been given by him in a short but important article on Newman, cited above in the historical study, "Newman's 'On Consulting the Faithful in Matters of Doctrine.'"

Walgrave had earlier discussed the importance in Newman's thought, of a certain freedom for the laity within the overall working of the Church, which would allow their sense of truth to be included in the process of doctrinal development.[555] In specifically discussing the *Rambler* controversy, Walgrave argues that both the article and Newman's responses to the controversy it caused show his concern for a Church characterized by an "organic unity and cooperation, combined with the idea of polarity, tension and conflict as necessary conditions of all life."[556] The human person experiences wholeness in this way, as does the body of Christ.[557] The members of the Church must work together, and thus Newman stresses that the sense of the faithful occurs in the *conspiratio* of laity and clergy.[558]

Walgrave notes that in actually discussing the nature of the *consensus fidelium*, Newman draws on five aspects that represent a diversity of contemporary and historical insights.[559] In this discussion Walgrave sees a precursor to Newman's treatment of "real" and "notional" assent in his *Grammar of Assent*.[560] Real assent is associated with faith and is primary, serving as a guide to notional assent which is the subject of theology.[561]

Musing over Newman's agreement with Ullathorne's description of the laity as a "peaceable set," Walgrave finds that the modern Catholic laity can hardly be assessed in the same way.[562] He observes that the social environment that allowed a distinct Catholic culture in Newman's day is gone, leaving a laity subject to the influences of materialism, hedonism, and "the all pervading influence of the modern media" carrying the predispositions of the modern world.[563] Walgrave describes the majority of Catholics as "worldly minded" and even "inwardly estranged from their traditional faith."[564] In the light of these developments, he asks where the faithful that could be consulted in the sense proposed by Newman might be found. Recognizing also that the magisterium might maintain traditional formulations "too fixedly," he sees "a conspicuous and dangerous conflict" between the hierarchy and the people. He thus ends by asking whether such consulting of the people "is still relevant and practicable."[565]

## Avery Dulles

The main elements of Avery Dulles's views are presented in his short article entitled, "*Sensus Fidelium*," already cited above. Dulles sets his own observations in the context of the official perspectives expressed by Robert Bellarmine, discussions at Vatican I, and *Lumen Gentium*. He notes the more disparate views that have influenced reflection, like those of Lamennais, and reviews some of the more important insights of the Patristic era and the Middle Ages.[566] Dulles acknowledges the impact of Newman and Moehler, especially at Vatican II, and then addresses the question, "Does the *sensus fidelium* still carry conviction in our day?"[567] He describes the current context as "hesitant to give full credit to the spontaneous convictions of the multitudes." He adds that to avoid "being rejected out of hand" the sense of the faithful "must today be explained with frank recognition of its limitations."[568]

Dulles observes that there is "no significant case" where there is "a truly universal consensus" to support the use of the sense of the faithful as a theological criterion. It has, in fact, provoked a "clash of opinions" where it has been introduced. He notes that historically, while a majority have at times supported orthodox belief, in some instances a minority has been either a "faithful remnant" or a "privileged vanguard" as new developments occurred.[569] Dulles cites John Paul II's observation, that "the supernatural sense of the faith" is not necessarily equivalent to a consensus view of the people, and suggests why this identification might not be possible when he says, "the whole subject of the *sensus fidelium* is complicated by the subjective element in human knowledge and especially by the historical and sociocultural conditioning of the knower."[570] Dulles notes how the sense of historical consciousness that was acknowledged officially in Roman Catholic theology after *Divino Afflante Spiritu* (1943) plays an important and complicating role in understanding Scripture and tradition. The sense of the faithful is not, for the most part, developed or expressed in terms of these complications. Thus Dulles advises that the laity are more apt to have a significant contribution in the areas that they are most in touch with, such as worship or "personal and family morality."[571]

In these areas too, Dulles sees limitations. Living in a secularized world, the Catholic faithful may reflect secular values. Dulles warns that opinion polls are as likely to reveal society's values as those of the Gospel. He advises, "We must look not so much at the statistics, as at the quality of the witnesses and the motivation for their assent."[572]

In considering the roles to be exercised by the hierarchy and the laity, Dulles cites Newman in saying "infallibility does not belong to the hierarchy alone or to the believing people alone," but is in the *conspiratio* of both. He adds that since the pastors are counted among the believers, "the distinction is an inadequate one."[573] Dulles observes that if Vatican I asserted that the pope speaks without needing the consent of the Church, he still teaches what has been given to the whole Church, "and thus all who are truly faithful should be able to find in the official doctrine an expression of their own faith."[574] He adds,

> For this reason, Vatican II was able to make a point not stated by Vatican I: that whenever the popes or bishops infallibly define matters of faith, "the assent of the church can never be wanting, on account of the activity of that same Holy Spirit, whereby the whole flock of Christ is preserved and progresses in unity of faith."[575]

He notes that historically both "devout believers" and "church authorities" have exercised "nonreception." Later magisterial teachings have superseded and changed earlier ones.[576]

In an article concerned with academic freedom and theological mission, Dulles deals more specifically with dissent. After discussing the responsibility Catholic theologians have to be "disposed to accepting" the teaching presented as "obligatory" by the hierarchy, he notes that the nature of theology may lead to judgments not in agreement with noninfallible teachings.[577] He asserts,

> Dissent should be neither glorified nor vilified. It is not necessarily an act of greater probity and courage to dissent than to assent. Whenever dissent is expressed, it tends to weaken the church as a sign of unity. Nevertheless dissent cannot be totally eliminated. It may be subjectively and even objectively justified. To deny its existence or to seek to suppress it would be more harmful than to acknowledge it and deal with it honestly.[578]

Though Dulles's statements here specifically address the responsibility of theologians in an academic setting, the implications of dissent for unity and the importance of honest treatment are justifiably extended to the wider body of believers, inasmuch as the debate on theological teachers is specifically concerned with the impact of such teachers on the larger community of faith. The notion that the faithful as a whole, as well as theologians, exercise both personal responsibilities and ecclesial ones in forming the consensus of the faithful or aiding magisterial expressions is made explicit by Dulles elsewhere.[579] Following Ladislas Orsy, he notes that the "religious submission of the mind" (*obsequium animi religiosum*) expected in regard to noninfallible magisterial teaching is a complex notion that speaks of "something more than a respectful hearing and something less than a full commitment of faith."[580] Dulles considers Vatican II to have legitimized dissent in such cases "implicitly by its action . . . but not explicitly by its words."[581] He makes a strong distinction between private and public dissent, with public dissent carrying added risks.[582] He also notes, however, the view of Richard McCormick that "organized" attempts to sway public opinion from official noninfallible teaching may be justified, if "other forms of less sensational dissent are ineffective" and if "circumstances are such that unopposed error would cause grave harm."[583] Dulles argues that "the church, as a society that respects the freedom of the human conscience, must avoid procedures that savor of intellectual tyranny."[584]

Dulles insists that the *sensus fidelium* is not some "supermagisterium"; the presumption is that the faithful will receive official teaching. Yet, they may "hear more than the teachers are conscious of saying," and in living out the teaching in an active way, they may develop and extend it. Problems in reception may themselves help the magisterium "to speak more accurately and convincingly." Dulles finds the sense of the faithful to be a "distinct theological font," but not one that is "autonomous and self-sufficient." It is, by its nature, interactive with the magisterium.[585]

In discussing the "successors" of the apostles, Dulles distinguishes apostolic, prophetic, and theological ministries in the Church in a way that sheds further light on the role of the sense of the faithful.[586] Peculiar to the prophetic role is that it "defies institutionalisation."[587] Each of the three has its own proper autonomy, and each has its own drawbacks. In regard to apostolic leadership, Dulles observes that in conserving the tradition, pastors may be prone to avoiding new developments "that call for fresh responses on the part of the Church," and which could enhance the Church's mission. Prophetic leaders may be "caught up in their own insights" and become "impatient and headstrong" assuming their views are "directives of the Holy Spirit." Intellectual leaders, Dulles says, "with their love of speculation, are often inclined to neglect the spontaneous piety of the people and the practical wisdom of the pastoral leaders."[588]

With his concern for a balance between the various elements of the Church, Dulles insists that the authoritative role of the hierarchy be understood.[589] In an article that specifically considers the teaching of Vatican II on the responsibilities that lay people exercise in the world through their secular vocations, he warns against adopting the view "that the tentative and consultative style adopted by the bishops in their recent social teaching should serve as a model for the revision of doctrines that have been proclaimed in a more binding manner."[590]

Dulles observes that in each essential ministry, of apostle, prophet and doctor, practitioners can become enthralled with their own perspectives, and thus need the balance provided by the others.[591] He encourages cooperation among the three groups even as they are present in different denominations, and predicts that "progress may be expected if a free and open exchange is permitted among the three types of leader . . . and if all alike are attentive to the movement of the Spirit in the Church as a whole."[592] He presents this point in a more poetic way elsewhere when he discusses the teaching function of the Church, and its need to "'tune in' on the theological wisdom that is found in the community and bring it to expression."[593] He writes:

> The official teaching of the Church emanates indeed from the episcopate, but not from the episcopate alone. The popes and bishops are, rather, the lens by which the light, issuing from all who are competent by faith and scholarship, is brought to focus and expressed. By gathering up and concentrating the diffused light, the hierarchy intensifies its splendor and enables it to be refracted, with greater power, into the world.[594]

## *Gerald O'Collins*

Several critical issues are raised by Gerald O'Collins concerning the consultation of believers that is recommended by many who place importance on the sense of the faithful.[595] Though acknowledging the importance of this source as described by Newman, and as used in the 1854 Marian definition, O'Collins cites an "obvious and persistent difficulty" in the Church's history; the majority have often been wrong.[596] During the famous Arian crisis, in certain areas, a minority of believers agreed with Athanasius.[597] After an historic period has past, it is possible to see in the events that transpired, the work of the Spirit. Yet O'Collins remarks, "It is too easy to be wise after the event."[598] The number of adherents to a doctrine in a given period is no guarantee of legitimacy, and thus he rejects the use of polls to assess public opinion.[599]

O'Collins's view here might be set in the context of his earlier treatment of dogma, where he cautioned that even in respect to major theological issues, St. Paul himself "appealed to the general consensus, scriptural testimony and a variety of arguments to persuade his readers of their own accord to return to the truth (1 Cor. 15)."[600] He sees the legitimate need for concrete support for faith as grounding the need for dogma. Its misuse has been evident when "the violence done to man's conscience and liberty in the name of dogmatic orthodoxy occurred because abstract principles supplanted the person of Jesus Christ."[601] He acknowledges too, that the expression of the faith in human language even when this is a dogmatic expression, is characterized by "an ineradicable ambiguity and plurality of meaning."[602] Further reflection and understanding in the Church must come to grips with both the original and contemporary meanings of doctrinal statements, even while those in the Church remain open to the possibility of new understandings that legitimately deepen the original insight into the faith expressed by dogma.[603]

In specifically addressing the role of the sense of the faithful, O'Collins does suggest some "signs" that may indicate that the Spirit is guiding the views of the people. To begin with, the whole Church must be considered. The insights of North Americans or Europeans are not to be stressed at the expense of those in Latin America, Africa or Asia. O'Collins further argues that particular attention should be paid to the "victims and losers of this world." He suggests that if Newman were writing today, he might add to his work a section entitled, "On

Consulting the Victims in Matters of Doctrine."[604] In urging that the Church look to "ordinary" believers, O'Collins connects the prophetic aspect of the sense of the faithful with the "folly of the saints." Naming Joan of Arc, Thomas More, William Wilberforce, Dietrich Bonhoeffer and Dorothy Day, he points out that those with saintly lives have at times been the voices of holiness and prophecy, and have received persecution from the majority.[605]

O'Collins offers two criteria of Old Testament prophets: a "deep loyalty to the inherited faith in God," and an upright, moral life.[606] These criteria are ratified in the New Testament; an interpretation of the Christian message must "clearly associate itself with the basic gospel" and the "Easter community," and must come from those who live lives of holiness.[607] Thus he suggests that in addition to victims, "consultation" should be engaged in with the saintly and the prophetic. He notes that one might ask just what matters might be subjects for consulting "that vast number of faithful who at a given moment do not prove to be markedly prophetic, saintly or victimized?"[608] Following Newman who spoke of their special "expertise" in the area devotion, O'Collins advises a focus on worship. More deeply, the insight of the laity should be considered in the understanding of "actions, the persons or the elements" that make up the signs and symbols used in worship. O'Collins suggests that the faithful might be consulted on the actual symbolic value they find in priestly celibacy for instance.[609] It is the symbols that express the faith in the actual life circumstance of the people that "could reveal hints of the genuine guidance of the Holy Saints."[610]

As part of a larger discussion of the interpretation of tradition, O'Collins has added some other insights on the *sensus fidei*.[611] He describes the difficulty of discerning this source, which requires knowledge of the faith of the whole Church to really establish its presence. Such agreement is not always present, and yet its absence may occur in periods where "genuine prophetic minorities" are contributing important insights for the good of the larger Church. For evaluating such contributions, O'Collins recommends "checking the visible fruits of the Spirit" as he has discussed above, and examining such contributions in comparison with several other important criteria in the Church.[612] These criteria include the magisterium, the elements of the Vincentian Canon, "universality, antiquity and consent," a living continuity with the past, the Creed, apostolicity, the Scriptures, and the Risen Christ.[613]

*James Heft*

James Heft has offered observations on the *sensus fidelium* in two areas where it is related to the magisterium. In an article focused on ecumenism and the dogmas of the Immaculate Conception and the Assumption, he reviews the basic characteristics of the sense of the faithful in current Roman Catholic thought, offering this source as evidence from within the Catholic tradition for a balanced view of both the doctrines and the role of the pope.[614]

Heft reviews the context of Vatican I's definition of infallibility, with attention to the limiting notions that the Council saw as applying to its expression by the pope, but which have not been popularly understood.[615] He next considers the *sensus fidelium* specifically in its connection with the promulgation of the two Marian dogmas. The "elusiveness" of the concept is pointed out, even as its "central role" in the definitions is emphasized.[616]

In reference to the two doctrines, Heft adopts a phrase of Newman's in saying that "the notion of the *sensus fidelium*, at least methodologically, seems to be 'an hypothesis to account for a difficulty,' namely, how to show that the recent Marian dogmas are indeed contained in the deposit of faith."[617] Heft notes the further complication of discerning the presence of the sense of the faithful in concrete situations. He suggests that in some cases Protestants and even Catholics might question the use of the *sensus fidelium* as arbitrary or even contrary Scripture.[618]

Heft draws attention to the practical aspects of determining the scope and presence of the source as they were illustrated by the suggestion of Cardinal Hume at the 1980 Synod on the Laity, that the experiences and views of the laity be considered in assessing the Church's teaching on issues concerning marriage and the family. Heft also cites Cardinal Ratzinger's response, that a balance was needed so that the "signs of the times" would be considered in doctrinal expression without allowing teachings to be determined by variable public opinion, when it is in fact the Church's mission to bring the Gospel to help the world.[619] Heft sees a substantial task remaining if the *sensus fidelium* is to be understood and used in current theological work. He continues his own discussion of the Marian dogmas in the ecumenical context with a treatment of the "hierarchy of truths."[620]

Heft's reserved and even tentative observations on the possibilities of the *sensus fidelium* for aiding the ecumenical process serve largely to mitigate common misconceptions concerning infallibility and the nature of doctrinal expression in Roman Catholicism. He offers stronger and much more practical observations in a later article that examines the relationship of the sense of the faithful to the internal discussions about war and economics in the U.S. Bishops' recent letters and the processes that preceded their presentation to the Church and other communities.[621] After a discussion of the teaching authority of bishops and episcopal conferences, Heft describes an "expanded role" for the *sensus fidelium*.[622] He considers the process used by the bishops in drafting their recent letters to be important in three areas; in illustrating "a new role for the laity," in appealing for "more persuasive teaching" and in showing "the importance of noninfallible teaching."[623]

Heft identifies in *Lumen Gentium* (# 12) four basic characteristics of the *sensus fidei* that support the role played by all the faithful in the Church's infallibility; their genuine acceptance of the word of God, their unfailing commitment to the faith, their insight into the meaning of revelation, and their ability to put their understanding of the faith into practice in their lives.[624] He sees the laity as having particular competence in the areas of war and economics, and the bishops as doing well to draw on them in developing their teachings. Heft refers again to the statements of Cardinal Hume at the 1980 Synod, where he spoke of the experience and insight of the people as an important theological source. Heft also points out the role of reception in the exercise of the sense of the faithful.[625]

The dual extremes of "democracy" and "autocracy" are both described as inadequate systems for ascribing authority to doctrine. Heft finds instead,

> There is rather a subtle but important interplay yet to be sufficiently worked out by theologians, between, on the one hand, formal (who says it) and material (what is said), and on the other hand, the way in which the acceptance of a teaching affects its authority.[626]

In order to achieve this interplay, "a deeper grasp of the nature and function of the 'sense of the faithful'" is needed.[627]

To develop the "more persuasive teaching" that is attempted by the bishops, Heft sees consultation as a key step. Those who are included in the process of developing a teaching are more apt to accept its outcome. Additionally, he sees the "discovery of the value of fallible teaching authority," especially in the North American context, as doubly important. It creates a climate where believers must develop responsible discernment, realizing that infallible statements alone cannot guide them. It acknowledges too, that there are many issues which the bishops should address even though infallible expressions are not appropriate and where the issues may in fact remain debatable.[628]

In the new approaches used by the U.S. bishops in recent teachings, Heft sees an opportunity for the sense of the faithful "to penetrate the gospel and apply it more thoroughly to life as it is actually experienced and lived."[629]

## *Jan Kerkhofs*

Jan Kerkhofs takes up the issue of the sense of the faithful and infallibility in the post-Vatican II context by first recalling that after Vatican I many in the Church thought that further councils would not be necessary. The pope could act on behalf of the *sensus fidelium* if new expressions of the faith were needed.[630] He adds that even if this view might be consistent with the approach of Pius IX himself, the participants at the First Vatican Council did not share it. He adds the observation that no expressions of the faith, either by the pope or the people, can be considered "once and for all" events.[631]

Kerkhofs observes that infallibility itself is most accurately spoken of in reference to God. It is necessary to attribute it to the Church as well, in order to avoid an "ecclesiological monophysitism."[632] Vatican II linked infallibility to the People of God and the *sensus fidelium* thus reconnecting the "magisteriums of bishops and theologians" to their foundation.[633]

Kerkhofs illustrates the importance of the topic with a brief historical and contemporary survey of how the sense of the faithful has been appropriated by theologians and the hierarchy. He sees particular importance in "the active reception (with the choosing that this implies) of the word of God that is continually addressed to his people in historical pilgrimage." He recalls the role of reception in the determination of the Scriptural canon, the veneration of saints, the effectiveness of councils and synods, and the establishment of canon law.

Conciliar history includes cases of "re-reception" as described by Congar, with the Christology of Chalcedon being reevaluated in recent theology and the minority view of Vatican I being accepted at Vatican II.[634]

He observes that the current context presents new questions and possibilities for the ancient concept, particularly with the modern acceptance of the importance of historical consciousness. Ideas raised by Moehler, Scheeben and Newman as well as more recent issues associated with the charismatic movement, process theology and base communities are all related to a newly found active understanding of the sense of the faithful.[635] Recent magisterial statements illustrate the important contributions that grassroot reflection has had in many areas of the world. Kerkhofs notes that the influence of base communities, ecumenical relations and women's issues have been acknowledged and encouraged at times by various episcopates, although some responses illustrate an ongoing ambiguity about these areas and the need for further progress.[636]

Kerkhofs asks the practical question of where the *sensus fidelium* is to be found. He recalls that at Vatican II, the bishop of Iceland suggested that public opinion should be sought from time to time through the use of polls. More recently, the 1980 Synod on the Laity considered the value of discerning such public views while cautioning against simply equating this source with the *sensus fidelium*.[637] However the relationship is to be understood, Kerkhofs describes how a recent survey of opinion illustrates a gap between the views of Catholics and official Church teaching. He recounts how a study done by the European Value System Study Group (reflecting the views of some 240 million Europeans) found that only 77% of practicing Catholics believed in an afterlife, 72% believed in heaven, and 60% believed in a "personal God."[638] Non-reception of *Humanae Vitae* was found to be "almost universal."[639] The majority of Europeans and even the most conservative country in the group, Belgium, expressed approval of abortion if the mother's health was at stake or if there was a risk of serious handicap in the child. Kerkhofs asks whether the magisterium or the faithful are in error here, or whether it might be both.[640]

Members of the clergy also disagree with the magisterium on a variety of positions including mandatory celibacy and other doctrines concerning sexuality. Although he sees no "trustworthy" studies on bishops, Kerkhofs offers a list of historical examples where the magisterium reversed previous teachings. He includes beliefs about the earth's position in the cosmos, the literal reading of the creation account in Genesis, the teaching of *"extra Ecclesium nulla salus,"* and teachings on religious liberty and usury.[641] Public opinion has changed the minds of individual popes, as in the example of John XXIII and his effort to require that Latin be used in priestly studies. Kerkhofs adds that the relationship of the *sensus fidelium* to public opinion is quite complex in regard to ecumenical relations, especially where other Christian churches have adopted policies different from those of the Roman Church in areas like ordination.[642]

The canonization of saints has been linked to the sense of the faithful and to infallibility. Here Kerkhofs raises questions about the universality of such judgments. He points out that most of the saints are male celibates from around the Mediterranean. Recalling that Hans Urs on Balthasar has described the saints as the "living tradition," he observes that if this is true, "this tradition is very selective."[643] Additionally, he observes, that connecting the use of the sense of the faithful to canonized saints would limit its use to witnesses from the past.[644]

Kerkhofs notes that finding consensus is another possible focus for the *sensus fidelium*, but one that is also problematic. New possibilities for developing widespread opinion exist because of improved intra-global communication. He adds that these have contributed to the acceptance of liberation theology and base communities as *"loci theologici."*[645] At the same time, not everyone among either "the faithful, or theologians or bishops" are in agreement about these areas.

Kerkhofs affirms though, "Consensus is not signified by unanimity."[646] The process of reception occurs over time and may include conflict.[647] He argues that to develop a "genuine consensus," both "a great freedom of expression and sufficient information" must be available.[648]

Kerkhofs details how this liberty is lacking in the Church. Bishops in attendance at several synods since Vatican II have expressed the desire to review such controversial issues as celibacy, *Humane Vitae* or communal absolution. Such efforts have been frustrated, however. Many bishops though, have not protested the limits placed on their own open discussion in order to avoid repercussions or conflicts within the hierarchy.[649] Kerkhofs suggests that the selection of bishops is itself suspect; candidates who will follow direction from above seem to be preferred.[650]

The possibility of communication within the Church that is free from interference and that could aid in developing the *sensus fidelium* is quite problematic. Kerkhofs identifies "fear and the desire for power" as serious problems in the Church's ability to roach honest dialogue within its many levels.[651] Despite declarations to the contrary, the Church does not nurture free expression. Kerkhofs recalls that in February of 1986 Pope John Paul II addressed a gathering of journalists saying, "It suffices to remark that the truth is indissolubly tied to the freedom of expression, and that it is the principal factor of progress in all domains of human life." Kerkhofs adds, "Unfortunately, this is not always the case in the interior of the Church itself."[652]

Kerkhofs goes on to say that even communication that is free from power issues is not itself a certain route to discerning the *sensus fidelium*. Neither the "*Volkgeist*" nor an "*Iglesia popular*" can be assumed to express the movement of the Spirit. Nevertheless, the "discernment of the community" must be recognized as a criterion that is certainly ancient, and also encouraged by Vatican II. The Council's insistence on ongoing synods and councils of regional and local nature has been clear, and has resulted in obvious successes in areas such as liturgical reform.[653]

The response found among many in the Church to teachings on birth control, general absolution, intercommunion, ordination and other topics indicate that the process of discernment is difficult. Kerkhofs asks how a "reciprocal non-reception" or even a "total impasse" between the faithful and those in authority can indicate "discernment." He notes that Vatican II's teaching on the "hierarchy of truths" may be a vital tool in further work on such problems.[654]

One post-conciliar phenomenon that offers a great deal of hope, is the proliferation of groups of Christians who have bonded together to work for specific causes.[655] Families, peace activists, and feminists, as well as those working for the marginalized or those concerned about ecology are among the many groups that exhibit the quality of "base" communities. They are creative networks of action and reflection, and exercise an influence on public opinion. Kerkhofs sees in such groups a creative attention to issues that need to be better understood in the Church and possible sources of the sense of the faithful. [656]

In such work the responsibilities of listening and interpretation are intertwined. Kerkhofs claims that a genuine respect for the role of the Holy Spirit requires an open and receptive context. To maintain such a climate, Kerkhofs sees the Church as needing the three ministries discussed by Avery Dulles.[657] Prophets are needed to discern the issues and insights emerging from the "pluriform base" that is "sometimes chaotic or polarized." These may be "lay, religious or cleric, male or female, young or old." [658] Theologians are also needed, who can communicate with other ecclesial bodies, the "great Tradition," and the human sciences. They must examine "the present and the past in view of the future," attending, Kerkhofs notes, to the "hierarchy of truths."[659] Leaders who are successors to the apostles are also needed to oversee the community, so that it retains the foundations of its tradition, and so "that by their decisions, always provisional, coherence is guaranteed."[660]

Kerkhofs recalls Newman's observation that the communication of an imperfect Church will itself be imperfect. Ministers of all three "types" are called "to take up this cross." Kerkhofs writes, "In the end, in each of us there will be a tension between our personal *sensus fidei* and the *sensus fidelium* being sought or temporarily recognized."[661] He sees the Holy Spirit present in both "diachronic" and "synchronic" dialogue. He adds that the movement of the Spirit occurs "primordially" in individual believers who are "more or less lucid, very historically determined, [and] more or less sinners." It is their task to continue to probe what God has revealed, while realizing their own words will never exhaust its meaning.[662]

## *Leo Scheffczyk*

Leo Scheffczyk takes a critical look at the contemporary uses made of the *sensus fidelium* as he attempts to recall its classical uses in "Sensus Fidelium—Witness on the Part of the Community."[663] He sees the unifying function of this source being ignored by those who would call on a "sense" or "instinct" of the faithful "to set the 'moral teaching of the Church' in opposition to the 'wisdom of the actually lived convictions of Christians.'"[664] If used correctly, this sense should move the faithful toward *conspiratio*, which Scheffczyk recalls is from *conspirare*, meaning "to breath together, to agree."[665] There are those who insist that "the obligatory nature of dogma is dependent upon its acceptance by the whole Church as the correct, appropriate and inerrant expression of its faith."[666] Such an insistence places the sense of the faithful in conflict with official Church teaching. Such misuses illustrate "a certain immanent problematic attached to the concept which must be seen and resolved."[667]

Scheffczyk gives an overview of the secular and Christian warrants for the legitimacy of the concept, stretching back to ancient times. Recalling the teaching of Vincent of Lerins, examples from Newman, and the views of Thomas Aquinas, he observes that the traditional uses of the *sensus fidelium* made it an inclusive tool, not an autonomous one.[668] He claims that properly understood, the association of the sense of the faithful and the priesthood of believers should have been strengthened by the challenge of the Reformation; the *sensus fidelium* is "obviously dependent upon a lively tension between the common priesthood and the teaching office and upon an equilibrium of both."[669] Yet too great an emphasis on the common priesthood in the era and the dependence on the notions of *sola scriptura* and *internum testimonium Spiritus Sancti* tended to separate the sense of the faithful from the "objective rule of faith."[670]

Thus with Cano, and others who would follow, a "stricter methodology" was used, and the *sensus fidelium* was seen as "unsuitable" as a criterion. Scheffczyk notes that additionally, the view was introduced that "the ultimate force of proof for a truth raised up out of the *sensus fidelium* can only be mediated through the infallibility of the Church."[671] This view reiterated the "necessary connection between the sense of the faith and hierarchical, ecclesial office."[672]

Scheffczyk recounts the "classical period" of the concept in the nineteenth century, where the influence of Moehler, the Roman School and Newman shaped the modern understanding of the concept.[673] Through the work of Perrone and others of the Roman School, he sees the fading of the "authoritative aspect" of ecclesiology, in favor of a "model of a differentiated, tension-filled polar interrelationship, in which formative significance is ascribed to the teaching office."[674] The "witness of the faithful" here came to be seen as a "confirmation and sealing of the teaching authority."[675] He sees Newman as providing a "deepening" of the concept in his insistence that the *sensus fidelium* be regarded "in relative independence and in immediacy to the Spirit of God." Rather than serving a merely passive function, it may even retain orthodox doctrine when those in the teaching office fail to do so.[676]

Scheffczyk next turns his attention to the "mystical basis" for the sense of the faithful.[677] He warns against using political models of discerning the "spirit of the people." The "intrinsic interrelationship" between the magisterium and the *sensus fidelium* "has no parallels in political life."[678] Neither should the sense of the faithful be used to "elevate the dignity of the laity a little" in the overall hierarchical view of the Church. Scheffczyk finds its most fundamental meaning "in the mystery of the Church, more specifically in its essence as the community of believers."[679]

He thus draws on the image of the body of believers with Christ as the head. This model is one where "salvation is to be mediated by the one (originally by the One), and received by the others." In the community established in this way, there continues to be a hierarchical structure where head and body are distinguished. These elements of a "hierarchically structured *communio*" are characterized by

> the distinction (not separation) between authoritative office in the Church, which is responsible for the ministry of mediating salvation, and those receiving the salvation ("receiving" is by no means to be equated here with passivity).[680]

Structured in this way, the Church is a visible symbol of the work of Jesus Christ. As Christ is the sacrament of the Father, the Church is the sacrament of Christ.[681]

Within the body of Christ, the Spirit is given to all. The faithful are not merely passive recipients of inerrant teaching, but are moved themselves to discern the truth, to witness to it and act upon it. In some ways they are teachers too.[682]

Here Scheffczyk sees the question of interrelationship of faithful and hierarchy as brought to a point. Are the two to be in "restless unity," where the magisterium is eventually "merged into the faithful," or is the resolution "a separation between superiors and subordinates" where ultimately "the testimony of the laity is recognized as supplementary to the teaching office?" He sees both as inadequate.

> The relationship is rather to be thought of as an organic, alternating relationship, a relatedness of two different capacities which, in working together, make real a higher order and unity (because a differentiated unity is always a higher one).[683]

In this relationship, the authority of the hierarchy is not to be ignored. Scheffczyk writes, "The witness of faith of the teaching office is juxtaposed to the witness of the laity and is ordered above it."[684] He thus claims that the witnesses of the laity and the magisterium do not conflict in "content and essence," but that they operate from different "levels" or "dimensions."[685] He adds:

> Such witness is carried out among the laity on the level of living, among the office holders on the level of the ministerial, the authoritative, and the juridical and legislative (which, of course, would also always be connected with the norm of life).[686]

The connection is not to be seen as merely giving the faithful the role of "a certain reinforcement and resonance of the proclamation of the teaching office." The Marian definitions illustrate "a relatively independent meaning to the witness of faith of the *sensus fidelium* as a means of proclamation for the living tradition in the Church."[687] This role is based in the baptism of the faithful and their share in the Spirit of God. Scheffczyk cautions that this role "remains a *relatively* independent one."[688] He cites Newman's view that the faithful and the magisterium "clarify" one another while always remaining intertwined.[689]

Scheffczyk returns finally to the "concrete expression" of the sense of the faithful. He recalls that in the current context, a shift sometimes occurs from the *sensus fidelium* with its objective reference, to the *sensus fidei* with its subjective character. Against this shift he prescribes care in distinguishing between the genuine action of the Spirit and the acceptance of novel ideas. Scheffczyk stresses that the sense of the faith is not the same as "public opinion," and he insists that it be distinguished from the "prevailing trends in theology and in Christian thought."[690] It resides not in "majority decisions," but in "the power of judgment and of witness" of believers who are open to the Spirit who is uniquely present in the community as a whole.[691] Against "merely private belief," Scheffczyk contrasts the sense of the faith that comes from "living communication and 'conspiration' of all believers, as well as out of the harmony of all organs, and above all out of agreement between the shepherds and the faithful."[692]

To make clear how this conspiration is to be identified, Scheffczyk asserts,

> In the present situation, it is appropriate to remind ourselves that the truth which is meant, which the sense of the faithful serves in the final analysis, is a substantially definite truth, filled with objective content, that it thus encompasses dogmatic faith and does not imply merely a feeling of human solidarity or pietistic edification.[693]

Scheffczyk adds that the sense of the faithful is more than an intellectual entity or "possession"; it engages the heart and is a "living capacity."[694] He closes with a call for growth, and stresses that his intent is to exclude no one "but to awaken responsibility and make known the commission which goes out to all."[695]

## Zoltán Alszeghy

In a short retrospective article examining the *sensus fidei* twenty-five years after the advent of Vatican II, Zoltán Alszeghy gives a comprehensive view of the key issues related to the topic.[696] Of particular interest to Alszeghy is the area of doctrinal development, and as a focal point he selects the text from section (# 8) of *Dei Verbum* that connects development to the religious experience of the faithful and their pastors.[697] He observes that the differences in translations that are extant for the passage illustrate the difficulty of understanding the concept. The passage in part asserts,

> There is a growth in insight into the realities and words that are being passed on. This comes about in various ways. It comes through the contemplation and study of believers who ponder these things in their hearts (cf. Lk. 2:19 and 51). It comes from *the intimate sense of spiritual realities which they experience.*[698]

Alszeghy notes that in the Latin text, "experience" is not a matter of the intellect, but rather is "an experimental knowledge based on what has been lived."[699] He organizes his own analysis of the concept into four reflections on "progress in knowledge of the faith," "the phenomenology of the *sensus fidei*," its epistemology, and the psychology of the concept.[700]

Alszeghy notes that the Council recognized the variety of elements that contribute to the development of doctrine, which include both the natural and supernatural. He emphasizes that the process of development involves all of the mundane activities of the Church and its members.[701] He maintains,

> The evolution of dogma is not some exceptional event; it is not expressed only in the solemn declarations of the magisterium, or in the great scientific works of famous thinkers. Rather, it is an aspect of everyday faith-life, in the same way that salvation history takes place both within general history as a whole, within the history of peoples, and within the events of the life of the

individual person who moves from sin, through justification, to glory.[702]

Contributing to the development of dogma are three elements that Alszeghy sees as "innate to the people of God": theological study, the work of the magisterium, and the *sensus fidei*.[703] These components overlap and work together in the Church, at times through the presence of conflict between them. Alszeghy relates these three elements to basic functions that he identifies in all human discourse: that which observes, that which elicits appropriate behavior, and that which expresses some interior reality. Scientific, legal or poetic contexts each emphasize one element, though not without some inclusion of the others. In the Church, theological discourse is concerned with observing revealed truths. "Magisterial discourse" proclaims the Gospel and calls the community to the truth. This is done in a concrete, definitive way.[704]

In the *sensus fidei* Alszeghy finds a source that neither offers new theological expressions of the faith nor is meant to elicit a direct, concrete response, but which gives voice to the experience of faith.[705] This experience does not pertain to some sort of objective knowledge, but rather to "something 'lived' . . . through which a personality is enriched and through which certain imprecisions are clarified."[706] Objective knowledge may be a by-product of such experience, but it is not the primary result. Thus such experience of faith "is not itself a *doctrine*," but neither is it unrelated to doctrine.[707] Religious experience involves an "interior picture" by which the believer "judges" doctrinal expressions and other matters.[708] Alszeghy observes,

> In my opinion, the *sensus fidei* is precisely this *capacity to recognize the intimate experience of adherence to Christ and to judge everything on the basis of this knowledge*. In this conception we find all the elements of the conciliar phrase.[709]

This intuition allows the individual to make judgments in practical matters of faith. It can also have a certain creative role. Alszeghy notes that in the same way that a scientist draws on common sense to aid his or her technical work, the *sensus fidei* can offer "hypothetical models for our verification" in matters of faith.[710]

Alszeghy draws on two epistemological models to explain the sense of the faith. The first he terms "transconceptualization." This is the process where the "symbolical and imaginary representations" that are familiar to the believer are compared with the expressions developed in other cultures, to determine their "correspondence or incompatiblity." The second model he calls "objective comprehension." From a foundation of "analytical assertions," the individual "conceives an objective and synthetic view of the whole order of salvation." This view is used to consider new expressions for the faith. Alszeghy sees this as the process by which the Marian dogmas were formed.[711]

Alszeghy observes that the practical judgment of the *sensus fidei* makes it more likely to address those areas of the faith that are related to personal behavior. In testing the congruence of an expression with the developed "view of the whole," it is less interested in "abstract essence," than with "the actual form in which it enters the common awareness within history."[712]

The judgments of the *sensus fidei* are by nature subject to reconsideration. Nonetheless, Alszeghy describes two criteria by which a "practically certain validity" can be attained. A presumably prophetic "inclination or aversion" to a given doctrinal expression must be checked against "what has been clearly proclaimed as the word of God." Alszeghy cites St. Paul's teaching in Romans 12:6, on judging the charism of prophecy in the light of faith: "Having gifts that differ according to the grace given to us, let us use them: if prophecy, in proportion to our faith." Alszeghy sees this advice as connecting subjective insight to the objective "rule of faith."[713]

Additionally, the results of any new insight must be examined to see if they lead to a holy, Christian life. Alszeghy here cites Matthew 7:16: "You will know them by their fruits." He observes, "The more the dictates of the Christian intuition bear the charismatic fruit of love of God and neighbor, the more we can assume that we are dealing with a true understanding of the order of salvation."[714]

Alszeghy demonstrates that Vatican II has taught that these two factors offer assurance of doctrinal validity through the presence of the *sensus fidei* only when they become evident to the Church as a whole. Genuine consensus may occur only after a view that began within a smaller segment of the Church expands to include the whole body. Consensus may be won only after a long period of time, as shown in the Arian crisis. Alszeghy's description of the fulfillment of the necessary criteria is not limited to a quantitative assessment of either the time span or the size of the group attesting to the truth of a doctrine, however. He writes:

> We can, therefore, say that the *sensus fidei* is sure when, presuming the other two criteria are met, a sufficiently large community of believers perseveres for an extended period in the spontaneous, effectively experienced, conviction that a doctrine is inseparably linked to the experience in which the believer freely and wholly entrusts himself to God, who is the source of salvation.[715]

Considering finally how the sense of the faith "works" Alszeghy describes it as a response to grace and as "an inclination that is both intellective and affective," with these two elements intertwined at such a "deep level of human existence" that it is useless to attempt an exact analysis of its dynamics.[716] Furthermore, it is in a series of acts of faith, that the operation of grace creates a consistent pattern.[717]

Alszeghy closes by warning against the assumption that the *sensus fidei* is somehow more accessible to the "simple" believer. He observes that the simplicity that comes from a lack of knowledge of the Church's teachings is actually a disadvantage to believers. He thus applauds current attempts to create a better educated laity, which should deepen their understanding of the faith, and "hone the *sensus fidei*."[718]

## Aidan Nichols

In a recent text on the nature and history of theology, Aidan Nichols has included a chapter on the sense of the faithful as part of his description of the sources for theology.[719] Linking the *sensus fidelium* to the *Ecclesia discens*, Nichols gives a brief sketch of the Patristic precedents for its use as a source in theologizing in the East and West, offering some detail on St. Augustine in particular and his references to the importance of the *dogma populare*.[720] Nichols recalls that Medieval treatments of the topic focused on its subjective side, or the development of the "habit of faith."[721]

Nichols suggests that while "some jaundiced views of the Catholic Reformation as a one-sided exaltation of the hierarchical Church over against the wider body" seemed to anticipate the loss of the *sensus fidelium* as vital source, it has been shown by Thils that theological appreciation for the role of the faithful was not lacking up through the modern era.[722] Nichols summarizes Thils's description of the function of the faithful in the understanding of the Church through Vatican I as one of an "infallible receiving" that completes the "infallible teaching" of the magisterium.[723] Citing *Lumen Gentium* (# 12), Nichols recalls Vatican II's understanding that the people as a whole operating with the hierarchy carry on the received tradition.[724]

Nichols finds the "fullest discussion" of the topic in the nineteenth century.[725] He recalls the gap between the laity and the clergy and the lack of any significant role given to the faithful. Newman's view, of course, saw the laity with an active part, which Nichols suggests may be one possible reason for his entry into the Roman Catholic communion.[726] He offers a brief history of the interaction of Newman with Perrone and Ullathorne, and recalls the main evidences and arguments of the *Rambler* article.[727] Nichols accepts the view that "[Newman's] teaching on the infallibility of the laity was . . . fully vindicated by the Second Vatican Council."[728]

Having thus offered a brief foundation for the importance of the *sensus fidelium*, Nichols turns to its problematic aspects, writing, "to state this teaching is one thing: to show what use it will have for the theological student is quite another." Determining the communal sense "is not the counting heads so much as the weighing of testimonies."[729] In looking for those in the body of believers who represent "the better-judging and thus weightier part of the Christian people" Nichols suggests following the lead of two nineteenth century disputants on the issue. With Ullathorne, he suggests looking to "the devout."[730] He adds that "the lives of the saints play a considerable part in the obtaining of the *sensus fidelium*."[731] Following Newman, he suggests that the greatest weight should be given to the testimony of those among the laity who suffer for their faith.[732]

Nichols points out that in some areas Christian faith is more likely to experience "corrosion" than prophetic challenge. He warns that "fluctuations in the *sensus fidelium*" may reflect responses to the Holy Spirit or to "the spirit of the age."[733] He suggests that "the voices of ordinary Christian experience echoing from the past" can serve as a tool of discernment in such contexts. He adds that the lives and words of the saints and martyrs provide "the strongest evidential value" for the *sensus fidelium*.[734]

Nichols adds that attention to the meaning of Christian experience is important to the task of theology.[735] Later in the same text he treats this experience at some length.[736] Of particular interest to the discussion here are the two criteria by which he suggests experience should be judged. Nichols first states that although experience is necessarily personal, it can include an affinity with others.[737] The experiences of others who are serving God in the Body of Christ are a central resource. He observes, however, that Christian experience "is only an aid to discernment" and does not constitute "the living source of enlightenment in Christian theology." He adds, "Only Scripture and Tradition understood by the norms of the Church herself can bring us to that source."[738] Thus he comes to his second criteria, the magisterium, which he finds "carries the greater responsibility." The Church's official teachers and the testimonies of experience are not be construed as "competing forces" as the contemporary media often portrays them.[739] The pastors serve a vital role in seeing that "the Church and each person within it will not misconstrue their experience of divine salvation."[740]

## *Karl Rahner*

One of the most frequently cited contemporary theologians in the post-Vatican II discussion of the sense of the faithful, is Karl Rahner. It would be impossible, even with an extended treatment here, to fully assess Rahner's influence on the theological reflection related to this topic in the last twenty-five years, or to examine all of his texts that would offer insight into the related concepts. What will be attempted is an indication of the main points brought out in his most frequently cited texts, and a description of some basic ideas of Rahner that bear directly on the sense of the faithful.

A work that preceded Vatican II, but which continued to have an influence after it, is Rahner's article "Free Speech in the Church."[741] Here Rahner discusses the role of "public opinion" in terms that anticipate in a striking way many of the post-conciliar issues that pertain to the *consensus fidelium*. Accepting the reality of public opinion in the Church, Rahner questions whether it should have a role that is analogous to that which it plays in the secular arena.[742] He finds that by its very nature as a human society, the Church must include public opinion. Noting Pius XII's admission of this reality, he calls for a clearer expression of its role. The *Syllabus of Errors* of Pius X is sufficient evidence that this source has not been universally welcomed or understood in the recent history of the Church.[743] Rahner stresses that the magisterium needs to know the views and issues that concern the faithful.[744] This implies that individual members should be free to express their views. This expression should not only be made to the leaders, but to the ecclesial community as well, so that those in authority may also see the responses such expressions elicit.[745]

Rahner encourages a truly free expression of ideas; the believer should be allowed "to talk his head off occasionally, so that one can judge from the way others react whether he is really saying anything of any general concern."[746] At the same time, the public opinion that develops in the Church should not be identified necessarily with the movement of the Holy Spirit.[747] Rahner claims, "Its justification is simply that this is the sole means of discovering what is really going on."[748] He asserts too, that in those areas where public opinion contributes a sense of "what is going on" the magisterium does not have special infallible insight.[749]

Rahner's pre-conciliar view shows both a great stress on the interdependence of hierarchy and laity, and insight into the style of expression that should characterize the laity. He asserts:

> If [the clergy] do not allow the people to speak their minds, do not, in more dignified language, encourage or even tolerate, with courage and forbearance and even a certain optimism free from anxiety, the growth of a public opinion within the Church, they run the risk of directing her from a soundproof ivory tower, instead of straining their ears to catch the voice of God, which can also be audible within the clamour of the times.[750]

Rahner insists that the expressions of individual believers should not contradict anything intrinsic to the Church, such as her dogmas or constitution.[751] Further, the final decision on what can be discussed belongs to the magisterium. At the same time, the range of such items must not be overly restricted, as has happened often in history.[752] In those areas where development may be appropriate, particularly in practical matters of piety or practice, "reforms . . . need the pressure of public opinion if they are not to be stifled by tradition."[753] As people attempt to discern new ways of expressing their own views and attempt to deepen the understanding of the faith, they may do so even in cases where the response "from above" is not expected to be favorable.[754] Rahner describes the range and foundation for responsibility in such situations:

> Ultimately no formal rule can be laid down as to how to achieve a concrete synthesis of what are apparently such opposing virtues. It will come about only when people truly seek, not their own will and opinions and self-justification, but the will of God and the Church—ultimately, in fact, when people are saints.[755]

Respect and patience are prerequisites to this process, as is the need for better education of laypeople to bring their knowledge of the faith to the level of sophistication attained in other areas.[756] The genuine teaching of the Church must be known.[757] Additionally though, the Church's tradition cannot be left at a legalistic level, but must be internalized to guide a living faith.[758] Lay people with such a living faith then have a responsibility to express themselves and to enrich the Church's public forum.[759] Rahner suggests that learning the fruits of this forum might be somewhat aided by polls, but "a rather more subtle kind" of assessment and response than is currently used would be preferred.[760] Rahner, in fact, does not say how the process of practical expression should be developed in detail, but argues rather for the development of responsibility among individual believers.[761]

Five years later, Rahner took up more directly the way the Holy Spirit works through the concrete expressions of the different gifts among members of the Church. *The Dynamic Element in the Church*, covers perhaps the widest range in any of his writings, of those issues that are most important for understanding the sense of the faithful. Rahner distinguishes first between "principles" and "prescriptions" as guides for behavior in the Christian's life. He discusses the role of providence in the interpretation of general principles in particular situations. Prescriptions apply to individuals in concrete cases and may, in fact, apply in a unique way to an individual with a specificity that is not possible with any principle.[762]

Because of the concrete nature of prescription, Rahner suggests the need for "a sort of modern 'probabilism'" or even a "tutiorism" that supports workable prescriptions but does not assume these can all be proven uniquely appropriate.[763] The believer must be able to use good judgment and act according to prescriptions while remaining open to new possible prescriptions too. Rahner advises that caution should guide behavior but should not stifle action.[764] He adds that the hierarchy's role is "for the most part not the task of discovering and defending the sort of prescriptions we are talking about."[765] It is not possible to give an exhaustive list of such guides. When they are lacking, believers are not exempt from using moral judgment and acting anyway.[766]

Rahner stresses that to develop the judgment needed to exercise their responsibilities as Christians, lay people should be "encouraged and educated" in discerning God's will.[767] He asserts in terms that recall his earlier work,

> practical prescriptions can only flourish in minds and hearts where there is proper freedom of opinion and inquiry, speech and discussion. According to Pope Pius XII, there must be a public opinion in the Church because the lack of it would be harmful to flock and shepherd.[768]

In a subsequent chapter, Rahner discusses "The Charismatic Element in the Church."[769] Here he describes the distinct though not independent nature of the various charisms. He notes that magisterial office itself must be seen as charismatic. It is not to be understood in solely juridical terms. The ultimate assurance of its success must be recognized as tied to "God's assistance alone."[770] Further, charismatic gifts are not confined to ecclesial offices.[771] When they appear outside of these offices, they may create conflict. Yet the Church may well be served by such challenges.[772] Rahner describes the support given by Pius XII in *Mystici corporis* for the notion that such gifts are not limited to the hierarchy. He adds too, that the "guarantee" of the proper use of the charisms that are distributed throughout the Church does not depend on magisterial authority. It is ultimately given by the Lord.[773]

Rahner later insists that ecclesial authorities should "cultivate the awareness" that they are not a "self-sufficient" base for everything that the Church might accomplish.[774] He also cautions against attempts to characterize the Church as a democracy according to a secular model.[775] Yet he adds that the initiative for some activities can be provided by the people themselves, as they are "guided directly by God."[776] Disagreement will also be found among the voices in the Church. Rahner claims that such tension "is not just to be regarded as a necessary evil."[777] In order to create a healthy context in the Church where a plurality of voices can be drawn upon, he recommends a strategy of "patience, tolerance and leaving another to do as he pleases as long as the error of his action is not established," rather than a "prohibition of all individual initiative until its legitimacy has been formally proved, with the onus of proof laid on the subordinate." Rahner sees such a "patient" approach as implied in "the very nature of the Church."[778]

Rahner describes the need for courage to accept those who would bring their gifts to the Church, observing that while it is laudable that prophets become "renowned and canonized" after their full impact has become clear, especially after their death,

> it is almost of greater importance to perceive such gifts of the Spirit on their first appearance so that they may be furthered and not choked by the incomprehension and intellectual laziness, if not the ill-will and hatred, of those around them, ecclesiastics included.[779]

He adds that the Church has to grapple continually with new expressions of its tradition in order for it to fulfill its original mission.[780]

In the final section of *The Dynamic Element in the Church*, Rahner gives a lengthy treatment of the way in which the Spiritual Exercises of St. Ignatius may help an individual develop the type of discernment that can fulfill the responsibilities he has described.[781] Where the previous sections argue for the importance of the sense of the faithful and offer insights into how the development of consensus may be enhanced, this section reflects on the possibilities for practical development of the *sensus fidei* in the individual believer.

Central to his discussion is the notion that elements in the believer's actual situation can be positive vehicles for the expression of the God's will. This personal context is "not merely . . . a limitation and restriction of a universal nature." It may serve in a direct manner with the same legitimacy as a universal principle.[782]

Rahner finds that "non-conceptual" aspects of the experience of God are assumed in the structuring of Ignatius's exercises on discernment.[783] In these exercises there is "a fundamental evidence and certainty" which operates in the same way as "the first principles of logic and ontology do for the rest of knowledge and which, distinct from the rules, makes them possible."[784] The stirrings of the soul that is drawn to God completely through love do not come mediated by conceptual knowledge. They have an "intrinsically and irreducibly self-evident self-sufficient character."[785] This sort of insight does not necessarily mean that one should expect dramatic or sudden mystical experiences.[786] Rather, in genuine discernment, the person doing the exercises should expect to examine and develop insights to understand any decision in the light of moral principles. This process involves time.[787]

Rahner sees in Ignatius's approach a means for discernment that can give the individual an insight into God's unique gifts and call. Of the role of the *Exercises* he says,

> It is a logic of concrete individual knowledge which can only be attained in the actual accomplishment of concrete cognition itself, in this instance knowledge of the particular will of God addressed to the individual as such.[788]

In this discussion of the means to discernment in practical, concrete existence, there is a clear connection with the transcendental theology that is the basis of much of Rahner's ongoing influence. The link between the "*sensus fidei* of the whole church," and Rahner's strong emphasis on dogma has been recognized by one author as being "presupposed by his transcendental method."[789] At the same time, Rahner retains a solid respect for the importance of the magisterium.[790]

Rahner develops a vision for the post-conciliar Church that stresses the interaction of ecclesial authorities and the people as a whole in *The Shape of the Church to Come*.[791] Here he observes that in the modern Church, complex issues exist because of the variety of groups within it that have different historical, cultural and social roots. Unity among them must be achieved through compromise.[792] He adds that at times, some groups may even have to temporarily postpone the pursuit of legitimate goals for the sake of unity.[793]

In striving to maintain orthodoxy, however, an "open Church" must be sought.[794] To help achieve this, Church authorities must be clear in their instructions about what "theological qualification" is attached to particular doctrines, so as not overstate any case.[795] In those areas where authority is exercised, it should not be with a simplistic dependence on the *fides implicita*, with the expectation of ready and complete acceptance.[796] Elsewhere, Rahner has suggested that the *fides implicita* may bear a wider meaning than it has had in the past. The nature of faith and revelation itself are founded in the God who is "unutterable mystery" but who is yet self-revealing. The mediate nature of the "signs" through which God is revealed and received do not eliminate mystery. Thus the faith of all believers retains an "implicit" quality. *Fides implicita* does not occur "only . . . when the *rudes* and the ignorant hear revelation and believe."[797] A pastoral approach that bases teaching and preaching in the basic beliefs of the faithful must be used. Rahner notes too, however, that pluralistic contemporary societies imbed within them views that are accepted by believers which are at variance with orthodoxy, but which will not be dislodged without difficulty.[798] He adds that from a foundation in basic beliefs there should be a development and defense of teaching authority as well as actual teachings.[799]

Rahner sees a greater need to develop a "Church from the roots." He confidently claims that, "The Church of the future will be one built from below by basic communities as a result of free initiative and association."[800] These communities would be places for living out the Christian life which would have connections with each other, but whose focus would be on serving the needs of members within them as individuals and families concerned for each other in practical ways.[801]

Conceived in this way, parishes or smaller groups within the Church "are not merely organs of the greater Church." They are themselves living expressions of the Church. Rahner suggests that the formation of the community based structure he describes would eliminate the problems connected with attempts to "democratize," the Church.[802] In some cases, the circumstances within communities would call for changes in the method used to select official leaders.[803] Decisions in these core communities should be made "at the lowest possible level."[804] The Church, understood on a large scale with its leaders, would then be able to enhance freedom within its own community and serve social needs outside of it.[805]

In these texts of Rahner's from the period preceding and following soon after the Council there is a clear foundation laid for exploring the role of the individual believer and the *sensus fidei* as well as the practical issues concerning the formation of public opinion in the Church with implications for the *consensus fidelium*. Rahner's work has continued to have an important influence on the contemporary understanding of the theological content of tradition and thus the *sensus fidelium*, particularly through his long interest in the development of doctrine.[806] Rahner has focused especially on the content of dogma, in contrast to the modern shift toward authority.[807] He sees the whole Church as responsible for doctrine and a deepening understanding of it through continual new experience and expression. The role of the Church at large in this process is exercised before the intervention of the magisterium. Ordinary life coupled with the work of the ordinary magisterium, results in the slow development of understanding in the faith. The magisterium and the pope in particular then perform the special function of giving voice to the faith of the community.[808]

Rahner discusses the tasks of dogma and the magisterium in the light of ecumenical questions in an important treatment entitled, "Open Questions in Dogma Considered by the Institutional Church as Definitively Answered."[809] He observes here that the exercise of infallibility by the pope is not to be done independently of the Church. He asserts, "In reaching *ex cathedra* definitions the pope acts as head of the Catholic Church and of the worldwide episcopate, as *an* instance that is conditioned by the church universal and its infallible faith."[810] The pope must consult the faith of the Church, or his definition would constitute a new revelation. Rahner describes him as the "authoritative spokesperson" who expresses the *sensus fidei* of the Church.[811] He observes,

> This connection with the consciousness of faith (*sensus fidei*) in the church universal has of course in various historical phases of the church shown itself in different ways, according to the possibilities that were available. For such an exercise of office today, there is a moral obligation, absolutely necessary objectively, to conduct some sort of inquiry among the worldwide episcopate.[812]

The process of research and consultation that precedes doctrinal teaching should be "clear to the public," though Rahner observes that such a stance has not yet been accepted in Rome.[813]

In an essay specifically on the development of dogma, Rahner has insisted that such development "is not a single process which can be adequately comprehended by formal laws."[814] Furthermore, as doctrine develops as the result of the several components in the Church that contribute to it, each of these components must itself develop.[815]

Rahner's treatment of these various factors continually seeks a balance both between them and within them. In "A Small Fragment 'On the Collective Finding of Truth,'" he describes the nature of formulations of faith in relation to their referent.[816] Human expressions, and especially those pertaining to faith in the God who is mystery, must remain open to further examination and development. Rahner notes that when a doctrinal statement is accepted by the body of believers it is precisely the statement rather than the understanding of it that is shared.[817] At the same time, such expressions are both "necessary and meaningful."[818] Doctrinal formulas that express common belief must be recognized for their important role. The Church, however, must avoid conceiving of them as the products to be pursued by human efforts or in an opposite distortion, as remote, perfected truths that would then paradoxically leave people alone with their own subjective interpretations of them.[819]

The goal of unity of expression must be accepted as a dynamic, ongoing task, open to development and fed by all levels of the Church. Rahner observes that in the past the Church has spoken with one voice at the cost of being "apologetic and defensive."[820] Though genuine movement occurred in the first half of this century, knowledge of it did not enter "the average awareness in the Church" due to a climate of "Pianic monolithism."[821] Rahner thus appeals for tangible, institutional vehicles to foster dialogue.[822]

Along with this dialogue, there must be an increase in awareness and education among all the members of the Church, and to a great extent, Rahner's own labors were undertaken to achieve this end. A particularly striking example of an attempt at gaining theological and pastoral clarity is an article in response to *Humanae Vitae*.[823] Rahner discusses magisterial statements of several popes as well as the current responses of the German bishops. He considers the theological context for the encyclical and the reactions to it, and takes up the issue of conscience and the responsibilities and options of lay believers. His encouragement of responsibility on each level and awareness of the larger context of the Church and its long tradition illustrates well a complex view of the Church, and the necessary interaction of its many members, charisms and offices as it grows in understanding and expressing the faith.[824] At the close of the article, Rahner explicitly places the controversy over *Humanae Vitae* in the context of the development of doctrine.[825] He maintains that such development has characterized the Church throughout its history. He claims that even if "over the last hundred years from the psychological point of view in the awareness of the average Catholic," such development may not have been acknowledged or expected, the

Church does not consider "dogmatic questions" to be closed or settled.[826] Rahner summarizes the process that can be discerned in history:

> On any true understanding there is, even in the Catholic Church, an open "system" in which the most varied factors (the "instinct" of the faithful, fresh insights on the part of individual Christians and theologians, fresh situations that arise in a particular age, the new questions to which these give rise and much else besides) work together to throw fresh light upon the Church's own awareness of her faith and to produce a development of doctrine.[827]

Within this open system, the magisterium has an indispensable role, but it is not to be understood as one of controlling the process in "any exclusive or totalitarian sense."[828] In one of his more pastoral works, Rahner earlier discussed the exercise of the conscience which was both self-critical and aware of its own legitimate role. He asserts that if the resources of such mature consciences were lacking "the Church would degenerate into a bureaucratic apparatus and a totalitarian system."[829] His views on the roles of people and their pastors clearly intend a balance that would enhance the functioning of each.

As mentioned earlier, to recount all of the places where Rahner has developed issues related to the sense of the faithful would be far beyond the scope of the present work.[830] It is instructive, however, to look at some observations made by Rahner in a later article that illustrates the unfinished business he saw in regard to the faith of "ordinary believers."[831]

Rahner sees a gap between the actual faith of Catholics and the teaching of the magisterium as well as a lack of ready acceptance of the authority of the magisterium, which make the use of the *fides implicita* problematic.[832] Such a gap has occurred he notes, even since New Testament times.[833] However, within the pluralistic climate which is the context for most contemporary Christian belief, a "fragmentary and imperfect faith" competes with an assortment of notions whose influence threatens the "formal principle of the faith, the formal authority of the Church."[834] Rahner faults the magisterium for failing to acknowledge the current situation and continuing to make its declarations in a style that assumes a uniform world view.[835] The Church's pastors speak as if their hearers were all characterized by a "clearly articulated Christian faith, together with a more or less absolute respect for the authority of the Church's magisterium."[836]

In contrast to official teaching, Rahner insists that *"the faith* that constitutes the Church" is that which "actually exists in heads and hearts."[837] In addition to the doctrinal formulas of the faith, saints, mystics and heroes throughout history contribute to the Church's understanding of its faith. Yet, Rahner insists:

> The Church does not consist only of its saints. The faith of the average Christian is not just a pitiable sketch of the official faith. It is a salutary faith borne by God's self-communication. It is really the faith that God's grace wishes to bring forth and keep alive in the Church.[838]

This faith may be lacking in "objective" terms, but it is the work of the Holy Spirit that moves the lives of ordinary believers.[839] Rahner calls this "the faith that actually saves . . . however pitiful and fragmentary its conceptualization may be."[840]

Rahner goes on to claim that such "actual faith . . . has a normative significance for the official faith of the Church."[841] He dismisses the use of inadequate methods (such as opinion polls) to try to determine its content, however, and insists that the magisterium also retains a normative role in the Church. Rahner describes the "normativeness" of the actual faith of the people and that of the teaching of the magisterium as "essentially different."[842] He adds, "These two influences *mutually* condition each other, although we must add that mutual does not mean equal."[843]

Rahner notes that history illustrates how the faith of ordinary believers precedes and sustains official expressions in doctrinal form by the hierarchy. Theologians have an active part in this process. The magisterium plays a unique role as it determines "what merely happens to be present" among the beliefs of the people and what should be considered binding.[844] Rahner asserts, however:

> It remains true that the faith of the People of God, as actually existing and not merely as officially approved, is a source of, and to some extent also a norm for, the official faith of the Church.[845]

He adds that the interdependence of these two entities is as old as the Church itself.[846]

"Feedback" of some sort should come from the faithful, according to Rahner, though "there can be no question in Catholic theology of withdrawing a defined doctrine because a considerable part of the faithful have refused to accept it."[847] At the same time, a response of "widespread non-reception" might lead pastors to reconsider the way they have expressed church teaching. Rahner observes that historically "the accent has shifted" in certain dogmas. He suggests that, "with an eye on the actual faith of the people in the Church," changes of this type should now be undertaken consciously."[848]

Rahner extends his focus on "actual faith" to note the significance it might have for future ecumenical progress. He notes that just as some "regional" churches in communion with Rome exercise "a certain autonomy" with regard to centralized authority, other ecclesial bodies with Reformation roots might be rejoined with the Roman Catholic Church while retaining "theologies which do not simply echo Roman theology."[849]

Rahner finally suggests that emphasizing authority as such may not be the most effective contemporary method for presenting the Gospel. He recommends a foundation in that faith which actually occurs among believers, advising, "This actual faith must certainly not be the whole of what is taught, but it should serve as a starting point."[850]

## "PRACTICAL" CONCERNS AND THE SENSE OF THE FAITHFUL

The main intent of the present work is to assess the way that post-Vatican II theology appropriates the *sensus fidelium* as a theological source in the clarifying of the received tradition. The authors considered thus far treat the topic directly, and attempt to define it in both its historical and theological contexts. These treatments are the most important in considering how the concept of the sense of the faithful has been understood in the Church in the two and a half decades since the Council.

Indirect uses and asides that refer to the sense of the faithful in the literature since the close of Vatican II are common. An exhaustive treatment of all such possible texts would be impossible. Yet it is important to offer some illustrations from the practical uses made of the sense of the faithful in addition to the main systematic treatments already discussed to indicate the extent to which this theological source informs and engages a significant range of viewpoints in theological discussions. Some illustrations will thus be given that further indicate the variety of understandings of the sense of the faithful that make up the post-conciliar context.

## PERSPECTIVES ON THE *SENSUS FIDEI*

Three authors will be considered here whose work focuses specifically on the sense of the faith in individual believers.

## John Glaser

The issue of moral judgment in the faithful has been an important focus of those reflecting on the *sensus fidei* since the Middle Ages. In the wake of Pope Paul VI's *Humanae Vitae*, this focus was reexamined by John Glaser in his article, "Authority, Connatural Knowledge, and the Spontaneous Judgment of the Faithful."[851] Here Glaser addresses the question of whether the view of "a loyal and faithful Catholic" who disagrees with authoritative teaching, has "theological weight."[852] Taking care to avoid a response that would have the teaching authority reverse itself in response to opposition or turn to opinion polls, he asks if the "conviction [of the faithful] should be considered one of the 'lights' of moral speculation."[853]

Glaser first outlines the role of the magisterium, whose main function he describes as helping the faithful to "overcome their own clouded vision."[854] The foundation for authority is an insight that is provided by the Spirit. He argues, however, that fallible magisterial assistance is "subsidiary, and only necessary and meaningful for the individual when he himself lacks the vantage point from which he could grasp the truth in question."[855] No one can probe the Gospel's meaning entirely without outside help. In some instances, however, clear understanding is possible. Glaser describes authority as "superfluous in any given concrete situation where an individual has already reached the vantage point from which he can grasp the truth."[856]

Glaser adds some qualifying observations. The individual in the concrete situation is not necessarily "independent of or in opposition to authority *taken as a whole.*" Authority may have provided the overall context for arriving at the needed "vantage point."[857] Further, an individuals specific disagreement with an authority does not imply the rejection of "genuine formal authority" but only disagreement with the "material instance which normally embodies and pronounces the valid insights of such authority."[858] Thus a concrete "exceptional" case should not be allowed to change the basic acceptance of authority by the believer.[859]

Historical cases like that of usury are recalled by Glaser to illustrate that the Church's authority has had to reconsider an originally flawed approach to specific problems. He notes that areas of "blindness" that affect human authorities, such as "cultural blindness, social and political prejudice, fear of undermining its own authority by a change of policy," can impede the operation of the Church's authority. He adds, however, that the magisterium receives more help from the Spirit in overcoming these problems than any believer who acts individually. Thus someone who rejects official teaching bears the "onus of proof."[860]

Within this context, Glaser examines the nature of "connatural knowledge."[861] He notes that the number of believers that might hold a contrary view is not as important as the "mature commitment to the central values of Christ's revelation," in those who disagree.[862] The Scriptural roots for the discernment of the faith that is given to the believer emphasize the knowledge of the heart. Glaser insists on the importance of seeing abstract knowledge in a wider context. He quotes Jacques Maritain.

> But we would have only a very incomplete picture of human knowledge if we did not take into account another type of knowledge, entirely different, which is not acquired through concepts and reasoning, but through *inclination*, as St. Thomas says, or through sympathy, congeniality or connaturality.[863]

Abstract or "systematic" understanding is then drawn from such primary knowledge. Glaser also recalls the insights of August Brunner, Josef Pieper, Joseph Fuchs and Karl Rahner, who from their own perspectives have each recognized and developed the distinction between these two types of knowing.[864]

Glaser maintains that when the two forms come into conflict, it is not possible to claim precedence a priori for either one. He adds, however, that when the "preconceptual" knowledge that opposes the formulations of official teaching is supported by "consistent systematic theological articulation," its importance "increases vastly."[865]

Glaser offers some observations on the "intuitive application of general moral principles to the concrete situation," inspired by Rahner's view of Ignatian Election.[866] He asserts that the state of grace places the individual in a new position with regard to consciousness. Even when it is not exercised conceptually, the believer's consciousness will resonate with what is good and reject evil which "clashes with and contradicts [the] fundamental peace and light" that characterizes the believer's perception. Glaser compares this sense of judgment to the exercise of taste which can assess the "fit" of a particular element in a larger work, as in a musical composition.[867]

This source has limitations. Yet Glaser remarks that this realization cannot "dare let us lose sight of the fact that such knowledge exists and has an importance which has too long been overlooked."[868] He adds that those who develop their views from contact with the "fullness of the concrete and specific reality" have the advantage of "richer insight" and thus have a legitimate authority. Glaser ends by making clear that his intention is to examine "only a small segment of the question of authority in the Church." He appeals for attention "to every source of truth available," claiming "this truth is ultimately none other than Christ Himself."[869]

## Harald Wagner

The *sensus fidei* is examined as the foundation for consensus in an article by Harald Wagner entitled "Glaubenssinn, Glaubenszustimmung und

Glaubenskonsensus."[870] He notes the importance of the sense of the faith is illustrated by its description in *Lumen Gentium* (# 12) which raised discussion of the topic to a level it had not reached since the 1950 definition of the Assumption.[871] Wagner notes that focusing on the aspect of "assent" with regard to the sense of the faithful can avoid its association with a "vague feeling." He observes that the actual functioning of the sense of the faithful is not to be understood in a way distinct from faith, but rather as what Rousselot termed "the eyes of faith."[872] It is the capacity by which the believer has a connatural knowledge of what is revealed. Wagner observes that without this received capacity a "truly human" faith would not in fact be possible. Through it the possibility for decision is also given.[873] With this function recognized in the Church's history and reiterated by Vatican II, there remains the issue of how this source operates not just in individuals, but in the Church as a whole.[874]

To understand the expression of the sense of the faith, Wagner suggests looking to the "normal" experience of believers. Certainly particular groups might be examined on their understanding of the faith. Examples from history can also be identified where the particular assessment of orthodoxy or error has changed. Wagner asserts that it is in the larger overview of Christians living in the common circumstances of the world that the faithfuls' experience and infallible sense of the faith will be found.[875] He adds that even in considering the foundational revelation of Jesus Christ, the common, everyday world is the central focus for experiencing faith.[876]

Wagner observes that though the message of the Gospel must be brought to each place and time in a fresh way, it still must be brought precisely to each individual person. The mind, will and heart of the believer will be used to develop "a certain *Gestalt* of the faith" in each occurrence in which revelation is realized.[877] The event, rooted in God's grace, whereby the meeting of the believer and God occurs is formed through human experience. Such an experience can thus be a "genuine 'locus' of revelation." When agreement is found among the different locations where expressions of faith have arisen in this way, it indicates a guarantee of freedom from error.[878]

From this foundation, Wagner confronts the question of how the sense of the faithful is to be related to the magisterium. Faith is more than an internally generated entity. It is also a response to teaching. It comes from hearing the truth. Wagner cites the view of H. J. Pottmeyer that it is "an open question" whether the sense of the faithful offers an "original contribution" to the Church's understanding of the faith or only expresses obedience to the magisterium.[879]

Pottmeyer claims, and Wagner agrees, that the Second Vatican Council diverged somewhat from the Church's earlier "closed system" which understood truth as coming "from the top down." The Council acknowledged that revelation that comes to believers through their human experience.[880] Just as the Word of God is found when the Logos takes flesh in Jesus, the Word of God becomes real in believers who experience the truth of revelation through the sense of faith that is given to them in human terms.[881]

Wagner cites Clement of Alexandria, Origen, and Augustine as understanding the working of the inner knowledge of faith, which he asserts must be seen in Christological terms as the work of the Logos. This same source is the foundation for the faith of believers and for the functioning of their pastors. Wagner asserts that the underlying issue to be considered is not the *consensus fidelium* but "the whole *Ecclesia credens*."[882] He quotes Moehler, who describes the necessary relationship of the individual believer to the faith of the whole historical community. Wagner stresses that the faith of the Church "is guaranteed by the Spirit of Christ himself." He advises that in seeking a unified community the contemporary Church should not reduce consensus to a juridical matter, or connect it solely with a particular segment or authority within the body of believers.[883] He adds that inasmuch as the hierarchy has the role of bringing the

"Christ-event" before the community, it should lead in forming the "collective finding of truth." Wagner asserts that it is in "the truth itself" that the genuine "criterion" of the *consensus fidelium* is to be found.[884]

## Eugen Biser

A bid to "rescue" the notion of the *sensus fidei* by examining it from the standpoint of both Medieval and modern perspectives is made in an article by Eugen Biser, "Der Glaubenssinn: Ein begriffskritischer Rettungsversuch."[885] He first cautions against simple attempts to understand the sense of the faithful. This sense is not sent down "from heaven" like a "revelation," but occurs through concepts and experiences that are more earthbound, although such human vehicles must be themselves carefully understood. Biser finds it useful to recall the words of Jesus to Nicodemus on how the Spirit, like the wind, "blows where it will," while at the same time noting the caution of Romano Guardini that the notion of the sense of the people is taken by Christianity from a secular source.[886]

Biser observes that current understandings of the concept of "sense" have suffered because of the modern secularized context.[887] He adds, however, that it is not so much "secularization" as modern "internalization" that should be considered in order to retrieve the "sense" as it was originally understood with respect to matters of faith.[888]

In the early scholastic period, this sense was identified as the *intellectus fidei*. This was not understood as an existential or merely human "sense" but as "the intelligible kernel of the mystery of faith." Biser observes, however, that this insight was developed in a period of "intellectual optimism." Within the "epoch making paradigm" of Anselm's *Cur Deus homo?* and its "quest" for theological understanding, the *sensus fidei* was seen as an "embodiment of . . . divine motivation."[889]

In the theology of the Middle Ages the claims made for this source were not without their problems, as evident in the differing views of Hugo of St. Victor and Bernard of Clairvaux on how this inner sense might or might not come to expression.[890] From such an unresolved state, the concept fell into disuse. Biser observes that with the later medieval "synthesis" of mystical and conceptual approaches, the "divine mysteries" were understood to be accessible through an "act of submission."[891]

Biser asserts, however, that "spiritual intuition and initiative" led a life of its own, exerting a "secret control" on conscious faith. It thus contributed to the theological approaches and appeals of Lessing and Kierkegaard and later to the work of Barth. Biser sees the modern era as lacking any solid understanding of the *intellectus fidei* in comparison with its earlier scholastic level, even though this sort of intuitive knowledge informed speculation like that of Hegel in another way. He observes that within Hegel's system the "mysteries of faith" are transformed into matters of knowledge.[892]

Biser notes that an "opposite" move from knowing to matters of faith came in the "anthropological turn."[893] He identifies the beginnings of this turn even before the negative views of Feuerbach in the work of Beethoven in which the mystical again became recognized as embodied in the hearts of believers. He finds in the different approaches of Bultmann, Tillich, Guardini and Rahner important contributions to the reappropriation of the notion that the human person is the image or "mirror" in which the divine can be found.[894]

Through such work there is now a renewed possibility of appropriating a direct contact with the mystery of the faith, particularly in the very question of how faith lies in the depth of human persons. The modern person realizes a deeper question of faith experientially, and in the experience of a "questioning sense" there can be a direct link to actual faith. It is in the combination of this internal question and the promise of freedom and fullness of being that is raised by the "question of God," that faith is possible.[895]

Biser cites Ignatius of Antioch, who spoke of Christ as "breaking the silence" of God. Through Christ, God takes up a place in the human heart, not as a "transcendent idea," but as a concrete presence bringing genuine reconciliation and hope.[896] Biser asserts that in the light of this presence, both Christologies from "above" or "below," as well as other theological descriptions, are inadequate to describe what occurs. He notes that Kierkegaard recovered an understanding of Jesus as "the unity of Helper and remedy, Person and work." In reference to this view, Biser adds that the divine action in Christ that transcends history is still accomplished in historical experience, when the believer embraces the source of faith in the experience of faith.[897]

Biser asserts then, that faith is not what it is often seen to be: an "alienated act of submission under the both incomprehensible and intense wisdom of God."[898] Rather, faith is a historically situated movement toward the self-giving Jesus, in whom the believer finds his or her own identity. At the same time, this is not a matter of an individual and God in a mere "vertical" relationship.[899] Faith is mediated in human context, in the "reciprocal give and take" that forms a "unity of the Spirit" in the community of believers.[900] Biser asserts that this community is not based merely on human efforts at consensus building. It is the result of God's initiative within this human context, drawing the members into a common faith and trust.[901]

Asking then, what final "sense" is to be given to the *sensus fidei*, Biser describes it as a source that offers more than "information"; from within the security of faith the *sensus fidei* expresses an openness that is born in questioning but which has had its burden relieved.[902]

## THE SENSE OF THE FAITHFUL AND MORAL THEOLOGY

The "practical" importance of the sense of the faithful has found substantial illustration in the post-conciliar discussions of morality and conscience. The authors discussed in the preceding section offer direct observations in this area. Still others develop the connection less directly.

It would be difficult to find a more dramatic event in the post-conciliar context than the promulgation of *Humanae Vitae*, since it had a very practical impact on the relationship of the laity and the magisterium, the general context of moral theology, and the different understandings and appropriations of the *sensus fidelium*.[903] In the present work, it is only possible to consider those authors whose direct concern is the *sensus fidelium*. Many authors could also be cited who refer to the sense of the faithful as part of a larger discussion of the promulgation or reception of *Humanae Vitae*. The encyclical has also engendered extended debates on the related topic of infallibility. With both topics, the variety of theological responses shows the significant differences that exist in the post-conciliar Church in regard to "models" for appropriating the Church's historical tradition. A few examples will be offered to illustrate this diversity.

John C. Ford and Germain Grisez have argued that the Church's teaching on artificial contraception should be considered as an expression of the infallibility of the ordinary magisterium.[904] In doing so they assert a clearly passive role for the sense of the faithful.

> The sense of the faith provides no mystical and privileged access to divine things which would permit the opinions of the faithful at a given time *insofar as these opinions conflict with received teaching* to become a criterion by which to measure the truth of that teaching.[905]

The authors also claim, that the "still-troubled consciences" of those who have used contraceptives at the instigation of dissenting theologians is evidence of "their genuine *sensus ecclesiae*, which the dissenting opinion of theologians has failed either to alter or reduce to silence."[906]

Others argue, however, that the troubled context that surrounds this issue is related to the larger questions of interpreting the doctrine of infallibility in the light of a historical understanding of Vatican I and the interpretation of the role of the faithful in the light of Vatican II. John T. Ford has observed, "In the absence of a critical hermeneutical understanding of *Pastor aeternus*, theologians may unsuspectingly have inherited a doctrinal teaching without a supporting theology."[907] Ford adds that "the absolutist monarchical ecclesiology" which previously contextualized this teaching "is no longer tenable," but he notes it has not been replaced by any model which adequately shows the place of infallibility in the Church.[908]

The importance of a careful hermeneutic of magisterial, and particularly papal statements, is well illustrated by the tendency of some authors to attribute an importance to *Humanae Vitae* that the pope himself did not claim for it. To offer but one example that followed quickly after the encyclical, Joseph Costanzo has claimed, "The technical formality of an *ex cathedra* definition would not add to the intrinsic validity that is, its certitude, and the obligatory force of *Humanae Vitae*."[909] This assertion is remarkable in the light of the official remarks made to the international press by Monsignor Ferdinando Lambruschini when the encyclical was first published, when he clearly described it as non-infallible, while adding strong clarifications about its authority.[910] With the volatile response that followed the encyclicals publication, however, it may not be surprising that some have supported its teaching with arguments that give it the most substantial possible authority.

From another standpoint, papal infallibility has itself been described as having "become an obstacle to developing a thinking Church."[911] Patrick Crowley observes,

> There is still a strong belief (at different levels of the Catholic community) that laity and theologians, even though part of the sensus fidelium, have no real share in the teaching function of the whole Church, and that any search for doctrinal consultation and consensus among them can only lead to chaos and loss of control.[912]

Both the tendency to exaggerate authority and the willingness to distrust or dismiss the authority of the magisterium illustrate the need for a more adequate foundation for criticism of the function of the magisterium in the context of the whole Church.

That this foundation must include a deepened understanding of the infallibility of the Church as expressed through both the magisterium and the faithful as a whole, as well as through the relationship between these sources, has only become clearer in the reflections that have followed *Humanae Vitae*. In the wake of the encyclical, Thomas F. O'Meara pointed out the uniquely modern problems created by "instant" communication that were illustrated in the immediate responses to the encyclical. He argues that in the attempt to understand response and reception, the process by which the whole community actually functions and communicates internally must be taken into account, before the content of a given topic can be understood. He insists that a key role for authority must remain, but that the "model of thinking" that should be used is now disputed.[913]

Five years after *Humanae Vitae*, Robert Dionne suggested that between the extremes of an excessive appeal to authority and a flat rejection of it, there is room for a carefully defined "talking back" to the pope which can aid in the development of doctrine. Genuine development must include both the "lived experience of the Church" and the "express approval of the Bishop of Rome."[914] In a ten year retrospective that examined responses to *Humanae Vitae*, Joseph Komonchak called for a use of all the "'bearers' of authority," including the magisterium and *sensus fidei* as well as the Scriptures, tradition, liturgy and other elements in the Church in a wholistic, organic way. He adds that these should be "interrelated organically and not hierarchically."[915]

Moral theology in the Roman Catholic Church has thus become notably different than it was before *Humanae Vitae*. The encyclical has been characterized as "the decisive moment in the transition from neo-Thomist to revisionist moral theology."[916] This "transition" to a new model is hardly accepted by everyone, however, and certainly not by all in authority. It is much more accurate to characterize the context of moral theology and moral practice in the Church as pluralistic. The theological event of *Humanae Vitae* is particularly important in that it is linked to an issue that is directly related to the lives of many ordinary believers. It is no surprise that in the contemporary context of moral theology, the *sensus fidelium* has become a lightening rod among those who want to claim the Church's history and tradition in support of diverse moral stances.

In direct confrontation with the magisterium, Daniel Maguire claims:

> Contrary to hierarchical pretensions, Catholic theology has already crossed the line into defending the morality of some direct abortions. It has done this with support from the *sensus fidelium*.[917]

In contrast, Cormac Burke, a priest of the Opus Dei Prelature and an auditor in the Roman Rota asserts:

> I do not see how a Catholic mind can avoid the conclusion that the traditional teaching on contraception enjoys a divine guarantee of truth—in virtue not so much of papal infallibility as of the

infallibility of the whole Church: of the ordinary and universal Magisterium, and also of the "sensus fidelium" for centuries right up to the post-conciliar period.[918]

Burke argues earlier for a distinction between the *sensus fidelium* and a majority view among Catholics, where practice is against Church teaching but where actual faith might be troubled.[919] He criticizes theologians who claim to express the faith of believers as in disagreement with the magisterium. He claims, "The bishops are pastorally and physically closer to the people, while the theologians tend to live in a more remote academic world."[920]

Richard McCormick has sought to maintain a central unifying role for the magisterium in moral teaching, while finding a nuanced relationship for the teaching office with the faithful as a whole.[921] He sees within the magisterium two ways in which the *sensus fidelium* is understood. In one approach, "The experience and reflection of the faithful (*sensus fidelium*) ought to be listened to, but it is the ultimate responsibility of authoritative teachers to determine the truth."[922] McCormick sees this tendency as present in the "Declaration on Certain Questions Concerning Sexual Ethics" of the Congregation for the Doctrine of the Faith. In an alternate approach, "The experience and reflection of the faithful ought to be listened to and it is absolutely essential to a certain and binding proclamation of moral truth."[923] In this view, when a significant number of the faithful

> do not see the arguments and conclusions of an authoritative teacher (particularly a ban or condemnation), it is a sign that the matter is not sufficiently clear, or that it is badly formulated, or is wrong.[924]

This approach is evident in the "Declaration on Euthanasia" of the same Congregation. McCormick summarizes his views: "to be a credible guarantor of unity in morals, even an accurate one, the teaching office must anchor its procedures in a thoroughly open and contemporary notion of the *magisterium*."[925]

Certainly, McCormick and those with similar views are not without critics. McCormick's views on *Humanae Vitae*, and the conditions that demand assent or dissent to magisterial teachings have been characterized as contributing to the "erosion of the magisterium."[926] His views on the *sensus fidelium* have come under fire from Thomas Dubay, who questions who McCormick includes among "the faithful."[927] Dubay suggests that "both theology and common sense would reply that 'the faithful' are precisely that, namely, faithful." The believers who should be consulted are "those who accept the whole Gospel, who are willing to carry the cross every day, who lead a serious prayer life, who accept the teaching magisterium commissioned by Christ." Dubay adds, "We could hardly call faithful those who reject knowingly anything Jesus has taught or established."[928]

In addition to motivating a great deal of reflection on the relationship of the sense of the faithful to the moral teaching of the Church, *Humanae Vitae* also touched off a virtual storm of writings on the topic of dissent.[929] Here too, the *sensus fidelium* has been appropriated in a variety of ways. In contextualizing the dissent of a number of Catholic theologians and philosophers to the teaching of *Humanae Vitae*, Charles Curran and Robert Hunt described the *sensus fidelium* as "a broadly based 'sense' in the Church."[930] Recalling that the early Church saw consensus as "a safe test of orthodoxy," they add,

> However, this was never understood to be a question of mere "majority rule." This notion of *sensus fidelium* shows a variety of historical forms depending on the theological and polemical context in which it is found.[931]

The authors go on to suggest that this source, expressed perhaps through dissent, might serve as a balance to the "trend toward establishing an *exclusive* teaching prerogative in the hierarchy."[932]

In criticizing the move away from authority and unanimity in the Church, Joseph Costanzo accuses Curran and Hunt and the other "subject professors" involved in the case of dissent at the Catholic University of America of relativism.[933] In his own argument, Costanzo asserts that the criteria of unanimity among all believers, reiterated in *Lumen Gentium* (# 12), is tautological: "Everyone is without error or everyone is in error."[934] Costanzo goes on to give counter arguments to examples offered in *Dissent In and For the Church*, where magisterial fallibility was to be illustrated.[935] He closes his review with some questions about the relationship of academic freedom and the issue of "teaching religious orthodoxy," while adding his own view that "the norm of orthodoxy in matters of Catholic faith and morals is the solemn definitive teachings of the papal magisterium whether *ex cathedra* or not and of the Councils approved and ratified by the Roman Pontiff."[936]

Some authors have been more circumspect, seeing the possibility of interaction between the faithful and their teachers as an outcome of dissent. Thus Joseph Bracken could write, "It is at least theoretically possible that the 'spontaneous judgment of the faithful,' based on the actual living-out of Catholic belief in daily life, can on occasion offer a valuable corrective to the judgment of the hierarchy."[937] Bracken cautions that the Church is not to be seen as a democracy, but he suggests that it can find in dissent "an indispensable means of self-criticism in the formulation of community policy." He claims that only if believers "perceive that it is both their right and their duty to express vigorous protest to any decision of the magisterium which they consider to be personally unjust and/or dangerous to their Catholic belief" will the *sensus fidei* be able to serve its role properly. Bracken further claims, "At stake is the integrity of the

Church's doctrine and their own sense of self-identity as members of the Roman Catholic community."[938]

Two decades after the promulgation of the encyclical, *Humanae Vitae*, neither the discussion nor repercussions of theological dissent had ended. In the summer of 1986, Charles Curran was declared to be "not suitable nor eligible to teach Catholic Theology" by the Congregation for the Doctrine of the Faith, because of his dissent from magisterial teachings.[939] In response to the suspension of Curran, attention has turned both to renewed discussion of dissent and to criticism of the process by which Curran was disciplined.[940]

The legitimacy of public dissent has been linked to the complex process of examining controversial ecclesial matters in the context of public opinion.[941] Margaret Farley argues that while there are risks in bringing such issues to the "public forum," there are more risks in not discussing them openly.[942] She asserts, "Open discussion . . . can be a necessary, but not a sufficient, condition for a faithful search for understanding."[943] Ecclesial debates must consider "substantive truths and moral obligations" in a way that is distinct from academic or political pursuits. She adds, however, that

> precisely because these truths are believed to "make sense" in the moral realm, and because their "sense" must be probed ultimately by each person and by the community as a whole, fidelity to the truth is served, not thwarted, by open public discourse.[944]

Commenting on the desire of some in the Church to protect the faithful from "confusion" in regard to controversial areas, Farley observes that such an approach "retards rather than fosters their moral development."[945]

This same point is taken up by Lisa Sowle Cahill who has maintained that the desire to avoid confusion in controversial areas of sexual morality has lead the Church's teachers to take too rigid a stance.[946] She asserts,

> Rhetoric deploring confusion of the faithful and scandal to the faithful caused by "dissent" hardly conceals the fact that greater confusion and scandal are caused by so-called guidance which is in conflict with the experienced moral obligations of persons, couples, and families attempting to live faithfully in Christian community.[947]

Others have argued that the organic relationship that should exist between hierarchy and faithful can be enhanced by the reemerging notion of reception. Thus Thomas Rausch describes reception as "the flip side of the theology of an authoritative magisterium, for authority can only teach what the whole Church itself believes; its role is to articulate what is the faith of the Church."[948] He recalls that there have been times where "a faithful remnant" has maintained orthodox belief, and other times where the magisterium has been prophetic in deepening the Church's understanding of the Gospel. The insight of the people and their pastors are thus both vital to the Church's ongoing discernment.[949] Elsewhere Rausch has observed, "The traditional doctrine of the *sensus fidelium* or sense of the faithful and the ecclesial reality of reception both imply an interdependence of teaching authority and the body of the faithful."[950]

There are difficulties in describing exactly how interdependence of laity and hierarchy, or even reception should look. Philip Kaufman has suggested that in contrast to earlier times, modern communications may make possible another source for discerning the sense of the faithful.

> Reliable and competently conducted surveys can inform us about what the faithful believe and what they reject as contrary to their faith experience. A wise church leadership will start to use this valuable tool.[951]

Most authors have been more wary of using such methods to assess the sense of the faithful.[952]

In an article that appeared early in the post-Vatican II discussion of this problem, Frans Haarsma addressed the difficulties inherent to the discernment of the sense of the faithful.[953] He asserts that because the *sensus fidei* itself is not knowable directly, it must be sought through "objectifying factors."[954] He adds though, that these are not "an adequate and unambiguous expression of the sense of the faith."[955] He considers several factors that make finding consensus difficult. One difficulty lies in identifying who the faithful are. In the light of Vatican II, Haarsma argues that other Christians must now be included, yet here again, appropriating their "sense" in the context of their differing beliefs poses a problem.[956] Turning over the interpretation of this source to ecclesial leaders ends up with a "vicious circle."[957] Focusing on the faithful raises the question of what areas are within their range of competence.[958] Haarsma comments that perhaps the faithful have the role of generating only negative criteria, but adds that then this role must be considered less than decisive in cases like the teaching of *Humanae Vitae*.[959]

Haarsma arrives eventually at what he sees as the "biggest difficulty" in discerning consensus:

> The consensus of the faithful is indeed presented as being brought about by the Holy Spirit, but still as a given *fact*, where as in reality it might well be a *task*—always to be desiderated, of course, yet never completely attained.[960]

When he examines the value of empirical examinations of religious questions, he finds that they fall short of giving "any direct answer to theological questions— including thus the theological question of what we are to understand by a consensus of the faithful."[961] They are more useful in showing areas of *dissensus*. He adds that questions which receive "an almost 100% unanimous reply are not questions of interest."⁹⁶² Those that reveal disagreement point to the areas where the Church must work for deeper understanding.⁹⁶³

Perhaps one important outcome of the contemporary controversy over dissent and its relation to the *sensus fidei*, is the deepening understanding of what constitutes a positive response of assent to Church teaching. Discussion of this issue has centered on the sort of assent that is called for in response to magisterial teaching as it is described in *Lumen Gentium* (# 25):

> In matters of faith and morals, the bishops speak in the name of Christ and the faithful are to accept their teaching and adhere to it with a religious assent of soul. This religious submission of will and of mind must be shown in a special way to the authentic teaching authority of the Roman Pontiff, even when he is not speaking ex cathedra.⁹⁶⁴

The difficulties of interpreting what the Council Fathers themselves intended by the term are described by Ladislas Orsy.⁹⁶⁵ A variety of interpretations of the key term, *obsequium*, have been offered since the Council.⁹⁶⁶ Orsy argues that the Fathers did not intend a precise meaning at all, but used the term as "seminal locution."⁹⁶⁷ This he defines as

> an expression which conveys an insight into the truth but without defining it with precision; it needs to be developed further. It is a broad and intuitive approach to a mystery that leaves plenty of room for future discoveries.⁹⁶⁸

He links this approach of the Council explicitly to the *sensus fidei* of the bishops themselves, asserting that it "helped them to identify, but not to dissect, analyze and classify, the seeds of truth which in due course can grow into a large tree."⁹⁶⁹

Orsy describes the Council Fathers as including the exercise of assent or obedience among the faithful itself as an active part in the development of understanding of the faith.[970] He describes *obsequium* as a "special expression" of *communio* in the area of doctrine.[971] It "ultimately signifies to be one with the church; one in mind and heart, which means one in belief and action." Rather than describing a particular type of response, it refers to an "attitude" of communion, that "may bind to respect, or to submission—or to any other attitude between the two."[972]

The connection between the believer's response to magisterial teaching and the sense of the faithful is also explicitly made by Bishop B. C. Butler.[973] After discussing the exercise of infallibility by the pope, the college of bishops and the whole Church, he briefly notes the importance of the *sensus fidelium* and its "latent infallibility."[974] From this source, the pope and other pastors may learn "aspects of developed gospel which they might otherwise overlook."[975] Butler then turns his attention to the response to be expected from believers to magisterial teaching. He first advises distinguishing between "*obsequium*" and "*assensus*."[976] The latter form of "assent" has the form of certainty that is embodied in an "internal act" of agreement that has no conditions.[977] Butler suggests that this use of the notion of assent be reserved for doctrines where no conditions are included. He adds the important point, that such assent is given to "the living reality that is Jesus Christ" which is referred to by doctrines, and not to the propositions themselves.[978]

In discussing the response due to teachings which may be conditioned in some sense, but which call the faithful to worshipful action and the expression of loyalty, Butler finds *obsequium* to be a better term. Some teachings are subject to further insight or may even be subject to error, and thus cannot be the subject of assent. At the same time, a dutiful response is warranted.[979] In *obsequium*, Butler finds an appropriate response, which he translates as "due respect."[980] He remarks,

> I have suggested that *obsequium* should be used to mean *due* respect. The advantage of this is that the quality of *obsequium* will

thus vary according to the situation in which it operates. A careful reading of LG n. 25 . . . will show that this variation in quality or degree of *obsequium* is operative in this most important passage of the Dogmatic Constitution on the Church. [981]

The respectful response of the faithful believer is particularly important in regard to the bishop in the believer's local church. Butler suggests, "The official teaching of the faith is done within a structured *koinonia*, and tends to build up the local church in which the universal koinonia is actualised."[982]

Butler goes on to say that "theoretical and practical respect" are included in *obsequium*. Both the will and the intellect are called to respond to official teaching. At the same time, he points out that both practical and intellectual agreement may "be limitable by other factors" in cases related to non-infallible teaching.[983] Butler closes his reflections by describing the *obsequium religiosum* as an appropriate response to *Humanae Vitae*.[984]

Many of the same issues are covered by Richard Malone, writing for the National Conference of Catholic Bishops' Committee on Doctrine, although he places more emphasis on the importance of the Church's teaching authority.[985] Carefully distinguishing the unique role of the pope and recalling the importance of the body of bishops as well, Malone then adds that revelation is not given to the magisterium in isolation, but to the Church as a whole.[986] He notes that *Lumen Gentium* (# 25) has "recurring references to the deposit of revelation *for the teaching that is done by the bishops* to be transmitted through the life and teaching of the Church."[987]

Malone later distinguishes the "certainty" of a teaching from its "infallibility."[988] A teaching may include a "serious moral obligation" without requiring "irrevocable assent."[989] Constant teaching of a doctrine may well be the basis for certainty, without guaranteeing infallibility.[990] In the case of such non-infallible teachings, dissent is possible, though Malone suggests it "should be rare."[991] He distinguishes too between private and public dissent; the latter may be more in league with "protest."[992] Malone warns that public dissent can turn bishops and theologians into adversaries. Dissent that is frequent places the individual's personal judgment over the magisterium as a "rule of faith."[993]

## DEMOCRATIZATION OF THE CHURCH

Concern over the proper role for authority in the Church characterizes discussion about the possibility of creating a more "democratic" Church. Christian Duquoc has seen in the *sensus fidei* the warrant for "an institutionalised correlate" in addition to the instinct for propositional faith, that should give the faithful an active role in the Church.[994] Duquoc argues that Vatican II made "recognized groups and pastoral councils" vehicles for "public opinion [that] not only exercises regulatory authority negatively through inertia or positively through resistance," but which "also enjoys institutional rights."[995] Involvement of the people in the selection of their own leaders is seen by Raymond Kottje as a practice by which the Church could reclaim its early tradition of participation, instead of relying solely on the procedures of the last seven hundred years.[996] Hervé-Marie Legrand has warned that simplistic appropriation of democratic processes is a "false trail" that "would lead to theological confusion."[997] He suggests a process where the people would be involved through early input, where elections would be handled by pastoral councils made up of both clergy and lay people, and where the candidates would be affirmed by the appropriate conferences of bishops and then the pope, as more faithful to the "ecclesiology of communion" in the early Church.[998]

Edward Kilmartin has suggested an approach that could lead to greater lay participation in the exercise of authority in the Church, by recommending a rethinking of the juridical system of authority that is based in a "Christocentric orientation" and the movement toward a fuller, "Trinitarian" base.[999] With such a view, the movement of the Spirit could be better appreciated as operating through the pastors and the people in the Church.[1000] A greater liturgical involvement in the consecration of bishops has been suggested by Joseph Lécuyer as another way of reappropriating the ancient practice of involving the faithful in the selection and approval of their leaders.[1001]

Respondents from a variety of theological perspectives have expressed the view that in its secular form, democracy cannot give an adequate structure to the Church community, even while calling for renewed structures that would increase interaction, communication and co-responsibility in decision making.[1002] John Heagle has called for a greater sensitivity to the *sensus fidelium*, claiming, "Whether we call this democracy or dialogue, consultation or collegiality, the institutional Church needs to listen to and trust the grassroots."[1003] Laurence J. O'Connell calls for greater reflection of the *sensus fidelium* in a Church whose leaders "may be too narrow-minded" and whose governmental structure may itself be less than adequate.[1004] Inasmuch as the Church relies on the foundational if "unrecognized" influence of the Holy Spirit, democracy will not provide a suitable alternate structure. At the same time, the teaching of Vatican II on co-responsibility and participation must foster a "reciprocal relationship" between pastors and people.[1005] O'Connell draws on the distinction between the bishops as *focus* of Church teaching and the People of God as *locus* "from which this teaching springs."[1006] More vital to the Church than democracy is the work of visionary leadership" that gives the faithful "a sense of full participation within the life of the Church."[1007]

## Reception

Both the difficulty and practical importance of achieving and discerning consensus in actual Church communities is illustrated well in those attempts to appropriate the sense of the faithful in the form of the reception of doctrinal teaching. In the post-conciliar context the importance of reception has been recognized especially following the important study of Congar discussed above.[1008] Congar stresses that reception is not a "juridical quality," but the response of believers to the content of a doctrine.[1009] The "confirmation" that reception gives to the expression of faith proposed by those in authority is not some sort of legal ratification, but rather is due to "the sense of the increased effectiveness that the consent of the affected parties gives to a decision."[1010]

In discussing the way in which Vatican II should be understood two decades after its close, Giuseppe Alberigo asserts that interpretation is a slow process, which cannot be left solely to the magisterium. He observes, "Only the *sensus fidei* of the Church as a whole can be the adequate interpreter of a major council."[1011] It may be debated as to when a pattern of interpretation has become sufficiently clear or has continued long enough to constitute reception. Luis M. Bermejo has argued, on the basis of a number of examples, that some expressions of doctrine may be accepted over long periods of time before finding "a final non-reception."[1012] Bermejo questions the extent to which Vatican I and its teachings on the papacy ought to be reexamined. He suggests that its reception may need reevaluation in the light of the ongoing *sensus fidei* operating in all the levels of the Church.[1013] Miguel M. Garijo Guembe has asked whether the long history of reception can be understood "coherently" in Catholic ecclesiology.[1014] Reception of magisterial teaching by the whole Church has not always been simple. Ultimately, discrepancies between official teaching and its reception by the faithful is resolved by the action of the Spirit who works in both elements in the

Church. Garijo points out that the Spirit has operated through tensions, corrections and even reversals during the Church's history.[1015]

The difficulties in establishing reception as the manifestation of the sense of the faithful are particularly obvious in the area of ecumenical dialogue. Paul O'Leary has described how the difficulty of forming and identifying consensus and reaching a genuine reception of doctrine between churches is tied to differing ecclesiologies and different readings of history.[1016] On the other hand, the very desire for unity has been identified as an important aspect of the *sensus fidelium* as it is exhibited in ecumenical work and reflection on the process of reception.[1017]

Thomas Rausch has described the importance of reception among participants in such dialogues. Those who take part have found some theological success in discussions with other communions, but they then face the difficult task of bringing their own churches into agreement.[1018] Rausch distinguishes between "classical" and "ecumenical" forms of reception. Classical reception developed in the first millennium. Before Constantine, churches used it to express acceptance of the teachings developed in the local or regional synods of other areas.[1019] In the era of the major councils, it referred to the process of acceptance of the teachings of earlier councils by later ones.[1020] Rausch stresses that this classical view of reception developed "in a church which understood itself as a communion of churches."[1021] He observes that with the newer, ecumenical form of reception, a more difficult task confronts separated communions. Agreement must now be reached between churches with different histories and traditions.[1022]

Rausch identifies several elements that should characterize a wider view of reception. He observes, "Reception cannot be reduced to a juridical determination, either of authority or on the part of the faithful; it is a process involving the whole Church."[1023] At the same time, formal decisions by leaders with authority play an important role.[1024] He notes reception is not only a matter of expressions of doctrine, but rather "involves the recognition and acceptance of a common faith."[1025] Finally, Rausch insists that the norm for reception "is not agreement with one's own ecclesial position but agreement with the apostolic tradition."[1026]

In order to achieve such response, Rausch recommends that education about the issues in ecumenical dialogue be brought into the "practical life of the churches."[1027] Further, Christians can best explore their common faith "through living and worshiping together."[1028] He urges churches at the local level to become involved in the actual reception process.[1029] Rausch notes too that at larger national and regional levels, representation from other communions could enhance the reflection of groups like the National Conference of Catholic Bishops.[1030] It is useful to compare the points made here by Rausch with the similar views expressed by the Orthodox theologian, John Zizioulas, on whom Rausch draws.[1031] Zizioulas emphasizes the role of all members of the Church in their lived faith and a focus on ecclesial communities rather than individuals, even where the latter are theologians. He suggests an active process of ecumenical progress where "*all* churches . . . re-receive and re-adjust themselves to the original Apostolic community."[1032]

Theologians from other Christian communions have clearly linked the process of reception with the sense of the faithful. Within the Lutheran tradition, Harding Meyer has discussed the role of the "magnus consensus ecclesiae," observing that its importance is noted in the first article of the Augsburg Confession.[1033] Lukas Vischer, an ecumenical officer of the Swiss Reformed Churches has described a "spirituality of reception" through which churches might examine their own need to change and move toward a common tradition in receiving the fruits of ecumenical efforts like the *Baptism, Eucharist and Ministry* document of the Faith and Order Commission of the World Council of Churches.[1034] George Lindbeck has proposed a reappropriation of a "biblically informed *sensus fidelium*" as a foundation for building community and unity in the churches.[1035] Episcopalian author Margaret O'Gara has noted that participants in Lutheran-Roman Catholic dialogue have found that *Lumen Gentium*'s description of the action of the Holy Spirit "whereby the whole flock of Christ is preserved and progresses in unity of faith" and the document's "emphasis on the *sensus fidelium*" help in creating an understanding that "'puts in proper context' Vatican I's *ex sese* clause."[1036] She suggests that the role of reception as an indicator of infallibility in church teaching is a key issue in Anglican-Roman Catholic dialogue.[1037]

Some of the more illuminating insights stemming from ecumenical discussions have come from Orthodox authors. Metropolitan Emilianos Timiadis, while recalling the important role of the laity in the stormy history of conciliar reception, claims:

> It is nevertheless important to stress that the faithful people do not sanctify the ecumenical councils nor do the bishops who compose these councils define doctrine in the name of the people, as if they were the agents of power who had received from the people the honor of proclaiming a truth protected by the people, as some Russian theologians seem to believe.[1038]

Timidias summarizes the wisdom of the Fathers on the differing roles in the Church: "The laity receive the faith and defend it while the episcopate defines and formulates it." He sees a need in the Western church to deepen its understanding of the connection between the laity and the bishops.[1039] Timiadis attributes the post-Vatican II "crisis of authority" fostered by "avant-garde" or "over-timid" interpretations of the Council's decrees, to a "naive conception of authority and obedience as if these were 'external' realities."[1040] He suggests that the *sensus fidei*, "the inner authority of the conscience and the inspiration of the Holy Spirit for *all* the people of God" should be reclaimed. The faithful should become more aware of their proper role.[1041]

At the same time, an emphasis on public opinion should not be allowed to lead to a "mob-ocracy, controlling spiritual matters, with the badly informed and badly trained masses monopolizing the discussion." The laity must be "spiritually mature and well-equipped."[1042] Consultation and participation must be carefully crafted, and "assaults from without and within" must be avoided.[1043] Elsewhere, Timiadis has made it clear that the final responsibility for reception or rejection of doctrine, lies with the Church's leaders. They are to listen to the *sensus fidelium*, but they themselves give the "decisive word."[1044]

The relationship between those with authority to teach in the Church and the greater number of the faithful whose role it is to receive Church teaching has been examined with particular attention to ecumenical ramifications by Dionne in *The Papacy and the Church* cited above. The scope of this study is too wide to allow a comprehensive treatment of it here. Yet, a brief view of the role given to the *sensus fidelium* can be included.[1045] In order to contribute to a better understanding of the papacy in the ecumenical context, Dionne addresses "the internal problem" of authority and infallibility in the Roman Catholic Church, which he describes as a "tension between Church as institution and Church as associations."[1046]

The result of Dionne's historical study of doctrinal development in regard to several modern issues (Catholicism and non-Christian religions, Church and state, religious freedom, and membership in the Church) is a foundation for judging that the Church's authority, in its actual practice and in its relation to the response in the Church as a whole, has demonstrated the characteristics of the *koinonia* as it was understood in the New Testament.[1047] This *koinonia* concept of Church is particularly rich in its possibilities for ecumenical dialogue.[1048]

The importance of *koinonia* as a model for the internal workings of the Roman Catholic Church is no less clear than is its importance for ecumenical dialogue. Rausch has noted that in Dionne's discussion of the Marian dogmas, the "associative elements based on the *sensus fidelium* were present in the process that led to both *ex cathedra* definitions."[1049] The consultation that preceded these definitions and the active influence of theologians "talking back" to the magisterium illustrate an active role in practice for the several levels that make up the Church.[1050] Dionne argues that the distinction between the *ecclesia docens* and the *ecclesia discens* that preceded Vatican II can hardly be considered as so "clear-cut" after the Council.[1051] This assertion is connected to his claim that the nature of the actual process of development of doctrine is active and involves the Church as a whole, even if ecclesial theory has not acknowledged this. Within this active process of development, an important role is played by reception. Dionne asserts, "A clear distinction must be made between reception as obedience and reception as functionally equivalent to an active *sensus fidelium*."[1052] Dionne sees the *sensus fidelium*, which has "talked back" to the hierarchy "respectfully and responsibly" in an effort to challenge or clarify what is taught by the ordinary magisterium, as possibly extending in practice even Newman's understanding of this source as expressed in *On Consulting the Faithful*.[1053] The practice of reception in the post-conciliar context as an active element in the development of doctrine may well have important precedents in the way the magisterium exercised its responsibilities in the recent past, even when its practice was inconsistent with its own dominant ecclesiology.[1054]

The issue of reception as discussed in ecumenical circles has provided one context for considering the practical influence of the sense of the faithful. An additional area of influence has been described by those who see the reception or interpretation of law as another expression of the same source. Rinaldo Bertolino has drawn on several of the historical and systematic studies of the *sensus fidelium* discussed above in arguing that the *sensus fidei* is vital to understanding and implementing canon law.[1055] Bertolino insists that contextualizing law in the whole Church, understood as a *communio* whose consensus is expressed in its laws, results in a legal framework that is not "extrinsic or formal, but intrinsic" to it.[1056] A practical interaction of the law with the customs of the people for whom it is written can allow the Church to discern the action of the Spirit through the practical living of the faith by all of the Church's members.[1057]

Before the new code of canon law was promulgated in 1983, James Coriden reexamined the legal context for shared responsibility in the light of Vatican II's ecclesiology.[1058] Relating the notion of shared decision making to several other issues, including a renewed understanding of the sacraments, the work of the Spirit, and the shared mission of the whole Church, he identified as "perhaps most pertinent and profound, the ancient and many-faceted concept of the Church" as *communio* or *koinonia*.[1059] Coriden asserted here that the general context of the law in the post-conciliar Church was one whose creative possibilities went beyond even an appeal to *epikeia* in fostering an openness and accountability in local churches, and particularly in the authority of bishops.[1060] A localized exercise of responsibility based in the Council's principle of subsidiarity could make possible "a return to the centuries-old principle, *quod omnes tangit ab omnibus approbetur*."[1061]

Ladislas Orsy has discussed the new code of canon law as it relates to the understanding of the Church community given in *Lumen Gentium*, in commenting on Canon # 27 of the new code, "Custom is the best interpreter of laws."[1062] Orsy argues that, in the light of "the recently achieved self-understanding of the Church," the community as a whole is responsible for giving the best possible interpretation of law. This interpretation by custom should occur through action, and "is the best because it goes beyond the authentic, beyond the judicial, and beyond the doctrinal."[1063]

At the same time, the actual development of the new code has received criticism from those who find its juridical style dominating the more wholistic ecclesiology of Vatican II. Eugenio Corecco finds a lack of the Council's emphasis on an ecclesiology of *communio*, with the participation of the whole People of God understood as foundational for the Church's life. This lack is reflected in "the *minimal utilisation of the sensus fidei of the faithful* (taken up in canon 750 in a seriously mutilated form *when compared to Lumen gentium* 12, 1) and of the *common priesthood* (can. 836)."[1064] Corecco finds that on the face of it, "the Code has received, in approximately equal measure" the ecclesiologies of the perfect society and the *communio*. Considered from a systematic standpoint, the code's use of the plurality of views found in the Council's documents has "made even clearer the unbridgeable gap between the two ecclesiologies."[1065] Corecco argues for a more nuanced approach that considers "the deeper tendencies at work in the Council" to properly implement the new law.[1066]

## LIBERATION MOVEMENTS

If the issue of reception of doctrine involves theologizing about the practical life of the Church, a definite shift in focus to the creation of theology through praxis may be found in the appropriation of the *sensus fidelium* in liberation theology. The notion of *koinonia*, recognized by many as an ecclesial model that can provide a solid context for understanding the active role of the sense of the faithful has also been linked specifically to the growing phenomenon of base communities.

Raymond Collins has shown the vital role played by small communities of believers in the early Church, and has described the continued importance of such groups through the Church's history, even in eras where they were not a dominant focus in ecclesiology.[1067] He notes that in the wake of Vatican II, small groups have taken on an important role in many areas, with those in Latin America being the most obvious examples.[1068] He observes that in such groups there is an important connection "between *koinōnia* and *kerygma—diakonia*, that is, between community and mission."[1069] These communities provide a vital place where the laity can take part in the life and mission of the Church. Collins notes that empowerment for this work is rooted in a renewed appreciation of the role of baptism in each believer's life.[1070]

Collins observes that basic communities have often grown in importance where there is a significant lack of clergy. He notes that within such communities "there is frequently a lack of adequate leadership, a lack of spiritual guidance, and a lack of sufficient and proper motivation in the formation." These problems also present a challenge to further growth.[1071] Collins finally cites comments made by Cardinal Basil Hume after the 1987 Synod of Bishops and the Synod document itself to suggest that the local church should become a "community of communities" where its smaller components can be nurtured even while they enliven the larger body.[1072]

The actual working out of the mutual influence between levels in the Church can be problematic. Virgil Elizondo, writing with special reference to the Hispanic churches of the United States, has described the tensions between smaller communities and the institutions of the Church that sometimes challenge the identity and life expressed in these churches.[1073] Elizondo recognizes that the institutions must help the smaller communities integrate themselves into the larger community. He asserts, however, "We do not want to form a separate church, but neither do we want to give up the faith treasures of our hearts—our tradition of faith or our particular *sensus fidelium*—in order to be a part of this Church."[1074] He sees the need for "a pluralistic church which will truly welcome the wealth which God has placed in the various people of the world."[1075]

Paulo Suess has described the importance of the sense of the faithful especially as it is developed in the popular religion of the poor. He asserts that such religion "reveals an authentic *sensus fidelium*, not only on a subjective and individual basis, but originating collectively and remaining a collective possession."[1076] The *sensus fidelium* found in the poor must be recognized as a wisdom given for the whole Church, specifically in its ability to disclose "a 'hierarchy of truths' in relation to their basic necessities of life."[1077]

The experience of the poor and the expressions of church life in all those whose faith is developed and nurtured in the "grassroots" of base communities can not be left at the level of smaller communities alone. Of its nature it calls for theological reflection and interpretation within the wider ecclesial context. The inclusion of the insights and experience of all the faithful as a key to interpreting the challenges of the modern Church are given an important place in theology by Johann Baptist Metz.[1078] In discussing how to consult or include the insights of the faithful, given the problems of the modern Church as well as those related to the *fides implicita* as originally described by Newman, Metz has asserted, "We can go beyond the Church of dependents only when the dependents transform themselves."[1079] An active laity must be encouraged. He adds that "the basic community church with its new culture of communication and solidarity" is

> neither a passing fad, nor an adaptation from the Third World, it is instead a legitimate ecclesial expression of the conciliar truth which calls for a subject church with a legitimate teaching authority of the faithful.[1080]

The understanding and experience that is achieved through the practical living of the faith especially by the poor and suffering must not be idealized or subsumed into a preset framework.[1081] Rather theology must "transcend the system of the Church of dependents in which the faithful must remain silent or merely reproduce a predetermined theology."[1082]

Leonardo Boff argues forcefully for the active participation of the faithful in the teaching mission of the Church: "The distinction between *Ecclesia docens* and *Ecclesia discens* is theologically valid only once socio-analytic reflection on religious division of labour has been assumed and surpassed."[1083] Teaching about the faith must overcome certain negative aspects of the "religious division of labour" that has characterized the history of theology. The Church's expression of its faith has been linked to the development of a hierarchical structure that must be critiqued from a sociological perspective.[1084] Interaction between the faithful and the hierarchy must then include genuine dialogue, "an attitude of mutual criticism," and an "outside" reference point in the world. Finally, the Spirit must be understood as the one "who embraces the world as well as the Church."[1085]

In discussing the way in which the experience of lay people might be included in the theological deliberations of those who teach in the Church, Monika Hellwig has observed that there is now a general tendency to include lay representatives in the work of special commissions at the papal and episcopal levels. These are meant to increase representation and give attention to praxis. Hellwig raises the question, however, as to "whose praxis" is being considered in the Church. She observes that

> sometimes it appears that certain few and a-typical persons are selected and thereafter move more and more in purely clerical circles where they become a special professional class of committee lay representatives.[1086]

She draws a connection to Newman's time, where the debate was similar to that of today: "whether the experience of Christians can be taken with theological and dogmatic seriousness as expressed by the laity themselves, or whether such experience is only to reach the process of reflection as reformulated by professional churchmen."[1087] Hellwig also draws attention to the "particularly urgent question" of whether there is a sufficient consideration of women's experience in the Church.[1088]

A special case where the *sensus fidelium* and the insights of women in particular were neglected has been cited by Eileen Flynn.[1089] Interestingly, Flynn refers to the process used by the U.S. Bishops to produce the 1983 pastoral letter, "The Challenge of Peace," as a case where along with other flaws, the "work was done from an almost completely masculinist perspective."[1090] This criticism is especially telling given the assertion of Heft and others, that the development of this pastoral represents a positive use of the sense of the faithful.

Feminist critiques of the hierarchical structure and the male dominated authority base in the Church cover a wide range of positions including both those who remain in the Church and those who are outside of it. The full range of these positions cannot be considered here.[1091] It is useful to observe though, that such treatments, even where they do not specifically reflect on the traditional concept of the *sensus fidelium*, still bear on the themes that are central to this subject. Many authors have described how a male-dominated Church has stifled the experience and expression of faith in women.

Elizabeth Schuessler Fiorenza has described the exercise of power in the Church as a system of patriarchal oppression in need of dramatic conversion.[1092] She describes the response expected by the patriarchical leaders of the Church from women as "submission of mind and will" and adds that these men are prepared to use force and even violence to insure compliance. She adds that in confrontations with those in power,

> no appeal is possible, no due process instituted. "Consensus fidelium" means unqualified, if necessary, forced compliance and obedience of the faithful. True, the Vatican no longer has the power to burn us at the stake or to incarcerate us in cloisters. Nevertheless its degrees and actions still use the power of threat and force rather than persuasion and consultation.[1093]

After describing the hierarchy's response to various actions and appeals by feminists who have sought correction of institutional wrongs, Schuessler Fiorenza characterizes the Vatican's response as a "take it or leave it" exercise of authority.[1094] Even among those who criticize the system from a feminist perspective and who have nevertheless stayed in the Church, there is a call for an end to patriarchy and to the treatment of women with an institutionalized version of the treatment given to "battered women."[1095]

Rosemary Radford Reuther has similarly argued that the "caste tendencies" of the hierarchical Church must be rethought in favor of an emphasis on the "local community . . . as the first reality founded by the Spirit."[1096] Reuther maintains that the structure as it stands requires a radical reshaping. What is required in the relationship of ministry and community is not a reform of individual parts, but a completely new vision or *"Gestalt."*[1097]

### STRATEGIES FOR DEVELOPING THE SENSE OF THE FAITHFUL

While many authors have reflected on how the *sensus fidelium* may be discerned in the actions or expressions of the laity, a few have turned their attention to consciously developing this "sense" in the ecclesial community.

Michael McGinniss has described one of the tasks of theology as "identifying and thematizing this unfolding *sensus fidelium*."[1098] He attempts to read the "signs of hope" offered by this source specifically in the United States in order to support a strategy for increased lay involvement.[1099] McGinniss sees a "fundamental shift" in many areas of the Church from an ecclesiology centered on clerical roles to one more widely based in the baptism of all believers.[1100] He describes how this shift is taking place in the active roles, problems and awareness of new possibilities in lay ministry, parish life and religious education.[1101] His use of the sense of the faithful as a paradigm for this new awareness and activity is illustrated in his description of a new consensus in those areas which are actually being influenced by more lay involvement.

> This consensus in theology contributes to the realization of those changes in the unfolding *sensus fidelium* by naming the developments in a substantial way, by critiquing inadequate realizations of that change, and by describing a horizon for future praxis and, hopefully, stimulating that praxis.[1102]

The hopeful signs that McGinniss finds it such developing communities are not found everywhere in the Church, however. He observes, "The winds of theological repression seem to be blowing again within Catholicism: those are not winds which make professional theologians hopeful."[1103] Yet, he sees reason to hope in the inroads made into the Church's structures so far. In these he identifies the roots for change even in a questionable climate.[1104] He concludes:

> The signs of hope in the *sensus fidelium* make it possible for real Catholics to proclaim "now is the time": the time to hope for ministries which arise from and really touch the lives of lay women and men throughout the church.[1105]

Unfortunately, even those who share McGinniss's hope for greater participation of the laity in the structures of the Church, may question whether his appropriation of the sense of the faithful is consistent with the traditional theological understanding of the concept. Certainly the changes he describes may be indicators of the work of the Spirit, operating through a renewed sense of the faith to create a new fundamental ecclesiology. On the other hand, by his own assessment this result is far from certain.

McGinniss's use of the term *sensus fidelium* is linked to a select segment of the Church. Early on he notes that he uses the terms "consensus of the community of faith" and *"sensus fidelium"* synonymously.[1106] In drawing on the traditional strength associated with "consensus" when it is more appropriate to speak of a new *sensus fidei* that may be evolving, McGinniss adds more weight to his appeal for hope in the future, but he does little to clarify the meaning of the *sensus fidelium*. When applied in a selective way, the work of the Spirit is claimed, and perhaps legitimately, but the function of the *sensus fidelium* as a criterion is lost. The actual dissonance that exists in the Church in regard to the structure of ministry is disregarded rather than addressed. McGinniss's approach illustrates the difficulties that come with a premature judgment that the sense of the faithful is present in a concrete situation, especially when it is connected only with a portion of the whole body of faithful.

The types of issues involved in nurturing the sense of the faithful in actual communities is discussed by Evelyn Eaton Whitehead and James D. Whitehead under the heading of "Ministering to the Sense of the Faithful."[1107] They first recount the traditional understanding of the sense of the faithful in both its individual and communal aspects. The intuitive aspect is studied in relation to the "instincts" described in the New Testament as being important to the believer.[1108] They give attention also, to the need to "season" and develop such instincts in the movement toward Christian maturity.[1109]

Equally important is the realization that such growth occurs in a community. The Whiteheads assert, "The challenge . . . is to bring the traditional and rhetorical category of the sense of the faithful into dialogue with a specific community's religious maturing."[1110] They then observe that while the "universal and unerring consensus about faith has usually been understood as a *received* sense," in *Lumen Gentium* and in the views of various theologians "a more active and generative aspect of this sense of faith can be discerned."[1111] The Whiteheads note that this emphasis found support in Scheeben and others before the Council, and they discuss also the elements described by Newman in his defense of consulting the faithful.[1112]

The Whiteheads recall the discussion of the *sensus fidelium* by Bishop Hume at the 1980 Synod on the Family and note the growing acceptance of the notion among other bishops. At the same time, they add,

> The official Church is today becoming more appreciative of what it has to learn from the lived faith of mature Christians. It has yet to fully appreciate that the sense of faith imbedded in maturing communities of faith is necessarily plural and divergent.[1113]

They maintain that in order to "rescue the sense of the faithful from its (largely) rhetorical status, we must acknowledge its pluralistic nature and examine its role in the life of particular and different faith communities."[1114]

The authors note that one of the most important elements in "ministering to the sense of the faithful" in a community is the belief that this source actually exists and can be found there. The community can then develop and form its "collective conscience" through liturgy, education, and exercising responsibility for its resources.[1115] An important aspect of its growth is brought out in the Whiteheads' observation:

> As with the individual conscience of a Christian, this collective conscience must not only be formed and purified, but also trusted. Maturity, for a community as well as for individuals, includes the ability to follow trustworthy instincts of faith.[1116]

The community must also deepen its understanding of its relationship to the whole Church. The local community is not merely subject to a "one-directional" sort of ministry from above, but may be called on to minister to those within the greater community.[1117] This may be in the form of challenges when a community's sense of the faith differs from existing attitudes in areas such as sexuality and social issues.[1118] The authors reiterate that such work "requires extraordinary maturity."[1119]

The Whiteheads close their reflections with a few "cautionary observations." While the goal of consensus is important, it "must be complemented by a greater awareness and appreciation of diversity."[1120] Conflict may help the community to face the areas in which it must grow. The authors also question whether "centuries of passivity" can be overcome. They reiterate their hope that religious maturity within communities can be enhanced precisely by reflection on the notion of the sense of the faithful.[1121]

## PERSPECTIVES FROM WITHIN THE MAGISTERIUM

Before evaluating the theological views that make up the contemporary understanding of the sense of the faithful, it will be useful to consider some recent approaches to the concept from the Church's magisterium. To describe the various views of bishops, popes and curial offices on this topic or on the related areas of conscience, morality, ecclesiology, and the role of the laity since Vatican II would be impossible. Only a few illustrations of specific remarks about the *sensus fidelium* from the Church's pastors will be offered here. These are chosen to demonstrate the presence of a diversity of perspectives within the hierarchy in the post-conciliar period and to indicate the context in which future confrontation or interaction in regard to this theological source may occur.

Not long after the close of Vatican II, the value of the *sensus fidelium* as an active contributor to the Church's expression of faith was expressed by Bishop Remi J. De Roo of Victoria, British Columbia, in a paper delivered to the Catholic Theological Society of America.[1122] Cautioning that the Church's authority was not to be seen as related to the people "in the superficial sense often ascribed to democracy," he nevertheless asserted, "There is an intimate bond between the *sensus fidelium* and enlightened public opinion."[1123] In this address he identifies the "moral unanimity of all the faithful" described in *Lumen Gentium* (# 12) as "the powerful criterion to determine authentic values and the best direction for the Church." De Roo calls the *sensus fidelium* "the most ancient manifestation of democratic freedom, since it is linked with the very Spirit of God moving the Church towards perfect liberty."[1124]

Addressing how this source might itself be nurtured, De Roo suggests the abandonment of secretive processes in decision making and the encouragement of genuine growth and freedom.[1125] Writing within the context of the response to *Humane Vitae*, he observes, "Since the truth of the gospel is not imposed but imposes itself, church leaders have cause to reflect when large bodies of the faithful express grave reservations or differ in opinion on issues which directly affect their lives."[1126] He later adds, "Even protest and challenge or contestation have a legitimate place in the ecclesial community, provided they are supported by gospel principles rather than mere numbers."[1127]

De Roo's main focus in this address is the interrelation of episcopal and petrine offices. He calls for shared responsibility and for an emphasis on the life of the Church as the foundation for the structures that serve it. Arguing for a balanced sense of responsibility in the magisterium itself, he recalls that in the early Church "unity was characterized by both elements of catholicity or communion of churches, and apostolicity or the episcopal principle. The one form of communion calls for the other."[1128] Describing how collegiality should be lived out he adds, "In this time of renewal greater priority should be given to the deepening and development of hierarchical communion than to assigning juridical categories to it."[1129]

De Roo points out that Vatican II's vision for the Church which gave importance to both hierarchical authority and the involvement of the whole Church in its many levels placed all of the Church's activity in the service of its main goal of being a saving community. He thus remarks, "Living communion is more essential than the ever necessary juridical powers, for this *koinonia* will survive into eternity."[1130]

The important role given to the sense of the faithful at Vatican II was reiterated in the 1973 document of the Sacred Congregation for the Doctrine of the Faith, *Mysterium Ecclesiae*.[1131] The document affirms, "Without doubt the faithful, who in their own manner share in Christ's prophetic office, in many ways contribute towards increasing the understanding of faith in the Church."[1132] It makes clear, however, that the actual role of teaching belongs to the pastors alone.[1133] The faithful are to give "an assent that is proportionate to the authority that they possess and that they mean to exercise." Even when the magisterium draws on the "contemplation, life and study of the faithful" it does not simply approve what the faithful believe; it can "anticipate or demand their assent."[1134]

The document does not leave doubt as to where the juridical right of teaching lies in the Church. At the same time, however, it acknowledges and gives an extended discussion of the "historical condition that affects the expression of Revelation."[1135] Francis Sullivan has described *Mysterium Ecclesiae* as the place "in which, for the first time, a document of the Roman magisterium clearly recognized the historically conditioned character of dogmatic statements."[1136] This, Sullivan notes, was done only eight years after Paul VI's encyclical *Mysterium Fidei*, which had a very different view of dogmatic formulations. Here the pope claimed that in such statements "concepts are expressed which are not tied to some definite human culture," adding "these formulas are well adapted to all men of all times and all places."[1137] Sullivan describes these two documents as illustrating Lonergan's distinction between classicist and historical-minded approaches to doctrine.[1138]

*Mysterium Ecclesiae* affirms that "it sometimes happens that some dogmatic truth is first expressed incompletely (but not falsely), and at a later date, when considered in a broader context of faith or human knowledge, it receives a fuller and more perfect expression."[1139] This does not mean that the meaning of dogma is in doubt, but that it may be expressed in better ways in the future. A dogmatic relativism that sees formulas as "indeterminate" or "approximations" can only "corrupt the concept of the Church's infallibility relative to the truth to be taught or held in a determinate way."[1140]

Elsewhere Sullivan has cited *Mysterium Ecclesiae* in underlining the unique role of the pope in correcting errors that may involve a large segment of the faithful.[1141] He insists, "The magisterial role of the pope cannot be reduced to merely announcing the results of a Church-wide opinion poll."[1142] He adds though, that in cases like the two modern Marian definitions, "the universal consensus of the Catholic faithful has in fact provided the only sufficient grounds for certitude that these particular doctrines were really contained in the deposit of revelation."[1143] He notes too that especially in a time where global communication has become easier, the pope must consult the college of bishops if he is to meet the "grave obligation to make use of every suitable means available to him in the preparation of an *ex cathedra* definition."[1144] Later Sullivan describes the use of the sense of the faithful as a common bond that connects the work of both the magisterium and theologians.[1145]

While taking care to avoid a relativizing of the importance of dogmatic formulations or magisterial authority, *Mysterium Ecclesiae* accepts into the magisterium's teaching about doctrine the notion that doctrine develops in history in concert with the faith of the whole Church. Perspectives on such a work-in-progress will vary among those who wish to interpret it. It should not be surprising then to find among those in the hierarchy, as in the body of theologians dealing with the role of the *sensus fidelium*, that there are indications of hermeneutical difficulties and some plurality of viewpoints in their descriptions and uses of it.

Clearly the bishops have a unique position in this process of interpreting the tradition. In a study of infallibility that consciously attempts to situate the issue in a historically contextualized approach to interpretation, Peter Chirico has described the difficulty of "tapping" the "implicit infallibility" that exists in the sense of the faithful, characterizing the view that it can be found by polls as "incredibly naive."[1146] On the other hand, he finds special value in the "apt articulation," most likely by pastors, of "the universal meanings implicit in the *consensus fidelium*" which the faithful can recognize but which they may not be able to put into words.[1147]

When such recognition is not immediately forthcoming, the process itself becomes the subject of interpretation and criticism. Joseph Moingt has claimed that the magisterium has "totally eclipsed" the critical ability of the *consensus fidelium* to serve as a criterion.[1148] He finds that a paternal attitude toward the laity has "only succeeded in provoking public expression of the *consensus fidelium* (the very thing it hoped to avoid)."[1149] He appeals for a common exercise of responsibility for the truth among the people and the bishops, even where the latter have the role of giving the faith its public expression.[1150]

Some bishops have themselves encouraged the interaction of the people and their pastors, even though practical realization of this goal is difficult. Archbishop Rembert Weakland of Milwaukee has described the *sensus fidelium* as an "elusive term" and yet argues that creating theology while consciously appropriating the experience of the faithful, especially insofar as they "have become a truly biblical people," may help to illuminate its meaning.[1151] He sees the church in the United States as having a particular contribution to make to theology with its "scientific and democratic background."[1152] As chair of the National Conference of Catholic Bishops' Ad Hoc Committee on Catholic Social Teaching and the U.S. Economy, Weakland created the structures for more involvement of church members in reflecting on economics and social justice during the process of developing the pastoral letter, *Economic Justice for All.*[1153] Weakland has also contributed personally to the ongoing theological reflection on the importance of interaction and practical structures needed for cooperation between clergy and laity.[1154]

The pluralism that has characterized church life and theology since the Council has directly affected the role of the bishops. In 1978 the U.S. Bishops' Committee on Doctrine addressed the issue of cooperation between bishops and theologians and addressed the difficulty of working in areas where a variety of theological opinions have developed.[1155] The bishops recognized their role of encouraging scholarship and finding genuine consensus. Their report affirms,

> The bishops, before teaching, have to engage in as broad a consultation of the whole people of God as possible in order to make the proclamation of the word effective. The magisterium has to exercise discernment between the real *sensus fidelium* and the voices of false prophets.[1156]

The turbulent nature of developing practical consultation may be illustrated by a specific example of over a decade later, when members of the Catholic Theological Society of America issued a statement that included the view that theological consultation on the part of those with the most authority in the Church was inadequate and "many possibilities for cooperation between the magisterium and theologians in keeping with the teaching of the council remain to be realized."[1157] In response to the document, Archbishop John Quinn of San Francisco suggested that the theologians would have better served the goal of dialogue if they had sought "to meet directly with officials of the Holy See, to air their concerns honestly, to collaborate in devising effective structures of dialogue."[1158]

Among bishops themselves there have been disagreements on the role of consultation. In the same year as the CTSA statement, Bishop Kenneth Untener of Saginaw, Michigan addressed the U. S. Bishops in regard to their proposed document on teachings concerning sexuality. He challenged the bishops to consider whether the Spirit is working not only through the magisterium but also through the whole Church as they prepare their teaching on birth control. Describing the *sensus fidelium* as "more than an opinion poll" or "a head count" he adds, "But the beliefs in the heads and hearts of our people must count for something." Untener asks, "Do we have adequate structures and procedures to listen to the *sensus fidelium*, particularly on this issue?"[1159] In response to Untener, Bishop James McHugh of Camden, New Jersey, suggested that the Church's teaching needs clearer explanation, and that listening to the faithful must include attention to experts in the areas of marriage and population including those who warn against permissiveness and instability due to sexual excess.[1160]

The willingness of some within the magisterium to consult in important if complex areas is illustrated again in the address of Bishop Matthew Clark of Rochester, New York, who, as chair of the National Conference of Catholic Bishops' Committee on Women in Society and the Church, addressed a symposium in Virginia in 1990 entitled "The Wisdom of Women."[1161] Clark spoke of the need to include conversion as part of the ongoing struggle of all individuals as the Church's understanding deepens and develops.[1162] He affirms that the faithful can aid their pastors in this task, and observes, "The bishop must learn from his people before he can be a good teacher or servant."[1163]

Treatment of the sense of the faithful has been more circumspect at higher levels of the magisterium. Cardinal Johannes Willebrands, the president of the Vatican Secretariat for Promoting Christian Unity in 1985 addressed the issue of how ecumenical developments are accepted into the life of the Church, by referring to the *sensus fidelium*.[1164] He asserts that it is the whole Church which "recognizes and accepts new insights, new witnesses of truth and their forms of expression" as part of the apostolic faith. Willebrands also adds some observations on specific roles exercised within the whole. He sees reception as bound up with *kerygma, didache* and *praxis pietatis*, and elaborates on these aspects:

> Inasmuch as the entire people of God partakes in the search for and the unfolding of the truth of God's word, all the charisms and services are involved according to their station: the theologians by means of their research activities, the faithful by means of their preserving fidelity and piety, the ecclesial ministries and especially the college of bishops with its function of making binding doctrinal decisions.[1165]

Cardinal Joseph Ratzinger, while addressing a workshop for bishops in Dallas, Texas, in 1984, discussed in a different context what happens when the reception of the laity within the Roman Catholic communion is not forthcoming.[1166] He describes dissent as a decision "which involves [the dissenter] in the taking of an intellectual stand with no claimable support from the enlightening Spirit of truth, but which nevertheless puts distance between the one that dissents and the ones who do not."[1167] He distinguishes its private and public varieties. Those who dissent privately may do so for a variety of reasons, which may mitigate the serious effects of the event. The dissent of a theological researcher may be based in views which differ from Church teaching, or which only seem to differ from official teaching. Ratzinger notes that such stances are tentative by nature and may not involve actual dissent.[1168] Dissent exercised by teachers, however, has a different level of seriousness, as Ratzinger points out.

> A person who teaches in the name of the church is taking what is basically a personal dissent and exaggerating its importance and its damage by propagating it. But the particularly grave damage here is not simply that he teaches his dissent, but that the teaches it in the name of the church.[1169]

In this context he comments on the difference between the *sensus fidei* and the *sensus fidelium*. He observes, "The single most salient feature of the *sensus fidei* is its catholicity." He then contrasts the genuine expression of the *sensus fidelium* with the claims made for "widespread dissent" on the basis of statistics as in the case of reactions to *Humanae Vitae*.[1170] Ratzinger again:

> What such percentages cannot show and which they would have to show to be the real *sensus fidelium*, is that the faithful of all times and places have shared the same or a similar belief. Statistics cannot be used to take the vote of those who have already preceded us, marked with the sign of faith.[1171]

Ratzinger adds that he finds it "all the more odd" that the polls which are taken among dissenting Catholics are "often used by those very theologians who organized the dissent in the first place."[1172] He affirms that genuine expressions of the *sensus fidei* are characterized by ecclesial unity.[1173]

Pope John Paul II has referred to the sense of the faithful in his Apostolic Exhortation, *Familiaris Consortio*, which followed the 1980 Synod on the Family. In a section addressing "evangelical discernment" the pope observes,

> The "supernatural sense of faith" however does not consist solely or necessarily in the consensus of the faithful. Following Christ, the Church seeks the truth, which is not always the same as the majority opinion. She listens to conscience and not to power, and in this way she defends the poor and the downtrodden. The Church values sociological and statistical research, when it proves helpful in understanding the historical context in which pastoral action has to be developed and when it leads to a better understanding of the truth. Such research alone, however, is not to be considered in itself an expression of the sense of faith [1174]

The pope's remarks carefully distinguish the sense of the faithful from a mechanical or juridical connection with polls. He also cautions against making it a source of judgment different from the magisterium. At the same time, he reaffirms the usefulness of research that includes a statistical or historical foundation for understanding the Church's teaching, and he maintains a specific focus on conscience, especially as it is linked to the "poor and downtrodden" over against the powerful.

In a note, this passage is connected with both *Lumen Gentium* (# 12) and the passage from *Mysterium Ecclesiae* cited above.[1175] The assertion that the *sensus fidei* "does not consist solely or necessarily" in consensus, may appear to contrast this source with the *consensus fidelium*. It appears more likely, however, that the next sentence restates the same thought in the way that it connects the opinions of the faithful with the judgment of the magisterium. It is worth noting that in this passage the Pope does not reduce the sense of the faithful to a simplistic response of the people to the magisterium, even though he maintains the central importance of the hierarchy. In the paragraph that follows he advises:

> Pastors must promote the sense of the faith in all the faithful, examine and authoritatively judge the genuineness of its expressions, and educate the faithful in an ever more mature evangelical discernment.[1176]

John Paul II's understanding of the *sensus fidelium* may be further illuminated by his use of the term in an address to the bishops of France during 1980, the same year as the Synod on the Family. While warning against the tendency within the Church to uncritically assimilate certain aspects of the secular world, he notes,

> Here also we see the huge task of pastors to keep the deposit of faith, to remain faithful to the mystery of Christ written in the whole history of man and also to remain faithful to that marvelous supernatural sense of the faith of the people of God as a whole, which generally is not the object of publicity on the part of the mass media and yet is expressed in the secret depths of hearts and of consciences in the authentic language of the Spirit.[1177]

Here he appeals to the sense of the faithful as it maintains the continuity of faith throughout history. It is a force that can aid in conserving the best of the tradition as the Church confronts secularization. The distinct usefulness of this source is suggested as he again advises: "Our doctrinal and pastoral mission should remain above all, in the service of the *sensus fidelium* according to the constitution *Lumen Gentium* (n. 12)."[1178]

The reference of the pope to the sense of the faithful in the context of the Synod on the Family may be considered in the light of some previously cited statements of bishops who attended the Synod. The view of Cardinal Hume, cited by several authors above, that the experience of married people should be considered in the Church's teaching, and the suggestion of Cardinal Carter of Toronto, that the people's actions might be a "non-reflexive expression of the *sensus fidelium*," represent an awareness on the part of leaders in the Church that an actively engaged laity can aid in the Church's understanding and teaching.[1179] To these could be added the appeal of Archbishop Derek Worlock of Liverpool to his own consultation of his people as a source for understanding the effects of technological change on marriages and families.[1180]

At the close of the Synod, the bishops proposed forty-three resolutions to the pope, offering their views on the various topics discussed. They included several resolutions which urged that attention be given to the sense of the faithful.[1181] Resolution Two in particular is worth examining for its closeness to the comments included in *Familiaris Consortio* by the pope.

> This "supernatural appreciation of the faith," *sensus fidei* is not just a consensus of all Christians. The church is not subject to majority rule. Christ's disciples seek truth, not numbers. Conscience, not power, moves them. That is why they defend even the weak and failing. Although the appreciation of the faith (*sensus fidei*) is not the result of opinion polls or statistics, the church does recognize the importance these methods have in a better investigation of the

truth, in setting up a right course of pastoral action and in exploring the signs of the times.[1182]

Resolution Three cites both the *Commonitoria* of Vincent of Lerins and Newman's *On Consulting the Faithful* before it describes the *sensus fidei* as "docile to the universal church and its magisterium" even while it adds that it "is not irrational but corresponds to that right reasoning with which the creator has endowed his creatures." Resolution Four describes this sense as "the fruit of a living faith" and notes that the magisterium should "cultivate this appreciation (*sensus*) and interpret it authentically."[1183]

After the Synod's close, Archbishop John Quinn of San Francisco reported on its proceedings to the national meeting of bishops in the United States, emphasizing the need for the Church to challenge the world with the Church's "sources of faith" even while it works "to remove [the] barriers to understanding and acceptance" of the Gospel.[1184]

The specific manner in which the work of both challenging and removing barriers is to be done has yet to be clarified, however, particularly in regard to the role of the sense of the faithful. An indication of this is given in the document prepared by the Bishops' conference of England and Wales for the 1985 Extraordinary Synod of Bishops, which observed:

> The exercise of the teaching office in the church is an area of difficulty calling for clarification. It operates in the context of community where dialogue is appropriate. Its relationship to the *sensus fidelium* and subsequent reception of teaching is not well understood. In its relationship with the work of theology, common interests need to be recognized and mutual respect built up. The controversies regarding *Humanae Vitae* are examples of these difficulties.[1185]

The document later cites the process of consultation used by the U.S. bishops in preparing their pastoral letter on peace, as having "lessons of wider importance about the exercise of authority with dialogue."[1186]

The Synod itself emphasized that an ecclesiology founded in the concept of *koinonia* "is the central and fundamental idea" of the documents of Vatican II.[1187] The Synod's final document did not discuss consultation of the faithful, though in its remarks on "participation and co-responsibility" it encouraged increased attention to the "collaboration of women in ecclesial activities," the efforts of younger people in the Church and the work of "basic communities."[1188] The bishops also suggested a study be undertaken "to examine whether the principle of subsidiarity in use in human society can be applied to the church and to what degree and in what sense such an application can and should be made."[1189]

Clarification of the role of the faithful in the Church's mission was to be a main focus of the Synod on the Laity convened two years later. In anticipation of the Synod, Cardinal Carter of Ontario again spoke of the *sensus fidei* as he appealed for an understanding of the priesthood of the laity that would neither ignore the active role of the people nor emphasize it "to the point of denigrating the ordained priesthood."[1190] Here Carter speaks specifically about the share the people have in "sanctification, teaching and administration." In regard to teaching, he cites Gilson, Maritain, Pegis, Chesterton and others as examples of lay people who have excelled in the area of scholarship. Yet he adds that it would be wrong to limit the understanding of the teaching role of the faithful to the work of such experts.

> What of the wisdom of the ordinary people who have the *sensus fidei* (the insight of faith). Why are lay people either so loath to speak up on matters which concern the church or why are they discouraged from doing so? There is a great deal of wisdom out there to be tapped.[1191]

Carter specifies that the local parish level is the best place to develop lay participation.[1192]

These remarks anticipate the view included in the "working paper" prepared by the Vatican general secretariat of the Synod of Bishops.[1193] In its section on "Communio and Participation in the Church," the document takes up the theme of Vatican II that describes the participation of the laity in the priestly, prophetic and kingly offices of Christ.[1194] In regard to the prophetic role, it cites *Lumen Gentium* (# 12) as a warrant for the view that the laity in their daily living "witness to their faith by announcing the Gospel in word and work."[1195] The whole Church is involved in this witness to the Gospel, though different members act in different ways. This is also true of the prophetic function which operates

> whether in a direct sense through the hierarchy who, by exercising their teaching office, teach in the name of and with the authority of Christ or, in an indirect sense through his witnesses, the laity, whom he provides with the appreciation of the faith (*sensus fidelium*) and the grace of the word.[1196]

The share that the laity have in the three offices of Christ is described again by Pope John Paul II in his apostolic exhortation following the Synod, *Christifideles Laici*.[1197] In his discussion of the faithful's part in these offices, the pope cites their "appreciation of the Church's supernatural faith" as the foundation for their prophetic role, as found in *Lumen Gentium* (# 12).[1198] He stresses that all of the offices are exercised by believers for the sake of the whole. He asserts, "The threefold mission of Christ requires that it be lived and realized *in communion* and *for the increase of communion itself.*"[1199]

This theme is reiterated in a later section that focuses on the involvement of the laity in the ongoing life of the Church, seen as a communion. John Paul II notes that the faithful can never remain in isolation from the community, but must live in a continual interaction with others, with a lively sense of fellowship, rejoicing in an equal dignity and common commitment to bring to fruition the immense treasure that each has inherited.[1200]

The pope stresses that the "diversity and complementarity" of callings among believers means that "every member of the lay faithful is seen *in relation to the whole body* and offers a *totally unique contribution* on behalf of the whole body."[1201]

In *Christifideles Laici* the pope describes the central role of an ecclesiology of communion in the forming of lay groups in the Church.[1202] In a list of "'Criteria of Ecclesiality' for Lay Groups," he offers the means for "discerning and recognizing" those groups that fulfill this ecclesiology.[1203] These characteristics include "the primacy given to the call of every Christian to holiness," "the responsibility of professing the Catholic faith," especially in obedience to the magisterium, "the witness to a strong and authentic communion" in relationship with the Pope as the "visible center of unity," "conformity to and participation in the Church's apostolic goals," and "a commitment to a presence in human society."[1204]

The identity of lay groups that fulfill the necessary characteristics of the *communio* is thus tied to the structural identity of the whole Church and its hierarchy. It is worth noting too though, that in the view of one commentator, the actual work of the Synod found one of its "more positive aspects" in the interaction of theologians, lay auditors and bishops in discussion groups.[1205] In the final liturgy of the Synod, the pope himself spoke of the involvement of lay people saying, "In a certain sense, the experience of this synod is unprecedented; and hopefully it will become a 'model,' a reference point for the future."[1206]

The contemporary approach to the role of the *sensus fidelium* on the part of the Church's pastors is colored by a diversity which is not as wide in range as the views expressed among theologians generally, but which still calls for further clarification. The positive role that the faithful may play as they share in the mission of the Church with the magisterium is seen in varying ways by those who make up the magisterium. In the central leadership of the Church the issue of unity is appropriately of great importance. Yet it is not clear how the pastoral responsibility, emphasized by the pope, of developing the *sensus fidei* and the practical inclusion of the faithful in the deliberation of the magisterium on specific issues is to be encouraged and structured in order to fully develop the vision of Vatican II for the sense of the faithful.[1207]

The pastoral context, like that of theology, awaits further clarification as to how the *sensus fidelium* may be recognized and brought into practical reflection and action in the Church. The relationship between the members of the hierarchy and theologians is of particular importance in work for greater clarification and involvement. The complex context within which contemporary efforts will be made to pursue better interaction on these issues will be illustrated by a final example that examines a recent document from the Congregation for the Doctrine of the Faith on the role of the theologian, with particular attention being given to the topic of dissent.

In 1990 the Congregation under the leadership of its prefect, Cardinal Joseph Ratzinger, issued a document entitled "Instruction on the Ecclesial Vocation of the Theologian." The document's intent is to show the role of theology in the understanding of the Church's faith. It affirms that theology has helped to deepen this understanding in the time preceding and following the Council, though not without experiencing "moments of crisis and tension."[1208] It is to such moments that the Congregation turns its focus, stressing the "unifying force" that the truth must exert in the Church, and including among the resources it cites the sense of the faith as described in *Lumen Gentium* (# 12).[1209]

In describing the work of theologians, the Instruction insists on the connection of reflection with the dynamic quality of the faith. The tools of theological study must be combined with prayer and set in an openness to the "supernatural sense of the faith" which "will appear to [the theologian] as a sure rule for guiding his reflections and helping him assess the correctness of his conclusions." In using resources from his or her cultural context, the theologian can better "illumine one or other aspect of the mysteries of faith." The document adds, "This is certainly an arduous task that has its risks, but it is legitimate in itself and should be encouraged." The final rule for judgment, however, is provided by revealed doctrine.[1210]

Directing its attention to the magisterium, the Instruction refers to the infallibility given by God to the Church, which the people of God share through the "supernatural sense of the faith" but which is interpreted "under the guidance of the church's living magisterium."[1211] It is the magisterium's role to give definitive decisions on formulations which are not themselves "truths of faith" but which are, however, "intimately connected with them in such a way that the definitive character of such affirmations derives the final analysis from revelation itself."[1212] Different levels of action of the magisterium are considered in the Instruction, with attention given to the type of acceptance to be expected in response to the weight of the teaching presented.[1213] It points out that "magisterial decisions in matters of discipline, even if they are not guaranteed by the charism of infallibility, are not without divine assistance and call for the adherence of the faithful."[1214] In its section on "collaborative relations" between the magisterium and theologians, it points out that the magisterium has the responsibility to warn the people and even intervene in discussions "of dangerous opinions which could lead to error."[1215]

The document emphasizes that "the willingness to submit loyally to the teaching of the magisterium on matters per se not irreformable must be the rule."[1216] At the same time, it recognizes that it may be appropriate for theologians to question "the timeliness, the form or even the contents of magisterial interventions." The Instruction recognizes that documents of the magisterium may in fact contain "deficiencies." This does not mean, however, that theologians should act as if official teaching "can be habitually mistaken in its prudential judgments or that it does not enjoy divine assistance in the integral exercise of its mission." Conflicts that come from a proper spirit, and not "from hostile and contrary feelings" may in fact help both hierarchy and theologians in their work.[1217]

When it considers "the problem of dissent" the document makes clear that "personal difficulties" are to be distinguished from "public opposition" to magisterial teaching.[1218] Secular values and the powerful influences of modern media must not be allowed to set the Church's agenda.[1219] The cultural pluralism which characterizes much of modern society can serve a positive role, but it can also lead to misunderstanding. Theologians are thus urged to use "critical, well-considered discernment as well as a true mastery of the issues" while working in such a climate.[1220]

In describing the "sociological" aspect of dissent, the document distinguishes between "opinions of the faithful" and the genuine *sensus fidei*. The gift of truth given to believers is that which is given to the Church. The individuals sense of the faith "implies then by its nature a profound agreement of spirit and heart with the church, *sentire cum ecclesia*." The document warns that the faithful "can be swayed by a public opinion influenced by modern communications media." It adds, "Not without reason did the Second Vatican Council emphasize the indissoluble bond between the *sensus fidei* and the guidance of God's people by the magisterium of the pastors." The Instruction affirms that "interventions" of the magisterium are thus made for the sake of ecclesial unity.[1221]

The document is clear in its teaching that alternative sources of authority are not to be placed over against the magisterium. Conscience is not to be asserted in an autonomous way, but must be joined to the commonly held "ecclesial heritage." Communal methods that attempt to establish alternatives are also not to be allowed. Thus the Instruction affirms, "Standards of conduct, appropriate to civil society or the workings of democracy, cannot be purely and simply applied to the church."[1222] Specifically,

> polling public opinion to determine the proper thing to think or do, opposing the magisterium by exerting the pressure of public opinion, making the excuse of a "consensus" among theologians, maintaining that the theologian is the prophetical spokesman of a "base" or autonomous community which would be the source of all truth, all this indicates a grave loss of the sense of truth and of the sense of the church.[1223]

The Congregation insists that the Church will gain credibility by striving for "concord and communion." It adds that permitting dissent "[allows] the 'leaven of infidelity to the Holy Spirit' to start to work."[1224] Theologians who "encounter difficulties due to the character of their research" are encouraged to "seek their solution in trustful dialogue with the pastors in the spirit of truth and charity which is that of the communion of the church."[1225]

The Instruction may be criticized more for what it omits than for what it includes. Responses to it indicate that there is still a need for better communication between the magisterium and theologians, and a better understanding of the role of the faithful in the Church. Ladislas Orsy has pointed out that the word "dissent" is used in different ways in countries whose language is English and in the document. He notes that the usual meaning of "dissent" in such countries is "to signify personal opinion different from the official one in matters where debate is permissible." In the Instruction, on the other hand, it describes "groups that have broken their basic communion with the church." Orsy observes that while theologians must be loyal to those in authority in the Church, they are also responsible to the people as a whole. He notes that the full presentation of the Gospel includes "the struggles, uncertainties and hesitations that are experienced in searching for the full meaning of the evangelical message." Orsy suggests that in facing such difficulties the whole Church can more surely recognize the guidance of the Spirit.[1226]

Joseph Komonchak criticizes the document in a similar way, suggesting that a "root problem" might be its uncritical view of the magisterium's formal authority which is untempered by a sense of its qualifying conditions. He affirms the vital role of the magisterial office. At the same time he points out the need for pastors to "remain within the apostolic faith," as well as the need to "respect the fundamental character of the Church and its structures," and with respect to reception, to "be concretely trusted by the faithful." Komonchak sees the issue of trust as a "condition" that is especially important to the exercise of authority, but one that is frequently not recognized.[1227]

Francis Sullivan remarks that the Instruction "lacks the equilibrium" exhibited in a similar statement issued by the International Theological Commission fifteen years earlier which was based in dialogues between representatives of the magisterium and theologians.[1228] Sullivan carefully examines the authority of the document itself, recalling the Instruction's own distinguishing of levels within magisterial teachings. He identifies the document itself as "an exercise of 'participated ordinary magisterium'" that has a teaching function rather than a legislative one.[1229] After reviewing the document's treatment of the responsibilities of theologians and the magisterium, Sullivan discusses their interaction. He argues specifically. that rather than deferring to their pastors in areas of "divergent opinions," theologians may legitimately use other avenues for debating such matters with their peers.[1230] Sullivan shows too, that the Congregation's use of the word "dissent" refers to the specific act of setting up an alternative to the magisterium.[1231] To illustrate the meaning of the word in the document, Sullivan quotes remarks attributed to Cardinal Ratzinger from a press conference where he discussed the Instruction:

> The instruction distinguishes between healthy theological tension and true dissent, in which theology is organized according to the principle of majority rule, and the faithful are given alternative norms by a "countermagisterium." Dissent thus becomes a political factor, passing from the realm of thought to that of a "power game." This is where a theologian's use of mass media can be dangerous.[1232]

Sullivan maintains that the Instruction does not deny the possibility of "legitimate dissent" of theologians from the ordinary magisterium. He adds that it does make it necessary to use the word "dissent" in a way that clarifies the difference between proper theological pursuits and organized opposition to legitimate authority.[1233]

What remains unclear after the document, is the extent to which the sense of the faithful, as it may be found among the larger population of the laity in the Church, can be expected to be a genuine *fons theologiae*, not developed or presented as an autonomous authority or as an alternative to the magisterium, but exhibiting nevertheless the characteristics of an active, living faith among believers who share the Church's mission in the modern world. What is lacking in the Instruction is a perspective that goes beyond those elements which are necessary for proper order and governance, to include the possibility of actual structures of interaction that can support creativity and even risk in engaging all levels of the Church in developing a common *sensus Ecclesiae*.

Thus in the current context of teaching in the Church, there is clarity about how problems may be corrected or even prevented. This context allows, too, for a certain tension to exist where theological discernment must continue among those specialists who treat controversial issues. It is not clear, however, how or whether the perspectives and structures that are in place are sufficient to prepare the faithful to develop that theological discernment that is necessary to their own living out of the Gospel in an age where faith itself is necessarily controversial.

# CHAPTER 6
# ADEQUATE AND INADEQUATE USES OF THE TRADITION OF THE *SENSUS FIDELIUM* IN POST-VATICAN II THEOLOGY

As indicated in the first chapter of this work, the plurality of views that characterizes contemporary study of the sense of the faithful presents a problem. Traditionally the consensus of believers has been linked with the identification and understanding of catholicity in the Church. This traditional role is challenged by the lack of unity among contemporary authors who have attempted to define or use the sense of the faithful as a theological source.

By drawing both on the history of this concept and the matrix of issues raised by participants in the contemporary discussion as described here, however, it is possible to indicate some underlying reasons for disagreement about the sense of the faithful. It is also possible to consider those deeper aspects of this source that may still operate in the contemporary Church to create unity even within an increasingly more diverse body of believers. The possibility of using the *sensus fidelium* as a source will be maintained here, after the array of contemporary voices concerning it has been considered in the light of the impact it has made in the Church's history.

## RECOVERING A HISTORICAL PERSPECTIVE

At one level, the plurality of current treatments is due to the variety of aspects in the life of the Church and its individual believers that are touched by the sense of the faithful. Individual authors in the contemporary discussion, as in the past, focus on the *sensus fidei*, *sensus fidelium* or *consensus fidelium* to better understand the way the Spirit may operate in the "instincts" of individuals or in the community as a whole in both "subjective" and "objective" areas. Each such focus does not deny the importance of other aspects of the sense of the faithful that would be given attention in a more comprehensive treatment of the topic. At the same time, authors who have examined history for a better understanding of the sense of the faithful have contributed insight and background to the current controversy. Historical expressions of the *sensus fidelium* challenge the more recent view, accepted to a large extent in the theology and practice of those with the most influence in the Church, that the *sensus fidelium* is a solely passive response to the magisterium.

Authors who wrote about the sense of the faithful around the time of the Second Vatican Council developed aspects of the topic that were missing from the ecclesial views that immediately preceded the Council. They reclaimed the insights of important theologians from the past, but they also recalled divergent views from the nineteenth century, and especially from the important contribution of Newman. Writers like Guitton or Biemer recalled Newman's insistence on the important role to be played by the faithful in practical development of the faith, even while the hierarchy was recognized as having responsibility for expressing and defining faith.[1] Coulson and Femiano emphasize that shared responsibility of the people and clergy is expressed in their *conspiratio*.[2] They suggest, as Newman did in his own day, that as this active source for development is recognized historically, it might be drawn on more explicitly to illuminate contemporary questions.

The difficulties of using this source are also recognized by these earlier, historically focused authors of the post-conciliar period. After examining the catalytic events and ideas found in Newman's situation, Patterson discussed the "pre-theological" nature of the sense of the faith, suggesting that Rahner's work in this area might bear fruit in a modern understanding of the concept. Patterson argued that recognition of this sense might motivate the practical involvement of the whole Church in current issues. At the same time, he described actual consensus as "illusive."[3] In an article within nearly a decade after these observations, Patterson claimed that such consensus must be achieved through growth and development, even though such efforts might be painful.[4]

Similarly, Penaskovic in his early work emphasized Newman's view of the Holy Spirit as an active force in the sense of the faithful and the development of doctrine. The expression of this sense is found "indirectly" in documents like the creeds. Penaskovic describes interaction of the people and the magisterium as necessary, but also as wholistic and mysterious in its actual operation.[5] Fifteen years later he addressed the way the *sensus fidei* might be seen as operating in more "differentiated" avenues such as liberation movements and through the influences of public opinion and reception.[6] He wrote that the process of reception is now more complicated because of the shortened time spans that occur between the expressions of and the responses to church teaching.[7]

Many authors whose views were considered in the historical review of this study have been motivated by a desire to encourage a more interactive exercise of responsibility in the Church by a reappropriation of earlier practices. Historians like Eno and King have informed the discussion by describing historical, practical precedents that might offer models for current practices.

Eno has also examined the historical shifts in the understanding of consensus itself that were variously expressed in the early Church as a past agreement in the Fathers, an agreement of contemporary views in the Church or the focus of authority in the traditions found in Rome. He observes that the conflicts that characterized the early Church, particularly as they occurred between charismatic and institutional elements, were resolved eventually by Roman centralization. He suggests that just as the *regula fidei* unified the ancient Church as it lived in the tension created between its charismatic and institutional elements, unity could be possible today. To achieve this the early Church might be a guide to tempering the centralization of authority by collegiality and shared responsibility within the community.[8]

In the area of law, King argues that reception can be understood and practiced in a more adequate way if it is freed from a juridical approach to law which is heir to ecclesiological battles since Trent that have emphasized the exercise of authority without sufficient acknowledgment of the community that contextualizes authority.[9]

John T. Ford has also begun his reflections on the sense of the faithful by examining Newman's impact in the *Rambler* controversy, and noting Newman's own use of Patristics in connection with Mariology and the more organic view embedded within such an approach. He characterizes Newman's article as "heuristic," allowing an understanding at several levels (historical, abstract or personal).[10] He describes the role of the *sensus fidelium* in the development of doctrine as circular, and suggests that a "functional analysis" might be useful in understanding how the Church interprets its faith.[11] In a later work he elaborates on the heuristic nature of dogma itself. He notes that through the process of reception the faithful may choose between several interpretations. They are not limited to one school of thought.[12]

Thus, authors who have begun with a historical focus have not merely contributed pieces to a larger picture of how the sense of the faithful has operated and might operate again in the Church if ecclesial structures were in place to allow more shared responsibility. The work of these authors has also illustrated how in practical, concrete operation, the sense of the faithful has exhibited its wholistic yet complex nature in history. The support for this point in the long history of the concept has already been presented in the discussion of the criteria selected above. What has also become clear again in the contemporary authors examined here, is the link between the interpretation given to the *sensus fidelium* within the tradition, and the approach a contemporary author assumes toward use of the source today.[13] Any contemporary appropriation is inseparable from the perspectives taken by modern authors on the exercise of authority by the magisterium, the meaning of infallibility and the practical conflicts that have surrounded these issues in modern times, especially since the middle of the nineteenth century.

Thus within the post-Vatican II discussion, there is a conflict between different residual influences. Though a centralized administration in the Church and the fostering of a passive laity developed over an extended part of the Church's history, these characteristics found rigorous expression in the period between the First and Second Vatican Councils.

Nonetheless, even with the success of the Roman School in theology and the strengthening of authority in the hierarchy in Church practice, the traditional understanding of the *sensus fidelium* was not lost. As Thils has demonstrated, it was not "collapsed" into a passive response of the people to the hierarchy. Theologians continued to discuss the role of the faithful in developing the expressions of faith, and the magisterium itself drew on the living faith of the people when other sources that fed magisterial pronouncements were not sufficient to support new doctrinal definitions. If magisterial theology and practice constricted the active expression of the sense of the faithful, they still neither ignored nor eliminated it.

With Vatican II, the active role of the laity was again encouraged. At the same time, as the Council retrieved this source and placed it alongside statements that reiterated the emphasis on hierarchy that had characterized the modern period, conciliar documents created a conflict of paradigms. The task of resolving the relationship between the various elements in the Church was left to post-conciliar efforts. As has been seen above, the Council's work did not result in a finished, consistent, univocal approach to its tasks or its resources.

The topics taken up in the conciliar documents indicate that the resolution of its problems and the pursuit of its mission is not possible without recognition of the role of many practical factors in the Church's engagement of the modern context. These issues include areas that affect Church governance, communication, and the development of a better educated laity.

An even greater theological impact has come from the Council's recognition of the historical conditioning of ecclesial expressions of faith. As has been discussed here already, with the Second Vatican Council the Church's magisterium opened a new perspective on how its own assertions may be interpreted. Much has been written about the repercussions of this perspective for understanding the development of doctrine. An adequate treatment of this impact, which would go beyond the historical observations already made, is beyond the scope of the present work. Yet it is important to recognize the influence in the contemporary Church and the understanding of the sense of the faithful that is clearly related to this historical shift. Whether or not Sanks's view can be borne out that a basic paradigm shift is underway in the Church, there are certainly now a variety of models in the Church whose differences can be seen as stemming from the way language is understood as subject to contextualization and development, even when it is the language of doctrine.

A plurality of views on how the modern context should be considered and how modern perspectives should be used is illustrated in the examples given at the end of the last chapter concerning approaches to the *sensus fidelium* among the Church's pastors. The attempts to implement the sense of the faithful and to define its relationship to the magisterium in both theological and practical ways indicate a work in progress. This work is being taken up by both those who are looking for innovative structures to develop consultation and shared responsibility and by those who are more cautious and who are concerned that magisterial authority not be undermined.

The acknowledgment of the historical context of doctrinal statements has created the task of widening and reorienting perspectives among the laity as well. While considering the topic of how expressions of the faith are conveyed in human terms, Piet Fransen has observed,

> The faithful are not sufficiently aware of how delicate and difficult it is to articulate satisfactorily the mystery of God's actions with people. A century of rationalism has left many Christians with the conviction that it is easy to work with concepts to express the truth. Nothing could be more wrong.[14]

Significantly, Fransen locates the responsibility for working out the meaning of the faith in the context of the whole church community. He adds, "This task of articulation is something for the whole of the believing Church, for the thinking and living of the entire ecclesial community in communion with its legitimate leaders."[15]

Fransen focuses on the Church seen as a community in direct contrast to a juridical view. This emphasis requires that the whole life of the Church be considered as foundational, with the specific solemn statements of the magisterium serving the faith of the Church. Against what others have called a "dogmatic mentality,"[16] he sees the magisterium as being responsible for protecting the actual faith of the Church from "alien" influences.[17]

The connection between the view an author takes on the *sensus fidelium* and a "hermeneutic of doctrine" that has been considered above under criterion eight is illustrated again in the range of contemporary authors whose views have been summarized here. Among these views are those who see the sense of the faithful as offering a unique contribution to the Church, with the recognition that through their baptism the laity contribute significantly to the *sensus Ecclesiae*. Others see the *sensus fidelium* as passive, with the response of the laity being dependent upon the explicit expressions of the magisterium.

Criterion five above maintains that the Church's history as well as the teaching of Vatican II do not support the notion of a passive *sensus fidelium*. Those approaches to authority, infallibility and the teaching of the magisterium which entail a passive *sensus fidelium* are considered here to be not only inconsistent with the long tradition of this source, but when seen within the larger question of interpretation of doctrine, they are also found to be inadequate for resolving the conflicts of interpretation that exist today.

To attempt to resolve the question of plurality of interpretation of the *sensus fidelium* by an authoritative decision rooted in the role of the magisterium alone, considered not just with respect to teaching but in reference to the possibility of further developments in the understanding and the expression of that teaching, is to beg the question. It resolves the question of sources in favor of only a portion of the resources available, and it does so in the face of a rich, if as yet underdeveloped ecclesiology received from Vatican II. The contemporary plurality of voices on the *sensus fidelium* is a necessary part of a deeper discernment in a Church that is still struggling to develop an ecclesiology moved by *aggiornamento*.

## THE POST-CONCILIAR CONTEXT

Following Vatican II, discussion soon widened from the question of whether the faithful should be included in the expression of the faith, to how co-responsibility should be exercised in practice. In its earliest stages the post-conciliar discussion of the sense of the faithful moved from an attempt to establish historical precedents that could illustrate its availability as a source for addressing contemporary theological issues to a deeper realization of the complex difficulties that meet any attempt at practical application. The various discussions of "democratization" that followed the Council, some of which have been considered here, are instructive on this point.

Duquoc has characterized democratization as the "institutionalised correlate" to the sense of the faithful in the individual.[18] Kottje has pointed out that involving the faithful in the selection of their own leaders would be a reclaiming of earlier Church tradition.[19] Yet Legrand warns against simplistic appropriation of democratic processes, which could "lead to theological confusion." He claims that the use of pastoral councils comprised of laity and clergy, with episcopal approval and reception of the choice by the pope, could better implement the "ecclesiology of communion" of the early Church.[20]

In considering the ongoing question of how lay people might be included in the selection of church leaders, it is useful to recall the suggestion of Eugui, that any system for choosing bishops, whether using the historical precedents of election or of hierarchical control, should maintain the goal that characterized both. Following the Fathers of Vatican II (*Christus Dominus*, # 20), he asserts that the best candidate should be selected by the "competent ecclesiastical authority."[21] The shift to a hierarchical process of selection occurred to a large extent to overcome abuses in the earlier system and insure a better candidate. "Competence" may itself be the notion that is being examined and expanded in the modern context. It may now be appropriate to ask whether the system should again be changed to select a candidate that more directly represents the people who will be led.

Kilmartin recommends rethinking the juridical system of authority from a Christocentric standpoint, with movement toward a fuller Trinitarian base.[22] Lécuyer points out the key role of liturgical involvement of the faithful.[23] In such perspectives, there is an emphasis on laying a truly theological foundation for the resolution of structural issues. Among several theologians who have called for greater dialogue and consultation to implement Vatican II's vision of co-responsibility, there is an awareness that while democratic structure is inadequate, a narrow governmental structure is equally unable to do justice to the sense of all the faithful. Heagle advises a return to the "grassroots" whether through "democracy or dialogue, consultation or collegiality."[24] Yet O'Connell emphasizes the importance of genuine, "visionary leadership."[25] Both he and Patterson have offered a useful heuristic distinction between the "locus" and "focus" of authority in the Church.[26] Such a distinction allows for practical structures of authority to be maintained, while a recognition of the foundation for authority in the entire Church rooted in the Spirit is retained.

Many authors have pointed out the need to overcome a predominantly juridical emphasis in the exercise of church authority. The issues involved are especially clear in the area that is most appropriately juridical, canon law. Both before and after the promulgation of the 1983 Code, theologians appealed for a contextualizing of church law in the responsible living of Christian life guided by the Spirit. Coriden describes how law must be related to other areas in the Church such as sacraments and shared mission. He sees the "many-faceted concept" of *koinonia* as providing the proper context for understanding responsibility and accountability.[27] After the Code was promulgated, Correco criticized its minimal attention to the sense of the faithful and noted its inclusion of the two ecclesiologies of *communio* and the "perfect society" as well as the "unbridgeable gap" between them.[28] Both individual and collective exercise of practical judgment are called for by those who have considered the way in which law is to be received. Bertolino describes the *sensus fidei* as vital to understanding and implementing canon law.[29] Orsy elaborates the role of custom for taking church practice past the "authentic," "judicial" or "doctrinal."[30]

Certainly, leadership based in genuine authority is vital to the Church. Yet leadership must support growth among believers and challenge them to take responsibility rather than assuming such responsibility for them. It is important to recall that even within the specific context of legal issues in the Church, the laity retain responsibilities and rights. Canon law includes among these roles the expectation of obedience to authority, but also the duty to participate in the life of the Church, to carry out its mission, to form associations, to assemble, to initiate apostolic activities and to express their views on ecclesial matters.[31]

Theological treatments of reception of doctrine follow a course similar to those concerned with the reception of law. In his foundational work, Congar pointed out the necessity of seeing reception in terms that are more comprehensive and nuanced than those that can be defined in juridical terms.[32] Twenty years after Vatican II, Alberigo claimed that only the whole Church in a slow process could adequately interpret a council.[33] Bermejo and Garijo Guembe both recall the need to look at the actual history of reception and non-reception in making judgments as to the nature of this process.[34]

Rausch too has described the need for understanding reception as a process that includes the whole Church, while not denying the indispensable role played by the formal decisions of those in authority. Speaking in reference to the ecumenical role of reception, Rausch insists that it is not a matter of ratifying formal doctrine, but a recognition of a commonly held faith.[35]

The contribution of other Christian thinkers to the understanding of *sensus fidelium* and the role of reception have similarly linked these concepts to the living response of faith among believers in community.[36] The perspectives of Orthodox Metropolitan Emilianos Timiadis are especially interesting, as he insists that the *sensus fidei* of all people should be reclaimed, while at the same time warning against an emphasis on public opinion that leads to "mob-ocracy." He affirms that the final responsibility for reception or rejection of doctrine remains with church leaders, but the laity must also be led to be "spiritually mature and well-equipped."[37]

Working with an ecumenical focus, but looking critically at the Roman Catholic perspective, Dionne convincingly argues that the "internal" problem of authority and infallibility is situated in the "tension between Church as institution and Church as association."[38] In a similar way, Crowley has stated that papal infallibility is a stumbling block for the development of a "thinking Church."[39] Dionne maintains that while the pre-conciliar period made a sharp distinction between *ecclesia docens* and *ecclesia discens*, the functional role of the *sensus fidelium* was an active one. He links the "talking back" to authorities that he recommends for the faithful to the models that come from the early Church. Dionne claims that these models support a more active use of the sense of the faithful than even Newman considered.[40]

Several authors whose influence was exercised prior to or during the Second Vatican Council drew on historical approaches to the sense of the faithful that were developed in the Patristic and Medieval periods. Such approaches were vital to the inclusion by the Fathers at the Council of the perspectives of historical consciousness and the more wholistic approaches to ecclesiology that characterized the thought and practice of the early Church. The work of Koster, Schmaus and Loehrer, specifically on the sense of the faithful, continued to influence systematic approaches after the Council. These authors emphasized that the whole Church is responsible for the faith. The Church's pastors have a unique role in expressing doctrine, yet their leadership should be exercised as an expression of the active faith of all. The various attempts at understanding the sense of the faithful in the post-conciliar period may be read as contributions to a deepening appreciation in theology of the need for interaction among different elements of the Church, and of the difficulties both of achieving such interaction and of "reading" the sense of the faith within it.

Some individual authors who have studied the topic over an extended period of time individually illustrate this growing appreciation. Congar, Beinert, Granfield, Thompson and Rahner are among those who must be added to the authors whose historical efforts have already been mentioned. The deepening complexity and struggle with issues of interpretation can also be observed, of course, in the disagreements between authors, disagreements which have continued to grow during the decades following the Council.

## EMPHASIS ON THE MAGISTERIUM

Most authors who have reflected on how the *sensus fidelium* is to be understood from a systematic standpoint have emphasized one of three positions. Some see the magisterium as the central focus for the faith and for the expression of the sense of the faith. Some stress the importance of the faithful and their experiences as primary, suggesting even major political or structural changes in the Church which could be accompanied perhaps by the use of different sociological tools so that this source might be both expressed and encouraged to develop. A third group comprising the largest body of theologians includes those who have emphasized in one way or another the importance of interaction between the faithful and their pastors. within this group, criticism of current activities among the laity, the hierarchy or theologians have, at times, led to an emphasis similar to one of the previous two groups. However, a more nuanced view, and recognition of the need to include all elements of the Church in expressing the *sensus fidelium* leads them to support an interactive model.

Among those considered here who focus on the role of the magisterium, the clearest proponent is Jesús Sancho Bielsa.[41] Sancho emphasizes that infallibility is attributable to God alone. Still, he insists that the magisterium is the organ in the Church that is given divine protection in proclaiming the truth. Acknowledging Vatican II's teaching that the whole Church expresses the faith, he recalls the unique role of the bishops, and the pope in particular, in setting limits and expressing the content of the faith, including the *sensus fidelium*. In formal definitions of faith, it is not the infallibility of the sense of the faithful that is expressed, but that of the whole Church with the magisterium as its guarantee. The infallibility of the people *in credendo* is not passive, but it is exercised in practical living. Interestingly, Sancho does not discuss the possibilities of dissension in the Church's response to official teaching in practice. Since the *sensus fidei* is the work of the Spirit, a positive response to the teaching is to be expected. Any attempts to contradict magisterial teaching by reference to individuals, groups or even the whole Church would by the very attempt show that the sense of the faithful was absent. No discussion is given by Sancho of those events in church history that other authors have offered as examples, where the sense of the faithful has balanced or challenged the magisterium or where in earlier times, the community as a whole directly contextualized the pastors' authority.

It is difficult to identify in Sancho's approach any sense that a contribution could be made by the *conspiratio* of people and pastors that is not reducible to the actions of the pastors alone. The role of the faithful is reduced to those responses and practical applications that are left when the magisterium's function of defining and expressing doctrines has been exercised. Sancho's views illustrate in the "purest" form the logical outcome of emphasizing the magisterium's role without a genuine interactive role for the faithful.

James Hitchcock presents a case for a strong magisterium with an unusual twist.[42] He argues that a total dependence on the consensus of the faithful, like that illustrated in the case of St. Thomas More, shows the innate conservative quality of the *consensus fidelium*. Such consensus needs the critical and even creative judgment of the magisterium in order to promote any prophetic insights or develop the faith and practice of the whole body of believers. Yet Hitchcock's argument can be used to show not just the need that the sense of the faithful has for the creative judgment and power of influence of the magisterium, but the converse as well: the need of the magisterium for the same sort of assistance from the faithful.

Hitchcock's example illustrates only one type of situation where an autonomous source within the Church is seen to be inadequate to the task of expressing the faith fully. It could be argued that a conserving, narrowly focused magisterium, if left in isolation, would also lack the creative challenge and prophetic insights available from the faithful. Essential to Hitchcock's logic is the isolation of a "consensus" from part of the Church. Yet if the magisterium were isolated it might also be unable to act on prophetic gifts that were given to the Church. Hitchcock's example seems more supportive of the notion that both the magisterium and the faithful must be acknowledged as sharing in the experience and expression of the faith, and that they have a fundamental responsibility for interacting with each other, than a demonstration that the *consensus fidelium* is necessarily a conservative agent in the Church. As argued under criterion three above, the magisterium is certainly responsible for teaching on behalf of the whole Church. Yet the inclusion of the faith of the whole Church in such teaching and further development of such teaching may be guaranteed precisely by the possibility of contributions from the whole Church to the process of development.

Hitchcock appears to assume that the magisterium would necessarily see the wisdom in the challenges and new insights of would-be prophets. Many events in the Church's history show that such charisms are given to other elements in the Church, and that at times the contributions of a variety of sources are appropriated by the magisterium only after a struggle.

A less stringent stance that still retains an emphasis on the hierarchy is taken by Jose Morales, when he stresses the need for strong leadership from the magisterium and theologians, in leading those of "simple faith."[43] The sense of the faithful is associated with the "instinct" or piety of the faithful. Yet in contrasting such faith with theological reflection, Morales appears to limit the possibilities of the *sensus fidelium*. He affirms that all levels in the Church are given for the good of the whole, and that balance between the levels is needed. Historical cases like the Arian crisis demonstrate that at times the faithful may in fact provide such balance. Morales acknowledges that tensions may occur in the Church, but claims that when the different elements listen to each other, they create the *sensus Ecclesiae*. What is missing in his description, however, are indicators of how tensions should be resolved or used to bear new fruit. Like Hitchcock, Morales finds that the magisterium must at times overcome the conservative inertia of the simple faithful. It is not clear, however, how the faithful might be expected to make a genuine theological contribution when theological responsibility is assumed to lie with the magisterium and the theologians. When a genuine theological role is not granted to the faithful it is difficult to see how any specifically theological resource can be found in the sense of the faithful.

Scheffczyk's stress on the Church as a "hierarchically structured *communio*" recalls some of the emphases present in Sancho and Morales.[44] He observes that with Cano and others the *sensus fidelium* came to be regarded as an "unsuitable" criterion for the tradition. With this assessment, it came to be seen as mediated in its infallible form through the magisterium. In its historical use, it is a tool of inclusion, not independence. Scheffczyk notes that nineteenth century theologians saw a creative role for conflict as part of the sense of the faithful. He is silent on how lay-initiated conflict might be legitimate.

Scheffczyk focuses rather on the *sensus fidelium* as an aspect of the mystery of the Spirit's activity in the Church. The hierarchy is not "merged" with the faithful nor is it separated from them. Both the magisterium and the faithful are inadequate to the task of expressing the tradition by themselves. They must work in an organic relationship, clarifying each other. He suggests that the Marian dogmas illustrate that the faithful offer a witness that is *"relatively* independent," but sees the value of their sense of the faith as it is expressed in the "conspiration" or harmony that is achieved with the Church's leaders. He stresses that the objective and subject elements, the *sensus fidelium* and *sensus fidei*, must be distinguished, and notes the importance of objective expression in doctrinal matters.

Scheffczyk also stresses that the *sensus fidelium* is not solely an intellectual entity, but a "living capacity" of the heart. His appeal for a distinct role for the sense of the faithful does much to distinguish his position from others who place an exclusive emphasis on the role of the magisterium in expressing the sense of the faithful. Still, by not addressing the role of the faithful as a possible critical agent, he seems to limit its scope and practical importance. The faithful may initiate insights that can reach completion within the larger context governed by the magisterium, but it is not clear that they can engage the expressions of the faith given by their pastors in an active, meaningful way once they are given. While he affirms that the lay witness is not just a matter of "reinforcement and resonance" of the hierachy's teaching, it does not appear that Scheffczyk sees it as one of genuine criticism or disagreement either.

The specific assumption of a dominant focus on the role of the magisterium has also been illustrated among authors that address particular practical questions. The support of John C. Ford and Germaine Grisez for the infallibility of *Humanae Vitae* is tied to a passive understanding of the sense of the faithful, and the view that the "genuine *sensus Ecclesia*" has not been affected by the dissent which has followed the encyclical.[45] Joseph Costanzo illustrates the tendency to tie doctrinal expression to the ordinary exercise of authority when he says that the "technical formality of an *ex cathedra* definition would not add to the intrinsic validity" of the encyclical.[46] Cormac Burke specifically identifies the teaching on birth control as infallible because of its connection to an infallible *sensus fidelium*. To support this claim, he argues that the sense of the faithful must be distinguished from the views of a majority, many of whose faith may in fact be disturbed and thus untrustworthy. He adds that identification of the views of the genuinely faithful must be decided by the pastors, who are closer to the people than the academic theologians are.[47]

## RELATED ISSUES

Focusing on the role of the pastors to resolve interpretative problems of the *sensus fidelium* has the advantage of clarifying church teaching in the face of the ambiguity of views that has now clearly become apparent. It is important to ask though, whether there is not a confusion among such authors between the legitimate responsibility of authority to clarify a teaching in a given context and the possibility of clarifying an issue for all time. Claiming finality in addition to clarity in reference to historically conditioned expressions may serve to avoid the responsibility shared by the whole Church, of continuing to accept the challenge of faith within the changing, pluralistic contexts of the modern world.

The way this challenge may be met while maintaining the authority of the magisterium and at the same time contextualizing interpretation within the tools and perspectives offered by modern hermeneutical theory has been developed well in the 1990 document of the International Theological Commission, "On the Interpretation of Dogmas."[48] Citing *Mysterium Ecclesiae*, the document asserts that "dogmas are historical in the sense that their meaning 'is partially dependent on the expressive power of the language used at a given time and under given circumstances.'" Further expressions will "preserve and confirm" earlier treatments of dogmatic truth. They will "illuminate them" as well, especially as "new questions or errors are being confronted" by them.[49]

The Commission suggests that the magisterium make clear the weight of particular teachings so that the faithful will be able distinguish the level of "binding force" behind them, inasmuch as the "religiously grounded obedience (*religiosum obsequium*)" admits of "varying degrees."[50] The process of defining doctrine should itself take into account the pastoral purpose of its authority. The document further affirms,

> In a pluralistically structured society and in a church shaping itself in different ways, the magisterium increasingly fulfills its pastoral office through persuasive argumentation. In this situation the legacy of the faith tradition can only be transmitted fruitfully if the magisterium and the other bearers of pastoral and theological responsibility are prepared for collaboration involving argument, especially prior to definitive decisions on the part of the church's magisterium.[51]

The Commission notes that the need on the part of the magisterium to focus on "one specific proposition" is rooted in "the concreteness and the decisiveness of Christian faith."[52] At the same time such focusing "contains the risk of both dogmatic positivism and dogmatic minimalism." To avoid these tendencies, there must be an understanding of dogma as interrelated to "the whole of the church's teaching and life," as well as an "integration of individual dogmas in that whole which is made up of all the dogmas."[53]

The Commission asserts that "theological interpretation . . . is not a purely intellectual process but a deeply spiritual event" that is "sustained by the Spirit of truth." Such interpretation "is inextricably linked" to "communion with Jesus Christ in the church."[54] The document later adds that it is the Holy Spirit that "awakens and nourishes the *sensus fidelium*" which leads the faithful to embrace the truth which is given expression by their pastors.[55] The interpretation of church teaching is itself meant to build up the *consensus fidelium*.[56]

In describing the relationship of the sense of the faithful and the magisterium in these ways, the Commission does not support a passive view of the faithful. It affirms, "Like the entire paradosis of the church, the contemporary interpretation of dogmas takes place *in* and *through* the whole life of the church."[57] This occurs in preaching, catechetical instruction, liturgy, prayer, the work of deacons and the ordinary living of the faithful, and even in areas of discipline. The document adds:

> The prophetic witness of individual Christians or groups is to be measured by whether and to what extent it is in communion with the life of the church as a whole; for example whether it can be received or accepted by the church, in a possibly lengthy and sometimes painful process.[58]

In closing the Commission reasserts the primary place of the "Christological axis" for interpretation.[59] In maintaining this foundational root of tradition, it recalls the importance of both "the criterion of origin, that is, apostolicity" and "the criterion of communion (*koinonia*) or catholicity." In a final "excursus" the document describes as "furthering and complementing" its own discussion of doctrinal development, the criteria of Newman in his *Essay*.⁶⁰ It closes by reasserting the apostolic authority of the magisterium, while recalling also the goal of interpretation as one of "eliciting from the letter of dogma 'spirit and life' in the church and individual Christians."⁶¹

The possibility of development in regard to expressions of faith, especially in new circumstances, and the possibility of clear changes in magisterial teachings in areas that ate not solemnly defined, requires a dynamic process for living, renewing and rethinking the faith. It is this process that Vatican II has described as the responsibility of the whole Church. John T. Ford has discussed how even solemnly defined statements are subject to continued reflection and new understandings.⁶² He asserts, as has been argued here, that the willingness to reconsider the meanings of doctrinal expressions as they are seen in new historical contexts is related to the stance that is taken on the historical contextualization of doctrine and the possibilities of doctrinal development. In regard to infallibility in particular, Ford writes:

> If infallibility is a genuine element in the mystery of the church, then, like any other divinely bestowed gift, it may function and be understood in a plurality of ways. Such a view is unlikely to be acceptable either to those who wish an unequivocal repudiation of infallibility or to those who wish to maintain an absolutistic concept of dogma in general and of infallibility in particular. Yet a commonality between absolutization and rejection should be recognized: neither admits the necessity or legitimacy of reconceptualization.⁶³

The complex relationship of the faithful to official teaching is illustrated well in those authors who have considered the issues of conscience and obedience, especially in reference to specific moral teachings. The issues raised by McCormick as well as the criticisms he has received indicate the array of problems involved.⁶⁴ In the area of authority and conscience, Margaret Farley and

Lisa Sowle Cahill have both warned against the danger of too rigid an approach on the part of leaders. Farley warns that "protection" of the faithful "retards rather than fosters" moral growth.[65] Cahill makes the important point that "rhetoric" about the need to avoid scandal that accompanies the adoption of a rigid stance ignores the larger scandal that occurs when the experience of the faithful is disregarded by those who propose to guide them.[66] Bracken sees the "sense of self-identity" of the believer as being based in a proper understanding of the role of the *sensus fidei.*[67]

The balancing role that may be played by the sense of the faithful is particularly well illustrated in the work of Rahner. In addition to his treatment of the roles of the magisterium and faithful, his distinction between principles and prescriptions in practical decision making lays a theological and psychological foundation for understanding how individual believers are called to exercise responsibility.[68]

Also important are the views of Orsy, Butler and others who have examined the meaning of *obsequium*, who have criticized a simplistic understanding of obedience while not denying the importance of authority. Orsy describes *obsequium* as an expression in the area of doctrine, of *communio*. Rather than prescribing a particular response, it indicates an "attitude" of communion that may be expressed in different responses ranging from respect to submission.[69] The *sensus fidei*, may serve the whole Church and the magisterium in particular, through both reception and corrective judgment. Bracken also has asserted that this sense can only be effective if individuals are aware of their responsibility to respond critically if necessary.[70]

Even when teaching is authoritatively given, the possibility of tension must be considered to be not only acceptable, but at times necessary to the Church's process of discernment. Reception and practical responses among the faithful that are legitimately discerned may include disagreement or dissonance.

Clarity with respect to teaching may in some sense be seen as less certain when the possibility of later developments is acknowledged. This does not deny legitimate authority, but requires, as several authors have argued, attention to the theological weight given to official teachings, and an active analysis and reception of their content.[71]

A reductionistic approach that sees all official teaching as retaining maximum weight because it issues from an official who possesses the ability to exercise decisive authority, even when such authority is not exercised in each case, or an approach which views obedience in solely juridical terms, disallows the legitimate exercise of discernment and conscience in the concrete living of the faithful. In terms of the characteristics of the *sensus fidelium* presented here, such approaches ignore criteria five and six.

### EMPHASIS ON THE FAITHFUL

Limiting the expression of the sense of the faithful to acceptance of what is given by the Church's pastors reduces this source to a passive response that adds nothing of a genuine theological character to the Church's understanding of the faith. A different reduction that is just as harmful to the traditional meaning of the *sensus fidelium* may be seen among authors who focus on the direct expressions of the faithful without sufficient regard for a genuine role of authority of the Church's pastors.

Certain contemporary positions have clearly broken from an interactive model where the faithful and the pastors deepen theological understanding together. Daniel Maguire's view that the *sensus fidelium* supports abortion reads the opinions of the faithful in a way that is as selective as Burke's view that the *sensus fidelium* clearly teaches that all artificial contraception is unacceptable.[72] Kaufman's appeal to the use of polls and his association of dissent with the sense of the faithful represent a form of interpretation that is found in more or less nuanced forms in several other authors.[73] The recent expression of the sense of the faithful is assumed not only to be present and at work, but available for direct access. Such identification of the sense of the faithful may be compelling and even prove true under more rigorous scrutiny. An assumption of its presence in the majority is too simplistic, however, as is argued even by many authors who support an active consultation of the laity.

In a way that is similar to the overconfidence expressed by some in the unchangeability of expressions of the magisterium, such an immediate identification of the views expressed by many of the faithful with the actual theological content of the *sensus fidelium* begs the question of how the sense of the faithful can be discerned by the whole Church, by reducing the process to the consultation of one dominant source. Consultation by sociological tools may be particularly problematic in that it limits the depth at which the sense of the faithful can actually be read. If this sense is really part of a dynamic process that integrates elements in the Church in a way that is qualitatively different than voting, the quantitative tools of polls or surveys may be inherently inadequate to the task of discovering the *sensus Ecclesiae* even while they offer some indicators of what the majority of the laity believes. Actual interplay of different levels in the community must occur to develop genuine understanding, let alone agreement. Even in the dynamics of small groups, the establishment of genuine consensus is much different than the weighing of different views. An extended dialectic process may be needed to move different parties beyond their initial views to find a deeper, shared understanding.

As seen in the example of Michael McGinniss, a selective reading of the faithful for input on issues of faith may answer some questions prematurely.[74] Premature judgment based in culturally conditioned lay expressions is similar to the premature finality sometimes given to magisterial statements. The practical concerns of "ministering" to the sense of the faithful that are presented by James and Evelyn Whitehead better illustrate the complex practical and theological task that appropriation of this source entails.[75] Feifel's educative agenda also indicates how the complex nature of "the faithful" warrants a sophisticated approach to developing the tools needed by believers to make possible the full exercise of their responsibilities.[76]

Authors who appeal for an ecclesial structure that is more "democratic" have, to a large extent, done so to redress the structural imbalance of the modern, highly centralized Roman Catholic Church. Yet in some authors like Ruether this appeal is not for a repair of the present system, but for a whole new image or "*Gestalt*" of what the Church should be.[77] Elisabeth Schuessler Fiorenza similarly rejects the patriarchical system within the Church's leadership which she finds reduces the *consensus fidelium* to mere obedience.[78]

As important as the message of these authors is for its emphasis on inclusion of all the faithful, and especially of women who arguably have been "disenfranchised" in the most unjust way for the longest time, the remedy offered often embodies rejection of the institutional Church altogether. Issues such as acceptance of women into the ordained ministry are proposed by some feminists as test issues in a "take it or leave it" manner that parallels the attitude identified in the magisterium by critics like Fiorenza. However much the theologically defensibility and appropriateness of ordaining women might continue to be the subject of further discussion, such ordination would not of itself clarify the interactive role to be played by the faithful and the magisterium (though in such a case, the talents of both genders would be available more fully in the various levels of further dialogue).

A sophisticated argument for "democratization" is presented by Leonard Swidler, who explicitly ties his critique of the current institutional structure to the historical power of the consensus of the faithful and to the innate meanings of democracy, consensus and church.[79] As many others have done, Swidler asks why the use of the sense of the faithful has been a useful source in teaching about the Assumption but not birth control. Recognizing the plurality within the *consensus fidelium*, he maintains that the diversity of expression within the Church's many cultures should be encouraged and celebrated. There are both "minimal" and "maximal" areas for agreement. As a foundation for developing the *consensus fidelium*, Swidler recommends that reflection on the faith should begin with the Jesus of history, and should develop a self-critical, dialogic relationship with God. Swidler then encourages dialogue within the different levels of the Church but warns that a "pre-Vatican II defensive model" has again been taken up, especially by the Congregation for the Doctrine of the Faith. He challenges the Congregation to take up true dialogue, which he adds, can only occur between equals.

Swidler roots his critique of modern institutional models in historical and scriptural contexts in which he identifies authority as operating "from the ground up." He warns against trying to base a hierarchical system on Jesus' own actions. Yet, it is here that Swidler's approach is limited in its ability to use practical elements from the tradition for current struggles with the interaction of the faithful and their pastors. It would seem more appropriate to recognize the ambiguity, described in the early chapters of the present study, in regard to the authority structures in the early Church. It is not always clear how early treatments of catholicity and leadership issues can be expressed in terms of modern ecclesial categories. Different strategies for interrelationship were, in fact, tried.

Both the solutions and failures that were experienced in historical attempts to resolve practical problems in implementing shared responsibility, especially of the churches of the Patristic period, must be considered further as models for the modern creation of balance among various elements of the Church. Both offices of authority and the structural inclusion of influence on the part of the faithful claim warrants in antiquity.

## RELATED ISSUES

Approaches to the sense of the faithful that involve a rejection of significant parts of its history, especially as the concept developed through practical problems in Patristic communities, the dogmatic debates in the great ecumenical councils, and the later theological reflections of Medieval and modern thinkers, raise questions of whether the source being appropriated and defined by some contemporary authors is in fact the same theological entity that has been identified in the Church's history. Approaches from the previous perspective that focused on the magisterium as the sole legitimate arbiter of this sense and those of the present group that accent the role of the faithful without a necessary acknowledgment of the role of authoritative leaders both can be criticized for ignoring important elements of the long history of the sense of the faithful.

The need for a modern balance that might be motivated by historically informed models is apparent in the views of both theologians and the hierarchy. The tensions and lack of real communication that sometimes characterizes relations between laity, theologians and bishops are certainly exacerbated by a polarization and entrenchment in camps like those described here. The current predominant lack of exercise of theoretical and practical models of interaction makes such polarization more likely in a Church that exists in a pluralistic context. This lack is more painful and frustrating when it is recognized that genuine interactive models are well supported by the Church's tradition.

An important though controversial contribution to the search for interactive models has been proposed by those whose work is collected under the heading of "liberation theology." Metz has argued that those who have been "dependents" in the Church must "transform themselves" to become a resource for new ways of thinking.[80] The wisdom of "grassroots" experience cannot be left at the ground level. The views expressed by Elizondo also show though, how a tension can exist between a desire to be true to a "particular *sensus fidelium*" and the efforts to share local insights with the larger Church.[81]

Some liberation theologians seem best placed in the following "group" that stresses interaction. Collins argues that the local church should be seen as "community of communities" where smaller groups both nourish and are energized by the whole.[82] Suess sees in the contribution of "popular wisdom" a refocusing of the "hierachy of truths" in terms of basic human needs.[83] Boff argues that the distinction between the Church as teacher and Church as learner must be overcome along with its hierarchical model at least partially through sociological analysis. Interaction between the faithful and the hierarchy must be based in open dialogue with the "outside" world acting as a reference point.[84]

The criticism that liberation theology has received is that it is at times connected to models of analysis that are foreign to the genuine tradition. A perceived dependence on class distinctions and Marxist analysis is found by some and seen as a foundation for undermining the Church's genuine mission.[85] For some critics, liberation theology should be seen as a movement that emphasizes the people at the expense of the Church's traditional theology and proper authority.

The impact of liberation theologies on the sources, method and content of theology is already significant. Their full contribution to both theology and practical ecclesial structures remains to be seen. The writings of Boff and Metz that link their theology with the sense of the faithful indicate that the challenge presented to theological reflection must be addressed through an interactive model, where pastors, laity and theologians draw each other into the development of new patterns of thought and concrete church life. This is especially important in regard to those whose experience may be crucial for understanding the modern call to holiness, the poor.

There is as yet no resolution as to how this theological source can be appropriated in a context that calls for social and political restructuring. Further work is needed to establish how this can be done with the appropriate involvement of ecclesial authority.

## EMPHASIS ON INTERACTION OF THE MAGISTERIUM AND THE FAITHFUL

Those modern treatments of the sense of the faithful which emphasize an interactive model have pursued the possibility of avoiding an unbalanced attraction to either "pole" as described by Congar and repeated also by Thompson.[86] The characteristics or "criteria" of the sense of the faithful that were drawn earlier from the long history of the source indicate the historical shortcomings in the two previously discussed approaches, that focus on either the magisterium or the faithful at the expense of the other. While seemingly giving respect to the notion that the sense of the faithful resides in the whole Church (criteria one and four), each approach involves a dependence on one element in the Church, while depriving another element of the voice and the force it has exercised in history. A legitimate partner in the process of development is thus reduced to acknowledging or repeating what is produced by the other dominant voice. In such approaches the multi-dimensional quality of the sense of the faithful (criterion two) is also ignored in practice. Limited focuses on the role of authority or on the sense of the faithful can lead to disunity when dialogue might be possible. They leave legitimate charisms within the Church unused.

Often in the contemporary Church those who disagree with the magisterium and who still claim genuine experience of the charisms given to all for living out and reflecting on the faith are left with a truncated list of options. They can deny their experiences and insights or reject authority. Those in authority who are confronted by dissent often respond with juridical demands or dismiss those who disagree as lacking any legitimate voice. They are then left to express the faith of the Church without understanding the depth of its experience.

The lack of interactive patterns can take a heavy toll. When theologians or groups among the faithful present the experiences or collective dissent of many in the Church in opposition to the magisterium in ways that at least appear to set the *sensus fidelium* up as an alternative to it, representatives within the hierarchy have responded by reinforcing their claim to teach on behalf of all, particularly in juridical modes. Conflicts have thus come to be conceived in terms of struggles over power and structure, and the opportunity for theological growth through creative tension is made much less likely. Contemporary fulfillment of Newman's fears, that without consultation and an active role the faithful might be left to indifference or superstition, is painfully obvious. The further result of rejection of part or all of the Church's teaching is another too frequent result.

When the substantial body of contemporary authors who argue for an interrelationship of magisterium and the faithful are examined, it is at once clear that they preserve the "wholistic" nature of the *sensus fidelium* more faithfully than those in the previous two groups. At the same time, it becomes apparent that the actual assessment of the expression of the sense of the faithful is more problematic within their more complex approach.

The authors in this third group are particularly adamant in insisting that the sense of the faithful is a quality of the whole Church (criterion one). Many of these authors take up common themes, drawing extensively on historical examples that illustrate interaction and shared responsibility. They recall the active theological contributions of the faithful to magisterial expressions and often emphasize Vatican II's statements about the responsibilities the laity. Many call for more open communication between laity and hierarchy and for increased education on the part of the laity that could enhance consultation by the bishops. The detailed treatments of these areas in the authors already discussed above will not be repeated here. Yet a recounting of some key points is needed to illustrate the way in which the authors of this "interactive focus" fulfill the criteria distilled above as they attempt to define and use the *sensus fidelium*, and to illustrate the particular aspects of this source that an interactive approach brings to light.

A stress on the importance of the whole Church (criterion one), which expresses the sense of the faithful through a variety of forms (criterion two), leads to the practical conclusion that an adequate expression of the *sensus fidelium* requires not just the realization of the importance of the magisterium and the faithful, but of their interaction as well (criterion three).

The interrelationship of these elements is illustrated particularly well in the work of Wolfgang Beinert.[87] Beinert specifically addresses the modern need for balance, claiming that Vatican II corrected the "Pian monolithism" and "magisterial positivism" that preceded it.[88] At the same time, he warns against a facile "democratization" that denies legitimate authority or accepts too readily influences from outside the Church.[89] After describing the lack of unanimity among authors after the Council on the topic and after reviewing a list of partial answers to the problem, Beinert suggests that a better understanding of the sense of the faithful would be as a "free charism" moving the Church to consensus.[90] The Logos cannot ultimately be reduced to human words. The influence of the *sensus Ecclesiae* is tied to the role the Church exercises as sacrament in the world. Significantly, Beinert does not answer the problem of concretely determining the sense of the faithful, but he calls for a continual reassessment of the forms of its expression. In later reflections, he has focused on the need for bishops and laity to interact and build models for consultation, linking the interaction of living and teaching with the ancient *regula fidei*.

Congar speaks of the need for interaction of magisterium and faithful as a communion, by contrasting this image with that of a mere "fusion" of elements.[91]

He considers reception in particular as a vehicle for creating and acknowledging interaction.

Patrick Granfield stresses unity within the diverse elements in the Church, beginning with his earliest writings on the "cybernetics" in the Church considered as a system of communication and continuing in his historical studies of Cyprian and the selection of bishops up until his recent discussion of the relationship of the *sensus fidelium* to the papacy. As observed earlier, an extended reflection on the topic has lead Granfield to a studied tentativeness about claiming too much for the *sensus fidelium*, even while he continues to argue for its importance for the ongoing understanding of the faith.[92]

Thompson, though following Congar in many respects, extends Congar's views in a way that is similar to Beinert, by saying that the *sensus fidelium* is a *regula fidei* when "properly understood and interpreted by the magisterium." At the same time, he sees the *sensus fidelium* as being a source that can "demythologize" the magisterium.[93] Tillard describes the practical tensions that exist between the hierarchy and the laity, and between "educated" and "popular" faith while still insisting on the *conspiratio* of laity and magisterium.[94] He describes the working of hierarchy and faithful as a "symbiosis," where the *sensus fidelium* and "remembrance" operate together.[95] Lamirande and Dumont find Tillard too optimistic and press for a still greater stress on interaction.[96] Dumont sees the best image of consensus as a "living dialectic."[97]

Fries is particularly critical of the magisterium as it is exercised in the contemporary Church and is skeptical of the possibilities for active consultation of the faithful. Yet he too insists on the value of the *conspiratio* stressed by Newman and sees an emphasis on the whole Church as the foundation needed for correcting current imbalances. He sees theologians in particular as having the responsibility for drawing on both the magisterium and the practical, living faith of the people as they seek a deeper understanding of doctrine.[98]

Dulles quite clearly acknowledges the lack of theological consensus on the meaning of the *sensus fidelium*. At the same time, he also appeals to Newman's notion of the *conspiratio* of faithful and hierarchy especially as the location of infallibility. Dulles describes the *sensus fidelium* as a "distinct" but "not autonomous" theological source, one which by its nature is interactive with the magisterium.[99]

O'Collins considers several central issues related to the consulting of the faithful, pointing out that while the ancient Church acknowledged the importance of consensus, the actual record of majority opinion as an indicator of what would be established as orthodox doctrine is shaky. A key step in indicating the presence of the Spirit in ecclesial expressions is found in consulting the whole Church, though a preference is given to its saints and victims. O'Collins also identifies an important interpretive problem in consulting the faithful, particularly with respect to those who come to be recognized as saints. Recognition of genuine faith is much easier with hindsight.[100]

Rahner, in particular, has considered a wide array of elements in the Church and in the faith of the individual believer that show the interdependence of the believer, the body of believers and the ongoing expressions of the tradition. He too insists on the responsibility of the whole Church for living out and reflecting on the mystery of God revealed to humanity in Jesus Christ. The scope of elements within Rahner's writing that pertain to the sense of the faithful illustrates vividly the scope of influence that this source might exercise in the Church. He is especially strong in his insistence on looking at the actual faith of believers as the faith that is genuinely expressive of the Church's message of salvation.[101]

Throughout the authors who have looked most deeply into the topic there is a deep appreciation of the genuine place of the *sensus fidelium* within the tradition. Tied directly to this perspective is a recognition of the difficulties of "reading" this source in any immediate way, and the need to focus on the process of interaction between the faithful and their pastors, if the full expression of this sense is to be found.

Precisely because it is tied to the catholicity of the Church, this *sensus Ecclesiae* cannot be separated from the diverse, interrelated elements that all contribute to the Church. In addition to arguing the need for an active relationship between the pastors and the faithful, the authors considered here describe the deep interdependence that exists between them. They also assume that acknowledgment of the mystery of the Spirit moving in the Church in different ways is foundational to an understanding of the "sense" that human respondents may gain into the meaning of faith and the ongoing re-expression of faith throughout history in the diverse vehicles of Christian tradition. In the current situation where conflict is common and practical expressions of cooperation are difficult to achieve, the sense of the faithful as a spiritual force is needed all the more. Yet this sense must be developed in believers who are not only pursuing the goal of sanctity, but who are doing so as critically thinking and acting agents in a complex world. For the Church in the modern world, the need is greater than ever for the faithful to exhibit that *phronesis* or practical judgment that has been recognized as the mark of mature believers since ancient times.

The first three criteria considered in the present study exhibit a unity that illustrates the wholistic, interrelational nature of the *sensus fidelium* as it is viewed historically. The next three criteria focus more directly on how the "inner life" of the Church (criterion four) whose mission has been clarified again by Vatican II as one of bringing the Gospel to the world by the participation of all of its members (criterion six), does so because of the inherent active nature of the sense of the faith (criterion five).

Theological treatments that focus on more "subjective" aspects of the source have illustrated the network of elements that are needed to allow a full appropriation of it. Thus, in the discussions of moral judgment and the *sensus fidei* as in Glaser, Wagner and Biser, the dynamic nature of the instinct for the faith in individual believers is seen to be connected to the lived faith of the whole community and the expression of doctrine by the magisterium. Yet this connection was also found to involve a reciprocal relationship between believers and those with authority within the community.

Wagner describes Vatican II as challenging the view that truth moves "from the top down" in the Church. He ties the expression of the *consensus fidelium* to the entire believing Church. Wagner asserts that the Church should find, in the hierarchy, leadership into a "collective finding of truth," rather than a setting for a juridical treatment of the Church's experience. Biser emphasizes that the Church is a community led by the Spirit. The *sensus fidei* is not a matter of information, but of an openness to the fundamental questions of human existence and to the release from real burdens through living faith. While beginning with the faith that is experienced in believers, Wagner and Glaser in particular have argued for an active interaction with and appropriation of such experience by those responsible for expressing the faith of the Church.[102]

The assertion of criterion six with respect to each believer is rooted in the very nature of faith in the Gospel. Yet this faith is given to the individual for the good of the community. It can neither be ignored in its individual integrity and prophetic possibility nor considered autonomous even when it is, in fact, prophetic.

The arguments of authors with an "interactive" focus have generally drawn on the complex way that the "instinctive" quality of the Church is exhibited in different ecclesial levels. As asserted in criterion two, whether it is considered as the instinct of believers, as the sense of the faith that can be articulated theologically, or as the consensus that may rise from a wide involvement of the whole Church and the inclusion of all the various aspects in the Church's expressions of faith, the interweaving of the "objective" and "subjective" elements of the source remain clear. This point is made especially by those contemporary authors who have discussed the appropriation of the *sensus fidelium* in practical ways.

## PRACTICAL ISSUES

While considering criteria for locating the sense of the faithful, Sartori has identified several that relate to both the "divine" and "human" aspects. In reference to the divine, he lists the primacy of faith, the dynamic character of the Spirit's gifts and the goal of consensus. These coincide well with the general characteristics that have been identified here as deriving from the history of the source. In considering the human elements, he places importance on communication and freedom. The *sensus fidelium* may be expressed in both consent and dissent. Interestingly, Sartori observes that ambiguity may characterize both responses. He sees "direct" response as more problematic in the contemporary Church than in earlier eras, and suggests that the move to a desired consensus should be recognized as a dialectical process. In working for this in practice, recognition of a more educated laity and a focus on practical issues are needed. He asserts too, that the quality of response from the faithful is more important than the quantity of response.[103]

Congar warns against reducing the sense of the faithful to official expressions considered at a juridical level. Yet he adds that the actions of the faithful must not be seen simplistically either. Non-reception, for instance, may not indicate that a teaching is false. It may show rather, that a more adequate or edifying expression is needed.[104]

This hesitancy to claim too much for the sense of the faithful or for the finality of particular dogmatic statements is expressed in strong terms by Sesboüé.

He criticizes those who would assume too quickly that *Humanae Vitae* has not been received. The many responses it has raised may indicate its importance in a way that is not yet understood. At the same time Sesboüé opposes the "dogmatic mentality" he finds in the Church since Trent, and criticizes the "ecclesial 'monophysism'" that does not appreciate the human, historical contextualization of dogmatic expressions. Sesboüé quite explicitly calls for a renewed sense of *koinonia*, and a dynamic interrelationship of communication between magisterium and the people. The Church's history shows that the entire *catholica* participates in the covenant with God.[105]

Several authors have raised the issue of whether the laity are prepared to take their place in contributing to the theological work of the *sensus fidelium*. Vorgrimler appeals to an active process involving the magisterium and the laity to find consensus as the result of concrete, practical proclamation of the faith. He questions whether the faithful are competent to teach the faith in theoretical matters. Yet, he adds, ordinary, living faith does not require expertise. He notes that in the early Church, the responsibility for preserving the tradition was given to experts. At the same time he recognizes the shift in Vatican II from Vatican I, moving the expression of the sense of the faith from a passive to an active matter. The responses of the laity to the Creed or to dogmatic expressions may be the expression of a will to agree, but such responses may not be an indication of actual understanding. Both renewal and discernment in the Church can be fostered by a concern for praxis.[106]

Walgrave, while retaining the view that the sense of the faith must be rooted in the *conspiratio*, further calls into question the competence of the laity, citing the secularization that characterizes the majority of believers. The "peaceable" laity of Newman's day does not now exist.[107] Walgrave warns that the magisterium might maintain some expressions of doctrine too rigidly, but he also questions where the laity are who might be consulted as a legitimate theological source. The current situation where communication between hierarchy and people is ineffective is hardly one that can be left unchallenged. Walgrave describes the relationship as one of "dangerous conflict."[108]

Alszeghy, after discussing the phenomenological, epistemological and psychological foundations for the sense of the faithful, warns against the assumption that the *sensus fidei* is more accessible to the "simple" believer. A simplicity that comes from a lack of knowledge of the teaching of the magisterium puts the faithful at a disadvantage. Efforts should be made to educate the laity so that their sense of the faith can be developed and deepened.[109]

The question of how to access the sense of the faithful through the mediation of "experts" has been addressed by Tillard and Vorgrimler, among others. Current practices have been criticized by Hellwig.[110] However, if, as several authors maintain, the *sensus fidelium* must be considered in functional terms,[111] it is difficult to see how a move can be made from a logic of interrelationship to an effective logistical exercise of interresponsibility that results in a genuine understanding of how the people as a whole experience faith in the world.

O'Collins and Thompson have both suggested turning to the "saints" or even to the oppressed as exemplars of the genuinely faithful. The approach of Boff and other liberation theologians would also support such a focus. At the same time, both philosophical and practical questions may be raised in regard to this form of consultation. Identifying and encouraging holiness within the faithful would not in itself resolve the question of how genuine informed consultation should be achieved.

The views of Aidan Nichols illustrate this point. Nichols provides a useful, succinct view of the role that the *sensus fidelium* has had in the past, and suggests that it can be the locus for innovation and criticism in the Church today. He also asserts quite clearly, that there are problems in determining which "fluctuations" in the common expressions of faith are the result of prophetic change or "corrosion" of the faith. He suggests following the focus of nineteenth century authors, who, like some modern counterparts, look to the saints and to those believers who suffer for their faith.[112] Nichols's approach seems concerned to protect roles for both the sense of the faithful and the magisterium, and to argue that they are not to be construed as "competing forces" especially as the secular media may be expected to do. However, while his cautious approach retains a clear acknowledgment of the traditional sources, it does little to offer insight into the problem of identifying the faithful who carry the *sensus fidelium*.

Heft adapts a statement of Newman's in describing the *sensus fidelium* as "an hypothesis to account for a difficulty," and discusses how this proposed source can be used in both ecumenical dialogue and the promulgation of Marian dogmas.[113] Use of the sense of the faithful encounters its own particular difficulty when theologians or church leaders try to discern its presence in concrete situations. Heft suggests nuancing the attention given to the *sensus fidelium* by comparing it to the notion of the "hierarchy of truths." Heft also sees consultation itself as a practical aid in making teachings more persuasive. Even in the concrete examples Heft uses, however, it is evident that a more discriminating approach will multiply the need for practical discernment in concrete contexts.[114]

Kerkhofs also suggests the use of the idea of the "hierarchy of truths." Following a comprehensive summary of the history and current questions relating to the sense of the faithful, he notes the particular complications that occur in the modern context because of the acceptance of historical consciousness. Practical measures that draw on modern methods of communication and tools of statistical analysis may be allies in the modern context too, but they do not insure success in arriving at consensus. Kerkhofs sees freedom of expression as a major requirement for such efforts. He also laments its absence in the Church. "Fear and the desire for power" impair efforts at genuine communication even within the hierarchy itself. He sees a genuinely spiritual task before all members of the Church, who must work to listen to and interpret each other even when such actions mean they must take up the cross of conflict. Kerkhofs observes that it is precisely in the tensions of a dialogue that is both "diachronic" and "synchronic" that the Holy Spirit is found.[115]

It thus appears that as more freedom and genuine dialogue are encouraged to appropriate the *sensus fidelium* as a theological source, both greater risks and an expanded tentativeness in the results will be encountered. Consultation on important topics will, at least initially, open up the field of theological discourse rather than close it.

### INTERRELATED ISSUES

What has become evident from the work of contemporary authors who argue for more involvement between the different levels within the Church, is that the *process* of interaction is vital to genuine expression of the *sensus fidelium*. In fact, the key to understanding the role of the *sensus fidelium* in the post-conciliar Church is in recognizing that the process of including the faithful is more concretely accessible than the results that emerge from the process, as finished doctrinal expressions. Haarsma, for instance, has described the "biggest difficulty" concerning the sense of the faithful as being that it is not so much a "fact" as a "task." He suggests that it is "always to be desiderated ... yet never completely attained."[116] The exercise of the *sensus fidelium* involves, by its appropriation of a living community, a necessarily open process of discernment.

Any consensus that is visible within the community and any expressions that are accepted as representative of the faith of the community will be developed over time and received over time. These may be redeveloped and re-received in more nuanced statements later. The fullest judgment of their legitimacy is an issue of quality not quantity of support.[117]

Biser has described the sense of the faithful as an issue of openness rather than information. Pursuing openness has its risks and ambiguities. Walgrave expresses doubts about the outcome of consulting the faithful in the current "dangerous" context of disagreement. Alszeghy, on the other hand, sees the danger of assuming a "simplicity" in the faithful that leaves them outside of the process. In the description of the tradition in Nichols, it is possible to see how the sources and genuineness of the sense of the faithful can be acknowledged without being able to define how actual interaction can take place.

Real interaction is needed. Yet along with practical steps to achieve it there must be an acceptance of certain "inadequacies" and practical blocks to closure in the treatment of specific issues. The process of consultation that embodies an appropriation of the *sensus fidelium* is an inherently open one. To recall the terms offered in the early work of Granfield, the Church that employs the sense of the faithful as a resource is an "open system" of communication.[118]

The authors who focus on an interrelationship of the hierarchy and the faithful as the best appropriation of its long tradition draw especially on models from the early Church that recognized the *regula fidei* as operating within the entire the *communio*. Above any simplistic authoritative structure that stressed juridical inter-responsibility, these early models and their modern analogues look for a higher form of operation—a "symbiosis" (Thompson), a genuine community rather than a "fusion" (Congar), and most importantly, a *conspiratio*.

To achieve this *conspiratio*, as several authors have stressed, there is the need for the *sensus fidelium* to be a "free charism" (Beinert). It employs the "spontaneous judgment of the faithful" acting in the Church (Bracken).[119] Its operation can be expected to cause tension (Fries). Caution must be exercised. The sense of the faithful cannot be immediately assumed to be equivalent to public opinion. Genuine faith and the growth toward holiness are its necessary root.

Development of the faith requires leadership within the Church (Wagner). Yet this leadership teaches the faith which is given to and recognized in the whole. Leadership may itself need the challenge of prophetic voices, even in response to official pronouncements. A circularity is embedded in the process of development and evaluation that recalls the "hermeneutical circle." Haarsma describes the situation where church officials are left the task alone as a "vicious circle" of interpretation.[120] Similar criticism can be made of the closed circle that might be formed by dependence on the faithful alone, as discussed above. Official teaching is needed, yet the faith of the whole Church must genuinely be represented in such teaching. A balanced understanding of the interpretive task of the whole Church is described well by Walgrave:

> Christian doctrine, then, in its more restricted sense is limited to the official teaching of the Church. That official teaching is supposed to voice the teaching of the apostolic Church. As such it is *semper eadem* and handed down from generation to generation within the Church. Dogma viewed in its undisturbed historical continuity is a tradition, and development of dogma is a characteristic of living tradition. As it passes through the chain of generations, each with its own spirit, its own controversial situations, intellectual problems, and spiritual needs, the continuous reflection of the faithful is constantly remolding and recasting its understanding of the mystery of Salvation according to the changing human focus from which the object of faith is illuminated.[121]

Walgrave also observes, "Dogmatic formalism tends to become the grave of the spirit."[122]

## Issues of Interpretation

The authors of the "interrelational" emphasis indicate a developmental quality in this source that is also suggested by modern hermeneutical theory. There is a need for "hermeneutical distance" in the area of doctrine, in order for the Church's expressions of belief to be read accurately. A plurality of views on a given topic may indicate a normal step in the process of interpretation. At the same time, it is still necessary to pursue a resolution of specific issues.[123] Schillebeeckx has observed,

> Pluralism in our interpretation of faith cannot, after all, be extended endlessly—at least, not in the sense that the mystery of faith must to some extent be present *in* the conceptualizations of faith, as an *aspect* of the total consciousness of faith, with the result that pluralism become an expression of unanimity on a deeper level and that a (collective) judgment about what does and what does not form part of orthodox faith really becomes possible, even though years or even centuries may pass (as the development of dogma clearly shows) before the Church is ready to make a decisive judgment in questions of faith.[124]

The work of Newman, in many ways the seed for much modern discussion of both the *sensus fidelium* and development of doctrine, is instructive here. His own recognition of the *consensus fidelium* in examples from the fourth, fifth, ninth and fourteenth centuries was accepted by his contemporaries. His nineteenth century appeal for consultation remains controversial even today.

The criteria that Newman suggested for identifying genuine doctrinal development can themselves be seen as theoretical or more easily used in retrospect.[125] The advantages of continual reflection over time are clear, as Newman's own ideas and influence are reconsidered in reference to Vatican I and Vatican II.[126]

Contemporary approaches to the *sensus fidelium* suggest that criteria for assessing the sense of the faithful might better focus on functional characteristics. What emerges from the present study is that a "tentativeness" at a secondary level of reflection on dogmatic statements is embedded in the issuing of such statements themselves in the ongoing history of the Church. From a larger hermeneutical perspective, the statements of the magisterium and the insights and responses of the faithful will continue to interact. The magisterium may expect further development from future magisteria. In the past, even where certain issues appeared to be settled, change has taken place. The history of teachings on the Beatific Vision, usury, the view that "outside the Church there is no salvation" and religious freedom illustrate the scope of doctrinal statements that may be reexamined. Historical examples indicate that disagreement on doctrine may be a prelude to deeper understanding.[127] Further, the Church as a whole, in its ongoing life down through history is the vehicle for further experience, reflection and revision of its own understanding.

The re-examination or re-reception of doctrine cannot itself be focused in the responsibility of only one segment of the Church. The magisterium retains its responsibility for voicing developing expressions just as the faithful retain their responsibility for living the faith and applying their insight in new situations. It is good to recall here the famous opening speech of John XXIII at the Second Vatican Council.[128] Failure to recognize the process of development of doctrine leads too easily to attempts to reduce legitimate expressions of either the hierarchy or the faithful to hardened stances.

## PRACTICAL DIRECTIONS

It is of equal importance to recognize that the process of development may be adequately or inadequately pursued. It is here that the long tradition of the sense of the faithful, particularly in its role as a foundation for practical involvement of the whole community in the doctrinal deliberations and the exercise of responsibility in the early Church, can contribute directly to improving the concrete interactions of the various elements in the contemporary Church.

If full knowledge about the durability of the content of doctrinal expressions is not accessible to the contemporary body of a Church as it attempts to meet the challenges of a modern world, there is in fact a genuine, immediate ability to tell whether the *process* of development is being carried on in good faith. More particularly, it is possible to see from the point of view of either the faithful or the hierarchy when the process is being harmed, even gravely, by a lack of development or interaction of those elements that are needed for the whole Church to exercise its responsibility for the tradition.

Vatican II has taken significant steps to enhance the healthy exercise of this process by recognizing the active role of the faithful in the modern world for spreading the Gospel, and by emphasizing the importance of coresponsibility through collegiality and subsidiarity.

The pursuit of these goals is possible through collaboration and the consultation of boards and councils in local churches, genuine participation in synods at the largest possible level, (as in the recent Synod on the Laity whose efforts were applauded by John Paul II)[129] and the wider use of listening sessions like those that preceded recent letters by the U.S. Bishops. As a foundation to these efforts, it will be helpful to reappropriate the image of the Church that characterized the early Church's communities: *koinonia* or *communio*. Many authors have suggested this model and have linked it to the sense of the faithful.

It seems clear that if efforts toward inclusion and involvement are not made under the leadership of the Church's pastors, the views of the faithful will find other avenues of expression in dissent or rejection of the Church itself. Such dissent is certainly far from ideal, yet it must be recognized that ignoring the genuine role of the faithful is far from ideal as well. A genuine openness on the part of the pastors is a necessary foundation for interaction, as well as for obedience and trust on the part of the people.

Acceptance of the view that doctrine may develop does not mean that all doctrinal expression is necessarily tentative. The magisterium is a defensive guard to prevent the Church from falling into error. Yet an overall approach to truth that is defensive at its core should not characterize the theological reflection of the Church. What is needed is a working balance between active parts. Authority and authoritative expressions retain an important role. Yet as response to these expressions are received, it must be recognized that genuine disagreement has its place. The Spirit may move within ambiguity and disagreement to bring more clarity to historically contextualized pronouncements. Diversity itself may indicate error and divisiveness as it has before in history. It may also be a necessary stage in arriving at a deeper insight. Haarsma's observation is valuable; the areas where the Church is not in unanimity indicate where it must work for deeper understanding of its faith.[130]

The need for a process of clarification of the Church's doctrinal expressions is not surprising if we accept the insight found in many authors, and expressed well by Rahner, that the initial "insight" of faith is "pre-thematic." Faith may come to expression in diverse contexts in a variety of valid forms.

In the contemporary Church, practical agreement remains difficult as different groups view the legitimacy of an open, active system differently. The difference in approaches to the task of theology may be seen in the documents discussed above, from the International Theological Commission and the Congregation for the Doctrine of the Faith. The concerns of these two documents are different, and they need not be seen as contradictory, yet they represent different levels of explicit recognition and active appropriation of the theological input from the *sensus fidelium*. Without recognition of the sense of the faithful as

a vital part of the ecclesial process, there is a danger of eliminating it.[131] Without recognition of the risks involved in using secular tools, the *sensus fidelium* could be left behind for mere public opinion without roots in the tradition.[132] Continued work is needed to resolve conflicts in the way the *sensus fidelium* and the laity are expected to contribute to theological reflection. It is also quite clear that those who are immersed in the influences of the modern world should be given active tools and active responsibility, rather than warnings, as they attempt to discern what is useful and dangerous in their cultures.[133]

Orsy has pointed out that the Fathers at Vatican II themselves retained ambiguous expressions within the Council's documents, which allow for a development of understanding of the teachings they presented.[134] With reflection over time, the Church may draw on the actions and reactions of the several charisms to create a fuller perspective. As noted above, Orsy has cited the efforts of the faithful to develop mature forms of obedience as part of the process by which those in the *communio* take an active part in developing the understanding of the faith.[135]

In a given context, if *consensus fidelium* as an expression of unity cannot be immediately claimed, *sensus fidelium* as one active element can be encouraged and recognized as a vehicle for movement within the Church serving the process of doctrinal development and the exercise of responsibility in the Church's practical pursuit of its mission.

The current plurality of views on the sense of the faithful is to some extent due to the variety of applications this source can have in a pluralistic context. It is not possible to immediately discern whether the *consensus fidelium* will result from the process of interaction among elements in the Church that is necessary for doctrinal development. The content of the *sensus fidelium* is best seen in hindsight. Some issues will be found to be important in the Church, and will be focused through ecclesial interaction and magisterial teaching. Others will be dismissed as of passing importance. At the same time, while issues are being considered in the Church, it is possible to tell whether the process itself is representative of the *sensus fidelium* or not.

The absence of such a representative process can be especially clear when there is a lack of involvement, consultation and collegiality. The absence of structures that allow the necessary interaction for the development and expression of the sense of the faithful can be seen in a given context. Movements toward emphases like those of the first two groups discussed here, where a necessary involvement of either the people or the pastors is ignored, can be seen for what they are.

The willingness to pursue a more nuanced approach, even with its attendant ambiguity, can be recognized too. Efforts at interaction and consultation can have immediately recognizable effects on those involved, even when the full impact on content and doctrinal expression remains unclear. The willingness to pursue a model of interaction, however halting or imperfect, takes up patterns that typified the early Church's understanding of itself as *koinonia*, a community characterized by unity within diversity.

To function effectively, the *sensus fidelium* must be based in the tradition. It is easier to continue to leave responsibility in the hands of experts. However, to leave the faithful in the position of being "simple believers," especially when little else in their lives is left in a simple state, is to deny them access to the tools they need for exercising their responsibility. Newman's warning about the repercussions of not consulting the faithful may be turned around. Those who are truly poor and ignorant in the worldly sense may hold the seeds of holiness, and a "preferential option" for serving and hearing them may anchor the hierarchy of truths. Those who are sophisticated in "worldly" ways must be given the tools of their tradition to genuinely confront the inner and outer challenges to their faith that are at least comparable to the tools they use for other "secular" challenges. If it is argued that the faithful are not sufficiently developed in their faith, or in their ability to reflect on or express their faith, to support their active consultation and involvement, then efforts for such development must be undertaken.[136]

The task of developing such a body of believers is enormous. It is, in fact, coextensive with the whole *diakonia* of the Church. It is not for this reason less necessary or urgent. The residual passive roles among the faithful must be overcome, even though this is a large practical and theological task. Central to the accomplishment of it is work on foundational, local levels to build genuine communities.

It may be necessary to attempt a variety of strategies and construct a variety of models to find ones that are effective. In this attempt, the example of the early churches is encouraging. A variety of models were used, and unity of purpose did not necessarily require uniformity of method. In the culturally rich environment of the contemporary Church, there are many resources for developing new models.[137]

In local settings, the stress should be on greater inclusion. When there is doubt as to whether or not responsibility should be extended to a larger group of people, preference should be given to more inclusion rather than less. When an interactive process is employed, the inter-critical efforts of a variety of elements can both bring out and purify the gifts of the community. Even before a consensus on content is reached, the *sensus fidelium* can be the foundation for unity in the process itself.

## Conclusion

Even with the difficulties that face the contemporary Church there is reason to believe that efforts to draw on the sense of the faithful can be fruitful.

The reason for hope lies in the foundation of the *sensus fidei*, the Spirit who brings a variety of gifts to the body of Christ.

There is reason to work too. Structures for realizing the influence of the *sensus fidelium* must be reconstructed in local churches as the understanding of the Church as a "community of communities" is regained.

The fact that most lay people in the contemporary Church would not recognize the phrase "sense of the faithful" is telling. Many would recognize the challenge to take responsibility for the tradition, however, if such a message was clearly presented to them. This has taken place in terms of concrete cases to a great extent in the post-Vatican II era. Such acceptance of genuine challenges indicates the real foundation of faith that is waiting to be developed further.

One of the most challenging assertions made by any theologian addressing the topic of the *sensus fidelium* is that of Karl Rahner, where he claims that the "actual faith" of real people is the faith by which the work of salvation is carried out in the Church.[138] This claim may strike the theologically educated as scandalous; such faith is an inadequate expression of the rich tradition that has come to the Church through its history.

The claim may be judged no less true for all that. The challenge to increase the theological sophistication of the faithful is, as Rahner points out, to build on the actual faith of the people first, recognizing its reality while not being content to leave it in its present form. Many modern members of the Church may be like the blind man described in the Gospel of Mark, who sees partially at first, and who must be touched again to gain the sight of a mature follower of Jesus (Mark 8: 22-26).

The need for developing insight among laity and pastors alike, will require a deep sense of humility, as partial and imperfect attempts are made to redress the imbalances in structure and communication that exist in the ecclesial community. All of the faithful might benefit from tempering their criticisms of each other with the advice given by Gamaliel to critics of the earliest bearers of the Christian tradition (Acts 5: 38-39).

The work of God cannot finally be prevented nor can its success be judged by human efforts. The recognition of the *sensus fidelium* as an active aspect of the Church's life is part of the unfinished task of implementing and receiving Vatican II. As such recognition occurs throughout the Church in its lay members and pastors, from the least known lay person to the most publicly acknowledged authority, the *sensus fidelium* will draw on the charisms that are given by the Spirit in a variety of ways and thus continue to serve as a source of unity.

# NOTES

## PREFACE

1. The translation used here is from *The Documents of Vatican II*, ed. Walter M. Abbott (New York: Guild Press, 1966), 199.

2. See James L. Heft, "'Sensus Fidelium' and the Marian Dogmas," *One in Christ* 28 (1992): 106-125, and Patrick J. Hartin, "*Sensus Fidelium*: A Roman Catholic Reflection on its Significance for Ecumenical Thought," *Journal of Ecumenical Studies* 28 (1991): 74-87.

3. Paul G. Crowley, "Catholicity, Inculturation and Newman's *Sensus Fidelium*," *Heythrop Journal* 33 (1992): 161-174. See particularly pp. 168-171.

4. See John J. Burkhard, "*Sensus Fidei*: Theological Reflection Since Vatican II: I. 1965-1984," and "*Sensus Fidei*: Theological Reflection Since Vatican II: II. 1984-1989," *Heythrop Journal* 34 (1993): 41-59, 123-136, as well as "*Sensus Fidei*: Meaning, Role and Future of a Teaching of Vatican II," *Louvain Studies* 17 (1992): 18-34.

## CHAPTER 1

1. A list of standard historical citations is given by Yves Congar in *Lay People in the Church* (London: Geoffrey Chapman, 1957; reprint, Frome and London: Butler and Tannen, 1962), 441-443 (page references are to reprint edition).

2. Tertullian, for instance, writes in his *Prescription Against the Heretics* (circa 200),

> Grant, then, that all have erred; that the Apostle was mistaken in bearing witness; that the Holy Spirit had no such consideration for

any one Church as to lead it into truth; although He was sent for that purpose by Christ, who has asked the Father to make Him the Teacher of truth; that the Steward of God and Vicar of Christ neglected His office, and permitted the Churches for a time to understand otherwise than He Himself had preached through the Apostles; now is it likely that so many and such great Churches should have gone astray into a unity of faith?

The original text is given by Congar, *Lay People*, 441. The translation used here is from William A. Jurgens, *The Faith of the Early Fathers* (Collegeville, Minn.: Liturgical Press, 1970-79), 1:121.

3. A variety of theological uses of the sense of the faithful will be examined here. These uses should be distinguished from the various terms that are associated with the concept throughout its history. These overlap in meaning, and authors will sometimes use them interchangeably. Patrick Granfield gives the following definitions of some key terms in "The Pope and the Catholic Faithful," chap. in *Limits of the Papacy* (New York: Crossroad, 1987), 135-136.

*sensus fidei*: "a subjective quality—a supernatural gift, graced sensitivity, or instinct—given to all believers, enabling them to perceive the truth of the faith."

*sensus fidelium*: "a more objective quality, referring rather to what is believed than to the believer." This is the "corporate presence of the *sensus fidei* in the community of believers." Similar to this term are *communis sensus fidei*, *sensus Ecclesiae* and *sensus Christi*.

*consensus fidelium*: "the unanimous agreement of the faithful in regard to a specific revealed truth."

4. Treatments of several aspects of the election of bishops are available in *Electing Our Own Bishops*, eds. Peter Huizing and Knut Walf (Edinburgh: T. & T. Clark, 1980). An example of research into the reception of canon law is available in an article by Geoffrey King, "The Acceptance of Law by the Community: A Study in the Writings of Canonists and Theologians, 1500-1750," *The Jurist* 37 (1977): 233-265. The role of the sense of the faithful in the establishment of doctrine is examined by William M. Thompson in "*Sensus Fidelium* and Infallibility," *American Ecclesiastical Review* 167 (1973): 450-486. A number of historical works that consider these areas in detail will be introduced in the following chapters, and may also be found in the bibliography.

5. Leonard Swidler, "*Dēmo-kratía*, The Rule of the People of God, or *Consensus Fidelium*," *Journal of Ecumenical Studies* 19 (1982): 226.

6. James Hitchcock, "Thomas More and the Sensus Fidelium," *Theological Studies* 36 (1975): 153-154.

7. Heinrich Fries, "Is there a *Magisterium* of the Faithful?" in *The Teaching Authority of the Believers*, eds. Johannes-Baptist Metz and Edward Schillebeeckx (Edinburgh: T. & T. Clark, 1985): 89-90.

8. Philip S. Kaufman, *Why You Can Disagree and Remain a Faithful Catholic* (Bloomington, Ind.: Meyer-Stone Books, 1989): 160.

9. Congregation for the Doctrine of the Faith, "Instruction on the Ecclesial Vocation of the Theologian," *Origins* 20 (1990): 125.

10. Ibid., 124.

11. See the discussion of Richard McCormick in "Dissent in the Church: Loyalty or Liability?" chap. in *The Critical Calling: Reflections on Moral Dilemmas Since Vatican II* (Washington, D.C.: Georgetown University Press, 1989), 25-46.

12. In 1983, *Theological Education* devoted an entire issue to a series of forums conducted by the Association of Theological Schools on the theme, "The Teaching Offices of the Church and Theological Education." Sessions were held in New York, St. Louis, and San Francisco, and were ecumenical in scope. Several times the roles of the *sensus fidelium* and *consensus fidelium* were discussed. Attention was given particularly to the issues involved in educating people in the churches to become more consciously the vehicles of the faith and its traditions. See David S. Schuller, "Editorial Introduction," *Theological Education* 19, no. 2 (Spring 1980): 5-6, for an introduction and background remarks. An assessment that is typical of the deliberations was reported by Joseph Komonchak in "Reflections on the New York Forum," 60-64. In regard to the New York forum Komonchak reports:

> There seemed to be agreement that the communal consensus and expression of the faith constitutes the immediate and always primary means by which the faith is transmitted from generation to generation. But it proved very difficult to turn this consensus into anything like a *locus theologicus*, . . . Still, it was widely agreed that reference to the whole community's faith is an essential

element for the exercise of the other functions and for training and selecting persons to carry them out. (p. 61.)

The other functions referred to here are the "communal," "pastoral," and "supervisory" aspects of the exercise of authority in ministry.

13. Ludwig Ott, for instance, distinguishes these roles in regard to the infallibility of the Church with the terms, *infallibilitas in docendo* for the teaching Church, and *infallibilitas in credendo* for the assent of the body of faithful members of the Church, in his *Fundamentals of Catholic Dogma* (St. Louis: Herder, 1957), 297.

14. Many passages could be cited from conciliar documents. The mandate for an active part for lay people is made quite clear in the "Decree on the Apostolate of the Laity," *Apostolicam Actuositatem* (# 13):

> The apostolate of the social milieu, that is, the effort to infuse a Christian spirit into the mentality, customs, laws, and structures of the community in which a person lives, is so much the duty and responsibility of the laity that it can never be properly performed by others.

The translation is from Abbott, 504. Emphasis on the wide array of tasks to be met and on the role lay people are to play as innovators is described at length in the Pastoral Constitution on the Church in the Modern World, *Gaudium et Spes*, especially in (# 43). The Fathers write, for example,

> Secular duties and activities belong properly although not exclusively to laymen. Therefore acting as citizens of the world, whether individually or socially, they will observe the laws proper to each discipline, and labor to equip themselves with a genuine expertise in their various fields. They will gladly work with men seeking the same goals. Acknowledging the demands of faith and endowed with its force, they will unhesitatingly devise new enterprises, where they are appropriate, and put them into action. (Abbott, 243-244)

15. Leonard Doohan, *The Lay-Centered Church* (Minneapolis: Winston Press, 1984), 28-29.

16. Avery Dulles, "*Sensus Fidelium,*" *America* 155 (1986): 241.

17. See, for instance, Thompson, "*Sensus Fidelium* and Infallibility," 451; Congar, *Lay People*, 441; and Dulles, "*Sensus Fidelium*," 240.

18. Johannes Quasten, *Patrology*, vol. 2, *The Ante-Nicene Literature After Irenaeus* (Utrecht-Antwerp: Spectrum, 1953; reprint, Westminster, Md.: Christian Classics, 1983), 270-272. See Thompson, "*Sensus Fidelium* and Infallibility," 451.

19. In his *Commonitoria* (2, 2b-3a), Vincent of Lerins writes,

> And thus, because of so many distortions of such various errors, it is highly necessary that the line of prophetic and apostolic interpretation be directed in accord with the norm of the ecclesiastical and Catholic meaning. In the Catholic Church herself every care must be taken that we may hold fast to that which has been believed everywhere, always, and by all. For this is, then, truly and properly Catholic. That is what the force and meaning of the name itself declares, a name that embraces all almost universally. This general rule will be correctly applied if we pursue universality, antiquity, and agreement.

The translation used here is from Jurgens, *Faith of the Early Fathers*, 3: 262-263.

20. From Vincent of Lerins's *Commonitoria* (23, 28); translated in Jurgens, *Faith of the Early Fathers*, 3: 265.

21. Ibid.

22. Thompson, "*Sensus Fidelium* and Infallibility," 453-455.

23. Ibid., 456-457.

24. Ibid., 475-486.

25. Congar cites the general trend toward centralization of authority since Trent in "The Historical Development of Authority," in *Problems of Authority*, ed. John M. Todd (Baltimore: Helicon Press, 1962), 144-145. Thomas P. Rausch contrasts the emphases on centralized authority and collegiality of Vatican I and Vatican II, in *Authority and Leadership in the Church* (Wilmington, Del.: Michael Glazier, 1989), 136-137.

26. The text of Newman's used here is John Henry Newman, *On Consulting the Faithful on Matters of Doctrine*, edited with an introduction by John Coulson (Kansas City: Sheed & Ward, 1961). The original article was printed in July of 1859 in the *Rambler*.

27. John Coulson describes the context for the writing of Newman's article, in his "Introduction," in Newman, *On Consulting*, 1-21.

28. Ibid., 55.

29. The main examples Newman cites are the Arian crisis of the 4th century, the definition of Mary as the Mother of God in the 5th, the definition of the real presence of Christ in the Eucharist in the 9th, the rejection of Pope John XXII's teaching on the Beatific Vision in the 14th, and the definition of the Immaculate Conception by Pope Pius IX in Newman's own day (1854). Ibid., 104-106.

30. See Coulson's discussion of the response Newman received. Coulson, "Introduction," 12-49.

31. A complete analysis of the hermeneutical issues involved in the interplay of interpretations of a past event, as viewed at the time of the event and as seen from the perspective of a later view, is beyond the scope of this paper. An interesting discussion of these issues as they apply to dogma is found in Thomas B. Ommen, *The Hermeneutic of Dogma* (Missoula, Mont.: Scholars Press, 1975), especially pages 223-233. In his discussion, Ommen draws on the hermeneutics of Hans-Georg Gadamer. A citation from Gadamer's *Truth and Method*, Second Revised Edition (New York: Crossroad, 1991), is suggestive of the point made here concerning the impact of hermeneutical distancing:

> In fact the important thing is to recognize temporal distance as a positive and productive condition enabling understanding. It is not a yawning abyss but is filled with the continuity of custom and tradition, in the light of which everything handed down presents itself to us. Here it is not too much to speak of the genuine productivity of the course of events. Everyone is familiar with the curious impotence of our judgment where temporal distance has not given us sure criteria (p. 297.).

32. The influence of Newman in Vatican II's understanding of the relationship of the laity and the hierarchy, and the issues that remain unresolved concerning the active involvement of the laity are discussed by Paul Chavasse in

"Newman and the Laity," in *Newman Today: The Proceedings of the Wethersfield Institute*, vol. 1, ed. Stanley L. Jaki (San Francisco: Ignatius Press, 1989), 68-75.

33. Walgrave, "Newman's 'On Consulting the Faithful on Matters of Doctrine,'" in *Teaching Authority of Believers*, 27-28.

34. Newman, *On Consulting*, 73.

35. Owen Chadwick, *From Bossuet to Newman*, 2d ed., (Cambridge: Cambridge University Press, 1987), 183-184.

36. Jean Bainvel, "Tradition and Living Magisterium," *Catholic Encyclopedia*, vol. 15, (New York: 1912), 9.

37. Ibid., 10.

38. Newman writes,

Each constituent portion of the Church has its proper functions, and no portion can safely be neglected. Though the laity be but the reflection or echo of the clergy in matters of faith, yet there is something in the "pastorum et fidelium *conspiratio*," which is not in the pastors alone. (Newman, *On Consulting*, 103-104.)

39. Of the Arian crisis, Newman writes,

I see, then, in the Arian history a palmary example of a state of the Church, during which, in order to know the tradition of the Apostles, we must have recourse to the faithful; for I fairly own, that if I go to writers, since I must adjust the letter of Justin, Clement, and Hippolytus with the Nicene Doctors, I get confused; and what revives and reinstates me, as far as history goes, is the faith of the people. (Ibid., 76).

Newman continued his treatment of the Arian controversy in an appendix entitled, "The Orthodoxy of the Body of the Faithful during the Supremacy of Arianism," in the 1871 (third) edition of his *The Arians of the 4th Century*. The appendix is reprinted in Newman, *On Consulting*, 109-118.

40. Pope Pius XII, *Apostolic Constitution on the Assumption of the Blessed Virgin Mary*, (Boston: St. Paul Editions, n.d.), 6-8. See sections 11-12.

41. *Lumen Gentium* (# 12). Abbott, 29. The passage quotes St. Augustine, *De praed. sanct.*, 14, 27.

42. Leonardo Boff uses this phrase and offers a concise discussion of the factors that show this "division" to be outmoded, particularly from the point of view of liberation theology in "Is the Distinction between the *Ecclesia docens* and *Ecclesia discens* Justified?" in *Who Has the Say in the Church?* eds. Juergen Moltmann and Hans Kueng (Edinburgh: T. & T. Clark, 1981), 49-50. This article is reprinted as the chapter, "*Ecclesia Docens* versus *Ecclesia Discens*," in Leonardo Boff, *Church: Charism & Power: Liberation Theology and the Institutional Church* (New York: Crossroad, 1988), 138-143.

43. Feminist authors in particular describe a growing tendency for lay people, and especially women, to challenge the hierarchy when it is seen as identifying itself too exclusively with the *Ecclesia docens*. Elisabeth Schuessler Fiorenza exhibits an aggressive stance in "Claiming our Authority and Power," in The *Teaching Authority of the Believers*, 45-51. Margaret A. Farley offers an analysis of the need for diversity of opinion in public discussion concerning church teaching in "Moral Discourse in the Public Arena," in *Vatican Authority and American Catholic Dissent: The Curran Case and its Consequences*, ed. William W. May (New York: Crossroad, 1987), 168-186. See especially, 176-179.

44. Doohan, 1-25 passim.

45. J. M. R. Tillard describes the debates as "difficult and delicate," in "*Sensus Fidelium*," *One in Christ* 11 (1975): 26. This article is a translation of J. M. R. Tillard, "A propos du '*sensus fidelium*,'" *Proche-Orient Chrétien* 25 (1975): 113-134. Reference here will be to the English version. Kaufman questions whether the teaching of the encyclical has been received, linking its reception explicitly with the response of the *sensus fidelium* in the Arian crisis, in the chapter, "Birth Control: A Teaching Not Received," in *Why You Can Disagree and Remain a Faithful Catholic*, 71-83. See especially, 82-83.

Bernard Sesboüé, on the other hand, remarks that it is much too soon to say that *Humanae Vitae* has not been "received" by the faithful. He says that paradoxically, this might have been easier to do if the encyclical had met with no response. As it stands, the continuing discussion must postpone any assessment of reception or non-reception. His remarks are in the appendix, "À propos de la 'réception' de 'Humanae Vitae,'" of his article, "Autorité du magistère et vie de foi ecclésiale," *Nouvelle Revue Théologique* 93 (1971): 361.

46. Pope John Paul II, *The Role of the Christian Family in the Modern World* (Boston: St. Paul Editions, n.d.), 16.

47. Ibid., 15-16.

48. In discussing *Humanae Vitae*, Kaufman writes that it may be more difficult to bring the laity "in line" than it would be to do so with theologians and bishops. He cites Cardinal G. Emmett Carter, Archbishop of Toronto, who asked the 1980 Synod on the Family to consider whether the response of the laity to the teaching on birth control was possibly "a non-reflexive expression of the *sensus fidelium*." (Kaufman, 83.) Carter's remarks are quite instructive in regard to the positions in which both the bishops and the laity find themselves, in the light of the reaction to the encyclical:

> In some of these matters is the Holy Spirit trying to say something to the whole church through this phenomenon or is this the beginning of a period of moral decadence among Christians, perhaps without parallel in history?
> Could this movement to the post-traditional level of moral reflection and concrete conduct be a non-reflexive expression of the *sensus fidelium*? In any case, . . . the magisterium must take account of this phenomenon or run the risk of speaking in a vacuum.

The passage is from G. Emmett Carter, "Spirit's Voice or Moral Decadence?" *Origins* 10 (1980): 277.

49. This need for new criteria is elaborated by Luigi Sartori in "What is the Criterion for the *Sensus Fidelium*?" in *Who Has the Say in the Church?*, 56.

50. John W. O'Malley, *Tradition and Transition* (Wilmington, Del.: Michael Glazier, 1989), 61.

51. Ibid., 59-61.

52. Yves M.-J. Congar, *Tradition and Traditions* (New York: Macmillan, 1966), 458. The French edition was originally published in two volumes, both carrying the title *La Tradition et les Traditions* in 1960 and 1963.

53. See *Dei Verbum* (# 8). The paragraph cited shows beautifully the intertwining of responsibilities in the Church, and is worth quoting in full. The translation is from *Vatican Council II: The Conciliar and Post Conciliar*

*Documents*, ed. Austin Flannery, New Revised Edition (Northport, N.Y.: Costello Publishing Company, 1984), 754.

The Tradition that comes from the apostles makes progress in the Church, with the help of the Holy Spirit.[5] There is a growth in insight into the realities and the words that are being passed on. This comes about in various ways. It comes through the contemplation and study of believers who ponder these things in their hearts (cf. Lk. 2:19 and 51). it comes from the intimate sense of spiritual realities which they experience. And it comes from the preaching of those who have received, along with their right of succession in the episcopate, the sure charism of truth. Thus, as the centuries go by, the Church is always advancing forward toward the plentitude of divine truth, until eventually the words of God are fulfilled in her.

---

5. Cf. First Vatican Council, *Dogm. Const. on the Catholic Faith*, c. 4 (On Faith and Reason): *Denz.* 1800 (3020).

## CHAPTER 2

1. Congar discusses the various names and their historical contexts in *Tradition and Traditions*, 315-321. Dillenschneider discusses the names in relation to Marian dogmas in P. Clément Dillenschneider, *Le Sens de la foi et le progrès dogmatique du mystère marial* (Rome: Academia Mariana Internationalis, 1954), 317-327.

2. The role of historical crisis in the development of doctrine is discussed in Jan Walgrave, *Unfolding Revelation* (London: Hutchinson & Co., 1972), especially, 31-33. In the historical portions of the present study, the views of many authors will be summarized and brought together. These authors will illustrate both historical and contemporary interpretations of the sense of the faithful.

3. Jesús Sancho Bielsa, *Infalibilidad del Pueblo de Dios: "Sensus Fidei" e Infalibilidad Organica de la Iglesia en la Constitución "Lumen Gentium" del Concilio Vaticano II* (Pamplona: Ediciones Universidad de Navarra, S.A., 1979). 191. Sancho cites Tertullian's, *Commonitorium*, 23, PL 50, 669.

4. Thompson, "*Sensus Fidelium* and Infallibility," 459-460.

5. Gustave Thils, *L'Infallibilité du peuple chrétien "in credendo": notes de théologie posttridentine* (Paris: Desclée de Brouwer, 1963).

6. M. Seckler, "Glaubenssinn," in *Lexicon fuer Theologie und Kirche*, vol. 4. (1960), 946.

7. M. Dominikus Koster, *Volk Gottes im Wachstum des Glaubens* (Heidelberg: Kerle, 1950), 13-14.

8. Dillenschneider, 267-269.

9. Abbott, 29.

10. Abbott, 30.

11. Ibid.

12. Kevin McNamara, ed., *Vatican II: The Constitution on the Church* (London: Geoffrey Chapman, 1968), 136-137.

13. Ibid., 133.

14. Ibid., 134.

15. *Lumen Gentium* (# 35); see Abbott, 61.

16. Ibid.

17. Abbott, 116, n. 19.

18. Jean Daniélou and Henri Marrou, *The First Six Hundred Years* (London: Darton, Longman and Todd, 1964), 115-121.

19. Hermann Wolfgang Beyer, "*EPISKOPOS* in the NT," in *Theological Dictionary of the New Testament*, vol 2. Edited by Gerhard Kittle and Gerhard Friedrich, (Grand Rapids, Mich.: Eerdmans, 1964-1974), 615-617.

20. Ibid., 615.

21. Ibid., 616-617.

## Notes to Chapter 2

22. Bas van Iersel, "Who According to the New Testament Has the Say in the Church?" in *Who Has the Say in the Church?* 14-15. Edited by Juergen Moltmann and Hans Kueng. (Edinburgh: T. & T. Clark, 1981).

23. Rudolf Pesch, "New Testament Foundations of Democratic Form of Life in the Church," in *Democratization of the Church*, 59. Edited by Alois Mueller. (New York: Herder and Herder, 1971).

24. Ibid., 56.

25. Ibid., 57.

26. Ibid.

27. Ibid., 59.

28. Claude Dagens, "Hierarchy and Communion: The Bases of Authority in the Beginning of the Church," *Communio* 9 (1982): 67-78.

29. Ibid., 74.

30. Ibid., 73. Emphasis in original.

31. A balanced view of this development is given by Rudolf Schnackenburg, in "Community Co-operation in the New Testament," *Election and Consensus in the Church*, 9-19. Edited by Giuseppe Alberigo and Anton Weiler. (New York: Herder and Herder, 1972). See especially pages 15 and 19.

32. Peter Stockmeier, "Congregation and Episcopal Office in the Ancient Church," in *Bishops and People*, edited and translated by Leonard Swidler and Arlene Swidler. (Philadelphia: Westminster, 1970), 85-86.

33. Rausch, *Authority and Leadership*, 56.

34. Ibid., 57.

35. Ibid., 58.

36. Ibid. Rausch cites 1 Clement 42: 1-4.

37. 1 Clement 42: 1-2a, 4-5. Translation is from *Ancient Christian Writers* Vol. 1, 34-35. *The Epistles of St. Clement of Rome and St. Ignatius of Antioch.* Translated by James A. Kleist. (New York: Newman Press, 1946).

38. Ibid., 34.

39. Rausch, *Authority and Leadership*, 58.

40. Ibid. 59. Rausch cites Raymond Brown's *The Community of the Beloved Disciple* (New York: Paulist Press, 1979), and *The Church the Apostles Left Behind* (New York: Paulist Press, 1984).

41. See Rausch, *Authority and Leadership*, 59.

42. Friedrich Hauck, "*KOINON* in the NT," in Kittel, vol. 3, 804-809.

43. Ibid., 804.

44. Ibid., 804-805.

45. Ibid., 805.

46. Ibid., 807.

47. Ibid., 807-808.

48. Ibid., 808. Hauck cites Rom. 15: 26 and 2 Cor. 8: 4.

49. Ibid., 807-808.

50. J. Coppens, "La *koinônia* dans l'Église primitive," *Ephemerides Theologicae Lovanienses* 46 (1970): 116-117.

51. Ibid., 118.

52. Ibid., 119-121.

53. Yves Congar, "Norms of Christian Allegiance and Identity in the History of the Church," in *Truth and Certainty*, 12. Edited by Edward Schillebeeckx and Bas van Iersel. (New York: Herder and Herder, 1973).

54. Ibid. Emphasis in original.

55. Ibid., 12-13. For (a), Congar cites Polycarp, for (b), Irenaeus and Origen.

56. Ibid., 13-14.

57. Ludwig Hertling, *Communio: Church and Papacy in Early Christianity*, 15. (Chicago: Loyola University Press, 1972).

58. Ibid., 16.

59. Ibid., 19.

60. Friedrich Buechsel, "*PARADOSIS*," in Kittel, vol 2, 172.

61. Ibid.

62. Marie-Louis Gubler, "Living Diversity in the NT Church," *Theology Digest* 37 (1990) : 115-119.

63. Ibid., 116.

64. Ibid., 117.

65. Ibid., 117-118.

66. Ibid., 118.

67. Ibid., 118-119.

68. Jean-Louis D'Aragon, "Le 'sensus fidelium' et ses fondements néotestamentaires," 44-47. In *Foi populair, foi savante*. J.-M. R. Tillard, et. al. (Paris: Éditions du Cerf, 1976).

69. See especially, Ibid., 43, 47-48.

70. Edward Schillebeeckx, "The Teaching Authority of All—A Reflection about the Structure of the New Testament," 19. In *The Teaching Authority of Believers*.

71. Ibid., 18.

72. *Didache*, 12:1. Quoted from *Ancient Christian Writers* Vol. 6. p. 23.

73. Schillebeeckx, "Teaching Authority," 18.

74. Alexandre Faivre, *The Emergence of the Laity in the Early Church*, 15. (Mahwah, N.J.: Paulist Press, 1990).

75. Ibid., 14, 16-17.

76. Ibid., 21.

77. Ibid., 22

78. Ibid., 7.

79. *Didache*, 15:1-4. *Ancient Christian Writers* Vol. 6. p. 24.

80. George MacRae, "Shared Responsibility—Some New Testament Perspectives," *Chicago Studies* 9 (1970): 122.

81. Ibid. MacRae contrasts his view with that of Rudolf Schnackenburg in *The Church in the New Testament* (New York: Herder and Herder, 1965), 74-75.

82. His theses are that the New Testament is not a "blueprint" for the contemporary Church, is not irrelevant to the contemporary Church, "is not uniform," and "does not invite us to choose a preferential 'canon within a canon' at least not in an exclusive sense." MacRae, 116-117.

83. Ibid., 118.

84. Ibid., 119-120.

85. Myles M. Bourke, "Collegial Decision-making in the New Testament," 1-13. In *Who Decides for the Church?* Edited by James A. Coriden. (Hartford, Conn.: The Canon Law Society of America, 1971).

86. Ibid., 3.

87. Ibid., 3-4. Bourke borrows the term from J. C. Hurd, *The Origin of I Corinthians* (New York: Seabury Press, 1965), 78.

88. Bourke, 4-5.

89. Ibid., 5-6.

90. Ibid., 7. Bourke cites W. D. Davies, *The Setting of the Sermon on the Mount* (Cambridge: University Press, 1964), 224.

91. Bourke, 7-8.

92. Ibid., 8-9.

93. Ibid., 9.

94. Ibid., 11-12.

95. Ibid., 12.

96. Ibid., 13.

97. Ibid.

98. MacRae, 123.

99. Ibid., 124. Emphasis in original.

100. Ibid., 124-126.

101. Ibid., 126.

102. Ibid. Emphasis in original.

103. Ibid., 118.

104. Jeremy Moiser, "The Role of the Laity in the Formation of the New Testament Canon." *Science et Esprit* 39 (1987): 301-317.

105. Moiser provides a list on pp. 302-303 of examples from the Gospels through St. Augustine.

106. Ibid., 303.

107. Ibid. See n. 7. Moiser cites Coulson's edition of Newman's *On Consulting the Faithful*, referring to pp. 65ff. Newman describes here how Perrone saw the pastors and the faithful as "distinct (not separate)" (p. 66.).

Drawing on Perrone, Newman looks to the "*conspiratio*" of both groups in determining the way the *sensus fidelium* contributes to the *sensus Ecclesiae*. Newman emphasizes their working together as evidenced in the particular examples he describes. Moiser seems to strongly contrast the clergy and the laity to more clearly see if the laity are obvious contributors to the process of defining canonicity. He seems interested in avoiding having a strong role for the laity read back into early periods in which no clear evidence is available. This is an important caution. Yet, it is not clear that the influence of the laity should be separated out of the examples that he gives. His distinguishing of the clergy and laity cannot speak to the historical relationship between them. To claim either a strong or weak interaction without sufficient information would beg the question.

108. Moiser, 316-317.

109. Ibid., 319.

110. MacRae, 116-117.

111. Ibid., 127.

112. Moiser, 317. See n. 33.

113. Ibid., 317.

114. Thomas P. Rausch, "The Church in the Sub-Apostolic Age," chap. in *The Roots of the Catholic Tradition*, 119-140. (Wilmington, Del.: Michael Glazier, 1986).

115. Ibid., 133-134.

116. Georges Tavard, "The Authority of Scripture and Tradition," in *Problems in Authority*, 38-39.

117. Ibid., 39-40.

118. Ibid., 40.

119. Ibid.

120. Monika Hellwig, "Living Tradition in the Living Church," *Chicago Studies* 19 (1980): 162.

121. Ibid.

122. Gerald Bray, "Authority in the Early Church," *Churchman* 95 (1981): 44.

123. Ibid., 44-45.

124. Ibid., 50.

125. Ibid.

126. Ibid., 50-51. Bray goes on to argue for a relativizing of hierarchical authority in the contemporary (Anglican) Church and for a greater dependence on Scriptural and credal faith. See Ibid., 51-52.

127. Eno, "Authority and Conflict in the Early Church," *Église et Théologie* 7 (1976): 42-43.

128. Eno notes that Julian left the Christians to their own devices, "knowing as he did from experience that no wild beasts are such enemies to mankind as are most Christians in their deadly hatred of one another." See Ibid., 43. The quote here is given by Eno from Ammianus Marcellinus, *Res Gestae*, 22, 5, 4 (*Loeb Classical Library* 2, 202).

129. Eno, "Authority and Conflict," 43. The quote is from *De Civitae Dei* 18, 51.

130. Eno describes two questions that focused the early Church:

1) In relation to the past, how are its traditions to be preserved and passed on? 2) Concerning the present, what is the relation between its traditions from the past and the structures which guard and transmit them and these immediate revelations from on high? Through whom does the Spirit speak? ("Authority and Conflict," 44.)

131. Ibid., 45.

132. Ibid.

133. Ibid., 46-48.

Notes to Chapter 2    511

134. Johannes Remmers, "Apostolic Succession: An Attribute of the Whole Church," 36-51. In *Apostolic Succession: Rethinking a Barrier to Unity.*

135. See especially Ibid., 40 and 46.

136. Remmers cites Edmund Schlink, "Die apostolische Sukzession," in *Der kommende Christus und die kirchlichen Traditionen* (Goettingen, 1961), pp. 160-195. Remmers, 40. See note 11.

137. Remmers cites the primary elements of the Church's mission given by Schlink as consisting in "faith in the apostolic message and obedience to the apostles' exhortations and instruction"; "bearing witness to the apostolic Gospel," a task given to each Christian; "preaching to and winning over the world," with each charism serving the whole community; and "caring for the community with all Christians and all the Churches throughout the world." Ibid., 40-41. Remmers cites Schlink, 192.

138. Remmers, 42.

139. Ibid.

140. Ibid., 43.

141. Ibid.

142. Ibid.

143. Peter Stockmeier, "The Election of Bishops of Clergy and People in the Early Church," 5. *In Electing Our Own Bishops.*

144. Remmers reference is in on page 43, to Cyprian's *Epistle* 66, 8, 3. The quote given here is taken from later in the same passage, and is from Jurgens, Vol. 1, 234.

145. Remmers, 43-44.

146. Ibid., 45. Remmers cites J. C. Groot, "Die horizontalen Aspekte der Kollegialitaet," in *De Ecclesia* (edited by G. Barauna) II, 86.

147. Remmers, 45.

148. Ibid., 46.

149. Remmers notes that in its Apostolic Constitution on the Laity, Vatican II emphasized that there is only one mission, though with many tasks, in the Church. Yet, for a century and a half before the Council, this insight was not recognized; Pius IX "never said a word about it," and Pius XII "mentioned it only with the greatest caution." Ibid., 48-49.

150. Ibid., 50.

151. Ibid., 51.

152. Bruno Kleinheyer, "Consensus in the Liturgy," 24-27. In *Election and Consensus in the Church*.

153. Ibid., 25.

154. Ibid., 24-25. Kleinheyer cites section 9 of the *Apostolic Tradition*.

155. Kleinheyer, 27.

156. Norbert Brox, "The Conflict between Anicetus and Polycarp," 41. In *The Unifying Role the Bishop*, edited by Edward Schillebeeckx. (New York: Herder and Herder, 1972).

157. Ibid.

158. Ibid., 41-45.

159. Jean-Marie Tillard, "Theological Pluralism and the Mystery of the Church," 62-63. In *Different Theologies, Common Responsibility: Babel or Pentecost*. Edited by Claude Geffré, Gustavo Gutierrez and Virgil Elizondo. (Edinburgh: T. & T. Clark, 1984).

160. Ibid., 63.

161. Herbert Vorgrimler describes the shift that took place in "From *Sensus Fidei* to *Consensus Fidelium*," 4. In *The Teaching Authority of the Believers*.

162. Quoted in Vorgrimler, 4.

163. O'Malley, *Tradition and Transition*, 14-18.

164. Ibid., 14.

165. On this topic, Julio Eugui gives some standard historical references, and states that there was a scarcity of materials before the Council. See Julio Eugui, *La Participatión de la Communidad Cristiana en la Elección de los Obispos: Siglos I-V* (Pamplona: Ediciones Universidad de Navarra, S.A., 1977.), 19-20. This view may be seen in contrast to that of Patrick Granfield in "Episcopal Elections in Cyprian: Clerical and Lay Participation," *Theological Studies* 37 (1976). Several such sources are given on p. 42, n. 6. Note too the sources mentioned by John E. Lynch, in "Co-Responsibility in the First Five Centuries: Presbyterial Colleges an the Election of Bishops." In *Who Decides for the Church?* 37, n. 105.

166. Cf. Thompson, *"Sensus Fidelium* and Infallibility," 451.

167. Eugui, 23-26.

168. Ibid., 25-26.

169. Ibid., 33.

170. Ibid., 34.

171. Ibid., 37-38.

172. Ibid., 39.

173. Robert B. Eno, "Shared Responsibility in the Early Church," *Chicago Studies* 9 (1970): 137-138.

174. Raymond Kottje, "Selection of Church Officials: Historical Facts and Experiences." In *Democratization of the Church*. Edited by Alois Mueller. (New York: Herder and Herder, 1971), 118-120.

175. Ibid., 118.

176. Stockmeier, "Election of Bishops," 3-9.

177. Ibid., 3.

178. Ibid., 8, n. 1. Stockmeier cites "Demokratisierung der Kirche." Ratzinger, J. and Maier, J. eds., *Demokratie in der Kirche. Moeglichkeiten,*

*Grenzen, Gefahren (Werdende Welt 16)* (Limburg 1970): 27-29. Ratzinger's more recent remarks that continue such criticism, written from his office as Prefect of the Congregation for Doctrine of the Faith, are cited above.

179. Stockmeier, "Election of Bishops," 8.

180. See Lynch, 37, for a description of this event. Lynch cites Eusebius, *Hist. Eccl.* 6, 11, in n. 108, p. 37.

181. Granfield, "Episcopal Elections," 41. Also see Eugui, 56.

182. Francine Cardman, "Cyprian and Rome: The Controversy over Baptism," in *The Right to Dissent*. Edited by Hans Kueng and Juergen Moltmann. (Edinburgh: T. & T. Clark, 1982.), 34.

183. Granfield, "Episcopal Elections," 44.

184. Ibid., 44-45.

185. Ibid., 52.

186. Ibid., 42-43.

187. Ibid., 42.

188. Eugui, 71.

189. Granfield, "Episcopal Elections," 43.

190. Ibid., 45.

191. See Granfield's discussion of these possibilities; Ibid., 45-49.

192. Ibid., 48.

193. Ibid., 48-49.

194. Ibid., 49.

195. Ibid., 45.

196. Ibid., 48-49. A detailed study of the Roman and ecclesial processes is available in Takeo Osawa, *Das Bischofseinsetzungsverfahren bei Cyprian* (Frankfurt am Main: Peter Lang, 1983).

197. Granfield, "Episcopal Elections," 49.

198. Kottje, 118-120.

199. Ibid., 119.

200. Ibid.

201. Hervé-Marie Legrand, "Theology and the Election of Bishops in the Early Church," in *Election and Consensus in the Church*, 40.

202. Ibid., 40-41.

203. Ibid., 40.

204. Ibid., 35.

205. Ibid., 35-36.

206. Ibid., 35. Legrand mentions Ambrose, Augustine, Martin of Tours, Gregory the Great and Basil.

207. Ibid., 36.

208. Ibid. Emphasis in original.

209. Ibid.

210. Francis A. Sullivan, *The Church We Believe In: One, Holy, Catholic and Apostolic* (New York: Paulist Press, 1988), 175-176.

211. Ibid., 175.

212. Ibid., 175-176.

213. Ibid., 234. See n. 145. Sullivan cites *The Apostolic Tradition* Edited with an English translation by Gregory Dix (London: SPCK, 1937). Sullivan also

cites the French translation by Bernard Botte, *Sources Chrétiennes* 11 bis, (Paris: Éditions du Cerf, 2nd ed., 1968).

214. Sullivan, *The Church We Believe In*, 176. See also p. 234, n. 148, where Sullivan cites Dix, xxxix-xl. Eugui notes the debate over the case of the church of Alexandria, which may have ordained its bishops with out interaction of other local bishops in the early centuries. Eugui, 39-40.

215. Ibid., 45.

216. Eno describes this example of acclamation in "Shared Responsibility," 138, citing and quoting from Epistle 213. Quotes from both Eno and Augustine are used here.

217. Gerard Bartelink, "Use of the Words *Electio* and *Consensus* in the Church until about 600," in *Election and Consensus in the Church*, 147.

218. Ibid., 149.

219. Ibid., 152.

220. Ibid., 154.

221. Eno, "Shared Responsibility," 139.

222. Quoted in Eno. Ibid., 140.

223. Bartelink, 150.

224. Eno, "Shared Responsibility," 140.

225. Ibid.

226. Kottje, 119-120.

227. Granfield, "Episcopal Elections," 52.

228. Described by Stockmeier in "Congregation," 79-80.

229. Ibid., 80-81.

230. Kottje, 119.

231. Eno, "Shared Responsibility," 139.

232. Lynch, 47.

233. Ibid.

234. Ibid. Lynch quotes Leo I, *Ep.* 12, 1-2.

235. Lynch, 47-48.

236. Granfield, "Episcopal Elections," 52.

237. Ibid.

238. Lynch, 51-52.

239. See the discussion, for instance, of Robert Benson, in "Election by Community and Chapter: Reflections on Co-Responsibility in the Historical Church." In *Who Decides for the Church?* 67-75.

240. Ibid., 68, 79-80.

241. Eugui, 198.

242. Ibid., 204-205.

243. Ibid., 205.

244. Ibid., 216-217. See also n. 55.

245. Ibid., 222-223.

246. Ibid., 223-224.

247. W. H. C. Frend, "The *Seniores Laici* and the Origins of the Church in North Africa," *Journal of Theological Studies* 12 (1961): 280.

248. Ibid., 281-282.

249. W. H. C. Frend, *The Rise of Christianity* (Philadelphia: Fortress Press, 1984), 412).

250. Frend, "*Seniores Laici*," 282.

251. Ibid., 283.

252. Ibid., 283-284.

253. Lynch, "Co-responsibility," 31-34.

254. Ibid., 32-33.

255. Ibid., 33.

256. Frend, *Rise of Christianity*, 413.

257. Robert B. Eno, "Consensus and Doctrine: Three Ancient Views," *Église et Theologie* 9 (1978): 473-474.

258. Karl Suso Frank, "Bishops and Laity in the Faith Tradition," *Theology Digest* 34 (1987): 40. Taken from "Bischoefe und Laien in der Glaubensueberlieferung," *Diakonia: Internationale Zeitschrift fuer die Praxis der Kirche* 17:3 (May, 1986): 149-156.

259. Frank, "Bishops and Laity," 40.

260. Ibid., 41. Quoted by Frank from *Joshua Hom.* 7, 6.

261. Patrick Granfield, "Concilium and Consensus: Decision Making in Cyprian," *The Jurist* 35 (1975): 404-405.

262. From *Epistle* 17:1, quoted by Granfield in "Concilium and Consensus," 405-406.

263. Ibid., 407.

264. Ibid.

265. Ibid., 408.

266. Avery Dulles, "The Magisterium in History: A Theological Reflection," *Chicago Studies* 17 (1978): 267.

267. Ibid.

268. Ibid., 267-268.

269. Ibid.

270. Maurice Bévenot, in "Introduction," *St. Cyprian: The Lapsed, The Unity of the Catholic Church* Vol. 25 of *Ancient Christian Writers* (New York: Newman Press, 1957), 5.

271. Adalbert Davids, "One or None: Cyprian on the Church and Tradition," in *The Unifying Role of the Bishop*, 47.

272. Dulles, "Magisterium," 268.

273. Dulles, *"Sensus Fidelium,"* 240.

274. Thomas Halton, "The Church, The People of God," chap. in *The Church* (Wilmington, Del.: Michael Glazier, 1985), 80.

275. Quoted by Halton, Ibid., 80-81.

276. Dulles, "Magisterium," 268-269.

277. Jakob Speigl, "Lay Participation in Early Church Councils," *Theology Digest* 28 (1980): 141. This article is a summary of "Zum Problem der Teilnahme von Laien an den Konzilien in kirchlichen Alterum," *Annuarium Historiae Conciliorum* 10:2 (1978): 241-248.

278. Speigl, "Lay Participation," 142.

279. Eno, "Consensus and Doctrine," 474.

280. Ibid. See n. 1.

281. Ibid., 474. See also n. 1.

282. Ibid., 475.

283. Ibid. Eno cites *Commonitoria*, 27.

284. Eno, "Consensus and Doctrine," 475-476.

285. Hellwig, 163.

286. Eno, "Consensus and Doctrine," 476. See also Hellwig, 163.

287. Eno, "Consensus and Doctrine," 476-477.

288. Ibid., 478.

289. Ibid., 478-479. Eno also notes the disagreement raised by Augustine's remark in *De baptismo contra Donatistas* II.3.4., that later councils could improve/correct earlier ones. Eno seems to prefer "improve" as the proper rendering of Augustine's thought. The less controversial reading is sufficient here to make the point that consensus was seen as key to the development of doctrinal insight.

290. Eno, "Consensus and Doctrine," 480.

291. Ibid. Eno adds, however, that "Vatican I was still fighting it in the guise of Gallicanism."

292. Ibid., 480-481. Eno observes that the Roman emphasis retains its priority today, even while its systematic approach to the ancient tradition is somewhat mitigated by the climate since Vatican II. See Ibid., 482.

293. Metropolitan Emilianos Timiadis, "Consensus in the Formulation of Doctrine," *Mid-Stream* 20 (1981): 178.

294. Ibid. Timiadis cites *De unitate*, 5. The quote used bore is from the translation in Jurgens, *Faith of the Early Fathers*, 1: 221.

295. Timiadis, "Consensus in the Formulation of Doctrine," 178-179.

296. Timiadis cites Socrates (*Hist. Eccl.* I.9.), Gregory the Great (*Epist.* I. 25; 3:10; 4:38), Ambrose (*De Fide* III, 15), Basil (*Epist.* 114) and others as witnesses to this idea. See Timiadis, "Consensus in the Formulation of Doctrine," 179.

297. Ibid., 179-181.

298. Ibid., 182.

299. Ibid.

300. Ibid., 182-183.

301. Ibid., 183.

302. Ibid., 188.

303. Dulles, "Magisterium," 269.

304. Ibid., 269-270.

305. Ibid., 269.

306. John Meyendorff, "Historical Relativism and Authority in Christian Dogma," *St. Vladimir's Seminary Quarterly* 11 (1967): 80.

307. Ibid., 79-80.

308. Faivre, 206. See also n. 43, p. 238.

309. Meyendorff, "Historical Relativism," 80.

310. Ibid.

311. Ibid.

312. Dulles, "Magisterium," 269.

313. Ibid.

314. Granfield, "Catholic Faithful," 138.

315. See Ibid., 137-140.

316. Jean Guitton, *The Church and the Laity: From Newman to Vatican II* (Staten Island, N.Y.: Alba House, 1965), 51.

317. *Dialogus contra Luciferianos* 19, the translation used here is from Jurgens, *Faith of the Early Fathers*, 2:190.

318. Coulson, "Introduction," 24.

319. Quoted by Newman in *On Consulting*, 106.

320. See Appendix II, in Congar, *Lay People*, 441-443.

321. Dillenschneider, 270-271.

322 Ibid., 272-273.

323. Ibid., 274. Dillenschneider points out that from the larger body of work of St. Augustine, it is clear that this claim is erroneous.

324. Ibid., 274-275.

325. Pierre Boglioni, "Pour l'étude de la religion populaire au Moyen Age: le problème des sources," in *Foi populare, foi savant*, 93-148.

326. Ibid., passim.

327. Ibid., 93-94.

328. R. A. Markus observes that a key cause of the characteristic centralization of power in the Middle Ages in Rome, is found in the lack of any important sees in the West that might "compete" with Rome, whereas in the East, balance was more easily kept. See "The Crisis of Authority in the Church: The Historical Roots," The *Modern Churchman* 10 (1967): 288.

329. Benson, 54-55.

330. Ibid., 55.

331. Ibid., 59-61.

332. Ibid., 61-62.

333. Ibid., 63-64.

334. Ibid., 64.

335. From *On the Sacraments of the Christian Faith* (2.2.2-4), quoted in Benson, 64.

336. Ibid., 65.

337. *Decretum* 63 dictum post c. 34, quoted in Benson, 66.

338. See Benson's review of medieval developments in pp. 67-80. He finally argues that contemporary political contexts could support a structure that would include "election by *clerus et populus*." In contrast to the Medieval situation, current systems of political involvement are much closer to the community orientation that existed in the early Church. Ibid., 80.

339. Jean Gaudemet, "Bishops: From Election to Nomination," *Electing Our Own Bishops*, 12.

340. *Dictum* on Distinction 62, c. 2; cited in Gaudemet, 12.

341. *Dictum* after c. 25, on Distinction 63; quoted in Gaudemet, 12.

342. Ibid., 12-13.

343. Yves Congar, "A Brief History of the Forms of the Magisterium," in *Readings in Moral Theology No. 3: The Magisterium and Morality* Edited by Charles E. Curran and Richard A. McCormick. (New York: Paulist Press, 1982), 316.

344. Ibid. Congar cites B. Haeggelund, "Die Bedeutung der 'regula fidei' als Grundlage theologischer Aussagen," *Studia Theologica* 12 (1958): 1-44.

345. Congar, "A Brief History," 317.

346. Ibid., 318.

347. Ibid., 321.

348. Ibid.

349. Ibid.

350. Yves M.-J. Congar, "Saint Thomas Aquinas and the Infallibility of the Papal Magisterium," *The Thomist* 38 (1974) : 81-105.

351. Ibid., 83.

352. Ibid., 91-92.

353. Ibid., 92.

354. Ibid., 95.

355. Ibid.

356. Ibid., 104-105.

357. Rausch, *Authority and Leadership*, 104.

358. Ibid.

359. Ibid., 104-105.

360. Ibid., 105. In this part of his discussion Rausch follows Ulrich Kuhn, "Reception—An Imperative and an Opportunity," *Ecumenical Perspectives on Baptism, Eucharist and Ministry*, ed. Max Thurian (Geneva: WCC, 1983) pp. 166-167.

361. Miguel M. Garijo Guembe, "El Concepto de 'Reception' y su Enmarque en el Seno de la Eclesiologia Catolica," *Lumen* 29 (1980): 321.

362. Rausch, *Authority and Leadership*, 105-106.

363. Ibid., 107-108.

364. Ibid., 106.

365. Ibid.

366. Edward J. Kilmartin, "Reception in History: An Ecclesiological Phenomenon and its Significance," *Journal of Ecumenical Studies* 21 (1984): 35.

367. Ibid., 35-36. See note 5. Yves Congar traces the history of this law in his article, "*Quod omnes tangit, ab omnibus tracteri et approbari debet*," in *Revue historique de droit français et étranger* 35 (1958): 210-259.

368. Kilmartin, "Reception in History," 36. See n. 5.

369. This point is developed by J. Robert Dionne in the context of Vatican II in *The Papacy and the Church: A Study of Praxis and Reception in Ecumenical Perspective* (New York: Philosophical Library, 1987). See specifically pp. 348-353.

370. Kilmartin, "Reception in History," 38.

371. Ibid.

372. Ibid. Emphasis added.

373. Ibid., 38-39. See n. 11

374. Garijo, 318-319.

375. Ibid., 319.

376. Ibid., 319-320.

377. Ibid.

378. Ibid., 321.

379. Ibid.

380. Yves Congar, "La 'réception' comme réalite ecclésiologique," *Revue des Science e philosophiques et theologiques* 56 (1972): 369-403. This article is translated and partially condensed as "Reception as an Ecclesiological Reality," in *Election and Consensus in the Church*, 43-68. Unless otherwise indicated, the English version will be cited here.

381. Ibid., 53.

382. Ibid., 53-54.

383. Ibid., 54-56.

384. Ibid., 54.

385. Ibid., 55.

386. Ibid., 57. Congar also poses the rejection by some Catholics of the dogma of infallibility from Vatican I and the response to *Humanae Vitae* by many Catholic lay people and theologians as connected to these other cases, and asks whether these are instances of "disobedience" or "non-reception." Ibid. 57-58.

386. 387. See Congar, "La 'réception' comme réalite ecclésiologique," 385-386.

388. Ibid., 386-388.

389. Congar, "Reception," 58-59.

390. Ibid., 59.

391. Ibid., 59-60.

392. Ibid., 60.

393. Kilmartin, "Reception in History," 48. Here Kilmartin draws on the ideas of Hermann-Josef Sieben in *Die Konzilsidee der Alten Kirche* Konziliengeschichte. Serie B: Untersuchungen (Paderborn: Schoeningh, 1979). Sieben gives a summary account of the early councils and the balance of secular and ecclesial powers in "On the Relation between Council and the Pope up to the Middle of the Fifth Century," in *The Ecumenical Council*, edited by Peter Huizing and Knut Walf. (New York: Seabury, 1983), 19-23. Here he discusses an "unstable equilibrium" of power evidenced in the Council of Chalcedon that capped a struggle involving the issue of papal influence. Sieben states that this equilibrium was possible as long as the Emperor could influence both the pope and the workings of the council, but adds that a new alignment of power "was bound to come into existence as soon as the papacy freed itself from the influence of both Eastern and Western Empires." Ibid., 23.

394. Kilmartin, "Reception in History," 49.

395. Ibid., 48-49.

396. Ibid., 49.

397. Ibid., 50.

398. Ibid., 52.

399. Jan Hendrik Walgrave, *Unfolding Revelation: The Nature of Doctrinal Development* (London: Hutchinson, 1972), 92.

400. Ibid.

## Notes to Chapter 2

401. Newman, *On Consulting*, 104.

402. Walgrave, *Unfolding Revelation*, 93.

403. Ibid., 92.

404. Ibid., 93.

405. Ibid.

406. N. M. Haring, "Paschasius Radbertus, St." in *New Catholic Encyclopedia* v. 10 (New York: McGraw-Hill, 1967), 1050.

407. In David Knowles with Dimitri Obolensky, *The Middle Ages* (New York: Paulist Press, 1969), 34.

408. Ibid.

409. Newman, *On Consulting*, 104.

410. Decima Douie, "John XXII and the Beatific Vision," *Dominican Studies* 3 (1950): 154-174.

411. Ibid., 154.

412. Ibid., 154-157, 171-172.

413. Quoted by Douie, Ibid., 157.

414. Ibid.

415. J. N. D. Kelly, "John XXII," in *The Oxford Dictionary of Popes* (Oxford: Oxford University Press, 1986), 215-216.

416. Quoted in Douie, 173.

417. Ibid., 172.

418. Douie himself notes that the response to the pope's sermons on the topic was that, "They scandalized many." Ibid., 162.

419. Dulles, "*Sensus Fidelium*," 240.

420. It occurs in III *Sent.* d 13 q 2 a 1 in a passage that probably comes from Alexander of Hales, according to Sancho, *Infalibilidad*, 62. See also n. 106.

421. Thompson, *"Sensus Fidelium* and Infallibility," 456.

422. Ibid., 455.

423. M. Dominikus Koster, "Der Glaubenssinn der Hirten und Glaeubigen," in *Volk Gottes im Werden: Gessamelte Studien.* Edited by Hans-Dieter Langer and Otto Hermann Pesch. (Mainz: Matthias-Gruenewald-Verlag, 1971), 136. See n. 7. Note, Thompson's references are to the same article printed originally in *Neue Ordnung* 3 (1949).

424. Quoted by Thompson in *"Sensus Fidelium* and Infallibility," 456, from Ménard *La Tradition: Révélation, Écriture, Église selon Saint Thomas D'Aguin* (1964), 160.

425. Thompson, *"Sensus Fidelium* and Infallibility," 456.

426. Congar, *Tradition and Traditions*, 317-319.

427. Ibid., 317-318.

428. Koster, "Glaubenssinn," 136. See n. 6.

429. The views of Thomas on the sense of the faithful as they were developed in the scholastic context are discussed by Sancho in *Infalibilidad*, 197-208.

430. Ibid., 202.

431. Ibid., 207-208. Sancho observes that St. Thomas uses the phrase *sensus spiritualis* in several places with a meaning that is similar to that of *sensus fidei*. He cites *III Sent.* d 13 q 3 obj. 2, *Super 1 ad Cor. 11*, lect. 1, no. 587, and *Super ad Gal 3*, lect. 1, no. 114. *Infalibilidad*, 207, n. 42. In n. 43 on the same page, Sancho also considers contemporaries and predecessors to Aquinas who employed analogous phrases for the sense of the faith.

432. Yves M.-J. Congar, *A History of Theology* (Garden City, N.Y.: Doubleday, 1968), 144.

433. Ibid., 154.

434. Ibid.

435. Lowell C. Green, "Erasmus, Luther and Melancthon on the *Magnus Consensus*: The Problem of the Old and the New in the Reformation and Today," *The Lutheran Quarterly* 27 (1975): 365.

436. Ibid., 365-366.

437. Ibid.

438. Ibid., 367.

439. Ibid.

440. Ibid., 368.

441. Ibid. The quote is Green's.

442. Ibid., 369.

443. Ibid., 370.

444. Ibid.

445. Ibid., 371.

446. Ibid., 372.

447. Ibid., 378-379.

448. Quoted in Green, Ibid., 378.

449. Ibid.

450. Ibid., 380-381.

451. Ibid., 381.

452. Thompson, "*Sensus Fidelium* and Infallibility," 457.

453. Ibid.

454. Quoted by Thompson. Ibid., 458.

455. Ibid.

456. Ibid.

457. Congar, *Lay People*, 266.

458. Ibid.

459. Ibid.

460. Thompson, "*Sensus Fidelium* and Infallibility," 457-458.

461. Ibid., 458.

462. Ibid. Here Thompson follows the emphasis of Hans Kueng in *Structures of the Church* (1964), 321.

463. Thompson, "*Sensus Fidelium* and Infallibility," 458-459.

464. Ibid., 459.

465. George H. Tavard, "Tradition as Koinonia in Historical Perspective," *One in Christ* 24 (1988): 98-100.

466. In addition to the conclusion of Green, 380-381, see, for instance, Hans Martin Mueller, "Magno consensus docent . . . Zum Konsensusbegriff nach evangelischem Verstaendnis," *Kerygma und Dogma* 28 (1982) : 113-126.

467. Tavard, "Tradition as Koinonia," 97.

468. Ibid., 97-98.

469. Translation by Tavard, Ibid., 98, n. 1.

470. Ibid., 99.

471. Quoted by Tavard, Ibid., 99.

472. Ibid.

473. Ibid., 100.

474. Quoted by Tavard, Ibid., 100.

475. Ibid.

476. Ibid., 101.

477. Ibid.

478. Dulles, "Magisterium," 274.

479. Robert E. McNally, "Freedom and Suspicion at Trent: Bonuccio and Soto," *Theological Studies* 29 (1968): 752-762.

480. Dulles argues that this need not be the case in the contemporary context. See "Magisterium," 274.

481. Jean Bernhard, "The Election of Bishops at the Council of Trent," in *Electing Our Own Bishops*, 24-30.

482. Ibid., 25-26.

483. Ibid., 26.

484. Ibid.

485. Ibid., 30.

486. Ibid.

487. Ibid.

488. Dulles, "Magisterium," 274.

489. Ibid.

490. Ibid., 274-275.

491. Ibid.

492. Ibid.

493. Frederick J. Parrella, "The Laity in the Church," *CTSA Proceedings* 35 (1980): 270.

494. Ibid. Parrella cites Congar's *L'Église du Saint Augustine à l'epoque moderne* (Paris: Éditions du Cerf, 1970), 382-383.

495. Parrella, 270.

496. From *De controversiis Christianae fidei adversus nostri temporis haereticos*, Vol. 2; *Prima Controversia generalis*, bk. 3, *De Ecclesia militante*, ch. 2: "de definitions Ecclesiae" (Ingolstadt, 1601 edition), col. 137-138. Quoted in Bernard P. Prusak, "The Theology of the Local Church in Historical Development," *CTSA Proceedings* 35 (1980): 298.

497. Giuseppe Alberigo, "L'unité de l'Église dans le service de l'Église romaine et la papauté (XIe-XXe siècle)," *Irénikon* 51 (1978): 58-63.

498. Quoted by Alberigo, Ibid., 58.

499. Ibid.

500. Ibid., 59-61.

501. Ibid., 62.

502. From [Denzinger-Schoenmetzer, *Enchiridion symbolorum*], # 1868. Hereafter cited as *DS*. Translation is from *The Christian Faith in the Doctrinal Documents of the Catholic Church*. Revised edition. dated by J. Neuner and J. Dupuis. (New York: Alba House, 1982), 21.

503. Alberigo, "L'unité," 62.

504. Ibid., 63.

505. Prusak, 297.

506. Ibid. Emphasis in original.

507. Ibid.

508. Ibid., 298.

## Notes to Chapter 2

509. Ibid.

510. See Walgrave, *Unfolding Revelation*, 129-131.

511. Ibid., 129.

512. Ibid.

513. Ibid., 129-130.

514. From A. Arnauld, "Seconde défense des professeurs en théologie de la faculté de Bordeaux," *Oeuvres completes*, vol. 21 (Paris: 1775-81), 167. Quoted in Walgrave, 130-131.

515. Ibid., 130.

516. Paul Schrodt, *The Problem of the Beginning of Dogma in Recent Theology* (Frankfurt am Main: Peter Lang, 1978), 157-158.

517. Ibid., 159. See especially n. 112.

518. Ibid., 158.

519. Tavard, "Tradition as Koinonia," 108.

520. Ibid.

521. Ibid.

522. Quoted by Dulles in *"Sensus Fidelium,"* 240.

523. Quoted in Thils, *L' infallibilité du peuple chrétien*, 18.

524. Sancho, *Infalibilidad*, 211.

525. Ibid.

526. *DS* 786. Translation is from *The Church Teaches: Documents of the Church in English Translation*. Edited by John F. Clarkson, et. al. (Rockford, Illinois: Tan Books, 1973), 46. Sancho's reference is in *Infalibilidad*, 211, n. 60.

527. George H. Tavard, "Tradition in Early Post-Tridentine Theology," *Theological Studies* 23 (1962): 384.

528. Ibid., 384-385.

529. Quoted in Tavard, Ibid., 385.

530. Ibid.

531. Ibid., 385.

532. Quoted by Tavard, Ibid., 385-386. Tavard modifies the quote from the text of John L. Murphy, *The Notion of Tradition in John Driedo* (Milwaukee: 1959), 91. See "Post-Tridentine Theology," 386, n. 42.

533. Congar, *Lay People*, 443.

534. Tavard, "Post-Tridentine Theology," 386.

535. Ibid.

536. Ibid., 386-387.

537. Ibid., 387.

538. Sancho, *Infalibilidad*, 211.

539. Ibid., 215-216.

540. From *De locis theologicis*, bk. 4, chap. 1 (Madrid: 1792), 187. Quoted in Sancho, *Infalibilidad*, 216. See n. 68.

541. Thils, *L'Infallibilité du peuple chrétien*, 14-15.

542. The discussion of this concept here is based in Lawrence J. Riley, *The History, Nature and Use of EPIKEIA in Moral Theology* (Washington, D.C.: Catholic University of America Press, 1948). (See p. 26.)

543. This description is based on Riley's own summary of Thomas's views. See Ibid., 52.

544. Ibid.

545. Franz Scholz, "Problems on Norms Raised by Ethical Borderline Situations: Beginnings of a Solution in Thomas Aquinas and Bonaventure." In *Readings in Moral Theology No. 1: Moral Norms and Catholic Tradition.* Edited by Charles E. Curran and Richard A. McCormick. (New York: Paulist Press, 1579), 166.

546. Ibid., 178. Scholz's approach involves examining the universality, or lack of it, in even the prescriptions of some of the ten commandments, and asking what might support the "'authorization' by appropriate weighty reason" for differences in judgment, that are considered in Aquinas's definition of *epikeia*. Scholz gives an extended discussion of Thomas's view on 161-175, and a summary on 178-179.

547. Ibid., 178-179.

548. Riley, 66-67.

549. Ibid., 67.

550. Ibid., 64-66.

551. Ibid., 100-101.

552. Ibid.

553. Ibid., 102.

554. King, 233.

555. Ibid., 233-234.

556. Ladislas Orsy, "General Norms, Introduction," in *The Code of Canon Law: A Text and Commentary.* Edited by James A. Coriden, Thomas J. Green and Donald E. Heintschel. (New York: Paulist Press, 1985), 25-26.

557. Ibid., 25. The book referred to is Book I, concerned with General Norms.

558. Ibid., 26.

559. Ibid.

560. Ladislas Orsy, "General Norms, Ecclesiastical Laws (cc. 7-22)." In *The Code of Canon Law: A Text and Commentary*, 29.

561. Ibid., 29-30.

562. King, 235. See n. 9.

563. Ibid., 235-236. See also pp. 257-258.

564. King refers to Sandeus's *Commentaria in Quinque Libros Decretalium* (Venice, 1570), Tom. I, col. 1241. King, 237.

565. Ibid.

566. Ibid., 238-244.

567. Ibid., 244.

568. Ibid., 245.

569. Ibid., 246.

570. Ibid.

571. Ibid., 247-249.

572. Ibid., 250-251. The text (of proposition 28) quoted in Latin by King is found in *DS* 2048. The translation used here is taken from Neuner and Dupuis, *The Christian Faith*, 586. See (# 2005).

573. Ibid., 251-256.

574. Ibid., 257.

575. From *Damnatae Theses*, Tom I: "Alexander VII," ed. 11 (Padua, 1727), 98. Quoted in King, 257.

576. Ibid.

577. Ibid., 258.

578. Ibid., 261.

579. Ibid., 264.

580. Ibid., 264-265.

581. Ibid., 265.

582. John T. Noonan, Jr. *The Scholastic Analysis of Usury* (Cambridge: Harvard University Press, 1957). Part Two, "Criticism and Revision of the Usury Theory, 1450-1750," in particular describes the development of the theory and teaching on the subject. See pp. 199-362.

583. Ibid., 11

584. Ibid., 312.

585. John T. Noonan, Jr. *Contraception: A History of Its Treatment by the Catholic Theologians and Canonists*, Enlarged Edition. (Cambridge: Harvard University Press, 1986), 341-342.

586. Ibid., 346.

587. Noonan, *Usury*, 381-382.

588. Noonan, *Contraception*, 346. See also, pp. 352-353, where Noonan observes that changes in the cultural context were allowed to affect the acceptance of usury but not contraception.

589. Quoted in Hans J. Hillerbrand, *Christendom Divided: The Protestant Reformation* (New York: Corpus, 1971), 182. Hillerbrand cites N. Harpsfield, *The Life and Death of Sir Thomas More* (London: Early English Text Society, 1963), 204.

590. Philip Sheldrake, "Authority and Consensus in Thomas More's Doctrine of the Church," *Heythrop Journal* 20 (1979): 147. Emphasis in original.

591. Ibid., 146.

592. Ibid., 147.

593. Ibid., 152-154.

594. Ibid., 153.

595. Knowles, *Middle Ages*, 207.

596. Sheldrake, 153.

597. Ibid.

598. Ibid., 154.

599. Ibid., 155.

600. Ibid.

601. Ibid., 157-158.

602. Ibid., 158.

603. Ibid.

604. Ibid., 159-160.

605. Ibid., 160.

606. Ibid.

607. Ibid., 162.

608. See for instance Sheldrake's remarks, Ibid., 161.

609. Hitchcock, 150.

610. Ibid., 146. In particular, Hitchcock cites More's writings against William Tyndale.

611. Ibid.

612. Ibid., 146-147.

613. Ibid., 149. Hitchcock cites Congar, *Tradition and Traditions*, 190, 298, 304. See n. 24 in Hitchcock.

614. From *Dialogue concerning Heresies*, ed. W. E. Campbell and A. W. Reed (London, 1927), 95-96. Quoted in Hitchcock, 149.

615. Ibid., 150.

616. Ibid., 151.

617. Ibid., 151-152.

618. Ibid., 152.

619. Ibid.

620. Ibid., 153.

621. Ibid.

622. Ibid., 154.

623. The implications of Hitchcock's position for a theological understanding of the *sensus fidelium* will be considered later, when contemporary views of the concept are examined.

624. Sheldrake, 161-162.

**CHAPTER 3**

1. Thompson, "*Sensus Fidelium* and Infallibility," 460-461.

2. Ibid., 461.

3. Thils, *L'Infallibilité du peuple chrétien*, 30.

4. Ibid., 31-32.

5. Ibid., 33.

6. Ibid., 34.

7. Ibid., 35-36.

8. This work is part of a larger work, the *Theologia Wirceburgensis*, published under the name of four Jesuits between 1766-1771. Thils, *L'Infallibilité du peuple chrétien*, 36.

9. Ibid., 36-37.

10. Ibid., 37-39.

11. Dulles, "Magisterium," 275.

12. Ibid.

13. Ibid., 276.

14. Ibid.

15. From *Pastor Aeternus* promulgated July 18, 1870. *DS* 1839. The translation used here is from Clarkson, *The Church Teaches*, 102.

16. *DS* 1836. See also Clarkson, *The Church Teaches*, 100-101.

17. Richard F. Costigan, "The Consensus of the Church: Differing Classical Views," *Theological Studies* 51 (1990): 25-48.

18. Ibid., 25-26. Vatican I is quoted by Costigan, 26. Article Four of the Gallican Declaration is from Henry Bettenson, ed. *Documents of the Christian Church*, second edition. (London: Oxford University Press, 1963), 271.

19. Costigan, 26.

20. Ibid., 27.

21. Ibid., 28. Costigan here cites with approval the assessment of M. Dubruel in "Gallicanisme," *DTC* 6/1, 1096-1137.

22. Costigan, 30.

23. From Tournély's *Praelectiones theologicae de ecclesia Christi* (Paris, 1765) 1.152. Quoted in Costigan, 30.

24. Ibid. Costigan quotes again from the same place.

25. Ibid., 31.

26. Ibid., 32.

27. Ibid. Emphasis is Costigan's. The passage draws on *Praelectiones* 2.28.

28. Costigan quotes from *Praelectiones* 1.266. Costigan, 33.

29. From *Praelectiones* 1.275. Quoted in Costigan, 33-34.

30. Ibid., 35.

31. Ibid., 37.

32. Ibid., 35.

33. Ibid.

34. Ibid.

35. Ibid., 37-38.

36. Ibid., 38.

37. Ibid., 39-40.

38. Quoted from *De vi ac ratione primatus romanorum pontificum, et de ipsorum infallibilitate in definiendis controversiis fidei* (Verona, 1766). Edited by E. W. Westhoff (Muenster: J. H. Deiters, 1845), 39. Quoted in Costigan, 40.

39. Ibid., 40-41.

40. From *De vi ac ratione*, 255. Quoted by Costigan, 41.

41. Ibid.

42. Ibid.

43. Ibid.

44. Ibid., 42.

45. Ibid., 43. Costigan cites *Appendix de infallibilitate pontificia in definiendis dogmaticis*, published with *De potestate ecclesiastica* (Rome: Congr. de Propaganda Fide, 1850). Costigan finds this work receiving too little attention in modern scholarship. See Costigan, 38-39, n. 86.

46. Ibid., 44.

47. Ibid.

48. From *Appendix*, 212. Quoted by Costigan, 44.

49. From *Appendix*, 231. Quoted by Costigan, 46.

50. Costigan, 45-46.

51. Ibid., 47. The capitalization is Costigan's.

52. Ibid., 47-48. Costigan cites Yves Congar, "Gallicanisme," *Catholicisme* 4 (1956): 1736, where Congar describes an important influence within Gallican ecclesiology: "One can, I believe characterize it in the history of ecclesiological doctrines as the will not to let the pole *Ecclesia* be absorbed by the pole *papacy*."

53. Thils, *L'Infallibilité du peuple chrétien*, 41-42.

54. Ibid., 45.

55. Dulles, "*Sensus Fidelium*," 240.

56. Richard Wightman Fox, "Lammenais' Understanding of the Spiritual and Temporal," *Chicago Studies* 8 (1969): 179.

57. Quoted in Fox, 178.

58. Ibid., 181.

59. Ibid., 181-182.

60. Ibid., 187.

61. Ibid.

62. Dulles, "*Sensus Fidelium*," 240.

63. Hellwig, 164.

64. Congar, *Tradition and Traditions*, 186.

65. Josef Rupert Geiselmann, *The Meaning of Tradition*, (Montreal: Palm Publishers, 1966), 52.

66. Chadwick, *Bossuet to Newman*, 109.

67. Ibid.

68. Ibid., 109-110. Chadwick sees this move to a more traditional stance as especially true in later editions. Ibid., 110.

69. Schrodt, 174.

70. Geiselmann, 72-73.

71. Ibid., 71.

72. Chadwick strongly asserts the change in Moehler's thought from *Einheit in der Kirche* to *Symbolik*, with respect to the relationship between faith and dogmas. Yet he notes Moehler's own claim of continuity in regard to his theory of the Church in these two works. See Chadwick, *Bossuet to Newman*, 110-111 and 227, n. 1.

73. Johann Adam Moehler, *Symbolism*, fifth edition, translated by J. B. Robertson. (London: Gibbings & Company, 1906), 261.

74. Ibid., 266.

75. Ibid., 307.

76. Ibid., 306-308.

77. Ibid., 308. See n. 1.

78. Ibid. Emphasis in original.

79. Ibid., 308.

80. Ibid.

81. Wolfgang Beinert, "Bedeutung und Begruendung des Glaubenssinnes (Sensus Fidei) als eines Dogmatischen Erkenntniskriteriums," *Catholica* 25 (1971): 281.

82. Moehler, *Symbolism*, 278.

83. Cited by Beinert, in "Bedeutung und Begruendung," 281. The translation use here is Robertson's from Moehler, *Symbolism*, 279.

84. Moehler, *Symbolism*, 279.

85. Ibid., 281.

86. An interesting description of the parties that supported and opposed the defining of papal infallibility immediately before Vatican I is given by Dom Edward Cuthbert Butler in "Eve of the Council: Controversy Among Catholics," in *The Vatican Council* (Westminster, Md.: The Newman Press, 1962), 85-107.

87. Congar, *Tradition and Traditions*, 196-197.

88. Chadwick, *Bossuet to Newman*, 111-119.

89. Ibid., 119.

90. Ibid., 112-113.

91. Congar, *Tradition and Traditions*, 186-187.

92. Hellwig, 164.

93. Congar, *Tradition and Traditions*, 324.

94. Thils, *L'Infallibilité du peuple chrétien*, 43.

95. Ibid., 44.

96. J. P. Mackey, *The Modern Theology of Tradition* (New York: Herder and Herder, 1961), vii.

97. Congar, *Tradition and Traditions*, 324-325.

98. Mackey, *Modern Theology*, viii.

99. Ibid., vii-viii.

100. Ibid., 16.

101. Ibid., 14.

102. Ibid., 14, n. 63.

103. Ibid., 14. See also n. 63. Here Mackey also asserts, "There is no mention of the Magisterium or of its authority in the tridentine context."

104. Ibid., 16.

105. Ibid., 16-17.

106. Ibid., 17.

107. Congar, *Tradition and Traditions*, 325. Emphasis in original.

108. Thils, *L'Infallibilité du peuple chrétien*, 42; Thompson, "*Sensus Fidelium* and Infallibility," 462.

109. Beinert, "Bedeutung und Begruendung," 281.

110. Thompson, "*Sensus Fidelium* and Infallibility," 462.

111. Ibid.

112. Thils, *L'Infallibilité du peuple chrétien*, 43.

113. Thompson, "*Sensus Fidelium* and Infallibility," 462. Emphasis in original.

114. Ibid., 462-463.

115. Ibid., 463.

116. Tillard, "*Sensus Fidelium*," 5. In the passage cited, Tillard refers to both the 1854 definition by Pius IX and that of the Assumption in 1950 by Pius XII.

117. Ibid.

118. Ibid.

119. Ibid., 6.

120. Eamon Carroll, "Papal Infallibility and the Marian Definitions, Some Considerations," *Carmelus* 26 (1979): 213-215.

121. Ibid., 213-214. Carroll cites Rene Laurentin, "The Role of the Papal Magisterium in the Development of the Dogma of the Immaculate Conception," in *The Dogma of the Immaculate Conception*; edited by E. D. Connor (Notre Dame, Ind.: 1958), 271-324.

122. Gerard Owens, "Historical Development of the Dogma of the Immaculate Conception: Obstacles Inhibiting Understanding and Acceptance," *CTSA Proceedings* 9 (1954): 77. This article offers a historical assessment of the other issues mentioned here as well.

123. Quoted in Carroll, "Marian Definitions," 214.

124. Ibid., 216-219.

125. Ibid., 218.

126. Ibid.

127. Ibid., 219.

128. Ibid. For the view expressed in quotes and the observation on the piety of Pius IX, Carroll cites Roger Aubert's *L'épiscopat belge et la proclamation du dogme de l'Immaculée Conception en 1854*, in *Virgo Immaculata* (Rome: 1956), II.

129. Carroll, "Marian Definitions," 221-222.

130. Ibid., 222.

131. Ibid., 223.

132. Ibid.

133. Ibid., 224.

134. Owens, 98.

135. Ibid., 98-99.

136. The view that the magisterium was characterized by a desire to consolidate authority has been argued recently by August Bernhard Hasler in his controversial *How the Pope Became Infallible* (Garden City, N.Y.: 1981), 177-178. In this book Hasler is interested in showing that the focus on papal infallibility in the Church was intended to give an "insurance" policy of certitude to believers. He argues that this politically generated attempt failed in that it isolated the papacy structurally from its base in the Church and left if open to great criticism on historical grounds as well. See for instance, 277-279.

137. From a personal letter of January 10, 1861. In Wilfrid Ward, *The Life of John Henry Cardinal Newman*, 2 vols. (London: 1913). I: 605. Quoted by Webster T. Patterson in *Newman: Pioneer for the Layman* (Washington, D.C.: Corpus Books, 1968), 15. Patterson discussed the relationship between the lay people and pastors in Newman's context in pp. 13-18.

138. From a personal letter of December 10, 1973. In Ward, II: 397-398. Quoted by Patterson in *Pioneer*, 16.

139. Richard J. Penaskovic, *Open to the Spirit: The Notion of the Laity in the Writings of J. H. Newman*, (Augsburg: W. Blasaditsch, 1972), 9-10.

140. Penaskovic cites the German edition of Guitton's work; J. Guitton, *Mitbuergen der Wahrheit: Das zeugnis der Laien in Fragen der Glaubenslehre* (Salzburg: 1964). Femiano's text is Samuel D. Femiano, *Infallibility of the Laity: The Legacy of Newman* (New York: Herder and Herder, 1967). Patterson's text is *Pioneer* as cited above.

141. Penaskovic, *Open to the Spirit*, 4-6.

142. Ibid., 7.

143. Ibid., 9.

144. Ibid., 2-3. Penaskovic cites Gadamer's *Warheit und Methode: Grundzuege einer philosophischen Hermeneutik* (Tuebingen: 1965), 284-290. See also Gadamer, *Truth and Method*, 300-307.

145. Penaskovic, *Open to the Spirit*, 2.

146. In addition to Guitton, Femiano, and Patterson mentioned already, additional authors who offer a specifically historical foundation for their views include Dulles, Koster, Thompson, Granfield, Beinert and others. The views of these authors will be discussed in detail later.

147. Karl Rahner describes a similar issue of interpretation when he discusses the difference between concrete moral prescriptions and universal moral principles in *The Dynamic Element in the Church* (New York: Herder and Herder, 1964), 13-29. Rahner discusses the situation in France after 1871, where neither the Bonapartists, the Monarchists nor the Republicans were obviously "'right' in their prescriptions," as an example of a situation where the Church did not (and could not) speak in terms of moral principles. Here moral responsibility on the part of Catholics was a duty that could be exercised within the guidelines of moral principles, but which might not necessarily be generated from those principles alone. (See especially, 27-28.) Rahner writes,

> It is evident from such an example, if it is carefully examined, that the very act of analysis itself alters the case—an idea of modern physics that can be transferred to this domain. The way the masses viewed the case, their interpretation, preference, taste, their individual decisions which coalesced into a collective will, were themselves also factors in the situation that was to be analysed, and this analysis itself, in the form of a preferred interpretation seeking acceptance, itself influenced the collective view of the case and so the situation itself that was in dispute. One ought really to recommend moral theologians to investigate for once in their casuistry real cases of some magnitude. (Ibid., 28-29.)

148. Coulson, "Introduction," 1-49.

149. Patterson, *Pioneer*, 21.

150. Ibid., 23.

151. See Patterson's detailed discussion, Ibid., 22-38.

152. Coulson, "Introduction," 2-3.

153. Quoted by Coulson, Ibid., 3-4.

154. Ibid., 4.

155. Ibid., 5-6.

156. Ibid., 6.

157. Ibid.

158. Ibid., 7.

159. Ibid., 8.

160. Ibid.

161. Quoted by Coulson, Ibid.

162. Ibid., 9.

163. Ibid., 12-13.

164. Ibid., 13.

165. Quoted by Coulson, 14.

166. Ibid., 8.

167. Femiano discusses the correspondence of Newman and Gillow, pp. 89-95. The quote is from a letter of Gillow to Newman of May 15, 1859, quoted in Femiano, 91.

168. Ibid.

169. Ibid., 91-92.

170. From a letter of Newman to Gillow, May 16, 1859, quoted in Femiano, 92. Femiano notes that the material of this letter with its link to Perrone is substantially repeated in Newman's *Rambler* article in July. Ibid., 91.

171. Ibid., 92. Emphasis is Newman's.

172. Letter from Newman to Gillow cited above, as quoted in Femiano, 93.

173. Ibid., 93-95.

174. Letter of Newman to Gillow, May 25, 1859. Quoted in Femiano, 95.

175. Patterson, *Pioneer*, 60.

176. Ibid., 60-61.

177. Quoted by Patterson, Ibid., 61.

178. Ibid.

179. Ibid., 61-62.

180. Ibid., 62.

181. Femiano, 98.

182. Ibid., 99.

183. See Newman, *On Consulting*, 54-62.

184. Patterson, *Pioneer*, 80.

185. Femiano, 99.

186. Patterson, *Pioneer*, 80.

187. Ibid., 81.

188. Newman, *On Consulting*, 62-63.

189. Ibid., 63.

190. Ibid.

191. Ibid.

192. Ibid., 63-64.

193. Ibid.

194. Ibid.

195. Ibid., 64-65. Newman's account of Perrone's work is found in pp. 65-73.

196. Patterson, *Pioneer*, 66. Emphasis in original.

197. Newman, *On Consulting*, 67. Emphasis is Newman's.

198. Ibid., 72. Emphasis in Newman's text.

199. Ibid., 72-73. Newman cites Ullathorne's text, pp. 172-173. In a recent reprint of Ullathorne's work, the passage quoted is found with the citations of Augustine identified. See The Right Reverend Bishop Ullathorne, *The Immaculate Conception of the Mother of God*. Reprinted, with an Introduction by Wilfred Schoenberg. (Westminster, Md.: Christian Classics, 1988), 135-136.

200. Ibid., 138.

201. Newman, *On Consulting*, 73.

202. Ibid., 73-74.

203. Ibid., 77.

204. Walgrave, "Newman's 'On Consulting,'" 28.

205. Ibid. Walgrave refers to Newman's *Grammar of Assent* (1970), 75-121.

206. Owen Chadwick, *Newman* (Oxford: Oxford University Press, 1983), 41-42. In his discussion in another place of the interaction of Newman and Perrone on the issue of doctrinal development, Chadwick notes that, "Newman's theory depended upon the validity of the analogy between the faith of the individual and the corporate faith of the Church." Chadwick, *Bossuet to Newman*, 182.

207. Chadwick, *Newman*, 42-43.

208. Kevin D. Bucher, "Newman on the Functions of the Church: A Prophetic Voice for Today?" *Louvain Studies* 7 (1978): 22.

209. Ibid.

210. Ibid., 23.

211. Quoted by Bucher from Newman's *Apologia pro Vita Sua* (London: 1890), 252.

212. Coulson, "Introduction," 25.

213. Quoted by Coulson, Ibid., 25. Newman's original statement is found in *On Consulting*, 103-104.

214. Ibid., 104.

215. Ibid.

216. Ibid., 106.

217. Ibid.

218. Coulson, "Introduction," 36.

219. Ibid.

220. Patterson, *Pioneer*, 71.

221. Ibid., 72.

222. Ibid., 73-75.

223. Coulson, "Introduction," 37.

224. Ibid., 37-41.

225. Ibid., 42.

226. Ibid., 43-45.

227. Ibid., 45.

228. Chadwick, *Bossuet to Newman*, 180-184.

229. Ibid., 182-183.

230. Ibid., 183. Emphasis in original.

231. Ibid.

232. C. Stephen Dessain, original ed., "Letter to Flanagan, 1868," in *The Theological Papers of John Henry Newman on Biblical Inspiration and on Infallibility*. Edited by J. Derek Holmes. (Oxford: Clarendon Press, 1979), 151-152. This article was originally published as "An Unpublished Paper by Cardinal Newman on the Development of Doctrine" in *The Journal of Theological Studies*, New Series, vol. IX, part 2, 1958. Dessain cites this letter as "Newman's clearest and shortest explanation" of his view of doctrinal development. He adds that this document supplies "as direct an answer as could be hoped for" to the question posed by Chadwick in *Bossuet to Newman*, as to how the "new doctrines of which the Church had a feeling or inkling" can be construed so as not to be in fact "new revelation." Dessain's comments are on pp. 151-152. For the quotes from Chadwick see *Bossuet to Newman*, 195.

233. Dessain, 152-154.

234. Ibid., 156-157.

235. Ibid., 157-159.

236. Ibid., 157.

237. Ibid.

238. Ibid., 157-158.

239. Ibid., 158

240. Ibid., 159-160.

241. Avery Dulles, "Newman on Infallibility," *Theological Studies* 51 (1990): 434-449.

242. Ibid., 434.

243. Ibid., 435.

244. Ibid., 434.

245. Ibid., 434. See also 444-445.

246. Ibid., 441-442.

247. Ibid., 444.

248. Ibid., 436.

249. Ibid., 437. Dulles notes the similarity in Newman's view at this time and the contemporary view of Hans Kueng.

250. Ibid.

251. Ibid., 438.

252. Ibid.

253. Ibid., 439.

254. Ibid., 441. For this view, Dulles cites a letter of Newman's to Alfred Plummer of April 3, 1871, in *Letters and Diaries of John Henry Newman* 25 (Oxford: Clarendon, 1973): 309.

255. Ibid., 441.

256. Ibid., 441-442.

257. Ibid.

258. Ibid., 442-443. Dulles cites Newman, *On Consulting*, 75-77.

259. Dulles, "Newman on Infallibility," 443.

260. Ibid., 445.

261. Ibid., 444-445.

262. Ibid., 445. Dulles cites Newman, *Letters and Diaries* 25: 310.

263. Ibid., 447.

264. Ibid., 448.

265. Ibid., 447.

266. Ibid., 447-448.

267. Joseph Hoffmann, "Théologie, magistère et opinion publique: Le discours de Doellinger au Congrès des Savants Catholiques de 1863." *Recherches de science religieuse* 71 (1983): 245-258.

268. Ibid., 246.

269. Ibid. Quoted by Hoffmann from the printed speech included in I. von Doellinger, *Kleinere Schriften*, edited by F. H. Reusch (Stuttgart: 1890), 184.

270. Hoffmann, "L'discours de Doellinger," 246.

271. Ibid., 247.

272. Ibid. See n. 4.

273. Ibid.

274. Ibid., 247-248.

275. Ibid., 248. Hoffmann cites M. Seckler, *Kirchliches Lehramt und theologische Wissenschaft*, Geschichtliche Aspekte, Probleme und Loesungselemente, in W. Kern, ed. *Die Theologie und das Lehramt*, Quaestiones Disputatae 91, (1982), 47.

276. Hoffmann, "L'discours de Doellinger," 248. Hoffmann cites *Kleinere Schriften*, 161.

277. Hoffmann, "L'discours de Doellinger," 248.

278. Ibid., 250-251.

279. Ibid., 251.

280. Ibid., 251-252.

281. Ibid., 252, n. 19. Hoffmann cites Doellinger's "Discourse of Linz (1850)" from *Kleinere Schriften*, 118-119.

282. Hoffmann, "L'discours de Doellinger," 252, note 19.

283. Ibid., 253-254.

284. Ibid., 257.

285. T. Howland Sanks, *Authority in the Church: A Study in Changing Paradigms* (Missoula, Mont.: American Academy of Religion, 1974), 21-22.

286. Ibid., 23, 28.

287. Ibid., 24-25.

288. Ibid., 24.

289. Ibid.

290. Ibid., 26. Sanks cites Perrone's *Praelectiones Theologicae*, (4 vols. revised edition Paris: Guame Fratres, 1856), IV, 139.

291. Sanks, *Authority in the Church*, 27.

292. Ibid., 28. Emphasis in original.

293. Ibid., 32.

294. Ibid., 33.

295. Ibid., 33-34. Sanks cites here Carlo Passaglia, *De Ecclesia Christi* 3 vols. (Ratisbone, 1853), III. 212-213.

296. Ibid., 34.

297. Ibid. Sanks cites Passaglia, III, 225.

298. Sanks, *Authority in the Church*. 34. Emphasis in original.

299. Ibid., 34-35.

300. Ibid., 37.

301. Ibid., 39.

302. Ibid., 40.

303. Ibid., 40-41.

304. Ibid., 41.

305. Ibid.

306. Ibid., 42.

307. Ibid., 42-43.

308. Ibid., 44. Emphasis in Sanks's text. Sanks draws on John Baptist Franzelin, *De Divina Traditione et Scriptura* (3rd ed.; Rome: S. C. de Propoganda Fide, 1882). For this particular passage, see pp. 11-12.

309. Sanks, *Authority in the Church*, 44.

310. Ibid., 44-45.

311. Ibid., 47-48.

312. Ibid., 52. The quote from Mackey is from *Modern Theology*, 12.

313. Sanks, *Authority in the Church*, 52-53.

314. Ibid., 53. Sanks cites Franzelin's *Divina Traditione*, 106.

315. Sanks, *Authority in the Church*, 53. Sanks refers here to *Divina Traditione*, 104.

316. Sanks, *Authority in the Church*, 53.

317. Ibid., 54.

318. Ibid., 54-55. The quote is from Franzelin's *Divina Traditione*, 117. Sanks notes that Franzelin cites Vatican I's *De Ecclesia Christi*, chapter IV for this notion.

319. Sanks, *Authority in the Church*, 55. Emphasis is Sanks's. Sanks cites Franzelin's *Divina Traditione*, 118, 148; and *De Ecclesia Christi* (Rome, 1887), 254, 386.

320. Sanks, *Authority in the Church*, 57.

321. Ibid.

322. Ibid., 57-58. Quoted from Franzelin's *Divina Traditione*, 118.

323. Sanks, *Authority in the Church*, 58.

324. Ibid.

325. Ibid., 60.

326. Ibid., 61.

327. Sanks sees this view of the magisterium as having "formed the attitude of a number of the hierarchy, the Curia, and recent popes, including Paul VI." Ibid., 103.

328. Ibid., 103. In Kuhn's usages these paradigms represent universally accepted models for organizing thought and reflection. The introduction of this idea is in Thomas S. Kuhn *The Structure of Scientific Revolutions* (Chicago: University of Chicago Press, 1962). Sanks stresses that he uses the term paradigm "analogously." His treatment of Newman and the modernists is found in Sanks, *Authority in the Church*, 146-161.

329. Ibid., 109-110.

330. Ibid., 116.

331. Ibid., 140-143. A short but powerful analysis of the same distinction between "classical" and "historical" approaches to doctrine and church structure is available in Bernard J. F. Lonergan, "The Transition from a Classicist World-View to Historical-Mindedness," in *A Second Collection*, edited by William F. J. Ryan and Bernard J. Tyrrell. (Philadelphia: Westminster Press, 1974), 1-9. On p. 1 of this article, Lonergan quotes a letter from James A. Coriden of July 22, 1966, which is reminiscent of the images used by Moehler, "The pattern of adaptation and change appears to be a mandate based on the very nature and mission of the

Church, just as growth and development are inherent in the nature of a living organism."

332. The importance of the pope's statement for the issue specifically considered here is dramatically clear when seen in the context of the speech itself:

> From the renewed, serene, tranquil adherence to all the teaching of the Church in its entirety and preciseness, as it still shines forth in the Acts of the Council of Trent and First Vatican Council, the Christian, Catholic, and apostolic spirit of the whole world expects a step forward toward doctrinal penetration and a formation of consciousness in faithful and perfect conformity to the authentic doctrine, which, however, should be studied and expounded through the methods of research and through the literary forms of modern thought. The substance of the ancient doctrine of the deposit of faith is one thing, and the way in which it is presented is another. And it is the latter that must be taken into great consideration with patience if necessary, everything being measured in the forms and proportions of a magisterium which is predominantly pastoral in character.

From "Pope John's Opening Speech to the Council," in Abbott, 715.

333. In *Vatican Council*, Butler gives an extensive discussion of the battles over infallibility inside and outside of the Council's meetings. The debates are well illustrated in his chapters "Infallibility Debate: Text of the Decree," 348-372; and "The Deputation *De Fide* and the Infallibility Decree," 373-385. On p. 385 Butler compares the alternate schemata proposed at the Council with the one that was actually adopted.

334. Andreas Lindt, "Aus dem Leben von Theologie und Kirche," *Reformatio* 19 (1970): 610.

335. Butler, *Vatican Council*, 416.

336. Ibid., 417.

337. John T. Ford, "Different Models of Infallibility," *CTSA Proceedings* 35 (1980): 219.

338. Ibid., 231.

339. See Paul K. Hennessy, "Infallibility in the Ecclesiology of Peter Richard Kenrick," *Theological Studies* 45 (1984): 702-714.

340. Ibid., 711. See n. 36.

341. Ibid., 713.

342. Ibid., 713-714.

343. John T. Ford, "Infallibility—From Vatican I to the Present," *Journal of Ecumenical Studies* 8 (1971): 770.

344. Ibid., 779.

345. Ibid., 775-778.

346. Ibid., 769.

347. Ibid., 777.

348. Ibid., 777. Ford quotes from C. Dessain, "What Newman Taught in Manning's Church," in *Infallibility in the Church* (London, 1968): 70.

349. Hennessy, 712-713.

350. Ford, "Vatican I to Present," 778.

351. Ibid., 779.

352. Ibid., 780.

353. Ibid., 780. Ford quotes from G. Wilson, "The Gift of Infallibility: Reflections Toward a Systematic Theology," *Theological Studies* 31 (1970): 625. Emphasis in original.

354. Giuseppe Alberigo, "The Authority of the Church in the Documents of Vatican I and Vatican II," *Journal of Ecumenical Studies* 19 (1982), 121-128.

355. Ford, "Vatican I to Present," 780-781.

356. Lindt, 611-612.

357. *DS* 3074. The translation here is from Neuner, *The Christian Faith*, 234.

358. Margaret O'Gara, "Listening to Forgotten Voices: The French Minority Bishops of Vatican I & Infallibility," *Theology Digest* 37 (1990): 3-15. A shorter paper by O'Gara that covers the same ground is "Infallibility and the French Minority Bishops of the First Vatican Council," *CTSA Proceedings* 35 (1980): 212-216. The citations here will be to the article in *Theology Digest*.

359. Ibid., 3.

360. Ibid., 4.

361. Ibid.

362. Ibid.

363. Ibid., 5.

364. Ibid.

365. Ibid., 5-6.

366. Ibid., 7.

367. Ibid., 8.

368. Ibid.

369. Ibid.

370. Ibid.

371. Ibid., 9.

372. Ibid., 10.

373. Ibid.

374. Ibid., 11.

375. Ibid.

376. Ibid., 12.

377. Ibid., 12-13.

378. Ibid.

379. Ibid., 14.

380. See Ibid., 14-15. O'Gara refers here to the article of Lonergan cited above.

381. Francis Schuessler Fiorenza, "Presidential Address: Foundations of Theology: A Community's Tradition of Discourse and Practice," *CTSA Proceedings* 41 (1986): 107-134. Fiorenza mentions the modern "turn" on p. 108 and Franzelin's role in *Dei Filius* on p. 110.

382. Ibid., 111-112.

383. See his subsection on this matter, Ibid., 109-115.

384. Ibid., 117. Fiorenza cites Sellars's "Empiricism and the Philosophy of the mind," in *Foundations of Science and the concepts of Psychology and Psychoanalysis*, edited by Herbert Feigl and Michael Scriven. (Minnesota Studies in the Philosophy of Science, Minn: University of Minnesota Press, 1956): 257.

385. George Dejaifve, "Ex Sese, Non Autem Ex Consensu Ecclesiae," *Eastern Churches Quarterly* 14 (1962): 360-378. A shorter version of this article is available as "Infallibility and Consent of the Church," *Theology Digest* 12 (1964): 8-13. References here will be to the longer version.

386. Ibid., 360. See Hans Kueng, *Infallibility? An Inquiry* (Garden City, New York: Doubleday, 1971). Originally, *Unfehlbar? Eine Anfrage* (Benziger: 1970).

387. Dejaifve, "Ex Sese," 361. Quoted by Dejaifve from Mansi, 51, 997D.

388. Dejaifve, "Ex Sese," 362. Quoted by Dejaifve from Mansi, 51, 1003C-D.

389. Dejaifve, "Ex Sese," 362-365.

390. Ibid., 370.

391. Ibid., 371.

392. Ibid.

393. Ibid., 372. Quotes from Freppel are cited from Mansi, 52, 1041A-C. Dejaifve's text includes other significant excerpts of Freppel's remarks as well.

394. Dejaifve, "Ex Sese," 372-373.

395. Ibid., 373.

396. Ibid., 374. Dejaifve refers to Mansi, 52, 1317A-B. He notes too that Mansi's text credits Pius IX with the addition of the words, "*non autem ex consensu Ecclesiae.*" Ibid., 1318A. See Dejaifve, "Ex Sese," 374, n. 55.

397. Ibid., 375. See also n. 57.

398. See Dejaifve's remarks on misinterpretation, Ibid., 375-376.

399. From Mansi, 52, 1213-1214. The translation used here is from Vincent Gasser, *The Gift of Infallibility: The Official Relatio on Infallibility of Bishop Vincent Gasser at Vatican Council I*, trans. with commentary, James T. O'Conner (Boston: St. Paul Editions, 1986), 43-44.

400. See Dejaifve, "Ex Sese," 376-377. A discussion which follows the same lines as Dejaifve, and that examines Gasser's *relatio* in detail, with attention to this passage in particular is given by Thomas A. Caffrey in "Consensus and Infallibility: The Mind of Vatican I," *The Downside Review* 88 (1970): 107-131. See especially 119-125. Caffrey presents the "mind of the Council" in a way that illustrates how the definition was meant to give the tradition of infallibility a respectful hearing, but which read it through Scholastic eyes.

401. Georg Denzler, "Bulletin: The Discussion about Bernhard Hasler's Publications on the First Vatican Council," in *Who Has the Say in the Church?* 85.

402. Ibid.

403. Beinert, "Bedeutung und Begruendung," 282.

404. Thompson, "*Sensus Fidelium* and Infallibility," 467.

405. Ibid., 468-469.

406. Ibid., 469. In note 61, Thompson quotes the full paragraph from Mansi, 49, 630C-D.

407. Thompson, "*Sensus Fidelium* and Infallibility." 469. Thompson cites Thils, *L'Infaillibilite pontificale* (1969): 12.

408. Thompson, "*Sensus Fidelium* and Infallibility," 469.

409. Alberigo, "Authority in Vatican I and Vatican II," 127.

410. Ibid., 127-128.

411. Ibid., 129.

412. The translation use here is from Pope Pius X, *Encyclical Letter of Pope Pius X On the Doctrines of the Modernists: Pascendi Dominici Gregis and Syllabus Condemning the Errors of the Modernists: Lamentabili Sane, July 3, 1907* (Boston: St. Paul Editions, n. d.), 71.

413. Alberigo, "Authority in Vatican I and Vatican II," 130.

414. John E. Thiel, "Theological Responsibility: Beyond the Classical Paradigm," *Theological Studies* 47 (1986): 586.

415. Ibid., 586-587.

416. From *Pascendi* (# 27), quoted from *The Papal Encyclicals 1903-1939*, ed. Claudia Carlen (Wilmington, N.C.: McGrath, 1981), by Thiel in "Theological Responsibility," 587.

417. Thiel, "Theological Responsibility," 587.

418. Ibid., 588.

419. Ibid., 591.

420. See Sanks, *Authority in the Church*, 140-144. An argument for the general applicability of Kuhn's theory to theology is offered by George A.

Lindbeck, "Theological Revolutions and the Present Crisis," *Theology Digest* 23 (1975): 308-319.

421. Sanks, *Authority in the Church*, 142.

422. Sanks notes that such rejection of new ideas only delayed the crisis of paradigms, rather than preventing it. Ibid.

423. Dulles, "Magisterium," 278.

424. Ibid., 279.

425. Ibid.

426. Ibid.

427. Ibid., 278.

428. Gabriel Daly, "The Dissent of Theology: The Modernist Crisis," in *The Right to Dissent*, 53-57.

429. Ibid., 54.

430. Ibid.

431. Ibid.

432. Ibid., 55.

433. See section 2, where the encyclical refers to the "partisans of error" both outside and within the Church. *On the Doctrines of the Modernists*, 7-8.

434. Alberigo, "L'unité," 66-67.

435. Ibid., 67.

436. Sanks, *Authority in the Church*, 140.

437. Ibid., 144.

438. Ibid. Sanks cites Schoof's *A Survey of Catholic Theology: 1880-1970*, translated by N. D. Smith (Glen Rock, N.J.: Paulist Newman Press, 1970), 152.

439. Sanks, *Authority in the Church*, 144.

440. Ibid., 145. This "preoccupation" continued up through mid-century. The work of several authors contemporary with *Humani Generis* (1950), including some who were under a cloud with respect to the magisterium, are discussed by John T. Galvin, in "A Critical Survey of Modern Conceptions of Doctrinal Development," *CTSA Proceedings* 5 (1950): 45-62. Examples of treatments that dealt with the development of doctrine just prior to the Second Vatican Council with an explicit look at an active role for the *sensus fidelium* and which continued to enhance study of the issue after the Council include, in addition to Mackey's *Modern Theology* cited already: Josef Rupert Geiselmann, *De Heilige Schrift und die Tradition* (Freiburg: Herder, 1962). An English translation of the first three chapters by W. J. O'Hara is available as *The Meaning of Tradition*, cited above. See also Henri Rondet, *Les Dogmes changent-ils?* (Librairie Arthème Fayard, 1960). ET, *Do Dogmas Change?* translated by Dom Mark Pontifex. (New York: Hawthorn Books, 1961).

441. Sanks, *Authority in the Church*, 145. Sanks cites Roman documents from the *Syllabus of Errors* (1864) through *Casti connubii* (1930) and "numerous responses of the Biblical Commission." See n. 1. More recent examples of statements by the Congregation for the Doctrine of the Faith in the areas of liberation theology and sexual ethics could be offered to illustrate that the "shift" or "shifts" are not yet over.

442. Sanks, *Authority in the Church*, 145. Sanks quotes Kuhn, 143-144.

443. Sanks, *Authority in the Church*, 146-161.

444. Ibid., 140. Sanks quotes Kuhn, 151.

445. Congar, *Tradition and Traditions*, 201.

446. Ibid.

447. Alberigo, "Authority in Vatican I and Vatican II," 130-131.

448. Ibid., 131.

449. Ibid., 132.

450. Ibid.

451. See "Crisis modernists y retorno a la terminología del 'sensus fidei,'" in Sancho, *Infalibilidad del Pueblo de Dios*, 219-235.

452. Ibid., 228-229.

453. Ibid., 229. Sancho notes that although Gardeil does not use the term *sensus fidei*, he refers to the "common sense of the faithful" (*sentido común de los fieles*), "the common faith" (*la fe común*), and "the living, social faith of the Church" (*la fe viviente y social de la Iglesia*).

454. Ibid., 229-230.

455. Ibid., 234.

456. Ibid., 234-235. A useful list of key pre-conciliar works on the sense of the faithful are given by M. Seckler in "Glaubenssinn," 948, and Mackey, *Modern Theology*, 209-216. For the works of such authors as cited by Sancho, note M. D Koster, *Volk Gottes im Wachstum des Glaubens*, (1950): J. Beumer, "Glaubenssinn der Kirche," *Trierer Theologische zeiteschrift* 61 (1952): 129-142; C. Balic, "Il Senso Cristiano e il progresso del dogma," *Gregorianum* 33 (1952): 105-134; C. Dillenschneider, *Le sens de la foi et le progrès dogmatique du mystère marial* (1954); Y. Congar, *Jalons pour une théologie du laicat* (1954) and *La Tradition et les traditions* (1960). A work that was published at the end of the Council, which has continued to be influential for its basic treatment of doctrinal development, is Herbert Hammans, *Die Neueren Katholischen Erklaerungen der Dogmentwicklung* (Essen: Ludgerus-Verlag Hubert Wingen KG, 1965). In his treatment of the sense of the faithful, Hammans draws on and criticizes the views of the more modern authors listed here. See his section, "Der Glaubenssinn," 242-262.

457. Congar, *Tradition and Traditions*, 204-205.

458. Ibid., 204. See n. 3.

459. Ibid., 205.

460. Carroll, "Marian Definitions," 231. The letter *Deiparae Virginis* was sent in 1946.

461. Pope Pius XII, *Munificentissimus Deus*, (# 12). The translation used here is from *Apostolic Constitution of Pope Pius XII on the Assumption of the Blessed Virgin Mary*, 7, cited above.

462. Ibid. The embedded quote is from *Ineffabilis Deus*. At the end of the citation given here, the pope cites Vatican I's *Dei Filius*, chapter 4.

463. Carroll, "Marian Definitions," 225. Carroll quotes *Munificentissimus Deus*.

464. Carroll, "Marian Definitions," 225. Carroll misquotes Tillard slightly, omitting the words given here in brackets. See Tillard, *"Sensus Fidelium,"* 7.

465. Later in the same section of the encyclical quoted above, the pope describes the doctrine as "a truth that has been revealed by God and consequently something that must be firmly and faithfully believed by all children of the Church." See Pius XII, *Assumption of the Blessed Virgin Mary*, 8.

466. A discussion of the response received by the pope's action in making the definition and an analysis of the religious and political context, and possible motives of the pope, are offered by Kilian Healy, in "Pope Pius XII and the Assumption," in *The Assumption of Mary* (Wilmington, Del.: Michael Glazier, 1982), 15-23.

467. Juniper B. Carol, "The Definability of Mary's Assumption," *The American Ecclesiastical Review* 118 (1948): 161-177.

468. Ibid., 161.

469. Ibid., 161-166.

470. Ibid., 166. Emphasis in original.

471. Ibid., 177.

472. Ibid. Emphasis in original.

473. Ibid. Emphasis in original.

474. Walter J. Burghardt, "The Catholic Concept of Tradition in the Light of Modern Theological Thought," *CTSA Proceedings* 6 (1951): 42-75.

475. Ibid., 44-65.

476. Ibid., 71.

477. Ibid., 71-75. A more thorough historical overview of teachings concerning the Assumption, written in the same general period as the works of Carol and Burghardt is Edward A. Wuenschel's "The Definability of the Assumption'" *CTSA Proceedings* 2 (1947): 72-102. Wuenschel's theological view of the conclusive role of the magisterium is close to Burghardt's although it anticipates the definition, and is asserted rather than argued.

478. Mackey, *Modern Theology*, 97.

479. Ibid., 101-102.

480. Ibid., 117.

481. Ibid., 115.

482. Ibid., 79, 131.

483. Ibid., 205.

484. Ibid.

485. Tillard, *"Sensus Fidelium,"* 9. Tillard does add, "To say this is not, however, to deny that, especially in the case of the Bull *Ineffabilis* of Pius IX, other factors may have played a part, in particular the desire to assert papal power." Ibid., 9-10.

## CHAPTER 4

1. Abbott, 29.

2. Ibid., 30.

3. Gérard Philips, "Le sens de la foi dans le foi dans le peuple fidèle," in *L'Eglise et son mystère au IIe Concile du Vatican*, Vol. 1., (Paris: Declee, 1967), 179.

4. Ibid.

5. Abbott, 61-62.

6. Ibid., 244.

7. See above, pp. 21-22.

8. Abbott, 116.

9. Parrella describes Vatican II as only beginning ecclesial reflection on the developing role of the laity in his "The Laity in the Church," 272-273.

10. Some of the repercussions of the ambiguity in the area of ecclesiology that is embedded in the Council's documents are described by Nicola Colaianni in "Criticism of the Second Vatican Council in Current Literature," in *The Ecumenical Council—Its Significance in the Constitution of the Church* (Edinburgh: T. & T. Clark, 1983): 106-110. Colaianni offers several examples here of passages and ideas that are used without reconciliation.

11. Thils, *L'Infallibilité du peuple chrétien*, 65.

12. Herwi Rikhof, *The Concept of Church: A Methodological Inquiry into the Use of Metaphors in Ecclesiology* (London: Sheed and Ward, 1981), 2. Rikhof introduces his use of the term "metaphor" on pp. 3-7.

13. Ibid., 3.

14. William P. Frost, "On Celebrating Newman's Faith in the Laity," *Horizons* 6 (1979): 260.

15. Ibid. Frost's references are to Femiano, 135-136.

16. Eduardo Molano, "Los Laicos en el Magisterio del Vaticano II," *Scripta Theologica* 17 (1985): 807-808.

17. Ibid., 810.

18. Patterson, *Pioneer*, 82. The quotes used here from *Lumen Gentium* are taken from Patterson.

19. Ibid., 82-83.

20. Joseph A. Komonchak, "Clergy, Laity, and the Church's Mission in the World," *The Jurist* 41 (1981): 427-428.

21. Ibid., 429-430.

22. Ibid., 430.

23. Also see Komonchak's reflections on the practical roles of clergy and laity, Ibid., 444-445.

24. Ibid., 446-447.

25. Alberigo, "Authority in Vatican I and Vatican II," 134.

26. Ibid.

27. Ibid.

28. Ibid., 135-137.

29. Peter Hebblethwaite, "Le discours de Jean XXIII à l'ouverture de Vatican II," *Recherches de science religieuse* 71 (1983): 203-212.

30. Alberigo, "Authority in Vatican I and Vatican II," 136.

31. Ibid., 137.

32. Ibid., 139.

33. Ibid., 141.

34. Granfield, "Catholic Faithful," 138.

35. Ibid., 138-139.

36. Ibid., 139.

37. Ibid., 140.

38. Jan Grootaers, "The Laity within the Ecclesial Communion," *Pro Mundi Vita*, Bulletin 106: 10.

39. Ibid.

40. Ibid., 12-34.

41. Ibid., 31.

42. Ibid., 32. This chapter contains section 35 cited above.

43. Ibid., 33. The phrase quoted is emphasized in Grootaers's text.

44. Ibid., 40.

45. George H. Tavard, "Is There a Catholic Ecclesiology?" *CTSA Proceedings* 29 (1974): 374-375.

46. Parrella, 265.

47. William M. Thompson, "Authority and magisterium in Recent Catholic Thought," *Chicago Studies* 16 (1977): 286-287.

48. Léon-Joseph Cardinal Suenens, *Coresponsibility in the Church* (New York: Herder and Herder, 1968), 29.

49. Ibid., 33.

50. Ibid.

51. Ibid., 204.

52. Ibid., 205.

53. Ibid., 206. Near to the time of Suenens's own reflections, Remi J. De Roo, Bishop of Victoria, British Columbia, wrote, "There is an intimate bond between the *sensus fidelium* and enlightened public opinion." See "Collegiality and the Petrine Office in the Pastoral Work of the Church," in *CTSA Proceedings* 25 (1970): 42. In a note De Roo adds that "Archbishop Amissah of Ghana suggested to the 1969 Synod that in certain cases the *sensus fidelium* and public opinion can be identified." See p. 42, n. 24. The diversity of views on the nature of the *sensus fidelium* even among those in the hierarchy will be considered below.

54. Suenens, 206. Suenens cites his own statements at the Council on the "charismatic dimension of the church," which he includes as an appendix to his book. In his intervention, he suggested that the Council invite practical witnesses to the charisms he discussed, in the persons of more auditors, including laity, and especially women, of whom he remarked "If I am not mistaken, they constitute half of humanity." He appealed also for the inclusion of religious brothers and sisters. Ibid., 218.

55. An interesting attempt to examine the theological implications of the inclusion of the laity in the mission of the Church, based in the teaching of Vatican II, is presented by Edward J. Kilmartin in "Lay Participation in the Apostolate of the Hierarchy," *The Jurist* 41 (1981): 343-370. Kilmartin gives attention to a "pneumatological" ecclesiology in pp. 362-366, and outlines the possibilities for a more wholistic, organic ecclesiology based in the "Image of the Trinity" in pp. 366-370.

56. Dulles, "Magisterium," 281.

57. Hellwig, 162.

58. See specifically Granfield, "Episcopal Elections," 52.

59. Eno, "Consensus and Doctrine," 474.

60. See for example, Congar, *Tradition and Traditions*, 315-320.

61. See the definitions of Granfield in "Catholic Faithful," 135-136.

62. Timiadis, "Consensus in Formulation," 178.

63. Markus, 288.

64. Walgrave, *Unfolding Revelation*, 92.

65. Kilmartin, "Reception in History," 38-39. See especially n. 11.

66. Walgrave, *Unfolding Revelation*, 129-130.

67. Congar, *Lay People*, 275.

68. A helpful summary of influential ecclesiologies both before and after the Council is given by Avery Dulles in "A Half Century of Ecclesiology,"

*Theological Studies* 50 (1989): 419-442. Dulles sees the Council as "the high point of Catholic ecclesiology" in that it brought the insights of decades of research together to challenge the Church to a deeper understanding of itself. He also asserts that much remains to be done after twenty-five years of post-conciliar ecclesiology. Dulles observes that the use of different "models" in the Final Report of the 1985 Extraordinary Synod "does not register any significant progress beyond Vatican II." Yet he adds, "The Extraordinary Synod made it clear that the favorite themes of particular schools can and must be harmonized in the interests of depth, completeness, and unity." Ibid., 442.

69. Edward Schillebeeckx, "Towards a Catholic Use of Hermeneutics," chap. in *God the Future of Man*, 1-49. (New York: Sheed and Ward, 1968).

70. Ibid., 44. An approach to hermeneutics that addresses the issue of infallibility in the light of Vatican I and Vatican II is offered by John J. Heaney in "Catholic Hermeneutics, the Magisterium, and Infallibility," *Continuum* 7 (1969): 106-119.

71. René Camilleri, *The 'Sensus Fidei' of the Whole Church and the Magisterium: From the Time of Vatican I to Vatican Council II*. (Rome: Pontificia Universitas Gregoriana, 1987). The text cited here is the published excerpt of a larger dissertation.

72. Ibid., 5.

73. Ibid.

74. O'Malley, *Tradition and Transition*, 55-56.

75. Ibid., 56-57.

76. The Reformation roots for the emergence of the larger field of modern hermeneutics are noted by Richard E. Palmer as he describes the evolution of issues that now characterize the study of interpretation in *Hermeneutics: Interpretation Theory in Schleiermacher, Dilthey, Heidegger, and Gadamer* (Evanston: Northwestern University Press, 1969). See especially pp. 34-45.

77. Tavard, "Tradition as Koinonia," 107-108.

78. Ibid., 108-109.

79. Ibid., 108.

80. Luis M. Fz. de Trocóniz y Sasigain, *"Sensus Fidei": Logica Connatural de la Existencia Cristiana* (Vitoria: Victoriensia, 1976), 110-122.

81. Heaney, "Catholic Hermeneutics," 111.

82. Piet F. Fransen, "Unity and Confessional Statements: Historical and Theological Inquiry of R.C. Traditional Conceptions," *Bijdragen* 33 (1972): 7-10.

83. Ibid., 7-8. Emphasis in original.

84. Ibid., 37.

85. Ibid., 10.

86. Tavard, "Post-Tridentine Theology," 403.

87. Ibid., 403-405.

88. Dulles, "Magisterium," 276.

89. See Costigan, especially 46-48.

90. Sanks, *Authority in the Church*, 57.

91. Thompson, *"Sensus Fidelium* and Infallibility," 469.

92. Camilleri, 93.

93. Ibid.

94. Sanks, *Authority in the Church*, 174-176.

95. Thiel, "Theological Responsibility," 591.

96. Nicholas Lash, *Change in Focus: A Study of Doctrinal Change and Continuity* (London: Sheed and Ward, 1973), 125.

97. Ibid., 125-126. Lash also observes that the same cultural elements also influence the Church's leaders.

98. O'Malley, *Tradition and Transition*, 88.

99. Ibid., 107.

100. Ibid., 123.

101. Ibid.

## CHAPTER 5

1. Congar, *Tradition and Traditions*, 314-338.

2. Ibid., 321.

3. Ibid., 317.

4. Ibid., 317-321.

5. Ibid., 326.

6. Ibid., 327.

7. Ibid.

8. The current discussion will continue to draw on the English translation, "Reception as an Ecclesiological Reality," cited above.

9. Ibid., 44-45.

10. Ibid.

11. Ibid. Congar cites *Lumen Gentium* (# 22) and *Christus Dominus* (# 4).

12. Congar, "Reception," 46-49.

13. Ibid., 49.

14. Ibid., 54.

15. Ibid., 54-58.

16. Ibid., 58-60.

17. Ibid., 61.

18. Ibid.

19. Ibid., 62.

20. Ibid., 64.

21. Ibid., 64-65.

22. Ibid., 66.

23. Ibid., 68.

24. Yves Congar, "Toward a Catholic Synthesis," in *Who Has the Say in the Church?* 68-80. Edited by Juergen Moltmann and Hans Kueng. (Edinburgh: T. & T. Clark, 1981).

25. Ibid., 71. The entire quote is emphasized in Congar's text.

26. Ibid., 72.

27. Ibid., 74-75.

28. Ibid., 74. Congar here refers to tests conducted by J. P. Deconchy. The reference (n. 24) is completely omitted from the end notes of the article cited here. The text referred to is likely that of Jean-Pierre Deconchy, *L'Orthodoxie religieuse: Essai de Logique psycho-sociale* (Paris: Les Editions Ouvrieres, 1971).

29. Yves Congar, "Magisterium, Theologians, The Faithful and the Faith," *Doctrine and Life* 31 (1981): 556-557.

30. Ibid., 556.

31. Ibid.

32. Ibid., 557.

33. Ibid.

34. Congar, "Catholic Synthesis," 78.

35. Coulson, "Introduction," 47.

36. Ibid., 47-49.

37. Quoted by Coulson from the Commission's Agreed Statement on *Authority in the Church*, in John Coulson, "Authority and the Revival of Theology," *The Downside Review* 95 (1977): 235. The emphasis is Coulson's.

38. John Coulson, *Newman and the Common Tradition: A Study in the Language of Church and Society* (Oxford: Clarendon Press, 1970), 129-130.

39. Guitton, *The Church and the Laity*, cited above.

40. Ibid., 32-33.

41. Ibid., 34.

42. Ibid.

43. Ibid., 34-35. Emphasis is Guitton's.

44. Guenter Biemer, *Ueberlieferung und Offenbarung. Die Lehre von der Tradition nach John Henry Newman* (Freiburg: Herder, 1961). Volume IV of *Die Ueberlieferung in der neuren Theologie*, edited by J. R. Geiselmann. Reference here will be to the revised English version, *Newman on Tradition* (Montreal: Palm Publishers, 1967).

45. Ibid., 113-114.

46. Ibid., 114.

47. Ibid., 111.

48. Ibid., 111-112.

49. Ibid., 112.

50. Ibid., 116-117.

51. Femiano, *The Infallibility of the Laity*, as cited above.

52. Ibid., 134-135.

53. Ibid., 135-136.

54. Ibid., 137.

55. Ibid.

56. In Patterson, Newman *Pioneer for the Layman*, cited above.

57. Ibid., 153.

58. Ibid., 153-154.

59. Ibid., 155.

60. Ibid., 155-158.

61. Ibid., 158.

62. Ibid., 159-162.

63. Ibid., 163.

64. Ibid., 164-167.

65. Ibid., 176.

66. Ibid., 178-179.

67. Ibid., 179.

68. Ibid., 180.

69. Webster Patterson, "Apologetics, Newman and the Teaching Church," in *Theology Confronts a Changing World*, 95-114. Edited by Thomas M. McFadden. (West Mystic, Conn.: Twenty-Third Publications, 1977).

70. Ibid., 101.

71. Ibid., 99-100.

72. Ibid., 102. Also see p. 113, n. 8.

73. Ibid., 102-103.

74. Ibid., 103.

75. Ibid., 105.

76. Ibid., 110. Here Patterson draws specifically on the ecclesiology of Thomas Aquinas.

77. Ibid., 110-112.

78. Ibid., 112.

79. Penaskovic, *Open to the Spirit*, 9.

80. Ibid., 210-214.

81. Ibid., 212-214.

82. Ibid., 214.

83. Ibid., 214-215.

84. Ibid., 191, n. 1. Penaskovic cites here the article of Beinert, "Bedeutung und Begruendung," to be discussed below.

85. Penaskovic, *Open to the Spirit*, 191, n. 1.

86. Ibid., 217.

87. Ibid., 252.

88. Ibid., 253.

89. Ibid., 254-255.

90. Ibid., 255.

91. Ibid.

92. Ibid., 255-256.

93. Ibid., 256.

94. Ibid., 256-257.

95. Ibid., 256.

96. Ibid., 257.

97. Richard Penaskovic, "Theology and Authority: The Theological Issues," in *Theology and Authority*, edited by Richard Penaskovic. (Peabody, Mass.: Hendrickson Publishers, 1987), 119.

98. Ibid., 118-120.

99. Ibid., 120.

100. Ibid., 121.

101. Ibid., 121-122.

102. Ibid., 122. For this last point, Penaskovic draws on F. Wolfinger, "Die Reception Theologischer Einsichten und Ihre Theologische und Oekumenische Bedeutung: Von der Einsicht zur Verwirklichung," *Catholica* 31 (1977): 204.

103. Penaskovic, "Theology and Authority," 122.

104. Ibid., 124.

105. Ibid.

106. Ibid. 124-125.

107. Ibid., 125-126.

108. Ibid., 127.

109. Ibid., 128.

110. The remarks made here are in reference to an unpublished manuscript; Denis W. Read, "How to Know the Faith: A Study of the Sensus Fidei in the Roman Catholic Church according to John Henry Cardinal Newman."

The manuscript obtained from the author at St. Florian's Monastery and Parish, West Milwaukee, Wisc.: n.d., is based on his dissertation, *Sensus Fidei: Practical Faith-Knowledge in Moral Theology* (Rome: 1968).

111. These points are made in Read's manuscript in the final section, "Conclusion IV: Faith-Knowledge of Charity Determines the Methodology of Moral Theological Elaboration." The section contains no page numbers.

112. Trocóniz y Sasigain, *"Sensus Fidei": Logica Connatural de la Existencia Cristiana*, cited above.

113. Ibid., 26-27.

114. Ibid., 108.

115. Ibid., 109.

116. Ibid., 110.

117. Ibid., 110-122.

118. John T. Ford, "Newman on '*Sensus Fidelium*' and Mariology," *Marian Studies* 28 (1977): 121.

119. Ibid., 122.

120. Ibid., 124.

121. Ibid., 133.

122. Ibid., 135.

123. Ibid.

124. Ibid., 135-137.

125. Ibid., 136. Ford quotes from Nicholas Lash, *Newman on Development* (Shephardstown, W. Va.: 1975), 22-23.

126. Ibid., 137-138.

127. Ibid., 138. Here Ford quotes Lash, *Newman on Development*, 17-19. See also p. 136, n. 61 in Ford's text.

128. Ford, "'*Sensus Fidelium*' and Mariology," 138-140.

129. John T. Ford, "'Dancing on the Tightrope': Newman's View of Theology," *CTSA Proceedings* 40 (1985): 140.

130. Ibid., 143. Ford's views on interpretation of doctrine as requiring reconceptualization are extended to the related issue of infallibility in his historical study, "Infallibility—From Vatican I to the Present," cited earlier.

131. Ford, "Newman's View," 142-143.

132. Ford, "*Sensus Fidelium* and Mariology," 143-144. Ford's article was initially presented as a lecture. In a question session which followed, the point was expressed by Alban Maguire, that "Newman's teaching of the *sensus fidelium* was closely intertwined with the idea of the Church as mystery." Maguire suggests that to deal with the problem of interpretation connected to Newman's treatment, which was "mixed up in a polemic on the relationship of the laity to the hierarchy," a better understanding of the *sensus fidelium* might be found by examining it through the medieval focus on the *sensus fidei*. Maguire suggests this would connect it more directly to the "sense of the Church as Mystery." See Alban A. Maguire, "Observations on Fr. Ford's Lecture," *Marian Studies* 28 (1977): 146-147.

133. Ford, "*Sensus Fidelium* and Mariology," 144.

134. Ibid.

135. Ibid., 144-145.

136. Ibid., 145.

137. Eno, "Consensus and Doctrine," 473-481.

138. Ibid., 481.

139. Ibid., 482.

140. Ibid., 483.

141. Eno, "Authority and Conflict," 59-60.

142. Eno, "Shared Responsibility," 140-141.

143. Ibid., 141.

144. Ibid., 136-141. In addition to the works cited here, a valuable summary of the development of authority in the early Church, as well as a useful collection of patristic texts pertaining to authority is available in Robert B. Eno, *Teaching Authority in the Early Church* (Wilmington, Del.: Michael Glazier, 1984).

145. See above, 111-112, 113-117.

146. King., 263-264.

147. Ibid., 264.

148. Ibid.

149. Ibid.

150. Ibid., 265.

151. Ibid.

152. Geiselmann, for instance, draws on Koster's *Volk Gottes im Wachstum des Glaubes* (1950) in *The Meaning of Tradition* (1966, original German edition, 1962). See "Tradition in Christianity," in Geiselmann, 9-38. Herbert Hammans, however, claims that Koster "makes his sources say may more than they contain," in "Recent Catholic Views on the Development of Dogma," in *Man as Man & Believer*, 125-126. Edited by Edward Schillebeeckx and Boniface Willems (New York: Paulist Press, 1966). Kevin McNamara describes Koster's introduction of the phrase "People of God' in his *Ekklesiologie im Werden* (1940), as a better ecclesial image than Moehler's "mystical body." See McNamara, 18-19.

153. See Koster, "Der Glaubenssinn der Hirten und Glauebigen," 131-150, as cited above. Citations here continue to be from this most recent printing.

154. Ibid. , 131-132.

155. Ibid., 132-133.

156. Ibid., 133.

157. Ibid., 134.

158. Ibid., 135.

159. Ibid., 135-136.

160. Ibid., 137.

161. Ibid., 137-138.

162. Ibid., 139.

163. Ibid., 141.

164. Ibid., 142.

165. Ibid., 142-143.

166. Ibid., 143-144.

167. Ibid., 144-145.

168. Ibid., 146.

169. Ibid., 147.

170. Ibid., 147-148.

171. Ibid., 149.

172. Ibid.

173. Ibid., 149-150.

174. Ibid., 150.

175. Michael Schmaus, *Katholische Dogmatik*. 5 volumes, bound in seven. (Munich: Hueber, 1948-1963.) Schmaus discusses the topic under the

minor heading "Die muendliche Ueberlieferung," in the section "Die heilshaften Funktionen der Kirche im einzelnen," (section 176b) in Volume III, part 1, *Die Lehre von der Kirche* (1958), 758-776.

176. Ibid., 772.

177. Ibid., 773.

178. Ibid., 774.

179. Michael Schmaus, "Eine Anmerkung zum Problem der Demokratisierung im Bereich der kirchlichen Lehrunfehlbarkeit," in *Kirche im Wachstum des Glaubens: Festgabe Mannes Dominikus Koster zum siebzigsten Geburtstag*, 255-265. Edited by Otto Hermann Pesch and Hans-Dieter Langer. (Freiburg: Paulusverlag Freiburg Schweiz, 1971). This volume appeared as *Freiburger Zeitschrift Fuer Philosophie und Theologie* 18 (1971).

180. See especially, Ibid., 263-265.

181. Michael Schmaus, *The Church: its Origin and Structure*, Volume IV in *Dogma*. (Sheed & Ward, 1972). Reprinted, (Westminster, Md.: Christian Classics, 1984). See especially the chapter, "The Laity," 120-131.

182. Ibid., 127.

183. Ibid., 206.

184. Ibid., 207-208.

185. Ibid., 210.

186. Ibid., 211-212.

187. Magnus Loehrer, "Glaubenssinn und Glaubenskonsens," in *Mysterium Salutis: Grundriss Heilsgeschichtlicher Dogmatik*. Vol. 1, 551-555. Edited by Johannes Feiner and Magnus Loehrer. (Einsiedeln: Benziger, 1965). Reference here will be to the French edition, "Sens de la foi et consensus de la foi," in *Mysterium Salutis: Dogmatique de l'histoire du Salut*. Vol. 3, 86-91. Edited by A. Darlap and H. Fries. (Paris: Les Éditions du Cerf, 1969.)

188. Ibid., 87.

189. Ibid., 87-88.

190. Ibid., 88.

191. Ibid., 89.

192. Ibid., 90-91.

193. Beinert, "Bedeutung und Begruendung des Glaubenssinnes (Sensus Fidei) als eines Dogmatischen Erkenntnis-Kriteriums," cited above.

194. Ibid., 271-272.

195. Ibid., 272.

196. Ibid.

197. Ibid., 272-288. His treatment has been cited above in reference to some historical figures.

198. Ibid. 287. Beinert cites Rahner, *Schriften zur Theologie* Vol. VII, (Einsiedeln-Zuerich-Koeln: 1967), 115.

199. Beinert, "Bedeutung und Begruendung," 287.

200. Ibid., 288.

201. Ibid.

202. Ibid.

203. Ibid., 288-289.

204. Ibid., 289.

205. Ibid.

206. Ibid., 289-290.

207. Ibid., 291.

208. Ibid., 291-292.

209. Ibid., 292-293.

210. Ibid., 294.

211. Ibid., 295.

212. Ibid., 296.

213. Ibid.

214. Ibid., 296-297.

215. Ibid., 297.

216. Ibid., 298.

217. Ibid., 298-299.

218. Wolfgang Beinert, "What Value Does the Laity Have in the Church?" *Theology Digest* 35 (1988): 39-44. Digested from "Was gilt der Laie in der Kirche?" *Stimmen der Zeit* 112 (1987): 363-378. Reference here will be to the English text.

219. Ibid., 43-44.

220. Ibid., 44.

221. Beinert, "Bedeutung und Begruendung," 300.

222. Ibid.

223. Ibid.

224. Ibid., 300-301. Beinert develops aspects of the *sensus fidelium* similar to those presented here in a discussion of the interrelationship of the sources of tradition in an ecumenical context in "Das Finden und Verkuenden der Wahrheit in der Gemeinshaft der Kirche," *Catholica* 43 (1989): 1-30. See especially pp. 22-24.

225. Beinert, "Bedeutung und Begruendung," 301-302.

226. Wolfgang Beinert, "Theologie - Tradition - Kirchliches Lehramt," *Catholica* 38 (1984): 185-198.

227. Ibid., 1904

228. Ibid.

229. Ibid.

230. Ibid., 191.

231. Ibid.

232. Ibid., 192-193.

233. Ibid., 193. Emphasis in original. Beinert cites here, B. Haegglund, "Die Bedeutung der 'regula fidei' als Grundlage theologischer Aussagen," *Studia Theologica* 12 (1958): 1-4.

234. Ibid., 194-195.

235. Ibid., 195.

236. Ibid., 197.

237. Ibid.

238. Ibid., 198.

239. Patrick Granfield. "Ecclesial Cybernetics: Communication in the Church," *Theological Studies* 29 (1968): 662-678. Granfield later expanded his study into *Ecclesial Cybernetics: A Systems Analysis of Authority and Decision-Making in the Catholic Church, with a Plea for Shared Responsibility* (New York: Macmillan, 1973).

240. Granfield, "Ecclesial Cybernetics," 663-667.

241. Ibid., 668-671.

242. Ibid., 673-675.

243. Ibid., 675-677. In *Ecclesial Cybernetics*, Granfield develops many of the points of his earlier article in greater detail. One interesting addition is included where he discusses the area of practical implementation. He makes special mention of the importance of a "creative minority" in seeding new insights during the process of development of theological understanding in the Church. See 238-242.

244. Granfield, "Ecclesial Cybernetics," 678.

245. In addition to the historical articles cited here, the chapter, "The Historical Development of Ecclesial Democracy," in *Ecclesial Cybernetics*, 139-170, gives a useful overview of key historical events and developments that pertain to the issue of democracy.

246. Granfield, "Concilium and Consensus," 398-403.

247. Ibid., 404-408.

248. Ibid., 405.

249. Ibid., 405-406.

250. Ibid., 406.

251. Ibid., 407.

252. Ibid., 408.

253. Ibid.

254. Granfield, "Episcopal Elections," 41-51.

255. Ibid., 52.

256. Ibid.

257. Ibid.

258. Ibid.

259. Patrick Granfield, "The *Sensus Fidelium* in Episcopal Selection," in *Electing Our Own Bishops*, 33.

260. Ibid., 33-34.

261. Ibid., 34.

262. Ibid., 35.

263. Ibid., 36.

264. Ibid.

265. Ibid., 37.

266. Ibid.

267. Patrick Granfield, "The Local Church as a Center of Communication and Control," *CTSA Proceedings* 35 (1980): 256-263.

268. See especially, Ibid., 261-262.

269. Patrick Granfield, "Presidential Address: The Uncertain Future of Collegiality," *CTSA Proceedings* 40 (1985): 100.

270. Ibid., 102-103.

271. Ibid., 103-104.

272. Ibid., 104.

273. Ibid., 104-105.

274. Granfield, "Catholic Faithful," 134-168.

275. Ibid., 140-141.

276. Ibid., 141.

277. Ibid., 142.

278. Ibid., 143.

279. Ibid.

280. Ibid., 143-144.

281. Ibid., 147.

282. Ibid., 147-152.

283. Ibid., 150. Dulles is quoted from *Teaching Authority and Infallibility in the Church: Lutherans and Catholics in Dialogue VI* Edited by Paul C. Empie, T. Austin Murphy and Joseph A. Burgess. (Minneapolis: Augsburg, 1978), 89. Ratzinger is quoted from *Das neue Volk Gottes* (Duesseldorf: Patmos, 1969), 144.

284. Granfield, "Catholic Faithful," 151.

285. Ibid., 152.

286. Ibid., 153-154.

287. Ibid., 158-167.

288. Sesboüé, "Autorité du magistère et vie de foi ecclésiale," cited above.

289. Ibid., 337.

290. Ibid., 338.

291. Ibid.

292. Ibid., 339.

293. Ibid., 340.

294. Ibid., 341-343.

295. Ibid., 344.

296. Ibid.

297. Ibid., 345.

298. Ibid., 345-347.

299. Ibid., 347.

300. Ibid., 347. Emphasis in original.

301. Ibid., 349. Emphasis in original.

302. Ibid.

303. Ibid., 351-353.

304. Ibid., 353-355.

305. Ibid., 355-356.

306. Ibid., 356.

307. Ibid., 357.

308. Ibid., 358.

309. Ibid., 358-359.

310. Ibid., 360-362.

311. Ibid., 360-361.

312. Ibid., 361.

313. Ibid.

314. Ibid.

315. Ibid., 362.

316. Ibid.

317. See Thompson's own summary of these historical views, "*Sensus Fidelium* and Infallibility," 466-467.

318. Ibid., 467-472.

319. Ibid., 471.

320. Ibid., 471-472.

321. See Ibid., 475, 480-483.

322. Ibid., 482-483.

323. Ibid., 484.

324. Ibid.

325. Ibid.

326. Ibid., 485-486.

327. Ibid., 486. Emphasis in original.

328. Ibid. Emphasis in original.

329. See William M. Thompson, *Fire and Light: The Saints and Theology: On Consulting the Saints, Mystics and Martyrs in Theology* (New York: Paulist Press, 1987). In the final chapter, "Consulting 'Everyday' Mystics," 178-198, he again suggests attention to Rahner's approach to knowledge.

330. Donald C. Maldari notes the importance of the concept in what has been another important interest in Tillard's writings, the theology of the religious life, in "The Identity of Religious Life: The Contributions of Jean-Marie Tillard Critically Examined," *Louvain Studies* 14 (1989): 325-326. Tillard has also spent a great deal of time in ecumenical work. In an article that examines the nature of the Church in an effort at better ecumenical relations, Tillard draws heavily on the early notion of *koinonia* and cites the *sensus fidelium* as one of the elements that serves the building up of the community. See "Church and Salvation: on the Sacramentality of the Church," *One in Christ* 20 (1984): 306-311. See especially 310-311.

331. Tillard edited the volume, *Foi populaire, foi savante* (1976), that includes the papers from the conference, some of which have been considered in several other places throughout the present work. His own address has been published in several places, as noted above. Reference here will be to the English translation, cited above as "*Sensus Fidelium.*"

332. Ibid., 2.

333. Ibid., 2-3.

334. Ibid., 4.

335. Ibid., 4-5.

336. Ibid., 5.

337. Ibid.

338. Ibid., 5-7. Emphasis in original.

339. Ibid., 7.

340. Ibid.

341. Ibid., 9.

342. Ibid., 9-10.

343. Ibid., 10.

344. Ibid., 11.

345. Ibid., 11-16.

346. Ibid., 16.

347. Ibid., 16-17.

348. Ibid., 17.

349. Ibid., 17-18.

350. Ibid., 19.

351. Ibid., 19-20.

352. Ibid., 20-21.

353. Ibid., 21-22.

354. Ibid., 22.

355. Ibid., 24-25. Tillard draws here on Congar's treatment of Blondel. See *Tradition and Traditions*, 359-368.

356. Tillard, "Sensus Fidelium," 25.

357. Ibid.

358. Ibid., 26.

359. Ibid., 26-27.

360. Ibid., 27.

361. Ibid.

362. Ibid.

363. Ibid., 27-28.

364. Ibid., 28.

365. Ibid., 28-29.

366. J. M. R. Tillard, "Autorité et mémoire dans l'Église," (part 1) *Irénikon* 61 (1988): 339.

367. See J. M. R. Tillard, "Autorité et mémoire dans l'Église," (part 2) *Irénikon* 61 (1988): 484.

368. Tillard, "Sensus Fidelium," 29.

369. J. M. R. Tillard, "'Reception': A Time to Beware of False Steps," *Ecumenical Trends* 14 (1985): 145.

370. Ibid., 145-146.

371. J. M. R. Tillard, *The Bishop of Rome* (Wilmington, Del.: Michael Glazier, 1983), 177.

372. Ibid. Tillard recalls that this notion is taught in *Mysterium Ecclesiae*.

373. J. M. R. Tillard, in "Theological Pluralism and the Mystery of the Church," 62-73, cited above.

374. Ibid., 62. Here he cites Congar's *Diversités et communion* (Paris: 1982).

375. Ibid., 63.

376. Ibid., 63-65.

377. Ibid., 65.

378. Ibid., 66.

379. Ibid., 67.

380. Ibid.

381. Ibid., 67-68.

382. Ibid., 68.

383. Ibid., 71-72.

384. Ibid., 71.

385. Ibid.

386. Emilien Lamirande, "La théologie du 'sensus fidelium' et la collaboration de l'historien," in *Foi populaire, foi savante*, 67-72.

387. Ibid., 69.

388. Ibid.

389. Ibid., 70.

390. Ibid., 71.

391. Ibid., 71-72.

392. Fernand Dumont, "Remarques critiques pour une théologie du 'consensus fidelium,'" in *Foi populaire, foi savante*, pp. 49-60.

393. Ibid., 49-50.

394. Ibid., 50-51.

395. Ibid., 51.

396. Ibid., 52.

397. Ibid.

398. Ibid.

399. Ibid., 52-53.

400. Ibid., 53.

401. Ibid., 53-54.

402. Ibid., 54.

403. Ibid.

404. Ibid., 55.

405. Ibid., 55-56.

406. Ibid., 57.

407. Ibid.

408. Ibid.

409. Ibid., 57-58.

410. Ibid., 58.

411. Ibid.

412. Ibid.

413. Ibid., 59.

414. Ibid.

415. Ibid., 59-60.

416. Hitchcock, 153.

417. Ibid., 152.

418. Ibid., 153.

419. Ibid., 153-154.

420. Ibid., 154.

421. Jose Morales, "Nota Historico-Doctrinal sobre las Relaciones entre Magisterio Eclesiastico, Oficio Teologico, y Sentido Popular de la Fe," *Scripta Theologica* 2 (1970): 481-499.

422. Ibid., 494.

423. See Ibid., 481-482, 486-488. Morales's interest in this article is actually more focused on the history and role of theologians than on the role of the sense of the faith as found distinctly in the laity. See 487-494, and 498-499. In his description of the functions of the various "levels" in the Church, the magisterium is described as the "active" source of doctrinal expression. See 481-482.

424. Ibid., 495.

425. See for instance, Ibid., 496.

426. Ibid., 497-498. See n. 68.

427. Ibid., 499.

428. Sancho, *Infalibilidad*, 14-16.

429. Ibid., 35-37.

430. Ibid., 52-53.

431. Ibid., 77.

432. Ibid., 86-87.

433. Ibid., 178-180.

434. Ibid., 184-185.

435. Ibid., 188.

436. Ibid., 257-263.

437. Ibid., 262.

438. Ibid.

439. Ibid., 263.

440. Ibid.

441. Ibid., 264-269.

442. Ibid., 264.

443. Ibid.

444. In his concluding chapter Sancho takes up the theme "The Organic Infallibility of the Church." Ibid., 271-284.

445. Neither the topical nor author indexes of Sancho's text carry listings for Newman or the Arian crisis. See his discussion on pp. 266-267, however, where he lists such standard examples in which "the magisterium intervened verifying and ratifying" what was held by the faithful. (p. 267.)

446. Ibid., 285.

447. Jesús Sancho, "*Sensus Fidei* e Interpretacion de la Ley Natural," in *Etica Y Teologia ante la Crisis Contemporanea.* Edited J. L. Illanes, et. al. (Pamplona: Ediciones Universidad de Navarra, S.A., 1980), 359.

448. Ibid., 359-360.

449. Ibid., 360-361. In support of this link between the *sensus fidei* and the magisterium, Sancho cites two speeches by Pope Paul VI, one of January 6, 1969 at the ordination of twelve bishops and one of April 16, 1969 at a Wednesday audience.

450. Ibid., 362.

451. Ibid., 364-366.

452. Ibid., 366.

453. Ibid., 367.

454. Jesus Sancho, "El *Sensus Fidei* en los Laicos," in *La Mision del Laico en la Iglesia y en el Mundo* Edited by Augusto Sarmiento, et. al. (Pamplona: Ediciones Universidad de Navarra, S.A., 1987), 545-551.

455. Ibid., 546.

456. Ibid., 547.

457. Ibid., 548.

458. Ibid., 548-549.

459. Ibid., 549-551.

460. Ibid., 550-551.

461. Ibid., 551.

462. Sartori, "What is the Criterion," 56.

463. Ibid.

464. Ibid.

465. Ibid., 57. In a later article, Sartori develops this point, as he argues that in the recognition of reception in doctrinal development, the active role of the laity is appropriated and the *sensus fidelium* is given its proper place. "Il 'Sensus Fidelium' del Popolo di Dio e il Concorso dei Laici nelle Determinzioni Dottrinali," *Studi Ecumenici* 6 (1988): 33-57.

466. Sartori, "What is the Criterion," 57.

467. Ibid., 57-58.

468. Ibid.

469. Ibid., 58-59.

470. Ibid., 59.

471. Ibid.

472. Ibid.

473. Swidler, "Dēmo-kratía," 226.

474. Ibid., 227.

475. Ibid., 228.

476. Ibid.

477. Ibid., 228-229.

478. Ibid., 228. Swidler here cites Hans Kueng, *The Church*, 72.

479. Swidler, "Dēmo-kratía," 228.

480. Ibid., 229.

481. Ibid.

482. Ibid., 230.

483. Ibid., 230-233.

484. Ibid., 233.

485. Ibid., 233-235.

486. Ibid., 235.

487. Ibid.

488. Ibid., 236. The quote is from Norbert Greinacher, "Der Vollzug der Kirche im Bistum," in *Handbuch der Pastoral-theologie* III (Freiburg: Herder, 1968), 106-107.

489. Swidler, "*Dēmo-kratía*," 236.

490. Ibid.

491. Ibid., 237. Swidler has argued in more popularly assessable contexts for the legitimacy of responsible dissent. See, for instance, Leonard Swidler, "Dissent an Honored Part of Church's Vocation," *National Catholic Reporter*, 22 September 1989, 14-15. Here Swidler asserts, "There can be no such thing as *con*sensus without the possibility of *dis*sensus." (p. 14. Emphasis in original.) Swidler also argued in favor of the resolution "Catholics Have a Right to Responsible Dissent to Non-Infallible Church Teaching" in a debate with James Hitchcock at Saint Louis University, on October 30, 1986.

492. Swidler, "*Dēmo-kratía*," 237.

493. Ibid., 238-239.

494. Ibid., 239.

495. Ibid.

496. Ibid. It is interesting to compare the emphasis here with that of an earlier article of Swidler's, where in a discussion of infallibility, he argues for situating Church teachings in their historical, cultural contexts. See Leonard Swidler, "*The* Ecumenical Problem Today: Papal Infallibility," *Journal of Ecumenical Studies* 8 (1971): 751-767. Here he stresses the renewed Roman Catholic focus on Scripture, on tradition "as the historicity of all aspects of man's life, including his thought, theology and religion," and "the absolute need of making religion speak effectively to the problems of the day." (p. 763.) Swidler is very concerned to develop a method as a way of affirming both discontinuity and continuity in the Church's understanding and expressions, and as a way to build a better ecumenical consensus. This continuing interest in finding consensus among diverse faiths is illustrated in the Winter 1980 edition of *Journal of Ecumenical Studies* 17 (# 1), where Swidler's article, "Dialogue: The Way toward Consensus," (iii-viii) introduces articles by Roman Catholic, Protestant, Orthodox, Jewish, Muslim, and Hindu authors.

497. Swidler, "Dēmo-kratía," 240-241.

498. Ibid., 241.

499. Ibid., 242.

500. Ibid., 242-243.

501. Ibid., 243.

502. Heinrich Fries, "Ex sese, non ex consensu ecclesiae," in *Volk Gottes: Zum Kirchenverstaendnis der Katholischen, Evangelischen und Anglikanischen Theologie. Festgabe fuer Josef Hoefer*, 480-500. Edited by Remigius Baeumer and Heimo Dolch. (Freiburg: Herder, 1967).

503. See especially Ibid., 495-496.

504. In Fries, "Is There a *Magisterium* of the Faithful?" cited above.

505. Ibid., 83-84. In his systematic approach to the sense of the faithful, Fries draws on the views of Seckler, "Glaubenssinn," 945.

506. Fries, "Is There a *Magisterium*?" 84.

507. Ibid., 84-85.

508. Ibid., 85.

509. Ibid., 86.

510. Ibid., 86-89.

511. Ibid., 89.

512. Ibid.

513. Ibid., 90.

514. Ibid. Quoted by Fries from *Lumen Gentium* (# 37).

515. Fries, "Is There a *Magisterium*?" 90.

516. Heinrich Fries, "Sensus Fidelium. Der Theologe Zwischen dem Lehramt der Hierarchie und dem Lehramt der Glaeubigen," in *Theologe und Hierarch*, 55-77. Magnus Loehrer, et. al. (Zurich: Benziger, 1988). Volume 17 of *Theologische Berichte*.

517. Fries, "Sensus Fidelium. Der Theologe," 61. (See 55-61 for Fries's historical illustrations.)

518. Ibid., 69-70.

519. Ibid., 69.

520. Ibid., 70.

521. Ibid.

522. Ibid., 71. Emphasis in original.

523. Ibid., 70.

524. Ibid., 71. The phrase quoted is emphasized in Fries's text.

525. Ibid.

526. Ibid., 72.

527. Ibid., 72-73.

528. Ibid., 73.

529. Ibid., 73-74.

530. Ibid., 74.

531. Ibid., 74-75.

532. Ibid., 75. Emphasis in original. Fries here cites Leonardo Boff, *Kirche: Charisma und Macht. Studien zu einer streitbaren Ekklesiologie* (Duesseldorf: 1985): 242-250. The English translation, *Church: Charism & Power*, has been cited in the present work.

533. Fries, "Sensus Fidelium. Der Theologe," 76. Fries cites *Lumen Gentium* (# 12 and # 25) as well as Vatican I's statement on infallibility (DS 3074).

534. Ibid.

535. Ibid., 76-77.

536. Ibid., 77.

537. Ibid.

538. Ibid., 77. Fries cites P. Neuner, *Der Laie und das Gottesvolk* (Frankfurt: 1988), 217f.

539. Vorgrimler, "From *Sensus Fidelium* to *Consensus Fidelium*," 3.

540. Ibid., 4.

541. Ibid., 4-5.

542. Ibid., 5.

543. Ibid., 6.

544. Ibid.

545. Ibid.

546. Ibid., 6-7.

547. Ibid., 7.

548. Ibid. Vorgrimler cites Rahner's "Heresies in the Church Today?" *Theological Investigations* 12 (London: 1974).

549. Vorgrimler, 7.

550. Ibid., 8.

551. Ibid.

552. Ibid., 8-9.

553. Ibid., 9-10.

554. Ibid., 10.

555. J.-H. Walgrave, *Newman the Theologian* (New York: Sheed & Ward, 1960), 179-196. See especially p. 185. It is worth noting too, that on p. 191 Walgrave describes Newman's view of the "infallible instinct" of the people as "mainly negative" and "far from being 'progressive.'" Rather, it is characterized as "ultraconservative, and quite unsuited to the creation of formularies hitherto unknown."

556. Walgrave, "Newman's 'On Consulting,'" 24.

557. Ibid., 25.

558. Ibid., 26.

559. Ibid., 27-28.

560. Ibid., 28.

561. Ibid.

562. Ibid., 28-29.

563. Ibid., 29.

564. Ibid.

565. Ibid.

566. Dulles, "*Sensus Fidelium*," 240.

567. Ibid., 240-241.

568. Ibid., 241.

569. Ibid.

570. Ibid., 241-242.

571. Ibid., 242.

572. Ibid.

573. Ibid. In a later article on Newman's view of infallibility, Dulles developed this point, saying that Newman "used the *sensus fidelium* not to offset the infallibility of the magisterium in teaching and defining, but rather to confirm the teaching of the magisterium when the latter is not uncontestably infallible." See Dulles, "Newman on Infallibility," 447. Dulles adds that even if Newman would accept the view that a lack of reception might cast doubt on a proposed "infallible" teaching, "he never suggested that the views of the faithful had infallible normative value apart from, or in opposition to, the teaching of the hierarchy." Ibid., 447-448.

574. Dulles, "*Sensus Fidelium*," 242, 263.

575. Ibid., 263. The quote is from *Lumen Gentium* (# 25).

576. Dulles, "*Sensus Fidelium*," 263.

577. Avery Dulles, "The Teaching Mission of the Church and Academic Freedom," *America* 162 (1990): 399.

578. Ibid.

579. See Avery Dulles, "Authority & Conscience: Two Needed Voices in the Church," *Church* 2 (# 3) (Fall, 1986): 10-11.

580. Ibid., 12-13. Dulles cites Orsy's "Reflections on the Text of a Canon," *America* May 17, 1986, pp. 396-399.

581. Dulles, "Authority and Conscience," 14.

582. Ibid., 14-15.

583. Ibid., 15. Dulles cites McCormick's "Notes on Moral Theology," *Theological Studies* 30 (1969): 652.

584. Dulles, "Authority and Conscience," 15.

585. Dulles, "*Sensus Fidelium*," 263.

586. Avery Dulles, "*Successio apostolorum—Successio prophetarum—Successio doctorum*," in *Who Has the Say in the Church?* 61-67.

587. Ibid., 62.

588. Ibid., 64.

589. See for instance, Dulles, "*Sensus Fidelium*," 263.

590. Avery Dulles, "Vatican II and the Purpose of the Church," in *The Reshaping of Catholicism: Current Challenges in the Theology of Church* (San Francisco: Harper & Row, 1988), 260, n. 24. (See also page 148.) Dulles cites here Dennis P. McCann, who suggests that the *sensus fidelium* be considered in regard to "birth control, abortion, divorce, sexual ethics in general, and the role of women in the church in particular." In *New Experiment in Democracy: The Challenge for American Catholicism* (Kansas City, Mo.: Sheed & Ward, 1987), 119-120.

591. Dulles, "*Successio apostolorum*," 66-67.

592. Ibid., 67. The portion quoted is emphasized in Dulles's text.

593. Avery Dulles, *The Survival of Dogma* (Garden City, N.Y.: Image Books, 1973), 108.

594. Ibid., 108-109.

595. Gerald O'Collins, "On Consulting the Faithful," *The Furrow* 37 (1986): 279-284.

596. Ibid., 279.

597. Ibid.

598. Ibid., 280.

599. Ibid.

600. Gerald O'Collins, *The Case Against Dogma* (New York: Paulist, 1975), 50.

601. Ibid. Some positive uses of dogma are discussed on pp. 52-54.

602. Ibid., 78. O'Collins is writing here specifically about conciliar statements.

603. Ibid., 78-85. The problems that O'Collins sees as inherent in dogmatic statements are further discussed in his last chapter, "The End of 'Dogma'?" 86-100.

604. O'Collins, "On Consulting the Faithful," 281.

605. Ibid., 282.

606. Ibid.

607. Ibid., 283.

608. Ibid.

609. Ibid., 283-284.

610. Ibid.

611. Gerald O'Collins, "Criteria for Interpreting the Traditions," in *Problems and Perspectives of Fundamental Theology* Edited by René Latourelle and Gerald O'Collins. (New York: Paulist Press, 1982), 327-339. See especially 333-334.

612. Ibid., 334.

613. See Ibid., 328-338 for O'Collins's extended discussion of these criteria.

614. James L. Heft, "Papal Infallibility and the Marian Dogmas: An Introduction," *One in Christ* 18 (1982): 309-340.

615. Ibid., 310-317.

616. Ibid., 318-320. Heft also stresses here the importance of considering the "hierarchy of truths" in relation to these dogmas.

617. Ibid., 320. Heft cites Ford, "'Sensus Fidelium' and Mariology," 136.

618. Heft, "Papal Infallibility and the Marian Dogmas," 320.

619. Ibid., 321-322.

620. Ibid., 322-327.

621. James L. Heft, "Episcopal Teaching Authority on Matters of War and Economics," in *Theology & Authority: Maintaining a Tradition of Tension*. Edited by Richard Penaskovic. (Peabody, Mass.: Hendrickson Publishers, 1987), 93-105.

622. Ibid., 100.

623. Ibid.

624. Ibid., 101.

625. Ibid.

626. Ibid., 102.

627. Ibid.

628. Ibid., 102-103. Heft makes a similar point in another context, where he connects dissent and the *sensus fidelium* with the way in which the faithful can "disagree in a responsible way with certain teachings not infallibly taught." See James L. Heft, "The Response Catholics Owe to Noninfallible Teachings," in *Raising the Torch of Good News: Catholic Authority and Dialogue with the World*. Edited Bernard J. Prusak. *The Annual Publication of the College Theology Society* 32 (1986): 120.

629. Heft, "Episcopal Teaching Authority," 104.

630. Jan Kerkhofs, "Le Peuple de Dieu est-il infaillible? L'importance du *sensus fidelium* dans l'Église postconciliaire," *Freiburger zeitschrift fuer Philosophie und Theologie* 35 (1988): 3.

631. Ibid.

632. Ibid., 4.

633. Ibid., 4-5.

634. Ibid., 5.

635. Ibid., 5-6.

636. Ibid., 7-8.

637. Ibid., 8.

638. Ibid., 8-9.

639. Ibid., 9.

640. Ibid.

641. Ibid., 9-10.

642. Ibid., 10-11.

643. Ibid., 11.

644. Ibid., 12.

645. Ibid.

646. Ibid.

647. Ibid., 12-13.

648. Ibid., 13.

649. Ibid.

650. Ibid., 13-14.

651. Ibid., 14.

652. Ibid., 15.

653. Ibid., 16.

654. Ibid., 17.

655. Ibid., 17-18.

656. Ibid., 18.

657. Ibid.

658. Ibid.

659. Ibid.

660. Ibid., 18-19.

661. Ibid., 19.

662. Ibid.

663. Leo Scheffczyk, "*Sensus fidelium*—Witness on the Part of the Community," *Communio* 15 (1988): 182-198.

664. Ibid., 182.

665. Ibid., 183.

666. Ibid. Here Scheffczyk cites Richard P. McBrien, *Catholicism*, vol, 1 (Minneapolis, Minn.: Winston Press, 1980), 71

667. Scheffczyk, 183.

668. Ibid., 184-186.

669. Ibid., 186.

670. Ibid.

671. Ibid., 187.

672. Ibid., 187-188.

673. Ibid., 188.

674. Ibid., 188-189.

675. Ibid., 189.

676. Ibid., 190.
677. Ibid.
678. Ibid., 190-191.
679. Ibid., 191.
680. Ibid., 192.
681. Ibid., 193.
682. Ibid., 193-194.
683. Ibid., 194.
684. Ibid.
685. Ibid., 194-195.
686. Ibid., 195.
687. Ibid.
688. Ibid. Emphasis is Scheffczyk's.
689. Ibid. Scheffczyk cites Newman's *On Consulting the Faithful.*
690. Scheffczyk, 196.
691. Ibid., 196-197.
692. Ibid., 197.
693. Ibid.
694. Ibid., 198.
695. Ibid.
696. Zoltán Alszeghy, "The *Sensus Fidei* and the Development of Dogma," in *Vatican II Assessment and Perspectives: Twenty-Five Years After*

*(1962-1987)* Vol. 1, 138-156. Edited by René Latourelle. (New York: Paulist Press, 1988).

697. Ibid., 138-139.

698. Ibid. Emphasis is Alszeghy's.

699. Ibid., 139. Alszeghy quotes from the original: "*ex intima spiritualium rerum quam experiuntur intelligentia.*"

700. Ibid.

701. Ibid., 140-142.

702. Ibid., 142.

703. Ibid.

704. Ibid., 142-144.

705. Ibid., 145.

706. Ibid.

707. Ibid., 145-146. Emphasis in original.

708. Ibid., 147.

709. Ibid. Emphasis in original.

710. Ibid., 147-148.

711. Ibid., 148-149.

712. Ibid., 149.

713. Ibid., 150.

714. Ibid., 151.

715. Ibid., 151-152.

716. Ibid., 152.

717. Ibid., 153.

718. Ibid., 153-154.

719. Aidan Nichols, "The Sense of the Faithful," chap. in *The Shape of Catholic Theology*, 221-231. (Collegeville, Minn.: The Liturgical Press, 1991).

720. Ibid., 221-222.

721. Ibid., 222.

722. Ibid.

723. Ibid., 223.

724. Ibid., 223-224.

725. Ibid., 224.

726. Ibid., 224-225.

727. Ibid., 225-229.

728. Ibid., 229.

729. Ibid.

730. Ibid.

731. Ibid., 230.

732. Ibid.

733. Ibid.

734. Ibid., 230-231.

735. Ibid., 231.

736. See the chapter, "Experience." Ibid., 235-247.

737. Ibid., 245.

738. Ibid., 246.

739. Ibid.

740. Ibid., 247.

741. Karl Rahner, "Free Speech in the Church," in *Free Speech in the Church* (New York: Sheed & Ward, 1959), 9-50.

742. Ibid., 9-14.

743. Ibid., 14-17.

744. Ibid., 22.

745. Ibid., 24.

746. Ibid..

747. Ibid., 24-25.

748. Ibid., 25.

749. Ibid.

750. Ibid., 26.

751. Ibid., 27.

752. Ibid., 27-30.

753. Ibid., 33.

754. Ibid., 36-37.

755. Ibid., 37.

756. Ibid., 39-40.

757. Ibid., 41.

758. Ibid., 41-42.

759. Ibid., 43-44.

760. Ibid., 46.

761. Ibid., 48-50.

762. See Rahner's chapter, "Principles and Prescriptions," in *Dynamic Element*, 13-41, especially, 15-18.

763. Ibid., 37.

764. Ibid., 38.

765. Ibid.

766. Ibid., 38-39.

767. Ibid., 40.

768. Ibid.

769. Ibid., 42-83.

770. Ibid., 44-46.

771. Ibid., 48-50.

772. Ibid., 48-49.

773. Ibid., 50-53.

774. Ibid., 70-71.

775. Ibid., 71-72.

776. Ibid., 72.

777. Ibid., 73.

778. Ibid., 75.

779. Ibid., 82.

780. Ibid., 83.

781. See Rahner's chapter, "The Logic of Concrete Individual Knowledge in Ignatius Loyola." Ibid., 84-170.

782. Ibid., 108.

783. Ibid., 129-130.

784. Ibid., 130.

785. Ibid., 143.

786. Ibid., 153-155.

787. Ibid., 159.

788. Ibid., 169.

789. Ronald Burke, "Reviewing Rahner's Rules for Theology," *Encounter* 37 (1976): 318.

790. Ibid., 320-321.

791. Karl Rahner, *The Shape of the Church to Come* (New York: Seabury, 1974).

792. Ibid., 35-37.

793. Ibid., 41.

794. Ibid., 93.

795. Ibid., 94-95.

796. Ibid., 97.

797. Karl Rahner, "Observations on the Concept of Revelation," chap. in *Revelation and Tradition*. Karl Rahner and Joseph Ratzinger. (New York: Herder and Herder, 1966), 20-21.

798. Rahner, *Shape of the Church*, 96-98.

799. Ibid., 99.

800. Ibid., 108.

801. Ibid., 116.

802. Ibid., 119.

803. Ibid., 120.

804. Ibid., 122.

805. Ibid., 127-131. The issues of "democracy" and the nature of the Church, as well as the practical issues that are developed in the text considered here, are also discussed in an earlier article of Rahner's, "Democracy in the Church," *The Month* 40 (1968): 105-119.

806. A useful discussion of Rahner's views in this area as they have developed through out his writings is given by Mary E. Hines in *The Transformation of Dogma: An Introduction to Karl Rahner on Doctrine*. (Mahwah, N.J.: Paulist Press, 1989).

807. Ibid., 44.

808. Ibid., 76. In her discussion, Hines draws particularly on Rahner's "Considerations on the Development of Dogma" in *Theological Investigations* 4:11-35. See especially pp. 32-34.

809. Karl Rahner, "Open Questions in Dogma Considered by the Institutional Church as Definitively Answered," *Journal of Ecumenical Studies* 15 (1978): 211-226.

810. Ibid., 221. Emphasis in original.

811. Ibid., 221-222.

812. Ibid., 222.

813. Ibid.

814. Rahner, "Considerations on the Development of Dogma," 7.

815. Ibid., 10.

816. Karl Rahner, "A Small Fragment 'On the Collective Finding of Truth,'" *Theological Investigations* 6:82-88.

817. Ibid., 86.

818. Ibid., 87.

819. Ibid., 87-88.

820. Karl Rahner, "Dialogue in the Church," *Theological Investigations* 10:107-108.

821. Ibid., 108.

822. Ibid., 113-117.

823. Karl Rahner, "On the Encyclical 'Humanae Vitae,'" *Theological Investigations* 11:263-287.

824. See especially, Ibid., 275-277.

825. Ibid., 285-287.

826. Ibid., 286.

827. Ibid.

828. Ibid., 287.

829. Karl Rahner, *Opportunities for Faith: Elements of a Modern Spirituality* (New York: Seabury, 1970), 222.

830. Rahner discusses aspects pertaining to the individual believer for instance in "The Faith of the Christian and the Doctrine of the Church," *Theological Investigations* 14:24-46; infallibility in "On the Concept of Infallibility in Catholic Theology," *Theological Investigations* 14:66-85; internal conflict in "Opposition in the Church," *Theological Investigations* 17:127-138; the hermeneutics of magisterial statements in "'*Mysterium Ecclesiae*.'"

*Theological Investigations* 17:139-155; and base communities in both Catholic and ecumenical contexts in "Basic Communities," *Theological Investigations* 19:159-165; to give just a few examples.

831. Karl Rahner, "What the Church Officially Teaches and What the People Actually Believe." *Theological Investigations* 22 (1991): 165-175. This article was originally published in 1981.

832. Ibid., 165.

833. Ibid., 166.

834. Ibid., 167.

835. Ibid., 167-168.

836. Ibid., 168.

837. Ibid., 169. Emphasis in original.

838. Ibid.

839. Ibid., 169-170.

840. Ibid., 170.

841. Ibid.

842. Ibid., 170-171.

843. Ibid., 171. Emphasis in original.

844. Ibid.

845. Ibid., 171-172.

846. Ibid., 172.

847. Ibid., 172-173.

848. Ibid., 173.

849. Ibid., 173-174.

850. Ibid., 175.

851. John W. Glaser, "Authority, Connatural Knowledge, and the Spontaneous Judgment of the Faithful," *Theological Studies* 29 (1968): 742-751.

852. Ibid., 742.

853. Ibid., 742-743.

854. Ibid. Glaser notes he is limiting his discussion to the magisterium's non-infallible teaching authority.

855. Ibid., 744.

856. Ibid.

857. Ibid. Emphasis in original.

858. Ibid., 744-745.

859. Ibid., 745.

860. Ibid., 745-746.

861. Ibid., 746-751.

862. Ibid., 747.

863. Ibid., 748. Glaser quotes from Jacques Maritain, *The Range of Reason* (New York, 1952), 16.

864. Glaser, 748-749.

865. Ibid., 749.

866. Ibid., 750. Glaser cites the German text of *The Dynamic Element in the Church* for the long section on knowledge in Ignatius discussed above.

867. Glaser, 750.

868. Ibid., 751.

869. Ibid.

870. Harald Wagner, "Glaubenssinn, Glaubenszustimmung und Glaubenskonsensus," *Theologie und Glaube* 69 (1979): 263-271.

871. Ibid., 263.

872. Ibid., 263-264.

873. Ibid., 264.

874. Ibid., 265.

875. Ibid., 265-266.

876. Ibid., 266-267.

877. Ibid., 267.

878. Ibid., 267-268.

879. Ibid., 268-269. Wagner cites Pottmeyer's "Theologie des Volkes. Ihr Begriff und ihre Bedingungen." In *Theologie des Volkes*. Edited by A. Exeler and N. Mette. (Mainz: 1978), 153.

880. Wagner, 269.

881. Ibid., 269-270.

882. Ibid., 270.

883. Ibid., 270-271.

884. Ibid., 271. Wagner quotes W. Kasper, *Einfuehrung in den Glauben* (Mainz: 1972), 131, in regard to the "collective finding of truth."

885. Eugen Biser, "Der Glaubenssinn: Ein begriffskritischer Rettungsversuch," *Stimmen der Zeit* 199 (1981): 678-684.

886. Ibid., 678. Biser refers to John 3:8 and to Guardini's, *Der Herr*.

887. Biser, 678-679.

888. Ibid., 679.

889. Ibid.

890. Ibid., 679-680.

891. Ibid., 680.

892. Ibid., 680-681.

893. Ibid., 681.

894. Ibid.

895. Ibid., 681-682.

896. Ibid., 682-683.

897. Ibid., 683.

898. Ibid.

899. Ibid.

900. Ibid., 683-684. Biser cites Eph. 4:3.

901. Ibid., 684.

902. Ibid.

903. The uniqueness of this event is asserted by John Mahoney in "The Impact of *Humanae Vitae*," which provides a useful summary of the events immediately preceding and following the publication of the encyclical. See *The Making of Moral Theology: A Study of the Roman Catholic Tradition* (Oxford: Clarendon Press, 1987), 259-301.

904. John C. Ford and Germain Grisez, "Contraception and the Infallibility of the Ordinary Magisterium," *Theological Studies* 39 (1978): 259.

905. Ibid., 300-301. Emphasis in original. In a note, the works of Congar (*Tradition and Traditions*), Geiselmann (*The Meaning of Tradition*), and Mackey (*The Modern Theology of Tradition*) are offered as sources for a "right understanding" of the concept. See p. 301, n. 92.

906. Ibid., 302.

907. John T. Ford, "Infallibility: A Review of Recent Studies," *Theological Studies* 40 (1979): 305.

908. Ibid., 305. Ford refers here to the work of Sanks, *Authority in the Church*, cited above. See Ford, "Infallibility," 305, n. 117. Sanks has himself cited the promulgation of *Humanae Vitae* by Paul VI over the advice of the "majority report" of the commission he authorized to study the issue, as the occasion for a rekindling of "the unresolved conflicts between the a-historical approach and the historical approach, as well as the issue of papal authority." See T. Howland Sanks, "Co-operation, Co-optation, Condemnation: Theologians and the Magisterium 1970-1978," *Chicago Studies* 17 (1978): 261.

909. Joseph F. Costanzo, "Papal Magisterium and 'Humanae Vitae,'" *Thought* 44 (1969): 398.

910. See Mahoney, 270-271.

911. Patrick Crowley, "Infallibility in a Teaching and Thinking Church," *Doctrine and Life* 32 (1982): 213.

912. Ibid., 199.

913. Thomas F. O'Meara, "Roman Catholicism: The Authority Crisis," *McCormick Quarterly* 23 (1970): 171-172.

914. Robert J. Dionne, "'Humanae Vitae' Re-examined: A Response," *Homiletic and Pastoral Review* (July 1973): 63.

915. Joseph A. Komonchak, "*Humanae Vitae* and its Reception: Ecclesiological Reflections," *Theological Studies* 39 (1978): 230.

916. John A. Gallagher, *Time Past, Time Future: An Historical Study of Catholic Moral Theology* (New York: Paulist Press, 1990) 223.

917. Daniel C. Maguire, "Catholicism and Modernity," *Horizons* 13 (1986): 366.

918. Cormac Burke, *Authority and Freedom in the Church* (San Francisco: Ignatius Press, 1988), 172.

919. Ibid., 161-163.

920. Ibid., 163.

921. Richard McCormick, "The Teaching Office as a Gaurantor of Unity in Morality," in *Christian Ethics: Uniformity, Universality, Pluralism*, 72-81. Edited by Jacques Pohier and Dietmar Mieth. (Mew York: Seabury Press, 1981).

922. Ibid., 76.

923. Ibid.

924. Ibid.

925. Ibid., 77.

926. E. J. Capestany, "McCormick and the Erosion of the Magisterium," *Catholicism and Crisis*, (June 1983): 23-28.

927. Thomas Dubay, "The State of Moral Theology: A Critical Appraisal.," in *Readings in Moral Theology, No. 3: The Magisterium and Morality*, 352.

928. Ibid.

929. An example of the diversity of views on dissent among theologians and those with an official teaching office can be found in the essays collected in *Readings in Moral Theology, No. 6: Dissent in the Church*. Edited by Charles E. Curran and Richard McCormick. (New York: Paulist Press, 1988).

930. Charles E. Curran and Robert E. Hunt, *Dissent In and For the Church: Theologians and Humanae Vitae* (New York: Sheed & Ward, 1969), 56.

931. Ibid.

932. Ibid., 86-87. Emphasis in original.

933. Joseph F. Costanzo, "Academic Dissent: An Original Ecclesiology," *The Thomist* 34 (1970): 646-647. This article is a review of Curran and Hunt's *Dissent In and For the Church*.

934. Costanzo, "Academic Dissent," 647.

935. Ibid., 648-651.

936. Ibid., 652.

937. Joseph A. Bracken, "Toward an Grammar of Dissent," *Theological Studies* 31 (1970): 455. Bracken draws here on the views of Glaser in "Authority, Connatural Knowledge, and the Spontaneous Judgment of the Faithful" cited above.

938. Bracken, 455. The creative value of dissent in the Church's history and contemporary context is illustrated well by Hermann Haering in "The Rights and Limits of Dissent," in *The Right to Dissent*, 95-107. A selection of texts and reflections that illustrate the impact of dissent during several eras of church history is given by José I. Gonzáles Faus in *Where the Spirit Breathes: Prophetic Dissent in the Church* (Maryknoll, N.Y.: Orbis, 1989).

939. The Congregation's letter to Curran is found in Charles E. Curran, *Faithful Dissent* (Kansas City: Sheed & Ward, 1986), 267-270. The quote given here is on p. 268. *Faithful Dissent* includes Curran's own history and analysis of his career and the controversial events within it, as well as his correspondence with the Congregation that pertains to the suspension of his canonical mission to teach theology at Catholic University.

940. A useful collection of responses to the "Curran affair" can be found in *Vatican Authority and American Catholic Dissent: The Curran Case and its Consequences*, cited above.

941. See Farley, "Moral Discourse in the Public Arena," 168-186.

942. Ibid., 177.

943. Ibid., 178.

944. Ibid.

945. Ibid., 179.

946. Lisa Sowle Cahill, "Catholic Sexual Teaching: Context, Function, and Authority," in *Vatican Authority*, 193-194.

947. Ibid., 194.

948. Thomas P. Rausch, "Authority and Credibility," in *Vatican Authority*, 122.

949. Ibid., 123. Rausch draws here on the work of Avery Dulles, citing his article, "*Sensus Fidelium*."

950. Rausch, *Authority and Leadership*, 140. Here Rausch cites Dionne's study of reception, *The Papacy and the Church*, as suggesting that "there is an element of interdependence in the church's very nature."

951. Kaufman, 160. See also his similar remarks on p. 79.

952. See for instance, Granfield's comments on the use of opinion polls in "Catholic Faithful," 141-142.

953. Frans Haarsma, "Consensus in the Church: Is an Empirical Inquiry Possible?" in *The Unifying Role of the Bishop*, 119-129.

954. Ibid., 120.

955. Ibid.

956. Ibid., 121-122.

957. Ibid., 122.

958. Ibid., 123.

959. Ibid.

960. Ibid., 125.

961. Ibid., 128.

962. Ibid.

963. Ibid., 129.

964. Abbott, 48.

965. Ladislas Orsy, *The Church: Learning and Teaching* (Wilmington, Del.: Michael Glazier, 1987), 82-89. Some of the same material from this text is used in an article by Orsy, "Magisterium: Assent and Dissent," *Theological Studies* 48 (1987): 473-497. Here he gives some historical and contemporary context for the discussion of assent and dissent.

966. Orsy, *The Church*, 85.

967. Ibid.

968. Ibid., 85-86.

969. Ibid., 86.

970. Ibid., 87-89.

971. Ibid., 89.

972. Ibid.

973. B. C. Butler, "Infallibile: Authenticum: Assensus: Obsequium. Christian Teaching Authority and the Christian's Response," *Doctrine and Life* 31 (1981): 77-89.

974. Ibid., 77-80.

975. Ibid., 80.

976. Ibid., 80-81.

977. Ibid., 81.

978. Ibid., 82. Butler notes that this form of assent is appropriately used in reference to infallible propositions.

979. Ibid., 83-84.

980. Ibid., 84.

981. Ibid.

982. Ibid., 85.

983. Ibid., 86.

984. Ibid., 88-89.

985. Richard Malone, "Magisterium and Dissent," *Euntes Docete* 39 (1986): 503-521.

986. Ibid., 508-509.

987. Ibid., 510. Emphasis in original.

988. Ibid., 512-515.

989. Ibid., 514.

990. Ibid., 515.

991. Ibid., 521.

992. Ibid., 519-521.

993. Ibid., 520-521.

994. Christian Duquoc, "An Active Role for the People of God in Defining the Church's Faith," in *The Teaching Authority of the Believers*, 73.

995. Ibid., 80.

996. Kottje, 126.

997. Legrand, 40.

998. Ibid., 41-42.

999. Edward J. Kilmartin, "Episcopal Election: The Right of the Laity," in *Electing Our Own Bishops*, 39-43. See especially p. 41.

1000. Ibid., 42.

1001. Joseph Lécuyer, "The Bishop and the People in the Rite of Episcopal Consecration," in *Electing Our Own Bishops*, 44-47.

1002. See the survey article of Candida Lund, "Would Democracy Solve the Problems of the Church?" *The Critic* 45 (1990): 2-21.

1003. Ibid., 6.

1004. Ibid., 14.

1005. Ibid., 15.

1006. Ibid.

1007. Ibid., 16. A useful selection of articles on the doctrinal and practical aspects of this topic that dates from a period of time nearer to the close of Vatican II, and which offers perspectives that are different and perhaps more speculative than those described here, may be found in Muller, *Democratization of the Church* cited above. See especially, Karl Lehmann, "On the Dogmatic Justification for a Process of Democratization in the Church," 60-86; and Norbert Greinacher, "A Community Free of Rule," 87-107.

1008. Congar, "La 'réception' comme réalité ecclésiologique." The English text used here is cited as "Reception."

1009. Ibid., 66.

1010. Ibid., 68.

1011. Giuseppe Alberigo, "The Christian Situation after Vatican II," in *The Reception of Vatican II*. Edited by Giuseppe Alberigo, Jean-Pierre Jossua, and Joseph A. Komonchak. (Washington, D.C.: The Catholic University of America Press, 1987), 24.

1012. Luis M. Bermejo, *Church Conciliarity, Communion* (Gujurat, India: Anand Press, 1990), 319.

1013. Ibid., 184. See Bermejo's extended discussion on pp. 184-211.

1014. Garijo, 323.

1015. Ibid., 326-327.

1016. Paul O'Leary, "Authority to Proclaim the Word of God, and the Consent of the Church," *Freiburger Zeitschrift fuer Philosophie und Theologie* 29 (1982). See pages 244-251.

1017. Emmanuel Sullivan, "Reception: Factor and Moment in Ecumenism," *Ecumenical Trends* 15 (1986): 109.

1018. Thomas P. Rausch, "Reception Past and Present," *Theological Studies* 47 (1986): 497.

1019. Ibid., 499.

1020. Ibid., 499-500.

1021. Ibid., 500.

1022. Ibid.

1023. Ibid., 501-502.

1024. Ibid., 503.

1025. Ibid., 504.

1026. Ibid.

1027. Ibid., 506.

1028. Ibid.

1029. Ibid., 507.

1030. Ibid., 508.

1031. See John Zizioulas, "The Theological Problem of 'Reception,'" *Bulletin/Centro Pro Unione* 26 (Fall 1984): 3-6.

1032. Ibid., 6. Emphasis in original.

1033. Harding Meyer, "Les présupposés de la réception ecclésiale ou le problème de la 'recevabilité,'" *Irénikon* 59 (1986): 11.

1034. Lukas Vischer, "The Process of 'Reception' in the Ecumenical Movement," *Midstream* 23 (1984): 228-229.

1035. George Lindbeck, "Scripture, Consensus, and Community," *This World* 23 (Fall 1988): 5-24. See p. 10 for the phrase quoted here.

1036. Margaret O'Gara, "Infallibility in the Ecumenical Crucible," *One in Christ* 20 (1984): 342.

1037. Ibid., 344-345.

1038. Timiadis, "Consensus in the Formulation of Doctrine," 182.

1039. Ibid., 188.

1040. Ibid., 188-189.

1041. Ibid., 189. Emphasis in original.

1042. Ibid.

1043. Ibid., 190.

1044. Metropolitan Emilianos Timiadis, "Reception, Consensus, and Unity," *The Greek Orthodox Theological Review* 26 (1981): 61.

1045. A useful introduction to Dionne's main themes is available in a short article, J. Robert Dionne, "An Interview With the Author of *The Papacy and the Church*" in *America* 160 (1989): 12-13, 22.

1046. Dionne, *The Papacy and the Church*, 29.

1047. Ibid., 293.

1048. See the remarks, for instance, of Emmanuel Sullivan in "Authority in the Church: Problem in Mystery." *Anglican Theological Review* 70 (1988): 179-180, where he discusses Dionne's use of the concept.

1049. Thomas P. Rausch, "Talking Back to Rome? J. R. Dionne on Papal Magisterium and the Church," *One in Christ* 24 (1989): 187.

1050. Ibid., 182.

1051. Dionne, *The Papacy and the Church*, 348.

1052. Ibid. The portion quoted is emphasized in Dionne's text.

1053. Ibid., 361-362. See also p. 472, n. 44 where Dionne suggests that this sort of active response may be implied in Newman's later writing.

1054. See Dionne, *The Papacy and the Church*, 360-366.

1055. Rinaldo Bertolino, "Sensus fidei et coutume dans le droit de l'Eglise," *Freiburger Zeitschrift fuer Philosophie und Theologie* 33 (1986): 227-243. Bertolino draws on the work of Granfield, Sartori, Congar, Dillenschneider, Sancho, Rahner and others.

1056. Ibid., 240.

1057. Ibid., 243.

1058. James A. Coriden, "Shared Authority: Rationale and Legal Foundation," *Chicago Studies* 9 (1970): 171-182.

1059. Ibid., 173-174.

1060. Ibid., 179.

1061. Ibid., 181-182.

1062. Ladislas Orsy, "General Norms, Custom (cc. 23-28)." In *The Code of Canon Law: A Text and Commentary*, 40.

1063. Ibid.

1064. Eugenio Corecco, "Ecclesiological Bases of the Code," in *Canon Law—Church Reality*. Edited by James Provost and Knut Walf. (Edinburgh: T. & T. Clark, 1986), 3-12. See especially p. 8. Emphasis in original.

1065. Eugenio Corecco, "Aspects of the Reception of Vatican II in the Code of Canon Law," in *The Reception of Vatican II*, 293-294.

1066. Ibid., 293-296. The practical implications for the participation of the laity in the Church, especially with reference to the use of power, are discussed by James H. Provost in the light of the ecclesiological conflicts and compromises embedded in the code of canon law, in "The Participation of the Laity in the Governance of the Church," *Studia Canonica* 17 (1983): 417-448.

1067. Raymond F. Collins, "Small Groups: An Experience of Church," *Louvain Studies* 13 (1988): 109-120.

1068. Ibid., 120-121.

1069. Ibid., 128.

1070. Ibid., 129.

1071. Ibid., 134-135.

1072. Ibid., 136. Collins cites B. Hume, "A Vast Canvas," *The Tablet* 241 (1987): 1225, and "Message to the People of God From the 1987 Synod of Bishops," *Origins* 17 (1987): 388. See nn. 107 and 108.

1073. Virgil Elizondo, "The Hispanic Church in the USA: A Local Ecclesiology," *CTSA Proceedings* 36 (1981): 155-170. See especially 166-170.

1074. Ibid., 169.

1075. Ibid.

1076. Paulo Suess, "The Creative and Normative Role of Popular Religion in the Church," in *Popular Religion*. Edited by Norbert Greinacher and Norbert Mette. (Edinburgh: T. & T. Clark, 1986), 126-127.

1077. Ibid., 127-128.

1078. See for example, Johann Baptist Metz, "Theology Today: New Crises and New Visions," *CTSA Proceedings* 40 (1985): 1-14.

1079. Ibid., 8.

1080. Ibid.

1081. Ibid., 9.

1082. Ibid., 10.

1083. Boff, "Is the Distinction between *Ecclesia docens* and *Ecclesia discens* Justified?" 48. The sentence quoted is emphasized in Boff's text.

1084. Ibid., 49. An interesting discussion of the *consensus fidelium* as it may be understood in the light of the work of Max Weber and the hermeneutics of Hans-Georg Gadamer and Max Horkheimer is given by Hans Waldenfels in "Authority and Knowledge," in *The Teaching Authority of the Believers*, 31-42.

1085. Boff, "Is the Distinction between *Ecclesia docens* and *Ecclesia discens* Justified?" 51.

1086. Hellwig, 166.

1087. Ibid., 166-167.

1088. Ibid., 166.

1089. Eileen P. Flynn, "The Bishops Bomb," *Theology Today* 40 (1983-84): 448-450.

1090. Ibid., 448.

1091. A helpful treatment of the key themes in the feminist critique is given by Anne E. Carr, in *Transforming Grace: Christian Tradition and Women's Experience* (San Francisco: Harper & Row, 1988).

1092. Fiorenza, "Claiming our Authority and Power," 45-53.

1093. Ibid.

1094. Ibid., 51.

1095. Ibid., 49-52.

1096. Rosemary Radford Ruether, "The Ministry of the People and the Future Shape of the Church," in *Toward A. D. 2000: Emerging Directions in Christian Ministry*. Edited by John I. Durham. Volume 1 of *Southeastern Studies* (Raleigh, N.C.: Edwards & Broughton, 1977), 84.

1097. Ibid., 92.

1098. Michael J. McGinniss, "*Sensus Fidelium*, USA: Laity and Church Structures for the Future," *Listening* 25 (1990): 72.

1099. Ibid., 72.

1100. Ibid., 73.

1101. Ibid., 74-82.

1102. Ibid., 77.

1103. Ibid., 82.

1104. Ibid., 82-84.

1105. Ibid., 84.

1106. Ibid., 71.

1107. Evelyn Eaton Whitehead and James D., Whitehead, "Ministering to the Sense of the Faithful," in *Community of Faith: Models and Strategies for Building Christian Communities*, 153-170. (New York: Seabury Press, 1982).

1108. Ibid., 153-159.

1109. Ibid., 159-162.

1110. Ibid., 162.

1111. Ibid., 162-163. Emphasis in original.

1112. Ibid., 163-164.

1113. Ibid., 165.

1114. Ibid., 166.

1115. Ibid.

1116. Ibid., 167.

1117. Ibid.

1118. Ibid., 168. The authors have in fact offered further reflections on the possibility of reformulating theological approaches to sexual issues in another work. See Evelyn Eaton Whitehead and James D. Whitehead, *A Sense of Sexuality: Christian Love and Intimacy* (New York: Doubleday, 1989). On pp. 15-18 they specifically link their reflections to the use of the sense of the faithful.

1119. Whitehead, "Ministering," 168.

1120. Ibid. Diversity in the experience of the faithful is given an important place in the approach of Erich Feifel, to theological education for adults in "Glaubenssinn und theologischer Lernprozess Funktion und grundlegende Strukturen theologischer Erwachsenenbildung," in *Erwachsenenbildung: Glaubenssinn und Theologischer Lernprozess*. Edited by Erich Feifel. (Zurich: Benziger, 1972), 13-14. Feifel argues that in developing a sense of responsibility in adult believers that goes beyond a "theological consumerism" the factors of differing age and experience should be taken into account. He also notes the importance of a spirit of openness and questioning.

1121. Whitehead, "Ministering," 168-169. The Whiteheads have included a discussion of the sense of the faithful in an earlier work that proposed a model for theological reflection in ministry. See James D. Whitehead and Evelyn Eaton Whitehead, *Method in Ministry: Theological Reflection and Christian Ministry* (New York: Seabury Press, 1980). There they write,

> The challenge is to develop means of critical access to this sense of the faithful—specific, practical means which rescue this category of *sensus fidelium* from its current rhetorical status and bring its religious information into the processes of pastoral decision making (p. 19).

1122. De Roo, "Collegiality and the Petrine Office in the Pastoral Work of the Church," cited above.

1123. Ibid., 42.

1124. Ibid.

1125. Ibid., 42-43.

1126. Ibid., 42.

1127. Ibid.

1128. Ibid., 52.

1129. Ibid.

1130. Ibid.

1131. Citations here will be from the translation printed as Sacred Congregation for the Doctrine of the Faith, "Declaration in Defence of the Catholic Doctrine on the Church Against Some Present-Day Errors," in *Vatican Council II: More Post Conciliar Documents*. Volume 2. General editor Austin Flannery. (Northport, N.Y.: Costello Publishing, 1982), 428-440.

1132. Ibid., 430.

1133. Ibid.

1134. Ibid., 431.

1135. Ibid., 433.

1136. Francis A. Sullivan, "Magisterium and Theology," *CTSA Proceedings* 43 (1988): 71.

1137. Ibid. Sullivan quotes here from *Mysterium Fidei* (1965).

1138. Sullivan, "Magisterium and Theology," 71.

1139. Sacred Congregation for the Doctrine of the Faith, "Catholic Doctrine on the Church," 433. See also Sullivan's further remarks on this passage in "Magisterium and Theology," 71-72.

1140. Sacred Congregation for the Doctrine of the Faith, "Catholic Doctrine on the Church," 434.

1141. Francis A. Sullivan, *Magisterium: Teaching Authority in the Catholic Church* (New York: Paulist Press, 1983), 104-105.

1142. Ibid., 104.

1143. Ibid., 105.

1144. Ibid.

1145. Ibid., 185-188.

1146. Peter Chirico, *Infallibility: The Crossroads of Doctrine* (Kansas City: Sheed Andrews and McMeel, 1977), 212. For Chirico's reference to historical method and his particular debt to Lonergan, see p. 3 in his text, and n. 3 on pp. 297-298.

1147. Ibid., 214.

1148. Joseph Moingt, "Authority and Ministry," *Journal of Ecumenical Studies* 19 (1982): 213.

1149. Ibid., 214.

1150. Ibid., 214-215.

1151. Rembert Weakland, "U.S. Contribution to the Theological Enterprise," *Origins* 19 (1989): 158.

1152. Ibid.

1153. National Conference of Catholic Bishops, *Economic Justice for All: Pastoral Letter on Catholic Social Teaching and the U.S. Economy* (Washington, D.C.: National Conference of Catholic Bishops, 1986).

1154. See for instance, Rembert G. Weakland, "The Church in Worldly Affairs: Tensions between Laity and Clergy," *America* 156 (1986): 201-205, 215-216.

1155. U.S. Bishops' Committee on Doctrine, "Report: An Ongoing Discussion of Magisterium," *Origins* 9 (1980): 543-544. This report covers meetings conducted by the bishops between 1977 and 1979.

1156. Ibid., 544.

1157. Catholic Theological Society of America, "Statement of Catholic Theological Society of America Members," *Origins* 20 (1990): 464.

1158. Quinn's remarks are included in Oscar Lipscomb and John Quinn, "Reaction to the CTSA Statement," *Origins* 20 (1990): 468.

1159. Untener's remarks are in Kenneth Untener and James McHugh, "Human Sexuality Document's Birth Control Section," *Origins* 20 (1990): 404.

1160. Ibid., 405.

1161. Matthew Clark, "On Hearing the Wisdom of the People," *Origins* 20 (1990): 445-452.

1162. Ibid., 447.

1163. Ibid., 450.

1164. Cardinal Johannes Willebrands, "The Impact of Dialogue," *Origins* 14 (1985): 722.

1165. Ibid.

1166. Cardinal Joseph Ratzinger, "Dissent and Proportionalism in Moral Theology," *Origins* 13 (1984): 666-669.

1167. Ibid., 667.

1168. Ibid., 668.

1169. Ibid.

1170. Ibid.

1171. Ibid.

1172. Ibid.

1173. Ibid., 669.

1174. Pope John Paul II, *The Role of the Christian Family*, 16.

1175. Ibid., 133, n. 13.

1176. Ibid., 16.

1177. Pope John Paul II, "Tensions of This Post-Conciliar Period," *Origins* 12 (1980): 53.

1178. Ibid.

1179. For Hume's remarks, see George Basil Cardinal Hume, "Synod '80: Development of Marriage Teaching," *Origins* 10 (1980): 275-276. For those of Cardinal Carter, see "Spirit's Voice or Moral Decadence," 277. A quote from Carter is given above in n. 48 of Chapter 1.

1180. Derek Worlock, "Marital Indissolubility and Pastoral Compassion," *Origins* 10 (1980): 273, 275. For a discussion of the uses of the sense of the faithful by some of the bishops at the Synod, see Kaufman, especially 81-82, 86, 156-159. Kaufman finds the pope unresponsive to many of the bishops' suggestions.

1181. These were reported as "secret resolutions" in the article, "Secret Resolutions Reveal Bishops . . . Rulings on Divorce, Celibacy, Sexuality," *National Catholic Reporter*, 12 December 1980, 20-22. The translation used here will be from this article.

1182. Ibid.

1183. Ibid.

1184. John Quinn, "Report on the Synod: Collegiality and Faith," *Origins* 10 (1980): 357.

1185. Bishops' Conference of England and Wales, "Vatican II and the 1985 Synod of Bishops," *Origins* 15 (1985): 184.

1186. Ibid.

1187. Synod of Bishops, "The Final Report," *Origins* 19 (1985): 448.

1188. Ibid., 449.

1189. Ibid.

1190. Cardinal Gerald Emmett Carter, "The Priesthood of the Laity," *Origins* 16 (1986): 386.

1191. Ibid.

1192. Ibid., 387.

1193. "Working Paper for the 1987 Synod of Bishops," *Origins* 17 (1987): 1-19.

1194. Ibid., 9-10.

1195. Ibid., 9.

1196. Ibid. This passage cites *Lumen Gentium* (# 35).

1197. Reference here will be to the Vatican translation published as John Paul II, *The Lay Members of Christ's Faithful People* (Boston: Daughters of St. Paul, 1988).

1198. Ibid., 33.

1199. Ibid., 34. Emphasis in original.

1200. Ibid., 50-51.

1201. Ibid., 48. Emphasis in original.

1202. Ibid., 72.

1203. Ibid., 73. The phrase quoted here is emphasized in the original text.

1204. Ibid., 73-75. Several phrases quoted here are emphasized in the text as introductions to explanatory passages.

1205. See the comments of Rausch in *Authority and Leadership*, 145.

1206. Quoted by Rausch, Ibid., from Pope John Paul II, "The Pope's Closing Homily," *Origins* 17 (1985): 390.

1207. The ongoing interaction between the pope and the bishops of the United States on topics that have been linked to the sense of the faithful are illustrated in the presentations made by four bishops to John Paul II during his 1987 visit to the United States. The topics of dissent, the role of women, sexual issues, and the relationship of the local and universal Church were taken up by Cardinal Joseph Bernardin of Chicago, Archbishop John Quinn of San Francisco, Archbishop Rembert Weakland of Milwaukee, and Archbishop Daniel Pilarczyk of Cincinnati, with responses to each speaker given by the pope. See John May, et., al., "Los Angeles Meeting of the Pope and U.S. Bishops," *Origins* 17 (1987): 253-267.

1208. Congregation for the Doctrine of the Faith, "Instruction," 119.

1209. Ibid.

1210. Ibid., 120.

1211. Ibid., 121.

1212. Ibid.

1213. Ibid., 122-123.

1214. Ibid., 122.

1215. Ibid.

1216. Ibid.

1217. Ibid., 123.

1218. Ibid.

1219. Ibid., 123-124.

1220. Ibid., 124.

1221. Ibid.

1222. Ibid., 125.

1223. Ibid.

1224. Ibid. The document quotes here from Pope Paul VI's *Paterna cum Benevolentia*, 2-3, (1974).

1225. Congregation for the Doctrine of the Faith, "Instruction," 125.

1226. Ladislas Orsy, "Magisterium and Theologians: A Vatican Document," *America* 163 (1990): 32.

1227. Joseph A. Komonchak, "The Magisterium and Theologians," *Chicago Studies* 29 (1990): 328.

1228. Francis A. Sullivan, "The Theologian's Ecclesial Vocation and the 1990 CDF Instruction," *Theological Studies* 52 (1991): 51.

1229. Ibid., 53-54.

1230. Ibid., 66.

1231. Ibid., 67.

1232. Ibid., 68. Sullivan cites *Origins* 20 (1990): 119.

1233. Sullivan, "Theologian's Ecclesial Vocation," 68.

**CHAPTER 6**

1. See pp. 259-260 above.

2. For Coulson, see pp. 258-259 above; for Femiano, pp. 260-261.

3. Patterson, *Pioneer*, 179.

4. Patterson, "Apologetics," 101-112.

5. See Penaskovic, *Open to the Spirit*, 252-256.

6. Penaskovic, "Theology and Authority," 120-122.

7. Ibid., 125.

8. See pp. 272-274 above.

9. See pp. 274-275 above.

10. Ford, "'*Sensus Fidelium*' and Mariology," 133.

11. Ibid., 144.

12. Ford, "Newman's View," 140.

13. See especially the discussion of criterion eight, pp. 240-251 above.

14. Piet Fransen, "The Exercise of Authority in the Church Today: Its Concrete Forms," *Louvain Studies* 9 (1982): 10.

15. Ibid.

16. See for instance, Sesboüé, 338.

17. Fransen, "Exercise of Authority," 11-14.

18. Duquoc, 73.

19. Kottje, 126.

20. Legrand, 40-42.

21. Eugui, 223-224.

22. See Kilmartin, "Episcopal Election," 41-42; and Kilmartin, "Lay Participation," 362-370.

23. Lécuyer, 44-47.

24. Lund, 6.

25. Ibid., 16.

26. Ibid., 15; Patterson, "Apologetics," 103.

27. Coriden, "Shared Authority," 174-175.

28. Correco, "Ecclesiological Bases of the Code," 8; and Correco, "Aspects of the Reception of Vatican II," 294.

29. Bertolino, 240-241.

30. Orsy, "Custom," 40.

31. See canons 211-218 of the new code. A useful discussion of consultation of the faithful with reference to canon law is given by James H. Provost in "Canon Law and the Role of Consultation," *Origins* 18 (1989): 793-799.

32. Congar, "Reception," 66-68.

33. Alberigo, "Christian Situation," 24.

34. See Bermejo, 184-211; Garijo, 323-326.

35. Rausch, "Reception Past and Present," 505-506. See also pp. 404-405 above.

36. See above, pp. 405-407.

37. Timiadis, "Consensus in the Formulation of Doctrine," 189.

38. Dionne, *The Papacy and the Church*, 29.

39. Crowley, 213.

40. See Dionne, *The Papacy and the Church*, 361-362, and pp. 407-408 above.

41. See pp. 317-322 above.

42. See pp. 315-316 above.

43. See pp. 316-317 above.

44. Scheffczyk, 192. See the discussion of Scheffczyk's views on pp. 354-358 above.

45. Ford, "Contraception and the Infallibility of the Ordinary Magisterium," 302. See also p. 388-389 above.

46. Costanzo, "Papal Infallibility and 'Humanae Vitae,'" 398.

47. Burke, *Authority and Freedom*, 161-164, 172.

48. International Theological Commission, "On the Interpretation of Dogmas," *Origins* 20 (1990): 1-14.

49. Ibid., 7.

50. Ibid.

51. Ibid., 7-8.

52. Ibid., 9.

53. Ibid.

54. Ibid., 10.

55. Ibid., 11.

56. Ibid., 12.

57. Ibid. Emphasis in original.

58. Ibid.

59. Ibid., 13.

60. Ibid.

61. Ibid., 14.

62. Ford, "Vatican I to the Present," 768-791.

63. Ibid., 790. In this passage Ford cites Karl Rahner, "Pluralism in Theology and the Oneness of the Church's Profession of Faith," *Concilium* [*The Development of Fundamental Theology*. Edited by Johannes B. Metz.] 46: 103-123; and J. Ford, "Ecumenical Convergence and Theological Pluralism," *Thought* 44 (1969): 540-545.

64. See pp. 392-393 above on the views of McCormick, Capestany and Dubay.

65. Farley, 179.

66. Cahill, "Catholic Sexual Teaching," 194.

67. Bracken, 455.

68. See above, pp. 365-379.

69. Orsy, *The Church*, 89.

70. Bracken, 455.

71. See for example, International Theological Commission, "On the Interpretation of Dogmas," 7; as well as the views of Heft, pp. 346-349 above and Kerkhofs, pp. 349-354 above on the need to consider the relative weight of church teachings. Also see the related observation of Fries that contributions of different charisms in the Church will occur at different times in what should still be an interrelated process. Fries, "Sensus Fidelium. Der Theologe," 75. Several authors who favor the "interactive" approach discussed below consider aspects of the "tentative" nature of historically contextualized expressions of faith.

72. See pp. 391-392 above.

73. For Kaufman's remark on polls, see p. 396 above.

74. See pp. 415-417 above.

75. See pp. 417-419 above.

76. See p. 639, n. 1120.

77. Ruether, 92.

78. Fiorenza, "Claiming our Authority and Power," 50.

79. See pp. 324-329 above.

80. Metz, 8.

81. Elizondo, 169.

82. Collins, 136. Here Collins cites the speech "Sharing the Mission of Christ," of Bishop Hume at the 1987 Synod of Bishops. Reprinted as "A Vast Canvas," in *The Tablet* 241 (1987): 1224-1226.

83. Suess, 127-128.

84. Boff, "Is the Distinction between *Ecclesia docens* and *Ecclesia discens* Justified?" 48-51.

85. See for instance the comments of Joseph Ratzinger in "A Certain 'Liberation,'" chap. in *The Ratzinger Report: An Exclusive Interview on the State of the Church.* Joseph Cardinal Ratzinger with Vittorio Messori. (San Francisco: Ignatius Press, 1985), 169-190.

86. Thompson, *"Sensus Fidelium* and Infallibility," 483; Congar, *Lay People*, 276-277.

87. See pp. 282-289 above.

88. Beinert, "Bedeutung und Begruendung," 287.

89. Ibid., 288.

90. Ibid., 293.

91. Congar, *Tradition and Traditions*, 320.

92. See the discussion of Granfield's work on pp. 290-296 above.

93. Thompson, *"Sensus Fidelium* and Infallibility," 484.

94. Tillard's views are discussed on pp. 303-310 above.

95. Tillard, "Autorité et mémoire dans l'Église," (part 1), 339.

96. See pp. 310-315 above.

97. Dumont, 54.

98. See pp. 329-335 above.

99. Dulles, *"Sensus Fidelium,"* 263. See the detailed discussion of Dulles's views on pp. 339-343 above.

100. See pp. 343-346 above.

101. Rahner's views are discussed on pp. 365-379 above.

102. The detailed views of Glaser, Wagner and Biser are given on pp. 380-387 above.

103. See pp. 322-324 above.

104. See pp. 254-257 above.

105. See the treatment of Sesboüé's views on pp. 296-300 above.

106. See pp. 335-337 above.

107. Walgrave, "Newman's 'On Consulting,'" 28-29.

108. Ibid., 29.

109. See pp. 362-363 above.

110. See Hellwig, 166.

111. For example, see Ford's views on p. 271 above and those of Dionne on pp. 407-408.

112. See the discussion of Nichols's views on pp. 363-365 above.

113. Heft, "Papal Infallibility and the Marian Dogmas," 320-321.

114. See pp. 346-349 above.

115. Kerkhofs's views are detailed on pp. 349-354 above.

116. Haarsma, 125.

117. See especially Sartori's discussion on pp. 322-324 above.

118. Granfield, "Ecclesial Cybernetics," 663-664.

119. Bracken, 455. Bracken draws here on Glaser's article.

120. Haarsma, 122.

121. Walgrave, *Unfolding Revelation*, 39.

122. Ibid.

123. See n. 31 in Chapter 1, p. 498 above.

124. Schillebeeckx, "Towards a Catholic Use of Hermeneutics," 41. Emphasis in original.

125. Discussion of Newman's criteria from the perspectives of Tavard and Trocóniz y Sasigain is given above, on pp. 243-244.

126. See the discussion above, pp. 183-184 on different interpretive phases described by John T. Ford in reference to the teaching of Vatican I on infallibility. Following the lead of modern biblical studies, Ford distinguishes the understandings of conciliar statements that have been expressed by "participants and contemporaries," "subsequent presentations," and those studying the Council a hundred years after its closing. Ford's views are suggestive of how the mechanism of "hermeneutical distancing" may operate in regard to other doctrinal statements. See Ford, "Vatican I to Present," 769-772.

127. Many authors have suggested that the response to *Humanae Vitae* is an indicator of the need for further reflection on its teaching or even that rejection of the teaching is the work of the *sensus fidelium*. It is interesting to note that in writing after the controversial response at Catholic University to the encyclical, Curran and Hunt observed that in some cases there is a need for more time in order for the whole Church to discern whether dissent is to be considered legitimate. They assert, however, that a contemporary critical response may be accurate and necessary, and they suggest that in the *Humanae Vitae* controversy such response was appropriate. The authors' discussion, given in the midst of conflict, further supports the view that the hermeneutics of ecclesial teachings involve a complex process. Curran, *Dissent in and for the Church*, 80-82.

128. See the discussion on pp. 216-217 above.

129. See p. 433 above.

130. Haarsma, 128-129. Haarsma specifically contrasts the goal of understanding and deepening the faith with a pursuit of consensus which is based in "a static conception of the Church."

131. Richard McCormick and Richard McBrien have warned, "The Vatican's view of today's laity seems to be captured in the odious term 'simple faithful.'" They describe Cardinal Ratzinger as promoting the view among other church authorities that "their primary responsibility is to protect the simple faithful against theologians who criticize in any way whatever an official teaching of the church." See Richard A. McCormick and Richard P. McBrien, "Theology as Public Responsibility," *America* 165 (1991): 204.

132. The Congregation for the Doctrine of the Faith has aptly pointed out the serious challenge to the modern Church that comes from secular media. See the Congregation's "Instruction," 124.

133. *Gaudium et Spes* describes the goal to be achieved in saying,

> In the exercise of all their earthly activities, [Christians] can thereby gather their humane, domestic, professional, social, and technical enterprises into one vital synthesis with religious values, under whose supreme direction all things are harmonized unto God's glory. (Abbott, 243).

134. Orsy, *The Church*, 83.

135. See the discussion above on pp. 398-399.

136. The directions offered in the recent document of the International Council for Catechesis, *Adult Catechesis in the Christian Community: Some Principles and Guidelines* (Vatican City: Liberia Editrice Vaticana, 1990) are encouraging, with their recognition of the need to consider adult issues of faith, and their acknowledgment that both adapting and remaining faithful to the tradition must characterize educational efforts in the Church. See pp. 16-19.

137. A hopeful approach to catechesis that stresses the role of the local church and that includes discussions of the role of liturgy and attention to social justice issues is offered by Michael Warren in *Faith, Culture and the Worshiping Community: Shaping the Practice of the Local Church* (New York: Paulist Press, 1989).

138. Rahner, "What the Church Officially Teaches, 169-172.

# WORKS CITED

## WORKS RELATED TO THE HISTORY OF THE *SENSUS FIDELIUM*

### Books

Bettenson, Henry, ed. *Documents of the Christian Church.* 2nd ed. London: Oxford University Press, 1963.

Biemer, Guenter. *Newman on Tradition.* Freiburg: Herder, 1967.

Butler, Dom Edward Cuthbert. *The Vatican Council.* Westminster, Md.: Newman Press, 1962

Chadwick, Owen. *From Bossuet to Newman.* 2nd ed. Cambridge: Cambridge University Press, 1987.

_____. *Newman.* Oxford: Oxford University Press, 1983.

Clarkson, John F., John H. Edwards, William J. Kelly, and John J. Welch, trans. *The Church Teaches: Documents of the Church in English Translation.* Rockford, Ill.: Tan Books, 1973.

Congar, Yves M.-J. *A History of Theology.* Garden City, N.Y.: Doubleday, 1968.

_____. *Lay People in the Church.* London: Geoffrey , 1957; reprint, Frome and London: Butler and Tannen, 1962.

_____. *Tradition and Traditions.* New York: Macmillan, 1967.

Daniélou, Jean, and Henri Marrou. *The First Six Hundred Years.* London: Darton, Longman and Todd, 1964.

Dillenschneider, P. Clément. *Le Sens de la foi et le progrès dogmatique du mystère marial.* Rome: Academia Mariana Internationalis, 1954.

Eno, Robert B. *Teaching Authority in the Early Church.* Wilmington, Del.: Michael Glasier, 1984.

Eugui Hermoso de Mendoza, Julio. *La Participación de la Communidad Cristiana en la Elección de los Obispos: Siglos I-V.* Pamplona: Ediciones Universidad de Navarra, S.A., 1977.

Faivre, Alexandre. *The Emergence of the Laity in the Early Church.* Mahwah, N.J.: Paulist Press, 1990.

Femiano, Samuel D. *Infallibility of the Laity: The Legacy of Newman.* New York: Herder & Herder, 1967.

Frend, W. H. C. *The Rise of Christianity.* Philadelphia: Fortress Press, 1984.

Gasser, Vincent. *The Gift of Infallibility: The Official Relatio on Infallibility of Bishop Vincent Gasser at Vatican Council.* Translated with commentary by James T. O'Conner. Boston: St. Paul Editions, 1986.

Geiselmann, Josef Rupert. *The Meaning of Tradition.* New York: Herder & Herder, 1966.

Guitton, Jean. *The Church and the Laity: From Newman to Vatican II.* Staten Island, N.Y.: Alba House, 1965.

Hasler, August Bernhard. *How the Pope Became Infallible: Pius IX and the Politics of Persuasion.* Garden City, N.Y.: Doubleday, 1981.

Hertling, Ludwig. *Communio: Church and Papacy in Early Christianity.* Chicago: Loyola University Press, 1972.

Hillerbrand, Hans J. *Christendom Divided: The Protestant Reformation.* New York: Corpus, 1971.

Jurgens, William A. *The Faith of the Early Fathers.* 3 Vols. Collegeville, Minn.: Liturgical Press, 1970-1979.

Kleist, James A. ed. *The Didache, The Epistle of Barnabas, The Epistles and the Martyrdom of St. Polycarp, The Fragments of Papias, The Epistle to Diognetus.* Vol. 6. Ancient Christian Writers. New York: Newman Press, 1948.

Knowles, David, with Dimitri Obolensky. *The Middle Ages.* London: Darton, Longman and Todd, 1969.

Koster, M. Dominikus. *Volk Gottes im Wachstum des Glaubens.* Heidelberg: Kerle, 1950.

Kueng, Hans. *Infallibility? An Inquiry.* Garden City, N.Y.: Doubleday, 1971.

Mackey, J. P. *The Modern Theology of Tradition.* New York: Herder & Herder, 1963.

Moehler, Johann Adam. *Symbolism.* Translated by J. B. Robertson. 5th ed. London: Gibbings & Company, 1906.

Neuner, J. and J. Dupuis, eds. *The Christian Faith in the Documents of the Catholic Church.* Rev. Ed. New York: Alba House, 1982.

Newman, John Henry. *On Consulting the Faithful in Matters of Doctrine.* Reprinted with an introduction by John Coulson. New York: Sheed & Ward, 1962.

Noonan, John T. *Contraception: A History of Its Treatment by the Catholic Theologians and Canonists.* Enlarged Ed. Cambridge: Harvard University Press, 1986.

————. *The Scholastic Analysis of Usury.* Cambridge: Harvard University Press, 1957.

Osawa, Takeo. *Das Bischofseinsetzungsverfahren bei Cyprian.* Bern/Frankfurt: P. Lang, 1983.

Ott, Ludwig. *Fundamentals of Catholic Dogma.* St. Louis: Herder, 1957.

Patterson, Webster T. *Newman: Pioneer for the Layman.* Washington: Corpus Books, 1968.

Penaskovic, Richard J. *Open to the Spirit: The Notion of the Laity in the Writings of J. H. Newman.* Augsburg: W. Blasaditsch, 1972.

Pius X, Pope. *Encyclical Letter of Pope Pius X On the Doctrines of the Modernists: Pascendi Dominici Gregis and Syllabus Condemning the*

658     Works Cited

*Errors of the Modernists: Lamentabili Sane, July 3, 1907.* Boston: St. Paul Editions, n.d.

Pius XII, Pope. *Apostolic Constitution of Pope XII on the Assumption of the Blessed Virgin Mary.* Boston: St. Paul Editions, n.d.

Quasten, Johannes. *Patrology.* Vol. 2, *The Ante-Nicene Literature After Irenaeus.* Utrecht-Antwerp: Spectrum, 1953; reprint, Westminster, Md.: Christian Classics, 1983.

Riley, Lawrence J. *The History, Nature and Use of EPIKEIA in Moral Theology.* New York: Paulist Press, 1948.

Sanks, T. Howland. *Authority in the Church: A Study in Changing Paradigms.* Missoula, Mont.: American Academy of Religion, 1974.

Schrodt, Paul. *The Problem of the Beginning of Dogma in Recent Theology.* Frankfurt am Main: Peter Lang, 1978.

Sullivan, Francis A. *The Church We Believe In: One, Holy, Catholic and Apostolic.* New York: Paulist Press, 1988.

Thils, Gustave. *L'Infaillibilité du peuple chrétien "in credendo": notes de théologie posttridentine.* Paris: Desclée de Brouwer, 1963.

Trocóniz y Sasigain, Luis M. Fz. de. *"Sensus Fidei": Logica Connatural de la Existencia Christiana: Un Estudio del Recurso al "Sensus Fidei" en la Teologia Catolica de 1950 a 1970.* Vitoria: Victoriensia, 1976.

Ullathorne, The Right Rev. Bishop. *The Immaculate Conception of the Mother of God.* 1855; reprinted with new Introduction by Wilfred Schoenberg. Westminster, Md.: Christian Classics, 1988.

Walgrave, Jan. *Newman the Theologian.* New York: Sheed & Ward, 1960.

### Articles

Alberigo, Giuseppe. "L'unité de l'Église dans le service de l'Église romaine et de la papauté (XIe-XXe siècle)." *Irénikon* 51 (1978): 46-72.

_____. "The Authority of the Church in the Documents of Vatican I and Vatican II." *Journal of Ecumenical Studies* 19 (1982): 119-145.

Bainvel, Jean. "Tradition and Living Magisterium." *Catholic Encyclopedia*. Vol. 15. New York: 1912.

Bartelink, Gerard. "The Use of the Words *Electio* and *Consensus* in the Church until about 600." In *Election and Consensus in the Church*, pp. 147-154. Edited by Giuseppe Alberigo and Anton Weiler. New York: Herder and Herder, 1972.

Benson, Robert L. "Election by Community and Chapter: Reflections on Co-Responsibility in the Historical Church." In *Who Decides for the Church?* pp. 54-80. Edited by James A. Coriden. Hartford, Conn.: The Canon Law Society of America, 1971.

Bernhard, Jean. "The Election of Bishops at the Council of Trent." In *Electing Our Own Bishops*, pp. 24-30. Edited by Peter Huizing and Knut Walf. Edinburgh: T. & T. Clark, 1980.

Bévenot, Maurice. "Introduction." In *St. Cyprian: The Lapsed, The Unity of the Catholic Church*, pp. 3-12. Vol 25. *Ancient Christian Writers*. New York: Newman Press, 1957.

Beyer, Hermann Wolfgang. "*EPISKOPOS* in the NT." In *Theological Dictionary of the New Testament*, Vol. 2. Edited by Gerhard Kittel and Gerhard Friedrich. Grand Rapids, Mich.: Eerdmans, 1964-1974. pp. 615-617.

Boglioni, Pierre. "Pour l'étude de la religion populaire au Moyen Age: le problème de sources." in *Foi populaire, foi savante*, pp. 93-148. J.-M. R. Tillard, et. al. Paris: Les Éditions du Cerf, 1976.

Bourke, Myles M. "Collegial Decision-Making in the New Testament." In *Who Decides for the Church?* pp. 1-13. Edited by James A. Coriden. Hartford. Conn.: The Canon Law Society of America, 1971.

Bray, Gerald. "Authority in the Early Church." *Churchman* 95 (1981): 43-53.

Box, Norbert. "The Conflict between Anicetus and Polycarp." in *The Unifying Role of the Bishop*, pp. 37-45. Edited by Edward Schillebeeckx. New York: Herder and Herder, 1972.

Bucher, Kevin D. "Newman on the Functions of the Church: A Prophetic Voice for Today?" *Louvain Studies* 7 (1978): 15-23.

Buechsel, Friedrich. "*PARADOSIS.*" In *Theological Dictionary of the New Testament*, Vol. 2. Edited by Gerhard Kittel and Gerhard Friedrich. Grand Rapids, Mich.: Eerdmans, 1964-1974. pp. 172-113.

Burghardt, Walter J. "The Catholic Concept of Tradition in the Light of Modern Theological Thought." *CTSA Proceedings* 6 (1951): 42-75.

Caffrey, Thomas A. "Consensus and Infallibility: The Mind of Vatican I." *The Downside Review* 88 (1970): 107-131.

Cardman, Francine. "Cyprian and Rome: The Controversy over Baptism." In *The Right to Dissent*, pp. 33-39. Edited by Hans Kueng and Juergen Moltmann. New York: Seabury Press, 1982.

Carol, Juniper B. "The Definability of Mary's Assumption," *The American Ecclesiastical Review* 118 (1948): 161-177.

Carroll, Eamon. "Papal Infallibility and the Marian Definitions, Some Considerations." *Carmelus* 26 (1979): 213-250.

Congar, Yves M. J. "A Brief History of the Forms of the Magisterium and Its Relations with Scholars." In *Readings in Moral Theology No. 3: The Magisterium and Morality*, pp. 314-331. Edited by Charles E. Curran and Richard A. McCormick. New York: Paulist Press, 1982.

_____. "The Historical Development of Authority in the Church. Points for Christian Reflection." In *Problems of Authority*, pp. 119-156. Edited by John M. Todd. London: Darton Longman & Todd, 1962.

_____. "Norms of Christian Allegiance and Identity in the History of the Church." In *Truth and Certainty*, pp. 11-26. Edited by Edward Schillebeeckx and Bas van Iersel. New York: Herder and Herder, 1973.

_____. "*Quod omnes tangit, ab omnibus tractari et approbari debet.*" *Revue historique de droit français e étranger* 35 (1958): 210-259.

_____. "Saint Thomas Aquinas and the Infallibility of the Papal Magisterium." *The Thomist* 38 (1974): 81-105.

Coppens, J. "La *koinônia* dans l'Église primitive." *Ephemerides Theologicae Lovaniensis* 46 (1970): 116-121.

Costigan, Richard F. "The Consensus of the Church: Differing Classical Views." *Theological Studies* 51 (1990): 25-48.

Coulson, John. "Introduction." In John Henry Newman, *On Consulting the Faithful in Matters of Doctrine*, pp. 1-49. Reprinted with an introduction by John Coulson. New York: Sheed & Ward, 1962.

Dagens, Claude. "Hierarchy and Communion: The Bases of Authority in the Beginning of the Church." *Communio* 9 (1982) : 67-78.

Daly, Gabriel. "The Dissent of Theology: The Modernist Crisis." In *The Right to Dissent*, pp. 53-57. Edited by Hans Kueng and Juergen Moltmann. New York: Seabury Press, 1982.

D'Aragon, Jean-Louis. "Le 'sensus fidelium' et ses fondements néotestamentaires." In *Foi populaire, foi savante*, pp. 41-48. J.-M. R. Tillard, et. al. Paris: Les Éditions du Cerf, 1976.

Davids, Adalbert. "One or None: Cyprian on the Church and Tradition." In *The Unifying Role of the Bishop*, pp. 46-52. Edited by Edward Schillebeeckx. New York: Herder and Herder, 1972.

Dejaifve, George. "Ex Sese, Non Autem Ex Consensu Ecclesiae." *Eastern Churches Quarterly* 14 (1962): 360-378.

_____. "Infallibility and Consent of the Church." *Theology Digest* 12 (1964): 8-13.

Denzler, Georg. "Bulletin: The Discussion about Bernhard Hasler's publications on the First Vatican Council." In *Who Has the Say in the Church?* pp. 81-86. Edited by Juergen Moltmann and Hans Kueng. Edinburgh: T. & T. Clark, 1981.

Dessain, C. Stephen, ed. "An Unpublished Paper by Cardinal Newman on the Development of Doctrine." In *The Theological Papers of John Henry Newman on Biblical Inspiration and on Infallibility*, pp. 151-160. Edited by J. Derek Holmes. Oxford: Clarendon Press, 1979.

Douie, Decima. "John XXII and the Beatific Vision." *Dominican Studies* 3 (1950): 154-174.

Dulles, Avery. "The Magisterium in History: A Theological Reflection." *Chicago Studies* 17 (1978): 264-281.

_____. "Newman on Infallibility." *Theological Studies* 51 (1990): 434-449.

Eno, Robert B. "Authority and Conflict in the Early Church." *Église et Théologie* 7 (1976): 41-60.

_____. "Consensus and Doctrine: Three Ancient Views." *Église et Théologie* 9 (1978): 473-483.

_____. "Shared Responsibility in the Early Church." *Chicago Studies* 9 (1970): 129-141.

Fernández de Troconiz, Luis M. "El 'sensus fidei' según Sto. Tomás de Aquino." *Scriptorium Victoriense* 40 (1993): 195-208.

Fiorenza, Francis Schuessler. "Presidential Address: Foundations of Theology: A Community's Tradition of Discourse and Practice." *CTSA Proceedings* 41 (1986): 107-134.

Ford, John T. "'Dancing on the Tightrope': Newman's View of Theology." *CTSA Proceedings* 40 (1985): 127-144.

_____. "Different Models of Infallibility?" *CTSA Proceedings* 35 (1980): 217-233.

_____. "Infallibility—From Vatican I to the Present." *Journal of Ecumenical Studies* 8 (1971): 768-791.

_____. "Newman on '*Sensus Fidelium*' and Mariology." *Marian Studies* 28 (1977): 120-145.

Fox, Richard Wightman. "Lamennais' Understanding of the Spiritual and Temporal." *Chicago Studies* 8 (1969): 177-187.

Frank, Karl Suso. "Bishops and Laity in the Faith Tradition." *Theology Digest* 34 (1987): 37-41.

Frend. W. H. C. "The *Seniores Laici* and the Origins of the Church in North Africa." *Journal of Theological Studies* 12 (1961): 280-284.

Galvin, John J. "A Critical Survey of Modern Conceptions of Doctrinal Development." *CTSA Proceedings* 5 (1950): 45-62.

Garijo Guembe, Miguel M. "El Concepto de 'Recepti ón' y su Enmarque in el Seno de la Eclesiología Católica." *Lumen* 29 (1980): 311-331.

Gaudemet, Jean. "Bishops: From Election to Nomination." In *Electing Our Own Bishops*, pp. 10-15. Edited by Peter Huizing and Knut Walf. Edinburgh: T. & T. Clark, 1980.

Granfield, Patrick. "Concilium and Consensus: Decision Making in Cyprian." *The Jurist* 35 (1975): 397-408.

_____. "Episcopal Elections in Cyprian: Clerical and Lay Participation." *Theological Studies* 37 (1976): 41-52.

Green, Lowell C. "Erasmus, Luther, and Melancthon on the *Magnus Consensus*: The Problem of the Old and the New in the Reformation and Today." *The Lutheran Quarterly* 27 (1975): 364-381.

Gubler, Marie-Louise. "Living Diversity in the NT Church." *Theology Digest* 37 (1990): 115-119.

Halton, Thomas. "The Church, The People of God." Chap. in *The Church*, pp. 62-93. Wilmington, Del.: Michael Glazier, 1985.

Hammans, Herbert. "Der Glaubenssinn." In *Die Neueren Katholischen Erklaerungen der Dogmenentwicklung*, pp. 242-262. Essen: Ludgerus, 1965.

Haring, N. M. "Paschasius Radbertus, St." *New Catholic Encyclopedia*, Vol. 10. New York: McGraw-Hill, 1967. p. 1050.

Hauck, Friedrich. "*KOINON* in the NT." In *Theological Dictionary of the New Testament*, Vol. 3. Edited by Gerhard Kittel and Gerhard Friedrich. Grand Rapids. Mich.: Eerdmans, 1964-1974. pp. 804-809.

Healy, Kilian. "Pope Pius XII and the Assumption." Chap. in *The Assumption of Mary*, pp. 15-23. Wilmington, Del.: Michael Glazier, 1982.

Hennessy, Paul K. "Infallibility in the Ecclesiology of Peter Richard Kenrick." *Theological Studies* 45 (1984): 702-714.

Hitchcock, James. "Thomas More and the Sensus Fidelium." *Theological Studies* 36 (1975): 145-154.

Hoffmann, Joseph. "Théologie, magistère, et opinion publique: Le discours de Doellinger au Congrès des Savants Catholiques de 1863." *Recherches de Science Religieuse* 71 (1983): 245-258.

Iersel, Bas van. "Who According to the New Testament Has the Say in the Church?" In *Who Has the Say in the Church?* pp. 11-17. Edited by Juergen Moltmann and Hans Kueng. Edinburgh: T. & T. Clark, 1981.

Kelly, J. N. D. "John XXII." In *The Oxford Dictionary of Popes*, pp. 214-216. Oxford: Oxford University Press, 1986.

Kilmartin, Edward J. "Reception in History: An Ecclesiological Phenomenon and its Significance." *Journal of Ecumenical Studies* 21 (1984): 34-54.

King, Geoffrey. "Acceptance of Law by the Community: A Study in the Writings of Canonists and Theologians, 1500-1750." *The Jurist* 37 (1977): 233-265.

Kleinheyer, Bruno. "Consensus in the Liturgy." In *Election and Consensus in the Church*, pp. 20-30. Edited by Giuseppe Alberigo and Anton Weiler. New York: Herder and Herder, 1972.

Kottje, Raymund. "The Selection of Church Officials: Some Historical Facts and Experiences." In *Democratization of the Church*, pp. 117-126. Edited by Alois Muller. New York: Herder and Herder, 1971.

Lécuyer, Joseph. "The Bishops and the People in the Rite of Episcopal Consecration." In *Electing Our Own Bishops*, pp. 44-47. Edited by Peter Huizing and Knut Walf. Edinburgh: T. & T. Clark, 1980.

Legrand, Hervé-Marie. "Theology and the Election of Bishops in the Early Church." In *Election and Consensus in the Church*, pp. 31-42. Edited by Giuseppe Alberigo and Anton Weiler. New York: Herder and Herder, 1972.

Lindbeck, George A. "Theological Revolutions and the Present Crisis." *Theology Digest* 23 (1975): 308-319.

Lindt, Andreas. "Aus dem Leben von Theologie und Kirche." *Reformatio* 19 (1970): 610-613.

Lynch, John E. "Co-Responsibility in the First Five Centuries: Presbyterial Colleges and the Election of Bishops." In *Who Decides for the Church?* pp. 14-53. Edited by James A. Coriden. Hartford, Conn.: The Canon Law Society of America, 1971.

McNally, Robert E. "Freedom and Suspicion at Trent: Bonuccio and Soto." *Theological Studies* 29 (1968): 752-762.

MacRae, George W. "Shared Responsibility—Some New Testament Perspectives." *Chicago Studies* 9 (1970): 115-127.

Maguire, Alban A. "Observations on Fr. Ford's Lecture." *Marian Studies* 28 (1977): 146-147.

Markus, R. A. "The Crisis of Authority in the Church: The Historical Roots." *The Modern Churchman* 10 (1967): 281-291.

Meyendorff, John. "Historical Relativism and Authority in Christian Dogma." *St. Vladimir's Seminary Quarterly* 11 (1967): 73-86.

Moiser, Jeremy. "The Role of the Laity in the Formation of the New Testament Canon." *Science et Esprit* 39 (1987) : 301-317.

O'Gara, Margaret. "Infallibility and the French Minority Bishops of the First Vatican Council." *CTSA Proceedings* 35 (1980) : 212-216.

_____. "Listening to Forgotten Voices: The French minority Bishops of Vatican I & Infallibility." *Theology Digest* 37 (1990): 3-15.

Owens, Gerard. "Historical Development of the Dogma of the Immaculate Conception: Obstacles Inhibiting Understanding and Acceptance." *CTSA Proceedings* 9 (1954): 67-101.

Parrella, Frederick J. "The Laity in the Church." *CTSA Proceedings* 35 (1980): 264-286.

Pesch, Rudolf. "The New Testament Foundations of a Democratic Form of Life in the Church." In *Democratization of the Church*, pp. 48-59. Edited by Alois Muller. New York: Herder and Herder, 1971.

Prusak, Bernard P. "The Theology of the Local Church in Historical Development." *CTSA Proceedings* 35 (1980): 287-308.

Rausch, Thomas P. "The Church in the Sub-Apostolic Age." Chap. in *The Roots of the Catholic Tradition*, pp. 119-140. Wilmington, Del.: Michael Glazier, 1986.

Remmers, Johannes. "Apostolic Succession: An Attribute of the Whole Church." In *Apostolic Succession: Rethinking a Barrier to Unity*, pp. 36-51. Edited by Hans Kueng. New York: Paulist Press, 1968.

Schillebeeckx, Edward. "The Teaching Authority of All—A Reflection about the Structure of the New Testament." In *The Teaching Authority of the Believers*, pp. 12-22. Edited by Johannes-Baptist Metz and Edward Schillebeeckx. Edinburgh: T. & T. Clark, 1985.

Schnackenburg, Rudolf. "Community Co-operation in the New Testament." In *Election and Consensus in the Church*, pp. 9-19. Edited by Giuseppe Alberigo and Anton Weiler. New York: Herder and Herder, 1972.

Scholz, Franz. "Problems on Norms Raised by Ethical Borderline Situations: Beginnings of a Solution in Thomas Aquinas and Bonaventure." In *Readings in Moral Theology No. 1: Moral Norms and Catholic Tradition*, pp. 158-183. Edited by Charles E. Curran and Richard A. McCormick. New York: Paulist Press, 1979.

Seckler, M. "Glaubenssinn." *Lexicon fuer Theologie und Kirche*, Vol. 4. 1960. 946-948.

Sheldrake, Philip. "Authority and Consensus in Thomas More's Doctrine of the Church." *Heythrop Journal* 20 (1979): 146-162.

Sieben, Hermann-Josef. "On the Relation between Council and Pope up to the Middle of the Fifth Century." In *The Ecumenical Council*, pp. 19-24. Edited by Peter Huizing and Knut Walf. New York: Seabury, 1983.

Slusser, Michael. "Does Newman's 'On Consulting the Faithful in Matters of Doctrine' Rest upon a Mistake?" *Horizons* 20 (1993): 234-240.

Speigl, Jakob. "Lay Participation in Early Church Councils." *Theology Digest* 28 (1980): 141-142.

Stockmeier, Peter. "Congregation and Episcopal Office in the Ancient Church." In *Bishops and People*, pp. 71-86. Edited and translated by Leonard Swidler and Arlene Swidler. Philadelphia: The Westminster Press, 1970.

_____. "The Election of Bishops by Clergy and People in the Early Church." In *Electing Our Own Bishops*, pp. 3-9. Edited by Peter Huizing and Knut Walf. Edinburgh: T. & T. Clark, 1980.

Tavard, Georges H. "The Authority of Scripture and Tradition." In *Problems of Authority*, pp. 27-42. Edited by John M. Todd. London: Darton, Longman & Todd, 1962.

_____. "Tradition as Koinonia in Historical Perspective." *One in Christ* 24 (1988): 97-111.

_____. "Tradition in Early Post-Tridentine Theology." *Theological Studies* 23 (1962): 377-405.

Thiel, John E. "Theological Responsibility: Beyond the Classical Paradigm." *Theological Studies* 47 (1986): 573-598.

Thompson, William M. "*Sensus Fidelium* and Infallibility." *American Ecclesiastical Review* 167 (1973): 450-486.

Walgrave, Jan. "Newman's 'On Consulting the Faithful in Matters of Doctrine.'" In *The Teaching Authority of the Believers*, 25-30. Edited by Johannes-Baptist Metz and Edward Schillebeeckx. Edinburgh: T. & T. Clark, 1985.

Wuenschel, Edward A. "The Definability of the Assumption." *CTSA Proceedings* 2 (1947) : 72-102.

## WORKS RELATED TO THE THEOLOGY OF THE *SENSUS FIDELIUM*

### Books

Abbott, Walter M., ed. *The Documents of Vatican II*. New York: Guild Press, 1966.

Bermejo, Luis M. *Church Conciliarity and Communion*. Gujarat, India: Anand Press, 1990.

Boff, Leonardo. *Church: Charism & Power: Liberation Theology and the Institutional Church*. New York: Crossroad, 1988.

Burke, Cormac. *Authority and Freedom in the Church*. San Francisco: Ignatius, 1988.

Camilleri, René. *The 'Sensus Fidei' of the Whole Church and the Magisterium: From the Time of Vatican I to Vatican Council II*. Rome: Pontificia Universitas Gregoriana, 1987.

Carr, Anne E. *Transforming Grace: Christian Tradition and Women's Experience*. San Francisco: Harper & Row, 1988.

Chirico, Peter. *Infallibility: The Crossroads of Doctrine*. Kansas City: Sheed Andrews and McMeel, 1977.

Coulson, John. *Newman and the Common Tradition: A Study in the Language of Church and Society*. Oxford: Clarendon, 1970.

Curran, Charles E. *Faithful Dissent*. Kansas City, Mo.: Sheed & Ward, 1986.

Curran, Charles E. and Robert E. Hunt. *Dissent In and For the Church: Theologians and Humanae Vitae*. New York: Sheed & Ward, 1969.

Curran, Charles E. and Richard A. McCormick, eds. *Readings in Moral Theology No. 6: Dissent in the Church*. New York: Paulist Press, 1988.

Deconchy, J. P. *L'Orthodoxie religieuse: Essai de Logique psycho-sociale*. Paris: Les Éditions Ouvrieres, 1971.

Dionne, J. Robert. *The Papacy and the Church: A Study of Praxis and Reception in Ecumenical Perspectus*. Now York: Philosophical Library, 1987.

Doohan, Leonard. *The Lay-Centered Church*. Minneapolis: Winston, 1984.

Dulles, Avery. *The Survival of Dogma*. Garden City, N.Y.: Doubleday, 1973.

Flannery, Austin, ed. *Vatican Council II: The Conciliar and Post Conciliar Documents*. New rev. ed. Northport, New York: Costello, 1984.

Gadamer, Hans-Georg. *Truth and Method*. 2nd Rev. ed. New York: Crossroad, 1989.

Gaillardetz, Richard R. *Witness to the Faith: Community, Infallibility, and the Ordinary Magisterium of Bishops.* New York: Paulist, 1992.

Gallagher, John A. *Time Past, Time Future: An Historical Study of Catholic Moral Theology.* New York: Paulist Press, 1990.

Garijo-Guembe, Miguel M. *Communion of Saints: Foundation, Nature, and Structure of the Church.* Collegeville, Minn.: Michael Glazier, 1994.

Geiselmann, Josef Rupert. *The Meaning of Tradition.* Freiburg: Herder, 1966.

González Faus, José I. *Where the Spirit Breathes: Prophetic Dissent in the Church.* Maryknoll, N.Y.: Orbis Books, 1989.

Granfield, Patrick. *Ecclesial Cybernetics: A Study of Democracy in the Church.* New York: Macmillan, 1973.

Hines, Mary E. *The Transformation of Dogma: An Introduction to Karl Rahner on Doctrine.* New York: Paulist Press, 1989.

Huizing, Peter, and Knut Walf, eds. *Electing Our Own Bishops.* Edinburgh: T. & T. Clark, 1980.

International Council for Catechesis. *Adult Catechesis in the Christian Community.* Vatican City: Liberia Editrice Vaticana, 1990.

John Paul II, Pope. *The Lay Members of Christ's Faithful People.* Boston: St. Paul Editions, n.d.

──────. *The Role of the Christian Family in the Modern World.* Boston: St. Paul Editions, n.d.

Kaufman, Philip S. *Why You Can Disagree and Remain a Faithful Catholic.* Bloomington, Ind.: Meyer-Stone Books, 1989.

Lash, Nicholas. *Change in Focus: A Study of Doctrinal Change and Continuity.* London: Sheed and Ward, 1973.

McNamara, Kevin, ed. *Vatican II: The Constitution on the Church: A Theological and Pastoral Commentary.* London: Geoffrey Chapman, 1968.

Mahoney, John. *The Making of Moral Theology: A Study of the Roman Catholic Tradition.* Oxford: Clarendon Press, 1987.

May, William W., ed. *Vatican Authority and American Catholic Dissent: The Curran Case and its Consequences.* New York: Crossroad, 1987.

Mouw, Richard J. *Consulting the Faithful: What Christian Intellectuals Can Learn from Popular Religion.* Grand Rapids, Mich.: Eerdmans, 1994.

Muller, Alois, ed. *Democratization of the Church.* New York: Herder and Herder, 1971.

National Conference of Catholic Bishops. *Economic Justice for All: Pastoral Letter on Catholic Social Teaching and the U.S. Economy.* Washington D.C.: National Conference of Catholic Bishops, 1986.

Nichols, Aidan. *The Shape of Catholic Theology.* Collegeville, Minn.: Liturgical Press, 1991.

O'Collins, Gerald. *The Case Against Dogma.* New York: Paulist Press, 1975.

O'Malley, John W. *Tradition and Transition.* Wilmington, Del.: Michael Glazier, 1989.

Ommen, Thomas G. *The Hermeneutic of Dogma.* Missoula, Mont.: Scholars Press, 1975.

Orsy, Ladislas. *The Church: Learning and Teaching.* Wilmington, Del.: Michael Glazier, 1987.

Palmer, Richard E. *Hermeneutics: Interpretation Theory in Schleiermacher, Dilthey, Heidegger, and Gadamer.* Evanston: Northwestern University Press, 1969.

Rahner, Karl. *The Dynamic Element in the Church.* New York: Herder & Herder, 1964.

_____. *Opportunities for Faith: Elements of a Modern Spirituality.* New York: Seabury, 1974.

_____. *The Shape of the Church to Come.* New York: Seabury, 1974.

Rausch, Thomas P. *Authority and Leadership in the Church.* Wilmington, Del.: Michael Glazer, 1988.

Read, Denis W. "How to Know the Faith: A Study of the Sensus Fidei in the Roman Catholic Church according to John Henry Cardinal Newman." Unpublished manuscript. St. Florian's Monastery and Parish, West Milwaukee, Wisc.: n.d. Based on the author's dissertation, *Sensus Fidei: Practical Faith-Knowledge in Moral Theology.* Rome, 1968.

Rikhof, Herwi. *The Concept of Church: A Methodological Inquiry into the Use of Metaphors in Ecclesiology.* London: Sheed and Ward, 1981.

Rondet, Henri. *Do Dogmas Change?* New York: Hawthorn, 1961.

Sancho Bielsa, Jesús. *Infalibilidad del Pueblo de Dios: "Sensus Fidei" e Infalibilidad Organica de la Iglesia en la Constitución "Lumen Gentium" del Concilio Vaticano II.* Pamplona: Ediciones Universidad de Navarra, 1979.

Sanks, T. Howland. *Authority in the Church: A Study in Changing Paradigms.* Missoula, Mont.: Scholars Press, 1974.

Scharr, Peter. *Consensus Fidelium: zur Unfehlbarkeit der Kirche aus der Perspektive einer Konsensustheorie der Wahrheit.* Wurzberg: Echter, 1992.

Schmaus, Michael. *Dogma* Vol. 4, *The Church: Its Origin and Structure.* Sheed and Ward, 1972; Westminster, Md.: Christian Classics, 1984.

Suenens, Leon-Joseph Cardinal. *Coresponsibility in the Church.* New York: Herder and Herder, 1968.

Sullivan, Francis A. *Magisterium: Teaching Authority in the Catholic Church.* New York: Paulist Press, 1983.

Thompson, William M. *Fire and Light: The Saints and Theology: On Consulting the Saints, Mystics, and Martyrs in Theology.* New York: Paulist Press, 1987.

Tillard, Jean M. R. *The Bishop of Rome.* Wilmington. Del.: Michael Glazer, 1983.

Walgrave, Jan Hendrik. *Unfolding Revelation: The Nature of Doctrinal Development.* London: Hutchinson, 1972.

Warren, Michael. *Faith, Culture, and the Worshiping Community: Shaping the Practice of the Local Church.* New York: Paulist Press, 1989.

Whitehead, Evelyn Eaton, and James D. Whitehead. *A Sense of Sexuality: Christian Love and Intimacy.* New York: Doubleday, 1989.

Whitehead, James D., and Evelyn Eaton Whitehead. *Method in Ministry: Theological Reflection and Christian Ministry.* New York: Seabury, 1980.

Wiederkehr, Dietrich, ed. *Der Glaubenssinn des Gottesvolkes - Konkurrent oder Partner de Lehramts?* Freiburg: Herder, 1994.

### Articles

Alberigo, Giuseppe. "The Christian Situation after Vatican II." In *The Reception of Vatican II*, pp. 1-24. Edited by Giuseppe Alberigo, Jean-Pierre Jossua, and Joseph A. Komonchak. Washington, D.C.: The Catholic University of America Press, 1987.

Alszeghy, Zoltán. "The *Sensus Fidei* and the Development of Dogma." In *Vatican II: Assessments and Perspectives Twenty-Five Years After (1962-1987).* Vol. 1, pp. 138-156. Edited by René Latourelle. New York: Paulist Press, 1988.

Beinert, Wolfgang. "Bedeutung und Begruendung des Glaubenssinnes (Sensus Fidei) als eines Dogmatischen Erkenntniskriteriums." *Catholica* 25 (1971): 271-303.

_____. "Das Finden und Verkuenden der Wahrheit in der Gemeinschaft der Kirche." *Catholica* 43 (1989): 1-30.

_____. "Theologie - Tradition - Kirchliches Lehramt." *Catholica* 38 (1984): 185-198.

_____. "What Value Does the Laity Have in the Church?" *Theology Digest* 35 (1988): 39-44.

Bertolino, Rinaldo. "Sensus fidei et coutume dans le droit l'Eglise." *Freiburger Zeitschrift fur Philosophie und Theologie* 33 (1986) 227-243.

Biser, Eugen. "Der Glaubenssinn: Ein begriffskritischer Rettungsversuch." *Stimmen der Zeit* 199 (1981): 678-684.

Bishops' Conference of England and Wales. "Vatican II and the Synod of Bishops." *Origins* 15 (1985): 177.

Boff, Leonardo. "Is the Distinction between *Ecclesia docens* and *Ecclesia discens* Justified?" In *Who Has the Say in the Church?* 47-51. Edited by Juergen Moltmann and Hans Kueng. Edinburgh: T. & T. Clark, 1981.

Bracken, Joseph A. "Toward a Grammar of Dissent." *Theological Studies* 31 (1970): 437-459.

Burke, Ronald. "Reviewing Rahner's Rules for Theology." *Encounter* 37 (1976): 315-325.

Burkhard, John J. "*Sensus Fidei*: Meaning, Role and Future of a Teaching of Vatican II." *Louvain Studies* 17 (1992): 18-34.

⎯⎯⎯⎯. "*Sensus Fidei*: Theological Reflection Since Vatican II: I. 1965-1984." *Heythrop Journal* 34 (1993): 41-59.

⎯⎯⎯⎯. "*Sensus Fidei*: Theological Reflection Since Vatican II: II. 1984-1989." *Heythrop Journal* 34 (1993): 123-136.

Butler, B. C. "Infallible: Authenticum: Assensus: Obsequium: Christian Teaching Authority and the Christian's Response." *Doctrine and Life* 31 (1981): 77-89.

Cahill, Lisa Sowle. "Catholic Sexual Teaching: Context, Function, and Authority." In *Vatican Authority and American Catholic Dissent: The Curran Case and its Consequences*, pp. 187-205. Edited by William W. May. New York: Crossroad, 1987.

Capestany, Edward J. "McCormick and the Erosion of the Magisterium." *Catholicism in Crisis* (June 1983): 23-28.

Carter, Gerald Emmett Cardinal. "The Priesthood of the Laity." *Origins* 16 (1986): 386.

_____. "Spirit's Voice or Moral Decadence?" *Origins* 16 (1980): 276.

Catholic Theological Society of America. "Statement of Catholic Theological Society of America Members." *Origins* 20 (1990): 461.

Chavasse, Paul. "Newman and the Laity." In *Newman Today: The Proceedings of the Wethersfield Institute*. Vol. 1. Edited by Stanley L. Jaki. pp. 49-78. San Francisco: Ignatius Press, 1989.

Clark, Matthew. "On Hearing the Wisdom of the People." *Origins* 20 (1990): 447.

Colaianni, Nicola. "Criticism of the Second Vatican Council in Current Literature." In *The Ecumenical Council—Its Significance in the Constitution of the Church*, pp. 106-110. Edited by Peter Huizing and Knut Walf. Edinburgh: T. & T. Clark, 1983.

Collins, Raymond F. "Small Groups: An Experience of Church." *Louvain Studies* 13 (1988): 109-136.

Congar, Yves M. J. "La 'réception' comme réalité ecclésiologique." *Revue des Sciences philosophiques et theologiques* 56 (1972): 369-403. Translated as "Reception as an Ecclesiological Reality." In *Election and Consensus in the Church*, pp. 43-68. Edited by Giuseppe Alberigo and Anton Weiler. New York: Herder and Herder, 1972.

_____. "Magisterium, Theologians, The Faithful and the Faith." *Doctrine and Life* 31 (1981): 548-564.

_____. "Toward a Catholic Synthesis." In *Who Has the Say in the Church?* pp. 69-80. Edited by Juergen Moltmann and Hans Kueng. Edinburgh: T. & T. Clark, 1981.

Congregation for the Defense of the Faith. "Declaration in Defence of the Catholic Doctrine on the Church Against Some Present-Day Errors." In *Vatican Council II: More Postconciliar Documents*, pp. 428-440. General Editor, Austin Flannery. Northport, N.Y.: Costello Publishing, 1982.

_____. "Instruction on the Ecclesial Vocation of the Theologian." *Origins* 20 (1990): 119.

Corecco, Eugenio. "Aspects of the Reception of Vatican II in the Code of Canon Law." In *The Reception of Vatican II*, pp. 249-296. Edited by Giuseppe

Alberigo, Jean-Pierre Jossua, and Joseph A. Komonchak. Washington D.C.: The Catholic University of America Press, 1987.

_____. "Ecclesiological Bases of the Code." In *Canon Law—Church Reality*, pp. 3-12. Edited by James Provost and Knut Walf. Edinburgh: T. & T. Clark, 1986.

Coriden, James A. "Shared Authority: Rationale and Legal Foundation." *Chicago Studies* 9 (1970): 171-182.

Costanzo, Joseph F. "Academic Dissent: An Original Ecclesiology: A Review Article." *The Thomist* 34 (1970): 636-653.

_____. "Papal Magisterium and 'Humanae Vitae.'" *Thought* 44 (1969): 377-412.

Coulson, John. "Authority and the Revival of Theology." *The Downside Review* 95 (1977): 231-238.

Crowley, Patrick. "Infallibility in a Teaching and Thinking Church." *Doctrine and Life* 32 (1982): 198-214.

Crowley, Paul G. "The *Sensus Fidelium* and Catholicity: Newman's Legacy in the Age of Inculturation." In *John Henry Newman: Theology and Reform*. Edited by Michael E. Allsopp and Ronald Burke. New York: Garland, 1992.

_____. "Catholicity, Inculturation and Newman's *Sensus Fidelium*." *Heythrop Journal* 33 (1992): 161-174.

De Roo, Remi J. "Collegiality and the Petrine Office in the Pastoral Work of the Church." *CTSA Proceedings* 25 (1970): 31-53.

Dobbin, Edmund J. "Sensus Fidelium Reconsidered." *New Theology Review* 2 (August 1989): 48-64.

Dionne, J. Robert. "'Humanae Vitae' Re-examined: A Response." *Homiletic and Pastoral Review* 73 (July 1973): 57-64.

_____. "An Interview with the Author of *The Papacy and the Church*." *America* 160 (1989): 12.

Dubay, Thomas. "The State of Moral Theology: A Critical Appraisal." In *Readings in Moral Theology No. 3: The Magisterium and Morality*, pp. 332-363. Edited by Charles E. Curran and Richard A. McCormick. New York: Paulist Press, 1982.

Dulles, Avery. "Authority and Conscience: Two Needed Forces in the Church." *Church* 2 (#3) (Fall 1986): 8-15.

_____. "A Half Century of Ecclesiology." *Theological Studies* 50 (1989): 419-442.

_____. "Sensus Fidelium." *America* 155 (1986): 240.

_____. "Successio apostolorum—Successio prophetarum—Successio doctorum." In *Who Has the Say in the Church?* 61-67. Edited by Juergen Moltmann and Hans Kueng. Edinburgh: T. & T. Clark, 1981.

_____. "The Teaching Mission of the Church and Academic Freedom." *America* 162 (1990): 397.

_____. "Vatican II and the Purpose of the Church." Chap. in *The Reshaping of Catholicism: Current Challenges in the Theology of Church*, pp. 132-153, 257-258. San Francisco: Harper & Row, 1988.

Dumont, Fernand. "Remarques critiques pour une théologie du 'consensus fidelium.'" In *Foi populaire, foi savante*, pp. 49-60. J.-M. R. Tillard, et. al. Paris: Les Éditions du Cerf, 1976.

Duquoc, Christian. "An Active Role for the People of God in Defining the Church's Faith." In *The Teaching Authority of the Believers*, pp. 73-81. Edited by Johannes-Baptist Metz and Edward Schillebeeckx. Edinburgh: T. & T. Clark, 1985.

Elizondo, Virgil. "The Hispanic Church in the USA: A Local Ecclesiology." *CTSA Proceedings* 36 (1981): 155-170.

Espin, Orlando O. "Tradition and Popular Religion: An Understanding of the Sensus Fidelium." In *Frontiers of Hispanic Theology in the United States*. Edited by Allan Figueroa Deck. Maryknoll, N.Y.: Orbis, 1992.

Farley, Margaret A. "Moral Discourse in the Public Arena." In *Vatican Authority and American Catholic Dissent*, pp. 168-186. Edited by William W. May. New York: Crossroad, 1987.

Feifel, Erich. "Glaubenssinn und theologischer Lernprozess. Funktion und grundlegende Strukturen theologischer Erwachsenenbildung." In *Erwachsenenbildung: Glaubenssinn und Theologischer Lernprozess*, pp. 13-77. Edited by Erich Feifel. Benziger, 1972.

Fiorenza, Elizabeth Schuessler. "Claiming our Authority and Power." In *The Teaching Authority of the Believers*, pp. 45-53. Edited by Johannes-Baptist Metz and Edward Schillebeeckx. Edinburgh: T. & T. Clark, 1985.

Flynn, Eileen P. "The Bishops Bomb." *Theology Today* 40 (1983-1984): 448-450.

Ford, John C. and Germain Grisez. "Contraception and the Infallibility of the Ordinary Magisterium." *Theological Studies* 39 (1978): 258-312.

Ford, John T. "Infallibility: A Review of Recent Studies." *Theological Studies* 40 (1979): 273-305.

Fransen, Piet F. "The Exercise of Authority in the Church Today: Its Concrete Forms." *Louvain Studies* 9 (1982): 3-25.

_____. "Unity and Confessional Statements: Historical and Theological Inquiry into Traditional Roman Catholic Conceptions." *Bijdragen* 33 (1972): 2-38.

Fries, Heinrich. "Ex Sese, Non Ex Consensu Ecclesiae." In *Volk Gottes: Zum Kirchenverstaendnis der Katholischen, Evangelischen un Anglikanischen Theologie*, pp. 480-500. Edited by Remigius Baeumer and Heimo Dolch. Freiburg: Herder, 1967.

_____. "Is There a *Magisterium* of the Faithful?" In *The Teaching Authority of the Believers*, pp. 82-91. Edited by Johannes-Baptist Metz and Edward Schillebeeckx. Edinburgh: T. & T. Clark, 1985.

_____. "Sensus Fidelium. Der Theologe zwischen dem Lehramt der Hierarchie und dem Lehramt der Glaeubigen." in *Theologische Berichte XVII: Theologe und Hierarch*, pp. 55-77. Magnus Loehrer, et. al. Zurich: Benziger, 1988.

Frost, William P. "On Celebrating Newman's Faith in the Laity." *Horizons* 6 (1979): 258-261.

Glaser, John. "Authority, Connatural Knowledge, and the Spontaneous Judgment of the Faithful." *Theological Studies* 29 (1968): 742-751.

Granfield, Patrick. "Ecclesial Cybernetics: Communication in the Church." *Theological Studies* 29 (1968): 662-678.

———. "The Local Church as a Center of Communication and Control." *CTSA Proceedings* 35 (1980): 256-263.

———. "The Pope and the Catholic Faithful." Chap. in *Limits of the Papacy*, pp. 134-168. New York: Crossroad, 1987.

———. "Presidential Address: The Uncertain Future of Collegiality." *CTSA Proceedings* 40 (1985): 95-106.

———. "The *Sensus Fidelium* in Episcopal Selection." In *Electing Our Own Bishops*, pp. 33-38. Edited by Peter Huizing and Knut Walf. Edinburgh: T. & T. Clark, 1980.

Greinacher, Norbert. "A Community Free of Rule." In *Democratization in the Church*, pp. 87-107. Edited by Alois Muller. New York: Herder and Herder, 1971.

Grootaers, Jan. "The Laity within the Ecclesial Communion." *Pro Mundi Vita* 106 (1986): 1-40.

Haarsma, Frans. "Consensus in the Church: Is an Empirical Inquiry Possible?" In *The Unifying Role of the Bishop*, pp. 119-129. Edited by Edward Schillebeeckx. New York: Herder and Herder, 1972.

Haering, Hermann. "The Rights and Limits of Dissent." In *The Right to Dissent*, pp. 95-107. Edited by Hans Kueng and Juergen Moltmann. Edinburgh: T. & T. Clark, 1982.

Hammans, Herbert. "Recent Catholic Views on the Development of Dogma." In *Man as Man & Believer*, pp. 109-131. New York: Paulist Press, 1967.

Hartin, Patrick J. "*Sensus Fidelium*: A Roman Catholic Reflection on its Significance for Ecumenical Thought." *Journal of Ecumenical Studies* 28 (1991): 74-87.

Heaney, John J. "Catholic Hermeneutics, the Magisterium, and Infallibility." *Continuum* 7 (1969): 106-119.

Hebblethwaite, Peter. "Le discours de Jean XXIII: à l'overture de Vatican II." *Recherches de science religieuse* 71 (1983): 203-212.

Heft, James L. "Episcopal Teaching Authority on Matters of War and Economics." In *Theology and Authority: Maintaining a Tradition of Tension*, pp. 93-105. Edited by Richard Penaskovic. Peabody, Mass.: Hendrickson Publishers, 1987.

_____. "Papal Infallibility and the Marian Dogmas: An Introduction." *One in Christ* 18 (1982): 309-340.

_____. "The Response Catholics Owe to Noninfallible Teachings." In *Raising the Torch of Good News: Catholic Authority and Dialogue with the World*. Edited by Bernard P. Prusak. *The Annual Publication of the College Theology Society* 32 (1986): 105-125.

_____. "'Sensus Fidelium' and the Marian Dogmas." *One in Christ* 28 (1992): 106-125.

Hellwig, Monika K. "Living Tradition in the Living Church." *Chicago Studies* 19 (1980): 161-170.

Hume, George Basil Cardinal. "Synod '80: Development of Marriage Teaching." *Origins* 10 (1980): 275.

International Theological Commission. "On the Interpretation of Dogmas." *Origins* 20 (1990): 1.

John Paul II, Pope. "Tensions of this Post-Conciliar Period." *Origins* 10 (1980): 49.

Kerkhofs, Jan. "Le Peuple de Dieu est-il infaillible? L' importance du sensus fidelium dans l'Église postconciliaire." *Freiburger Zeitschrift fuer Philosophie und Theologie* 35 (1988): 3-19.

Kilmartin, Edward J. "Episcopal Election: The Right of the Laity." In *Electing Our Own Bishops*, pp. 39-43. Edited by Peter Huizing and Knut Walf. Edinburgh: T. & T. Clark, 1980.

———. "Lay Participation in the Apostolate of the Hierarchy." *The Jurist* 41 (1981): 343-370.

Komonchak, Joseph A. "Clergy, Laity, and the Church's Mission in the World." *The Jurist* 41 (1981): 422-447.

———. "*Humanae Vitae* and its Reception: Ecclesiological Reflections." *Theological Studies* 39 (1978) : 221-257.

———. "The Magisterium and Theologians." *Chicago Studies* 29 (1990): 307-329.

———. "Reflections on the New York Forum." *Theological Education* 19 (Spring 1983): 60-64.

Koster, M. Dominikus. "Der Glaubenssinn der Hirten und Glaeubigen." In *Volk Gottes im Werden: Gessamelte Studien*, pp. 131-150. Edited by Hans-Dieter Langer and Otto Hermann Pesch. Mainz: Matthias-Gruenewald Verlag, 1971.

Lamirande, Emilien. "La théologie du 'sensus fidelium' et la collaboration de l'historien." In *Foi populaire, foi savante*, pp. 67-72. J.-M. R. Tillard, et. al. Paris: Les Éditions du Cerf, 1976.

Lehmann, Karl. "On the Dogmatic Justification for a Process of Democratization in the Church." In *Democratization in the Church*, pp. 60-86. Edited by Alois Muller. New York: Herder and Herder, 1971.

Lindbeck, George. "Scripture, Consensus, and Community." *This World* 23 (Fall 1988): 5-24.

Lipscomb, Oscar, and John Quinn. "Reaction to the CTSA Statement." *Origins* 20 (1990): 467.

Loehrer, Magnus. "Glaubenssinn und Glaubenskonsens." In *Mysterium Salutis: Grundriss Heilsgeschichtlicher Dogmatik.* Vol. 1. *Die Grundlagen Heilsgeschichtlicher Dogmatik*, pp. 551-555. Edited by Johannes Feiner and Magnus Loehrer. Einsiedeln: Benziger, 1965. Translated as "Sens de la foi et consensus de la foi." In *Mysterium Salutis: Dogmatique de l'histoire du Salut*. Vol. 3, 86-91. Edited by A. Darlap and H. Fries. Paris: Les Éditions du Cerf, 1969.

Lonergan, Bernard J. "The Transition from a Classicist World-View to Historical-Mindedness." In *A Second Collection*, pp. 1-9. Philadelphia: The Westminster Press, 1974.

Lund, Candida. "Would Democracy Solve the Problems of the Church?" *The Critic* 45 (1990): 2-21.

McCormick, Richard A. "Dissent in the Church: Loyalty or Liability?" Chap. in *The Critical Calling: Reflections on Moral Dilemmas Since Vatican II*, pp. 25-46. Washington, D.C.: Georgetown University Press, 1989.

_____. "The Teaching Office as a Guarantor of Unity in Morality." *Christian Ethics: Uniformity, Universality, Pluralism*, pp. 72-81. Edited by Jacques Pohier and Dietmar Mieth. New York: Seabury Press, 1981.

McCormick, Richard A. and Richard P. McBrien. "Theology as Public Responsibility." *America* 165 (1991): 184.

McGinniss, Michael J. "*Sensus Fidelium*, USA: Laity and Church Structures for the Future." *Listening* 25 (1990): 71-85.

McClelland, Vincent A. "Sensus Fidelium: The Developing Concept of Roman Catholic Voluntary Effort in Education in England and Wales." In *Christianity and Educational Provision*. Edited by Witold Tulasiewicz and Colin Brock. London: Routledge, 1988.

Maguire, Daniel C. "Catholicism and Modernity." *Horizons* 13 (1986): 355-370.

Maldari, Donald C. "The Identity of Religious Life: The Contributions of Jean-Marie Tillard Critically Examined." *Louvain Studies* 14 (1989): 325-345.

Malone, Richard. "Magisterium and Dissent." *Euntes Docete* 39 (1986): 503-521.

May, John, et. al. "Los Angeles Meeting of the Pope and U.S. Bishops." *Origins* 17 (1987): 253.

Metz, Johann Baptist. "Theology Today: New Crises and New Visions." *CTSA Proceedings* 40 (1985): 1-14.

Meyer, Harding. "Les présupposés of la réception ecclésiale ou le problème de la 'recevabilité.'" *Irénikon* 59 (1986): 5-19.

Miller, E. J. "Newman's *Sensus Fidelium* and Papal Fundamentalism." *Annual Publication of the College Theology Society* 35 (1989, ed. 1993): 289-304.

Moingt, Joseph. "Authority and Ministry." *Journal of Ecumenical Studies* 19 (1982): 202-225.

Molano, Eduardo. "Los Laicos en el Magisterio del Vaticano II." *Scripta Theologica* 17 (1985): 805-811.

Morales, Jose. "Nota Historico-Doctrinal Sobre las Relaciones entre Magisterio Eclesiastico, Oficio Teologico, y Sentido Popular de la Fe." *Scripta Theologica* 2 (1970): 481-499.

Mouw, Richard J. "Ending the Cold War between Theologians and Laypeople." *Christianity Today* 18 July 1994: 26-31.

Mueller, Hans Martin. "Magno Consensu Docent . . . Zum Konsensusbegriff nach evangelischem Verstaendnis." *Kerygma und Dogma* 28 (1982): 113-126.

O'Collins, Gerald. "Criteria for Interpreting the Traditions." In *Problems and Perspectives of Fundamental Theology*, 327-339. Edited by René Latourelle and Gerald O'Collins. New York: Paulist Press, 1982.

_____. "On Consulting the Faithful." *The Furrow* 37 (1986) : 279-284.

O'Gara, Margaret. "Infallibility in the Ecumenical Crucible." *One in Christ* 20 (1984): 325-345.

O'Leary, Paul. "Authority to Proclaim the Word of God, and the Consent of the Church." *Freiburger Zeitschrift fuer Philosophie und Theologie* 29 (1982): 239-251.

O'Meara, Thomas F. "Roman Catholicism: The Authority Crisis." *McCormick Quarterly* 23 (1970): 168-180.

Orsy, Ladislas. "General Norms, Custom (cc. 23-28)." In *The Code of Canon Law: A Text and Commentary*, pp. 38-40. Edited by James A. Coriden, Thomas J. Green and Donald E. Heintschel. New York: Paulist Press, 1985.

_____. "General Norms, Ecclesiastical Laws (cc. 7-22)." In *The Code of Canon Law: A Text and Commentary*, pp. 29-38. Edited by James A. Coriden, Thomas J. Green and Donald 9. Heintschel. New York: Paulist Press, 1985.

_____. "General Norms, Introduction." In *The Code of Canon Law: A Text and Commentary*, pp. 25-26. Edited by James A. Coriden, Thomas J. Green and Donald E. Heintschel. New York: Paulist Press, 1985.

_____. "Magisterium and Theologians: A Vatican Document." *America* 163 (1990): 30.

_____. "Magisterium: Assent and Dissent." *Theological Studies* 48 (1987): 473-497.

Patterson, Webster. "Apologetics, Newman and the Teaching Church." In *Theology Confronts a Changing World*, pp. 95-114. Edited by Thomas M. McFadden. West Mystic, Conn.: Twenty-Third Publications, 1977.

Penaskovic, Richard. "Theology and Authority: The Theological Issues." In *Theology & Authority: Maintaining a Tradition of Tension*, pp. 118-130. Edited by Richard Penaskovic. Peabody, Mass.: Hendrickson Publishers, 1987.

Philips, Gérard. "Le sens de la foi dans le peuple fidèle." In *L'Eglise et son mystère au IIe Concile du Vatican* Vol. 1, pp. 167-179. Paris: Declée, 1967.

Provost, James H. "Canon Law and the Role of Consultation." *Origins* 18 (1989): 793.

_____. "The Participation of the Laity in the Governance of the Church." *Studia Canonica* 17 (1983): 417-448.

Quinn, John. "Report on the Synod Collegiality and Faith." *Origins* 10 (1980): 355.

Rahner, Karl. "Basic Communities." In *Theological Investigations* Vol. 19, pp. 159-165. New York: Crossroad, 1983.

_____. "Considerations on the Development of Dogma." In *Theological Investigations* Vol. 4, pp. 3-35. London: Darton, Longman & Todd, 1974.

———. "Democracy in the Church?" *The Month* 40 (1968): 105-119.

———. "Dialogue in the Church." *Theological Investigations* Vol. 10, pp. 103-121. New York: Seabury, 1977.

———. "The Faith of the Christian and the Doctrine of the Church." In *Theological Investigations* Vol. 14, pp. 24-46. New York: Seabury, 1976.

———. "Free Speech in the Church." In *Free Speech in the Church*, pp. 9-50. New York: Sheed & Ward, 1959.

———. "'*Mysterium Ecclesiae*.'" In *Theological Investigations* Vol 17, pp. 139-155. New York: Crossroad, 981.

———. "Observations on the Concept of Revelation." In *Revelation and Tradition*, pp. 9-25. Karl Rahner and Joseph Ratzinger. New York: Herder and Herder, 1966.

———. "On the Concept of Infallibility in Catholic Theology." In *Theological Investigations* Vol. 14, pp. 66-84. New York: Seabury, 1976.

———. "On the Encyclical 'Humanae Vitae.'" In *Theological Investigations* Vol. 11, pp. 263-287. New York: Crossroad, 1982.

———. "Open Questions in Dogma Considered by the Institutional Church as Definitively Answered." In *Readings in Moral Theology No. 3: The Magisterium and Morality*, pp. 129-150. Edited by Charles E. Curran and Richard A. McCormick. New York: Paulist Press, 1982.

———. "Opposition in the Church." In *Theological Investigations* Vol. 17, pp. 127-138. New York: Crossroad, 1981.

———. "A Small Fragment 'On the Collective Finding of Truth.'" In *Theological Investigations* Vol. 6, pp. 82-88. New York: Crossroad, 1982.

———. "What the Church Officially Teaches and What the People Actually Believe." In *Theological Investigations* Vol. 22., pp. 165-175. New York: Crossroad, 1991.

Ratzinger, Joseph Cardinal. "Dissent and Proportionalism in Moral Theology." *Origins* 13 (1984): 666.

Ratzinger, Joseph Cardinal, with Vittorio Messori. "A Certain 'Liberation.'" Chap. in *The Ratzinger Report: An Exclusive Interview on the State of the Church*, pp. 169-190. San Francisco: Ignatius Press, 1985.

Rausch, Thomas P. "Authority and Credibility." In *Vatican Authority and American Catholic Dissent*, pp. 115-126. Edited by William W. May. New York: Crossroad, 1987.

_____. "Reception Past and Present." *Theological Studies* 47 (1986): 497-508.

_____. "Talking Back to Rome? J. R. Dionne on Papal Magisterium and the Church." *One in Christ* 24 (1988): 180-189.

Riedel-Spangenberger, Ilona. "Der Verkuendigungsdienst (munus docendi) der Kirche und der Glaubenssinn des Volkes Gottes (sensus fidelium)." In *Wege der Evangelisierung: Heinz Feilzer zum 65 Geburtstag*. Edited by Andreas Heinz. Trier: Paulinus, 1993.

Ruether, Rosemary Radford. "The Ministry of the People and the Future Shape of the Church." In *Toward A. D. 2000: Emerging Directions in Christian Ministry*. Vol. 1. *Southeastern Studies*. pp. 81-93. Edited by John I. Durham. Wake Forest, N.C.: Southeastern Baptist Theological Seminary, 1977.

Sacred Congregation for the Defense of the Faith. "Declaration in Defence of the Catholic Doctrine on the Church against Some Present-Day Errors." In *Vatican Council II: More Post Conciliar Documents*, Vol. 2. pp. 428-440. Edited by Austin Flannery. Northport, N. Y.: Costello, 1982.

Sancho, Jesús. "*Sensus Fidei* e Interpretacion de Ley Natural." In *Etica y Teologica ante le Crisis Contemporanea*. pp. 359-367. Edited by P. Alves de Sousa, T. Lopez, et al., 1980.

_____. "El *Sensus Fidei* en los Laicos." In *La Mision del Laico en la Iglesia y en el Mundo*, pp. 545-551. Edited by Augusto Sarmiento, et. al. Pamplona: Ediciones Universidad de Navarra, S. A., 1987.

Sanks. T. Howland. "Co-operation, Co-optation, Condemnation: Theologians and the magisterium 1870-1978." *Chicago Studies* 17 (1978): 242-263.

Sartori. Luigi. "Il 'sensus fidelium' del popolo di Dio e il concorso dei laici nelle determinazioni dottrinali." *Studi Ecumenici* 6 (1988): 33-57.

_____. "What is the Criterion for the *Sensus Fidelium?*" In *Who Has the Say in the Church?* pp. 56-60. Edited by Juergen Moltmann and Hans Kueng. Edinburgh: T. & T. Clark, 1981.

Scheffczyk, Leo. "Sensus Fidelium: Witness on the Part of the Community." *Communio* 15 (1988): 182-198.

Schillebeeckx, Edward. "Toward a Catholic Use of Hermeneutics." Chap. in *God the Future of Man*, pp. 1-49. New York: Sheed & Ward, 1968.

Schmaus, Michael. "Eine Anmerkung zum Problem der Demokratisierung in Bereich der kirchlichen Lehrunfehlbarkeit." In *Kirche im Wachstum des Glaubens: Festgabe Mannes Dominikus Koster zum siebzigsten Geburtstag*, pp. 255-265. Edited by Otto Hermann Pesch and Hans-Dieter Langer. Freiburg: Paulusverlag Freiburg, 1971. This volume appeared as *Freiburger Zeitschrift Fuer Philosophie und Theologie* 18 (1971).

_____. "Die heilshaften Funktionen der Kirche im einzelnen." In *Katholische Dogmatik* Vol. III., 1. *Die Lehre von der Kirche*, pp. 740-797. Munich: Max Hueber, 1958.

Schuller, David S. "Editorial Introduction." *Theological Education* 19 (Spring 1983): 5-6.

"Secret Resolutions Reveal Bishops . . . Rulings on Divorce, Celibacy, Sexuality." *National Catholic Reporter* 12 December 1980: 20-22.

Sesboüé, Bernard. "Autorité du magistère et vie de foi ecclésiale." *Nouvelle Revue Théologique* 93 (1971): 337-362.

_____. "Le 'sensus fidelium' en morale à la lumière de Vatican II." *Le Supplément* 181 (1992): 153-166.

Suess, Paulo. "The Creative and Normative Role of Popular Religion in the Church." In *Popular Religion*, pp. 122-131. Edited by Norbert Greinacher and Norbert Mette. Edinburgh: T. & T. Clark, 1986.

Sullivan, Emmanuel. "Authority in the Church: Problem in Mystery." *Anglican Theological Review* 70 (1988): 177-185.

_____. "Reception: Factor and Moment in Ecumenism." *Ecumenical Trends* 15 (1986): 105-110.

Sullivan, Francis A. "Magisterium and Theology." *CTSA Proceedings* 43 (1988): 65-75.

_____. "The Theologian's Ecclesial Vocation and the 1990 CDF Instruction." *Theological Studies* 52 (1991) : 51-68.

Swidler, Leonard. " *Demō -kratía*, The Rule of the People of God, or *Consensus Fidelium*." *Journal of Ecumenical Studies* 19 (1982): 226-243.

_____. "Dialogue: The Way toward Consensus." *Journal of Ecumenical Studies* 17 (1980): iii-viii.

_____. "Dissent an Honored Part of Church's Vocation." *National Catholic Reporter* 22 September 1989: 14-15.

_____. "*The* Ecumenical Problem Today: Papal Infallibility." *Journal of Ecumenical Studies* 8 (1971): 751-767.

Synod of Bishops. "The Final Report." *Origins* 19 (1985): 444.

Tavard, George H. "Is There a Catholic Ecclesiology?" *CTSA Proceedings* 29 (1974): 367-380.

Thompson, William M. "Authority and Magisterium in Recent Catholic Thought." *Chicago Studies* 16 (1977) : 278-298.

Tillard, Jean M. R. "Autorité et mémoire dans l'Église." (part 1) *Irénikon* 61 (1988): 332-346.

_____. "Autoritité et mémoire dans l'Église." (part 2) *Irénikon* 61 (1988): 481-484.

_____. "Church and Salvation: On the Sacramentality of the Church." *One in Christ* 20 (1984): 290-314.

_____. "'Reception': A Time to Beware of False Steps." *Ecumenical Trends* 14 (1985): 145-148.

_____. "*Sensus Fidelium.*" *One in Christ* 11 (1975): 2-29.

———. "Theological Pluralism and the Mystery of the Church." In *Different Theologies, Common Responsibility: Babel or Pentecost?* pp. 62-73. Edited by Claude Geffré, Gustavo Gutiérrez and Virgil Elizondo. Edinburgh: T. & T. Clark, 1984.

Timiadis, Metropolitan Emilianos. "Consensus in the Formulation of Doctrine." *Mid-Stream* 20 (1981): 177-190.

———. "Reception, Consensus, and Unity." *The Greek Orthodox Theological Review* 26 (1981): 47-61.

Untener, Kenneth, and James McHugh. "Human Sexuality Document's Birth Control Section." *Origins* 20 (1990): 404.

U. S. Bishops' Committee on Doctrine. "Report: An Ongoing Discussion of Magisterium." *Origins* 9 (1980): 543.

Vischer, Lukas. "The Process of 'Reception' in the Ecumenical Movement." *Mid-Stream* 23 (1984): 221-233.

Vorgrimler, Herbert. "From *Sensus Fidei* to *Consensus Fidelium*." In *The Teaching Authority of Believers*, pp. 3-11. Edited by Johann Baptist Metz and Edward Schillebeeckx. Edinburgh: T. & T. Clark, 1985.

Wagner, Harald. "Glaubenssinn, Glaubenszustimmung und Glaubenskonsens." *Theologie und Glaube* 69 (1979): 253-271.

Waldenfels, Hans. "Authority and Knowledge." In *The Teaching Authority of Believers*, pp. 31-42. Edited by Johann Baptist Metz and Edward Schillebeeckx. Edinburgh: T. & T. Clark, 1985.

Weakland, Rembert G. "The Church in Worldly Affairs: Tensions between Laity and Clergy." *America* 156 (1986): 201.

———. "U.S. Contribution to the Theological Enterprise." *Origins* 19 (1989): 157.

Whitehead, Evelyn Eaton, and James D. Whitehead. "Ministering to the Sense of the Faithful." In *Community of Faith*, pp. 153-170. New York: Seabury, 1982.

Willebrands, Johannes Cardinal. "The Impact of Dialogue." *Origins* 14 (1985): 720.

_____. "The Ecumenical Dialogue and its Reception." *One in Christ* 21 (1985): 217-225.

"Working Paper for the 1987 Synod of Bishops." *Origins* 17 (1987): 1.

Worlock, Derek. "Marital Indissolubility and Pastoral Compassion." *Origins* 16 (1980): 273.

Zizioulas, John. "The Theological Problem of 'Reception.'" *Bulletin/Centro Pro Unione* No. 26. (Fall 1984): 3-6.

# SUBJECT INDEX

abortion, 350-351, 391, 463, 609n. 590
Acton, John, Lord, 141, 152-153, 182
Ambrose, 52, 56, 515n. 206, 520n. 296
Anglican-Roman Catholic International Commission, 259
Aquinas, Thomas, 7, 74, 77-78, 82, 87-89, 107, 108-110, 145, 237, 254, 269, 276, 278, 285, 303, 305, 318, 321, 355, 381, 580n. 76
Arian controversy, 11, 70, 72, 81, 88, 122, 151, 161, 163, 165, 226, 260, 304, 317, 344, 362, 456, 498n 29, 499n. 39, 500n. 45, 600n. 445
Aristotle, 87, 108, 168, 237; Aristotelian "turn" of the *sensus fidelium*, 87
assent, 54, 56, 61, 130, 132, 137, 161, 172, 191, 193, 194, 199, 217, 220, 224, 263, 338, 340, 341, 383, 393, 398-400, 421, 496n. 13
Athanasius, 41, 70, 344
Augustine, 29, 42, 47, 54, 60, 64, 66, 72, 73, 107, 152, 154, 160, 161, 225, 272, 280, 363, 384, 500n. 41, 508n. 105, 515n. 206, 551n. 199
autocracy, 348

Ballerini, Pietro, 133-135
base communities, 292-293, 329, 350, 351, 353, 372-373, 410-412,

base communities (*continued*), 431, 437, 450, 467-468, 621-622n 830
beatific vision, 86-87, 164, 231, 278, 484, 498n. 29
Bellarmine, Bobert, 100, 101, 105, 127, 339
birth control (contraception), 118, 332, 337, 353, 388-389, 391-392, 425, 458, 463, 466, 500n. 45, 501n. 48, 609n. 590
Boniface VIII, Pope, 104

Cano, Melchior, 18, 38, 104, 105, 106, 107-108, 127, 231, 243, 280, 304, 318, 355, 457
canon of New Testament, 5, 22, 35-36, 37, 38, 39, 81, 223-224, 229, 255, 349; interpretation and canon, 254, 328
canon law, 1, 79, 82, 111-117, 119-120, 132, 215, 329, 349, 408-410, 450-451, 494n. 4
Catholic Theological Society of America, 207, 419, 424
*Christifidelis Laici*, 432-433
*Christus Dominus*, 449, 576n. 11
Clement of Alexandria, 33, 72, 287, 384
Clement of Rome. 25, 32, 33, 48, 62, 65, 72
*communio*, 29, 39, 44, 46, 135, 218, 223, 226, 293, 330, 334, 356, 399, 408, 409, 410, 432, 433, 451, 456, 462, 481, 485, 487

Congregation for the Doctrine of the Faith, 392-393, 395, 421, 434-439, 466, 486, 513-514n. 178, 566n. 441, 654n. 132; (formerly as) Holy Office, 202
connatural knowledge, 87, 88, 124, 238, 301, 381, 383
*conspiratio* of pastors and faithful, 10, 163, 205, 219-221, 224, 234, 235, 241, 258, 261, 307-308, 315, 334, 338, 340, 354, 358, 442, 454, 457, 472, 473, 477, 481, 499n. 38, 508-509n. 107
coresponsibility, 25, 34, 35-36, 40, 47, 49, 74, 292, 326, 402, 431, 449, 450, 485, 513n. 165, 517n. 239
creeping infallibilism, 181
criteria for interpreting the *sensus fidelium*, 4-5, 9, 12-14, 19-20, 160-161, 222, 223-252, 269, 313, 322-324, 345-346, 348, 361-363, 364-365, 460-461, 474, 476, 483-484
Cyprian, 43-44, 49-52, 59-60, 61-62, 63, 64, 66, 67, 97, 224-225, 291-292, 472, 513n. 165

*Dei Verbum*, 21, 104, 213, 218, 330, 359, 501n. 53
democracy, 1, 2, 23, 49, 52, 68, 69, 135, 137, 233, 266, 280, 283, 292, 293, 324-326, 329, 331, 348, 369, 373, 394, 401-402, 419, 420, 423, 437, 449, 450, 465-466, 471, 590n. 245, 620n. 805
dissent, 12, 42, 49, 193, 194, 200, 203, 238, 239, 295, 323, 327, 341-342, 389, 393-396, 397-398, 400-401, 426, 427, 434, 436-437, 439, 454, 458, 463-464, 469-470,

dissent (*continued*), 476, 485, 611n. 628, 628n. 938, 644-645n. 1207, 653n. 127
Doellinger, Ignaz von, 141, 146, 152, 154, 172-175, 330
dogmatic mentality, 67, 296-299, 300, 344, 448, 476-477, 482
Driedo, John, 106-107, 114

Easter dating controversy, 46
*Ecclesia discens/Ecclesia docens*, 11, 97, 99, 143, 155, 158, 164, 165, 166, 206, 208, 231, 236, 259, 322, 327, 329, 363, 408, 412, 452, 500n. 43
*Ecclesia in credendo*, 127, 128, 136, 141, 196, 301; infallibility of the faithful *in credendo*, 18, 127, 130, 141, 142, 179, 213, 232, 236, 319, 454; infallibility *in docendo*, 178, 319; of bishops and doctors, 128; infallibility *in credendo* and *in docendo* compared, 136, 141, 178, 496n. 13
ecclesial "monophysism", 297, 349, 477
echo (the *sensus fidelium* as an "echo" of official teaching), 143, 163, 217, 499n. 38
ecumenical implications of the *sensus fidelium*, 21, 79, 81, 94-95, 220, 255, 257-258, 262, 283-284, 288, 293, 302, 308, 323, 329, 334, 346-347, 350, 351, 373-374, 378, 404-408, 425-426, 451-452, 479, 495-496n. 12, 588n. 224, 594n. 330, 603n. 496, 621-622n. 830
Ephesus, Council of, 69, 71, 164
*epikeia*, 108-111, 114, 116, 120, 231-232, 234, 238, 409

Index 693

*ex cathedra* statements, 185, 193, 373, 389, 394, 398, 408, 422, 458

failures of the *sensus fidelium* in history, 68, 70, 228, 239, 305, 311, 339, 343-344, 473, 486
feedback (talking back), 290, 327, 378, 390, 408, 452
*fides implicita*, 165, 372, 376, 412
focus/locus distinction for *sensus fidelium*, 264, 402, 450
Franzelin, Johann Baptist, 141-143, 166, 175, 177-180, 189, 202, 207, 246, 247, 280, 301
French minority bishops at Vatican I, 185-189, 190
functional aspects of the *sensus fidelium*, 123-124, 272, 286, 292, 444, 452, 478, 484; functional role of consensus among teachers, 323; reception as functionally equivalent to *sensus fidelium*, 408

Gallicanism, 82-83, 97, 102, 115-116, 128, 129, 130-135, 136, 144, 174, 179, 185-186, 233, 246, 520n. 291
Gasser, Vincent, 182, 192-194, 196, 563n. 400
*Gaudium et Spes*, 13, 212, 237, 322, 496n. 14, 654n. 133
gestalt, *sensus fidelium* as, 383, 415, 465
Gillow, John, 154-156, 165
Gratian, 75, 76, 82, 113

hermeneutical implications, 4-5, 6, 8, 14, 18, 41, 62-63, 105, 135-136, 147, 148, 150-151, 171, 183, 188-190, 194-195, 201, 206-207, 208, 222, 240-251, 268, 270-272, 283-284, 299, 312, 389, 397, 422-423,

hermeneutical implications (*continued*), 445-446, 448, 451, 453, 459-461, 482, 483-484, 498n. 31, 574nn. 70, 76, 583nn. 130, 132, 621-622n. 830, 637n. 1084, 650n. 71, 653nn. 126, 127
heuristic qualities of the *sensus fidelium*, 215, 251, 270, 271, 444, 450
*Humanae Vitae*, 12, 267, 273, 281, 288, 300, 304, 313, 314, 327, 330, 333, 350, 375, 380, 388-392, 393-395, 397, 400, 427, 430, 458, 477, 501n. 48, 525n. 386, 626n. 908, 653n. 127
*Humani Generis*, 203, 566n. 440

International Theological Commission, 268, 438, 459, 486, 650n. 71
Irenaeus, 42, 43, 46, 62, 64-65, 66, 134, 506n. 55

John XXII, Pope, 85-87, 164, 498n. 29

Kenrick, Peter Richard, 182, 183, 187
Kleutgen, Joseph, 196
*koinonia*, 26, 27, 29, 94-95, 104, 243, 245, 297, 299, 309, 400, 407, 409, 410, 421, 431, 450, 460, 477, 485, 488, 594n. 330

Lammenais, Félicité de, 136-137
*Lamentabili*, 197, 203, 234,
*Lumen Gentium*, 11, 18, 19-21, 45, 211-212, 213-215, 217, 218, 219, 223, 237, 261, 267, 290, 317, 322, 329, 331, 339, 348, 363, 383, 394, 398, 400, 406, 409, 410, 417, 420, 428, 429, 432, 434, 576n. 11,

*Lumen Gentium (continued)*, 606n. 533, 608n. 575, 644n. 1196
liberation theology, 337, 351, 410-415, 443, 467-469, 478, 500n. 42, 566n. 441
Luther, Martin, 89-93, 105, 107, 330

*magnus consensus*, 90-92, 405
Marian dogma and the *sensus fidelium*, 270, 304-306, 313, 346-347, 357, 361, 407-408, 422, 457, 479, 502n. 1
Mary; as *theotokos*, 71, 164, 270; Immaculate Conception of, 11, 135, 141, 143, 144-148, 153, 155, 159, 160, 163, 165, 179, 205, 220, 233, 246, 261, 278, 343, 346, 498n. 29; Assumption of, 11, 204-207, 234, 249, 278, 311, 313, 327, 330, 346, 383, 466, 498n. 29, 545n. 116, 569n. 477; devotion to, 21, 265
mob-ocracy, 407, 452
Moehler, Johann Adam, 9, 88, 137-141, 161, 175, 214, 233, 234, 236, 238, 246, 254, 269, 280, 339, 350, 355, 384, 558-559n. 331, 584n. 152
More, Thomas, 118-124, 228, 315-316, 345, 455
*motus caritatis*, 88, 238
*Mysterium Ecclesiae*, 421-422, 428, 459, 596n. 372, 621-622n 830

Newman, John Henry; and the *Rambler*, 8, 141, 148-162, 165-166, 170, 173, 201, 242, 258, 259, 260, 261, 265, 270, 303, 338, 364, 444, 498n. 26, 549n. 170;

Newman, John Henry (*continued*), citations to Newman's influence on the notion of the *sensus fidelium* occur in the theological treatments of the following authors (listed in the authors index); Beinert, Biemer, Congar, Coulson, Dulles, Dumont, Eno, Femiano, Ford, Fries, Granfield, Guitton, Heft, Kerkhofs, Nichols, O'Collins, Patterson, Penaskovic, Read, Scheffczyk, Schmaus, Tillard, Trocóniz y Sasigain, Walgrave

*obsequium*, 341, 398-400, 414, 459, 462
opinions of the faithful (also related use of polls, surveys, statistics); not to be equated with the *sensus fidelium*, 2, 4, 12, 155, 157, 162, 173-175, 197, 216, 220, 228, 250, 257-258, 263, 282, 285, 294, 305, 311, 316, 322, 339-340, 341-342, 344, 347, 350-351, 358, 364, 365-368, 377, 380, 396, 397-398, 388, 407, 419-420, 422, 423, 425, 427-428, 429-430, 436-437, 463-464, 479, 481-482, 487, 443, 452, 473, 629n. 952 ; as closely associated with *sensus fidelium*, 350, 396, 572n. 53; practical development and views of the faithful, 12, 173-175, 263, 267, 341-342, 352-354, 365-368, 373, 395-396, 401, 415-419, 420-421, 422, 425, 435, 437-438, 452, 473, 487, 495n 12, 500n. 43
Origen, 50, 61, 63-64, 72, 280, 384, 506n. 55

*paradosis*, 28. 29, 43, 81, 90, 94, 223, 460; *traditio*, 39
*Pascendi Dominici Gregis*, 197-198, 199-200, 203
Paschasius Radbertus, 84-85
Passaglia, Carlo, 159-159, 175, 176-177, 200
Perrone, Giovanni, 9, 10, 141, 150, 155, 158-160, 161, 166-167, 175-176, 200, 202, 233, 246, 270, 280, 304, 330, 355, 364, 508-509n. 107, 551n. 206, 556n. 290
*phronema*, 9, 161, 214, 238, 292, 301, 305
*phronesis*, 474
Pian monolithism, 283, 375, 471
pneumatology and the *sensus fidelium*, 292, 573n. 55

reception; by the community of the faithful, 1, 72, 78-88, 124, 188, 224, 230, 231, 234, 237, 281, 282, 284, 255-256, 267-268, 295, 296, 297, 298, 302, 308-309, 330-331, 333, 342, 348, 349-350, 352, 390, 396, 403, 410, 426, 430, 438, 443, 444, 451-452, 462-463, 472, 601n. 465, 629n. 950; of law, 111-121, 230, 232, 444, 494n. 4; of conciliar teaching, 69-70, 72; by bishops, 233; by magisterium, 449; and ecumenism, 94, 274-274, 308; of *Humanae Vitae*, 299-300, 350, 388, 430, 500n. 45; in Newman, 171-172; non-reception, 68, 230, 275, 288, 289, 295, 340, 350, 353, 378, 476, 525n. 386, 608n. 573; re-reception, 255, 350, 484
real presence. doctrine of, 84-85, 164, 231, 278, 498n. 29; cf., 101-102

*regula fidei* (rule of faith), 28, 40-41, 46, 76, 65, 90, 93, 96, 129, 202, 218, 289, 355, 361, 444, 471, 481; magisterium considered as "proximate" rule of faith, 273; individual's judgment seen as rule of faith, 401; *sensus fidelium* as rule of faith, 472

saints; canonization of, 81, 82, 255-256, 351, 370; cult of, 311; veneration of, 349; as witnesses to the *sensus fidelium*, 364, 377, 473, 479
Scheeben, Mattheas Joseph, 143-144, 202, 246, 254, 269, 280, 301, 330, 350, 417
Schrader, Clemens, 175, 176-177, 201
selection of leaders by the faithful; historical precedents, 1, 33, 39, 47-59, 69, 74-76, 97-98, 124, 494n. 4; modern considerations, 224-225, 274, 291-293, 326, 352, 373, 401-402, 472, 449-450, 523n. 338
*seniores laici*, 59-60
*sentire cum ecclesia*, 2, 284, 436
simple faithful (*simplices, rudes*), 44, 99, 242, 262, 266, 267, 307, 316, 317, 362-363, 372, 456, 478, 481, 488, 654n. 13
*sola scriptura*, 95-96, 142, 169, 245, 246, 355

terms, diverse meanings of the sense of the faithful, 1, 17, 494n. 3, 502n 1, at Council of Trent, 105
Tertullian, 5, 18, 33, 42, 59, 62, 63, 64, 65, 66, 90, 287, 493n. 2
Tournély, Honoré, 128-129, 131-133, 135

Trent, Council of, 7, 22, 79, 96-103, 105, 107, 127, 129, 142, 170, 195, 206, 232, 242-243, 248, 267, 298, 301, 314, 335, 444, 447, 497n 25, 559n. 332

Ullathorne, W. B., Bishop, 153, 154, 156-157, 159, 160, 165, 338, 364
*Unam Sanctum*, 104
U. S. Bishops, pastorals on war and peace and economics, 268, 288, 347-348, 414, 423-424, 431
usury, 117-118, 231, 351, 381, 484

Vincent of Lerins, 6, 18, 64, 65-66, 72, 90, 225, 272, 280, 355, 430; *Commonitoria*, 6, 65, 430, 497n. 19

Vincentian Canon, 6, 63, 67, 102, 103, 122, 191, 346;

Wiseman, Nicholas Cardinal, 152, 153
women and the *sensus fidelium*; collaboration within the church's structure, 431, 500n. 43, 572n. 54, 44-645n. 1207; consulting of women, 425, 609n. 590; feminist critiques of ecclesial structure, 414-415; feminist theology, 336, 350, 353, 637n. 1091; historical issues, 24, 30; women as disenfranchised, 465; women's experience, 413; women in ministry, 332, 465

# INDEX OF AUTHORS

Alberigo, Giuseppe, 100-101, 184, 196, 197, 200, 202-203, 216, 217, 403, 451
Alszeghy, Zoltán, 359-363, 478, 481

Bainvel, Jean, 10
Balic, C., 204, 207, 284, 567n. 456
Bartelink, Gerard, 54-55
Beinert, Wolfgang, 139-140, 143, 282-289, 453, 471, 472, 481, 548n. 146, 580n. 84
Benson, Robert L., 74-75, 517n. 239, 523n. 338
Bermejo, Luis M., 403, 451, 632n. 1013
Bernhard, Jean, 97-98
Bertolino, Rinaldo, 408-409, 451
Beumer, J, 204, 284
Biemer, Guenter, 260, 442
Biser, Eugen, 385-387, 475, 481
Boff, Leonardo, 412-413, 468, 478, 500n. 42
Boglioni, Pierre, 73
Bourke, Myles, 34-36
Bracken, Joseph A., 394-395, 462, 481
Bray, Gerald, 41
Brown, Raymond, 26
Bucher, Kevin D., 162-163
Buechsel, Friedrich, 29
Burghardt, Walter J., 206-207, 569n. 477
Burke, Cormac, 391-392, 458, 463

Burke, Ronald, 619n. 789
Burkhard, John J., xx
Butler, B. C., 399-400, 462
Butler, Dom Edward C., 544n. 86, 559n. 333

Caffrey, Thomas J., 563n. 400
Cahill, Lisa Sowle, 395-396, 462
Camilleri, René, 242, 247-248
Capestany, Edward J., 627n. 926, 649n. 64
Cardman, Francine, 514n. 182
Carol, Juniper B., 205-206, 207, 569n. 477
Carr, Anne E., 637n. 1091
Carroll, Eamon, 145-146, 205
Carter, Gerald Emmett Cardinal, 429, 431-432, 501n. 48, 643n. 1179
Chadwick, Owen, 10, 137-138, 140-141, 162, 166-167, 543n. 72, 551n. 206, 553n. 232
Chavasse, Paul, 498-499n. 32
Chirico, Peter, 423, 641n. 1146
Clark, Matthew, 425
Colaianni, Nicola, 510n. 10
Collins, Raymond F., 410-411, 468, 636n. 1072, 650n. 82
Congar. Yves, 12, 28, 72, 76-78, 81-83, 88, 89-90, 93, 99, 107, 135, 137. 141, 142, 143, 171, 202, 204, 227. 228, 239, 253-258, 280, 284, 302. 350, 403, 451, 453, 469.

Congar, Yves (*continued*), 471-472, 476, 481, 493n. 1, 497n. 25, 502n. 1, 524n. 367, 542n. 52, 596n. 355, 597n. 374, 626n. 905, 635n. 1055
Coppens, J., 27-28, 205
Corecco, Eugenio, 409-410
Coriden, James A., 409, 450, 558n. 331
Costanzo, Joseph F., 389, 394, 458
Costigan, Richard F., 130-135, 246
Coulson, John, 71, 151-152, 153-154, 163, 165, 166, 258-259, 442-443, 498nn. 27, 30, 508n. 107
Crowley, Patrick, 390, 452
Crowley, Paul G., xx
Curran, Charles, 393-394, 395, 628nn. 939, 940, 653n. 127

Dagens, Claude, 23-24
Daly, Gabriel, 199-200
D'Aragon, Jean-Louis, 31, 33
Davids, Adalbert, 63
Deconchy, J.P., 577n. 28
Dejaifve, George, 190-193
Denzler, Georg, 194-195
De Roo, Remi J., 419-421, 572n. 53
Dessain, C. Stephen, 553n. 232, 560n. 348
Dillenschneider, P. Clément, 19, 72-73, 204, 207, 502n. 1, 567n. 456, 635n. 1055
Dionne, J. Robert, 390-391, 407-408, 452, 524n. 369, 629n. 950, 634nn. 1045, 1048
Douie, Decima, 86, 87
Dubay, Thomas, 393, 649n. 64
Dulles, Avery, 3-4, 62-63, 68, 69-70, 87, 97, 98-99, 129-130, 136, 169-172, 198-199, 221, 246, 295, 339-343, 353, 473, 531n. 480, 548n.

Dulles, Avery, (*continued*), 146, 573-574n. 68, 608n. 573, 629n. 949
Dumont, Fernand, 312-315, 472
Duquoc, Christian, 401, 449

Elizondo, Virgil, 411, 467-468
Eno, Robert B., 41-42, 48-49, 54, 55, 57, 64-65, 66-67, 225, 272-274, 443, 444, 584n. 144
Eugui Hermoso de Mendoza, Julio, 47-48, 50, 54, 58-59, 449, 513n. 165, 516n. 214

Faivre, Alexandre, 32-33, 45, 69
Farley, Margaret A., 395, 461-462, 500n. 43
Feifel, Erich, 465, 639n. 1120
Femiano, Samuel, 149, 150, 157, 214, 260-261, 265, 442-443, 548n. 146, 549nn. 167, 170
Fiorenza, Elizabeth Schuessler, 414-415, 465, 500n. 43
Fiorenza, Francis Schuessler, 189-190
Flynn, Eileen P., 414
Ford, John C., 388-389, 458
Ford, John T., 182, 183-184, 270-272, 389, 444, 461, 610n. 617, 652n. 111, 653n. 126
Fransen, Piet F., 244-245, 447-448
Frend, W. H. C., 59-60
Fries, Heinrich, 329-335, 472, 481, 495n. 7, 650n. 71
Frost, William P., 214

Gadamer, Hans-Georg, xx, 150, 498n. 31, 547n. 144, 637n. 1084
Galvin, John J., 566n. 440
Garijo Guembe, Miguel M., 79, 81, 403-404, 451

Gaudemet, Jean, 76
Gieselmann, Josef Rupert, 137, 138, 566n. 440, 584n. 152, 626n. 905
Glaser, John, 380-382, 475, 628n. 937
González Faus, José I., 628n. 938
Granfield, Patrick, 50-51, 55, 57, 61-62, 70, 217-218, 225, 290-296, 453, 472, 481, 494n. 3, 513n. 165, 548n. 146, 629n 952, 635n. 1055
Green, Lowell C., 90-92, 530n. 466
Greinacher, Norbert, 326, 603n. 488, 632n. 1007
Grisez, Germain, 388-389, 458
Gubler, Marie-Louise, 30-31
Guitton, Jean, 149-150, 152, 259-260, 442, 547n. 140, 548n. 146

Haarsma, Frans, 397-398, 480, 482, 486
Haering, Herbert, 628n. 938
Hammans, Herbert, 567n. 456, 584n. 152
Hartin, Patrick J., xx
Hasler, August Bernhard, 547n. 136
Hauck, Friedrich, 26-27
Heagle, John, 402, 450
Healy, Kilian, 568n. 466
Heaney, John J., 244, 574n. 70
Hebblethwaite, Peter, 216
Heft, James L., xx, 346-349, 414, 479, 650n. 71
Hellwig, Monika K., 40-41, 65, 137, 141, 223, 413, 478
Hennessy, Paul K., 182
Hertling, Ludwig, 29
Hillerbrand, Hans, 118-119
Hines, Mary E., 620nn. 806, 808
Hitchcock, James, 121-124, 315-316, 455-456, 603n. 491
Hoffmann, Joseph, 172-175, 190

Hume, George Basil Cardinal, 347, 348, 411, 418, 429, 650n. 82
Hunt, Robert E., 393-394, 653n. 127

Iersel, Bas van, 23

John XXIII, Pope, 13, 82, 181, 200, 216, 217, 259, 264, 351, 484
John Paul II, Pope, 2, 12, 257, 328, 332, 339, 352, 427-429, 432-433, 485, 644-645n. 1207

Kaufman, Philip S., 396, 463, 464, 500n. 45, 501n. 48, 643n. 1180
Kelly, J. N. D., 86
Kerkhofs, Jan, 349-354, 479-480, 650n. 71
Kilmartin, Edward J., 79-80, 83-84, 231, 401-402, 450, 573n. 55
King, Geoffrey, 111-112, 113-117, 274-275, 443, 444, 494n. 4
Kleinheyer, Bruno, 45-46
Knowles, David, 85, 119-120
Komonchak, Joseph A., 215-216, 218, 391, 438, 495n. 12, 571n 23
Koster, M. Dominikus, 19, 87, 88, 204, 207, 275-279, 280, 452-453, 548n. 146, 567n. 456
Kottje, Raymund, 49, 51-52, 401, 449
Kueng, Hans, 190, 530n 462, 554n. 249, 602n. 478
Kuhn, T. S., 180, 198, 200-201, 248

Lamirande, Emilien, 310-312, 472
Lash, Nicholas, 249, 270-271
Lécuyer, Joseph, 402, 450
Legrand, Hervé-Marie, 52-53, 401, 449
Lehmann, Karl, 632n. 1007

Lindbeck, George A., 405-406, 565n. 420
Lindt, Andreas, 181, 184-185
Loehrer, Magnus, 281-282, 452-453
Lonergan, Bernard J., 268-269, 421, 558n. 331, 562n. 380, 641n. 1146
Lund, Candida, 632n. 1002
Lynch, John E., 57-58, 60, 513n. 165, 514n. 180

Mackey, J. P., 142-143, 178, 207-208, 566n. 440, 567n. 456, 626n. 905
MacRae, George W., 33-34, 36-37, 38
Maguire, Alban A., 583n. 132
Maguire, Daniel, 391, 463
Mahoney, John, 625n. 903
Maldari, Donald C., 594n. 330
Malone, Richard, 400-401
Marín-Sola, F., 203, 269
Maritain, Jacques, 381, 431, 623n. 863
Markus, R. A., 230, 522n. 328
McBrien, Richard P., 613n. 666, 654n. 131
McCormick, Richard A., 341-342, 392-393, 461, 495n. 11, 608n. 583, 654n. 131
McGinniss, Michael J., 415-417, 464
McHugh, James, 425
McNally, Robert E., 97
McNamara, Kevin, 20-21, 584n. 152
Metz, Johann Baptist, 336, 412, 467, 468
Meyendorff, John, 68-69
Meyer, Harding, 405
Moingt, Joseph, 423
Moiser, Jeremy, 37, 38
Molano, Eduardo, 214-215
Morales, Jose, 316-317, 456

Mueller, Hans Martin, 530n. 466
Nichols, Aidan, 363-365, 478-479, 481
Noonan, John, 117-118

O'Collins, Gerald, 343-346, 473, 478
O'Connell, Laurence J., 402, 450
O'Gara, Margaret, 185-189, 190, 406
O'Leary, Paul, 404
O'Malley, John W., 13, 47, 242-243, 249-250
O'Meara, Thomas F., 390
Ommen, Thomas G., 498n. 31
Orsy, Ladislas, 112-113, 341, 398-399, 409, 437-438, 451, 462, 487, 608n. 580
Osawa, Takeo, 515n. 196
Ott, Ludwig, 496n. 13
Owens, Gerard, 145, 147

Palmer, Richard E., 574n. 76
Parrella, Frederick J., 99-100, 219, 570n. 9
Paul VI, Pope, 12, 100, 220, 273, 332, 380, 421, 558n. 327, 601n. 449, 626n. 908, 645n. 1224
Patterson, Webster, 149, 150, 152, 156-157, 159, 215, 261-264, 265, 443, 450
Penaskovic, Richard, 149-150, 264-268, 443,
Pesch, Rudolf, 23
Philips, Gérard, 212, 284
Pius IX, Pope, 11, 135-136, 144, 145-146, 181, 182, 183, 184, 195, 201, 233, 246-247, 270, 349, 498n. 29, 512n. 149, 545n. 116, 563n. 396, 569n. 485
Pius X, Pope, 197, 366

Pius XII, Pope, 11, 204, 234, 330, 366, 368, 369, 512n. 149, 545n. 116
Pottmeyer, H. J., 384
Provost, James H., 635n. 1066, 648n. 31
Prusak, Bernard P., 101-102

Quinn, John, 424, 430, 644n. 1207

Rahner, Karl, 170, 262, 267, 282, 286, 301-302, 336, 365-379, 381, 382, 386, 443, 453, 462, 473, 486, 490, 548n. 147, 587n. 198, 594n. 329, 635n. 1055, 649n. 63
Ratzinger, Joseph Cardinal, 2, 5, 49, 295, 347, 434, 439, 426-427, 513n. 178, 654n. 131, 651n. 85
Rausch, Thomas P., 24-26, 39, 78-79, 396, 404-405, 407-408, 451, 497n. 25, 644n. 1205
Read, Denis, 268-269
Remmers, Johannes, 43-45
Rikhof, Herwi, 214
Riley, Lawrence, 108-109, 110-111
Rondet, Henri, 566n. 440
Ruether, Rosemary Radford, 415, 465

Sancho Bielsa, Jesús, 18, 88-89, 105-106, 107-108, 203-204, 317-322, 454-455, 456, 528nn. 420, 429, 635n. 1055
Sanks, T. Howland, 175-181, 198, 199, 200-201, 247, 248, 446, 626n. 908
Sartori, Luigi, 322-324, 476, 501n. 49, 635n. 1055
Scheffczyk, Leo, 354-358, 456-458
Schillebeeckx, Edward, 31-32, 240-241, 483

Schmaus, Michael, 279-281, 452-453
Schnackenburg, Rudolf, 504n 31, 507n. 81
Scholz, Franz, 109
Schoof, T. M., 201
Schrodt, Paul., 104, 138
Schuller, David S., 495n. 12
Seckler, M., 19, 173, 284, 567n. 456, 604n. 505
Sesboüé, Bernard, 296-300, 476-477, 500n. 45, 647n. 16
Sheldrake, Philip, 119, 120-121, 123
Sieben, Hermann-Josef, 526n. 393
Slusser, Michael
Speigl, Jakob, 64
Stockmeier, Peter, 43-44, 49
Suenens, Leon-Joseph Cardinal, 219-221
Suess, Paulo, 411-412, 468
Sullivan, Emmanuel, 633n. 1017, 634n. 1048
Sullivan, Francis A., 53, 421, 422, 438-439, 640n 1139
Swidler, Leonard, 324-329, 465-466

Tavard, George H., 39, 94-97, 104-105, 106, 107, 219, 243, 245, 653n. 125
Thiel, John E., 197-198, 201, 248-249
Thils, Gustave, 18, 105, 108, 127-129, 136, 141, 143, 195, 213-214, 232, 363, 445
Thompson, William M., 6-7, 87-88, 92-94, 127, 143-144, 195-196, 219, 227, 247, 301-303, 453, 469, 472, 478, 481, 494n.4, 528n. 423, 548n. 146

Tillard, Jean M. R., 46, 144, 205, 208, 303-310, 312, 315, 472, 478, 500n. 45
Timiadis, Metropolitan Emilianos, 67-68, 406-407
Trocóniz y Sasigain, Luis M. Fz. de, 244, 269

Untener, Kenneth, 424-425

Vischer, Lukas, 405
Vorgrimler, Herbert, 335-337, 477, 478, 521n. 161

Wagner, Harald, 382-385, 475, 482
Waldenfels, Hans, 637n. 1084

Walgrave, Jan, 9-10, 84, 85, 102-103, 161, 230-231, 232, 337-339, 477-478, 481, 482, 502n. 2
Warren, Michael, 654n. 137
Weakland, Rembert G., 423-434, 644n. 1207
Weber, Max, 144, 304, 637n. 1084
Whitehead, Evelyn Eaton & James D., 417-419, 464-465
Willebrands, Johannes Cardinal, 425-426
Worlock, Derek, 429
Wuenschel, Edward A., 569n. 477

Zizioulas, John, 405

www.ingramcontent.com/pod-product-compliance
Lightning Source LLC
Chambersburg PA
CBHW052038290426
44111CB00011B/1540